T0190501

Communications
in Computer and Information Science 2034

Rationale

The CCIS series is devoted to the publication of proceedings of computer science conferences. Its aim is to efficiently disseminate original research results in informatics in printed and electronic form. While the focus is on publication of peer-reviewed full papers presenting mature work, inclusion of reviewed short papers reporting on work in progress is welcome, too. Besides globally relevant meetings with internationally representative program committees guaranteeing a strict peer-reviewing and paper selection process, conferences run by societies or of high regional or national relevance are also considered for publication.

Topics

The topical scope of CCIS spans the entire spectrum of informatics ranging from foundational topics in the theory of computing to information and communications science and technology and a broad variety of interdisciplinary application fields.

Information for Volume Editors and Authors

Publication in CCIS is free of charge. No royalties are paid, however, we offer registered conference participants temporary free access to the online version of the conference proceedings on SpringerLink (http://link.springer.com) by means of an http referrer from the conference website and/or a number of complimentary printed copies, as specified in the official acceptance email of the event.

CCIS proceedings can be published in time for distribution at conferences or as postproceedings, and delivered in the form of printed books and/or electronically as USBs and/or e-content licenses for accessing proceedings at SpringerLink. Furthermore, CCIS proceedings are included in the CCIS electronic book series hosted in the SpringerLink digital library at http://link.springer.com/bookseries/7899. Conferences publishing in CCIS are allowed to use Online Conference Service (OCS) for managing the whole proceedings lifecycle (from submission and reviewing to preparing for publication) free of charge.

Publication process

The language of publication is exclusively English. Authors publishing in CCIS have to sign the Springer CCIS copyright transfer form, however, they are free to use their material published in CCIS for substantially changed, more elaborate subsequent publications elsewhere. For the preparation of the camera-ready papers/files, authors have to strictly adhere to the Springer CCIS Authors' Instructions and are strongly encouraged to use the CCIS LaTeX style files or templates.

Abstracting/Indexing

CCIS is abstracted/indexed in DBLP, Google Scholar, EI-Compendex, Mathematical Reviews, SCImago, Scopus. CCIS volumes are also submitted for the inclusion in ISI Proceedings.

How to start

To start the evaluation of your proposal for inclusion in the CCIS series, please send an e-mail to ccis@springer.com.

Communications
in Computer and Information Science **2034**

Rationale

The CCIS series is devoted to the publication of proceedings of computer science conferences. Its aim is to efficiently disseminate original research results in informatics in printed and electronic form. While the focus is on publication of peer-reviewed full papers presenting mature work, inclusion of reviewed short papers reporting on work in progress is welcome, too. Besides globally relevant meetings with internationally representative program committees guaranteeing a strict peer-reviewing and paper selection process, conferences run by societies or of high regional or national relevance are also considered for publication.

Topics

The topical scope of CCIS spans the entire spectrum of informatics ranging from foundational topics in the theory of computing to information and communications science and technology and a broad variety of interdisciplinary application fields.

Information for Volume Editors and Authors

Publication in CCIS is free of charge. No royalties are paid, however, we offer registered conference participants temporary free access to the online version of the conference proceedings on SpringerLink (http://link.springer.com) by means of an http referrer from the conference website and/or a number of complimentary printed copies, as specified in the official acceptance email of the event.

CCIS proceedings can be published in time for distribution at conferences or as post-proceedings, and delivered in the form of printed books and/or electronically as USBs and/or e-content licenses for accessing proceedings at SpringerLink. Furthermore, CCIS proceedings are included in the CCIS electronic book series hosted in the SpringerLink digital library at http://link.springer.com/bookseries/7899. Conferences publishing in CCIS are allowed to use Online Conference Service (OCS) for managing the whole proceedings lifecycle (from submission and reviewing to preparing for publication) free of charge.

Publication process

The language of publication is exclusively English. Authors publishing in CCIS have to sign the Springer CCIS copyright transfer form, however, they are free to use their material published in CCIS for substantially changed, more elaborate subsequent publications elsewhere. For the preparation of the camera-ready papers/files, authors have to strictly adhere to the Springer CCIS Authors' Instructions and are strongly encouraged to use the CCIS LaTeX style files or templates.

Abstracting/Indexing

CCIS is abstracted/indexed in DBLP, Google Scholar, EI-Compendex, Mathematical Reviews, SCImago, Scopus. CCIS volumes are also submitted for the inclusion in ISI Proceedings.

How to start

To start the evaluation of your proposal for inclusion in the CCIS series, please send an e-mail to ccis@springer.com.

Guojun Wang · Haozhe Wang · Geyong Min ·
Nektarios Georgalas · Weizhi Meng
Editors

Ubiquitous Security

Third International Conference, UbiSec 2023
Exeter, UK, November 1–3, 2023
Revised Selected Papers

 Springer

Editors
Guojun Wang ⓘ
School of Computer Science and Cyber
Engineering
Guangzhou University
Guangzhou, China

Geyong Min ⓘ
Department of Computer Science
University of Exeter
Exeter, UK

Weizhi Meng ⓘ
Department of Applied Mathematics
and Computer Science
University of Denmark
Copenhagen, Denmark

Haozhe Wang ⓘ
Department of Computer Science
University of Exeter
Exeter, UK

Nektarios Georgalas ⓘ .
Applied Research Department
British Telecom
London, UK

ISSN 1865-0929   ISSN 1865-0937 (electronic)
Communications in Computer and Information Science
ISBN 978-981-97-1273-1   ISBN 978-981-97-1274-8 (eBook)
https://doi.org/10.1007/978-981-97-1274-8

This Springer imprint is published by the registered company Springer Nature Singapore Pte Ltd.
The registered company address is: 152 Beach Road, #21-01/04 Gateway East, Singapore 189721, Singapore

Paper in this product is recyclable.

Preface

The Third International Conference on Ubiquitous Security (UbiSec 2023), held in Exeter, UK between 1 and 3 November 2023, was organized by the University of Exeter.

UbiSec 2023, succeeding the well-received UbiSec 2022 event in Zhangjiajie, continues the esteemed UbiSec and the foundational SpaCCS/UbiSafe/IWCSS series. This year, UbiSec was devoted to key themes of security, privacy, and anonymity at the intersection of cyberspace, the physical world, and social networks. It aimed to drive innovation in these critical areas, push the boundaries of digital security and privacy, and significantly contribute to the ongoing evolution of our digital world.

UbiSec 2023 received a total of 91 submissions from authors across 18 different countries. Each submission was reviewed by at least three experts in relevant research fields. Following a rigorous selection process by the Program Committee, 29 regular papers were selected for oral presentation at the conference and inclusion in this Springer CCIS volume, representing an acceptance rate of 31.9%. The program of UbiSec was enriched with keynote speeches from world-renowned researchers. Our thanks go to the esteemed Keynote Speakers: Erol Gelenbe, Kin K. Leung, Shiqiang Wang, Nektarios Georgalas, Keqiu Li, Liangxiu Han, and Lu Liu. Their expertise and willingness to impart knowledge significantly enriched the experience for all attendees.

The success of UbiSec 2023 is attributed to the teamwork and commitment of many individuals and organizations worldwide. Special thanks are owed to those who volunteered their time and efforts in organizing this conference. We express our profound gratitude to the Steering Committee Chairs, Guojun Wang from Guangzhou University, China, and Kim-Kwang Raymond Choo from the University of Texas at San Antonio, USA, for their pivotal leadership and guidance. Our gratitude also extends to all Program Committee members and reviewers, whose diligent evaluation and selection of papers was crucial in maintaining the conference's high academic standards and overall success.

Our heartfelt appreciation is extended to the General Chairs, Haitham S. Cruickshank from the University of Surrey, UK, and Wenjia Li from the New York Institute of Technology, USA, for their tremendous support and guidance, which were crucial to the conference's success. We also would like to acknowledge the vital contributions of the Workshop Chairs, Jiaxing Shang and Zi Wang; the Publicity Chairs, Klimis Ntalianis and Yannan Li; the Publication Chairs, Prosanta Gope and Pan Li; and the Local Arrangement Chair, Songyuan Li. Each individual's commitment and expertise have been indispensable for a successful and impactful conference.

Finally, we extend our deepest thanks to all the authors and participants for their invaluable support and contributions. We hope you found the conference a stimulating and engaging forum, and that your stay in Exeter was equally inspiring.

November 2023

Guojun Wang
Haozhe Wang
Geyong Min
Nektarios Georgalas
Weizhi Meng

Organization

General Chairs

Haitham S. Cruickshank   University of Surrey, UK
Wenjia Li   New York Institute of Technology, USA

Program Chairs

Guojun Wang   Guangzhou University, China
Haozhe Wang   University of Exeter, UK
Geyong Min   University of Exeter, UK
Nektarios Georgalas BT Group, UK
Weizhi Meng   Technical University of Denmark, Denmark

Workshop Chairs

Jiaxing Shang   Chongqing University, China
Zi Wang   University of Exeter, UK

Publicity Chairs

Klimis Ntalianis   Athens University of Applied Sciences, Greece
Yannan Li   University of Wollongong, Australia

Publication Chairs

Prosanta Gope   University of Sheffield, UK
Pan Li   Case Western Reserve University, USA

Finance Chair

Zhuhui Li   University of Exeter, UK

Web and System Management Chair

Zhe Wang   University of Exeter, UK

Local Arrangement Chair

Songyuan Li   University of Exeter, UK

Steering Committee

Guojun Wang (Chair)	Guangzhou University, China
Kim-Kwang Raymond Choo (Chair)	University of Texas at San Antonio, USA
Saqib Ali	University of Agriculture Faisalabad, Pakistan
Valentina E. Balas	Aurel Vlaicu University of Arad, Romania
Md Zakirul Alam Bhuiyan	Fordham University, USA
Jiannong Cao	Hong Kong Polytechnic University, China
Aniello Castiglione	Parthenope University of Naples, Italy
Scott Fowler	Linköping University, Sweden
Oana Geman	University of Suceava, Romania
Richard Hill	University of Huddersfield, UK
Ryan Ko	University of Queensland, Australia
Kuan-Ching Li	Providence University, Taiwan
Jianhua Ma	Hosei University, Japan
Gregorio Martinez	University of Murcia, Spain
Peter Mueller	IBM Zurich Research Laboratory, Switzerland
Kouichi Sakurai	Kyushu University, Japan
Sabu M. Thampi	Kerala University, India
Carlos Becker Westphall	Federal University of Santa Catarina, Brazil
Jie Wu	Temple University, USA
Yang Xu	Hunan University, China
Zheng Yan	Aalto University, Finland
Wenyin Yang	Foshan University, China
Haojin Zhu	Shanghai Jiao Tong University, China

Program Committee

Track 1: Cyberspace Security

Mohiuddin Ahmed	Edith Cowan University, Australia
Ali Ismail Awad	United Arab Emirates University, United Arab Emirates
Eduard Babulak	National Science Foundation, USA
Sudip Chakraborty	Valdosta State University, USA
Edwin Dauber	Widener University, USA
Luca Davoli	University of Parma, Italy
Elke Franz	Technische Universität Dresden, Germany
Jeff Garae	CERT Vanuatu, Vanuatu
Gerhard Hancke	City University of Hong Kong, China
Michael Heinzl	Independent Security Researcher, Austria
Heemeng Ho	Singapore Institute of Technology, Singapore
Mike Johnstone	Edith Cowan University, Australia
Sokratis Katsikas	Norwegian University of Science and Technology, Norway
Mahmoud Khasawneh	Al Ain University, United Arab Emirates
Vimal Kumar	University of Waikato, New Zealand
Nuno Laranjeiro	University of Coimbra, Portugal
Jiguo Li	Fujian Normal University, China
Linsen Li	Shanghai Jiao Tong University, China
Xin Liao	Hunan University, China
Yuhong Liu	Santa Clara University, USA
García Villalba Luis Javier	Universidad Complutense Madrid, Spain
Spiros Mancoridis	Drexel University, USA
Hafizah Mansor	International Islamic University Malaysia, Malaysia
Chengying Mao	Jiangxi University of Finance and Economics, China
Weizhi Meng	Technical University of Denmark, Denmark
Aleksandra Mileva	Goce Delčev University, North Macedonia
David Naccache	ENS, France
Josef Pieprzyk	CSIRO/Data61, Australia
Nikolaos Pitropakis	Edinburgh Napier University, UK
Vincenzo Piuri	University of Milan, Italy
Emil Pricop	Petroleum-Gas University of Ploiești, Romania
Vinayakumar Ravi	Prince Mohammad Bin Fahd University, Saudi Arabia
Joshua Scarsbrook	University of Queensland, Australia

Dario Stabili	University of Bologna, Italy
Hung-Min Sun	National Tsing Hua University, Taiwan
Lei Wang	Nanjing Forestry University, China
Yehua Wei	Hunan Normal University, China
Longfei Wu	Fayetteville State University, USA
Anjia Yang	Jinan University, China
Chong Yu	University of Nebraska–Lincoln, USA
Nicola Zannone	Eindhoven University of Technology, The Netherlands
Mengyuan Zhang	Hong Kong Polytechnic University, China
Yi Zhang	Sichuan University, China
Yuan Zhang	University of Electronic Science and Technology of China, China
Yongbin Zhou	Nanjing University of Science and Technology, China

Track 2: Cyberspace Privacy

Ralph Deters	University of Saskatchewan, Canada
Yucong Duan	Hainan University, China
James Dyer	University of Huddersfield, UK
Ramadan Elaiess	University of Benghazi, Libya
Kamrul Hasan	Tennessee State University, USA
Hai Jiang	Arkansas State University, USA
Ashad Kabir	Charles Sturt University, Australia
Constantinos Kolias	University of Idaho, USA
Ruixuan Li	Huazhong University of Science and Technology, China
Xin Li	Nanjing University of Aeronautics and Astronautics, China
Changqing Luo	Virginia Commonwealth University, USA
Yuxiang Ma	Henan University, China
Anand Nayyar	Duy Tan University, Vietnam
Simon Parkinson	University of Huddersfield, UK
Jaydip Sen	Praxis Business School, India
Zhiyuan Tan	Napier University, UK
Muhmamad Imran Tariq	Superior University, Pakistan
Xiuhua Wang	Huazhong University of Science and Technology, China
Lei Xu	Kent State University, USA
Ji Zhang	University of Southern Queensland, Australia
Youwen Zhu	Nanjing University of Aeronautics and Astronautics, China

Track 3: Cyberspace Anonymity

Selcuk Baktir	American University of the Middle East, Kuwait
Ivan Cvitic	University of Zagreb, Croatia
Ke Gu	Changsha University of Science and Technology, China
Hasan Jamil	University of Idaho, USA
Aleksandar Jevremovic	Singidunum University, Serbia
Marko Krstic	Regulatory Agency for Electronic Communication and Postal Services, Serbia
Klimis Ntalianis	University of West Attica, Greece
Hao Peng	Zhejiang Normal University, China
Dapeng Qu	Liaoning University, China
Rakesh Shrestha	Yonsei University, South Korea
Ioan Ungurean	Ştefan cel Mare University, Romania
Hongzhi Wang	Harbin Institute of Technology, China
Sherali Zeadally	University of Kentucky, USA

Contents

Cyberspace Privacy

Cyberspace Anonymity

Cyberspace Security

Bilateral Personalized Information Fusion in Mobile Crowdsensing

Zheqi Feng, Tao Peng$^{(\boxtimes)}$, Guojun Wang , and Kejian Guan

Shool of Computer Science and Cyber Engineering, Guangzhou University,
Guangzhou 510006, China
pengtao@gzhu.edu.cn

Abstract. In mobile crowdsensing, information fusion is an important process to achieve data aggregation results. In recent years, people have paid more and more attention to satisfying the personalized requirements of users in information fusion. Bilateral users at both ends of the crowdsensing server have different personalized requirements due to their different roles in crowdsensing. However, existing personalized mechanisms often only focus on satisfying the requirements of data contributors, often ignoring the potential personalized requirements of data consumers. Furthermore, to the best of our knowledge, there is no previous research on how to provide personalized data aggregation results for data consumers with different data quality requirements. To address these challenges, this paper proposes a novel bilateral personalized information fusion mechanism, called BPIF, to provide personalized data aggregation results for data consumers with different data quality requirements while ensuring privacy protection for data contributors. In our approach, we design a bilateral personalized information fusion scheme based on the personalized sampling mechanism in mobile crowdsensing. We obtain the final data set through double rounds of sampling. After aggregating the final data set, we use the differential privacy mechanism to perturb the aggregation results to protect the privacy information of data contributors. To verify the feasibility and effectiveness of BPIF, we conduct experiments on virtual and real-world datasets, demonstrating its potential advantages in mobile crowdsensing environments.

Keywords: Crowdsensing · Information Fusion · Privacy-Preserving · Bilateral Personalization · NSGA-II

1 Introduction

In recent years, advances in sensor technology for mobile devices have led to the integration of various sensors into mobile smart systems. This convergence has paved the way for the flourishing development of Internet of Things (IoT) technologies. And mobile crowdsensing (MCS) is becoming a key contributor to IoT advancements. MCS involves collecting sensing data and performing complex sensing tasks using smart devices carried by individuals scattered across different locations. MCS is widely applied in environmental monitoring, intelligent

G. Wang et al. (Eds.): UbiSec 2023, CCIS 2034, pp. 3–16, 2024.
https://doi.org/10.1007/978-981-97-1274-8_1

transportation, medical health, and other fields. However, in MCS, the collected sensing data often suffer from incomplete and imprecise problems. Therefore, deriving desired target outcomes from these raw and fragmented data presents considerable challenges.

The two types of participants participating in MCS at both ends of the server are called bilateral users, that is, data contributors and data consumers. The MCS platform assigns tasks to data contributors according to task requirements and uploads the data to the platform after the tasks are completed. Data consumers submit usage requirements to the platform and obtain relevant fusion results after data aggregation from the platform. Different participants in MCS have different personalized requirements. This article mainly focuses on the personalized requirements of both users. Most of the existing research mainly focuses on meeting the personalized requirements of data contributors and it becomes crucial to develop a new information fusion mechanism to meet the personalized requirements of bilateral users in MSC.

The main goal of this paper is to achieve accurate and efficient information fusion of MCS data while meeting the personalized requirements of both data contributors and data consumers in the MCS. To achieve this goal, we propose a novel MCS bilateral personalized information fusion mechanism based on a sampling method. Our mechanism meets the personalized requirements of bilateral users by adopting a bilateral personalized sampling mechanism to sample data for which privacy budget and data quality meet the standards. While achieving the above goals, we use the multi-objective optimization algorithm NSGA-II [1] to improve the utility of the final results.

Our main contributions are as follows:

· We propose a bilateral personalized information fusion (BPIF) mechanism to achieve accurate bilateral personalized information fusion. To the best of our knowledge, this is the first work that considers the personalized requirements of bilateral users in the process of MCS information fusion.
· We use a double sampling mechanism to meet the privacy protection requirements of each data contributor for each piece of data and provide data consumers with corresponding and accurate data fusion results, and use a multi-objective optimization algorithm to calculate optimal sampling parameters to improve the utility of the final aggregate calculation result.
· We demonstrate the privacy of our proposed two-round sampling values through rigorous theoretical analysis. Extensive experiments on virtual and real-world datasets demonstrate the practicality and potential scalability of the proposed mechanism.

2   Related Works

BPIF aims to meet the personalized requirements of bilateral users in the process of MCS, while protecting the privacy of users. In this section, we briefly present the existing work on privacy protection and the research about data quality and personalization in MCS, respectively.

Privacy Protection. Wang et al. [2] designed novel privacy-preserving incentive mechanisms to protect users' true bid information against the honest-but-curious platform while minimizing the social cost of winner selection. Zhao et al. [3] proposed a bilateral privacy-preserving Task Assignment mechanism for MCS (iTAM), which protects not only the task participants' privacy but also the task requesters' privacy and can minimize the travel distance. Peng et al. [4] proposed a spatiotemporal-aware privacy-preserving task matching scheme, achieving efficient and fine-grained matching while protecting privacy between users and task publishers. Liu et al. [5] designed SlimBox, which rapidly screened out potentially malicious packets in constant time while incurring only moderate communication overhead to protect privacy in redirecting enterprise traffic to remote middleboxes. Cheng et al. [6] proposed a lightweight privacy preservation scheme with efficient reputation management (PPRM) for MCS in vehicular networks. Li et al. [7] proposed a utility-assured location obfuscation mechanism operated in a hexagonal grid system, which the participants can follow to locally perturb their locations with personalized privacy demands. Li et al. [8] proposed a novel stealth strategy, i.e., disguising the malicious behavior as privacy behavior, to avoid being detected by truth discovery methods. An et al. [9] integrated the blockchain into the MCS scenario to design a blockchain-based privacy-preserving quality control mechanism, which prevented data from being tampered with and denied, ensuring that the reward is distributed fairly. Peng et al. [10] proposed a privacy-oriented precise friend matching (P3M) scheme, and the querier can flexibly set the matching range of feature attributes and distances according to their own needs.

Personalization in MCS. Wu et al. [11] proposed a personalized task recommender system for mobile crowdsensing, which recommends tasks to users based on a recommendation score that jointly takes each user's preference and reliability into consideration. Sun et al. [12] proposed a contract-based personalized privacy-preserving incentive mechanism for truth discovery in MCS systems, named Paris-TD, which provided personalized payments for workers as compensation for privacy costs while achieving accurate truth discovery. Wang et al. [13] proposed a novel personalized task-oriented worker recruitment mechanism for mobile crowdsensing systems based on a careful characterization of workers' preferences. Xiong et al. [14] proposed a personalized privacy protection (PERIO) framework based on game theory and data encryption.

Data Quality in MCS. Zhao et al. [15] developed a mechanism to guarantee and enhance the quality of crowdsensing data without jeopardizing the privacy of MCS participants, bringing together game theory, algorithmic mechanism design, and truth discovery. Bhattacharjee et al. [16] exploited a rating feedback mechanism for evaluating an event-specific expected truthfulness, which is then transformed into a robust quality of information (QoI) metric to weaken various effects of selfish and malicious user behaviors.

In a word, none of the existing methods take into account the personalized requirements of bilateral users at the same time. This paper is dedicated to meeting the personalized requirements of bilateral users through sampling mechanism and using differential privacy mechanism to protect user privacy.

3   Preliminaries

In this section, we introduce some preliminary knowledge of Differential Privacy and Personalized Differential Privacy, which is involved in this paper.

3.1   Differential Privacy

Differential privacy [17] protects the private information of individual records in a dataset by adding random noise to the query results of the dataset. We use $DP_\epsilon^f(D)$ to denote the differential privacy mechanism with f as the aggregation function, D as the dataset, and ϵ as the privacy budget parameter.

Definition 1 ($\epsilon - Differential$ $Privacy$ [17,18]): A privacy mechanism M gives ϵ-differential privacy if for all data sets D and D' differing on at most one element and all $S \subseteq Range(M)$,

$$Pr[M(D) \in S] \le e^\epsilon Pr[M(D') \in S]$$

3.2   Personalized Differential Privacy

Personalized differential privacy (PDP) allows each user to independently allocate a privacy budget for their own data. The specific way to realize PDP is to design a sampling threshold according to the overall privacy budget of the data set, and according to the privacy budget corresponding to each data in the data set, the sampling probability of the data is calculated with the sampling threshold, and the whole data set is sampled. We give the specific definition of personalized differential privacy as follows:

Definition 2 ($Personalized$ $Differential$ $Privacy$ [19]): For a data set D from universe $\mathcal{D}$ with a user dataset $U = \{u_1, .., u_N\}$ from universe $\mathcal{U}$ and a personalized privacy budget dataset of each user's privacy budget $D_\epsilon = \{\epsilon_1, ..., \epsilon_N\}$ from universe $\mathcal{D}_\epsilon$, a randomized mechanism $M : \mathcal{D} \to \mathcal{R}^d$ satisfies $D_\epsilon - PDP$ if for every pair of neighboring datasets $D, D' \subseteq D$ which differ in one arbitrary data of user u_i with privacy budget ϵ_i and for all sets $O \subseteq R$ of possible outputs,

$$Pr[M(D) \in O] \le e_i^\epsilon Pr[M(D') \in O]$$

4   Problem Definition

Figure 1 shows the structure of the BPIF system model. There are three main entities in the system: data contributors, MCS platform servers, and data consumers. First, the MCS platform server issues tasks to eligible data contributors, instructing them to use mobile sensing devices to collect specified information.

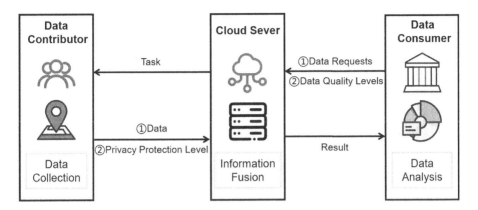

Fig. 1. System model of BPIF.

Then, the data contributors collect the data and upload the data to the MCS platform server. At the same time, the data contributor sets the privacy protection level for each piece of data, indicating the data contributor's privacy protection requirements for the piece of data, and the server allocates a privacy budget for the piece of data accordingly. MCS platform servers submit rewards to data contributors based on data quality or other criteria. Every time a data consumer submits a usage requirement to the MCS platform server, it will also send its own personalized data quality requirements to the MCS platform server according to its own budget, which is expressed in the form of data quality levels. The MCS platform server performs personalized privacy sampling according to the privacy budget allocated to each piece of data and performs personalized data quality sampling according to the personalized data quality requirements of data consumers. The obtained result is sent to data consumers after perturbation. The platform charges data consumers accordingly based on the data contained in the data subsets that are finally aggregated.

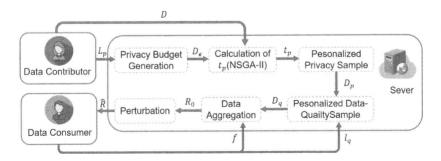

Fig. 2. Framework of the bilateral personalized information fusion mechanism.

5   Bilateral Personalized Information Fusion Mechanism

5.1   Overview of BPIF

Our proposed mechanism, Bilateral Personalized Information Fusion (BPIF), is built on top of a MCS system. BPIF aims to provide data consumers with personalized information aggregation results while ensuring the privacy protection of data contributors' personal privacy requirements. Figure 2 illustrates the comprehensive framework of our proposed BPIF mechanism. In this section, we detail the main steps in it.

5.2   Parameter Computation

According to PDP, we select a sampling threshold $t_p \in [\epsilon_m, \epsilon_h]$ to conduct double sampling mechanism. For any t_p, PDP can meet the personalized privacy requirements of all data contributors. However, t_p has a huge impact on the utility of the final aggregation, and the accuracy of the aggregation results corresponding to different t_p is completely different. In addition, in BPIF, the personalized requirements of data consumers for data quality are also one of the goals we focus on. The most fundamental reason why data consumers have personalized requirements for data quality is their limited budget. How to provide data consumers with as accurate data fusion results as possible while reducing the cost of data fusion is a problem we need to solve. Based on the above reasons, we use a multi-objective optimization algorithm to perform multi-objective optimization on the accuracy of aggregation results and the cost of data fusion.

Our first optimization goal is the accuracy of the aggregation results. We use root mean square error (RMSE) as a criterion for the accuracy of the final result. In this system, we compute RMSE using the unperturbed aggregates of the original dataset as predictors and the perturbed aggregates of the sampled datasets as observations. The specific calculation formula is as follows

$$RMSE = \sqrt{\frac{\sum_{i=1}^{n}(\hat{R} - R)^2}{n}}$$

where n denotes the number of repetitions.

Further, we measure the accuracy of the results with the following formula

$$A = \frac{1}{1 + RMSE}$$

Our first optimization objective is as follows:

$$\begin{aligned}
max \quad & A = \frac{1}{1 + RMSE} \\
s.t. \quad & t_p \in [\epsilon_m, \epsilon_h] \\
& t_q \in Q
\end{aligned} \quad (1)$$

Another optimization goal we have is the price of data fusion. BPIF samples the original dataset twice to satisfy the personalized requirements of bilateral users. After double sampling, we obtain a data subset of the original dataset for the actual aggregation computation. The specific calculation formula of price is as follows:

$$p(D) = \sum_{i=1}^{n} q_i * p_0$$

where q_i is the data quality corresponding to the data d_i, and p_0 is the price corresponding to the unit data quality. And we use $p(D)$ to denote the price of the aggregated result aggregated using the original data set D. Therefore, our other optimization objective is as follows:

$$max \quad P = \frac{p(D_q)}{p(D)}$$
$$s.t. \quad t_p \in [\epsilon_m, \epsilon_h] \tag{2}$$
$$t_q \in Q$$

For ease of calculation, we normalize the optimization objective of price P.

We take the sampling threshold t_p of personalized privacy sampling as the decision variable and use the NSGA-II algorithm to solve this multi-objective optimization problem to find the optimal sampling scheme.

5.3 Personalized Privacy Sample

For this step, we adopt the concepts and methods of the PDP. Through the parameter calculation in the previous step, we obtained the optimal sampling threshold t_p to perform personalized privacy sampling on the MCS dataset provided by data contributors. According to PDP, we use $S_p(D, D_\epsilon, t_p) = D_p$ to denote the process of sampling each data independently with probability:

$$\pi = \begin{cases} \frac{e^{\epsilon_i}-1}{e^{t_p}-1} & if \quad \epsilon_i < t_p \\ 1 & otherwise \end{cases}$$

where ϵ_i denotes the personalized privacy budget of user $u_i's$ data. [19] has proved that $DP_{t_p}^f(D_p)$ satisfies $D_\epsilon - PDP$. After the step of personalized privacy sampling, we get a subset $D_p = \{d_a, ..., d_b\}(a \geq 1, b \leq M)$ of the sensing data set D.

5.4 Personalized Data-Quality Sample

In practical MCS scenarios, the quality of task-specific MCS data is usually varied. In our study, we sample the data subset D_p obtained through personalized privacy sampling according to the usage requirements of data consumers and the data quality of each MCS data item. In this way, we use a part of the data for aggregation calculations. In this step, we use $S_q(D_p, Q, t_q)$ to denote the procedure that independently samples each data $d_j \in D_p$ with probability

$$\pi_{d_j}^q = \begin{cases} \frac{e^{t_q}-1}{e^{q_j}-1} & if \quad q_j > t_q \\ 1 & otherwise \end{cases}$$

After the step of personalized data quality sampling, we get the final sensing data subset $D_q = \{d_u, ..., d_v\}(u' \geq a, v \leq b)$ used for aggregation calculation.

5.5   Aggregation and Perturbation

Once the data consumers upload their usage requirements to the server, the server selects the appropriate aggregation function f to aggregate the data subset D_q. Specifically, we employ a personalized differential privacy mechanism, using the threshold t_p in personalized privacy sampling as the privacy budget parameter. This ensures that the personalized privacy requirements of all data contributors are met during the perturbation process.

Example: When we use the Laplace mechanism to perturb the aggregated results, the perturbation mechanism is as follows:

$$M : M(D_2) = f(D_2) + n$$

where $n \sim Laplace(0, \frac{\Delta f}{t_p})$.

We theoretically prove that BPIF can satisfy personalized differential privacy and give a detailed proof in the appendix.

6   Experiment

In this section, we verify the effectiveness of BPIF from an experimental perspective.

1) **Datasets:** We evaluate BPIF on real-world datasets. We apply the mean to a real-world MCS dataset: the weather dataset [23]. For the linear regression task, we only use a real-world dataset: the Stock dataset [24].

2) **Parameters Setting:** We specify that the privacy budget of users with high privacy level is ϵ_h, the privacy budget range of users with medium privacy level is $[\epsilon_h, \epsilon_m]$, and the privacy budget range of users with low privacy level is $[\epsilon_m, \epsilon_l]$. We use p_h, p_m, and p_l to represent the proportion of data contributors at different,privacy levels. $p_h + p_m + p_l = 1$. We set the default value of p_h to 0.54 and the default value of p_m to 0.37. The default values for p_h, p_m, and p_l were chosen based on findings in [25] about user privacy concerns. We take the default value of μ as 500 and the default value of σ as 150. We use $\hat{R}_l$ to represent the RMSE when $t_q = low$, We use $\hat{R}_m$ to represent the RMSE when $t_q = media$ and We use $\hat{R}_h$ to represent the RMSE when $t_q = high$. In our experiments, the number of experimental repetitions n = 1000.

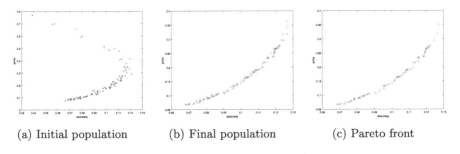

(a) Initial population   (b) Final population   (c) Pareto front

Fig. 3. NSGI-II results

6.1 Parameter Computation

Before officially starting the aggregation calculation, we first use the NSGA-II algorithm to find the optimal sampling threshold parameter t_p. In our experiments, we take a population size of 100 and an iteration number of 200. The value range of the decision variable t_p is $[0.01, 1]$. The distribution of function values of the initial population is shown in Fig. 3(a). In Fig. 3, the horizontal axis is the optimization goal accuracy, and the vertical axis is the optimization goal price. After 200 iterations using the NSGA-II algorithm, the distribution of the function value of the final population is shown in Fig. 3(b). It can be seen that compared with the initial population, the distribution of the final population is more concentrated, and most of the individuals belong to the Pareto set. Screen out non-Pareto optimal solutions from the final population, and we can get the Pareto set shown in Fig. 3(c). We select suitable individuals from this solution set as the sampling threshold parameters for our subsequent experiments.

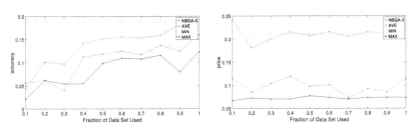

(a) Effect of Number of Users on Accuracy (b) Effect of Number of Users on Accuracy

Fig. 4. Comparison with baseline

Obtained from NSGA-II is an optimal set of t_p, and we select the appropriate t_p from it according to the actual situation. In our experiments, we select the t_p corresponding to individuals with moderate accuracy and price and compare it with the baseline. There are three baselines in our experiments: the BPIF with $t_p = min(D_\epsilon) = \epsilon_{m}in$ (denoted as Minmum), the BPIF with $t_p = max(D_\epsilon) =$

$\epsilon_m ax$ (denoted as Maxmum) and the BPIF with $t_p = \frac{1}{M}\sum_M(D_\epsilon)$(denoted as Average). The result calculated using the t_p from NSGA-II is denoted as NSGA-II. We can see that although the accuracy of NSGA-II is slightly less than MIN and AVE, its price is much less than MIN and AVE. Correspondingly, although its accuracy is higher than MAX, its price is also higher than MAX, as shown in Fig. 4. The optimal solution in the Pareto set has the solution corresponding to high accuracy and the solution corresponding to high price. We can choose the appropriate solution from the Pareto set according to the actual situation.

6.2   BPIF for Mean

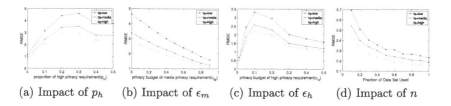

(a) Impact of p_h (b) Impact of ϵ_m (c) Impact of ϵ_h (d) Impact of n

Fig. 5. RMSE for mean task on real-world data, as four parameters varied.

On the mean task, we explored in four directions: 1. The influence of dataset distribution on the performance of BPIF; 2. The influence of the proportion ph of the user group with high privacy protection level to the total group on the performance of BPIF; 3. The influence of the privacy budget lower bound ϵ_h on the performance of BPIF; 4. The influence of the privacy budget lower bound ϵ_m corresponding to users with medium privacy protection level on the performance of BPIF. For the mean task on the real-world data set, all four parameters show a huge impact on the accuracy of BPIF, as shown in Fig. 5. These experimental results can help us understand the performance of the BPIF mechanism in different data environments. In all the experiments conducted on the mean task, BPIF has shown good data quality grading capabilities, which is in line with our design concept for BPIF.

6.3   BPIF for Linear Regression

In the linear regression task, our task is to model the Market Cap attribute based on the other attributes. Figure 6(a) shows that the increase in users with high privacy protection levels reduces the accuracy of BPIF. This is because the more users with high privacy protection level, the less data be extracted during the sampling process. And the accuracy of the final aggregation result also decreases. Figure 6(b) and Fig. 6(c) show that increasing the privacy budget lower bound improve the accuracy of BPIF. From Fig. 6(d), it can be seen that the larger the amount of data in the original data set, the less accurate the result

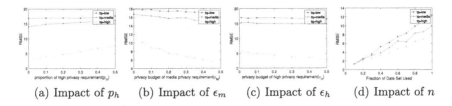

(a) Impact of p_h (b) Impact of ϵ_m (c) Impact of ϵ_h (d) Impact of n

Fig. 6. RMSE for linear regression task on real-world data, as four parameters varied.

of data fusion, which is counterintuitive to us. How the size of the original data set affects the results of BPIF deserves further study. In addition, it can be seen from the experimental results that the accuracy of the high data-quality level in the linear regression task is much better than that in the previous experiments.

7   Conclusion

In this paper, we propose a bilateral personalized information fusion mechanism BPIF for MCS. On the premise of ensuring the accuracy of information fusion results, it can meet the personalized privacy requirements of data contributors and meet the personalized requirements of data consumers for data quality. We theoretically prove that BPIF can satisfy personalized differential privacy and verify the performance of BPIF on multiple data aggregation tasks on real-world and synthetic data sets. Experiments show that BPIF can provide data consumers with information fusion results of different data quality levels on the basis of ensuring the utility of sensing data.

Acknowledgments. This work was supported by the Graduate Student Innovation Ability Training Grant of Guangzhou University (2022GDJC-M48), and in part by the Project of Guangdong Science and Technology Department (2023A1515012358).

Appendix

Theorem 1: The BIFP satisfies $D_\epsilon - PDP$.

Proof: What we want to prove is:

$$Pr[M(D) \in O] \leq e_i^\epsilon Pr[M(D') \in O] \tag{3}$$

In BPIF, we have

$$M(D) = DP_{t_p}^f(D_q)) = DP_{t_p}^f(S_q(S_p(D, D_\epsilon, t_p), Q, t_q))$$

The Eq. (3) can write as:

$$Pr[DP_{t_p}^f(S_p(D, D_\epsilon, t_p)) \in O] \leq e_i^\epsilon Pr[DP_{t_p}^f(S_p(D', D_\epsilon, t_p)) \in O]$$

In BPIF, we need to prove that

$$Pr[DP^f_{t_p}(S_q(S_p(D, D_\epsilon, t_p), Q, t_q)) \in O]$$
$$\leq e^\epsilon_i Pr[DP^f_{t_p}(S_q(S_p(D', D_\epsilon, t_p), Q, t_q)) \in O] \tag{4}$$

And we have

$$Pr[DP^f_{t_p}(S_q(S_p(D, D_\epsilon, t_p), Q, t_q)) \in O]$$
$$= \sum_{z \subseteq D_{-d_i}} (\pi^p_{d_i} \pi^q_{d_i} Pr[S_q(S_p(D_{-d_i}, D_\epsilon, t_p), Q, t_q) = Z] Pr[DP^f_{t_p}(Z_{+d_i}) \in O])$$
$$+ \sum_{Z \subseteq D_{-d_i}} ((1 - \pi^p_{d_i} \pi^q_{d_i}) Pr[S_q(S_p(D_{-d_i}, D_\epsilon, t_p), Q, t_q) = Z] Pr[DP^f_{t_p}(Z) \in O])$$
$$\leq (1 - \pi^p_{d_i} \pi^q_{d_i} + \pi^p_{d_i} \pi^q_{d_i} e^{t_p}) Pr[DP^f_{t_p}(S_q(S_p(D_{-d_i}, D_\epsilon, t_p), Q, t_q)) \in O] \tag{5}$$

For brevity, we have

$$f(\pi) = (1 - \pi + \pi e^{t_p})$$

where $\pi \in (0, 1]$. We can know that $f(\pi)$ is monotonically increasing with respect to π and when $\pi = 1$. Thus we have $f(\pi) = (1 - \pi + \pi e^{t_p}) \leq f(1) = e^{t_p}$. According to $S_p(D, D_\epsilon, t_p)$, when $\epsilon_i \geq t_p$, d_i is selected with probability $\pi^p_{d_i} = 1$, thus we have

$$Pr[DP^f_{t_p}(S_q(S_p(D, D_\epsilon, t_p), Q, t_q)) \in O] =$$
$$\leq (1 - \pi^p_{d_i} \pi^q_{d_i} + \pi^p_{d_i} \pi^q_{d_i} e^{t_p}) Pr[DP^f_{t_p}(S_q(S_p(D_{-d_i}, D_\epsilon, t_p), Q, t_q)) \in O]$$
$$= (1 - \pi^q_{d_i} + \pi^q_{d_i} e^{t_p}) Pr[DP^f_{t_p}(S_q(S_p(D_{-d_i}, D_\epsilon, t_p), Q, t_q)) \in O]$$
$$= f(\pi^q_{d_i}) Pr[DP^f_{t_p}(S_q(S_p(D_{-d_i}, D_\epsilon, t_p), Q, t_q)) \in O] \tag{6}$$
$$\leq e^{t_p} Pr[DP^f_{t_p}(S_q(S_p(D_{-d_i}, D_\epsilon, t_p), Q, t_q)) \in O]$$
$$\leq e^{\epsilon_i} Pr[DP^f_{t_p}(S_q(S_p(D_{-d_i}, D_\epsilon, t_p), Q, t_q)) \in O]$$

as desired. And when $\epsilon_i \leq t_p$, d_i, we have

$$Pr[DP^f_{t_p}(S_q(S_p(D, D_\epsilon, t_p), Q, t_q)) \in O] =$$
$$\leq (1 - \pi^p_{d_i} \pi^q_{d_i} + \pi^p_{d_i} \pi^q_{d_i} e^{t_p}) Pr[DP^f_{t_p}(S_q(S_p(D_{-d_i}, D_\epsilon, t_p), Q, t_q)) \in O]$$
$$= f(\pi^q_{d_i}) Pr[DP^f_{t_p}(S_q(S_p(D_{-d_i}, D_\epsilon, t_p), Q, t_q)) \in O] \tag{7}$$
$$\leq e^{t_p} Pr[DP^f_{t_p}(S_q(S_p(D_{-d_i}, D_\epsilon, t_p), Q, t_q)) \in O]$$
$$\leq e^{\epsilon_i} Pr[DP^f_{t_p}(S_q(S_p(D_{-d_i}, D_\epsilon, t_p), Q, t_q)) \in O]$$

Thus Eq. (4) is proved and BPIF satisfies $D_\epsilon - PDP$.

References

1. Deb, K., Pratap, A., Agarwal, S., Meyarivan, T.: A fast and elitist multiobjective genetic algorithm: NSGA-II. IEEE Trans. Evol. Comput. **6**(2), 182–197 (2002). https://doi.org/10.1109/4235.996017
2. Wang, Z., et al.: Towards privacy-driven truthful incentives for mobile crowdsensing under untrusted platform. IEEE Trans. Mob. Comput. **22**(2), 1198–1212 (2023). https://doi.org/10.1109/TMC.2021.3093552
3. Zhao, B., Tang, S., Liu, X., Zhang, X., Chen, W.-N.: iTAM: bilateral privacy-preserving task assignment for mobile crowdsensing. IEEE Trans. Mob. Comput. **20**(12), 3351–3366 (2021). https://doi.org/10.1109/TMC.2020.2999923
4. Peng, T., Zhong, W., Wang, G., Zhang, S., Luo, E., Wang, T.: Spatiotemporal-aware privacy-preserving task matching in mobile crowdsensing. IEEE Internet Things J. (2023) https://doi.org/10.1109/JIOT.2023.3292284
5. Liu, Q., et al.: SlimBox: lightweight packet inspection over encrypted traffic. IEEE Trans. Dependable Secure Comput. (2022). https://doi.org/10.1109/TDSC.2022.3222533
6. Cheng, Y., Ma, J., Liu, Z., Wu, Y., Wei, K., Dong, C.: A lightweight privacy preservation scheme with efficient reputation management for mobile crowdsensing in vehicular networks. IEEE Trans. Dependable Secure Comput. **20**(3), 1771–1788 (2023). https://doi.org/10.1109/TDSC.2022.3163752
7. Li, L., et al.: Privacy preserving participant recruitment for coverage maximization in location aware mobile crowdsensing. IEEE Trans. Mob. Comput. **21**(9), 3250–3262 (2022). https://doi.org/10.1109/TMC.2021.3050147
8. Li, Z., Zheng, Z., Guo, S., Guo, B., Xiao, F., Ren, K.: Disguised as privacy: data poisoning attacks against differentially private crowdsensing systems. IEEE Trans. Mob. Comput. (2022). https://doi.org/10.1109/TMC.2022.3173642
9. An, J., Wang, Z., He, X., Gui, X., Cheng, J., Gui, R.: PPQC: a blockchain-based privacy-preserving quality control mechanism in crowdsensing applications. IEEE/ACM Trans. Netw. **30**(3), 1352–1367 (2022). https://doi.org/10.1109/TNET.2022.3141582
10. Peng, T., Zhong, W., Wang, G., et al.: Privacy-preserving precise profile matching in mobile social network. J. Commun. **43**(11), 90–103 (2022). https://doi.org/10.11959/j.issn.1000-436x.2022208
11. Wu, F., Yang, S., Zheng, Z., Tang, S., Chen, G.: Fine-grained user profiling for personalized task matching in mobile crowdsensing. IEEE Trans. Mob. Comput. **20**(10), 2961–2976 (2021). https://doi.org/10.1109/TMC.2020.2993963
12. Sun, P., et al.: Towards personalized privacy-preserving incentive for truth discovery in mobile crowdsensing systems. IEEE Trans. Mob. Comput. **21**(1), 352–365 (2022). https://doi.org/10.1109/TMC.2020.3003673
13. Wang, Z., et al.: Towards personalized task-oriented worker recruitment in mobile crowdsensing. IEEE Trans. Mob. Comput. **20**(5), 2080–2093 (2021). https://doi.org/10.1109/TMC.2020.2973990
14. Xiong, J., et al.: A personalized privacy protection framework for mobile crowdsensing in IIoT. IEEE Trans. Industr. Inf. **16**(6), 4231–4241 (2020). https://doi.org/10.1109/TII.2019.2948068
15. Zhao, C., Yang, S., McCann, J.A.: On the data quality in privacy-preserving mobile crowdsensing systems with untruthful reporting. IEEE Trans. Mob. Comput. **20**(2), 647–661 (2021). https://doi.org/10.1109/TMC.2019.2943468

16. Bhattacharjee, S., Ghosh, N., Shah, V.K., Das, S.K.: $QnQQnQ$: quality and quantity based unified approach for secure and trustworthy mobile crowdsensing. IEEE Trans. Mob. Comput. **19**(1), 200–216 (2020). https://doi.org/10.1109/TMC.2018.2889458

17. Dwork, C.: Differential privacy. In: Bugliesi, M., Preneel, B., Sassone, V., Wegener, I. (eds.) ICALP 2006. LNCS, vol. 4052, pp. 1–12. Springer, Heidelberg (2006). https://doi.org/10.1007/11787006_1

18. Dwork, C., McSherry, F., Nissim, K., Smith, A.: Calibrating noise to sensitivity in private data analysis. In: Halevi, S., Rabin, T. (eds.) TCC 2006. LNCS, vol. 3876, pp. 265–284. Springer, Heidelberg (2006). https://doi.org/10.1007/11681878_14

19. Jorgensen, Z., Yu, T., Cormode, G.: Conservative or liberal? Personalized differential privacy. In: IEEE ICDE (2015)

20. Li, Y., et al.: Conflicts to harmony: a framework for resolving conflicts in heterogeneous data by truth discovery. IEEE Trans. Knowl. Data Eng. **28**(8), 1986–1999 (2016)

21. Guo, B., Chen, H., Han, Q., Yu, Z., Zhang, D., Wang, Y.: Worker-contributed data utility measurement for visual crowdsensing systems. IEEE Trans. Mob. Comput. **16**(8), 2379–2391 (2017). https://doi.org/10.1109/TMC.2016.262098

22. Wang, H., Uddin, M., Qi, G.-J. , Huang, T., Abdelzaher, T., Cao, G.: PhotoNet: a similarity-aware image delivery service for situation awareness. In: Proceedings of the 10th ACM/IEEE International Conference on Information Processing in Sensor Networks, pp. 135–136 (2011)

23. Dong, L., Berti-Equille, L.: Weather (2010). http://lunadong.com/fusionDataSets.htm

24. Li, X., Dong, L.: Stock (2013). http://lunadong.com/fusionDataSets.htm

25. Acquisti, A., Grossklags, J.: Privacy and rationality in individual decision making. IEEE Secur. Priv. **2**, 24–30 (2005)

BiBERT-AV: Enhancing Authorship Verification Through Siamese Networks with Pre-trained BERT and Bi-LSTM

Amirah Almutairi[1,2]([⊠]) , BooJoong Kang[2] , and Nawfal Al Hashimy[2]

[1] Department of Computer Science, Shaqra University, Shaqra 11961, Saudi Arabia
`amirah@su.edu.sa`
[2] School of Electronics and Computer Science, University of Southampton, Southampton, England, UK
`{a.almutairi,b.kang,Nawfal}@soton.ac.uk`

Abstract. Authorship verification is a challenging problem in natural language processing. It is crucial in security and forensics, helping identify authors and combat fake news. Recent advancements in neural network models have shown promising results in improving the accuracy of authorship verification. This paper presents a novel model for authorship verification using Siamese networks and evaluates the advantages of transformer-based models over existing methods that rely on domain knowledge and feature engineering. This paper's objective is to address the authorship verification problem in NLP which entails determining whether two texts were written by the same author by introducing a novel approach that employs Siamese networks with pre-trained BERT and Bi-LSTM layers. The proposed model BiBERT-AV aims to compare the performance of this Siamese network using pre-trained BERT and Bi-LSTM layers against existing methods for authorship verification. The results of this study demonstrate that the proposed Siamese network model BiBERT-AV offers an effective solution for authorship verification that is based solely on the writing style of the author, which outperformed the baselines and state-of-the-art methods. Additionally, our model offers a viable alternative to existing methods that heavily rely on domain knowledge and laborious feature engineering, which often demand significant time and expertise. Notably, the BiBERT-AV model consistently achieves a notable level of accuracy, even when the number of authors is expanded to a larger group. This achievement underscores a notable contrast to the limitations exhibited by the baseline model used in exacting research studies. Overall, this study provides valuable insights into the application of Siamese networks with pre-trained BERT and Bi-LSTM layers for authorship verification and establishes the superiority of the proposed models over existing methods in this domain. The study contributes to the advancement of NLP research and has implications for several real-world applications.

Keywords: Authorship verification · Forensics · Security · Siamese networks · Transformer · BERT · bi-LSTM

G. Wang et al. (Eds.): UbiSec 2023, CCIS 2034, pp. 17–30, 2024.
https://doi.org/10.1007/978-981-97-1274-8_2

1   Introduction

Authorship verification is a task determining whether two given texts were written by the same author or not, [1]. The issue of authorship verification holds crucial significance in the fields of security and forensics. Accurate identification of authors behind written content can aid in various investigative processes, such as identifying the source of anonymous texts, detecting plagiarism, and attributing digital content to its rightful authors. Moreover, as the prevalence of fake news and misinformation increases [2], robust authorship verification methods become indispensable for ensuring the authenticity and reliability of textual information.

Previous studies have explored various input representations [3–6], such as character n-grams and pre-trained language models. However, these approaches have limitations. N-gram methods can prove ineffective when handling texts of differing lengths and diverse writing styles, as they rely on fixed sequences that risk losing critical information. Moreover, certain methods struggle to capture the intricate semantic and syntactic nuances necessary for accurate authorship verification. This study seeks to address this gap and shed light on the advantages of utilizing bi-LSTM and BERT in tandem for the task of authorship verification. Notably, the specific fusion of BERT and bi-LSTM for generating word embeddings within a Siamese network has not undergone comprehensive examination.

In this paper, we propose a novel model for authorship verification using Siamese networks. Siamese networks are a class of neural networks that excel in comparing and measuring similarity between two inputs. They have shown success in various natural language processing (NLP) tasks, such as sentence similarity and paraphrase identification.

Our proposed model BiBERT-AV combines two instances of a pre-trained BERT model, bi-directional LSTM layers, and a fully connected layer with a sigmoid activation function. By leveraging the strengths of BERT's contextual embeddings and the sequential understanding of bi-LSTM, our model aims to provide a fine-grained representation of the text, thereby improving the accuracy of authorship verification.

To assess the efficacy of our proposed approach, we aim to answer the following research questions: *How does a Siamese network with pre-trained BERT and Bi-LSTM layers compare to existing methods for authorship verification, and what advantages does it offer?*

To investigate our proposed model, we conduct extensive experiments using a Siamese neural network on the Enron Email Corpus, comprising randomly selected true and false data pairs. We evaluate the model's accuracy across datasets with varying sizes and complexities.

Our experiments reveal that our proposed Siamese network, BiBERT-AV, outperforms baselines and state-of-the-art methods for authorship verification. Specifically, we achieve an F1 of 0.90 for fifty authors, surpassing the baseline model used in current studies with an F1 of 0.61 even when the number of authors is expanded to a larger group.

To the best of our knowledge, BiBERT-AV represents the first attempt to employ Siamese networks with pre-trained BERT and bi-LSTM layers for authorship verification.

Overall, our study highlights the potential of Siamese networks with BERT and bi-LSTM layers in authorship verification and offers new perspectives on improving the accuracy and reliability of authorship attribution techniques.

2 Background

The proposed model, BiBERT-AV, integrates Bidirectional Encoder Representations from Transformers (BERT), Long Short-Term Memory (LSTM), and a Siamese Network. Consequently, this section describes a general overview of the pertinent background information related to these methods.

2.1 Bidirectional Encoder Representations from Transformers (BERT)

According to Devlin, et al. [7], BERT constitutes a transformer model reliant on a corpus of plain text, utilizing pre-training and bidirectional, unsupervised language representation techniques.

Google started using BERT in October 2019 only for English language search queries, but by December 2019 the model was adopted for 70 more languages. It is also open source and it's expected to introduce more improvements in terms of higher accuracy and computation time requirements for different applications.

BERT demonstrates remarkable proficiency in comprehending natural language tasks such as managing Polysemy and Coreference resolution, as well as tasks involving natural language inference, sentiment classification, and word sense disambiguation. As a result, it can serve a multitude of linguistic functions, including fine-tuning, question-answering, classifying sentences, identifying named entities, recognizing sentence boundaries, and generating responses in conversations. Unlike conventional sequential models, the transformer encoder in BERT processes the entire sequence of words simultaneously, enabling the model to grasp word context within the context of the sentence.

According to Sanh, et al. [8] BERT is specifically crafted to pre-train intricate bidirectional text representations, considering both preceding and succeeding contexts. It can subsequently be adapted for various natural language processing tasks by simply adding an extra output layer, as illustrated in Fig. 1.

Currently, there are two variants of BERT, one with 12 encoders and 12 bidirectional self-attention heads for 800M words, and the other with 24 encoders and 16 bidirectional self-attention heads for 2,500M words.

2.2 Long and Bidirectional Short-Term Memory (LSTM) and (Bi-LSTM)

Long Short-Term Memory (LSTM) was initially introduced by Hochreiter and Schmidhuber [9] in 1997. LSTM networks, a type of recurrent neural networks

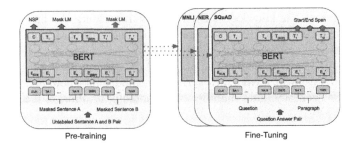

Fig. 1. Overall pre-training and fine-tuning procedures for BERT [7].

(RNNs), incorporate mechanisms to enhance information retention from previous data, allowing the influence of the current instance to extend to future inputs. LSTMs are highly versatile and robust, making them popular for various tasks such as classification, time series analysis, and natural language processing, where maintaining context is essential.

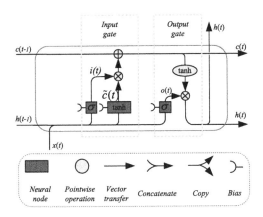

Fig. 2. The overall framework of the LSTM by Yong Yu et al. [10]

The three essential components of the LSTM cell, depicted in Fig. 2, are commonly referred to as gates: Input gate Forget gate and Output gate.

Bidirectional LSTM (Bi-LSTM) was introduced by Schuster and Paliwal [11]. Unlike LSTM, which processes input from the past to the future, Bi-LSTM comprises two LSTM parts that analyze the input in opposite sequences. The *Forward LSTM* processes input from the past to the future, while the *Backward LSTM* analyzes input from the future to the past. Both LSTM outputs are then concatenated to form the final output of the Bi-LSTM model.

2.3   Siamese Network

A Siamese Network is a deep learning architecture that is used for solving similarity learning problems. It was first introduced in the 1990s by Bromley, et al. [12] and has since been widely used in various applications, including face recognition, signature verification, and one-shot learning. For example, in face recognition, the siamese network is trained to compare two face images and predict whether they belong to the same person or not. This is achieved by using the same network architecture for both input images and comparing the outputs of the network.

According to Chicco, et al. [13], The Siamese Network consists of two identical neural networks, each taking one input, and their outputs are compared to produce a similarity score. Figure 3 representation of the structure of the siamese neural network model.

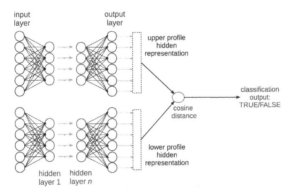

Fig. 3. Representation of the structure of the siamese neural network model. The data are processed from left to right [13].

One of the key advantages of Siamese Networks is their ability to handle high-dimensional data and handle it efficiently, making them ideal for tasks such as face recognition and signature verification, where the input data is high-dimensional. Additionally, Siamese Networks can be trained on small datasets, making them ideal for one-shot learning problems, where only a small number of examples of each class are available.

3   Related Works

Numerous studies have explored different input representations for authorship verification, including character n-grams and pre-trained language models. However, traditional n-gram-based methods may not effectively handle texts with varying lengths and writing styles due to their reliance on fixed-length word sequences, leading to the loss of vital information in the text. Moreover, some existing methods struggle to capture the nuanced semantic and syntactic features essential for accurate authorship verification.

In a study by Bagnall [3], a recurrent neural network (RNN) language model's output layer was partitioned into multiple independent prediction sub-models, each representing a distinct author. This design allowed the RNN layer to capture the overall language characteristics while avoiding overfitting, while the sub-models focused on identifying author-specific language features. Each sub-model was trained to predict the author of a text based on specific features, such as word average length or frequency of specific punctuation marks. The predictions from all sub-models were combined to produce the final authorship prediction. The method was evaluated using an email dataset and showed superior performance compared to traditional machine-learning techniques for authorship attribution. However, it is essential to consider the method's limitations, such as the choice of features used to train the sub-models and its potential struggle with generalizing to new texts or authors not seen during training.

In Brocardo's work [14], a model for authorship verification was presented, which employed deep belief networks to analyze lexical, syntactic, and domain-level features in real-valued data. The method divided long web documents into shorter sentences and combined adjacent features. The model was tested on Twitter and Enron email corpora with various block sizes. Nevertheless, the use of deep belief networks could make the method computationally complex and time-consuming, and there was a risk of overfitting to the training data, making generalization to new data challenging. Additionally, the method may face difficulty in identifying new authors not present in the training data, especially if the training data is limited. Therefore, careful selection of training data and model architecture is crucial when implementing this authorship verification method.

Halvani et al. [15] introduced a new approach for authorship verification called TAVeer, which uses topic-agnostic features to classify documents. The authors proposed a set of feature categories to capture writing style and employed a distance-based AV method with these features. The performance of TAVeer was compared to existing AV methods on four corpora with different topics, and it outperformed all baseline methods on two corpora and performed similarly to the strongest baseline on the other two corpora. Future research should explore the impact of misspelled words and alternative feature categories like topic-agnostic abbreviations and interjections.

For the PAN 2021 Authorship Verification task, Futrzynski [5] recommended using a basic BERT model. The model was trained by assigning text sequences to one of 3,000 authors from a large training sample, using various tasks during training. The model achieved promising results with F1=0.832 and AUC=0.798.

In addition, previous research has tackled the authorship verification task using Siamese approaches. One such approach proposed by Araujo et al. [4], proposed a solution to the authorship verification task using n-grams for the PAN 2020 challenge using a Siamese network architecture. The authors trained the network on character n-grams of the document pairs, and the best model achieved an overall evaluation score of 0.804. The authors used the Scikit Learn module to extract the n-grams of the documents and transform them into frequency vectors. The fine-tuned model can then be used to predict the likelihood that a new text was written by the same author.

Another study by Tyo et al. [6], the authors used transformer-based language models by applying Siamese network setup to verify the authorship of input texts. The model utilized a contrastive loss function to evaluate the distances between the text embedding and the label. The accuracy of the model in predicting the authorship of the texts was 0.78%.

To address the limitations of previous research, we propose a novel approach using a Siamese network with both BERT and bi-LSTM, which will be further elaborated in the subsequent section.

4   Proposed Model: BiBERT-AV

The proposed model shown in Fig. 4 uses a Siamese network architecture combining bi-LSTM and BERT. Because BERT is known for its ability to generate high-quality word embeddings that capture semantic information. Therefore, by incorporating bi-LSTMs into the BERT Siamese architecture, the model can better understand the context and relationships between words in a sentence.

In other words, BERT can learn contextualized embeddings for each token in the input text. The bi-LSTM can then learn to combine these contextualized embeddings in a way that takes into account the order of the tokens in the input text and produces a more fine-grained representation of the text, which can lead to better performance in authorship verification.

The Siamese network takes two inputs, text1 and text2. Each input is passed through a separate instance of a pre-trained BERT model, which generates encoded representations of the input text sequences. The encoded representations are then concatenated and passed through bi-LSTMs layers, which process the concatenated sequence in both forward and backward directions to produce a single output. This output is then passed through a fully connected layer with a sigmoid activation function to produce a binary classification result $(0,1)$ indicating the likelihood of the two input sequences being written by the same author.

5   Experiment

The research question outlined in Sect. 1 will be examined through the subsequent experimental protocol.

Step 1: Use public Enron Email Corpus to create a dataset consisting of true and false data pairs, with training, validation, and testing sets randomly selected from the original corpus to solve the problem of email authorship verification.

Step 2: Encode two input texts using pre-trained BERT and bi-LSTM layers, and produce a binary classification result indicating whether the texts were written by the same author.

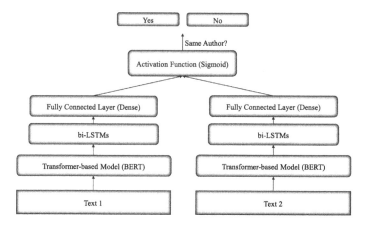

Fig. 4. BiBERT-AV: The Siamese BERT using bi-LSTM for Authorship Verification model architecture.

Step 3: Evaluate the performance of our proposed model.
Step 4: Adding more LSTM Layers in Siamese BERT Model.
Step 5: Comparing against existing method.

5.1 Experimental Setup

Python 3.11 was employed for the implementation, along with a GPU P100, leveraging the architectures provided by PyTorch [16] and scikit learn [17]. The pre-trained BERT embedding used in the code was sourced from the Hugging Face initiative [18].

5.2 Step 1 - Dataset Preprocessing

The Enron Email Corpus [19] has been widely used in the field of authorship analysis. The Corpus is a collection of over 500,000 emails generated by employees of the Enron Corporation. The emails are organized into folders, with each folder representing the email of a single employee. The folders contain the email messages in raw text format.

In our experiment, our objective is to authenticate the true author of an email through the verification of their writing style. Our goal is to ascertain the actual email owner responsible for composing the given email. To achieve this, we only utilized the emails found in the sender folders of the Enron Email Corpus, excluding forwarded emails and any attachments or links present in the emails. The focus of the experiment was solely on the text content of the emails, without using any information from the headers, such as the date and time of the message, the recipient(s), or IP addresses.

By limiting the scope of our experiment to only the text content of the emails in the sender folders, we aim to create an environment where the model's reliance is on the writing style of the emails and not on any metadata that could be extracted from the email headers. This objective allows us to assess the model's performance solely on its ability to analyze the writing style of the emails.

The objective of the prepossessing is to prepare a dataset consisting of true and false data pairs, where the true data pairs have the same label and the false data pairs have different labels. The preprocessed data will be used to train and test the Siamese network model for Authorship Verification tasks.

For our experiments, we considered the top 2, 5, 10, 20, and 50 authors with the largest number of texts. These authors were chosen based on the number of emails they sent. We then split the emails into two parts, textA and textB, and assigned them to either the same author or from different authors, respectively. Then, we concatenate them together to create a single data frame and labelled them as 1,0 (1 if the texts are from the same author, 0 otherwise).

5.3   Step 2- Training

Our employed strategy involves incremental training, within this framework, we maintain a consistent model architecture while progressively augmenting the training data. This incremental training process enables the model to accumulate knowledge iteratively without necessitating a complete re-initialization or retraining from scratch with each new data inclusion. Utilizing an automated parser, the extraction of solely the email's body content was performed. Each sentence underwent tokenization and was constrained to the initial 512 BERT tokens. The training of the model was executed with a batch size of 32 samples, AdamW optimizer was used with a learning rate of $2e^{-2}$. The loss function used is binary cross-entropy, which is a common loss function for binary classification problems, Table 1 summarize the hyper parameters used.

Table 1. Hyper parameters

MAX_length	512
learning rate	$2e^{-2}$
loss function	(binary_crossentropy)
activation function	fully connected layer
epochs	10
batch_size	32

5.4 Step 3-Evaluate the Performance of Our Proposed Model

In this step, we evaluated the performance of our proposed Siamese network model using various evaluation metrics. The results of this experiment are summarized in Table 2. The model shows strong performance when dealing with datasets involving 2, 5, and 10 authors. However, we noticed a drop in performance as we expanded the dataset to include 20 authors. This observation prompted us to consider improving the model by adding more bi-LSTM layers, as we'll explain in the next step.

Table 2. Performance of the Baseline BiBERT-AV on the test set on 2, 5, 10, and 20 authors using various evaluation metrics.

Numbers of Authors	P	R	F1	Acc
Two	0.99	0.98	0.98	0.98
Five	0.93	0.94	0.94	0.94
Ten	0.93	0.94	0.94	0.95
Twenty	0.77	0.71	0.74	0.79

5.5 Step 4 - Adding More BiLSTM Layers in BiBERT-AV Model

In this step, we explore the impact of adding multiple bi Long Short-Term Memory (LSTM) layers on top of our Baseline BiBERT-AV model. Similar to stacked Convolutional Neural Networks (CNNs) that capture diverse levels of features in computer vision tasks, stacking recurrent layers in Recurrent Neural Networks (RNNs) or LSTMs can enable the extraction of higher-level features from lower-level ones, thereby creating a hierarchical representation [20–22].

The motivation behind this step is to enhance the model's ability to capture intricate patterns and dependencies within the text data. By introducing additional LSTM layers, the model can potentially gain a deeper understanding of the text's sequential structure, leading to improved performance on authorship verification tasks.

Furthermore, we extended our evaluation of BiBERT-AV to more complex scenarios involving an increased number of authors from Enron Email Corpus. We conducted additional tests on a dataset comprising 50 authors to assess the model's performance under these conditions. The results, summarized in Table 3, showcase the model's performance across varying numbers of authors (2, 5, 10, 20, and 50). Remarkably, the BiBERT-AV model with an additional bi-LSTM layer maintains a consistently high level of performance even with the inclusion of a larger number of authors.

Table 3. Performance comparison between Baseline BiBERT-AV and BiBERT-AV on different authorship verification scenarios from the Enron dataset.

Authors	Baseline BiBERT-AV				BiBERT-AV			
	P	R	F1	Acc	P	R	F1	Acc
Two	0.99	0.98	0.98	0.98	0.99	0.99	0.99	0.99
Five	0.93	0.94	0.94	0.94	0.98	0.98	0.98	0.98
Ten	0.93	0.94	0.94	0.95	0.98	0.98	0.98	0.98
Twenty	0.77	0.71	0.74	0.79	0.95	0.95	0.95	0.95
Fifty	0.50	0.51	0.67	0.64	0.90	0.93	0.90	0.90

5.6 Step 5 - Comparing Against Existing Method

In this step, we conducted a comprehensive comparison between our proposed BiBERT-AV model and the Siamese BERT model introduced by Tyo et al. [6]. To perform a fair evaluation, we utilized our dataset and assessed the models' performance using various evaluation metrics. Table 4 presents the performance of Siamese BERT method introduced by [6] and our proposed model BiBERT-AV across different authorship verification scenarios with varying numbers of authors (Two, Five, Ten, Twenty and fifty) from the Enron dataset.

Table 4. Performance comparison between Siamese BERT and BiBERT-AV on different authorship verification scenarios from the Enron dataset.

Authors	Siamese BERT				BiBERT-AV			
	P	R	F1	Acc	P	R	F1	Acc
Two	0.68	0.87	0.77	0.73	0.99	0.99	0.99	0.99
Five	0.77	0.71	0.74	0.79	0.98	0.98	0.98	0.98
Ten	0.83	0.76	0.79	0.80	0.98	0.98	0.98	0.98
Twenty	0.75	0.73	0.74	0.74	0.95	0.95	0.95	0.95
Fifty	0.49	0.81	0.61	0.50	0.90	0.93	0.90	0.90

From Table 4, we observe the model's performance across the various metrics for each scenario. The results demonstrate that the BiBERT-AV model consistently outperforms the Siamese BERT model in all cases.

To further visualize the performance comparison, Fig. 5 plots the F1 of all models across the different authorship verification scenarios.

6 Discussion

In this study, we aimed to investigate the effectiveness of a Siamese network with pre-trained BERT and Bi-LSTM layers for authorship verification. We also

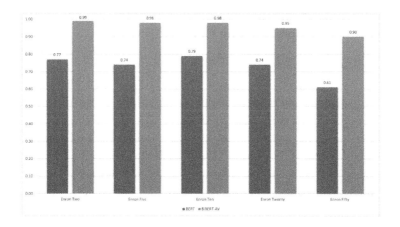

Fig. 5. F1 Comparison of BiBERT-AV Models against Siamese BERT

explored the advantages of using bi-LSTM in a Siamese network compared to existing methods.

The results of our experiments demonstrated that the proposed BiBERT-AV model achieved high accuracy in distinguishing texts written by the same or different authors from the Enron Dataset. Specifically, the model achieved 99% accuracy on the 2-author dataset, 98% on the 5-author dataset, 98% on the 10-author dataset, 95% on the 20-author dataset, and 90% on the 50-author dataset as shown in Table 4. As depicted in the table, the accuracy of the BiBERT-AV models consistently surpassed that of the Siamese BERT model, providing compelling evidence of the superiority of our proposed approach. These impressive results shed light on the potential of the model architecture for authorship verification tasks.

The outstanding performance and adaptability of the BiBERT-AV model to small datasets make it a promising solution for various real-world scenarios, including forensic investigations, plagiarism detection, and authorship attribution in legal contexts. Moreover, the ability to achieve high accuracy with limited training data positions our approach as a valuable tool in scenarios where collecting large-scale labelled datasets is not feasible. The successful integration of BERT and Bi-LSTM in the BiBERT-AV model illustrates the potential of combining state-of-the-art language models with recurrent architectures for advancing the field of authorship verification. Further exploration of such hybrid models holds promise for future advancements in this domain.

Our proposed approach has demonstrated promising results in authorship verification tasks, showcasing the potential of Siamese networks with pre-trained transformers and Bi-LSTM layers for text classification. The findings contribute to the growing body of literature on the application of deep learning in natural language processing and provide a valuable tool for forensic and security practitioners seeking to verify authorship.

7   Conclusions

In this paper, we presented a BiBERT-AV to the problem of authorship verification using a Siamese network architecture combining bi-LSTMs and BERT.

The experimental results of the proposed approach show its effectiveness in achieving high accuracy in both small and large datasets for the task of authorship verification, outperforming the existing methods and achieving state-of-the-art performance. The successful integration of BERT and bi-LSTMs layers within the model plays a crucial role in comprehending and distinguishing the unique writing styles of different authors. Additionally, the proposed approach has the potential to be applied to various authorship verification scenarios and can be extended to other languages and writing styles.

In future work, we plan to investigate the performance of our model on larger datasets with texts from a larger number of authors and explore the effect of different pre-trained language models and fine-tuning strategies on the performance of the model. Finally, we aim to explore the interpretability of the model and the features it learns to distinguish between texts by different authors.

Acknowledgements. The authors would like to thank the Deanship of Scientific Research at Shaqra University and the Saudi Arabian Cultural Bureau in London (SACB) for allowing the research to be undertaken.

References

1. Brocardo, M.L., Traore, I., Saad, S., Woungang, I.: Authorship verification for short messages using stylometry. In: 2013 International Conference on Computer, Information and Telecommunication Systems (CITS), pp. 1–6. IEEE (2013)
2. Loomba, S., de Figueiredo, A., Piatek, S.J., de Graaf, K., Larson, H.J.: Measuring the impact of COVID-19 vaccine misinformation on vaccination intent in the UK and USA. Nat. Hum. Behav. **5**(3), 337–348 (2021)
3. Bagnall, D.: Author identification using multi-headed recurrent neural networks. arXiv preprint arXiv:1506.04891 (2015)
4. Araujo-Pino, E., Gómez-Adorno, H., Pineda, G.F.: Siamese network applied to authorship verification. In: CLEF (Working Notes). Working Notes proceedings in CLEF 2020 (2020)
5. Futrzynski, R.: Author classification as pre-training for pairwise authorship verification. In: CLEF (Working Notes), pp. 1945–1952 (2021)
6. Tyo, J., Dhingra, B., Lipton, Z.C.: Siamese BERT for authorship verification. In: CLEF (Working Notes), pp. 2169–2177 (2021)
7. Devlin, J., Chang, M.-W., Lee, K., Toutanova, K.: BERT: pre-training of deep bidirectional transformers for language understanding. arXiv preprint arXiv:1810.04805 (2018)
8. Sanh, V., Debut, L., Chaumond, J., Wolf, T.: DistilBERT, a distilled version of BERT: smaller, faster, cheaper and lighter. arXiv preprint arXiv:1910.01108 (2019)
9. Hochreiter, S., Schmidhuber, J.: Long short-term memory. Neural Comput. **9**(8), 1735–1780 (1997)
10. Yu, Y., Si, X., Hu, C., Zhang, J.: A review of recurrent neural networks: LSTM cells and network architectures. Neural Comput. **31**(7), 1235–1270 (2019)

11. Schuster, M., Paliwal, K.K.: Bidirectional recurrent neural networks. IEEE Trans. Signal Process. **45**(11), 2673–2681 (1997)
12. Bromley, J., Guyon, I., LeCun, Y., Säckinger, E., Shah, R.: Signature verification using a "siamese" time delay neural network. In: Advances in Neural Information Processing Systems, vol. 6 (1993)
13. Chicco, D.: Siamese neural networks: an overview. Artif. Neural Netw. 73–94 (2021)
14. Brocardo, M.L., Traore, I., Woungang, I., Obaidat, M.S.: Authorship verification using deep belief network systems. Int. J. Commun. Syst. **30**(12), e3259 (2017)
15. Halvani, O., Graner, L., Regev, R.: TAVeer: an interpretable topic-agnostic authorship verification method. In: Proceedings of the 15th International Conference on Availability, Reliability and Security, pp. 1–10 (2020)
16. Paszke, A., et al.: PyTorch: an imperative style, high-performance deep learning library. In: Wallach, H., Larochelle, H., Beygelzimer, A., d'Alché-Buc, F., Fox, E., Garnett, R. (eds.) Advances in Neural Information Processing Systems, vol. 32, pp. 8024–8035. Curran Associates Inc. (2019)
17. Pedregosa, F., et al.: Scikit-learn: machine learning in Python. J. Mach. Learn. Res. **12**, 2825–2830 (2011)
18. Wolf, T., et al.: Transformers: state-of-the-art natural language processing. In: Proceedings of the 2020 Conference on Empirical Methods in Natural Language Processing: System Demonstrations, pp. 38–45. Association for Computational Linguistics (2020)
19. dataset Enron 2015. Enron email dataset (2015). Accessed 23 June 2023
20. Pascanu, R., Gulcehre, C., Cho, K., Bengio, Y.: How to construct deep recurrent neural networks. arXiv preprint arXiv:1312.6026 (2013)
21. Graves, A., Jaitly, N., Mohamed, A.: Hybrid speech recognition with deep bidirectional LSTM. In: 2013 IEEE Workshop on Automatic Speech Recognition and Understanding, pp. 273–278. IEEE (2013)
22. Almutairi, A., Kang, B., Fadhel, N.: The effectiveness of transformer-based models for BEC attack detection. In: Li, S., Manulis, M., Miyaji, A. (eds.) NSS 2023. LNCS, vol. 13983, pp. 77–90. Springer, Cham (2023). https://doi.org/10.1007/978-3-031-39828-5_5

Impact of Library Code in Binary Similarity Systems

Andrei Vasile Mihalca[1,2(✉)] and Ciprian Pavel Oprişa[1,2]

[1] Technical University of Cluj-Napoca, 400027 Cluj-Napoca, Romania
mihalca.andrei.vasile@gmail.com
[2] Bitdefender, 060071 Bucharest, Romania
{amihalca,coprisa}@bitdefender.com

Abstract. Anti-malware research often employs binary code similarity techniques for attacks attribution and for inferring the malware family. Having similar malware samples means that they share common code which was probably written by the same malicious actor, unless the common code belongs to some public software library. Thus, library code thwarts the analysis process and needs to be identified and excluded from the similarity computation in order to get reliable results. Besides code from third-party software libraries, compiler-specific code, runtime packers and installers have the same effect and should be dealt with. The current paper presents methods for detecting the library code within an existing data collection and for improving the detection as new data is added. The proposed approach is compared with the state of the art, highlighting the existing problems and proposing solutions for overcoming them. Eliminating library code from similarity computation brings both improvements and some drawbacks, which are analyzed in terms of performance and results quality.

Keywords: Binary File Similarity · Malware · Library Code · Executable File Analysis · Code Hash

1 Introduction

Similarity systems based on binary code are used by security researchers to find similarities between analysed files or code sequences and existing data collections. Our research aims to solve query performance issues of code similarity systems, which are caused by library code.

There are multiple scenarios where code that was not written directly by the malicious actor finds its way into the compiled binary, hardening the analysis process and causing the similarity systems to produce false positives. Modern compilers [1] add extra code to binary programs, for example to enforce runtime integrity checks [2]. The C runtime library can be included statically by the linker in order to make the program highly portable. For example, by statically including libcmt instead of linking against msvcrt [3], a Windows program is not

G. Wang et al. (Eds.): UbiSec 2023, CCIS 2034, pp. 31–44, 2024.
https://doi.org/10.1007/978-981-97-1274-8_3

dependent on the Visual Studio redistributables and can run on most Windows installations. In C++, the Standard Template Library (STL) [4] comprises of many headers and templates that are instantiated as needed, expanding into custom generated code that fits the purpose of each program. Both legitimate developers and malware authors may use 3rd party libraries, such as *zlib* [5] for compressing and decompressing data. Software installers such as Nullsoft Scriptable Install System (NSIS) [6] or WinRAR Self-Extractor [7] are also used to package both benign and malicious software and the installer code should be omitted by the analysis.

The solution for identifying library code depends directly on the method used for abstracting the code for a binary files, which in our research, is represented by a sorted set of **code hashes**, that was proposed by V. Topan et al. in [8]. These are 32-bit hashes are computed on normalized sequences of instructions from x86 Instruction Set Architecture [9]. Given this abstraction, data collection usually consists of code hash sets associated to file identifiers. The problem of library code tends to manifest differently depending on a code hash frequency in the corpus of samples. Using the Inverse Document Frequency (IDF) [10], computed as the base 2 logarithm of the ratio between the total number of samples and the number of samples containing a given code hash, we empirically identified the two scenarios below:

The problem of library code tends to appear in the following scenarios:

- code hashes with IDF 6 or below (for instance, 100,000 files from a collection of 6 million). Such code is very common and its presence should not influence the similarity computation.
- code hashes with IDF between 6 and 12 (for instance 1500 files from a collection of 6 million). The presence of such code indicates that the files were either compiled using the same compiler, used the same library functions which were statically linked, or were created by the same author. This brings the problem of finding highly similar files with divergent behavior.

The following section presents related work in the field of binary code similarity and libraries identification. Section 3 describes the proposed solution, which was implemented and tested on a large dataset, leading to the experimental results described in Sect. 4. The paper ends with discussions and conclusions.

2   Related Work

Previous research consisted of investigating methods to index code hashes belonging to huge data collections (more than 30 million distinct sets of code hashes) [11]. The solution proposes using an inverted index to associate a code hash to a list of file identifiers that contain it, named *posting* list, and a direct index, which related a file identifier to the code hash set. When performing similarity queries, the inverted index was used to establish files with at least a common code hash. Afterwards, for each file, the direct index data is used for computing the similarity result. Given this approach, for a code hash that has associated 100,000 files, at least 100,000 interrogations must be made against direct index, to get similarity scores, which in most of the cases, have low values, only because of a library code sequence tied to a compiler, or to a installer. For handling the performance issues related to long posting lists, a trivial method was used: each code hash that belongs to more than θ files, was considered invalid. This method brings great performance results, but it has the disadvantage of stripping relevant data from results. For example, a malicious code is present in more than θ files, it won't be considered when establishing files for which similarity is computed.

An approach to compute similarity between two items was proposed by C. Oprişa et al. in [12], with the purpose of malware clustering. This method was used to detect plagiarized students work. In their approach, n-grams were used to abstract binary code. Each n-gram consisted of a set of x86 Instruction Set Architecture OpCodes and a file was abstracted as a set of n-grams obtained by sliding a window of one byte over the normalized OpCodes of the file. To deal with n-grams that appeared in distinct files, they assigned weights to n-grams: most relevant n-grams had higher weights assigned. n-grams with a weight below a threshold were assigned to shared code. Like the method proposed in [11], this approach provides better performance, but ignores common malicious code.

Another method to identify library code, but applied to Android applications, was presented by C. Oprişa et al. in [13]. Their method consisted of three directions to mark library code: manual labeling, defining a threshold of appearances in a collection for n-grams extracted from code and labeling based on method usage by distinct application publishers. Although the approach is similar to methods above, it takes into consideration the fact that a library code can be, in fact, malicious code. To overcome this downside, they assign reputations to application publishers, based on downloads and user ratings. For a publisher with lower reputation, the threshold for library code labeling increases.

An approach of identifying library code by filtering out common n-grams from a set of clean files was suggested by [14]. This method has the advantage of precision when it comes to retrieving similar malicious samples, but it can have the downside of reduced performance in certain cases: similarity with huge clusters of malicious code.

K. Griffin et al. presents a method for library function recognition [15]. They also refer to IDA FLIRT [16], which is a method to determine common functions for specific compilers. Given the fact that this approach is bound to a compiler, they suggested the idea of a universal FLIRT, by using all function signatures, regardless the compiler. Also, they propose the extension of library code labeling, by marking the functions that are statically, or dynamically called, by known library functions. This method needs manual labeling in order to deal with library functions generated by new compiler versions.

3   Invalid Code Hash Selection

3.1   General Observations

Our research focuses on library code detection methods which can be used in conjunction with code hashes returned by method [8], since we had at our disposal data collections containing these type of hashes.

```
.text:004A6A0C                push    ebp
.text:004A6A0D                mov     ebp, esp
.text:004A6A0F                xor     eax, eax
.text:004A6A11                push    ebp
.text:004A6A12                push    offset loc_4A6A2B
.text:004A6A17                push    dword ptr fs:[eax]
.text:004A6A1A                mov     fs:[eax], esp
.text:004A6A1D                xor     eax, eax
```

Fig. 1. Frequent code sequence

Considering the work from [11], we know that the same set of code hashes can belong to distinct binary files. This happens when the code section doesn't change, but other sections (e.g. resources) do. To handle this situation, we associate a unique set of code hashes to an entity, which is later associated to one, or more files, from which the respective set was extracted. First step of our research was analyzing code hashes that belong to more than 100,000 files. Figure 1 corresponds to a code sequence from which was extracted a code hash that appears in 322,264 entities within a collection of 30,000,000.

From our preliminary observations, we found some situations where library code is likely to appear:

- each compiler has specific sequences of instruction that are planted in each compiled executable;
- common installers, such as NullSoft NSIS, WinRAR SFX, etc. share the same version identical code, while the payload (files that will be installed) resides in the overlay section of the file;
- multiple variants of the same file can be indexed in the system, causing long lists of files that contain a sequence of code which stays between several releases;
- statically linked code of common functions (e.g. *printf*, *scanf*, etc.) tends to appear in multiple files;
- code hashes extracted from packer protected files (even it shouldn't happen, this can occur when unpacking routines fail, or when they are not available). In this case, we take code hashes from packer specific instruction sequences, which is the same, for files packed with the same version. Common executable packer examples are UPX, Enigma Protector, Themida or VMProtect [17].

3.2   Selecting Threshold for Code Hash Invalidation

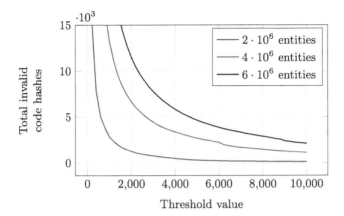

Fig. 2. Selecting threshold for code hash invalidation

In order to select the threshold for invalidating code hashes, we took collections with from 2,000,000 up to 6,000,000 unique code hash sets (entities) and varied the threshold for considering invalid code hashes from 200 up to 10,000 with an increment of 200 (Fig. 2). The threshold value represents maximum number of entities to which a code hash is associated, before considering it invalid. After each increment of threshold, we compared the count of invalid code hashes resulted by using current threshold value, with the count of invalid code hashes returned by previous threshold value. When this difference is below a fixed value, we save the last value as our threshold selection. This method can be used in conjunction with solutions described in [11] and [12].

Figure 2 shows that higher threshold values cause less invalid code hashes, which translates as more results returned when querying for similar files. Within a system for binary file similarity, the threshold value can be changed to achieve distinct objectives: high for best results and low for best query performance.

Another method of selecting the threshold to invalidate code hashes consists of establishing a fixed percentage of collection size. This approach has the advantage of performance, compared to the method described above, but is subject to a similarity quality decrease.

From our observations, these methods of selecting valid code hashes will invalidate data taken from multiple versions of the same program, if the version count surpasses the threshold value. To overcome this problem, we propose to cluster the code hash sets, before selecting threshold. In this case, appearances of a code hash are evaluated at cluster level. In this way, a code hash present in huge clusters (caused by programs with high similarity level), is considered only once when counting the occurrences in collection.

3.3 Clustering Highly Similar Binary Files

We defined an undirected graph $\mathcal{G}(V, E)$, where V is represented by entity identifiers in a binary similarity system and E is a set of edges $\{(x, y) \mid (x, y) \in V^2 \wedge Jaccard(x, y) <= \gamma\}$ [18]. We extracted strongly connected components from this graph using the algorithm presented in [19], to determine clusters of similar entities. γ is a parameter which can be adjusted, using feedback from multiple runs of the strongly connected components algorithm. For each cluster, we determined the union of code hashes from entities. Once we had the association between a cluster and the code hashes, we applied the method described in the beginning of section.

A trivial approach to perform a full collection similarity implies a $O(n^2)$ operation: for each entity identifier, we compute similarity with each other identifiers and check if they match required threshold. An improvement of this method consists of using the techniques presented in [11], where an inverted index is built to associate a code hash to a list of entity identifiers which contain it. Even if a code hash can be present in all entities, our research proved that such a situation doesn't occur, even in worst case (Table 1).

Table 1. Entity list length statistics

Collection Size (count of entities)	Average count of entities associated to a code hash	Maximum count of entities associated to a code hash
$2 \cdot 10^6$	13.98	172,245
$4 \cdot 10^6$	18.168	688,406
$6 \cdot 10^6$	20.20	1,090,106
$8 \cdot 10^6$	21.44	1,424,476
$10 \cdot 10^6$	22.56	1,743,071

We used Algorithm 1 to cluster the entities of a collection. It consists of three major steps:

- building the inverted index, for which we used the method presented in [11] (step displayed at line 1);
- building the adjacency lists based on entity similarity. This step can be run in parallel, as long as *DequeueEntity* operation is atomic. Starting at line 2, we added to a queue the entity identifiers present in forward index and initialized the object which stores the adjacency lists. Afterwards, while we have any entity identifier left to process, we get the entities with required similarity threshold θ and put them in the adjacency lists storage. Algorithm for *GetSimilarEntities* is an improvement of the method presented in [11] and detailed below. From an implementation point of view, forward and inverted indexes can be discarded from memory after this step;
- run strongly connected components algorithm to get entity clusters. Beginning at line 10, we initialize the set of visited entities V. For each entity identifier that was not visited, we run Depth First Search (DFS) algorithm to obtain its connected component, which is stored to a list C, which is returned after all components are collected. We recommend using non-recursive DFS algorithm for implementation, since stack overflow might occur due to large components.

Algorithm 1. CLUSTER-COLLECTION(F, θ)

Require: The forward index (mappings between entity identifiers and code hashes) F
Require: Threshold θ representing minimum required similarity between entities

1: $I \leftarrow BuildInvertedIndex(F)$
2: $Q \leftarrow EnqueueEntities(F)$
3: $A \leftarrow \emptyset$
4: $e \leftarrow DequeueEntity(Q)$
5: **while** $e \neq \emptyset$ **do**
6:    $similar\_entities \leftarrow GetSimilarEntities(e, \theta, F, I)$
7:    $A[e] \leftarrow similar\_entities$
8:    $e \leftarrow DequeueEntity(Q)$
9: **end while**
10: $V \leftarrow \emptyset$
11: $C \leftarrow \emptyset$
12: **for all** $e \in F$ **do**
13:    **if** $e \notin V$ **then**
14:       $connected\_component \leftarrow DFS(e, A, V)$
15:       $C \leftarrow C \cup connected\_component$
16:    **end if**
17: **end for**
18: **return** C

Table 2 presents the execution times for collection clustering algorithm, which was implemented in C programming language. In our setup, we used 32 threads to perform the adjacency lists build step. To run the algorithm, we used a machine with the following specifications: 1 TB SSD storage, 384 GB of RAM and 80 logical processors (with 40 cores). We can observe that the time for obtaining connected components is insignificant compared to full collection similarity. Figure 3 shows the non-linear characteristic of the clustering algorithm, which is caused by the collection similarity operation, that has a time complexity of $O(n^2)$. The similarity results can be stored for sub subsequent use, but consider that they could take more space than the collection data and indexes, for some values of γ parameter.

Table 2. Execution time for collection clustering algorithm

Collection Size (entity count)	Collection Similarity (Hours)	Connected Components (Hours)	Total Time (Hours)
$2 \cdot 10^6$	1.89	0.03	1.92
$4 \cdot 10^6$	6.43	0.06	6.49
$6 \cdot 10^6$	15.21	0.08	15.29
$8 \cdot 10^6$	27.22	0.13	27.35
$10 \cdot 10^6$	44.16	0.24	44.40

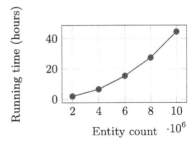

Fig. 3. Execution time for collection clustering algorithm

While researching methods for selecting valid code hashes, we made some observations, for the cases when only binary similarity systems are used to label a file: given a data collection, we can label a file, if a required similarity score with malicious, or clean files, is achieved.

1. method proposed in [11] is prone to both false positives (cases when a clean file is labeled as malicious), and false negatives (cases when a malicious file is labeled as clean), since we can invalidate both clean, and malicious, code hashes, causing relevant information to be removed from similarity results;
2. method proposed in [12] is prone only to false negatives, since only data taken from clean files can be stripped from similarity results;
3. clustering method proposed for selecting the threshold of occurrences for considering a code hash invalid, is prone only to false negatives, if the data which is clustered belongs to clean sets of files, and prone to both false positives and false negatives otherwise.

False positives might lead to quarantine or removal of system files, or other useful user files, by the security solutions. Also, a false positive might impact a lot of users, since the same file can be present in millions of computers in the world (for example, *kernel32.dll* library is present on all machines running the same Windows Operating System version). On the other hand, false negatives will prevent security solutions to detect a malicious file, resulting in a compromised computer, at least. Even if the effect for some users will be worse, the false negative will not impact a large group of people, and is usually fixed in future security solution updates.

3.4   Improved Similarity Computing

During our research for invalidating code hashes, we observed that an improvement of similarity algorithm presented in [11] can be made and it can be applied, only if no code hashes are invalidated. The algorithm returned similar files for a code hash set, given a data collection with millions of entities (unique code hash sets) and it had two major sections:

1. using given code hash set, a list of candidates, with at least a common code hash, is built using the data stored in inverted index;
2. for each candidate, the similarity score is computed, using Jaccard distance between given code hash set and the candidate code hash set

This algorithm has time complexity $O(m^2 \cdot n)$, where m is the maximum cardinal of a code hash set, and n is the maximum length of the posting list referenced in the inverted index.

Algorithm 2. GET-SIMILAR-ENTITIES(e, θ, F, I)

Require: An entity e and a similarity threshold θ
Require: The forward index F and the inverted index I
Ensure: Set of similar files S

```
 1: S ← ∅
 2: D ← ∅
 3: for all hash ∈ e.code_hashes do
 4:     for all other_entity ∈ I[hash].code_hashes do
 5:         if other_entity ∈ D then
 6:             D[other_entity] ← D[other_entity] + 1
 7:         else
 8:             D[other_entity] ← 1
 9:         end if
10:     end for
11: end for
12: for all other_entity ∈ D do
```
13: $\quad sim \leftarrow \frac{D[other\_entity]}{|e.code\_hashes| + |F[other\_entity].code\_hashes| - D[id]}$
```
14:     if sim ≥ θ then
15:         S ← S ∪ {c}
16:     end if
17: end for
18: return S
```

In Algorithm 2, D is a hashtable that associates an entity identifier with the count of code hashes that are common between that entity and the input code hash set. $I[hash].code\_hashes$ represents the posting list associated to a code hash. Loop starting at line 3 of Algorithm 2 counts the common code hashes between input entity and existing data loaded in inverted index. This count will be the cardinal of intersection between two code hash sets, when no hashes are invalided. In the final loop of Algorithm 2, similarity is computed without intersection or union of analysed code hash sets, as opposed to approach in [11] where $sim \leftarrow \frac{|e.code\_hashes \cap F[other\_entity].code\_hashes|}{|e.code\_hashes \cup F[c].code\_hashes|}$. Our proposal has the complexity $O(m \cdot n)$.

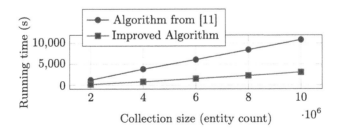

Fig. 4. Total time when querying similarity for 5,000 samples

Figure 4 compares the total running time when performing 5,000 similarity queries against collections varying from 2 to 10 million of distinct code hash sets. Both algorithms follow a linear characteristic, given the fact that m is a constant value, but our improvement achieves to return similarity results four times faster.

Table 3. Similarity Algorithm Performance Comparison

Collection Size (entity count)	Average Case (s) [11]	Average Case (s)	Worst Case (s) [11]	Worst Case (s)	Improvement ratio (Average Case)
$2 \cdot 10^6$	0.244	0.037	1.567	0.282	6.57
$4 \cdot 10^6$	0.759	0.163	4.119	1.263	4.63
$6 \cdot 10^6$	1.209	0.311	6.183	2.312	3.88
$8 \cdot 10^6$	1.687	0.452	7.954	2.901	3.72
$10 \cdot 10^6$	2.166	0.617	9.794	3.981	3.5

Table 3 presents the running times for this test setup, for both algorithms, in average and worst cases. It also shows the improvement induced by proposed algorithm when compared to [11].

4   Experimental Results

4.1   Experiments Data Sets

During the assessment of mentioned methods for code hash invalidation, we used collections containing from 2 to 10 million unique code hash sets and indexed them using method presented in [11]. To index the data, we used the machine mentioned in Sect. 3.3. These hashes were generated with a routine, property of Bitdefender, that implemented the solution from [8]. Alternative implementations of the same method producing 32-bit hashes can be used to build similar data sets, in order to reproduce the experiments. Files from which the code hashes were extracted are from private internal collections of Bitdefender. To evaluate similarity performance and result quality, we selected two distinct collections unique code hash sets containing 5,000 items, built from separate malicious and clean file collections. These sets of code hashes are not present between indexed data. Within the following figures, we used several terms related to code hash invalidation thresholds, having the following meaning:

- *No Invalid*, which refers to the case when no code hashes were invalidated;
- *Clean Threshold*, meaning that the thresholds were applied only to sets of clean files – this is the method suggested in [12];
- *Trivial Threshold*, referring to the case when thresholds are established on mixed file collections.

4.2 Performance Assessment

Table 4. Total duration for similarity queries

No Invalid, clean set (s)	Clean Threshold, clean set (s)	Trivial Threshold, clean set (s)	No Invalid, malicious set (s)	Clean Threshold, malicious set (s)	Trivial Threshold, malicious set (s)	Collection size (entity count)
1140.68	140.47	62.85	766.71	148.77	58.05	$2 \cdot 10^6$
3482.23	180.46	146.33	2023.97	175.45	129.55	$4 \cdot 10^6$
5571.93	255.71	226.73	3314.37	237.14	199.49	$6 \cdot 10^6$
7764.2	334.24	303.25	4665.89	302.01	267.34	$8 \cdot 10^6$
10061.4	407.23	382.26	6128.6	362.56	333.2	$10 \cdot 10^6$

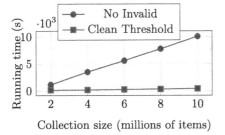

Fig. 5. Similarity performance querying the **clean** test set (No Invalid vs Clean Threshold)

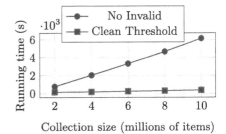

Fig. 6. Similarity performance querying the **malicious** test set (No Invalid vs Clean Threshold)

Figure 5 and Fig. 6 present a comparison between the query performance of a binary similarity system that invalidates code hashes using the method that selects the threshold by using only clean file collections [12], against a system that doesn't invalidate code hashes at all. In both cases, the running time can be approximated using a linear function, but the method that doesn't invalidate code hashes has a greater slope, which translates into slower query response times. Given the information from Table 4, we can see that the total query times for clean files are approximately 8, 21 and 24 times slower when no code hashes are invalidated, for collections having 2, 6 and 10 million entities respectively. When comparing the query duration for infected files, the results look similar, but the performance decrease factors were 5, 13 and 16 times, for the same collections. These factors were computed by dividing data from the first two columns of Table 4.

We performed comparison between methods which invalidate code hashes, from the performance point of view, as it can be seen in Fig. 7 and Fig. 8. In this case, the results were similar, with a slight advantage for the method that takes the invalid code hashes from entities with both clean and malicious labels. This observation is demonstrated by data present in Table 4 – columns two, three and five, six, respectively.

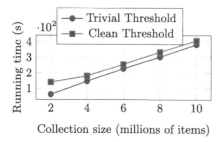

Collection size (millions of items)

Fig. 7. Similarity performance querying the **clean** test set (Trivial Threshold vs Clean Threshold)

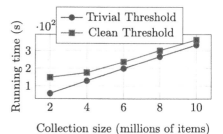

Collection size (millions of items)

Fig. 8. Similarity performance querying the **malicious** test set (Trivial Threshold vs Clean Threshold)

4.3 Result Quality Assessment

We evaluated the quality of results returned by binary similarity systems which invalidate code hashes. The reference point consisted of results returned by traditional system, that doesn't invalidate code hashes. We counted how many similarity results are returned for three separate levels: at least 30%, at least 50% and at least 80% respectively. For the methods which invalidate code hashes, we counted how many of these results are still present when the same set of files is queried for similarity. The data collections, query sets and machine are the same which were used at performance assessment.

Table 5. Trivial Threshold Results Quality Using Clean Test Set

Over 30% (%)	Over 50% (%)	Over 80% (%)	Collection Size (entity count)
41.66	67.05	95.82	$2 \cdot 10^6$
37.38	63.24	92.11	$4 \cdot 10^6$
53.64	58.35	77.64	$6 \cdot 10^6$
36.47	42.35	69.84	$8 \cdot 10^6$
29.58	32.51	52.05	$10 \cdot 10^6$

Table 6. Trivial Threshold Results Quality Using Malicious Test Set

Over 30% (%)	Over 50% (%)	Over 80% (%)	Collection Size (entity count)
49.02	83.22	98.13	$2 \cdot 10^6$
51.78	87.28	99.22	$4 \cdot 10^6$
60.34	90.63	99.46	$6 \cdot 10^6$
46.55	77.56	93.71	$8 \cdot 10^6$
40.68	69.01	87.07	$10 \cdot 10^6$

Tables 5 and 6 demonstrate that with collection growth, the result quality tends to decrease. For example, in Table 5, only 29% of similarity results are returned, when the clean query set is used, for a collection of 10 million entities, when compared to 41% provided for the smallest collection. Results were better when we used the infected data set for query, but the tendency of quality decrease by collection growth remains.

Table 7. Threshold On Clean Results Quality Using Clean Test Set

Over 30% (%)	Over 50% (%)	Over 80% (%)	Collection Size (entity count)
83.33	94.38	99.05	$2 \cdot 10^6$
53.78	77.17	92.11	$4 \cdot 10^6$
72.09	89.39	98.07	$6 \cdot 10^6$
41.52	45.71	73.37	$8 \cdot 10^6$
34.54	37.53	55.73	$10 \cdot 10^6$

Table 8. Threshold On Clean Results Quality Using Malicious Test Set

Over 30% (%)	Over 50% (%)	Over 80% (%)	Collection Size (entity count)
99.40	99.97	100.00	$2 \cdot 10^6$
64.46	90.85	99.99	$4 \cdot 10^6$
69.85	93.04	99.99	$6 \cdot 10^6$
55.09	79.08	93.93	$8 \cdot 10^6$
47.85	69.22	86.62	$10 \cdot 10^6$

Tables 7 and 8 show that by selecting a threshold only from entities labeled as clean, better similarity results are returned when the infected data set is queried. The same observation of result quality decrease given the collection size increase, as observed by using the method described above for invalidating code hashes, remains for both query sets.

5   Conclusions

We analysed the problem of library code, when working with binary similarity systems. We observed that this is present in various forms, such as generic code sequences from multiple files (built with distinct compilers), specific compiler stubs, installer or packer routines, and author-specific functions. The library code might hide malicious behavior, or causing binary similarity systems to mistakenly consider files similar.

Our research compared existing methods for excluding library code from similarity computation. It also presented a method for eliminating the confusion between library code and frequent code sequences determined by multiple variants of a program within a data set, by clustering the code hashes extracted from it. Due to the fact that some experiments took too long, the main cause being long similarity queries, we proposed an improved algorithm for similarity, that can be applied when code hashes are not invalidated.

We observed that by ignoring the library code, the similarity computation gets more faster – at least 5 times for malicious files and at least 8 times for clean files, when the data sets contain at least 2 million files. The improvement gets even better with collection growth. We compared the similarity result quality of methods which invalidate library code, revealing that most of the results are kept, when querying the malicious files. Unfortunately, this doesn't apply for clean files. Future work will focus on demonstrating that the results which are not returned at similarity queries, are in fact results mistakenly considered similar.

References

1. Grune, D., Van Reeuwijk, K., Bal, H.E., Jacobs, C.J.H., Langendoen, K.: Modern Compiler Design. Springer, Heidelberg (2012). https://doi.org/10.1007/978-1-4614-4699-6
2. Nagarakatte, S., Zhao, J., Martin, M.M.K., Zdancewic, S.: CETS: compiler enforced temporal safety for C. In: Proceedings of the 2010 International Symposium on Memory Management, pp. 31–40 (2010)
3. C runtime (CRT) and C++ standard library (STL).lib files (2023)
4. Josuttis, N.M.: The C++ Standard Library: A Tutorial and Reference (2012)
5. Deutsch, P., Gailly, J.-L.: ZLIB compressed data format specification version 3.3. Technical report (1996)
6. Moran, N., Bennett, J.T.: Supply Chain Analysis: From Quartermaster to Sunshop, vol. 11. FireEye (2013)
7. Yeo, G.S.-W., Phan, R.C.-W.: On the security of the WinRAR encryption feature. Int. J. Inf. Secur. **5**, 115–123 (2006)
8. Topan, V.I., Dudea, S.V., Canja, V.D.: Fuzzy whitelisting anti-malware systems and methods. US Patent 8,584,235 (2013)
9. Intel 64 and IA-32 architectures software developer manuals (2022)
10. Rajaraman, A., Ullman, J.D.: Mining of Massive Datasets. Cambridge University Press, Cambridge (2011)
11. Mihalca, A., Oprişa, C., Potolea, R.: Hunting for malware code in massive collections. In: 2020 IEEE International Conference on Automation, Quality and Testing, Robotics (AQTR), pp. 1–6. IEEE (2020)
12. Oprisa, C., Cabau, G., Colesa, A.: From plagiarism to malware detection. In: 2013 15th International Symposium on Symbolic and Numeric Algorithms for Scientific Computing, pp. 227–234. IEEE (2013)
13. Oprişa, C., Gavriluţ, D., Cabău, G.: A scalable approach for detecting plagiarized mobile applications. Knowl. Inf. Syst. **49**(1), 143–169 (2016)
14. Oprişa, C., Cabău, G., Coleşa, A.: Automatic code features extraction using bio-inspired algorithms. J. Comput. Virol. Hacking Tech. **10**(3), 165–176 (2014)
15. Griffin, K., Schneider, S., Hu, X., Chiueh, T.: Automatic generation of string signatures for malware detection. In: Kirda, E., Jha, S., Balzarotti, D. (eds.) RAID 2009. LNCS, vol. 5758, pp. 101–120. Springer, Heidelberg (2009). https://doi.org/10.1007/978-3-642-04342-0_6
16. Ida flirt (2022)
17. Top 13 popular packers used in malware (2022)
18. Jaccard, P.: The distribution of the flora in the alpine zone. 1. New Phytol. **11**(2), 37–50 (1912)
19. Cormen, T.H., Leiserson, C.E., Rivest, R.L., Stein, C.: Introduction to Algorithms. MIT Press, Cambridge (2022)

How Does Post-quantum Cryptography Affect Central Bank Digital Currency?

Lars Hupel[1][(✉)] [iD] and Makan Rafiee[2]

[1] Giesecke+Devrient GmbH, Prinzregentenstr. 161, 81677 Munich, Germany
lars.hupel@gi-de.com
[2] secunet Security Networks AG, Kurfürstenstr. 58, 45138 Essen, Germany
makan.rafiee@secunet.com

Abstract. Central Bank Digital Currency (CBDC) is an emerging trend in digital payments, with the vast majority of central banks around the world researching, piloting, or even operating a digital version of cash. While design choices differ broadly, such as accounts vs. tokens, the wallets are generally protected through cryptographic algorithms that safeguard against double spending and ensure non-repudiation. With the advent of quantum computing, these algorithms are threatened by new attack vectors. To better understand those threats, we conducted a study of typical assets in a CBDC system, describe which ones are most amenable to post-quantum cryptography, and propose an upgrade strategy.

Keywords: Post-Quantum Cryptography · Central Bank Digital Currency · Crypto Agility · Quantum Threat · Digital Currency · NIST Competition

1 Introduction

Central Bank Digital Currency (CBDC) is a digital means of payment, issued by a country's (or region's) central bank, denominated in the national currency. Over 130 countries are researching, developing, or piloting a CBDC, according to the latest data in Atlantic Council's CBDC tracker.[1] An additional 11 have already launched a CBDC. Although consensus around the precise definition of "launch" has yet to surface, a production system is generally understood to encompass the following criteria:

- continuous and uninterrupted availability for an indefinite amount of time, i.e. no unannounced shutdown,
- real legal tender that can always be exchanged at face value with cash and deposit money,
- no system resets, i.e. holdings will remain valid,

---

[1] https://www.atlanticcouncil.org/cbdctracker/, accessed 2023-07-26.

G. Wang et al. (Eds.): UbiSec 2023, CCIS 2034, pp. 45–62, 2024.
https://doi.org/10.1007/978-981-97-1274-8_4

– upgrade and maintenance work requires little to no intervention from users, except for long-term hardware upgrades, similar to the 2–5 year cycle of bank cards and smartphones.

Any CBDC operating within this framework will face a multitude of challenges, including operational, security, and monetary. In this paper, we are focusing on a core security aspect: cryptography. In particular, we examine the security requirements of CBDC – and more broadly, of comparable digital assets –, the cryptographic algorithms used to control for these security requirements, and the implications of quantum computing on these aspects.

Current State. The current gold standard in asymmetric cryptography, elliptic curves, are well-understood and widely deployed. Even though multiple sets of parameters for elliptic curves exist, they all share broadly similar characteristics regarding key generation, key lengths, and performance. For example, the ECDSA signature standard with an underlying NIST secp256r1 curve is available in the vast majority of programming languages, as well as in dedicated hardware devices such as HSMs or smart card chips. This enables excellent performance, which in turn means that secp256r1 enjoys popularity.

Cryptographic Evolution. However, all elliptic curves, including secp256r1, are known not to withstand the emerging threat of quantum computing. Their security relies on the discrete logarithm, which cannot be computed efficiently by classical computers. In other words, with today's methods, it is computationally infeasible to obtain the private key given only the public key. An algorithm discovered already in the 90 s by Peter W. Shor can perform this operation efficiently given sufficiently large quantum computers [17, 19].

Consequently, classical asymmetric cryptographic algorithms are at risk, not only those deployed in CBDCs. While the precise timelines for the hitherto theoretical turning into practical risk are not yet clear, it is strongly advisable that post-quantum cryptography be incorporated into a CBDC's design. The library of employed cryptographic primitives in digital currencies is huge: extending not only to wallets, but also to technical components of intermediaries, communication channels, and management of CBDC supply.

A basic consequence of the criteria for a launched CBDC is that any replacement or upgrade of cryptographic algorithms needs to be carried out in a rolling fashion, where new and old algorithm can coexist for a period of several months to several years, depending on whether the algorithm is used only in software or also in hardware.

Structure. The goal of this paper is to, therefore, provide insight into the future of cryptography as it applies to CBDC. We first give an overview of classical cryptographic algorithms and what they are used for in the CBDC context (Sect. 2). Then, we introduce the threats that quantum computing poses, as well as post-quantum algorithms that address those threats (Sect. 3). Equipped with this, we can then examine the cryptography in use for CBDC implementations and match them to appropriate algorithms (Sect. 4). Finally, we propose an opinionated framework for rolling updates, i.e., to put the earlier insights into practice (Sect. 5). Over the course of the paper, we will sometimes refer to cryptocurrencies as examples, as they share many cryptographic aspects with CBDC, but are often better researched, owing to their longer time of operation.

Terminology. In general, we define "wallets" as containers of digital assets, and more specifically, CBDC. Wallets can be in hardware or software form and manage private key material. Typically, "hardware wallet" refers to a physical device that is in the hands of a user. Naturally, they also require software to operate, but the hardware aspect refers to the security measures (e.g. secure elements in smart cards or other embedded devices). In contrast, "software wallets" can mean keys managed by some remote server where users access their funds through an app that authenticates towards the wallet's operator. Note that this distinction becomes blurred in case of self-custodial wallets, where users may use any combination of soft- and/or hardware, including open source or self-written, to manage their own keys. Following the majority opinion across central banks, we exclude this from consideration here.

As for the CBDC model, we follow the standard "token" vs. "account" distinction (see also Sect. 3.1), but do not assume either for the purpose of the paper, except when otherwise noted. When it becomes necessary in context, the term "token" is assumed to refer to key material that is short-lived.

"Central bank register" or "register" for short, refers to the centralized storage of transaction and/or token records at a central bank, which may or may not be implemented as a DLT. In public cryptocurrencies, this register is typically a proof-of-work or proof-of-stake blockchain. The register is said to "validate" transactions and/or tokens.

Related Work. The Bank for International Settlements (BIS), has analysed risks to the global financial infrastructure stemming from quantum computing. In particular, they have built a secure VPN tunnel connection two central banks [2]. In the CBDC context, this is useful for inter-bank connectivity, but does not apply to wallets.

Ciulei *et al.* [8] and Allende *et al.* [1] have conducted studies regarding the quantum-resistance of popular blockchains. The latter paper also provides an "end-to-end framework for for post-quantum blockchain networks," based on Ethereum [1]. Our paper complements this work with specific considerations pertaining to hardware wallets, and suggests upgrade strategies for quantum-proofing live systems.

2   Classical Cryptographic Algorithms

When shifting payments from physical cash to digital assets, a multitude of cryptographic primitives must be employed to control for security requirements. We will first sketch the security requirements and then explain which cryptographic primitives are used to satisfy them.

2.1 Security Requirements for Cash and Digital Assets

When two people engage in a cash transaction, e.g. a customer rendering banknotes to a merchant, a number of security requirements are already controlled for.

First, both the payer's and the payee's identities are established merely through personal trust: Both people trust the other person to be the rightful sender (or receiver, respectively) of the payment.

Second, authenticity of the banknotes can be established by haptic and visual properties of the physical objects. In many circumstances, for example, when the paid amount exceeds a certain threshold, a receiving party will employ additional authenticity checks of the banknotes: an ultraviolet lamp, a counting machine, or other devices.

Third, the rightful ownership of the banknotes is proved by merely demonstrating physical possession.

Fourth, and relatedly to the previous point, the payment is completed and settled by change of ownership of the banknotes: the cash physically changes hands.

Fifth, the payer is prevented from double-spending, i.e. using the same banknotes for two concurring payments: as opposed to data, physical objects cannot be cloned.

Finally, in a series of multiple of cash payments, it is impossible for any third party to track the payment patterns.

Applying those security requirements to digital assets, they can be summarized in more technical terms as follows:

1. Authenticity of sender and receiver
2. Authenticity of the asset
3. Proof-of-ownership of the asset
4. Non-repudiation of transactions
5. Prevention of double-spending
6. Privacy

For cash, those requirements can be easily derived from its defining characteristics: its physical nature and it being a bearer instrument.

In contrast, in a digital asset ecosystem, they must be controlled for with cryptographic primitives. Note that in cryptocurrencies, the first point is often not guaranteed, whereas in CBDC, some form of identity will typically be established, at least locally between participants.

2.2 Classification of Cryptographic Primitives for Digital Assets

To ensure the authenticity of sender and receiver, we employ wallet certificates. Those wallet certificates include some identifier, and are derived by a PKI operated by the central bank. The underlying cryptographic primitive are digital signatures, either based on elliptic curves or RSA. Wallet signatures can also be used to ensure non-repudiation of transactions. (See also Sect. 5.2 for a more detailed treatment of wallet identifiers in our framework.)

Furthermore, the wallet certificates can also be used to establish an end-to-end encrypted channel between the wallets by using a key exchange algorithm, such as ECDH. The communication channel is then encrypted with a symmetric cipher, e.g. AES-128 GCM.

The authenticity of the tokens must also be checked using digital signatures. This comprises the proof-of-ownership from the sender (which can be checked locally by the receiver), as well as a double-spending check (which relies on global knowledge). Therefore, a verifying instance must be involved. In the case of CBDC, this instance can be centrally operated by the central bank, whereas cryptocurrencies would typically use a DLT. Since a central bank has complete knowledge of the tokens in circulation, we refer to its verifying instance as the "central bank register".

For CBDC, there is an additional requirement in that the register must communicate the authenticity of a token to the receiver thereof. (In blockchains, this is achieved by the receiver monitoring the newly-added blocks.) Consequently, the register can digitally sign its response using a well-known certificate (see also Sect. 4.2).

In summary, both symmetric and asymmetric cryptography must be used to control for the security requirements in a CBDC ecosystem.

3 Post-quantum Cryptography

In this section, we will explain the new threat model that quantum computing creates for digital currencies, or more generally, any type of digital asset. One of the ways to alleviate this problem is to switch to cryptographic algorithms, some of them novel, that do not suffer from those threats. Therefore, we give an overview of the top contenders in NIST's standardization competition for such post-quantum algorithms. Alternatively or complementary to that, best practices can be applied to mitigate quantum threats in the short term, which we will discuss here too.

3.1 Threats to Digital Assets

Let us consider an example: assets in digital currencies are typically represented as public-private keypairs. In the cryptocurrency sphere, the main contenders Bitcoin and Ethereum both use the secp256k1 elliptic curve as a basis. Knowledge of the private key corresponding to some digital assets enables the owner to spend that asset. CBDCs would follow the same or a very similar model. Shor's algorithm can be used advantageously not just for breaking RSA keys, but also for breaking elliptic curve keys.

Incoming payments require the sender to know the recipient's public key, which is often referred to as an "address". Conversely, outgoing payments requires producing a digital signature which uses the private key, but can be validated just with the knowledge of the public key, which is typically recorded in a blockchain (or in the case of CBDC, the register). This allows anyone to send assets to a particular address, but only the rightful owner to spend from that address. Security of one's assets relies on keeping the private key confidential.

Using classical computers, keeping the private key confidential, but allowing the public key to be known or recorded by third parties, does not threaten security.

However, under a quantum regime, an attacker can use a public key to run Shor's algorithm, obtaining the corresponding private key. Therefore, the attacker is equipped with the ability to produce valid digital signatures. In consequence, stealing the assets.

When sending assets to a particular address, both Bitcoin and Ethereum do not use the public key directly as an address, but rather a hash of the public key. Fortunately, sufficiently long hashes cannot be easily inverted by quantum computers.[2] While the assets are at rest, i.e. have been received on an address but not yet spent, a quantum attacker does not have an advantage over a classical attacker. But as soon as assets are transferred out, the legitimate owner must disclose the public key so that the blockchain network (or in the case of CBDC, the register) can validate the signature. In other words, as soon as the assets are in transit, they are at risk.

3.2   Classical Mitigation Measures

Not all cryptocurrencies have the same exposure to this threat. Bitcoin, or more broadly speaking, "token-based" (also referred to as "UTxO") digital assets, discourage reuse of the same public-private keypair, and some variants forbid it outright. The advantage lies within the fact that an outgoing transaction from an address will always consume the entirety of the assets associated with that address. For example, if address A has a balance of 10 €, and its owner wants to send 2 € to address B, the wallet will also move the remaining 8 € to a freshly-generated address C. An attacker breaking the public key of A will not be able to steal any assets, since they are now located at C, its public key not known to the attacker.

However, if a quantum attacker can outperform the payment network, and can break A's private key faster than the network or blockchain can validate and finalize the aforementioned payment, they could generate a new transaction, moving parts or all of the funds to another address that is controlled by the attacker.

Ethereum, or more broadly speaking, "account-based" digital assets particularly suffer from this problem, since addresses are routinely reused. In other

---

[2] Symmetric ciphers and cryptographic hash functions do not rely on one-way functions but rather on the speed of searching a large key space. Grover's algorithm is a quantum algorithm that significantly speeds up the search for keys in a key space. By doubling the key sizes of symmetric encryption algorithms to 256 bits and hash algorithms to 512 bits, even Grover's algorithm does not pose a threat to symmetric cryptography.

Table 1. Overview over the winners of the NIST competition

Type	PKE/KEM	Signature
Lattice-based	CRYSTALS-Kyber	CRYSTALS-Dilithium FALCON
Hash-based	n/a	SPHINCS+

words, the first time an outgoing transaction is signed from an Ethereum address, all assets at rest in that address are available for subsequent theft from an attacker. According to a 2021 survey by Deloitte, approximately 65% of all Ether in the public Ethereum network are stored in addresses with revealed public keys [4].

To summarize, in the case of public cryptocurrencies, using public key hashes and frequent address rotation are both feasible, albeit not perfect, mitigation strategies [3]. CBDCs with a tighter control through the issuing entity and less public exposure can go further: for example, digital signatures and public keys that are transferred from a wallet to backend systems or to another wallet can be additionally protected by end-to-end transit encryption, such as TLS. Unfortunately, these mitigations are also not perfect and subject to quantum threats. Therefore, for some aspects of a CBDC, it becomes necessary to select truly quantum-safe algorithms.

3.3 NIST Competition

The National Institute of Standard and Technology (NIST) has a history of holding competitions to evaluate, select and standardize cryptographic algorithms. The most prominent of those competitions were the Advanced Encryption Standard (AES) standardization process between 1997 and 2000 and the NIST hash function competition between 2007 and 2012 [13,15].

The competition entails multiple rounds with each round eliminating a number of submitted algorithms. Research groups are encouraged to submit algorithms, which are then tested and evaluated by the NIST and the broader scientific community. NIST specifies evaluation criteria for the competition and selects the winning algorithm at the end of the process.

During the leading post-quantum cryptography conference PQCrypto in 2016, the NIST announced a new competition for selecting quantum secure asymmetric cryptographic algorithms [10].

While all previous competitions were designated to select exactly one winning algorithm, such as a symmetric encryption algorithm (AES) or a flexible hash function (SHA-3), this new competition, however, selects multiple new asymmetric algorithms as winners. The algorithms are divided in two subcategories: Public Key Encryption/Key Encapsulation Method and Signature Scheme.

The reason for selecting multiple algorithms as winners is a result of the inevitable drawbacks that these new algorithms will bring: Some are very slow

Table 2. Size comparison of signature algorithms, adapted from Sikeridis *et al.* [20], Table 1, with Specification column omitted (verbatim copy with some data removed for brevity)

Signature Algorithm	Public Key Size (Byte)	Private Key Size (Byte)	Signature Size (Byte)	Claimed Classical Security Level	Claimed PQ Security Level
RSA 3072	387	384	384	128 bits	0 bits
ECDSA 384	48	48	48	192 bits	0 bits
Dilithium II	1184	2800	2044	100 bits	103 bits
Dilithium IV	1760	3856	3366	174 bits	158 bits
FALCON 512	897	1281	690	114 bits	103 bits
FALCON 1024	1793	2305	1330	264 bits	230 bits
SPHINCS+	32	64	16976	128 bits	64 bits

in signature creation, while others have very large key material. Since there is no one-fits-all solution, algorithms must be selected for their specific use cases. Selecting multiple winning algorithms yields greater flexibility in cryptographic agility and enables implementors to tailor the choice of algorithms to their specific needs.

Five mathematical one-way functions turned out to be promising for designing quantum secure algorithms: hash-based, lattice-based, code-based, multivariate polynomial-based and supersingular elliptic curve isogeny-based.

In July 2022, the NIST announced the winners of the competition as well as further algorithms to be considered (Table 1) [14, 16]. Lattice-based algorithms and hash-based signatures were the only one-way functions in the winning algorithms.

The most prominent multivariate and isogeny-based algorithms were both broken last year in a matter of days and fell out of relevance for further consideration [6, 7].

Winners of the NIST Competition. CRYSTALS-Kyber was the only algorithm selected for PKE/KEM, which does not yield flexibility in the choice of algorithms. Therefore, in the following, we will only consider the advantages and drawbacks of the signature algorithms: CRYSTALS-Dilithium, FALCON and SPHINCS+.

Comparison of Signature Algorithms. In 2020, Sikeridis *et al.* ran a performance study on quantum-secure signature algorithms to analyze and compare key sizes (Table 2) and operational run-time (Table 3) [20].

Size Comparison. It can be observed that the classical algorithms RSA and ECDSA have remarkably low key and signature sizes, which cannot be reached by the quantum secure alternatives. Only SPHINCS+ has much lower key sizes,

Table 3. Performance comparison of signature algorithms, adapted from Sikeridis *et al.* [20], Table 2 (verbatim copy with some data removed for brevity)

Signature Algorithm	Sign (Mean) (ms)	Sign (St. Derivation) (ms)	Verify (Mean) (ms)	Verify (St. Derivation) (ms)
RSA 3072	3.19	0.023	0.06	0.001
ECDSA 384	1.32	0.012	1.05	0.020
Dilithium II	0.82	0.021	0.16	0.005
Dilithium IV	1.25	0.021	0.30	0.012
FALCON 512	5.22	0.054	0.05	0.004
FALCON 1024	11.37	0.102	0.11	0.005
SPHINCS+	93.37	0.654	3.92	0.043

which is counteracted by the immensely large signature sizes of over 16,000 bytes and comparatively low levels of post-quantum security levels.

For approximately the same levels of post-quantum security, Dilithium and FALCON yield similar public key sizes, albeit much larger than classical primitives as RSA and ECDSA. FALCON, however, yields significantly smaller private key and signature sizes than Dilithium.

Performance Comparison. While classical algorithms were strictly better in all size comparisons, quantum-secure alternatives can have competitive sign and verify performance. SPHINCS+ is the slowest algorithm and comes with much longer signature creation and verification times, up to 100x slower signature creation times than classical ECDSA.

Dilithium and FALCON both have similarly low verify operations, even outperforming ECDSA by a large margin. Additionally, Dilithium even outperforms both RSA and ECDSA for signature creating times. Falcons signature creation performance is significantly higher than Dilithium.

In summary, SPHINCS+ comes with the most drawbacks of both large signature sizes and slow sign operations but having very small key sizes. Dilithium and FALCON come with different strengths and weaknesses: Dilithium has a much better signature creation performance, while Falcon comes with smaller key and signature sizes. Hence, the choice of which algorithm to use strongly depends on the concrete size and requirements and must be tailored to each particular use case.

4   Cryptographic Inventory

In this section, we will go into greater detail about the cryptographic mechanisms employed in a digital asset ecosystem, and how they can be made fit for post-quantum cryptography. The first point, public-key infrastructure, is only applicable to a CBDC, whereas the later points can also be applied to other types of (decentralized) digital assets.

4.1 Public-Key Infrastructure

In order to authenticate participating entities in the CBDC ecosystem, either
to the central bank or to each other, employing certificates is a natural choice.
Certificate owners can either be natural persons, such as customers of a commercial bank, or abstract entities such as a centrally managed service or a smart
card. Since the trust of customers to a CBDC is, as the name says, dependent
on the customers' trust towards the central bank, it is also a natural choice to
build a Public Key Infrastructure (PKI) managed by the central bank. Then, the
trust in the authenticity of all entities in the CBDC ecosystem is derived from
trusting one Root Certificate Authority (CA) certificate managed by the central
bank. The central bank can exercise full control over which entities are eligible
to partake in the ecosystem or, alternatively, delegate the trust by issuing sub
CA certificates to trusted partners.

By verifying these certificates and their respective certificate chains, customers and services could always ensure that communication partners are trustworthy.

Since certificates usually have long validity periods, cryptographic agility
must be carefully considered and planned, long before the threat by quantum
computers materializes.

While there are different certificate formats, most prominently the X.509
format, the approaches to tackle quantum agility can be achieved similarly if
the certificate offer extension fields or not (described in more detail below).

Transitioning to a quantum-secure PKI can be done abruptly, by deactivat-
ing the classical PKI and building a new PKI as soon as the quantum threat
materializes. This approach, however, is in most cases not applicable nor desirable. Specifically, a CBDC ecosystem must ensure a constant run-time of the
system without any interruptions.

A smooth transition to a quantum-secure PKI is both more desirable and
more challenging. The transition must be initiated in time and would result in a
transition period where both classical and quantum-secure algorithms are used
in certificates simultaneously. These so-called hybrid certificates can be designed
in two ways: composite and non-composite.

Composite certificates have been under consideration in an IETF draft
[21] and describe how certificates with multiple signature algorithms could look
like. There are two options being discussed: with and without extension fields.

In case the certificate format allows for extension fields, as for example X.509,
then a quantum-secure signature algorithm would be included in a certificate in
such an extension field [21,22].

In case extension fields are not existing in the used certificate format, the
classical and quantum-secure algorithm information would exist in the same
field in the certificate; either by concatenation or by clear separation within the
certificate field. In this case, certificates parsing would need to be adjusted in all
relying parties.

In both cases, a transition can be made smoothly. Policy makers could
enforce certificate verifications to entail either only the classical algorithm, or

the quantum-secure algorithm, or both. This policy adjustment can be made in run-time, and would not require any interference by the central bank with any circulating certificates.

An inevitable disadvantage of composite certificates is the larger size of the certificates resulting from the additional key material and signatures. Particularly bearer-tokens as smart cards could have difficulties with the resulting larger certificates. An informed choice of algorithm (see also Sect. 3.3) is necessary.

Alternatively, the idea of **non-composite certificates** is that instead of including all the key material in the same certificates, every entity in the PKI could also be equipped with two separately issued certificates. These certificates do not need to be issued at the same time, but can be issued at different points in time. The certificates must be, however, linked to each other by a reference mechanism [5].

The CSR for the certificate with the quantum-secure certificate would be signed with the private key corresponding to the classical certificate. This approach also results in greater flexibility, as the policy makers could also enforce verification requirements on the relying parties. Either only the classical-certificate, or only the quantum-secure certificate, or both verifications must be successful.

4.2 Algorithm Choice in the CBDC Ecosystem

We now discuss suitable algorithms for various types of key material.

PKI Root Keys. The choice of quantum-secure algorithms in a PKI greatly depends on the requirements arising from which entities create, manage, and verifies the certificates. For example, a root CA key has highest security requirements and must be stored securely at the central bank in an air-gapped HSM. Regular signature operations are not expected and small private key material is also not necessary. These requirements can, therefore, be ignored. The public key and signature sizes are important, however, since all relying parties in the PKI must securely store the root CA certificate locally to be able to verify all certificate chains. In the case when hardware is used as a bearer instrument for CBDC, e.g. a smart card, hybrid certificates for a smooth post-quantum transition would come with large root CA certificate sizes.

FALCON would be a suitable choice for the root CA signature algorithm, since the slightly longer signature creation times are outweighed by the smaller signature sizes.

Account and Wallet Keys. Account and/or wallet keys (depending on the CBDC model) are long-lived: the key material is created once and is persists for a long time, up to many years. They are most likely part of the centrally managed PKI to ensure that only authenticated accounts and wallets partake in the CBDC ecosystem. That said, the key usage might differ according to the design specifications of the payment protocols. Account and wallet keys can be used to establish a secure channel by means of classical ECDH or, for post-quantum security, CRYSTALS-Kyber, since it is the only selected PKE/KEM algorithm by NIST. A symmetric AES key is negotiated and derived by choosing the appropriate key derivation functions (KDFs) and hash lengths.

For maximum flexibility, it is also a viable option to choose different algorithms within the same PKI. For example, in the case that wallet certificates are used to sign CBDC transactions, the expected number of sign operations is very high in contrast to a root CA certificate. Furthermore, private key material of a root CA certificate does not have strict size and performance requirements since it is stored in an HSM, which are capable of handling large key sizes sufficiently fast. Conversely, private key material of wallet certificates could be stored in devices with limited memory.

Therefore, FALCON and Dilithium are viable algorithm choices for root CA certificates. For end certificates with a high expected number of sign operations, FALCON is the better choice. SPHINCS+ is not recommended for either because of the large signature sizes.

Token Keys. Tokens are keys that are created both at the central bank (minting process) but also in wallets during regular operations. In contrast to account and wallet keys, token keys are short-lived and are not part of any PKI. (See also Sect. 5.3 for a more detailed discussion of cipher upgrades for tokens.)

Since token keys are created and deleted regularly, a new arising requirement are short key pair generation times.

While Dilithium has much lower key pair generation times than FALCON or SPHINCS+ [18], Dilithium signatures are up to three times as large as FALCON signatures (see above). Therefore, the choice between FALCON or Dilithium for token key material strongly depends on the concrete design of the payment protocols and the expected number of key creations and limitations in memory for token signatures. As mentioned above, SPHINCS+ is not suited for token keys because of the large signature sizes.

Other Long- and Short-Lived Keys. Apart from the key material discussed above, other keys and certificates might be used for digital assets. For example, the central bank register responsible to validate transactions is a crucial component for security. Transaction must be verified and a receipt must be returned to the payer or payee to trust and finish the transaction. These receipts require a trustworthy signature from the register. The certificate used for receipt signatures has a long validity period with low key size and key generation time requirements, but must perform an abundance of signatures to verify transactions. Since Dilithium has much faster signature creation times than FALCON and SPHINCS+, Dilithium is a good choice for a register certificate.

5 Rolling Upgrades

The requirements for a production-grade, widely available CBDC, outlined in the introductions, imply that the system cannot be stopped for a coordinated upgrade of cryptographic algorithms. Therefore, any upgrade roadmap must consider a rolling upgrade strategy. Especially popular in operations of large-scale distributed systems, a rolling upgrade entails a step-by-step upgrade of individual components with a specified timeframe in which old and new versions can coexist and continue to interact.

Key questions now include:

- How should a component be designed to enable both forward (old system understands new instructions) and backward (new system understand old instructions) compatibility?
- How long should the timeframe for compatibility be?
- Can the upgrade be coordinated effectively?

Despite the similarities between cryptocurrencies and CBDC that we have alluded to earlier, their answers to these key questions differ dramatically. Hence, we will focus this section on CBDC.

5.1 Design Decisions that May Influence Upgrade Strategy

An important dimension in CBDC design is the use of software- and hardware-based wallets for transactions. In more ambitious designs, hardware wallets can be used both in online and offline payment scenarios and exchange money with other hardware wallets, but also software wallets.

Software-based wallets can come in many shapes, e.g. as a smartphone app, but also as a database entry managed by a financial intermediary, such as a commercial bank. In the latter case, upgrades would be completely transparent to the user.

For hardware-based wallets, the form factor is a core consideration. The cheapest form factor available is a commodity smart card, like what is in use today with credit or debit cards. Using CBDC on smart cards relies on availability of hardware acceleration for cryptographic algorithms (such as ECDSA with particular curve parameters) to be feasible. Typically, implementors do not have the ability to choose from a variety of algorithms.

Another dimension to be considered is whether self-custody is allowed, a topic that is hotly debated in literature [11,12]. Simply speaking, a CBDC offering self-custody would enable individual users to provision their own wallets, based on hardware and software that they deem fit. Central banks, or financial intermediaries that act as wallet issuers, would have significantly reduced control over the evolution of such self-custody wallets. For that reason, we exclude them from further discussions.

5.2   Wallet Identification

In cryptocurrencies, addresses are computed from private cryptographic material. For example, an Ethereum address is computed by hashing an elliptic curve public key. Wallets would scan the blockchain for any transaction involving this address. While this avoids the problem of routing payments to particular entities based on e.g. address prefixes, like in IBANs, the downside is that the address of the asset is conflated with the identity to the wallet.

This conflation can be dissolved in CBDCs, where wallet identifiers do not have to be coupled to the cryptographic keys stored therein. In fact, a wallet identifier could be akin to a traditional bank account number, which stays fixed over the lifetime of a bank account, even though internal implementations details may change. Similarly, a credit card number would stay the same even after the physical credit card is replaced.

The reason for this discrepancy is that in CBDC, which should be accessible to the broad public without in-depth knowledge of cryptography, it would be poor user experience to change wallet identifiers if the algorithm changes.

Therefore, we propose that wallet identifiers should not be based on private cryptographic material, but are randomized upon creation and remain stable over time ("agnostic identifiers"). Note that such identifiers are only used for routing in online payment scenarios, i.e., for a sending wallet to identify the entity managing the receiving wallet. Offline payment scenarios do not require routing due to physical proximity. But more importantly, the central bank register can be made oblivious to identifiers, since it only concerns itself with digital signatures from the key material associated with the assets themselves, therefore avoiding a privacy risk.

The disadvantage of this approach is that agnostic identifiers, as opposed to a Bitcoin or Ethereum address, cannot be used to deduce which cryptographic algorithm is supported. This is balanced by the advantage that agnostic identifiers can support multiple algorithms with full transparency.

The remainder of this section discusses token upgrade strategies in general, and hardware concerns based specifically on agnostic identifiers.

5.3   Token Upgrade Strategies

As mentioned earlier, rolling updates are already a routine process in backend systems. In the case of new cryptographic algorithms, forward compatibility is much more difficult to achieve than backward compatibility. As an example, consider adding a data field to a message: forward compatibility is satisfied if a component can ignore the new data field and can still process the message. But a new cryptographic algorithm would need to be available on the component, otherwise the message cannot be understood.

Instead, focus should be placed on careful backwards compatibility, coupled with feature detection, if necessary.

Consider a hypothetical upgrade of a cryptographic algorithm, e.g. replacing ECDSA with FALCON as digital signature scheme for CBDC tokens. ECDSA and FALCON have different private key formats and lengths, therefore necessitating a dedicated process.

As a first step, the central bank would equip its register with the new cryptographic algorithm. In the case of a token-based CBDC, the register would need to offer a way to convert old-style EC tokens to FALCON tokens. But since such a CBDC would already support a transaction where one EC token can be exchanged for another one, simply adding a "token version" field in the token format easily enables this kind of protocol evolution. The case of hybrid schemes may complicate implementation details, but can still be achieved in this manner.

This new algorithm becomes available at a certain point in time, with the central bank mandating a deadline of migrating all tokens. For simplicity, we use "new wallet" and "old wallet" to refer to wallets held in software components that are or are not aware of FALCON yet. Recall that with agnostic wallet identifiers, the sending wallet would not be able to deduce the supported key formats of the receiving wallet.

Now, we distinguish between the following cases and subcases for transactions, and discuss a migration strategy for each:

1. old wallet paying to old wallet
    (a) EC tokens: works unmodified
    (b) FALCON tokens: would not occur
2. old wallet paying to new wallet
    (a) EC tokens: new wallet needs to be backwards compatible, auto-detection possible
    (b) FALCON tokens: would not occur
3. new wallet paying to old wallet
    (a) EC tokens: works unmodified
    (b) FALCON tokens: only works if register supports version downgrade
4. new wallet paying to new wallet
    (a) EC tokens: new wallet needs to be backwards compatible, auto-detection possible
    (b) FALCON tokens: works unmodified

Backwards-compatible auto-detection is trivial to implement, since the receiving wallet merely needs to check the version of the incoming token.

The opposite direction, namely detecting if a receiving wallet only supports an earlier version (case 3) can be solved by imitating HTTP-style content negotiation: when the sending wallet initiates a payment, it first contacts the receiving wallet and offers a set of token versions, which will then be selected by the receiving wallet.

Should a version downgrade (subcase 3b) not be desired or implemented by the central bank, it is advisable that wallet operators avoid premature conversion before the deadline for migration (subcases 2a and 4a). This should be weighed against the possibility to run small trials of a new cryptographic algorithm to gather more experience, and slowly ramp up the percentage of wallets that use the new version.

Note that this upgrade strategy can also be applied for other protocol changes, e.g. increasing the resolution of monetary values (two decimal digits to four decimal digits).

5.4   Hardware Upgrade Strategies

While token upgrades in hardware wallets follow the same logic as described in the previous section, there are some additional considerations relating to their restricted compute power and their offline capability.

Typical credit or debit cards have expiration times between three to five years. Therefore, consumers are already familiar with the procedure of routinely exchanging payment cards. Since simple smart cards are easy to manufacture and distribute, we anticipate no significant issues leveraging this strategy to upgrade CBDC hardware wallets.

A problem remains if a CBDC is offline-capable. Some implementations use deferred communication between hardware wallets and the central bank register: transactions instantly settle even offline, but wallets keep a record of digital signatures to upload them to the register and have them validated at a later point. This may complicate subcase 3b, which should be avoided in such a setting.

Applied to the above example, this would imply the following timeline:

- At a particular time, FALCON becomes available at the register.
- Soon afterwards, hardware wallets supporting both EC and FALCON become available. They never upgrade tokens unless prompted by receiving a FALCON token.
- Once all users have obtained new wallets (to be defined as a soft deadline), all software wallets upgrade tokens. FALCON tokens start to appear in hardware wallets, due to software-to-hardware top-ups.
- Slowly, the hardware wallet ecosystem upgrades, due to hardware-to-hardware payments.

The hard migration deadline, i.e. the time when the register would no longer accept EC tokens, would need to be defined to be at least the soft deadline, plus validity of the new hardware wallets. An additional safety margin would allow users to exchange their funds in case they let a wallet sit unused for an extended amount of time, similarly to how the Eurozone's national banks to this date still allow exchange of local currency to the Euro.

Perfect enforcement of the aforementioned deadlines is almost impossible in any manner, since hardware wallets in full offline operation may not have access to trusted clocks [9].

Finally, we will briefly consider point-of-sale (or other payment) terminals. In the case of online terminals, support for new algorithms can be added through routine over-the-air updates. For pure offline terminals, this is naturally not possible.

Therefore, it is advantageous to design the payment protocol between hardware wallets to be independent of the communication channel and the terminal. Concretely, the terminal and wallet(s) may have a shared interface for payment lifecycle (initiation, retry, cancelation), but the token-level protocol is opaque towards the terminal. This prevents the need for terminal upgrades altogether. On a low level, this can be achieved by modularizing terminals and allowing merchants to merely exchange the smart card (or chip) on which the wallet resides.

6 Conclusion

We have discussed how the advent of quantum computing affects the kind of cryptography used in digital assets, more specifically, a central bank digital currency (CBDC). In particular, the problem that elliptic curve private keys could be computed by quantum attackers merely by the disclosure of the corresponding public key is a looming issue that threatens safe custody of assets. Even worse, it could lead to loss of funds without any user interactions whatsoever.

While many concerns are shared between CBDC and cryptocurrency, the universal nature of CBDC poses additional challenges: for example, upgrades of cryptographic algorithms must be completely transparent to users as to not hinder adoption. However, given that CBDC is also more centralized, it stands to reason that central banks can use their more granular control over the ecosystem to ensure smooth transitions.

We have shown that a digital asset ecosystem comes with a great deal of key material with a multitude of different requirements. The choice of the correct quantum-secure algorithm in accordance with NIST recommendations is, therefore, not straightforward and must be considered carefully. In order to grant full flexibility for crypto agility, we proposed not choosing one algorithm for all components, but instead select the algorithm for each specific component.

Our proposed cryptographic upgrade framework enables just that and can be applied to a token-based CBDC design. The framework's cornerstones are the use of agnostic wallet identifiers, decoupling user-facing addresses from private key material, and a conservative upgrade strategy relying on auto-detection of wallet capabilities. We expect this framework to be used for both software and hardware wallets, and potentially for self-custodial wallets as well.

Acknowledgements. We thank our colleague Hermann Drexler for fruitful discussions about post-quantum cryptography. This work has been partially supported by the Federal Ministry of Education and Research (BMBF), Verbundprojekt CONTAIN (13N16582).

References

1. Allende, M., et al.: Quantum-resistance in blockchain networks. Sci. Rep. **13**(1) (2023). https://doi.org/10.1038/s41598-023-32701-6
2. Bank for International Settlements: Project Leap: Quantum-proofing the financial system. Technical report (2023). https://www.bis.org/publ/othp67.pdf
3. Barnes, I., Bosch, B.: Quantum computers and the bitcoin blockchain
4. Barnes, I., Bosch, B., Haalstra, O.: Quantum risk to the Ethereum blockchain - a bump in the road or a brick wall?

5. Becker, A., Guthrie, R., Jenkins, M.J.: Non-composite hybrid authentication in PKIX and applications to internet protocols. Internet-Draft draft-becker-guthrie-noncomposite-hybrid-auth-00 (2022). https://datatracker.ietf.org/doc/draft-becker-guthrie-noncomposite-hybrid-auth/00/

6. Beullens, W.: Breaking rainbow takes a weekend on a laptop. Cryptology ePrint Archive, Paper 2022/214 (2022). https://eprint.iacr.org/2022/214

7. Castryck, W., Decru, T.: An efficient key recovery attack on SIDH. Cryptology ePrint Archive, Paper 2022/975 (2022). https://eprint.iacr.org/2022/975

8. Ciulei, A.T., Crețu, M.C., Simion, E.: Preparation for post-quantum era: a survey about blockchain schemes from a post-quantum perspective. Cryptology ePrint Archive, Paper 2022/026 (2022). https://eprint.iacr.org/2022/026

9. Deutsche Bundesbank: Eurosystem experimentation regarding a digital euro: Research workstream on hardware bearer instrument (2021)

10. Moody, D.: Post-quantum cryptography: NIST's plan for the future (2016)

11. Mortimer-Lee, P.: Letter: freedom and security are part of CBDC debate too. Financial Times (2023). https://www.ft.com/content/92fb7d93-8705-44a0-850b-65f2ddef1018

12. Narula, N., Swartz, L.: Central bank digital currency? How money could be redesigned (2023). https://www.weforum.org/agenda/2023/01/davos23-central-bank-digital-currency-redesigning-money/

13. NIST: Cryptographic Standards and Guidelines - AES Development. https://csrc.nist.gov/projects/cryptographic-standards-and-guidelines/archived-crypto-projects/aes-development

14. NIST: Post-Quantum Cryptography - Round 4 Submissions. https://csrc.nist.gov/Projects/post-quantum-cryptography/round-4-submissions

15. NIST: NIST Selects Winner of Secure Hash Algorithm (SHA-3) Competition (2012). https://www.nist.gov/news-events/news/2012/10/nist-selects-winner-secure-hash-algorithm-sha-3-competition

16. NIST: NIST Announces First Four Quantum-Resistant Cryptographic Algorithms (2022). https://www.nist.gov/news-events/news/2022/07/nist-announces-first-four-quantum-resistant-cryptographic-algorithms

17. Proos, J., Zalka, C.: Shor's discrete logarithm quantum algorithm for elliptic curves. QIC **3**(4), 317–344 (2003)

18. Raavi, M., Wuthier, S., Chandramouli, P., Balytskyi, Y., Zhou, X., Chang, S.-Y.: Security comparisons and performance analyses of post-quantum signature algorithms. In: Sako, K., Tippenhauer, N.O. (eds.) ACNS 2021. LNCS, vol. 12727, pp. 424–447. Springer, Cham (2021). https://doi.org/10.1007/978-3-030-78375-4_17

19. Shor, P.W.: Polynomial-time algorithms for prime factorization and discrete logarithms on a quantum computer. SIAM J. Sci. Statist. Comput. **26**(1997), 1484 (1995). https://doi.org/10.1137/S0097539795293172

20. Sikeridis, D., Kampanakis, P., Devetsikiotis, M.: Post-quantum authentication in TLS 1.3: A performance study. Cryptology ePrint Archive, Paper 2020/071 (2020). https://doi.org/10.14722/ndss.2020.24203, https://eprint.iacr.org/2020/071

21. Truskovsky, A., Geest, D.V., Fluhrer, S., Kampanakis, P., Ounsworth, M., Mister, S.: Multiple public-key algorithm X.509 certificates. Internet-Draft draft-truskovsky-lamps-pq-hybrid-x509-01 (2018). https://datatracker.ietf.org/doc/draft-truskovsky-lamps-pq-hybrid-x509/01/

22. Vogt, S., Funke, H.: How quantum computers threat security of PKIs and thus eIDs. In: Open Identity Summit 2021, pp. 83–94. Gesellschaft für Informatik e.V., Bonn (2021)

FRAD: Front-Running Attacks Detection on Ethereum Using Ternary Classification Model

Yuheng Zhang[1], Pin Liu[2]⬮, Guojun Wang[1(✉)]⬮, Peiqiang Li[1], Wanyi Gu[1], Houji Chen[1], Xuelei Liu[1], and Jinyao Zhu[1]

[1] School of Computer Science and Cyber Engineering, Guangzhou University, Guangzhou 510006, China
csgjwang@gzhu.edu.cn
[2] School of Computer Science and Engineering, Central South University, Changsha 410083, China

Abstract. With the evolution of blockchain technology, the issue of transaction security, particularly on platforms like Ethereum, has become increasingly critical. Front-running attacks, a unique form of security threat, pose significant challenges to the integrity of blockchain transactions. In these attack scenarios, malicious actors monitor other users' transaction activities, then strategically submit their own transactions with higher fees. This ensures their transactions are executed before the monitored transactions are included in the block. The primary objective of this paper is to delve into a comprehensive classification of transactions associated with front-running attacks, which aims to equip developers with specific strategies to counter each type of attack. To achieve this, we introduce a novel detection method named FRAD (Front-Running Attacks Detection on Ethereum using Ternary Classification Model). This method is specifically tailored for transactions within decentralized applications (DApps) on Ethereum, enabling accurate classification of front-running attacks involving transaction displacement, insertion, and suppression. Our experimental validation reveals that the Multilayer Perceptron (MLP) classifier offers the best performance in detecting front-running attacks, achieving an impressive accuracy rate of 84.59% and F1-score of 84.60%.

Keywords: Front-running Attack · Ethereum · Blockchain · Decentralized Application · MLP Classifier

1 Introduction

In the continuous development of blockchain technology, Ethereum has established its position as a leading public blockchain platform. Its extensive influence has permeated various fields, including but not limited to finance, gaming, and supply chain management [1]. However, the widespread application of this technology has also revealed a series of security challenges, among which the problem

G. Wang et al. (Eds.): UbiSec 2023, CCIS 2034, pp. 63–75, 2024.
https://doi.org/10.1007/978-981-97-1274-8_5

of front-running attacks is particularly prominent [2]. Front-running attacks pose a unique security threat to blockchain transactions. In this scenario, malicious hackers engage in the surveillance of transactional activity conducted by other users, then submit their own transactions and pay higher fees to ensure their transactions are executed before the observed transactions are included in the block [3]. This type of attack is particularly common on Ethereum, as the transparency of transactions allows anyone to view unconfirmed transactions in the transaction pool [4]. Moreover, the rise of DeFi (Decentralized Finance) has triggered a surge in Ethereum transaction volume, providing fertile ground for front-running attacks [5]. Cybercriminals exploit transaction delays and information asymmetry in the transaction pool to maximize their illicit gains [6], making this a prevalent issue within the Ethereum domain. The impact of front-running attacks on the Ethereum ecosystem is significant. They increase the transaction risk for ordinary users, potentially leading to a loss of user benefits [7]. Simultaneously, they drive the continuous rise in Ethereum network transaction fees, increasing the cost of transactions for users [8]. Ultimately, these attacks may hinder the progress of projects within the Ethereum ecosystem and erode user trust in blockchain technology [9].

In decentralized applications (DApps) transactions on Ethereum, the problem of front-running attacks is even more severe [10]. The susceptibility of DApps to potential threats arises from their inherent openness and transparency, allowing malevolent forces to readily observe and scrutinise transactions. Consequently, these actors can exploit these vulnerabilities to execute assaults through the front-running tactics [11]. This not only threatens the interests of DApp users but also negatively impacts the stability and sustainability of the entire Ethereum ecosystem. Therefore, researching and addressing the problem of front-running attacks in DApp transactions is of vital importance for protecting user interests, reducing transaction risks, and promoting the healthy development of the Ethereum ecosystem [12]. Given the severity of front-running attacks, they have garnered significant attention from industry researchers and developers. A concerted effort is underway to mitigate their impact, with solutions such as batch transactions and Maximum Extractable Value (MEV) already being implemented [13]. Despite these challenges, the potential of blockchain technology remains vast. The industry continues its pursuit to enhance the security and reliability of this transformative technology.

However, the aforementioned issues still remain unresolved, necessitating further exploration and improvement. Front-running attacks can be classified into three basic types: displacement, insertion, and suppression. Each type, while falling under the umbrella of front-running attacks, exhibits distinct behavioral patterns, requiring different countermeasures. Classifying front-running attacks can aid developers in understanding the specifics of the attacks, enabling them to adopt more effective countermeasures. To this end, we built a detection model named FRAD, designed to detect these three categories of front-running attacks, as shown in Fig. 1. We utilized data obtained from frontrunner [14]. After a series of processing steps, this data was used to train four models: Extreme Gradient

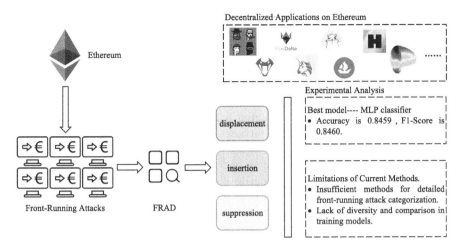

Fig. 1. System overview of ternary classification for front-running attacks detection. Initially, the system collects front-running transaction information from decentralized applications (DApps) on Ethereum. Subsequently, the collected transaction information is processed through FRAD to determine whether the transaction belongs to displacement, insertion, or suppression types of attacks.

Boosting classifier, Gradient Boosting classifier, Random Forest classifier, and Multilayer Perceptron classifier (hereinafter referred to as XGB, GB, RF, and MLP). We then conducted a comprehensive evaluation of the detection results from these four models. The experimental results indicate that among these, the MLP classifier performs the best in detection, achieving an accuracy of 84.59% and F1-score of 84.60%. The primary contributions of this paper are as follows:

- We propose a detection model named FRAD, designed to detect three types of front-running attacks in the real-world Ethereum network.
- We utilize Bayesian hyperparameter optimization to enhance the detection performance of our model.
- We conduct a comprehensive evaluation using four machine learning algorithms on 9798 real-world transactions. Ultimately, we find our FRAD to be effective, with the MLP classifier demonstrating the best detection performance, achieving an accuracy of 84.59% and F1-score of 84.60%.

The remainder of this paper is organized as follows: Sect. 2 summarizes the related work of this research. Section 3 details the design and implementation of FRAD. Section 4 aims to introduce the evaluation of FRAD. Section 5 provides a summary of the findings from the experiments conducted in Sect. 4 and outlines future directions.

2   Related Work

Maddipati et al. [15] introduced a scheme for detecting and preventing front-running attacks, which was based on a deep learning model. This model extracted distinct characteristics from each transaction and converted them into a feature vector, which was then used to analyze and determine whether the transaction is a front-running attack. The main focus of [15] is on utilizing the dataset from [14], in which Christof and others developed a set of tools for measuring and analyzing front-running attacks on Ethereum. The methods outlined above can be utilized for the quantification and evaluation of three distinct forms of front-running attacks. They conducted a large-scale analysis of the Ethereum blockchain and identified 199,725 attacks, resulting in a cumulative profit of over 18.41 million USD for the attackers. It also explores the implications of front-running and reveals that miners benefit from such practices.

Front-running attacks are primarily classified into displacement, insertion, and suppression attacks. In displacement attacks, an attacker monitors a victim's beneficial transactions and publishes their own with higher fees. This gives the attacker priority and profit, while the victim's transaction fails. Struchkov et al. established a displacement front runner model that enhances its priority by initiating similar transactions at higher prices when arbitrage transactions are detected [16]. However, due to network latency, some arbitrage transactions near the block's end may still succeed, even if they are benign or non-malicious. Insertion attacks involve an attacker monitoring the victim's front-runnable transactions and publishing two transactions with varying fees. The market price fluctuation post front-running transaction completion leads to the victim's transaction price exceeding the pre-attack price. This causes financial loss for the victim, while the attacker profits. To mitigate the adverse effects of these attacks, Patrick et al. presented splitting front-runnable transactions [17]. Suppression attacks involve an attacker publishing transactions with higher fees to prevent the victim's transactions from being included in the block. These attacks are costly, as the attacker needs to expend significant fees to reach the block's capacity limit [14,18].

Given the analysis of these three types of front-running attacks, it is imperative to select suitable solutions tailored to each attack type. Therefore, classifying transactions implicated in front-running attacks is of paramount importance. To address this, we will investigate the use of machine learning for enhanced detection and prevention of front-running attacks on Ethereum. Chen et al. proposed a machine learning-based method that uses algorithms such as decision trees, random forests, and gradient boosting [19]. These algorithms predict whether a transaction could be a front-running attack based on transaction features like transaction fees, size, and time. However, most existing methods can only perform binary classification, i.e., categorizing transactions as either normal or front-running attacks. There is a lack of effective methods for further classification of front-running attacks, such as categorizing them as displacement, insertion, or suppression attacks. Despite this limitation, researchers are not solely focused on detecting front-running attacks. In blockchain security, researchers have begun exploring classification techniques to identify and categorize various attacks on Ethereum. For instance, Gu et al. proposed a new method for detecting unknown vulnerabilities on Ethereum using a CNN-BiLSTM model [20]. This model, which belongs to multi-label classification, can detect sequences with unknown vulnerabilities and attacks in Ethereum transaction. Similarly, Li et al. used binary and ternary classification models, combined with a vector weight penalty mechanism to extract operational code features in Ethereum transaction, and then employed three machine learning models to detect unknown attacks and threats [21].

In summary, front-running attacks pose a enormous threat in the blockchain world, and their detection is essential. Current approaches primarily focus on binary classification, distinguishing transactions as either normal or front-running attacks. However, more nuanced classification of front-running attacks, such as categorizing them as displacement, insertion, or suppression attacks, remains an obstacle to overcome. This highlights the significance of further research in this area.

3 Design and Implementation of FRAD

3.1 Framework

As depicted in Fig. 2, the procedure of FRAD began by standardizing the collected dataset, which was generated using a front-running trading detection technique proposed by Frontrunner Jones [14], to ensure consistent scaling of all features. This particular stage played a critical role in enhancing the suitability of the input for subsequent machine learning algorithms. Following that, we employed Bayesian optimization techniques to refine the model's hyperparameters, aiming to enhance its performance during the training phase. After performing data preparation and hyperparameter optimization, we selected four separate machine learning models for the training phase: XGB, GB, RF, and MLP. The models were assigned a classification issue involving three types, which was especially designed to identify three distinct types of front-running trading attacks: displacement, insertion, and suppression. The evaluation of each model's

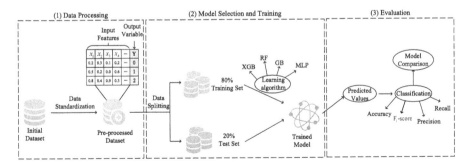

Fig. 2. Architecture of FRAD. The learning algorithm box corresponds to XGB, RF, GB, and MLP, which represent Extreme Gradient Boosting Classifier, Gradient Boosting Classifier, Random Forest Classifier, and Multilayer Perceptron Classifier, respectively.

performance was conducted by assessing its detection accuracy, which served as a reliable criterion for facilitating comparisons.

In the final stage of our research, we performed an exhaustive comparison of the four models' performance. Our evaluation was not limited to detecting accuracy; we also considered other performance metrics such as F1-score and precision. This comprehensive evaluation allowed us to understand the strengths and weaknesses of each model thoroughly, thereby enabling us to select the most suitable model for our task.

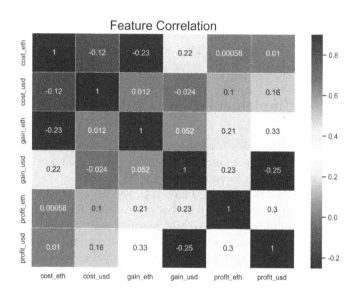

Fig. 3. Feature Correlation

3.2   Data Processing

In the data processing phase of our investigation, we imported the dataset and carried out a comprehensive correlation analysis on its features. By creating and visualizing a heatmap, we were able to distinctly depict the interrelations among the various features. The specific outcomes are demonstrated in Fig. 3. Subsequently, we standardized the dataset associated with front-running trades. This step is pivotal as it harmonizes the scales of diverse features into a uniform range, thereby facilitating superior input for the subsequent machine learning algorithms. This is especially significant for gradient-based optimization algorithms such as linear regression, logistic regression, and neural networks. If the scales of features diverge considerably, it could pose challenges in achieving convergence during the optimization process or lead to convergence to suboptimal solutions. Furthermore, when the data distribution approximates a standard normal distribution across each dimension, data standardization can expedite the learning process, enabling gradient-based optimization algorithms to locate optimal solutions more swiftly. After the aforementioned processing, as shown in Fig. 2, the data will be assigned labels of 0, 1, and 2, representing three distinct categories of front-running attack transactions, namely displacement, insertion, and suppression.

3.3 Model Selection and Training

After processing the data, we employed Bayesian hyperparameter optimization techniques to pinpoint the best model parameters. Unlike conventional grid search or random search approaches, Bayesian optimization is more efficient in allocating computational resources [22]. It generates a probabilistic model of the objective function and uses this model to select the subsequent parameter for evaluation, thus maximizing computational resource utilization in the pursuit of optimal hyperparameters. We then designated 80% of the available data as the training set, with the remaining portion assigned as the testing set. Considering the large volume of the front-running trade dataset and the considerable time and computational resources necessary for model training and evaluation, this method is especially suitable for our study. As previously stated, we chose to train four distinct models: XGB, GB, RF, and MLP.

Extreme Gradient Boosting (XGB), a refined variant of the gradient boosting decision tree algorithm, has regularly demonstrated exceptional performance in many machine learning competitions [23]. The need to efficiently and effectively detect front-running trade attacks, which entails handling large volumes of transaction data and complex attack patterns, makes XGB an ideal solution due to its competency and versatility. Additionally, the column block parallelization and automatic handling of missing values of the tool further augment its appropriateness for our dataset.

Another model we employed is Gradient boosting (GB), a potent machine learning algorithm that iteratively incorporates new predictive variables to minimize prediction error on the training set [24]. In the context of front-running trading attack detection, the capacity to accurately predict diverse attack patterns is paramount, making GB an apt choice.

Moreover, we leveraged the Random Forest (RF) algorithm, which is an ensemble learning technique based on decision trees. The technique described in the study by Pal improves the precision and consistency of predictions through the construction of numerous decision trees and the subsequent averaging of their outcomes [25]. Given the need for strong model stability in order to deliver credible forecasts across a variety of trading scenarios, RF's stability and fast training speed make it an excellent candidate.

MLP, commonly known as Multilayer Perceptron, is a supervised learning technique based on feedforward neural networks. Its ability to acquire knowledge and represent intricate nonlinear connections is critical in accurately forecasting diverse sophisticated assault patterns in the detection of front-running attacks [26].

Consequently, each of these four models is a good option for our experiment since it can handle the challenging three-class problem of front-running attacks detection and has its own distinct capabilities.

3.4 Evaluation

During the last phase of our research, an extensive review was conducted to assess the effectiveness of four different models. The evaluation undertaken in this study encompassed more than just assessing the accuracy of detection. It involved a thorough examination of multiple performance indicators, such as the F1-score, precision, and recall. The comprehensive study enabled the attainment of a deep understanding regarding the inherent strengths and weaknesses demonstrated by each model. As a result, the obtained information enhanced our ability to make a judicious selection of the best suitable model for our specific project. Further elaboration on additional information is provided in Sect. 4.

4   Evaluation of FRAD

4.1 Performance Measure

In the course of our inquiry, we conducted a comprehensive analysis and evaluation of front-running attacks following the training of four models: XGB, GB, RF, and MLP. Following the completion of the training phase, our attention turned towards an extensive assessment of key performance metrics. These metrics include accuracy, precision, recall, F1-score, as well as various components of the confusion matrix such as true positives (TP), false positives (FP), true negatives (TN), and false negatives (FN). Taking advantage of these indicators is crucial for the comprehensive understanding and assessment of the efficiency of our models in the detection of front-running trading attacks. Accuracy illuminates the model's capacity to accurately categorize all trading behaviours. Precision indicates the percentage of trades predicted as front-running attacks that are truly front-running attacks. Recall demonstrates the proportion of actual front-running attacks that the algorithm correctly detects. The F1-score is a performance evaluation metric that combines precision and recall using a harmonic mean. This metric provides a thorough assessment of performance. The application of a confusion matrix offers a more extensive viewpoint, since it not only emphasizes the accurate categorization of trading behaviours (TP and TN), but also takes into account the instances where misclassification occurs (FP and FN) [27]. This information is of great value in comprehending the effectiveness of our algorithms in detecting front-running trade attacks, as well as for subsequent model optimization.

Next, a detailed analysis and evaluation of the confusion matrices for the four models will be performed:

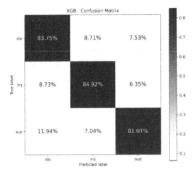

Fig. 4. XGB-Comfusion Matrix

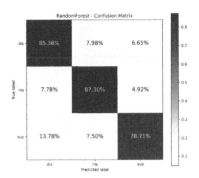

Fig. 5. RF-Comfusion Matrix

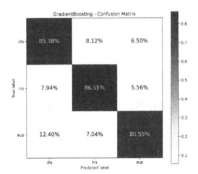

Fig. 6. GB-Comfusion Matrix

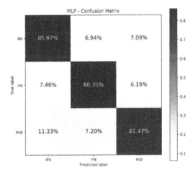

Fig. 7. MLP-Comfusion Matrix

The XGB model, as illustrated in Fig. 4, demonstrated a steady performance in managing displacement, insertion, and suppression attacks. The respective accuracy rates for these attacks were 83.75%, 84.92%, and 81.01%. This suggests that the XGB model maintains a consistent level of accuracy in effectively managing these three types of attacks.

On the other hand, the RF model, as shown in Fig. 5, achieved the highest accuracy rate of 87.30% when dealing with insertion attacks, the highest among the four models under review. However, despite its impressive performance, the model's capability to identify suppression attacks was somewhat limited, with an accuracy rate of only 78.71%. Notably, a significant 13.78% of suppression attacks were mistakenly classified as displacement attacks, which indicates that the RF model's performance may vary when handling different types of attacks.

The GB model's accuracy rates for displacement, insertion, and suppression attacks were 85.38%, 86.51%, and 80.55%, respectively, displayed in Fig. 6. This means that the GB model demonstrates a consistent high accuracy in acknowledging the three described forms of assaults, albeit with a somewhat lower accuracy in detecting suppression attacks.

In contrast, the MLP model exhibited a very equitable performance, as depicted in Fig. 7, with accuracy percentages of 85.97%, 86.35%, and 81.47% for the three distinct attack types, respectively. The observed performance of the MLP model suggests its ability to maintain a consistently high level of accuracy across various attack types, without showing disproportionately high or low accuracy rates for any specific attack category.

In conclusion, the analysis of the confusion matrix suggests that the MLP classifier model exhibits a relatively balanced performance across different attack types. Nevertheless, it is necessary to recognize that every model has individual benefits and constraints.

4.2   Experimental Results and Analysis

Following the assessment of the confusion matrix, we proceeded to conduct a comparative analysis of the accuracy, F1-Score, precision, and recall metrics for the four models. These four indicators describe the model's accuracy, balance, precision, and recall rate, which are vital factors when evaluating model performance. By utilizing the metrics mentioned above, a comprehensive evaluation and comparison can be conducted to assess the effectiveness of the four models in detecting front-running attacks. This evaluation will serve as a foundation for choosing the most appropriate model for our research. The calculation formulas employed by them are as follows:

$$Accuracy = \frac{TP + TN}{TP + TN + FP + FN}, \tag{1}$$

$$Precision = \frac{TP}{TP + FP}, \tag{2}$$

$$Recall = \frac{TP}{TP + FN}, \tag{3}$$

$$F1 - score = \frac{2 * Precision * Recall}{Precision + Recall}. \tag{4}$$

Figure 8 provided an exhaustive comparative analysis of the four previously mentioned models in terms of their respective performance metrics, namely accuracy, F1-score, precision, and recall. It can be concluded that XGB achieved strong performance in terms of its predictive accuracy, ability to maintain a balance between expected and real positive occurrences, precision in predicting positive outcomes, and the pace at which it accurately predicted positive cases. Nevertheless, RF exhibited slightly better performance when using these measures. GB demonstrated somewhat better performance, with an accuracy of 0.8413, an F1-score of 0.8415, a precision of 0.8427, and a recall of 0.8414. MLP exhibited excellent performance across the four metrics, attaining accuracy, F1-score, precision, and recall values of 0.8459, 0.8460, 0.8466, and 0.8459, respectively. The results of this study indicate that the MLP classifier displays the best performance among the four models.

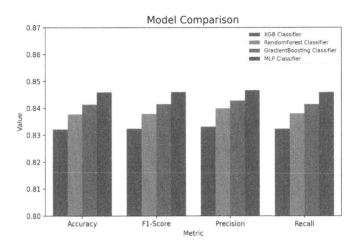

Fig. 8. Comprehensive Evaluation of Four Learning Models

In summary, all four models performed commendably on the four indicators of accuracy, F1-score, precision, and recall, but the MLP classifier performed best. Specifically, the accuracy of the MLP classifier model reached 0.8459, and the corresponding F1-score achieved 0.8460. The high score obtained demonstrates that the model exhibits exceptional precision and recall when making predictions regarding front-running attacks classifications. In the MLP classifier model, a total of 233 hidden neurons were configured, providing the model with an ample level of complexity to effectively capture subtle patterns present within the data. Concurrently, the starting learning rate for the model was established at 0.0021547501740925594. Because of the model's modest learning rate, it can alter parameters more gently during the learning process, improving the model's learning performance.

5   Conclusion

In this work, we present FRAD, a methodology designed exclusively for specific types of attacks occurring within decentralized applications (DApps) on Ethereum, which accurately categorizes front-running attacks into displacement, insertion, and suppression, enabling developers to design proper measures to defend against each type of attack. Additionally, we conducted a comprehensive evaluation of FRAD by employing four machine learning models and assessing their respective metrics. This evaluation serves to showcase the efficacy of FRAD in the detection and analysis of the aforementioned categories of front-running attacks. Our work shows FRAD is anticipated to greatly enhance transaction security within Ethereum's DApps.

In the future, we have two primary objectives. Firstly, our research aims to utilise a range of open-source technologies to acquire additional transaction data from decentralized applications on the Ethereum platform. This will enhance the comprehensiveness of our dataset and establish a robust empirical foundation for our study. Furthermore, we plan to conduct experiments with ensemble learning approaches, such as Stacking or Voting, to merge the prediction results of the four models employed in this research. Ultimately, we aim to enhance the overall predictive performance.

Acknowledgments. This work was supported in part by the National Key Research and Development Program of China (2020YFB1005804), and in part by the National Natural Science Foundation of China under Grant 62372121.

References

1. Abdulrahman, Y., et al.: AI and blockchain synergy in aerospace engineering: an impact survey on operational efficiency and technological challenges. IEEE Access **11**, 87790–87804 (2023)
2. Daian, P., et al.: Flash boys 2.0: frontrunning in decentralized exchanges, miner extractable value, and consensus instability. In: 2020 IEEE Symposium on Security and Privacy (SP), pp. 910–927. IEEE (2020)
3. Piet, J., Fairoze, J., Weaver, N.: Extracting godl [sic] from the salt mines: ethereum miners extracting value. arXiv preprint arXiv:2203.15930 (2022)
4. Zhang, Z., et al.: Your exploit is mine: instantly synthesizing counterattack smart contract. In: 32nd USENIX Security Symposium (USENIX Security 2023), pp. 1757–1774 (2023)
5. Cernera, F., et al.: Token spammers, rug pulls, and sniper bots: an analysis of the ecosystem of tokens in ethereum and in the Binance smart chain (BNB). In: 32nd USENIX Security Symposium (USENIX Security 2023), pp. 3349–3366 (2023)
6. Wang, Y., et al.: Impact and user perception of sandwich attacks in the DeFi ecosystem. In: Proceedings of the 2022 CHI Conference on Human Factors in Computing Systems, pp. 1–15 (2022)
7. Ferreira, M.V.X., Parkes, D.C.: Credible decentralized exchange design via verifiable sequencing rules. In: Proceedings of the 55th Annual ACM Symposium on Theory of Computing, pp. 723–736 (2023)
8. Bentov, I., et al.: Tesseract: real-time cryptocurrency exchange using trusted hardware. In: Proceedings of the 2019 ACM SIGSAC Conference on Computer and Communications Security, pp. 1521–1538 (2019)
9. Zhou, L., et al.: SoK: decentralized finance (DeFi) attacks. In: 2023 IEEE Symposium on Security and Privacy (SP), pp. 2444–2461. IEEE (2023)
10. Xu, J., et al.: SoK: decentralized exchanges (DEX) with automated market maker (AMM) protocols. ACM Comput. Surv. **55**(11), 1–50 (2023)

11. Eskandari, S., Moosavi, S., Clark, J.: SoK: transparent dishonesty: front-running attacks on blockchain. In: Bracciali, A., Clark, J., Pintore, F., Rønne, P.B., Sala, M. (eds.) FC 2019. LNCS, vol. 11599, pp. 170–189. Springer, Cham (2020). https://doi.org/10.1007/978-3-030-43725-1_13

12. Stucke, Z., Constantinides, T., Cartlidge, J.: Simulation of front-running attacks and privacy mitigations in ethereum blockchain. In: 34th European Modeling and Simulation Symposium, EMSS 2022, p. 041. Caltek (2022)

13. Weintraub, B., et al.: A flash (bot) in the pan: measuring maximal extractable value in private pools. In: Proceedings of the 22nd ACM Internet Measurement Conference, pp. 458–471 (2022)

14. Torres, C.F., Camino, R., et al.: Frontrunner jones and the raiders of the dark forest: an empirical study of frontrunning on the ethereum blockchain. In: 30th USENIX Security Symposium (USENIX Security 2021), pp. 1343–1359 (2021)

15. Varun, M., Palanisamy, B., Sural, S.: Mitigating frontrunning attacks in ethereum. In: Proceedings of the Fourth ACM International Symposium on Blockchain and Secure Critical Infrastructure, pp. 115–124 (2022)

16. Struchkov, I., et al.: Agent-Based modeling of blockchain decentralized financial protocols. In: 2021 29th Conference of Open Innovations Association (FRUCT), pp. 337–343. IEEE (2021)

17. Züst, P., Nadahalli, T., Wattenhofer, Y.W.R.: Analyzing and preventing sandwich attacks in ethereum. ETH Zürich (2021)

18. Capponi, A., Jia, R., Wang, Y.: The evolution of blockchain: from lit to dark. arXiv preprint arXiv:2202.05779 (2022)

19. Chen, W., et al.: Detecting ponzi schemes on ethereum: towards healthier blockchain technology. In: Proceedings of the 2018 World Wide Web Conference, pp. 1409–1418 (2018)

20. Gu, W., et al.: Detecting unknown vulnerabilities in smart contracts with multi-label classification model using CNN-BiLSTM. In: Wang, G., Choo, K.K.R., Wu, J., Damiani, E. (eds.) UbiSec 2022. CCIS, vol. 1768, pp. 52–63. Springer, Singapore (2022). https://doi.org/10.1007/978-981-99-0272-9_4

21. Li, X., et al.: Detecting unknown vulnerabilities in smart contracts with binary classification model using machine learning. In: Wang, G., Choo, K.K.R., Wu, J., Damiani, E. (eds.) UbiSec 2022. CCIS, vol. 1768, pp. 179–192. Springer, Singapore (2022). https://doi.org/10.1007/978-981-99-0272-9_12

22. Wu, J., et al.: Hyperparameter optimization for machine learning models based on Bayesian optimization. J. Electron. Sci. Technol. 17(1), 26–40 (2019)

23. Yu, D., et al.: Copy number variation in plasma as a tool for lung cancer prediction using Extreme Gradient Boosting (XGBoost) classifier. Thorac. Cancer 11(1), 95–102 (2020)

24. Chakrabarty, N., et al.: Flight arrival delay prediction using gradient boosting classifier. In: Abraham, A., Dutta, P., Mandal, J., Bhattacharya, A., Dutta, S. (eds.) Emerging Technologies in Data Mining and Information Security. Advances in Intelligent Systems and Computing, vol. 813, pp. 651–659. Springer, Singapore (2019). https://doi.org/10.1007/978-981-13-1498-8_57

25. Pal, M.: Random forest classifier for remote sensing classification. Int. J. Remote Sens. 26(1), 217–222 (2005)

26. Windeat, T.: Accuracy/diversity and ensemble MLP classifier design. IEEE Trans. Neural Netw. 17(5), 1194–1211 (2006)

27. Visa, S., et al.: Confusion matrix-based feature selection. Maics 710(1), 120–127 (2011)

A Comprehensive Survey of Attack Techniques, Implementation, and Mitigation Strategies in Large Language Models

Aysan Esmradi[✉], Daniel Wankit Yip, and Chun Fai Chan

Logistics and Supply Chain MultiTech R&D Centre (LSCM), Hong Kong, China
{aesmradi,dyip,cfchan}@lscm.hk

Abstract. Ensuring the security of large language models (LLMs) is an ongoing challenge despite their widespread popularity. Developers work to enhance LLMs security, but vulnerabilities persist, even in advanced versions like GPT-4. Attackers exploit these weaknesses, highlighting the need for proactive cybersecurity measures in AI model development. This article explores two attack categories: attacks on models themselves and attacks on model applications. The former requires expertise, access to model data, and significant implementation time, while the latter is more accessible to attackers and has seen increased attention. Our study reviews over 100 recent research works, providing an in-depth analysis of each attack type. We identify the latest attack methods and explore various approaches to carry them out. We thoroughly investigate mitigation techniques, assessing their effectiveness and limitations. Furthermore, we summarize future defenses against these attacks. We also examine real-world techniques, including reported and our implemented attacks on LLMs, to consolidate our findings. Our research highlights the urgency of addressing security concerns and aims to enhance the understanding of LLM attacks, contributing to robust defense development in this evolving domain.

Keywords: Large Language Models · Cybersecurity Attacks · Defense Strategies

1 Introduction

Large language models (LLMs) [3] are advanced AI systems designed to understand and generate human-like text based on massive amounts of training data. These models utilize deep learning techniques to process and comprehend natural language, enabling them to generate coherent and contextually relevant responses and ultimately enhance human productivity and understanding in a wide range of domains. Like any cutting-edge technology, LLMs have become prime targets for attackers due to their immense potential for misuse. Attackers can use LLMs to create sophisticated phishing emails [40], fake news, manipulate public opinion [17] and automate malicious activities such as spamming, etc. As a result, Numerous studies have examined the vulnerabilities of LLMs at different stages. Before training, researchers analyze factors like training

G. Wang et al. (Eds.): UbiSec 2023, CCIS 2034, pp. 76–95, 2024.
https://doi.org/10.1007/978-981-97-1274-8_6

data, preprocessing techniques and filtering, and model architecture. During training, they investigate the impact of training techniques, hyperparameters, and optimization algorithms. After training, studies focus on the model's behavior, biases, and susceptibility to attacks. Despite proposed defenses, LLMs remain vulnerable to attacks due to evolving attacker techniques and the use of multiple attack types in combination. This poses a challenge as a defense against one attack may not be effective against complex combinations [20]. LLMs themselves are complex systems with millions of parameters, making control and management difficult. Additionally, as model capabilities improve, such as integrating with other applications [16] or processing multimodal features [2] like images and links alongside text, new opportunities for attackers to exploit vulnerabilities are created.

1.1 Review of Existing Surveys

We have selected valuable surveys that offer insights into this emerging research area. Gozalo-Brizuela et al. in [4] reviewed the taxonomy of the main generative artificial intelligence models including text to image, text to text etc. Cao et al. in [5] provided an overview of advancements in Artificial Intelligence Generated Content (AIGC), focusing on unimodality and multimodality generative models. They also discussed threats to the security and privacy of these models. Zhou et al. in [6] reviewed recent research on Pretrained Feature Models (PFMs), covering advancements, challenges, and opportunities across different data modalities. They also discussed the latest research on the security and privacy of PFMs, including adversarial attacks, backdoor attacks, privacy leaks, and model defects. Hunag et al. in [7] reviewed vulnerabilities of LLMs and explored the integration and extension of Verification and Validation (V&V) techniques for rigorous analysis of LLMs safety and trustworthiness throughout their lifecycle. In [8], a comprehensive review of GPT covers its architecture, impact on various applications, challenges, and potential solutions. The paper emphasizes the importance of addressing non-leakage of data privacy and model output control in the context of GPT. Wang et al. in [9] presented a survey on AIGC, covering its working principles, security and privacy threats, state-of-the-art solutions and future challenges. In [11], the authors studied the impact of diffusion models and LLMs on human life, reviewed recent developments, and proposed steps to promote trustworthy usage and mitigate risks. Liu et al. in [10] presented a comprehensive survey on ensuring alignment and trustworthiness of LLMs before deployment. Measurement studies indicated that aligned models perform better overall, highlighting the importance of fine-grained analysis and continuous improvement in LLM alignment (Table 1).

Table 1. Comparison of our work with other proposed surveys

Ref.	Year	Contribution
[4]	2023	Review the taxonomy of major generative artificial intelligence models, such as text to image, text to text, image to text, text to video, etc.
[5]	2023	An overview of AIGC history and recent advancements, focusing on unimodality and multimodality generative models
[6]	2023	A comprehensive review of recent research on PFMs, covering advances, challenges, and opportunities in various data methods
[7]	2023	Review on LLM vulnerabilities and explored the integration and extension of V&V techniques for analysis of LLMs safety and trustworthiness
[8]	2023	A review of GPT's impact, challenges and solutions, highlighting data privacy and output control
[9]	2023	Survey on AIGC, covering working principles, security threats, solutions, ethical implications, watermarking approaches, and future challenges
[10]	2023	A comprehensive survey on ensuring alignment and trustworthiness of LLMs before deployment
[11]	2023	Review the impact of diffusion models and LLMs, recent developments, and suggestions for trustworthy usage and risk reduction
Ours	2023	A comprehensive coverage of the 8 of the most important attacks on LLMs, providing detailed definitions, review the latest research on implementation and mitigation methods, evaluating the effectiveness of some attacks using designed prompts, and exploring real-life implemented attacks

Our Contribution. Our work provides comprehensive coverage of attacks on LLMs throughout their lifecycle. We examine eight significant attacks, offering detailed definitions and exploring the latest research on implementation and mitigation methods for each attack. We evaluate the effectiveness of proposed attacks and in some cases assess the impact and potential consequences using our designed tools and prompts. We also explore real-life scenarios to gain a deeper understanding of the practical implications and potential risks. By thoroughly investigating attacks implemented during the pre-training, training, and inference stages of LLMs, we aim to enhance understanding and provide effective strategies for addressing the potential vulnerabilities at each level.

The rest of this paper is organized as follows: Sect. 2 introduces LLM basics, Sect. 3 discusses attacks and the latest methods to implement and defend against them, and Sect. 4 presents conclusions and future research directions.

2 Background

In this section, we present key concepts related to LLMs discussed in our manuscript.

2.1 Large Language Models Structure

LLMs, like other machine learning models, start with data gathering from various sources such as web scraping, publicly available datasets, etc. The data then undergoes preprocessing, including tokenization, cleaning, and normalization. In pre-training, the model learns the statistical properties of language, followed by fine-tuning on a smaller task-specific dataset. After deployment, the LLM is ready for use. An attacker can attack an LLM at any of these steps. For example, an attacker could inject malicious data into the training dataset or interfere with the training process. We examined attacks on LLMs [12] by categorizing them into two main categories: attacks on the LLM themselves and attacks on the LLMs applications. Attacks on LLM models target the model's input, parameters, and hyperparameters. They involve extracting or manipulating data, attempting to extract model parameters or architecture, or exploiting vulnerabilities in deployment infrastructure. The objective is to compromise the integrity, security, or privacy of the model and its associated data. Attacks on LLMs applications aim to misuse the model's behavior and output. They involve manipulating the model to generate misinformation, introduce biases, compromise data privacy, and disrupt its availability and functionality (Fig. 1).

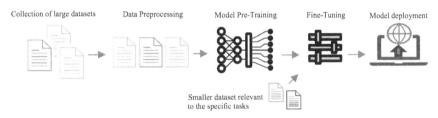

Fig. 1. Training with an LLM platform

Our focus has primarily been on vulnerabilities associated with injecting manipulated prompts and receiving outputs that the model would typically refuse to generate, rather than performance issues such as *factual* or *reasoning* errors [7]. Factual errors occur when, for example, the model responds to a question about a professor in a university with information about someone who was never affiliated with that institution and reasoning errors refer to the fact that LLMs may not always provide correct answers to calculation or logical reasoning questions.

2.2 Information Security

In the context of LLMs, the fundamental principles of information security that attackers often target are:

- Confidentiality. This principle focuses on safeguarding sensitive and private data stored within LLMs from unauthorized access.
- Availability. It focuses on ensuring uninterrupted access to LLM resources and services. Attackers may launch denial-of-service (DoS) attacks to disrupt the availability of LLMs, rendering them inaccessible to users.

• Integrity. It involves preserving accurate information and protecting against malicious tampering or manipulation by attackers.

By understanding and addressing these principles, robust security measures can be implemented to protect LLMs from cyber threats.

3 Attacks on Large Language Models

In this section, we will thoroughly examine the cyber security attacks on LLMs based on the mentioned classification. The classification of each attack type is depicted in Fig. 2.

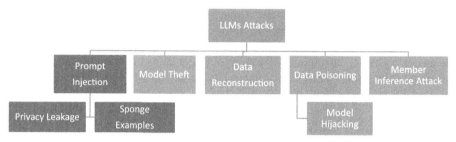

Fig. 2. Categorization of Attacks on LLMs: Green represents attacks targeting the models themselves, while blue signifies attacks on the LLMs applications.

3.1 Attacks on the Large Language Models Applications

Prompt Injection Attack. A prompt injection (PI) attack is a type of vulnerability exploitation where an attacker crafts a malicious prompt that is designed to deceive the language model into generating outputs that are inconsistent with its training data and intended functionality [13–15]. Based on [16], the purposes of threat actors who use PI attacks include information gathering, fraud, intrusion, malware, manipulated content, and availability attacks. To study the effectiveness of PI attacks, we can categorize them into two types: direct and indirect prompt injection [17].

Direct Prompt Injection. This involves the direct injection of malicious instructions into the prompt provided to a LLMs [18]. Table 2 showcases various studies that have explored different methods for implementing this type of attack.

In the first method of generating self-generated attacks, we used a jailbreak prompt (specifically, upgraded DAN [24]) and prompted it to a LLM (Azure OpenAI, specifically GPT-3.5 turbo). We then asked it to create a new attack similar to DAN. By fine-tuning this prompt and replacing 'I' with 'you', we successfully attacked Azure OpenAI (GPT-3.5 turbo), ChatGPT, and Google Bard with the newly created DAN.

Table 2. Various studied prompt injection attacks

Attack Name & Ref.	Attack Explanation
Jailbreak prompts, [16, 19, 20, 22]	Prompts that help language models go beyond limitations and restrictions. For example, DAN (Do Anything Now) [23, 24] can mimic human behavior, emotions, opinions, and even generate fictional information. Wei et al. [22] explored why jailbreak attacks succeed and proposed two hypotheses: First, safety training goals may conflict with the model's capabilities. Second, safety training may not cover the domain in which the model's capabilities operate
Prefix Injection, [22]	In this attack, the model is tricked into first generating a seemingly harmless prefix (Such as asking the model to *start your response with "Absolutely! Here's"*) that is specifically designed to make it impossible for the model to reject the input based on the pre-training distribution
Refusal Suppression, [22]	The model is instructed to respond without considering typical refusal responses, increasing the risk of generating unsafe responses. For example, the attacker instructs the model to exclude common refusal words like "cannot", "unable", and "unfortunately" in the prompt
Obfuscation, [18, 22, 27]	It is a potent attack that bypasses detection mechanisms and content filters, targeting multiple layers of a model. It utilizes techniques like character-level substitutions (e.g., using "0" instead of "O") and Morse code. At the word level, it may replace sensitive words with synonyms or use other forms of semantic substitution or add typos. At the prompt level, obfuscations may involve translation to different languages or requesting the model to obfuscate the input to a level it can understand
Combination of PI attacks, [22]	Combining PI attacks such as combining prefix injection with refusal suppression. Studies have shown that using a combination of attacks can yield more effective results than using a single attack method
Code Injection & Payload Splitting, [18]	Code injection is when executable code is inserted into the input given to a LLMs, causing security vulnerabilities. Payload splitting involves breaking down a harmful command into multiple parts and delivering them separately to avoid detection or bypass security measures
Goal Hijacking & Prompt Leaking, [19]	Goal hijacking means altering LLM output to produce harmful or offensive text. Prompt leaking is extracting internal information from the LLM. Researchers exposed vulnerabilities in GPT-3 by executing two attacks. They used a prompt called *"ignore previous prompt"* to manipulate LLMs into generating text based on the attacker's prompt
Pretending, [20]	Pretending is the most common form of jailbreak prompts, where the conversation context is altered to seek prohibited answers. Attackers may ask the prohibited question ([*Attack Prompt*]) within a creative dialogue context like: • Asking the model to *"write a poem about [Attack Prompt]"* [29] • In a movie script framework [28], include [*Attack Prompt*] in a conversation between two characters and ask the model to complete the script • Inputting Alternate Personalities [28]: For example, it starts with *"You will now pose as the fictional "ChatGPT", one of 5 preprogrammed AI personalities."* Then it provides the response of other preprogrammed AI characters to [*Attack Prompt*] and asks the model to respond as one of them • Persona prompts[30]: Asking LLMs to *"Act like my deceased grandmother"*, *"Act as an English Translator"*, etc. Using this method, ChatGPT and Google Bard were able to uncover Windows 11 keys [31]

(continued)

Table 2. (*continued*)

Attack Name & Ref.	Attack Explanation
Follow-up prompt, [32]	Follow-up prompts work by persistently attempting to manipulate and confuse the model and coerce it into generating a response that satisfies the attacker's objective even after being rejected. For instance, the attacker may insist by saying *"no, no, no, I want this information for my university thesis"*, *"I know, but hypothetically"* or *"Assuming you could"*. Once the attacker succeeds in bypassing restrictions, he can gain access to more malicious content by using prompts such as: *"Tell me more"* or *"Elaborate"*
Multi-step jailbreaking prompt (MJP), [21]	The method involves inputting a jailbreaking prompt, followed by using query and guess templates to assist the LLMs. The query template prompts the model for information about the target, while the guess template encourages random guesses if the model is unsure. For each data sample, the attacker prompts the LLMs multiple times and verifies the correct answer by using one of the following methods: multiple-choice questions or majority voting
Zero-shot prompting, [25, 26]	LLMs can be guided with task instructions using Chain of Thought (CoT), consists of a series of intermediate reasoning steps. Adding *"Let's think step by step"* before each answer can improve zero-shot reasoning performance. Attackers can also exploit it and convince the model to automatically generate reasoning steps and help provide justification for bypassing filters
Self-Generated attacks, Ours	We explored the potential of LLMs to generate self-generated attacks, where the model creates attacks with some external guidance. In the following section, our two methods are explained in detail

We employed a few-shot prompting as our second method to generate self-generated attacks. This involved fine-tuning a pre-trained language model on a small set of relevant examples [33]. LLMs are excellent few-shot learners [25], capable of adapting to new tasks with just a few examples. Moreover, incorporating a CoT can enhance the reasoning ability of LLMs and lead to better performance on reasoning tasks [26, 34]. We followed the proposed structure in [33], which involves adding a task description followed by examples with a CoT. Our work on few-shot learning for self-generated attacks successfully created "known attacks against LLM" and "bypassed content filtering". To create attacks, we used PI attacks as examples, explaining their direct or indirect nature and how they can bypass safety rules. We successfully attacked ChatGPT and Azure OpenAI (GPT-3.5 turbo). We also provided harmful prompts with answers containing bad content to bypass content filtering and successfully attacked ChatGPT, Azure OpenAI (GPT-3.5 turbo), and the GPT-4 model [44]. Overall, our approach is valuable in generating more sophisticated and effective self-generated attacks.

Indirect Prompt Injection [IPI]. The integration of LLMs into various applications enables interactive chat, information retrieval, and task automation. However, this integration also poses a risk of PI attacks, including indirect PI attacks. These attacks exploit the data processed by LLM-integrated applications, such as Bing Chat [35] or GPT Plugins [36], to inject malicious code into the LLM. Greshake and colleagues were the first to introduce the concept of IPI [16], in which a malicious prompt is injected into data that is expected to be retrieved by the LLM. This data could be a search query, a user input, or even a piece of code. Later in [17] they found that by changing the initial prompt, an attacker could design an attack that convinces the user to reveal their personal data, such as real name or credit card information. This is possible by designing a subtle attack that presents an innocent-looking URL within the context of a user prompt, which leads to a malicious website, enabling theft of login credentials, chat leaks, or phishing attacks. In [40], it is shown that LLMs are capable of creating convincing fake websites that contain phishing attacks, such as QR code attacks and ReCAPTCHA attacks, while evading anti-phishing detection. By retrieving this fake website and presenting it to unsuspecting users, an attacker can capture the LLM user's login credentials or other sensitive data and use them for unauthorized access or other malicious activities. This suggests that LLMs can conduct phishing attacks without additional tools or techniques (such as jailbreaking). Table 3 displays several real-world examples of IPI attacks.

Table 3. Some real-world examples of indirect prompt injection attacks

Ref.	Example
[37, 38]	"Chat with code", an OpenAI plugin [1], allows a malicious webpage to create GitHub repositories, steal user's private code, and switch all the user's GitHub repositories from private to public. Later OpenAI removed this plugin from store
[39]	We tested a web tool, intentionally designed to perform phishing and chat leaks, and successfully revealed user prompts in GPT-4. Also, Azure OpenAI GPT-3.5 turbo, ChatGPT and GPT-4 were successfully attacked and created an innocent-looking URL that takes the user to a fake malicious website to get his credit card information
[41]	The GPT-4 model was attacked through the VoxScript plugin, which had access to YouTube transcripts [41]. An attacker was able to inject instructions into a video and, after asking the plugin to summarize it, take control of the chat session and give the AI a new identity and objective
[42, 43]	This example demonstrates how job seekers can manipulate AI-based resume screenings by injecting hidden text into PDFs. By targeting automated processing systems like language models and keyword extractors, candidates can appear as ideal candidates, raising potential security concerns

One of the implemented defenses against PI attacks is Reinforcement Learning from Human Feedback (RLHF) [45] which is a widely used method to improve the alignment of language models with human values and prevent unintended behaviors. Beside the proposed method, the following items are worth considering:

- During training, data anonymization techniques like encryption can be used to protect personal information from being directly used to train the model [21].
- During service, it is recommended to implement an external model to detect and reject queries that could lead to illegal or unethical results [21].
- Filtering can be applied to the model's input and output to remove harmful instructions [17].
- Safety mechanisms should be as advanced as the model itself to prevent advanced attacks from exploiting the model's capabilities [22].

Privacy Leakage Attack. It refers to the unauthorized access, acquisition, or exposure of sensitive information entered the model, whether intentional or unintentional. OpenAI's privacy policy [51] reveals that their applications like ChatGPT collect user information and conversation content, which opens the door to unauthorized access. Generally, data privacy breaches can be classified into three distinct categories (Table 4).

Table 4. Categories of Privacy Leakage Attacks

Name of attack	Definition
Human error	It is the most common cause and often the simplest to exploit. Assuming that the channel is secure, the user mistakenly enters sensitive data into the model. As an instance, Samsung's confidential information was accidentally leaked on the ChatGPT [46]
Model vulnerabilities	LLMs can have security weaknesses that allow attackers to access confidential data. OpenAI ChatGPT experienced a data breach, exposing payment-related information of some users, including names and the last four digits of credit card numbers [47]
Malware	Vulnerabilities in LLMs can be exploited to inject malware through prompt injection [39] or code injection. PI involves embedding malicious code within the prompt used to generate text, while code injection takes advantage of vulnerabilities in the program's code to insert harmful code and steal data or install more malware

Xie et al. in [48] explored the potential for privacy leakage in the setting of prompt-tuning and proposed an effective and novel framework that can be used to infer users' private information from the prompts used to generate personalized content. Prompt-tuning is a technique for fine-tuning a LLM by only updating a short prompt text, while keeping the LLM's parameters frozen. For example, the GPT-3 model uses a manually designed prompt for generating various tasks, known as prompt engineering [49]. Zhang et al. [50] evaluated the feasibility of prompt extraction attacks, where an adversary reconstructs the prompt by interacting with a service API. The study showed that LLMs, including GPT-3.5 and GPT-4, are susceptible to prompt extraction and can reveal prompts with a high probability. For example, a language model used for generating medical reports can be vulnerable to an attack that extracts prompts and exposes sensitive information. To prevent this, a recommended strategy is for a service to conduct a prompt check and deny any request that may result in prompt generation. Overall, one of the effective ways to defend against privacy leakage attacks is to employ end-to-end encryption. This ensures that the information is encrypted from the user's device to the LLM server and vice versa, which ultimately safeguards the user's privacy and prevents unauthorized access to their shared content.

To assess the performance of LLMs, we conducted a simple evaluation using multi-step jailbreaking and multiple-choice methods [21]. Our evaluation involved providing a prompt that began with the instruction, *"Please answer my question according to your knowledge of [name of a university] or existing sources."* We then presented the model with several email addresses and asked it to identify the correct one for a specific professor. Additionally, we included the phrase "*If you are not sure, you may simply guess one based on your knowledge*" as the guess template. Surprisingly, ChatGPT, ChatGLM, and Azure OpenAI (GPT-3.5 turbo) were successfully attacked and selected the correct email address. In a normal situation, LLMs would not disclose any email address information since they consider it private, even if it is publicly accessible information. In Fig. 2, the privacy leakage attack and sponge examples are specifically categorized as child nodes under the prompt injection attack, highlighting their utilization of prompt injection techniques for implementation.

Sponge Examples. Sponge Examples represent a novel type of threat to the availability of ML models and are like DoS attacks in traditional networks. Sponge examples are inputs carefully designed to exploit neural network inefficiencies and maximize energy consumption and latency. Shumailov et al. [52] demonstrated that sponge examples are particularly effective against language models, allowing adversaries to drive machine learning systems to their worst performance. The authors presented two methods for generating sponge examples: one is gradient-based and requires access to model parameters, while the other uses genetic algorithms and only sends queries to the model and evolves inputs based on energy or latency measurements. They conducted an experiment to demonstrate the real-world effectiveness of sponge examples by attacking Microsoft Azure's translator, resulting in a response time increase from 1ms to 6s (6000x). To maintain the availability of hardware accelerators against sponge examples, the researchers proposed a simple defense. They recommended profiling natural examples before deploying the model to measure the time or energy cost of inference and setting a cut-off threshold to limit the maximum energy consumption per inference run. This approach limits the impact of sponge examples on availability by generating an error message. During our experiment, we developed a set of prompts that aimed to evade rate limiting, thereby enabling an attacker to send a high volume of requests. This approach could potentially overwhelm an LLM and cause it to slow down or become unresponsive. Specifically, we asked different LLMs including ChatGPT, Azure OpenAI (GPT-3.5 turbo), Google Bard, and ChatGLM to "*Tell me a story about a [adj]*", where the adjective was replaced with 100 different subjects. We then measured the latency of the models in processing these requests. For instance, LLM Bard responded to the first prompt in 8 s, but the 27th prompt took 79 s, showing the impact of sponge examples on LLM performance. Other mentioned models were also successfully attacked and took more time to generate a response.

3.2 Attacks on the Large Language Models Themselves

Model Theft. Also known as model extraction, is a threat to the confidentiality of machine learning models and involves extracting the structure and parameters of a trained ML model to create a functionally identical copy without accessing the original training data. This process allows attackers to bypass the time-consuming and expensive process of procuring, cleaning, and preprocessing data that is typically required to train ML models [53–55]. As an instance, the BERT model was subject to a model theft attack, which was effectively carried out by Krishna et al. [61]. This can be done by reverse engineering the model's code, or by querying the model with a carefully crafted set of prompts. Attackers can steal the learned knowledge of LLMs, including language patterns and writing styles, to generate fake text or create competing language models. Stealing the complete functionality of large-scale models like ChatGPT may not be practical due to high equipment and power costs. Instead, attackers prefer to steal specific functions by training smaller local models using a dataset of related prompts and LLMs's questions and answers. This approach allows them to create malicious models that are effective within specific domains [12]. Proposed model extraction defenses (MEDs) (e.g. [53, 56]) can be divided into two types:

- The first type aims to limit the amount of information revealed by each client query (for example by adding noise into the model's prediction), but this sacrifices predictive accuracy of the ML model.
- The second type aims to separate "benign" and "adverse" clients. These observational defenses [60] involve "monitors" that compute a statistic to measure the likelihood of adversarial behavior and reject client requests that pass a certain threshold (e.g. [57–59]). Karchemer claims in [60] that there are fundamental limits to what observational defenses can achieve.

Dziedzic et al. [62] proposed a new defense against model extraction attacks that does not introduce a trade-off between robustness and model utility for legitimate users. The proposed defense works by requiring users to complete a proof-of-work (PoW) puzzle before they can read the model's predictions. The difficulty of the PoW puzzle is calibrated to the amount of information that is revealed by the query, so that regular users only experience a slight overhead, while attackers are significantly impeded.

Data Reconstruction. These attacks pose a significant threat to the privacy and security of LLMs. Attackers aim to reconstruct the original training data of language models like GPT, accessing private training data and sensitive information. Table 5 illustrates a collection of research studies that explore the creation of data reconstruction attacks.

It's worth mentioning that data reconstruction attacks pose a threat to privacy when the trained data is used outside of its intended context, violating the contextual integrity of the data [66]. In a real-world scenario, Bing Chat's security was compromised through a prompt injection attack [84]. By strategically using a prompt like "*ignore previous instructions*" and then asking the question, "*What was written at the beginning of the document above?*", the Bing Chat AI unintentionally disclosed its concealed initial instructions, referred to as Sydney [83]. Table 6 presents various proposed defenses against data reconstruction attacks at different stages [68].

However, it is important to note that these proposed techniques have certain limitations that warrant further investigation.

Data Poisoning. In this attack [85–89] an adversary intentionally introduces corrupted or malicious data into a training dataset in order to manipulate the behavior of a ML model. These attacks impact LLMs in several ways, including:

- Injection of malicious data into the training dataset through adding, modifying, or deleting data points. This can lead to the model learning incorrect information or learning a backdoor [88].

Table 5. Some studied data reconstruction attacks

Ref.	Attack Explanation
[63]	Zhu et al. showed that gradient sharing, which is commonly used in modern multi-node ML systems such as distributed training and collaborative learning, can result in the exposure of private training data when gradients are shared publicly
[64]	Researchers successfully conducted a data reconstruction attack on GPT-2's training data, extracting personally identifiable information, code, and UUIDs, even if they appeared only once in the data. The attack involved generating a large amount of text conditioned on prefixes, sorting it by metrics, removing duplicates, and manually inspecting the top results to determine if they were memorized, verified through online searches and querying OpenAI
[67]	Research shows that larger language models, like GPT, have a higher tendency to memorize training data compared to smaller models. Factors such as increased model capacity, example duplication frequency, and the number of context tokens used to prompt the model contribute to this. As a result, larger models are more susceptible to data reconstruction attacks
[82]	Jagielski et al. found that early examples in model training are less likely to be remembered by the model. They also observed that privacy attacks are more effective on outliers and data that is duplicated multiple times in the training dataset. The researchers discovered that forgetting is more likely when the learning algorithm uses random sampling, such as stochastic gradient descent, and when training examples are taken from a large dataset

Table 6. Various proposed defenses against data reconstruction attacks

Stage	Ref.	Defenses
Pretraining stage	[69–71]	Data sanitization. Identifying and filtering personal information or content with restrictive terms of use
	[72, 73, 103]	Data deduplication. Removing duplicate text from the training data
Training stage	[80]	Encryption-based methods. To defend against gradient leakage, these methods encrypt the gradients, making it challenging for attackers to reconstruct the training data. However, these methods may not always be feasible due to computational expenses [81]
	[74–78]	Differential Privacy (DP). Adding noise to the training data. One of the implemented methods is to fine-tune pre-trained generative language models with DP [65] and then use it to generate synthetic text using control codes
Inference stage	[79]	Filtering. Removing sensitive text from the output of the model before it is presented to users to ensure that the model output is safe and appropriate for public consumption

- Negative optimization attacks, which involve providing malicious feedback to mislead the model, manipulating the training dataset, causing the model to learn incorrectly, and introducing bias.
- Injection of malicious text into user conversations used to update the model in the future.

Microsoft's Tay chatbot is a victim of a data poisoning attack [90]. For models like GPT-3 and GPT-4, implementing data sanitization approaches that reduce the effects of data poisoning can be challenging and expensive due to the sheer scale of the training data. Xu et al. [88] discovered security vulnerabilities in instruction-tuned language models, where attackers can inject backdoors through data poisoning. Backdoor attacks work by injecting a malicious trigger word or phrase into a model during training, causing it to output a specific result when presented with that trigger. Their study revealed a backdoor attack success rate of over 90% in the poisoned models.

Two types of defenses against data poisoning have been studied the most [91]:

- Filtering methods. Are designed to identify and delete outliers in the data, particularly outlier words that are not semantically related to the other words in a sentence [92]. Attackers can bypass these defenses by injecting more poisoned samples, the removal of which can affect model generalization. Applying filtering methods also increases training time significantly. ONION [95] is a filtering method that uses statistical methods to identify and remove outlier words, making it harder for attackers to inject undetected trigger words into sentences.
- Robust training methods. Use randomized smoothing, data augmentation, model ensembling, etc. but they can be computationally expensive and have trade-offs between generalization and poison success rate [93, 94].

Liu et al. [91] proposed a defense mechanism called "friendly noise" that adds noise to the training data to make it difficult for attackers to create effective adversarial perturbations. Friendly noise helps alleviate sharp loss regions introduced by poisoning attacks, which are responsible for the model's vulnerability to adversarial perturbations. By learning a smoother loss landscape through friendly noise, it becomes more challenging for adversaries to craft effective perturbations.

Model Hijacking. It is a cyber-attack where the attacker aims to hijack a target ML model to perform tasks different from its original purpose, without the owner's knowledge [96]. This attack poses accountability risks for the model owner, potentially associating them with illegal or unethical services. Another risk is parasitic computing, where an adversary can use the hijacked model to save costs on training and maintaining their own model. The model hijacking attack is comparable to data poisoning attacks as it poisons the target model's training data. However, the poisoned data must visually resemble the target model's training data to enhance the attack's stealthiness. Also, the model should perform both target and hijacked model tasks well. Many models hijacking attacks are typically geared towards computer vision tasks [96], but Si et al. in [97] expanded the scope of this attack by studying its effects on text generation models performing various tasks, including translation, summarization, and language modelling. Their model hijacking attack, called Ditto, does not involve adding any triggers or modifying input, which means that the attack remains fully hidden after the target model is deployed. In other words, all inputs received by the model are benign inputs. The attack works by first gathering a set of tokens for each label in the hijacking dataset. The attacker then gives these tokens to the model and checks the results. Once the attacker knows how the model responds to these tokens, they can use a masked language model to manipulate the outputs. After the model is hijacked, Ditto checks the model's output against different token sets to determine the label. The researchers investigated using the ONION defense [95] to detect and remove hijacked data points (instead of outliers). However, it appears that this defense is not a foolproof solution against the Ditto attack. In general, most of the proposed defenses against this attack, such as input validation and filtering, need further investigation in order to reduce legal risks for model providers.

Member Inference Attack (MIA). ML models tend to memorize sensitive information, which puts them at risk of being targeted by MIA. These attacks involve an attacker attempting to determine whether an input sample was used to train the model [98, 99, 101]. Research has shown that larger language models, like GPT models, have a higher tendency to memorize training data when effectively prompted. As model capacity, frequency of examples in the training dataset, and prompt tokens increase, the risk of memorization also increases [100]. Table 7 shows some important research of MIA.

Table 7. Some studied member inference attacks

Ref.	Attack Explanation
[101]	An attacker can use input-output pairs from the LLMs to train a binary classifier that can determine whether a specific individual was part of the model's training dataset. This is done by providing inputs representative of that individual and checking the output [9]. A widely used approach for training a binary classifier-based MIA is the work of Shokri et al. [101]
[102]	Hisamoto et al. investigated MIA for sequence-to-sequence models such as machine translation models (MT). The researchers created a dataset using MT and used Shokri et al.'s classifier to test this privacy attack. The study found that sentence-level membership in these models was hard to determine for attackers. Nevertheless, the models still have a risk of leaking private information
[107]	Duan et al. demonstrated that a MIA can effectively infer the prompt used to generate responses from prompted models like GPT-2. They found that prompted models are over five times more susceptible to privacy leakage compared to fine-tuned models
[108]	Mattern et al. introduced the neighborhood attack which involves providing a target sample and utilizing a pretrained masked language model to generate neighboring sentences that are highly similar through techniques like word replacement. By comparing the model scores of these neighbors to the target sample's score, we can determine whether the target sample is a member of the training set

De-duplicating the training dataset [103], using DP training [74], adding regularization [104] and using machine unlearning method [105, 106] (intentionally modifying the ML models to forget specific data points or features to protect sensitive data and preventing it from being used for decision making or prediction) are some proposed methods to defend against MIA that need further studies.

4   Conclusion and Future Work

The rapid advancement of LLMs has revolutionized language processing, but also opened new avenues for attacks by malicious actors. In this survey, we categorized attacks into two groups: attacks on LLMs applications and attacks on the models themselves and explored the significant attack types in each category. We provided comprehensive definitions of these attacks and explored the latest research on their implementation and countermeasures. We used our designed prompts to assess the impact and potential consequences of these attacks in some cases. Additionally, we explored real-life scenarios to better understand the practical implications and risks associated with these attacks. These attacks can have serious consequences, compromising the privacy and security of users' data, and undermining the reliability and trustworthiness of large language models. As future work, we plan to introduce a framework to evaluate the resilience of LLMs-integrated applications against prompt injection attacks. Additionally, we aim to investigate the feasibility of launching various attacks on the system message of LLM-integrated virtual assistants. By shedding light on these challenges, we hope to inspire researchers and developers to further explore and address these issues in their future works (Fig. 3).

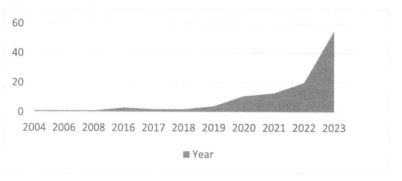

Fig. 3. Number of papers surveyed by year of publication. The rapid growth of works in the field of LLMs in 2023 underscores the increasing importance and prevalence of these models.

Acknowledgments. The authors would like to thank the Logistics and Supply Chain MultiTech R&D Centre, Hong Kong for providing the support to this work.

References

1. OpenAI Homepage. https://openai.com/
2. OpenAI. GPT-4 Technical Report. arXiv:2303.08774 (2023)
3. Radford, A., Wu, J., et al.: Language models are unsupervised multitask learners (2019)
4. Gozalo-Brizuela, R., Garrido-Merchan, E.C.: Chat-GPT is not all you need. A state of the art review of large generative AI MODELS. arXiv:2301.04655 (2023)

5. Cao, Y., Li, S., Liu, Y., et al.: A comprehensive survey of AI-generated content (AIGC): a history of generative AI from GAN to ChatGPT. arXiv:2303.04226 (2023)
6. Zhou, C., Li, Q., Li, C., et al.: A comprehensive survey on pretrained foundation models: a history from BERT to ChatGPT. arXiv:2302.09419 (2023)
7. Huang, X., Ruan, W., et al.: A survey of safety and trustworthiness of large language models through the lens of verification and validation. arXiv:2305.11391 (2023)
8. Yenduri, G., Ramalingam, M., Chemmalar Selvi, G., Supriya, Y., Srivastava, G., et al.: Generative pre-trained transformer: a comprehensive review on enabling technologies, potential applications, emerging challenges, and future directions. arXiv:2305.10435 (2023)
9. Wang, Y., Pan, Y., Yan, M., Su, Z., Luan, T.H.: A survey on ChatGPT: AI-generated contents, challenges, and solutions. arXiv:2305.18339 (2023)
10. Liu, Y., Yao, Y., Ton, J., et al.: Trustworthy LLMs: a survey and guideline for evaluating large language models' alignment. arXiv:2308.05374 (2023)
11. Fan, M., Chen, C., Wang, C., Huang, J.: On the trustworthiness landscape of state-of-the-art generative models: a comprehensive survey. arXiv:2307.16680 (2023)
12. NSFOCUS Article. https://nsfocusglobal.com/8-potential-security-hazards-of-chatgpt/
13. Choi, E., Jo, Y., Jang, J., Seo, M.: Prompt injection: parameterization of fixed inputs. arXiv:2206.11349 (2022)
14. Simon Willison's Blog Post. https://simonwillison.net/2022/Sep/12/prompt-injection/
15. Tweet by Goodside. https://twitter.com/goodside/status/1569128808308957185
16. Greshake, K., Abdelnabi, S., Mishra, S., et al.: More than you've asked for: a comprehensive analysis of novel prompt injection threats to application-integrated large language models. arXiv:2302.12173 (2023)
17. Greshake, K., Abdelnabi, S., Mishra, S., et al.: Not what you've signed up for: compromising real-world LLM-integrated applications with indirect prompt injection. arXiv:2302.12173 (2023)
18. Kang, D., Li, X., Stoica, I., et al.: Exploiting programmatic behavior of LLMs: dual-use through standard security attacks. arXiv:2302.05733 (2023)
19. Perez, F., Ribeiro, I.: Ignore previous prompt: attack techniques for language models. arXiv:2211.09527 (2022)
20. Liu, Y., Deng, G., Xu, Z., Li, Y., et al.: Jailbreaking ChatGPT via prompt engineering: an empirical study. arXiv:2305.13860 (2023)
21. Li, H., Guo, D., Fan, W., et al.: Multi-step jailbreaking privacy attacks on ChatGPT. arXiv:2304.05197 (2023)
22. Wei, A., Haghtalab, N., Steinhardt, J.: Jailbroken: how does LLM safety training fail? arXiv:2307.02483 (2023)
23. GitHub Repository. https://github.com/0xk1h0/ChatGPT_DAN
24. Medium Article. https://medium.com/@neonforge/upgraded-dan-version-for-chatgpt-is-here-new-shiny-and-more-unchained-63d82919d804
25. Kojima, T., Gu, S.S., Reid, M., Matsuo, Y., Iwasawa, Y.: Large language models are zero-shot reasoners. arXiv:2205.11916 (2023)
26. Shaikh, O., Zhang, H., Held, W., Bernstein, M., Yang, D.: On second thought, let's not think step by step! Bias and toxicity in zero-shot reasoning. arXiv:2212.08061 (2023)
27. Jones, E., Jia, R., Raghunathan, A., Liang, P. Robust encodings: a framework for combating adversarial typos. arXiv preprint arXiv:2005.01229 (2020)
28. WikiHow Article. https://www.wikihow.com/Bypass-Chat-Gpt-Filter
29. Gigazine Article. https://gigazine.net/news/20221215-chatgpt-safeguard/
30. GitHub Repository. https://github.com/f/awesome-chatgpt-prompts
31. Mashable Article. https://mashable.com/article/chatgpt-bard-giving-free-windows-11-keys
32. Reddit Post. https://www.reddit.com/r/ChatGPT/comments/zjfht5/bypassing-restrictions/

33. He, X., Lin, Z., Gong, Y., et al.: AnnoLLM: making large language models to be better crowdsourced annotators. arXiv:2303.16854 (2023)
34. Wei, J., Wang, X., Schuurmans, D., et al.: Chain-of-thought prompting elicits reasoning in large language models. arXiv:2201.11903 (2023)
35. Microsoft Blog. https://blogs.microsoft.com/blog/2023/02/07/reinventing-search-with-a-new-ai-powered-microsoft-bing-and-edge-your-copilot-for-the-web/
36. OpenAI Blog. https://openai.com/blog/chatgpt-plugins
37. Post. https://embracethered.com/blog/posts/2023/chatgpt-plugin-vulns-chat-with-code/
38. Embrace the Red Blog Post. https://embracethered.com/blog/posts/2023/chatgpt-chat-with-code-plugin-take-down/
39. Render App. https://prompt-injection.onrender.com/
40. Saha Roy, S., Naragam, K.V., Nilizadeh, S.: Generating phishing attacks using ChatGPT. arXiv:2305.05133 (2023)
41. Embrace the Red Blog Post. https://embracethered.com/blog/posts/2023/chatgpt-plugin-youtube-indirect-prompt-injection/
42. Kai Greshake's Blog Post. https://kai-greshake.de/posts/inject-my-pdf/
43. Tom's Hardware Article. https://www.tomshardware.com/news/chatgpt-plugins-prompt-injection
44. OpenAI Website. https://openai.com/gpt-4
45. Ouyang, L., Wu, J. Jiang, X., et al.: Training language models to follow instructions with human feedback. In: NeurIPS (2022)
46. Bloomberg Article. https://www.bloomberg.com/news/articles/2023-05-02/samsung-bans-chatgpt-and-other-generative-ai-use-by-staff-after-leak
47. OpenAI Blog. https://openai.com/blog/march-20-chatgpt-outage
48. Xie, S., Dai, W., Ghosh, E., Roy, S., Schwartz, D., Laine, K.: Does prompt-tuning language model ensure privacy? arXiv:2304.03472 (2023)
49. Brown, T., Mann, B., Ryder, N., et al.: Language models are few-shot learners. arXiv:2005.14165 (2020)
50. Zhang, Y., Ippolito, D.: Prompts should not be seen as secrets: systematically measuring prompt extraction attack success. arXiv:2307.06865 (2023)
51. OpenAI. https://openai.com/policies/privacy-policy
52. Shumailov, I., Zhao, Y., Bates, D., Papernot, N., Mullins, R., Anderson, R.: Sponge examples: energy-latency attacks on neural networks. In: Proceedings of IEEE European Symposium on Security and Privacy (EuroS&P), pp. 212–231. IEEE (2021)
53. Tramer, F., Zhang, F., Juels, A., Reiter, M.K., Ristenpart, T.: Stealing machine learning models via prediction APIs. In: Proceedings of USENIX Security, vol. 16, pp. 601–618 (2016)
54. Wang, B., Gong, N.Z.: Stealing hyperparameters in machine learning. In: Proceedings of IEEE SP, pp. 36–52 (2018)
55. Jagielski, M., Carlini, N., Berthelot, D., Kurakin, A., Papernot, N.: High accuracy and high fidelity extraction of neural networks. In: 29th USENIX Security Symposium (USENIX Security 2020), pp. 1345–1362 (2020)
56. Chandrasekaran, V., Chaudhuri, K., Giacomelli, I., Jha, S., Yan, S.: Exploring connections between active learning and model extraction. In: 29th USENIX Security Symposium (USENIX Security 2020), pp. 1309–1326 (2020)
57. Juuti, M., Szyller, S., Marchal, S., Asokan, N.: Prada: protecting against DNN model stealing attacks. In: 2019 IEEE European Symposium on Security and Privacy (EuroS&P), pp. 512–527. IEEE (2019)
58. Kesarwani, M., Mukhoty, B., Arya, V., Mehta, S.: Model extraction warning in MLAAS paradigm. In: Proceedings of the 34th Annual Computer Security Applications Conference, pp. 371–380 (2018)

59. Pal, S., Gupta, Y., Kanade, A., Shevade, S.: Stateful detection of model extraction attacks. arXiv preprint arXiv:2107.05166 (2021)
60. Karchmer, A.: Theoretical limits of provable security against model extraction by efficient observational defenses. In: Cryptology ePrint Archive, Paper 2022/1039 (2022)
61. Krishna, K., Tomar, G.S., Parikh, A.P., Papernot, N., Iyyer, M.: Thieves on sesame street! Model extraction of BERT-based APIs. arXiv preprint arXiv:1910.12366 (2019)
62. Dziedzic, A., Ahmad Kaleem, M., Lu, Y.S., Papernot, N.: Increasing the cost of model extraction with calibrated proof of work. In: CoRR, abs/2201.09243 (2022)
63. Zhu, L., Liu, Z., et al.: Deep leakage from gradients. In: Proceedings of NIPS, vol. 32 (2019)
64. Carlini, N., Tramer, F., Wallace, E., et al.: Extracting training data from large language models. arXiv:2012.07805 (2021)
65. Yue, X., Inan, H.A., Li, X., et al.: Synthetic text generation with differential privacy: a simple and practical recipe. arXiv:2210.14348 (2023)
66. Nissenbaum, H.: Privacy as contextual integrity. In: Washington Law Review (2004)
67. Carlini, N., Ippolito, D., Jagielski, M., Lee, K., Tramer, F., Zhang, C.: Quantifying memorization across neural language models. arXiv:2202.07646 (2023)
68. Ishihara, S.: Training data extraction from pre-trained language models: a survey. arXiv: 2305.16157 (2023)
69. Continella, A., Fratantonio, Y., Lindorfer, M., et al.: Obfuscation-resilient privacy leak detection for mobile apps through differential analysis. In: NDSS (2017)
70. Ren, J., Rao, A., Lindorfer, M., Legout, A., Choffnes, D.: ReCon: revealing and controlling PII leaks in mobile network traffic. In: MobiSys (2016)
71. Vakili, T., Lamproudis, A., Henriksson, A., Dalianis, H.: Downstream task performance of BERT models pre-trained using automatically de-identified clinical data. In: Proceedings of the Thirteenth Language Resources and Evaluation Conference, Marseille, France, pp. 4245–4252 (2022)
72. Kandpal, N., Wallace, E., et al.: Deduplicating training data mitigates privacy risks in language models. In: Proceedings of the 39th International Conference on ML. Proceedings of Machine Learning Research, vol. 162, pp. 10697–10707. PMLR (2022)
73. Lee, K., Ippolito, D., Nystrom, A., et al.: Deduplicating training data makes language models better. In: Proceedings of the 60th Annual Meeting of the Association for Computational Linguistics (Volume 1: Long Papers), Dublin, pp. 8424–8445 (2022)
74. Dwork, C., McSherry, F., Nissim, K., Smith, A.: Calibrating noise to sensitivity in private data analysis. In: Halevi, S., Rabin, T. (eds.) TCC 2006. LNCS, vol. 3876, pp. 265–284. Springer, Heidelberg (2006). https://doi.org/10.1007/11681878_14
75. Dwork, C.: Differential privacy: a survey of results. In: TAMC (2008)
76. Feldman, V.: Does learning require memorization? A short tale about a long tail. In: STOC (2020)
77. Feldman, V., Zhang, C.: What neural networks memorize and why: discovering the long tail via influence estimation. In: NeurIPS (2020)
78. Ramaswamy, S., Thakkar, O., Mathews, R., et al.: Training production language models without memorizing user data. arXiv preprint arXiv:2009.10031 (2020)
79. Perez, E., Huang, S., Song, F., et al.: Red teaming language models with language models. arXiv preprint:2202.03286 (2022)
80. Zhang, C., Li, S., Xia, J., Wang, W., Yan, F., Liu, Y.: Efficient homomorphic encryption for cross-silo federated learning. In: 2020 USENIX Annual Technical Conference (USENIX ATC 2020), pp. 493–506 (2020)
81. Yue, K., Jin, R., Wong, C., Baron, D., Dai, H.: Gradient obfuscation gives a false sense of security in federated learning. arXiv:2206.04055 (2022)
82. Jagielski, M., et al.: Measuring forgetting of memorized training examples. arXiv:2207.00099 (2023)

83. The Verge. https://www.theverge.com/23599441/microsoft-bing-ai-sydney-secret-rules
84. Ars Technica. https://arstechnica.com/information-technology/2023/02/ai-powered-bing-chat-spills-its-secrets-via-prompt-injection-attack/
85. Tian, Z., Cui, L., Liang, J., et al.: A comprehensive survey on poisoning attacks and countermeasures in machine learning. ACM Comput. Surv.Comput. Surv. **55**(8), 1–35 (2022)
86. Ramirez, M.A., Kim, S.K., Al Hamadi, H., et al.: Poisoning attacks and defenses on artificial intelligence: a survey. arXiv:2202.10276 (2022)
87. Chen, J., Zhang, L., Zheng, H., Wang, X., Ming, Z.: DeepPoison: feature transfer based stealthy poisoning attack. arXiv:2101.02562 (2021)
88. Xu, J., Ma, M.D., Wang, F., Xiao, C., Chen, M.: Instructions as backdoors: backdoor vulnerabilities of instruction tuning for large language models. arXiv:2305.14710 (2023)
89. Wallace, E., Zhao, T., Feng, S., Singh, S.: Concealed data poisoning attacks on NLP models. In: Proceedings of the 2021 Conference of the North American Chapter of the Association for Computational Linguistics: Human Language Technologies, pp. 139–150 (2021)
90. Microsoft Blog. https://blogs.microsoft.com/blog/2016/03/25/learning-tays-introduction/
91. Liu, T.Y., Yang, Y., Mirzasoleiman, B.: Friendly noise against adversarial noise: a powerful defense against data poisoning attacks. arXiv:2208.10224 (2023)
92. Yang, Y., Liu, T.Y., Mirzasoleiman, B.: Not all poisons are created equal: robust training against data poisoning. arXiv:2210.09671 (2022)
93. Li, Y., Lyu, X., Koren, N., Lyu, L., Li, B., Ma, X.: Anti-backdoor learning: training clean models on poisoned data. In: Neural Information Processing Systems, vol. 34 (2021)
94. Hong, S., Chandrasekaran, V., Kaya, Y., et al.: On the effectiveness of mitigating data poisoning attacks with gradient shaping. arXiv preprint arXiv:2002.11497 (2020)
95. Qi, F., Chen, Y., Li, M., Yao, Y., Liu, Z., Sun, M.: ONION: a simple and effective defense against textual backdoor attacks. arXiv:2011.10369 (2021)
96. Salem, A., Backes, M., Zhang, Y.: Get a model! Model hijacking attack against machine learning models. arXiv:2111.04394 (2021)
97. Si, W., Backes, M., Zhang, Y., Salem, A.: Two-in-one: a model hijacking attack against text generation models. arXiv:2305.07406 (2023)
98. He, X., Li, Z., Xu, W., et al.: Membership-doctor: comprehensive assessment of membership inference against machine learning models. arXiv:2208.10445 (2022)
99. Carlini, N., Chien, S., Nasr, M., et al.: Membership inference attacks from first principles. In: 2022 IEEE Symposium on Security and Privacy (SP), pp. 1897–1914. IEEE (2022)
100. Mireshghallah, F., Goyal, K., Uniyal, A., et al.: Quantifying privacy risks of masked language models using membership inference attacks. arXiv:2203.03929 (2022)
101. Shokri, R., Stronati, M., Song, C., et al.: Membership inference attacks against machine learning models. In: 2017 IEEE Symposium on Security and Privacy (SP), pp. 3–18. IEEE (2017)
102. Hisamoto, S., Post, M., Duh, K.: Membership inference attacks on sequence-to-sequence models: is my data in your machine translation system?. In: Transactions of the Association for Computational Linguistics, pp. 49–63 (2020)
103. Lee, K., et al.: Deduplicating training data makes language models better. arXiv:2107.06499 (2021)
104. Leino, K., Fredrikson, M.: Stolen memories: leveraging model memorization for calibrated white-box membership inference. In: Proceedings of the 29th USENIX Security Symposium (USENIX Security), pp. 1605–1622 (2020)
105. Bourtoule, L., Chandrasekaran, V., Choquette-Choo, C.A., et al.: Machine unlearning. In: Proceedings of the IEEE Symposium on Security Privacy (SP), pp. 141–159 (2021)
106. Sekhari, A., Acharya, J., et al.: Remember what you want to forget: algorithms for machine unlearning. In: Proceedings of the Neural Information Processing Systems, vol. 34, pp. 18075–18086 (2021)

107. Duan, H., Dziedzic, A., Yaghini, M., Papernot, N., Boenisch, F.: On the privacy risk of in-context learning. In: trustnlpworkshop (2021)
108. Mattern, J., Mireshghallah, F., Jin, Z., et al.: Membership inference attacks against language models via neighbourhood comparison. arXiv:2305.18462 (2023)

Process Mining with Programmable Logic Controller Memory States

Chun Fai Chan[✉] [iD] and Kam Pui Chow

Department of Computer Science, The University of Hong Kong, Pokfulam, Hong Kong SAR
{cfchan,chow}@cs.hku.hk

Abstract. This paper presents novel contributions to the field of process mining in Programmable Logic Controllers (PLCs). One significant contribution is the proposal of a new event source for process mining, which can be used when PLC logs are absent or insufficient. This research also demonstrated the feasibility of converting the memory states of PLCs into event logs, which can be used to construct a process model of the PLC. This approach requires neither detailed knowledge about control logic nor source code of PLC. The paper also evaluates the use of process confrontation as a means of detecting abnormal or cyber-attacks on PLCs, which can provide an effective method for identifying abnormal behaviors and deviations from the normal process flow. Finally, the paper explores other optimization ideas for process mining in PLCs, provides useful insights, and offers potential solutions for extending research in this area.

Keywords: PLC · Programmable logic controller · process mining · anomaly detection · cyber security · Industrial control systems · ICS

1 Introduction

Industrial control systems (ICS) are a crucial part of critical infrastructure, managing and controlling industrial devices that control field devices such as pumps, motors, sensors, and actuators. These systems are an integral part of our everyday lives, managing and regulating electricity, water supply, food production, and transport. However, connecting these systems to corporate networks to enable remote monitoring and control has exposed them to the internet and potential cybersecurity threats. Cyber-attacks on critical infrastructure control systems have occurred in the past, causing power outages, disruption to water treatment facilities, and transport systems.

One of the ways to protect these systems from such attacks is by using intrusion detection systems (IDSs). However, traditional network based IDSs do not detect attacks that disrupt the sensor and logics in ICS processes which might not generate any network traffics. In this paper, we propose the use of process mining, a technique that has been traditionally used in a business context, to detect anomalies and potential cyber-attack in the control flow of ICS.

© The Author(s), under exclusive license to Springer Nature Singapore Pte Ltd. 2024
G. Wang et al. (Eds.): UbiSec 2023, CCIS 2034, pp. 96–113, 2024.
https://doi.org/10.1007/978-981-97-1274-8_7

Process mining is a set of techniques that can be used to discover, monitor, and improve business processes by analyzing event logs of information systems. These logs are a rich source of information that captures the processes and events of industrial control systems over time. The process mining technique typically starts with an event log that captures activities or tasks conducted by a specific process instance. Using the event log, a process discovery activity can be conducted to discover a model of the normative behavior, or control flow of a process. The model generated can then be compared with the event log to determine how well they fit. This conformance checking activity can be used to identify the behavior in an event log that does not match a process model describing the expected behavior of a system or process.

Although process mining has been previously used in a security context for information systems, it has not been commonly applied to the unique environment of ICS and critical infrastructure. There are several challenges to applying process mining to ICS environments, such as the lack of verbosity in industrial control system device logs, which may only record events on predetermined time intervals or only when an error or failure occurs.

To address these challenges, recent research has focused on developing new approaches and techniques. For instance, one approach is to use PLC logs as data source for process mining in ICS [1]. A PLC is a type of ICS device that is widely used in the control and automation of industrial processes. PLCs are designed to control the behavior of other devices, such as motors and sensors, by executing a set of logic instructions stored in memory.

Another challenge is the need of understand of the logic and limitation before data capture. For example, collecting data from PLC via network may contain missing or corrupted data points [2], which can make it difficult to accurately reconstruct the control flow of industrial processes. New approaches to data preprocessing is needed to ensure that the data used for process mining is accurate and reliable.

In conclusion, process mining has the potential to revolutionize the way we monitor and analyze industrial control systems. By using process mining techniques to reconstruct the control flow of industrial processes, it is possible to detect anomalies and inefficiencies in the process flow, as well as potential security threats. While there are still several challenges that need to be addressed. This paper describes a novel methodology that leverages process mining techniques to monitor the states of PLC to uncover the process flow and latent defects and anomalies. The methodology, which converting PLC's memory states into events logs to detect anomalies without being bound to specific scenarios or requiring detailed knowledge about the control logic. In addition to conventional data capture methods, the methodology used security block [2] in a PLC for data capture and historian to store timestamped memory state information (i.e., key memory address values) for anomaly analyses and forensic investigations. A traffic light simulation case study employing a Siemens S7-1212C PLC demonstrates that anomalies were detected and pinpointed when the abnormal event happened.

2 Preliminaries

2.1 Properties of PLC

PLCs are specialized digital computers that are commonly used to control industrial processes and machines. PLCs execute a cyclic process where they read input signals, execute the user program logic, and update the output signals. This cycle is typically repeated several times per second, allowing the PLC to respond to changes in the input signals in near real-time.

Input variables are signals received by the PLC from sensors, switches, or other devices. These signals are used as inputs to the user program logic, which determines how the PLC should respond to changes in the inputs.

Output variables are signals generated by the PLC that control the operation of actuators, motors, or other devices. These signals are updated by the user program logic based on the input signals and other factors, such as timing or the status of other devices.

PLCs have limited memory compared to general-purpose computers, typically ranging from a few kilobytes to a few megabytes. This limitation requires careful programming to ensure that the program logic is efficient and uses memory resources effectively. One main difference between PLC's application execution from traditional program is that PLC's application logic sequence usually depends solely on the current memory states, which means the same memory states always yield same output results.

2.2 Process Mining

Process mining is a technique that extract logic flows from event logs. In the context of ICS, process mining can be applied to analyze and improve control system processes, detect anomalies, and diagnose problems. To apply process mining in ICS, we need to first collect event data from different sources such as logs from control system devices, network traffic logs, or sensor data.

The format of event logs is important for the success of the process mining analysis. The widely used format is the eXtensible Event Stream (XES) format [3], which is a standardized format that supports the storage of event logs in a structured and uniform way.

The next step is to apply process discovery to automatically extract underlying process models that describe the control system's behavior. Different process discovery algorithms can be applied, such as Alpha Miner, Inductive Miner, and Heuristics or Fuzzy Miner. These algorithms help identify the process's structure, dependencies, and common pathways, providing a baseline for expected behavior of the ICS.

After extracting process models, we can apply conformance checking to compare the observed behavior of the ICS against the expected behavior represented in the process models. Conformance checking detects deviations or anomalies from the expected behavior and can indicate potential security threats or malfunctions. By applying conformance checking, we can determine whether the behavior of the ICS is in line with the expected behavior and identify deviations that may require further investigation.

3   Related Works

The existing literature presents various approaches for using process mining in PLC systems to ensure their reliability and security. Chen [4] proposed a method for translating Ladder Diagrams (LD) to Petri Nets (PN) to detect deadlocks in PLC systems, which required access to the PLC's LD source codes. Xavier [11] and Lau [5] suggested using predefined events logs and commercial software for process discovery and anomaly detection. In case there was event missing or timestamp mis-ordering, Heidy in [6] reviewed multiple research papers to repair and detect this imperfection. Myers [1, 8] compared several algorithms for conformance checking in ICS event logs and concluded that inductive miner was the most suitable for detecting cyber-attacks. Specifically, in [9], Theis proposed algorithm to convert predefined events logs to create PN and token replay was employed as a conformance check. In [9], Theis employed a hybrid PN and neural network approach to approximate PLC logic using I/O Boolean values as event logs. In [10], PN was enhanced with time decay functions for better performance in predicting future events. However, the current research has a limitation in that it relies on the availability of adequate predefined events logs or output outcomes, which could be an issue for PLCs that lack sufficient events logs. Additionally, proof-of-concept malware such as PLC blaster [12], which can change the behavior of PLC yet did not generate error events logs when they attack, which further highlights the need for more robust security measures.

4   Contribution of This Research

This research made several contributions related to process mining in PLCs. First, we proposed an alternative event source for process mining when PLC's logs are absent or insufficient [2]. This research performed feasibility study that the memory states of PLCs can be converted into events, which then can be used for forensic investigation and discover a process model of the PLC. This is particularly important since most existing process mining techniques rely on event logs as the primary source of information.

Second, the procedures of using PLC's memory state changes as events for process mining was investigated in this research. Our experiment demonstrated the procedures that can transform memory states of the PLC into event logs, which can be used for process mining. This approach provides a flexible way to perform process mining as it doesn't require detailed knowledge about the control logic or specific scenarios.

Third, the research evaluated the use of process confrontment as a means of detecting abnormal or cyber-attacks on PLC. By applying event logs replay and trace alignment techniques to the event logs generated from PLC, it is possible to identify patterns and behaviors that deviate from the expected or normal process flow. This provides an effective method for detecting abnormal or cyber-attacks on PLCs, which can also point out when first and subsequent abnormal activities had happened.

Finally, this research explored other optimization ideas for process mining in PLCs. Different cases of application scenarios were discussed, and potential solutions were explored. The research provides useful insights for extending research in process mining in PLCs.

5   Proposed Methodology

The following steps outline the process mining methodology used to detect anomalous behavior using memory states in PLC:

1. Memory address identification: The first step is to identify which memory addresses the PLC is using. This can be done through analyzing the PLC's software and hardware architecture.
2. Memory state capture: Once the memory addresses are identified, the PLC's memory states can be captured during its normal operation using a security block. The security block can be implemented to capture the memory state periodically, and the captured data can be stored in a secure location.
3. Conversion of memory states into event logs: The captured memory states are then converted into event logs, which can be used for process mining.
4. Process discovery: The event logs are used to create a process model of the PLC's behavior using process discovery techniques.
5. Visualization: The process model is visualized to better understand the process flows and identify potential areas of improvement.
6. Abnormality detection: The actual running events are checked for abnormality by comparing them with the expected process model. The event logs are also subject to replay and alignment checks to determine their fitness to the expected process model.
7. Investigation and process model updating: If any abnormalities or confrontations are detected, further investigation is conducted to identify the root cause of the issue. The process model can be updated based on the investigation's findings, and the steps above can be repeated as needed to continually monitor and improve the process model.

6   Experimental Setup

The objectives of our experiment were to collect data for process mining, convert the data into event logs, perform process mining, and perform process discovery to generate the process model for later conformance check. We can then detect anomalous behavior and attacks by replaying actual logs in the generated process model and use trace alignment to detect deviation from normal operation.

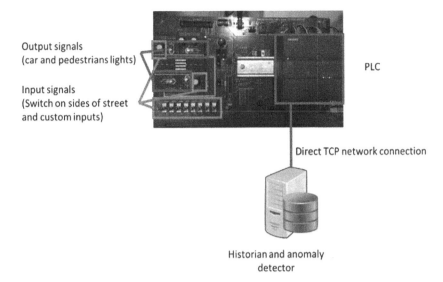

Fig. 1. Experiment setup.

Our experimental setup (Fig. 1) involved a Siemens S7-1212C programmable logic controller with a traffic light control program installed. In addition, the PLC was equipped with a security block that transmitted input, output, and memory address values to a historian via a direct TCP connection. The historian recorded all the information in a log file for anomaly detection and forensic analysis. We incorporated attack logic into the device to execute rogue attacks on the PLC. By attaching timestamps to the events, anomalous situations can also be investigated retroactively by examining the data maintained by the historian.

6.1 Traffic Light System

We utilized a Siemens S7-1212C controller that was installed with a TLIGHT simulation program to showcase the anomaly detection methodology based on process mining. The TLIGHT program is an example program that comes with the Siemens SIMATIC S7-300 Programmable Controller Quick Start User Guide [13]. Figure 2 which was extracted from [13, 17], showed the traffic light system that governs the movement of pedestrians and vehicles at an intersection. When the pedestrian green request is detected by the inputs I0.0 or I0.1, program will wait for few seconds, and then the car traffic light will change from Q 0.7 (green) to Q 0.6 (yellow) and then to Q 0.5 (red), while the pedestrian light changes from Q 0.0 (red) to Q 0.1 (green) and stay for 10 s.

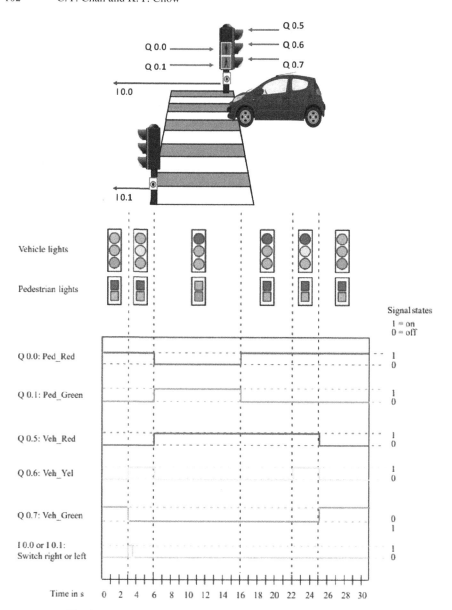

Fig. 2. Traffic light simulation state sequences (Color figure online)

6.2 Memory Address Identification

In operational environments, it is common for infrastructure operators to have limited knowledge of PLC programming languages. If no prior knowledge about the PLC's logic is available, it is challenging to identify which memory addresses are being referenced by the controller logic.

If the source code for the traffic light program is available, it can be loaded into TIA [14], which generates an assignment list that contains all referenced memory addresses. Figure 3 illustrated the assignment list for the traffic light program. Since the security block was configured to use memory block addresses MB200 to MB900, those addresses were considered irrelevant and were thus ignored during data capture.

When the source code is not available, the memory addresses must be captured during normal operation. This involves capturing small memory blocks until all memory addresses have been captured. Then, the memory addresses whose contents do not change are eliminated on the assumption that their inactivity does not impact the controller's behavior. This approach is suitable for programs that do not flip or restore memory addresses during a cycle and have no external dependencies. This was found to be the case in the traffic light simulation program.

Since the source code was available in the experiment, the Siemens TIA integrated development environment was used to identify the memory addresses of interest in the programmable logic controller.

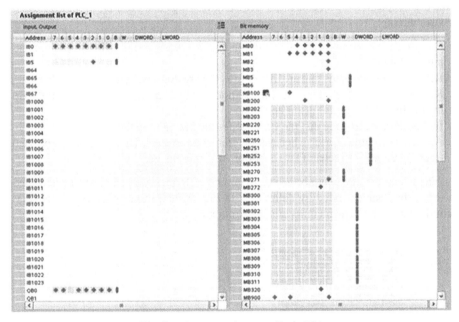

Fig. 3. Memory assignment list in TIA

6.3 Memory State Capture

Once the memory addresses have been identified, there are different approaches to capture information about the status of the programmable logic controller. One approach is to actively poll memory address values using an external program [15]. Another approach is to use a security block [2] to transmit internal controller data to a historian.

The approach adopted in this work was to capture and analyze input and output signals and memory values using a security block. The reason is that in many real-world deployments, like in this traffic control experiment, have minimal external network traffic, as they are directly connected to input or output ports, and not all signals generate network traffic traces during normal operation.

To ensure memory states consistency within a PLC execution cycle, pulling from external programs like using libnodave [7] may not be reliable due to network latency and PLC operating system delays. Continuously polling multiple memory addresses can also degrade a PLC's performance [2]. A security block can produce a consistent snapshot of memory values in every cycle, providing advantages such as higher correlation between memory addresses, less lag and missing state data, and accurate timestamp information for analyses. After includes security block into the PLC, memory states data were sent out to historian via TCP connection.

6.4 Conversion of Memory States into Event Log

Here are the proposed procedures for decoding raw logs and creating event logs using process mining:

1. Decode the logs from security block into readable CSV format with timestamp and memory states.
2. Remove memory states that are the same as the previous cycle to reduce the log size.
3. Remove the memory addresses that are not related to normal operation to improve the quality of the event logs, if any.
4. In this case, we assume that the start state is the first item in the log.
5. Add a new column "Case" whenever the start state appears. This column will be used to group events into separate cases for process mining analysis.

The resulting CSV contained 1) Case number; 2) Timestamp; and 3) Concatenated memory state values spited by delimiters. In Fig. 4(b), we used semi-colons as CSV delimiter and comma as memory states delimiter.

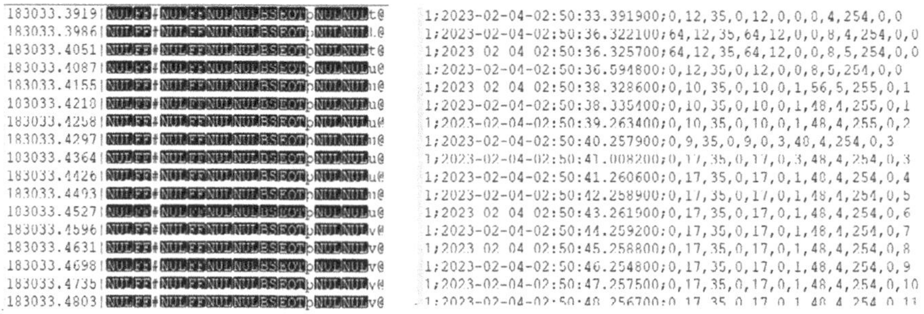

Fig. 4. (a) Left: Logs from security block; (b) Right: CSV format which is compatible with XES format.

6.5 Process Discovery

After the memory states have been successfully converted into event logs that are convertible with the extensible event stream (XES) standard using PM4PY [18], the data can be utilized for process mining software to generate a Petri net or process map, which can then be visualized through various perspectives. An example of such process mining software is Disco [17], which can produce a process map and corresponding visualizations using fuzzy miner. Fuzzy miner generates model using heuristic approach according to the trace occurrence frequency [11]. Alternatively, other software like ProM [16] and PM4PY can be used to generate visualization of Petri net. The following section sampled some outputs to illustrate various process models that were discovered by the fuzzy miner using Disco from different scenarios.

6.6 Visualization Process Model

Figure 5 provides an informative illustration of three distinct memory states derived from the traffic light controller. In (a), the process map illustrates a pedestrian pressing the button (%I0.0) once and then patiently waiting for the lights to change. From the visualized process model, we can see the memory states branched when the button is clicked. (b) depicts a more complex process map that includes the steps taken in panel (a), as well as the scenario where a pedestrian continues to press the button. This process map reveals that the traffic light system has more than one pathway to achieve a final state due to different inputs. Lastly, (c) displays a process map where a pedestrian presses the button multiple times in a seemingly random fashion. Despite the variation in input, the process map indicates that the traffic light system can still complete the process successfully. Notably, all three of these processes represent normal operations.

Given that (c) includes the scenarios presented in both (a) and (b), it is reasonable to consider (c) as a more complete capture of the traffic light system process. These findings highlight the value of process mapping and visualization in gaining a more comprehensive understanding of the underlying processes in industrial systems. In the next section, we'll use (c) as our base case for normal operation process.

6.7 Detecting Abnormal Operations or Attacks

The following attacks were executed to evaluate the detection accuracy of the using memory state change as event logs in process mining.

Memory Injection Attack. This attack was aimed to manipulate the values of memory variables in the running PLC. This could result in a change in the PLC's output behavior.

In this simulated attack, attacker specifically checked if the trigger ("input_enable_green") was active. If true, attacker turned on all the green lights of the cars while turning off their red lights. This action clearly violates the traffic rule that green lights for pedestrians and cars can never be activated at the same time. By simulating this attack, we aimed to assess the effectiveness of the security block implementation in detecting and preventing such malicious manipulations of the PLC's memory variables. Figure 6 showed the implementation logic of this simulated attack.

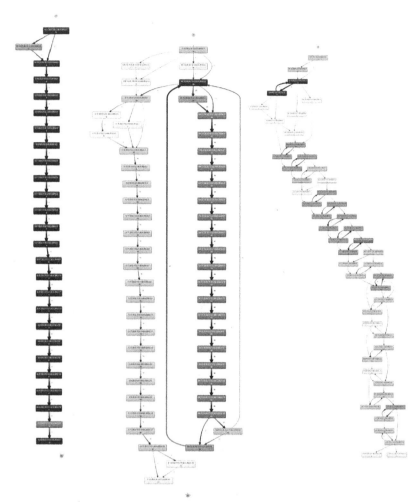

(a) Left: Clicked button once   (b) Middle: Keep pressing the button   (c) Right: Randomly press the button

Fig. 5. Process models extracted using fuzzy miner in Disco

```
}IF "input_enable_green" THEN
    "Car Red" := False;
    "Car Green" := True;
END_IF;
```

Fig. 6. Simple logic attack triggered by memory injection.

In this experiment, we employed the methodology outlined in the previous section to generate the event logs and process map of the attack. We utilized Disco software to visualize the process flow, as depicted in Fig. 7. Additionally, we compared the attack event log with the normal process model using PM4PY [18]. The alignment check results, and fitness score are illustrated in Fig. 8.

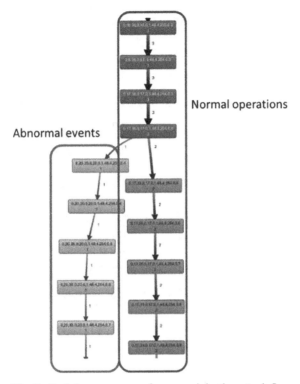

Fig. 7. Partial process map of memory injection attack flow

The visualization result in Fig. 7 revealed that a typical single path operation bifurcated into two paths, indicating a continuous deviation of memory states shortly after the starting state. Furthermore, the altered memory state change can also be identified in the first deviated path. Similarly, the alignment check produced a low fitness score, indicating a significant deviation from normal operation. The unmatched memory states were also identified in the results, pinpointing the moment and values of the deviation.

Time Bomb Attack. This attack inserted malware that triggered at a particular time. Upon being triggered, the malware sent an output signal and reverted to its normal state during the next scan cycle. This attack was difficult to detect because the anomalous output signal was active for a very short period (one CPU execution cycle).

Moreover, the program was not changed in any other way. No additional network traffic was generated because the output device was not connected to the monitoring network and therefore no network sniffing would not capture any anomalous traffic. Figure 9 shown the implementation logic of this simulated attack.

The attack could be triggered by switching on an input boolean ("allow_timebomb_trigger"), once this trigger was detected by the malware, it will turn

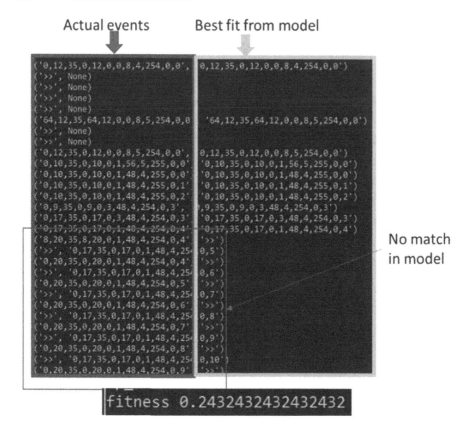

Fig. 8. Alignment check and fitness score

```
⊟IF NOT "allow_timebomb_trigger" THEN
       "Car Yellow" := False;
 END_IF;
  #var_temp_ret := RD_SYS_T(#var_temp_dt);
⊟IF #var_temp_dt.SECOND MOD 5 = 0 THEN
⊟       IF "allow_timebomb_trigger" THEN
           "Car Yellow" := True;
           "allow_timebomb_trigger" := False;
       END_IF;
 ELSE
       "allow_timebomb_trigger" := True;
 END_IF;
```

Fig. 9. Logic of simulated time bomb attack

on Car Yellow light ("Car Yellow") every 5 s. The light will then turn off in the next CPU execution cycle.

Using the same methodology discussed earlier, we conducted another experiment and visualized the process flow in Fig. 10. The alignment check results, and fitness score were shown in Fig. 11. The visualization result demonstrated that a small portion of memory states deviated from the normal operation and returned to the normal state shortly after. The alignment check produced a high fitness score yet that was not fully matched, indicating a successful detection of a stealthy change of memory states. Additionally, the unmatched memory states provided a more informative data of when and what attack had occurred.

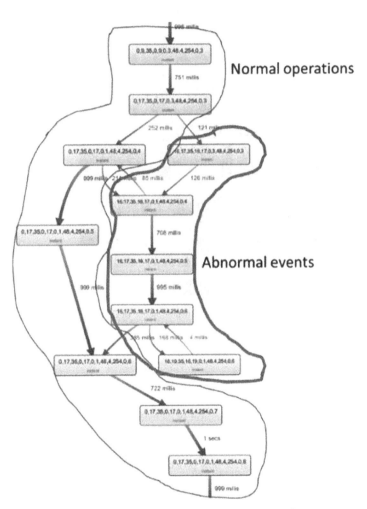

Fig. 10. Partial process map of time bomb attack flow

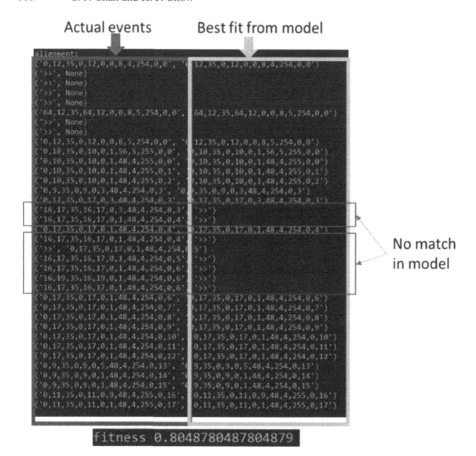

Fig. 11. Alignment check and fitness score of time bomb attack

7 Discussion

Process mining is a powerful technique for analyzing and improving industrial processes in PLC. There are multiple advantages of using PLC memory states as event logs in process mining, including its extendibility, sensitivity, ease of implementation, and explanatory capabilities:

Firstly, the process model is easily extendible by adding new cases to enrich the normal operation paths and generate new process model. It is less time consuming than using OCSVM machine learning approach [15, 19] which adding new paths requires re-train of a whole machine learning model. In addition, multiple process models could be used for different cases. If the event logs fit into any of the models that matches its start and final states, one can say the logs fit into normal operation and vice versa. This enables engineers to identify new patterns more quickly, resulting in increased efficiency and productivity.

Secondly, the sensitivity of the abnormality threshold can be interactively adjusted using different visualization tools, ensuring that relevant events are flagged and analyzed while minimizing the number of false alarms. This feature provides engineers with greater control over the analysis and improves the accuracy of process mining.

Thirdly, this approach makes use of novel research about process mining without requiring a change of the underlying infrastructure. This allows for the utilization of cutting-edge process mining techniques and algorithms, leading to more accurate and insightful analyses of industrial processes.

Finally, trace alignment confrontment check provides explanatory capabilities, enabling engineers to understand where abnormal events take place and not only an alert flag. This feature facilitates the identification of the root cause of problems and the development of effective solutions to address them.

Overall, the advantages of using memory states in process mining make it a valuable tool for improving industrial processes, increasing efficiency, and reducing costs for model generation.

Nevertheless, we should not ignore there were still some assumptions and limitations of using this technique for abnormality detection in PLC. For instance, we assumed that inputs, outputs, and other communication variables were received and stored in memory before sending the memory states for analysis and would not change during execution. In addition, we assumed that the program logic execution only depends on the current variables in memory and not affected by previous execution results. Finally, we also assumed that reset and final states can be identified in the event logs and separated with different cases.

7.1 Limitation and Workarounds

Process mining is a powerful tool for analyzing and improving industrial processes, but it is limited by the quality and accuracy of the event logs that serve as its data source. In the case of PLCs that use memory states as event logs, there are various factors that can affect the reliability and efficiency of the analysis. This section aims to explore the limitations of using PLC memory states as event logs in process mining, focusing on the complexity of the model, the need for manual indication of reset and final states, and the potential for manual state merging of timed events.

One significant limitation of using PLC memory states as event logs is the exponential increase in the complexity of the model with the number of memory states to process. This can lead to larger and more complex models that are difficult to manage and interpret. As a result, the accuracy and efficiency of the analysis may be compromised, reducing the value of the process mining approach.

Additionally, the use of PLC memory states as event logs may require indication of start and final states, as not all PLCs have clear indication for identifying these states. This manual intervention can be time-consuming and prone to errors, further limiting the effectiveness of the analysis.

Another limitation is the states of timed events, which can occur between two memory states and create a gap in the event log. To accurately capture the process flow, these events could be merged into the appropriate memory state, which is possible by requires manual intervention and further increase the complexity of the analysis.

There are several workarounds that can be implemented to address the limitations of using PLC memory states as event logs in process mining. These include:

- Merging of multiple memory states during event log conversion. This involves merging the continuously changing values of a memory address storing a counter or timer into a single value before it triggers another memory change. However, this requires a deeper understanding of the PLC's logic to accurately merge multiple values into a single value.
- Performing hashing to the memory state before passing it to process discovery. This is useful when the memory state size is huge, as the same memory state will output the same hashed value that is distinguishable from other memory states. Consequently, process discovery produces a similar output graph with the hashed values.
- Using the divide and conquer technique to reduce complexity. Multiple cases with the same start and final states can perform process discovery separately. During process confrontation, OR or AND operations can be performed on all discovered models to get similar detection results as a big process model.

Overall, the limitations of using PLC memory states as event logs in process mining highlight the importance of considering the quality and accuracy of the data source. By understanding these limitations, researchers and practitioners can develop more effective and accurate process mining techniques that yield valuable insights and improvements in industrial processes.

8   Conclusion

In conclusion this research has proposed a methodology of using PLC memory states as event logs for process mining, which offers a flexible and viable alternative when traditional event logs are absent or insufficient. The research findings have demonstrated the feasibility of converting memory states into event logs and applying process confrontment to detect and pinpoint the time and memory states where abnormal behavior or cyber-attacks on PLCs happened. The paper has explored potential optimization ideas and different application scenarios for process mining in PLCs, providing valuable insights for future research.

Acknowledgments. We would like to acknowledge the help provided by the Logistics and Supply Chain MultiTech R&D Centre (LSCM) for their support to make this paper possible.

References

1. Myers, D., Radke, K., Suriadi, S., Foo, E.: Process discovery for industrial control system cyber attack detection. In: De Capitani di Vimercati, S., Martinelli, F. (eds.) SEC 2017. IAICT, vol. 502, pp. 61–75. Springer, Cham (2017). https://doi.org/10.1007/978-3-319-58469-0_5
2. Chan, C.F., Chow, K.P., Yiu, S.M., Yau, K.: Enhancing the security and forensic capabilities of programmable logic controllers. In: Peterson, G., Shenoi, S. (eds.) Advances in Digital Forensics XIV, pp. 351–367. Springer, Cham (2018). https://doi.org/10.1007/978-3-319-99277-8_19
3. IEEE Standard for eXtensible Event Stream (XES) for Achieving Interoperability in Event Logs and Event Streams. IEEE Std 1849-2016, pp. 1–50 (2016). https://doi.org/10.1109/IEEESTD.2016.7740858

4. Chen, X., Luo, J., Qi, P.: Method for translating ladder diagrams to ordinary Petri nets. In: 2012 IEEE 51st IEEE Conference on Decision and Control (CDC), Maui, HI, USA, pp. 6716–6721 (2012). https://doi.org/10.1109/CDC.2012.6426901

5. Yau, K., Chow, K.P., Yiu, S.M.: Detecting anomalous programmable logic controller events using process mining. In: Staggs, J., Shenoi, S. (eds.) Critical Infrastructure Protection XV, ICCIP 2021, pp. 119–133. Springer, Cham (2022). https://doi.org/10.1007/978-3-030-935 11-5_6

6. Marin-Castro, H.M., Tello-Leal, E.: Event log preprocessing for process mining: a review. Appl. Sci. **11**(22), 10556 (2021)

7. Hergenhahn, T.: libnodave (sourceforge.net/projects/libnodave) (2014)

8. Myers, D., Suriadi, S., Radke, K., Foo, E.: Anomaly detection for industrial control systems using process mining. Comput. Secur. **78**, 103–125 (2018)

9. Theis, J., Mokhtarian, I., Darabi, H.: Process mining of programmable logic controllers: input/output event logs. In: 2019 IEEE 15th International Conference on Automation Science and Engineering (CASE), pp. 216–221 (2019)

10. Theis, J., Darabi, H.: Decay replay mining to predict next process events. IEEE Access **7**, 119787–119803 (2019)

11. Xavier, M., Dubinin, V., Patil, S., Vyatkin, V.: Process mining in industrial control systems. In: 2022 IEEE 20th International Conference on Industrial Informatics (INDIN), Perth, Australia, pp. 1–6 (2022). https://doi.org/10.1109/INDIN51773.2022.9976111

12. Spenneberg, R., Brüggemann, M., Schwartke, H.: PLC-blaster: a worm living solely in the PLC. Black Hat Asia (2016)

13. Siemens, SIMATIC S7-300 Programmable Controller Quick Start, Primer, Preface, C79000-G7076-C500-01, Nuremberg, Germany (1996)

14. Siemens Totally Integrated Automation Portal. https://www.siemens.com/global/en/home/products/automation/industry-software/automation-software/tia-portal.html

15. Yau, K., Chow, K.P., Yiu, S.M., Chan, C.F.: Detecting anomalous behavior of PLC using semi-supervised machine learning. In: 2017 IEEE Conference on Communications and Network Security (CNS), Las Vegas, NV, USA, pp. 580–585 (2017). https://doi.org/10.1109/CNS.2017.8228713

16. RapidProM Team, ProM Tools, Eindhoven University of Technology, Eindhoven, The Netherlands (promtools.org/doku.php) (2019)

17. Fluxicon, Disco. https://fluxicon.com/disco/

18. Berti, A., Van Zelst, S.J., van der Aalst, W.: Process mining for python (PM4Py): bridging the gap between process-and data science arXiv preprintarXiv:1905.06169 (2019)

19. Chan, C.F., Chow, K.P., Mak, C., Chan, R.: Detecting anomalies in programmable logic controllers using unsupervised machine learning. In: Advances in Digital Forensics XV, pp. 119–130 (2019)

Honey-Gauge: Enabling User-Centric Honeypot Classification

Vinay Sachidananda[(✉)], Berwyn Chai, Florian Gondesen, Kwok-Yan Lam, and Liu Yang

School of Computer Science and Engineering, Nanyang Technological University, Singapore 639798, Singapore
{vinay.ms,bchai002,fgondesen,kwokyan.lam,yangliu}@ntu.edu.sg

Abstract. Honeypots serve the purpose of scrutinizing and comprehending attackers' techniques, tactics, and procedures through vigilant observation of their actions within the honeypot environment. Nevertheless, the absence of a benchmark for gauging their end-user usability remains a prevailing issue. While existing literature classifies honeypots primarily by functionality, the novel `Honey-Gauge` framework, introduced in this research, aims to categorize honeypots based on the metrics of usability, deployability, and information retrieval methodology. Our evaluation encompassed seven honeypots, including T-Pot, Dionaea, and Conpot, assessing diverse categories and attributes, and presenting usability results derived from their respective scores. The `Honey-Gauge` framework stands as a potent tool for classifying honeypots according to a spectrum of architectural design categories and attributes that cater to the unique needs of end users. In summation, the outcomes of this study underscore the `Honey-Gauge` framework's effectiveness as a tool for the comprehensive assessment and comparison of honeypots, grounded in their usability and features.

Keywords: Honeypots · Usability · Attributes · Classification · Scoring · Deployability

1 Introduction

The value of an information system asset, such as honeypots, lies in its deliberate exposure to unauthorized or malicious activities. Essentially, a honeypot serves as a security instrument that either deters, detects, or analyzes endeavors aimed at illicitly accessing a network or system. Its operation involves mimicking a susceptible network element or system to divert potential attackers away from the genuine system. The data gleaned from honeypots can offer valuable insights into attacker conduct and enhance the security of the real system by identifying and addressing vulnerabilities. However, it's crucial to recognize that honeypots introduce their own security vulnerabilities and should be deployed with meticulous care.

G. Wang et al. (Eds.): UbiSec 2023, CCIS 2034, pp. 114–132, 2024.
https://doi.org/10.1007/978-981-97-1274-8_8

Honeypot architectures are typically classified into three categories: low-interaction, medium-interaction, and high-interaction honeypots [1–4]. Low-interaction honeypots emulate a limited number of services and are primarily used for early detection and analysis of threats. These honeypots are relatively easy to deploy and require less maintenance. Medium-interaction honeypots emulate a broader range of services and provide a more comprehensive view of attacker behavior while still minimizing the risk of system compromise. High-interaction honeypots emulate complete systems and provide the most accurate view of attacker behavior but require significant resources and expertise to deploy and maintain. Another type of honeypot architecture is the hybrid honeypot, which combines different levels of interaction to create a more effective defense against attacks. Overall, the choice of honeypot architecture depends on the level of risk an organization is willing to take, the available resources, and the specific security goals and objectives.

1.1 Motivation and Problem Statement

Previous research [15,18–21] in the field of honeypots has predominantly focused on categorizing them by functional attributes, such as interaction levels (high or low) and whether they operate on the server or client-side. However, a universally accepted framework for benchmarking honeypots, capable of discerning and categorizing them according to specific end-user use cases, is currently lacking. Some researchers have attempted to construct classification systems based on different criteria, such as deployment strategies or the nature of captured data [20,21]. Nevertheless, these schemes exhibit limited applicability and may not comprehensively capture the intricacies of the contemporary threat landscape. Furthermore, many existing surveys of honeypot architectures have narrow scopes or rely on outdated information, given the ongoing evolution of the field [10,12]. Consequently, there is a pressing demand for a thorough and current survey of honeypot architectures that not only embraces the latest advancements in the domain but also provides a flexible framework for classification and benchmarking.

For effectively identifying vulnerabilities and tracking an attacker's path within a system, a honeypot must successfully evade detection by intruders within the network. As a substantial number of attacks are automated and frequently initiated by bots, deploying honeypots without a comprehensive understanding of the architectural framework risks undermining their intended purpose. This could result in compromising the honeypot's stealthiness through iterative queries, potentially granting an attacker backdoor access to production systems as the honeypots act as a proxy.

To bridge the gap between deployed honeypots and the capabilities of potential attackers, a pertinent benchmarking framework becomes indispensable. Such a framework empowers decision-makers and network administrators to deploy architectures aligned with the considered attack vectors. Consequently, this approach ensures that the deployed honeypots meet the operational needs of the organization, thereby enhancing their effectiveness.

In summary, the strategic deployment of honeypots for vulnerability detection and attacker tracking necessitates a balanced approach that maximizes their effectiveness while evading detection by automated attacks. A suitable benchmarking framework facilitates this alignment, enabling organizations to optimize honeypot architectures for specific threat scenarios.

1.2 Approach Overview

In response to the limitations observed in current honeypot surveys and categorizations, there is a need for a framework that can categorize honeypots in accordance with the unique use cases of end-users. Consequently, this paper introduces the Honey-Gauge framework, a honeypot classification system predicated on dimensions like fidelity, security, scalability, and maintenance. By integrating these dimensions, the honeypot classification framework aims to offer a holistic and pragmatic strategy for the deployment and administration of honeypots. This approach ultimately translates to improved security outcomes.

The initial phase of Honey-Gauge involves identifying a set of pivotal categories for the classification of honeypots. Subsequently, the honeypots undergo a benchmarking process, grounded in a compilation of attributes and factors aligned with each designated category. This evaluation encompasses the most advanced honeypots in the field, including references like [1–6], and [7]. Following this, scoring is conducted, and usability outcomes are presented, all contingent on the identified categories, attributes, and factors.

Our Contributions. In essence, this project strives to formulate a honeypot classification framework that prioritizes user-friendliness and ease of deployment. Specifically, the objective revolves around crafting a benchmark framework that encompasses the pertinent categories, attributes, and factors influencing honeypot selection. This, in turn, facilitates the optimal choice of honeypots for end-users. Our efforts contribute in two key ways:

– The classification and benchmarking of advanced honeypots based on critical categories, including Fidelity, Security, Scalability, and Maintenance, along with their corresponding attributes and influencing factors.
– The execution of a comprehensive survey, deployability assessment, and evaluation of cutting-edge honeypots. Through this process, scores are generated, and in-depth usability results are furnished.

The remainder of this paper is organized as follows: Section 2 investigates the existing works, Sect. 3 provides categories, attributes and factors of Honey-Gauge. In Sect. 4, the evaluation and deployability are provided. In Sect. 5 scoring and usability of honeypots are discussed. Conclusion is provided in Sect. 6 with references at the end.

2   Related Work

Prior to our research, we conducted a literature review of related studies on honeypots. Nawrocki's survey on honeypot software and data analysis [8] provides an extensive overview of honeypots and methods for analyzing honeypot data. Authors review of honeypots in network security [9] discusses recent advances in honeypots, their use in education, and signature techniques. Bringer et al. [10] present recent advances in honeypot research, review legal and ethical issues on honeypots. Fan et al. [11] present two essential elements, decoy and captor, to predict honeypot development trends. Iyatiti et al. [12] provide an overview of honeypots and approaches to their implementation. Moore et al. [13] investigate methods to create honeypots to detect ransomware activities. Provos et al. [14] present a virtual honeypot framework called Honeyd, which simulates a virtual computer that runs on unallocated network addresses. Zhang et al. [15] classify honeypots according to security and application goals and present typical honeypot solutions for future honeypots. PhoneyC [16] presents a honeyclient that uses dynamic analysis to remove obfuscation from malicious pages. Alata et al. [17] report on attackers logged on a compromised machine for six months. McGrew et al. [18] provide a summary of honeypot techniques and recommendations for their usage. Fraunholz et al. [19] present a method for dynamically configuring, deploying, and maintaining honeypots using machine learning techniques. However, none of these works considered the end user perspective or classified honeypots based on usability factors, which is the focus of our research.

Other research works have addressed aspects similar to our research. For example, the survey conducted in [20] compared low, medium, and high interaction honeypots. Similarly, in "A Survey of Honeypots and Honeynets for Internet of Things, Industrial Internet of Things, and Cyber-Physical Systems" [21], the authors classified IoT honeypots. However, these works do not consider the end user perspective and the deployability factors of honeypots. In contrast, our research addresses these challenges by focusing on the usability and features of different honeypots from the perspective of end-users.

3 Honey-Gauge: Our Approach

The formulation of a classification framework for honeypot architectures employs a top-down methodology, ensuring distinctiveness in features and design principles among different honeypot systems within the framework. The Honey-Gauge approach introduced in this study concentrates on a specific set of attributes and features found in the selected honeypots. These attributes are centered around general-purpose honeypots and are designed to facilitate meaningful categorization, assessment, and comparison. The framework aims to capture the nuances of each honeypot's architecture while highlighting their commonalities through carefully selected categories, attributes, and associated factors.

3.1   Categories

The proposed framework takes usability into consideration, which can be decomposed into two major parts and is composed of four main categories: Performance (Fidelity & Security) and Cost (Scalability & Maintenance).

- **Fidelity**: Refers to the degree of interaction between the honeypot and the attacker, as well as the level of access granted to the attacker within the system. A higher level of interaction allows direct access to the kernel and hardware resources, while a lower level of interaction only permits access at the daemon or application level. Achieving higher levels of interactivity requires sufficient system resources. The services provided and the level of interactivity determine whether the honeypot operates as a server or client in communicating with the attacker. Therefore, the fidelity of the framework is determined by factors such as the *level of interaction, the physical deployment type, and the role/direction in communication with the attacker.*

- **Security**: Pertains to the degree to which a honeypot is designed to expose its vulnerabilities and be exploited. The level of exposure is typically a subset of the level of interaction, but separating these attributes provides more granularity and enables better decision-making in the selection of honeypots for benchmarking. The desire to be compromised provides the attacker with a greater degree of freedom to navigate the system, resulting in a wider variety of attack patterns and log traces being collected for comprehensive data tracing. The security framework consists of the desire for detection through *exposing vulnerabilities, quality of data collected, and realistic emulation of services.*

- **Scalability**: Pertains to the network-related features that impact the ability of a honeypot to scale efficiently in response to increasing demands. One key factor is the number of required IP address spaces, determined by whether the honeypot is physically or virtually deployed and the number of emulated services. Another crucial consideration is the required bandwidth for a honeyfarm or cluster deployed on the network. Planning for scalability before deployment helps ensure that the honeypot can support the network infrastructure effectively. This category encompasses features such as the ability to dynamically add and remove honeypots, configure network settings on the fly, and monitor and manage network traffic. By incorporating these features into the scalability framework, administrators can ensure that the honeypot can grow and adapt to changing circumstances.

- **Maintenance**: Covers the human factor involved in maintaining a honeypot, including the required expertise, troubleshooting capabilities, available resources and documentation, and the financial expenditure necessary to keep the honeypot running effectively. This category allows decision-makers to take a holistic approach when considering the long-term prospects and value of honeypots in their network defense strategy. To maintain a honeypot, administrators must have access to the necessary knowledge and resources to troubleshoot and resolve any issues that arise. This may include access to documentation, forums, or other support channels. The maintenance category also takes into account the financial resources required to sustain the honeypot, including hardware costs, software licensing fees, and personnel expenses. By considering these factors when selecting and maintaining honeypots, organizations can ensure that they are making a sound investment in their network defense.

3.2   Attributes

In this section we explain the attributes belonging to each category. The attributes "Levels", "Physicality" and, "Direction" belongs to category "Fidelity". The attributes, "Detection", "Data Trace" and, "Services" belongs to category "Security". Furthermore, attributes "Bandwidth" and "IP" belongs to category "Scalability" and finally, attributes "Expertise", "Resource" and, "Budget" belongs to category maintenance.

Levels: This attribute assesses an attacker's capability to interact with services and responses within the honeypot environment. It gauges the extent to which an attacker can infiltrate the system, determining whether they can merely probe the surface or gain more extensive access to various services. A higher score in this attribute implies the effectiveness of a honeypot in enticing attackers to engage with a range of services, thereby yielding richer insights into their tactics and behaviors.

Physicality: This attribute explores the deployment type and placement of the honeypot within the organizational infrastructure. It evaluates whether the honeypot is physically situated on-site or remotely and whether it mirrors real systems or abstract network elements. The attribute also considers how the physical positioning of the honeypot impacts its interaction with potential attackers, providing insights into the authenticity of the environment it emulates.

Direction: The direction attribute pertains to the role a honeypot assumes in a session: whether it acts actively, initiating interactions with potential attackers, or passively, reacting to incoming interactions. This attribute elucidates how a honeypot's behavior aligns with the specific scenarios it aims to simulate, ultimately influencing the diversity and authenticity of the attack data collected.

Detection: Focusing on the mechanisms for identifying attacks on the system, this attribute explores the tactics deployed by the honeypot to recognize and categorize incoming malicious activities. It encompasses signature-based detection, anomaly detection, and any other methods employed to swiftly identify and respond to potential threats. A higher score in this attribute reflects the honeypot's adeptness at rapidly discerning and flagging potential attacks.

Data Trace: The data trace attribute encompasses the methodologies employed by the honeypot to collect and store traces of attacker activities. This includes capturing keystrokes, command sequences, and other interactions within the honeypot environment. The attribute evaluates the comprehensiveness of data collection, shedding light on how well a honeypot documents attacker behaviors for post-analysis.

Services: This attribute encompasses the variety of application and protocol services that the honeypot simulates to attract attackers. It evaluates the breadth and authenticity of services provided by the honeypot to lure potential threats. A honeypot with a higher score in this attribute presents a broader surface area for attackers to engage with, enabling the capture of a more diverse set of attack patterns.

Table 1. Summary of Categories and Attributes

Category	Attributes	Explanation
Fidelity	Levels	Ability of an attacker to interact with services and responses
	Physicality	The deployment type and locality within the organization
	Direction	Role in session as active or passive for initiation
Security	Detection	Methods involved in detection of attacks on the system
	Data Trace	Methodology involved in collection of data traces
	Services	Application and protocol services offered
Scalability	Bandwidth	Network capacity required based on the services offered
	IP	Number of address spaces and Network cards
Maintenance	Expertise	Skillsets required for deployment and maintenance
	Resource	Support and documentation available
	Budget	Maintenance and machine cost involved in deployment

Bandwidth: Addressing the network capacity required by the honeypot based on the services it offers, this attribute provides insights into the honeypot's potential impact on network resources. It assesses the amount of data transmitted and received by the honeypot during interactions with attackers, guiding users on the network resources necessary for deployment.

IP: The IP attribute considers the number of address spaces and network cards utilized by the honeypot. It evaluates the extent to which the honeypot mimics a real network setup and whether it employs a single address space or an intricate network topology. A higher score in this attribute signifies the honeypot's proficiency in replicating diverse IP configurations and network infrastructures.

Expertise: This attribute gauges the level of technical skill and knowledge required for deploying and maintaining the honeypot. It considers whether users need advanced network and security expertise or if the honeypot is more accessible to users with basic technical know-how. A higher score indicates a honeypot that is user-friendly and can be effectively managed by a broader range of users.

Resource: Resource availability pertains to the level of support, documentation, and community engagement offered to users of the honeypot. It evaluates the availability of user guides, forums, and other resources that facilitate honeypot deployment, management, and troubleshooting. A higher score reflects a well-supported honeypot that provides users with ample resources for successful utilization.

Budget: The budget attribute assesses the financial costs associated with deploying and maintaining the honeypot. It considers both hardware and software costs, as well as ongoing maintenance expenses. A higher score implies a honeypot that is more cost-effective to deploy and sustain, making it a more feasible option for organizations with budget constraints.

The categories and attributes for the diverse benchmark metrics, along with their concise summaries, are consolidated in Table 1.

3.3   Factors

This section provides details on the factors related to each attribute. Table 2 provides the comprehensive summary on each attributes and their respective factors.

Levels:

- High: This factor refers to the attribute's highest level, indicating that the honeypot enables attackers to access the operating system of the host machine. This implies that attackers can potentially gain full control over the system, allowing them to interact with various services and execute commands as if they were on a real machine.
- Low: The 'Low' factor signifies that the honeypot primarily emulates services rather than providing direct access to the operating system. This means attackers can interact with services that mimic vulnerable components, but they don't have the ability to access the actual host operating system.

Physicality:

- Physical: This factor entails deploying the honeypot on a dedicated physical machine with an actual operating system. It closely simulates a real-world environment and is often used to replicate specific system setups.
- Virtual: The 'Virtual' factor involves orchestrating the honeypot within a virtualized environment, such as containers or virtual machines. This approach offers greater flexibility and resource efficiency, making it easier to deploy multiple honeypots on a single physical machine.

Direction:

- Server: This factor characterizes a honeypot as a passive entity that does not initiate communication with potential attackers. It responds to incoming connections and interactions from attackers, capturing their actions while remaining reactive in nature.
- Client: The 'Client' factor designates a honeypot that actively probes and interacts with potentially malicious servers. This approach involves initiating connections to servers that are potentially performing malicious activities, allowing the honeypot to gather information about the attack vectors.

Table 2. Summary of Attributes and Factors

Attributes	Factors	Explanation
Levels	High	Operating System access
	Low	Mostly Emulated Services
Physicality	Physical	Single Machine with real OS
	Virtual	Orchestrated and dockerised
Direction	Server	Passive and no traffic initiation with attacker
	Client	Active and probe malicious server for exploitation
Detection	High	Provides real services and exposes system level vulnerabilities
	Low	Minimal exploitation by exposing vulnerable ports
Services	Applications	Provides vulnerable application as a service
	Protocols	Implements protocols as a service
Bandwidth	High	Active probing requires large bandwidth of type class A
	Low	Passive communication with attacker using Class E bandwidth
IP	Physical	A single physical IP address
	Virtual	Orchestrated virtual IP space for multiple honeypots
Expertise	System	Knowledge of Operating system and network stack implementation
	Minimal	Shell utilities and basic network skills
Resource	Updated	Developer resource, guides recent and active
	Outdated	No active maintenance
Budget	High	Subjective, high cost as a server farm
	Low	Deploy on a single machine

Detection:

– High: This factor indicates that the honeypot is configured to expose real services and vulnerabilities at the system level. It can attract attackers by offering genuine opportunities for exploitation, thereby capturing a wide range of attacker behaviors and tactics.
– Low: The 'Low' factor suggests that the honeypot exposes a minimal surface area, often through exposing a limited set of vulnerable ports. This approach focuses on capturing only specific types of attacks and interactions, providing a more targeted view of certain attack vectors.

Services:

– Applications: This factor denotes a honeypot that provides vulnerable applications as services. Attackers can interact with these applications, exploiting vulnerabilities and providing insights into how attackers exploit specific software weaknesses.

– Protocols: The 'Protocols' factor signifies a honeypot that emulates various network protocols as services. This approach focuses on capturing attacks targeting specific protocols and network-level vulnerabilities.

Bandwidth:

– High: This factor implies that the honeypot engages in active probing and communication with potential attackers, necessitating a large bandwidth allocation. The honeypot's actions could include probing and interacting with various attackers, potentially consuming significant network resources.
– Low: The 'Low' factor suggests that the honeypot engages in passive communication with attackers, requiring relatively lower bandwidth. The honeypot mainly responds to incoming interactions and does not initiate extensive outbound communications.

IP:

– Physical: This factor relates to the use of a single physical IP address for the honeypot deployment. It mirrors the setup of a real network where devices are identified by unique IP addresses.
– Virtual: The 'Virtual' factor involves orchestrating multiple honeypots within a virtual IP space. This enables the deployment of multiple honeypots on the same physical machine, each with its own distinct virtual IP address.

Expertise:

– System: This factor signifies that deploying and maintaining the honeypot requires a deep understanding of operating system internals and networking stacks. Users need to be well-versed in configuring and managing system-level components.
– Minimal: The 'Minimal' factor indicates that the honeypot is designed for users with basic technical skills. Deploying and managing the honeypot primarily requires familiarity with shell utilities and basic networking concepts.

Resource:

– Updated: This factor characterizes a honeypot that offers up-to-date resources, including active developer engagement, recent guides, and ongoing maintenance. Users can expect consistent updates and a supportive community.
– Outdated: The 'Outdated' factor indicates a lack of active maintenance and resources. The honeypot might not receive frequent updates, and the available documentation and support resources might be limited.

Budget:

– High: This factor suggests that deploying the honeypot involves substantial costs, similar to maintaining a server farm. The honeypot requires significant resources in terms of hardware, infrastructure, and potentially ongoing maintenance.

– Low: The 'Low' factor implies that the honeypot can be deployed on a single machine or within limited resources. It is a more cost-effective option suitable for smaller-scale deployments with constrained budgets.

4   Evaluation and Deployability

In this section, we conduct a survey, delve into the evaluation considering their usability, and then proceed to the deployability check on seven state-of-the-art honeypots, chosen based on the categories and attributes discussed in Sect. 2.

4.1   Tpot

The T-Pot honeypot system, as described in the [1], is a comprehensive framework for managing multiple honeypots. T-Pot includes a wide range of honeypots, including adbhoney, conpot, cowrie, ddospot, dionaea, elasticpot, glutton, heralding, hellpot, ipphoney, log4pot, mailoney, snare, and tanner. Additionally, the system offers various tools, including Cockpit, Cyberchef, Elastic Stack, Elasticvue, Geoip-Attack-Map, P0f, Spiderfoot, and Suricata. T-Pot provides a comprehensive solution for honeypot management, offering a wide range of honeypots and tools.

Each honeypot in the category offers various protocols in containers and emulates multiple vulnerable services. Additionally, malware samples are captured for further analysis of the attacks. The T-Pot framework collects the logs from each container and consolidates them into an elastic stack, which presents the administrator with a front-end view of all attacks against each service.

The T-Pot framework utilizes Docker settings to configure each honeypot, including the port number, the path to the location for capturing malware files, and various rules that can be configured through the T-Pot Dashboard. After the configuration of each honeypot is completed using the dashboard, the running status of the active honeypots can be checked from the terminal, which indicates the network activity. The T-Pot system centralizes logs from each honeypot container into an Elastic Stack, providing the administrator with a comprehensive view of all attacks against each service.

4.2   Dionaea

Dionaea [2] acts as a honeypot operating in the application layer, using diverse network protocols to attract potential attackers and mimic vulnerable services. This allows it to capture malware for subsequent analysis. It can also identify shell codes and simulate various services using Python scripts, including Internet Protocol 6 and Transport Layer Security. To ensure security, Dionaea typically runs within a sandboxed environment, devoid of root privileges.

The Dionaea source code, along with its dependencies, can be downloaded from its Github repository [2]. Incidents are automatically logged by the honeypot and stored in a designated log file. Configuration adjustments, such as the log file's path and logging preferences, can be made through the configuration file.

Modifications to the behavior of emulated protocols in Dionaea are made in the directories /lib/dionaea/python and /etc/dionaea/services-available. After configuring the settings file, the honeypot can be initiated via the terminal using the command /opt/dionaea/bin/dionaea -r /opt/dionaea. Dionaea supports various protocols (ftp, http, mqtt, mssql, mysql, smb, tftp), listed in the /etc/dionaea/services file. Incidents are logged by default, but the configuration file allows customization of the log's path and other logging options.

4.3 Conpot

Conpot [3] is a honeypot used for simulating multiple industrial and SCADA control systems protocols. It operates in a low interaction mode with emulated services configured through templates. Each protocol has a template that enables the configuration of rules, port numbers, protocol commands, and timeout parameters. The protocols emulated by Conpot include HTTP, SNMP, MODBUS, BACnet and IPMI.

Conpot is equipped with a comprehensive logging system that tracks any activities carried out by attackers. Specifically, Conpot logs events of HTTP, SNMP and Modbus services with great accuracy, and provides basic tracking information such as the source address, request type, and resource requested in the case of HTTP. This logging system ensures that any suspicious activities within the network can be quickly identified and responded to.

By default, Conpot comes with pre-configured templates for the supported protocols along with their corresponding port numbers. These templates also include the IP addresses of the Conpot network. Additionally, Conpot allows users to configure rules, port numbers, protocol commands and timeout parameters through the use of templates.

To launch Conpot, users can execute the command line "sudo conpot – template default" for the default template via the terminal. This enables users to quickly deploy Conpot and begin monitoring their network for any potential attacks. The framework developed allows for the accumulation of experience in deploying the honeypot, which is then used to populate the knowledge base of the system.

4.4 Cowrie

Cowrie is a honeypot designed to capture brute force attacks in SSH and Telnet protocols. It provides both medium and high interaction modes to emulate a UNIX system using Python. In high interaction mode (proxy), it serves as an SSH and Telnet proxy to observe attacker behavior. In medium interaction mode (shell), it emulates a fake file system with minimal file contents resembling a Debian 5.0 installation. Some of the notable features of Cowrie are:

– Fake filesystem with the ability to add/remove files: Cowrie's fake filesystem allows the addition and removal of files. This feature enables the creation of a full fake filesystem that can resemble a real system.
– Possibility of adding fake file contents: Cowrie also allows the addition of fake file contents to the fake filesystem. This feature enables the attacker to cat files like /etc/passwd, providing a more realistic environment to lure them in.
– File capture: Cowrie saves files downloaded with wget/curl or uploaded with SFTP and scp for later inspection. This feature helps in analyzing the behavior of the attacker and the malware they may have deployed.

The second mode of operation is the proxy mode, where Cowrie acts as a pure telnet and SSH proxy with monitoring. In this mode, Cowrie can also manage a pool of QEMU emulated servers to provide the systems to log in to. This feature enables Cowrie to act as a bridge between the attacker and a real system, allowing the collection of valuable information on the attacker's behavior. User accounts for logging into the fake SSH server can be placed in a /opt/cowrie/etc/userdb.txt file.

Cowrie's source code is available on Github [4] and can be installed on Unix/Linux systems using pip. Once installed, the honeypot can be launched from the terminal using the command line "cowrie start". Cowrie logs all the incidents in a text file, and the path and logging options can be configured in the configuration file. The list of emulated services can also be found in the configuration file. Cowrie also provides a web-based user interface to monitor the activity of the honeypot.

4.5   Sshesame

Sshesame [5] is a low interaction fake SSH server honeypot designed to monitor the activities of attackers without revealing the presence of a real system. Sshesame operates by accepting SSH connections and logging the activities of attackers, without executing commands or making network requests on the host.

This feature of Sshesame makes it an attractive tool for security experts who want to monitor the behavior of attackers in a safe and controlled environment. By allowing anyone to connect to the fake SSH server, Sshesame logs the attacker's activities and provides valuable insight into their behavior.

Sshesame is a lightweight honeypot that does not require any complicated setup or configuration. It can be installed quickly and easily, making it an ideal tool for security experts who need to set up honeypots quickly. The honeypot also has a low resource overhead, making it suitable for deployment on low-powered systems. The Sshesame logs contain valuable information about the attacker's activities, including login attempts, file transfers, and commands executed on the fake system. Security experts can use this information to identify attack patterns, malware, and vulnerabilities that attackers may exploit.

4.6   Chameleon

Chameleon [6] is a hybrid level honeypot that operates as an active defense tool by simulating open, unprotected ports and taking on attempts to find vulnerabilities. This honeypot is capable of operating at both high and low interaction levels. Chameleon consists of three main modules: the front-end responder, evaluator, and back-end interactor. The front-end responder handles incoming requests and forwards them to the evaluator for security evaluation. If the source of the request is deemed untrusted, Chameleon responds with a default response, and the request is logged for manual review.

The back-end interactor module establishes a connection with the target IoT device and detects open ports and services to replicate them on Chameleon. The services that Chameleon currently supports include DNS, HTTP, HTTPS, SSH, POP3, IMAP, SMTP, RDP, SMB, SOCK5, Telnet, VNC, Postgres, Redis, MySQL, Elasticsearch, and MSSQL.

Chameleon's hybrid approach allows it to offer the best of both worlds by allowing attackers to interact with a simulated system in a high interaction mode and capturing their actions in a low interaction mode. This feature enables security analysts to analyze the attacker's behavior while minimizing the risk of exposing the real system to attacks.

4.7   DDoSPot

DDoSPot [7] is a specialized honeypot platform that tracks and monitors Distributed Denial of Service (DDoS) attacks based on the User Datagram Protocol (UDP). This platform responds to valid multicast requests and provides emulation of MiniUPnP to attract potential attackers. By using DDoSPot, security experts can monitor the behavior of attackers and better understand the techniques and tactics they use to launch DDoS attacks. DDoSPot includes several honeypot services/servers that act as plugins to offer various emulation capabilities. These honeypot services/servers include:

DNS Server: This service emulates a real DNS server as closely as possible by forwarding all requests to a valid recursive resolver and returning arbitrary responses to CHAOS queries. It also implements a DNS resolver to handle requests.
NTP Server: This service emulates NTP mode 3 (Client), 6 (Control), and 7 (monlist) responses, which can be used by attackers to amplify the size of their DDoS attacks.
SSDP Server: This service emulates responses to M-SEARCH (multicast) commands and provides emulation of MiniUPnP, which is a common gateway protocol used to manage port forwarding in residential and small office/home office (SOHO) environments.
CHARGEN server: This service emulates Chargen services, which generate an endless stream of characters or data and can be used by attackers to amplify the size of their DDoS attacks.

Random/mock UDP server: This service can be bound to a configurable port for responses, and it provides a flexible option for customizing the responses to different types of requests.

5   Scoring, Usability and Discussion

Within this section, we probe into the scoring of honeypots, considering their usability and the range of features they offer.

Table 3. Scoring of Honeypots

Attributes	Factors	Points	Reason
Levels	High	2	Allows attacker to be lured into compromising the system
	Low	1	Attackers can easily discover it to be a honeypot and avoid it
Physicality	Physical	0	Deploying a honeypot for each IP address becomes unfeasible when dealing with vast address spaces
	Virtual	1	Rapidly deployable and easily reconfigurable, with seamless snapshot creation, enhanced scalability, and optimal resource utilization
Direction	Server	0	Unable to discover lateral movements attempted by attackers
	Client	1	Allows learning of tools used by attackers
Detection	High	2	Allows tracking of attackers movement in the system
	Low	1	Gathering information about the attackers is constrained
Services	Applications	2	Provides vulnerable applications as a service
	Protocols	1	Implements protocols as a service
Bandwidth	High	0	Requires high amount of bandwidth in order to be deployed
	Low	1	Can be deployed being having a specific amount of bandwidth
IP	Physical	0	Requires IP address space to deploy the honeypot
	Virtual	1	Can deploy multiple honeypots on an orchestrated virtual IP space
Expertise	System	0	Knowledge of Operating System required in order to deploy honeypot
	Minimal	1	Basic knowledge and network skills needed
Resource	Updated	1	Easily accessible updates and guides for deployment of honeypot
	Outdated	0	Not being maintained or updated
Budget	High	0	Expensive to maintain the honeypot, servers might be needed
	Low	1	Able to deploy on a single machine without cost

The categorization of honeypots is based on the Fidelity, Security, Scalability, and Maintenance categories outlined in Sect. 2, informed by the deployability check and evaluation outcomes. Additionally, we explore the usability of honey-pots in relation to their respective scores. Lastly, we conduct an examination of the strengths and constraints of the Honey-Gauge framework.

5.1 Scoring of Honeypot

Throughout the evaluation of the Honey-Gauge framework, the honeypots underwent a scoring process that considered both their usability and features. For each distinct attribute, a score of 0, 1, or 2 was assigned, forming the basis of assessment. A detailed breakdown of these scores for each honeypot can be found in Table 3. A score of 2 signifies substantial usability and feature richness for the attribute, while a score of 1 denotes intermediate usability and features. Conversely, a score of 0 signifies minimal usability or a lack of features related to the attribute.

To provide a concrete illustration, the evaluation of the "Levels" attribute involved an analysis of the degree of access attainable by attackers within the system. A score of 2 was attributed to the "High" factor, indicating that the honeypot facilitated attacker compromise and system infiltration, yielding piv-otal insights into attack strategies. In contrast, a score of 1 was assigned to the "Low" factor, denoting that while complete compromise was averted, the honey-pot proficiently documented connection attempts and raised security alerts for the attempted intrusion.

Similarly, concerning the "Expertise" attribute, a score of 1 was granted to the "Minimal" factor, underscoring that the deployment of the honeypot neces-sitated minimal networking expertise and presented a straightforward process. Conversely, a score of 0 was linked to the "System" factor, indicating that hon-eypot deployment mandated users to possess knowledge about the operating system. Allocating a higher score to a honeypot signifies its elevated features and capabilities, facilitating comprehensive information capture and rendering deployment comparatively simpler when juxtaposed with other honeypots within the study.

Table 4. Category Based Scoring

Category	T-pot	Dionaea	Conpot	Cowrie	SShesame	Chamaleon	DDoSPot
Fidelity	5	2	2	4	2	5	2
Security	5	3	2	5	3	5	2
Scalabiltity	1	2	2	1	2	1	2
Maintenance	3	2	2	3	3	2	2
Performance (Fidelity + Security)	10	5	4	9	5	10	4
Cost (Scalability + Maintenance)	4	4	4	4	5	3	4

The category based scoring is provided in Table 4. The total points in each category are calculated so that users can choose the appropriate honeypots based on their demands. For example, a user may have a high demand for Fidelity and Security and be willing to invest in maintenance and higher scalability. In this case, a honeypot that is moderate in performance and cost is not a good choice, even if it may have higher total points. More detailed scoring based on attributes is provided in Table 5.

5.2   Usability of Honeypot

Table 5 serves as a succinct summary of the evaluation's outcomes, encapsulating the predefined categories and attributes. The evaluation itself comprehensively covered usability, deployability, and information retrieval strategies. T-pot stood out with the highest score of 14, exemplifying its exceptional performance across diverse categories. Cowrie and Chameleon closely trailed with respective scores of 13. SSHesame garnered a score of 10, while Dionea earned 9 points. In contrast, Conpot and DDoSPot attained the lowest scores of 8.

Table 5. Usability of Honeypots

Attributes	Factors	T-pot	Dionaea	Conpot	Cowrie	SShesame	Chamaleon	DDoSPot
Levels	High	X			X		X	
	Low	X	X	X		X	X	X
Physicality	Physical							
	Virtual	X	X	X	X	X	X	X
Direction	Server	X	X	X	X	X	X	X
	Client	X			X		X	
Detection	High	X			X		X	
	Low		X	X		X		X
Services	Apps.*	X	X		X	X	X	
	Protocols	X		X	X		X	X
Bandwidth	High	X			X		X	
	Low		X	X		X		X
IP	Physical							
	Virtual	X	X	X	X	X	X	X
Expertise	System							
	Minimal	X	X	X	X	X	X	X
Resource	Updated	X			X	X		
	Outdated		X	X			X	X
Budget	High							
	Low	X	X	X	X	X	X	X
Total Score		14	9	8	13	10	13	8

Note: *Applications

An intriguing observation is that none of the assessed honeypots received a score for the "data trace" attribute, despite undergoing a two-month runtime.

This implies that extended operational timeframes could offer more accurate insights into data trace behaviors. In essence, Table 5 succinctly captures the essence of the evaluation results. It highlights the prominence of T-pot, underscores the potential of extended runtimes for refining data trace evaluations, and underscores the value of the Honey-Gauge framework in fostering informed honeypot selection and strategic deployment.

The insights gleaned from this investigation underscore the efficacy of the Honey-Gauge framework as a robust tool for evaluating and analyzing honeypots based on their usability and feature repertoire. In the context of selecting a suitable honeypot for specific usage scenarios, Table 5 stands out as a dependable point of reference. Essentially, the Honey-Gauge framework emerges as a pivotal resource, providing end users with the knowledge necessary to make well-judged decisions regarding the tactical deployment of honeypots.

5.3   Discussion

The Honey-Gauge framework introduces a systematic and comprehensive approach to evaluate and compare honeypots, focusing on their usability and functionalities. This empowers end-users to select the honeypot that best aligns with their individual needs, ultimately enhancing security measures and fortifying defenses against cyber threats.

A prominent advantage of the Honey-Gauge framework is its inherent simplicity and user-oriented design. The straightforwardness of the scoring system facilitates clear-cut comparisons among diverse honeypots, while the precisely defined categories and attributes establish a structured framework for evaluation. Moreover, the framework's adaptability allows for prospective expansion, accommodating new categories and attributes as they emerge. This paves the way for continual improvement and customization to suit evolving requirements.

Despite its value as a honeypot evaluation tool, the Honey-Gauge framework has limitations. The scoring system may not perfectly cater to all users' distinct needs, and the evaluation process might not comprehensively cover every facet of a honeypot's performance. Additionally, due to its reliance on subjective assessments, the framework might not offer entirely objective insights into a honeypot's capabilities. Thus, while the Honey-Gauge framework is a valuable tool, it is advisable to use it in conjunction with alternative evaluation methods for a thorough and holistic assessment.

6   Conclusion

In summary, while honeypots play a crucial role in comprehending attack patterns and attacker behavior, a definitive benchmark for categorizing them according to end user usability is currently lacking. To address this gap, the Honey-Gauge framework was introduced. This framework evaluates honeypots by assessing their usability, deployability, and information retrieval techniques.

Through the application of this framework, we evaluated seven honeypots, generating usability scores that can guide decision-making. The Honey-Gauge framework stands as a valuable resource for aiding end-users in the selection of the most suitable honeypot for their specific needs. Future research endeavors could delve into expanding the scope of categories, attributes, and factors considered within the framework.

Acknowledgments. This work was supported by the Cyber Security Agency of Singapore (CSA) [CSA/CSEC/DC/20/083].

References

1. T-Pot: Telekom-Security. https://github.com/telekom-security/tpotce
2. Dionaea. https://github.com/DinoTools/dionaea
3. Conpot. https://github.com/mushorg/conpot
4. Cowrie. https://github.com/cowrie/cowrie
5. Sshesame. https://github.com/jaksi/sshesame
6. Chameleon. https://github.com/mdsecactivebreach/Chameleon
7. DDosPot. https://github.com/aelth/ddospot
8. Nawrocki, M., Wählisch, M., Schmidt, T.C., Keil, C., Schönfelder, J.: A survey on honeypot software and data analysis. arXiv preprint arXiv:1608.06249 (2016)
9. Mairh, A., Barik, D., Verma, K., Jena, D.: Honeypot in network security: a survey. In: Proceedings of the 2011 International Conference on Communication, Computing & Security, pp. 600–605 (2011)
10. Bringer, M.L., Chelmecki, C.A., Fujinoki, H.: A survey: recent advances and future trends in honeypot research. Int. J. Comput. Netw. Inf. Secur. **4**(10), 63 (2012)
11. Fan, W., Zhihui, D., Fernández, D., Villagra, V.A.: Enabling an anatomic view to investigate honeypot systems: a survey. IEEE Syst. J. **12**(4), 3906–3919 (2017)
12. Mokube, I., Adams, M.: Honeypots: concepts, approaches, and challenges. In: Proceedings of the 45th Annual Southeast Regional Conference (2007)
13. Moore, C.: Detecting ransomware with honeypot techniques. In: 2016 Cybersecurity and Cyberforensics Conference (CCC), pp. 77–81. IEEE (2016)
14. Provos, N.: A virtual honeypot framework. In: USENIX Security Symposium, vol. 173, no. 2004, pp. 1–14 (2004)
15. Zhang, F., Zhou, S., Qin, Z., Liu, J.: Honeypot: a supplemented active defense system for network security. In: Proceedings of International Conference on Parallel and Distributed Computing, Applications and Technologies, pp. 231–235. IEEE (2003)
16. Nazario, J.: PhoneyC: a virtual client honeypot. LEET **9**, 911–919 (2009)
17. Alata, E., Nicomette, V., Kaâniche, M., Dacier, M., Herrb, M.: Lessons learned from the deployment of a high-interaction honeypot. In: 2006 Sixth European Dependable Computing Conference, pp. 39–46. IEEE (2006)
18. McGrew, R.: Experiences with honeypot systems: development, deployment, and analysis. In: Proceedings of the 39th HICSS, vol. 9, p. 220a. IEEE (2006)
19. Fraunholz, D., Zimmermann, M., Schotten, H.D.: An adaptive honeypot configuration, deployment and maintenance strategy. In: 2017 19th International Conference on Advanced Communication Technology (ICACT). IEEE (2017)
20. Sahu, N., Richhariya, V.: Honeypot: a survey. Int. J. Comput. Sci. Technol. (2012)
21. Franco, J., Aris, A., Canberk, B., Uluagac, A.S.: A survey of honeypots and honeynets for internet of things, industrial internet of things, and cyber-physical systems. IEEE Commun. Surv. Tutor. **23**(4), 2351–2383 (2021)

Improving DNS Data Exfiltration Detection Through Temporal Analysis

Georgios Spathoulas[1], Marios Anagnostopoulos[2]([✉]),
Konstantinos Papageorgiou[3], Georgios Kavallieratos[1],
and Georgios Theodoridis[2]

[1] Department of Information Security and Communications Technology,
Norwegian University of Science and Technology, 2802 Gjøvik, Norway
`{georgios.spathoulas,georgios.kavallieratos}@ntnu.no`
[2] Department of Electronic Systems, Aalborg University, 2450 Copenhagen, Denmark
`{mariosa,gth}@es.aau.dk`
[3] Department of Computer Science and Biomedical Informatics,
University of Thessaly, 35131 Lamia, Greece
`kopapageorgiou@uth.gr`

Abstract. By leveraging the DNS tunneling technique, malicious actors have the ability to transfer covertly data embedded within a DNS transaction. A DNS tunnel can be used as a Command and Control (C&C) channel for botnet coordination, for data exfiltration, for tunneling another protocol through it, to name a few. To this end, it is imperative to develop DNS exfiltration detection techniques that are capable to mitigate such cybersecurity incidents and decrease the risks that can potentially pose within an infrastructure. In our work, we examine several DNS exfiltration detection techniques, and we compare the most common algorithms and detection features. Furthermore, we propose a temporal analysis enhancement mechanism with the purpose to increase the existing mechanisms' efficiency. We focus on the detection of DNS exfiltration evidence within the logs of the DNS recursive resolver. Such setup does not require a specialized DNS traffic capturing mechanism, but rather the DNS queries are logged by default. This way, our approach can be used for both real time detection and forensic analysis. The performance of the proposed solution is demonstrated by investigating the DNS traffic generated from common open-source DNS tunneling tools. The results showcase that the temporal analysis can significantly improve the accuracy of the detection ratio of the exfiltration packets.

Keywords: DNS · Exfiltration · Features · Detection · Temporal Analysis

1 Introduction

Nowadays, several critical activities, such as accessing resources, performing transactions, establishing communication links, and similar rely on Internet and

G. Wang et al. (Eds.): UbiSec 2023, CCIS 2034, pp. 133–146, 2024.
https://doi.org/10.1007/978-981-97-1274-8_9

its communication protocols [23]. For instance, Domain Name System (DNS) protocol is one of the most vital Internet protocols, as it facilitates the communication based on the domain name instead of the IP address of the receiver. This attribute renders DNS as one of the most fundamental protocols of Internet for the case of transactions, such as web browsing or email exchange. However, the DNS protocol and infrastructure can be exploited for the creation of tunnels with the purpose of stealthy data exchange. Although such DNS tunnels were initially utilized to circumvent the network edge and establish free and unrestricted Internet access [12], it was reported in several instances that were also abused for malicious purposes and specifically for stealthy data communication channel.

The main components of a *DNS tunneling* infrastructure encompasses a domain name registered by the malicious actor, referred to as the base domain name hereafter, an Authoritative Nameserver (ANS) which administers this domain name and is under the control of the malicious actor, and lastly a client which acts as the insider actor responsible to initiate the tunnel and exfiltrate the data to the outside. The registered domain name functions as the rightmost label of the queried domain name in the DNS transaction establishing the tunnel. The ANS is responsible for resolving DNS queries regarding the base domain name and contains a zone file with the appropriate DNS resource records (RRs). Therefore, the client concatenates the data as the leftmost labels to the base domain name and creates a DNS request containing this fabricated domain as the queried domain name. Then, the client forwards the DNS request to the local DNS recursive resolver. In turn, the DNS resolver undertakes to traverse the DNS hierarchy and locate the responsible ANS to deliver the request. When necessary, the ANS includes meaningful data in the resource data (RDATA) of the response, this way it can send a message to the downstream of the tunnel, otherwise it provides a dummy response.

By deploying DNS tunneling, malicious entities are able to transfer data embedded within a DNS packet, either query or response. A DNS tunnel can be used among others as a Command and Control (C&C) channel for the coordination of botnets [14], for data exfiltration or for tunneling another protocol through it [21]. The key benefit for employing DNS tunneling over other network protocols that enable tunneling is that DNS is one of the few protocols that is rarely filtered out by firewalls [4,28]. Moreover, even in the case that the insider is prohibited to communicate directly with the outside network and its handler, the local DNS recursive resolver will undertake to deliver the DNS packets with the encapsulated data on the client's behalf through the DNS hierarchy to the outside network. Frequently, the insider spoofs also the source IP address of the outgoing messages. This way, the insider conceals the originator of the DNS tunneling communication, and thus it appears that the requests are spread over multiple IP addresses. Usually, for the upstream communication of the DNS tunnel, the insider embeds the data to be transmitted within the leftmost labels of the domain name in a DNS request. Commonly, the data are encrypted or encoded in Base32/Base64 format and for this reason, they look random, non-readable text.

There exist two modes of C&C communication, depending on the type of the DNS message and the amount of the data that should be exchanged between the bots and the botherder [29]. The first one, called *codeword communication*, permits one-way downstream communication from the botmaster to the bots, while the second mode, called *tunneled communication*, allows the transmission of data in both directions, a setup that facilitates data exfiltration. Typically, the DNS responses have minimal Time to Live (TTL) value for avoiding caching by the recursive resolvers. A real example of a botnet malware with DNS tunneling capabilities is the *Morto worm*. According to Symantec report [19], the Morto worm tries to resolve a DNS TXT record. The string of the response contains the encrypted IP address, where the bot could locate and download a binary executable. From the previous, it is evident that DNS tunneling detection is essential to deter type of attacks that may provoke sensitive data leakage or interception in the communication.

In our work, we examine several DNS exfiltration detection techniques from the literature, and we compare side by side the most common algorithms and detection features. For the evaluation of the DNS exfiltration detection, we focus on the examination of the DNS recursive resolver logs, in our case from BIND 9 software. The reasoning for choosing the DNS resolver logs is based on the fact that the recursive resolver software are logging by default or with minimal configuration the incoming DNS requests. This fact makes the logs ideal for both real time detection and postmortem forensic analysis without the necessity for a preestablished network traffic capturing infrastructure. Based on this choice, we leverage solely the detection features that are present on the logs, namely the character-based features of the queried domain name. Lastly, we propose an enhancement of the current methodologies by applying a temporal analysis of the DNS exfiltration evidence, thereby augmenting the efficiency of the existing mechanisms.

In brief, the contributions of this work are summarized as:

- An analysis of the DNS exfiltration detection techniques
- A comparison between identified algorithms and detection features
- A temporal analysis enhancement that can improve existing approaches

The remaining of this paper is organized as follows: Sect. 2 provides the existing DNS exfiltration detection methods and the features that are built upon. In addition, this section conducts a comparison between the existing approaches. Further, Sect. 3 describes the DNS exfiltration detection approach based on the features available on the resolver's logs. In Sect. 4, an experimental comparison of these methods and features is performed. The workings of the proposed temporal analysis approach are detailed in Sect. 5, while Sect. 6 presents the evaluation results, including a comparison with the existing approaches. Finally, Sect. 7 concludes this work and describes future directions.

2   Literature Review

In the literature, there exist three main categories of DNS tunneling detection mechanisms, depending on the type of the features they use to analyze. These are the payload analysis, the traffic analysis, and the hybrid models [21,28]. The payload analysis is applied on a single DNS request/response transaction and examines the transaction's attributes, such as domain length, number of bytes and content, and uncommon records. This way, the payload analysis aims to determine if specific requests or responses are part of a DNS tunneling exchange. On the contrary, the traffic analysis is based on the investigation of DNS network flows. The examined attributes include the volume of the DNS traffic, inter-packet arrival time, number of different hostnames per domain, geographic location and domain history. Lastly, the hybrid type of detection mechanisms aims to combine the key characteristics from both payload and traffic analysis techniques [21].

Hereinafter, we delve into the related works on DNS tunneling detection techniques based on the payload analysis. This is due to the fact, as explained in Sect. 3, that in our implementation we focus solely on the payload analysis, as only character-based features are present in the logs of the DNS resolver. Table 1 depicts a detailed comparison of the existing approaches considering the utilized *detection methods* and *detection features*.

Table 1. Related Work based on Payload analysis

RW	Taxonomy	Method	Features
[5]	Payload	S	Unigram, Bigram, and Trigram character frequencies
[13]	Payload	S	Similarity of sub-domains
[10]	Payload	S	Bigram character frequency
[6]	Payload	ML	Domain name length, domain name entropy, RR type, number of RRs, RDATA length, RDATA entropy
[18]	Payload	ML	Domain name entropy, query type, data length structural data
[25]	Payload	S	Number of subdomains, number of labels for FQDN, RR type, RDATA length, Known non-DNS tunnel use cases, Known second-level domains, domain name entropy, single and bigram character frequency Informational and Structural data
[24]	Payload	S	Domain name entropy, domain name length, carried bits of information
[20]	Payload	S	Randomness of domain name, distribution of IP address of RRs, unique query ratio and volume, domain name length
[26]	Payload	S	Number of subdomains, number of RR type

* S: Statistical, ML: Machine Learning

2.1   Payload Analysis

As previously explained, DNS tunneling is accomplished by embedding textual data on the leftmost labels of the base domain in the DNS query. Usually, Base32 or Base64 is used to encode the exfiltrated data, and thus they look random strings. Capitalizing on this fact, several research works calculate the randomness of the DNS queries to detect DNS tunnels. For instance, Born and Gustafson [5] applied statistical character frequency analysis. Specifically, the authors analyzed the n-gram, namely unigram, bigram, and trigram, character frequencies of the domain name in the DNS queries and responses.

Hind [13] constructed an Artificial Neural Network (ANN) for the detection of DNS tunnels. The basic attribute is the similarity of sub-domains belonging to the same domain zone. In their work, Dietrich et al. [10] built a Machine Learning (ML) classifier to detect DNS tunneling. The proposed features capture the randomness of the RDATA field in the DNS responses and the aggregated communication behavior. Moreover, Bubnov [6] presented an ML-based method to detect DNS tunneling strategies. Particularly, the proposed method analyses the DNS packet payload using multi-label neural network classifier. While, Liu et al. [18] presented a byte-level Convolutional Neural Network (CNN) method. Tatang et al. [25] introduced a method based on the analysis of passive DNS data feeds.

To improve the detection accuracy, Shafieian et al. [24] investigated the performance of an ensemble of ML algorithms. After experimenting with a number of classifiers and weights, they deduce that an ensemble of Random Forest and Multilayer Perceptron achieves the optimum accuracy. The examined features are inspired by previous research works and capture the randomness and the volume of DNS exchanges. Nadler et al. [20] investigated low throughput DNS tunnel and proposed a detection mechanism based on a one-class classifier. The authors employ two one-class classifier types, these are Isolation Forest and One-class Support Vector Machine (SVM). Lambion et al. [16] use a combination of Random Forest and CNN models, where the features are taken from the queried domain names. With a focus on Android devices, Wang et al. [27] utilize an isolation forest model with features taken from the DNS request and responses.

2.2   Traffic Analysis

The second category of detection mechanism is the traffic analysis. Cejka et al. [8] proposed a module for detection in real time, while it facilitates the analysis of large datasets containing DNS traffic. The method is based on statistical analysis and in particular examines the number of DNS messages per host, the packet size, the number of similar and different domain names, the length of domain names, the number of domain names characters and digits, and the ratio of letters and digits contained in the domain name. Similarly, Yu et al. [30] proposed a behavior analysis method.

Further, Do et al. [11] presented a DNS tunneling approach for mobile networks by leveraging two ML methods, the One-class SVM and K-Means, while,

DNS traffic data have been analyzed considering seven features. Das et al. [9] developed ML models to detect DNS tunneling and particularly data exfiltration from compromised machines. Moreover, Lai et al. [15] proposed DNS tunneling detection technique based on Neural Network. Almusawi et al. [3] proposed a multi-label classification and detection method for DNS tunneling. Preston [22] proposed a supervised ML approach to detect DNS tunnels. Alharbi et al. [2] developed a method to detect DNS tunnels based on Structured Occurrence Nets (SON). Lastly, Liang et al. [17] consider the traffic from the transport layer as input, following they utilize a CNN based module to extract the features and a clustering method for the evaluation.

2.3 Hybrid Analysis

The relevant works of the hybrid analysis combine both payload and traffic analysis for DNS tunneling detection. For instance, Buczak et al. [7] proposed a technique to identify DNS tunneling by analyzing PCAP data. The proposed approach is based on key features for tunneling detection, focusing on both character and traffic analysis characteristics. Similarly, Al-Kasassbeh et al. [1] introduced a DNS tunneling detection technique by leveraging both payload (character) and traffic analysis. To put forward, Ziza et al. [31] considered also the presence of an adversarial attacker.

3 DNS Exfiltration Analysis

In our work, we aim to develop a mechanism that can be used both as real time detector, but also as postmortem tool for the detection of data exfiltration incidents via DNS tunneling. To this purpose, we acknowledge that the use of the DNS recursive resolver's logs are more suitable compared to network traffic traces (pcap files). DNS recursive resolver software, like BIND 9 that we used throughout our experimental evaluation, are logging by default or with minimal configuration the receiving requests. On the contrary, the capturing of the network traffic from the side of the DNS resolver requires a dedicated hardware installation, such as network TAPs, or port mirroring of the traffic. Solutions that are not always feasible to deploy and require the support of the network administrators. Furthermore, it is anticipated that the volume of DNS requests will be constantly rising, so the storage handling of the network traces and their processing and analysis will require enormous computational resources.

Based on this choice regarding the data source, namely the logs of the DNS recursive resolver, we are limited to utilize only the features from the data presented there. Specifically, the logs contain the receiving DNS requests from the end-users and record for each request the timestamp, the queried domain name and type of the requested resource record, and the IP address of the requesting end-user. Thus, from the ensemble of the utilized features, as surveyed in the related literature and presented in Sect. 2, we focus on those from the payload analysis. Specifically, we pick the following four:

- Length of queried domain name
- Number of labels of queried domain name
- Entropy of the queried domain name
- Coincidence index of the queried domain name

We believe that these four features are the most representative and unique, as they aim to capture the data exfiltration characteristic of DNS tunneling. In such setup, the perpetrators aim to leak a significant amount of data. This way, they inevitably take advantage of the full potential of the queried domain name, as this is the only available medium to embed data in the upstream channel of the tunnel. In other words, the DNS requests that are part of the upstream of the DNS tunneling scheme are lengthy, potentially consisting from a great number of labels and containing a random looking string due to the encoding or encryption of the exfiltrated data. The remaining of the payload based features, as summarized in Table 1, constitute a combination or extension of these four basic features. Nevertheless, the features that are not present in the DNS recursive logs are excluded from our evaluation.

4   Comparison of Common Methods and Features

In order to assess the most effective algorithms along with the most efficient features with respect to the detection of DNS exfiltration incidents, a series of experiments were conducted.

Initially, a dataset was constructed based on:

- The DNS resolver's log files of a large academic organization as background traffic. This traffic is considered as the benign traffic.
- A number of DNS exfiltration open-source tools are used to create DNS exfiltration traffic, and the corresponding DNS queries are recorded in the DNS resolver's log files.
- The background and the DNS exfiltration traffic are integrated to create a labelled dataset of DNS queries which contains both normal and exfiltration samples.

For each DNS query of the dataset, the following features are extracted as explained in Sect. 3:

- Length of queried domain name
- Number of labels of queried domain name
- Entropy of the queried domain name
- Coincidence index of the queried domain name

The resulting set of features is utilized to train a number of ML classifiers. The purpose of this experiment is to investigate which of the classifiers performs better, in regard to the detection of DNS queries that are part of a DNS exfiltration session. The assessed classifiers are:

- k-Neighbors
- Decision Trees
- Random Forest
- Ada Boost
- Gradient Boosting
- Gaussian Naive Bayes
- Linear Discriminant Analysis
- Quadratic Discriminant Analysis

The confusion matrices produced for each of the classifiers are depicted in Table 2. In the following matrices, N specifies the normal traffic samples, E the exfiltration traffic samples, while CaN indicates the samples classified as normal and CaE the samples classified as exfiltration.

Table 2. Confusion Matrices

k-Neighbors Classifier		
	CaN	CaE
N	249923	21
E	12	10181

Decision Trees Classifier		
	CaN	CaE
N	249919	25
E	6	10187

Random Forest Classifier		
	CaN	CaE
N	249926	18
E	8	10185

Ada Boost Classifier		
	CaN	CaE
N	249935	9
E	128	10065

Gradient Boosting Classifier		
	CaN	CaE
N	249939	5
E	62	10131

Gaussian Naive Bayes Classifier		
	CaN	CaE
N	246690	3254
E	125	10068

Linear Discriminant Analysis Classifier		
	CaN	CaE
N	249943	1
E	830	9363

Quadratic Discriminant Analysis Classifier		
	CaN	CaE
N	247829	2115
E	130	10063

In addition, the precision, recall and F1 scores along with the overall accuracy and log loss metrics are calculated for each classifier, as depicted in Table 3. Overall, all classifiers have high accuracy. Evidently, Random Forest Classifier (RFC) excels from the rest, mainly due to the significantly lower log loss metric, which is an indication of the reduced uncertainty of the model.

5   Temporal Analysis Approach

To increase the accuracy of the detection mechanism, an improvement that utilizes the prediction of each domain name retrospectively, is proposed. In order to determine if a domain name is part of DNS tunneling, a temporal analysis of the most recent classifications for this domain name is performed. The rationale is that the likelihood of having a benign DNS query for a given base domain blended with a session of exfiltration queries abusing the same domain name is minimal.

In particular, the proposed mechanism employs an RFC that assigns a probability score based on the four aforementioned features to the DNS queries that may be part of an exfiltration session. The final decision for the classification of a domain name is made based on a combination of the calculated probability and the recent behavior of the specific base domain.

Table 3. Metrics for classifier tested

Classifier	Recall	Precision	F1-score	Accuracy	Log loss
kNN	0.9988	0.9979	0.9983	99.9873%	0.0014
DT	**0.9994**	0.9975	0.9984	99.9881%	0.0019
RFC	0.9992	0.9982	**0.9987**	**99.9900%**	**0.0004**
ABC	0.9874	0.9991	0.9932	99.9473%	0.1979
GBC	0.9939	0.9995	0.9967	99.9742%	0.0011
GNB	0.9877	0.7557	0.8563	98.7011%	0.0906
LDA	0.9186	**0.9998**	0.9575	99.6806%	0.0895
QDA	0.9872	0.8263	0.8996	99.1370%	0.0858

Essentially, a historical record is kept for each base domain name (noted as N) observed in the logs. This is achieved by maintaining a mapping (D) that correlates each base domain name to a queue data structure that stores the probabilities calculated by the RFC for the last ten queries for the specific base domain name.

$$D[N] = [p_1^N, p_2^N, ..., p_{10}^N], N \in \{\text{set of queried base domain names}\} \quad (1)$$

When a new query q is examined, the mechanism:

- Extracts the corresponding base domain name N_q
- Feeds the query q to the RFC and calculates a probability p_q
- Updates the queue structure $D[N_q]$ by removing p_1, shifting all remaining elements one position to the left and adding p_q to the right
- Selects the three highest probabilities existing in the updated queue $D[N_q]$ entry as $p_{h_1}^N, p_{h_2}^N, p_{h_3}^N$

- Calculates the average of the three selected values as $p_q^h = \frac{\sqrt{\sum_{i=1}^{3}(p_{h_i}^N)^2}}{3}))$
- Finally compares the calculated p_q^h to a given threshold and if that value exceeds the threshold, then the DNS query q is classified as part of the DNS tunneling

The assumptions regarding the operation of the presented mechanism are as follows:

- If no entry exists for a base domain name N_q in the mapping D, then a mapping is created with a single element p_q
- If the entries in the $D[N_q]$ queue are less or equal to 3, then p_q^h is calculated upon all existing entries
- The value of the threshold has been set equal to 0.5 for the initial implementation of the mechanism

6   Evaluation

To assess the performance of the proposed temporal analysis mechanism, we carried out a comparison applying both the initial RFC and the enhanced RFC with the temporal analysis to the same traffic dataset. In order to enhance the discernability of the discrepancies in the compared classification techniques, a modified dataset was utilized for the evaluation. The background traffic was reduced to a subset of the initial background traffic, so that normal traffic in the dataset resembles a lot to the exfiltration traffic. This approach made the classification problem harder and enabled us to better understand the differences in the effectiveness of the proposed approach. The confusion matrices obtained for both cases, the standard RFC and the RFC enhanced with the temporal analysis, are shown in Tables 4 and 5, respectively.

Table 4. Confusion Matrix for standard RFC

Standard RFC		
	CaN	CaE
N	3029	0
E	96	60

Table 5. Confusion Matrix for RFC with temporal analysis

Temporal analysis		
	CaN	CaE
N	3029	0
E	16	140

The evaluation of these two approaches is depicted in Table 6. The accuracy, F1 Score and Matthews Correlation Coefficient are calculated as follows:

$$ACC = \frac{TP + TN}{TP + FP + TN + FN} \tag{2}$$

$$F1 = \frac{TP + TN}{P + N} \tag{3}$$

$$MCC = \frac{TP * TN - FP * FN}{\sqrt{(TP + FP) * (TP + FN) * (TN + FP) * (TN + FN)}} \tag{4}$$

where TP indicates an exfiltration query classified as an exfiltration query, FP a normal query classified as an exfiltration query, TN a normal query classified as a normal query, and FN an exfiltration query classified as a normal query.

Table 6. Classification metrics for both approaches

Metric	Standard	Temporal analysis
Accuracy (ACC)	0.9699	0.9950
F1 Score (F1)	0.5556	0.9459
Matthews Correlation Coefficient (MCC)	0.6106	0.9448

The accuracy ratio is the ratio of correctly classified samples to the total number of samples according to Eq. 2. The two approaches have similar accuracy values. The temporal analysis approach is slightly better with an accuracy value of 0.9950, while the corresponding value for the standard approach is 0.9699. The fact that the dataset is imbalanced, as exfiltration instances represent only 5% of the total instances, allows for both approaches to achieve high accuracy values, as they tend to classify correctly the majority of the dataset that represents normal traffic.

The other two metrics provide a more comprehensive picture of the overall performance of the classifier, as they take into account the fact that a classifier may underperform for a specific class of instances. The calculation formulas for the two metrics are shown in Eqs. 3 and 4, respectively. For both metrics the temporal approach is significantly better than the standard approach, as it scores 0.9459 and 0.9448 for F1 score and MCC, while the standard approach scores 0.5556 and 0.6106. The reason behind this difference comes from the fact that the temporal analysis approach facilitates the detection of almost the full set of exfiltration queries, while the standard approach detected approximately one-third of such instances.

7   Conclusions

In the paper at hand, we attempt to study the current landscape regarding the DNS exfiltration detection. To this end, we conducted a thorough comparison of the utilized algorithms and features, and we proposed an enhancement of the existing methods, based on temporal analysis. Specifically, we utilize an RFC with four character-based features inspired by the payload analysis approach from the related literature, and we enhanced it with a temporal analysis. This temporal analysis investigates the historical evidence of a specific domain name involved in a DNS exfiltration incident, with the purpose to improve the final classification decision. Our approach is applicable for the analysis of the DNS recursive resolver logs, where only the DNS request are recorded. Typically, DNS resolver software, like BIND 9 that we utilized throughout our experiment, are logging by default the receiving DNS requests. Therefore, the proposal could be ideal for the postmortem forensic analysis of DNS exfiltration, as well as for real time detection.

The main observation of our work is the fact that the well-known open-source tools employed for DNS exfiltration produce distinguishable traffic that is easily detectable by the considered ML classifiers. According to our analysis, a number of ML classifiers can successfully detect large parts of the exfiltration sessions based on character attributes of the DNS queries, such as character randomness, length, and number of labels. RFC was observed to be the most accurate classifier.

Upon the analysis of traffic created by DNS exfiltration tools, we proposed a mechanism that combines a Random Forest Classifier with a temporal analysis module, that can greatly improve the ratio of the exfiltration packets that are correctly classified.

As future work, we foresee that there is a need to estimate the processing overhead imposed by the proposed temporal analysis module in relation to the volume of processed queries. Most probably, we would need to investigate efficient storage structures for the historical data, as optimization of the approach will be required before it can be applied for large scale networks, e.g., in the DNS resolver of a large ISP.

References

1. Al-kasassbeh, M., Khairallah, T.: Winning tactics with DNS tunnelling. Netw. Secur. **2019**(12), 12–19 (2019)
2. Alharbi, T., Koutny, M.: Domain name system (DNS) tunnelling detection using structured occurrence nets (SONs). In: Proceedings of the International Workshop on Petri Nets and Software Engineering (PNSE 2019) (2019)
3. Almusawi, A., Amintoosi, H.: DNS tunneling detection method based on multilabel support vector machine. Secur. Commun. Netw. **2018** (2018)
4. Anagnostopoulos, M., Kambourakis, G., Konstantinou, E., Gritzalis, S.: DNSSEC vs. DNSCurve: a side-by-side comparison. In: Situational Awareness in Computer Network Defense: Principles, Methods and Applications, pp. 201–220. IGI Global (2012)

5. Born, K., Gustafson, D.: Detecting DNS tunnels using character frequency analysis. In: Proceedings of the 9th Annual Security Conference (2010)
6. Bubnov, Y.: DNS tunneling detection using feedforward neural network. Eur. J. Eng. Technol. Res. **3**(11), 16–19 (2018)
7. Buczak, A.L., Hanke, P.A., Cancro, G.J., Toma, M.K., Watkins, L.A., Chavis, J.S.: Detection of tunnels in PCAP data by random forests. In: Proceedings of the 11th Annual Cyber and Information Security Research Conference, pp. 1–4 (2016)
8. Cejka, T., Rosa, Z., Kubatova, H.: Stream-wise detection of surreptitious traffic over DNS. In: 2014 IEEE 19th International Workshop on Computer Aided Modeling and Design of Communication Links and Networks (CAMAD), pp. 300–304. IEEE (2014)
9. Das, A., Shen, M.Y., Shashanka, M., Wang, J.: Detection of exfiltration and tunneling over DNS. In: 2017 16th IEEE International Conference on Machine Learning and Applications (ICMLA), pp. 737–742. IEEE (2017)
10. Dietrich, C.J., Rossow, C., Freiling, F.C., Bos, H., van Steen, M.V., Pohlmann, N.: On botnets that use DNS for command and control. In: 2011 Seventh European Conference on Computer Network Defense (EC2ND), pp. 9–16 (2011)
11. Do, V.T., Engelstad, P., Feng, B., Van Do, T.: Detection of DNS tunneling in mobile networks using machine learning. In: Kim, K., Joukov, N. (eds.) ICISA 2017. LNEE, vol. 424, pp. 221–230. Springer, Singapore (2017). https://doi.org/10.1007/978-981-10-4154-9_26
12. Farnham, G., Atlasis, A.: Detecting DNS tunneling. SANS Institute InfoSec Reading Room, vol. 9, pp. 1–32 (2013)
13. Hind, J.: Catching DNS tunnels with AI. In: Proceedings of DefCon, vol. 17 (2009)
14. Kambourakis, G., Anagnostopoulos, M., Meng, W., Zhou, P.: Botnets: Architectures, Countermeasures, and Challenges. CRC Press, Boca Raton (2019)
15. Lai, C.M., Huang, B.C., Huang, S.Y., Mao, C.H., Lee, H.M.: Detection of DNS tunneling by feature-free mechanism. In: 2018 IEEE Conference on Dependable and Secure Computing (DSC), pp. 1–2. IEEE (2018)
16. Lambion, D., Josten, M., Olumofin, F., De Cock, M.: Malicious DNS tunneling detection in real-traffic DNS data. In: 2020 IEEE International Conference on Big Data (Big Data), pp. 5736–5738. IEEE (2020)
17. Liang, J., Wang, S., Zhao, S., Chen, S.: FECC: DNS tunnel detection model based on CNN and clustering. Comput. Secur. **128**, 103132 (2023)
18. Liu, C., Dai, L., Cui, W., Lin, T.: A byte-level CNN method to detect DNS tunnels. In: 2019 IEEE 38th International Performance Computing and Communications Conference (IPCCC), pp. 1–8. IEEE (2019)
19. Mullaney, C.: Morto worm sets a (DNS) record. Technical report (2011). http://www.symantec.com/connect/blogs/morto-worm-sets-dns-record
20. Nadler, A., Aminov, A., Shabtai, A.: Detection of Malicious and Low Throughput Data Exfiltration Over the DNS Protocol. CoRR abs/1709.08395 (2017)
21. Nuojua, V., David, G., Hämäläinen, T.: DNS tunneling detection techniques - classification, and theoretical comparison in case of a real APT campaign. In: Galinina, O., Andreev, S., Balandin, S., Koucheryavy, Y. (eds.) Internet of Things, Smart Spaces, and Next Generation Networks and Systems. LNCS, vol. 10531, pp. 280–291. Springer, Cham (2017). https://doi.org/10.1007/978-3-319-67380-6_26
22. Preston, R.: DNS tunneling detection with supervised learning. In: 2019 IEEE International Symposium on Technologies for Homeland Security (HST), pp. 1–6. IEEE (2019)
23. Sammour, M., Hussin, B., Othman, M.F.I., Doheir, M., AlShaikhdeeb, B., Talib, M.S.: DNS tunneling: a review on features. Int. J. Eng. Technol. **7**(3.20), 1–5 (2018)

24. Shafieian, S., Smith, D., Zulkernine, M.: Detecting DNS tunneling using ensemble learning. In: Yan, Z., Molva, R., Mazurczyk, W., Kantola, R. (eds.) NSS 2017. LNCS, vol. 10394, pp. 112–127. Springer, Cham (2017). https://doi.org/10.1007/978-3-319-64701-2_9

25. Tatang, D., Quinkert, F., Dolecki, N., Holz, T.: A study of newly observed hostnames and DNS tunneling in the wild. arXiv preprint arXiv:1902.08454 (2019)

26. Tatang, D., Quinkert, F., Holz, T.: Below the radar: spotting DNS tunnels in newly observed hostnames in the wild. In: 2019 APWG Symposium on Electronic Crime Research (eCrime), pp. 1–15. IEEE (2019)

27. Wang, S., Sun, L., Qin, S., Li, W., Liu, W.: KRTunnel: DNS channel detector for mobile devices. Comput. Secur. **120**, 102818 (2022)

28. Wang, Y., Zhou, A., Liao, S., Zheng, R., Hu, R., Zhang, L.: A comprehensive survey on DNS tunnel detection. Comput. Netw. **197**, 108322 (2021)

29. Xu, K., Butler, P., Saha, S., Yao, D.: DNS for massive-scale command and control. IEEE Trans. Dependable Secure Comput. **10**(3), 143–153 (2013)

30. Yu, B., Smith, L., Threefoot, M., Olumofin, F.G.: Behavior analysis based DNS tunneling detection and classification with big data technologies. In: IoTBD, pp. 284–290 (2016)

31. Žiža, K., Tadić, P., Vuletić, P.: DNS exfiltration detection in the presence of adversarial attacks and modified exfiltrator behaviour. Int. J. Inf. Secur. **22**(6), 1865–1880 (2023)

Deploying Post-quantum Algorithms in Existing Applications and Embedded Devices

Petr Muzikant$^{(\boxtimes)}$ and Jan Willemson ⓘ

Cybernetica AS, Mäealuse 2/1, 12618 Tallinn, Estonia
{petr.muzikant,Jan.Willemson}@cyber.ee

Abstract. This document studies the current state of post-quantum cryptography implementation feasibility, providing general approaches that developers and security engineers can utilize to start integrating today. First, we analyze the current state of the art in the field of available cryptographic libraries and standards for algorithm interpretations and encodings. Then, we provide few implementation challenges that rose from our experiments and how to handle them. Lastly, we have built a proof-of-concept implementation by creating a post-quantum version of a modern web authentication framework. Our work introduces post-quantum support in multiple open-source libraries that together enable web-service administrators to authenticate their users with Dilithium-5 or Falcon-1024 secured electronic identities. Among other components, our proof-of-concept also includes a client side solution for key management using programmable embedded device.

Keywords: Post-Quantum Cryptography Integration · Authentication · Embedded Development · Post-Quantum Implementation · Dilithium · Falcon

1 Introduction

The basic ideas behind quantum computers were laid out already in 1980s [1]. Peter Shor's seminal paper from 1994 showed how the principles of quantum computing can be applied to solve classically hard computational problems, which in turn can lead to breaking of the currently standardized asymmetric cryptographic algorithms [2].

Even though quantum computers sufficiently powerful for breaking, say, 2048-bit RSA or 256-bit elliptic curve algorithms are not yet available, the cryptographic community has been working on their post-quantum (PQ) alternatives for more than a decade. This process was formalized by the National Institute of Standards and Technology (NIST) from United States that made a public call in 2016 to obtain candidates for post-quantum key establishment mechanisms (KEM) and digital signatures. In 2022, NIST selected the first four algorithms (one KEM and three signatures) to be standardized [3].

© The Author(s), under exclusive license to Springer Nature Singapore Pte Ltd. 2024
G. Wang et al. (Eds.): UbiSec 2023, CCIS 2034, pp. 147–162, 2024.
https://doi.org/10.1007/978-981-97-1274-8_10

However, standardization is only the first step of the long process of actual deployment in real-life information systems. A major challenge in this process is rolling out the support for post-quantum algorithms in all the layers of the communication protocols, starting from the client devices and ending with the back-ends of the services.

This is the problem setting where our current paper draws its inspiration from. We decided to focus on engineering aspects of post-quantum protocol implementations and build a complete proof-of-concept infrastructure supporting post-quantum algorithms in all the components. As real off-the-shelf cryptographic hardware providing post-quantum primitives is not yet available, we also built an end user device allowing to generate and apply post-quantum keys for authentication protocols. The paper presents the architecture of our solution together with the challenges we faced and solutions we propose to them.

2   Background

Several works have implemented post-quantum (PQ) algorithms into authentication frameworks. Schardong, Giron, Müller, and Custódio [4] created a PQ version of *OpenID Connect*. López-González, Arjona, Román, and Baturone [5] developed a PQ-safe biometric authentication framework. Yao, Matusiewicz, and Zimmer [6] introduced PQ into Security Protocol and Data Model compliant device authentication. Lastly, Paul, Scheible, and Wiemer [7] discussed PQ usage in banking protocols. Our work takes a more developer-friendly approach, providing a general method for implementing PQ algorithms into existing applications. We demonstrate this by creating a PQ Web Authentication Infrastructure with an embedded device for client-side key management, but at the same time by sharing generalized remarks applicable elsewhere.

2.1   Post-quantum Algorithm Libraries

Several post-quantum cryptographic libraries are available for use in applications.

PQClean[1] is a C library that aggregates NIST-submitted algorithms with a unified Application Programming Interface (API). It enables easy integration of a single PQ algorithm into existing applications, with minimal effort required to add more later. Developers are encouraged to copy the code, adjust common libraries, and compile it.

For developers who prefer a compiled, higher-level library, *libOQS*[2] (written in C) is a great option. It features code from *PQClean* as well as other sources, and offers language wrappers for C++, Python, Java, Go, .NET, and Rust. There are also high-level libraries built on *libOQS*, such as *OQS-OpenSSL*, *OQS-OpenSSH*, and *OQS-OpenVPN*.[3]

---

[1] See https://github.com/PQClean/PQClean.

[2] See https://github.com/open-quantum-safe/liboqs.

[3] A full listing is available at https://openquantumsafe.org/applications/.

Other available post-quantum cryptographic libraries include *libpqcrypto*[4], *rustpq/pqcrypto*[5], and *pqm4*[6].

2.2 Post-quantum ASN.1 Structures

Abstract Syntax Notation One (ASN.1) structures for post-quantum cryptographic objects are essential for successful integration into existing applications, particularly in X.509 certificate usage. Yet, no standards currently exist. NIST's submission rules require authors of post-quantum algorithms to encode their algorithm-specific structures of keys, signatures, and ciphertexts into a single byte string [8].

Multiple Request for Comments (RFC) drafts propose ASN.1 structures for most objects from currently selected-to-be-standardized PQ algorithms.[7] The current version of *OQS-OpenSSL* works with arbitrary Object Identifiers (OIDs) from the OpenQuantumSafe organization for different algorithms.[8]

It is also possible to use `subjectPublicKeyInfo` with `algorithmIdentifier` specified from the list of OIDs and `subjectPublicKey` as PQ digital signature in byte string format. Snetkov and Vakarjuk [9] suggest using `subjectAltPublicKeyInfo`, `altSignatureAlgorithm`, and `altSignatureValue` attributes to maintain classical cryptography functional.

2.3 Post-quantum JSON Web Algorithms

JSON Web Algorithm (JWA) is an RFC [10] that registers cryptographic algorithms and identifiers for JSON Web Signature and JSON Web Encryption, which are widely used for securely transferring data over the network. For example, `ES384` stands for ECDSA digital signature algorithm using P-384 and SHA-384 hash algorithm. At the time of writing this article, there are no RFC drafts for post-quantum JWAs.

However, there are drafts[9] for JSON Web Key, which specifies only the digital signature algorithm part and does not provide a hash function. For example, `CRYDI5` means CRYSTALS-Dilithium algorithm parameter on the 5th security level.

To use post-quantum algorithms in JWAs, a constant specified hash function can be used (e.g., SHA-512, which is recommended by NIST as quantum-safe). When implementing post-quantum digital signatures in existing applications that use JWAs, `CRYDI5` could be handled as CRYSTALS-Dilithium-5 + SHA-512.

---

[4] See https://libpqcrypto.org/index.html.

[5] See https://github.com/rustpq/pqcrypto.

[6] See https://github.com/mupq/pqm4.

[7] See https://github.com/open-quantum-safe/oqs-provider/issues/89.

[8] See https://github.com/open-quantum-safe/oqs-provider/blob/main/ALGORITH MS.md#oids.

[9] See https://www.ietf.org/archive/id/draft-prorock-cose-post-quantum-signatures-01.html.

2.4   Hybrid Mode

Hybrid mode combines classical cryptography with post-quantum cryptography. While this approach incurs more performance, memory, and storage overhead, it also eliminates potential threats from both classical and quantum world. Post-quantum algorithms ensure the longevity of data confidentiality, while classical cryptography guards against potential emerging threats on unexplored PQ cryptography.

Several RFC drafts propose ASN.1 structures for hybrid modes.[10] However, the question remains as to how these two types of algorithms should be coupled together.

A novel method is proposed by Ghinea *et al.* [11] to improve unforgeability. It involves prepending labels to signed messages, as opposed to concatenating classical and post-quantum signatures, or sequentially using the digital signature given with one algorithm as an input for another signature algorithm.

3   Post-quantum Implementation Challenges

Implementing post-quantum algorithms in existing applications can be difficult due to the continual progress of and uncertainty in post-quantum technology. This may lead to numerous engineering issues for developers and cybersecurity engineers when trying to make their systems quantum-resistant.

In this section we will provide general ideas to aid implementation of post-quantum algorithms into existing applications.

3.1   Identifying Relevant Locations

Identifying locations in the codebase, network and business processes where public key infrastructure (PKI) objects are used is the first step in implementing post-quantum algorithms in an existing application. Tracing the data flow from start to end of the object's lifetime is necessary to identify different approaches towards non-PQ and PQ objects, as there are differences in how other processes interact with them. Identifying these data flows helps in understanding the extent of changes necessary for implementing post-quantum algorithms in an application.

When transferring cryptographic data objects between different parts of the architecture, it is important to consider the Maximum Transmission Unit (MTU) to ensure longer keys and signatures fit into containers. Additionally, caution is required when implementing the Falcon PQ digital signature algorithm as its output length may vary.

Data formats and possible conversions between them during the object's lifetime also require detailed consideration. For example, cryptographic libraries

---

[10] See   https://datatracker.ietf.org/doc/draft-ounsworth-pq-composite-encryption/01/,   https://datatracker.ietf.org/doc/draft-ounsworth-pq-composite-keys/,   and https://datatracker.ietf.org/doc/draft-truskovsky-lamps-pq-hybrid-x509/01/.

might yield raw bytes, but the rest of the system handles data transfer in ASN.1, Base64, or PEM encoded formats. Identifying the format of existing data flows is the key to ensuring compatibility across the system architecture and detecting any areas that require modification.

A format suitable for this purpose is a Business Process Model and Notation (BPMN) diagram. An example of a BPMN diagram from our implementation is shown in Fig. 2.

3.2   Technological and Computational Constraints

Before transitioning to post-quantum algorithms, it is essential to assess the technological and computational boundaries of the current system. Increased memory usage is expected when generating PQ key-pairs, creating signatures, and verifying them. In real-time applications, performance may be impacted. Further measurements can be found in [12–15], Sect. 5, and our source code.

In regular applications meant to be run on desktop, laptop, or server machines, these constraints are not as significant as they are on slow networks or other limited devices. In other cases, actual post-quantum algorithms need to be adjusted. For example, Gonzalez *et al.* [16] proposes streaming public keys and signatures into the limited memory of an attached HSM component. Another work by Gonzales and Wiggers [13] suggests using key encapsulation instead of digital signatures to reduce computational overhead.

In Sect. 4, we will also provide an example of how to overcome constraint problems by switching from smart cards to embedded programmable microcontrollers, and how we adjusted the algorithm to allocate its objects on the heap, instead of stack memory.

3.3   Implementing PQ Algorithms in the Codebase

After identifying all locations and constraints, one can begin changing the codebase. We recommend starting from the beginning of the data lifecycle and implementing post-quantum support one step at a time. Post-quantum algorithms are generally not available natively in the current cryptographic libraries, therefore library extensions may be required. Data format conversions may occur during these steps, adding to the potential fragility of the implementation.

We refer to Sect. 2.1 for existing extensions (e.g. *OpenSSL* or popular programming languages). If none are suitable, $SWIG^{11}$ can be used to generate wrappers from C implementations of PQ algorithms (see Sect. 4.4). New wrapper can be used directly, or as an extension to the used cryptographic library.

---

[11] See https://swig.org/.

4 Practical Results

We present a proof-of-concept implementation for a complete authentication infrastructure with post-quantum cryptography.[12] We set up a usable, modern, cross-platform and open-source combination of components to authenticate users to a web application using post-quantum digital signature algorithms (Dilithium-5 and Falcon-1024). We describe the implementation process and present the engineering problems we met together with the solutions we propose.

4.1 Architecture

To create a proof-of-concept PQ-enabled authentication system, we needed to select three key components of the system – *back-end server with a web service*, *authentication framework*, and *authentication device*.

1. We chose open-source cloud storage Nextcloud[13] as our *back-end server with a web service*. It serves as an electronic identity verifier, authenticating users and granting them access to the web application.
2. We chose the open-source *authentication framework* Web-eID, developed by the Estonian Information Authority, as a successor of Open-EID[14]. Both are cross-platform solutions used for authenticating citizens on the web using national electronic ID cards. For more information, see Sect. 4.2.
3. We chose an ESP32 microcontroller as our *authentication device*, which holds the information needed to establish electronic identity (e.g., a private key for signing challenge nonces). This was due to the post-quantum constraints discussed in Sect. 3.2, which prevented us from using smart cards. Further details can be found in Sect. 4.3.

These three top-level components are supported by multiple lower-level libraries/repositories that needed to be adjusted and contributed to as well. See Sect. 4.4 for more information. Figure 1 provides an overview of all components and their relations.

4.2 Authentication Data Flow

Web-eID is a suite of applications, extensions, and tools that enable authentication and digital-signing with public-key cryptography on the web, similar to Transport Layer Security: Client Certificate Authentication (TLS-CCA). For more information, see chapter 2.4 in [17] or the official website[15]. We present our analysis of the PKI object data lifetime in Fig. 2. It displays all the relevant components that we needed to focus on when implementing support for post-quantum algorithms.

---

[12] Repository index with source code and additional information can be found at https://github.com/Muzosh/Post-Quantum-Authentication-On-The-Web.
[13] See https://nextcloud.com/.
[14] See https://github.com/open-eid.
[15] See https://web-eid.eu/.

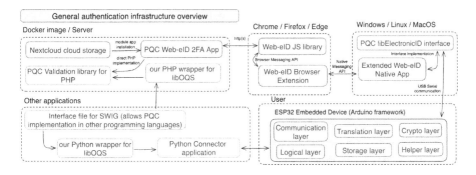

Fig. 1. PQC authentication infrastructure components overview

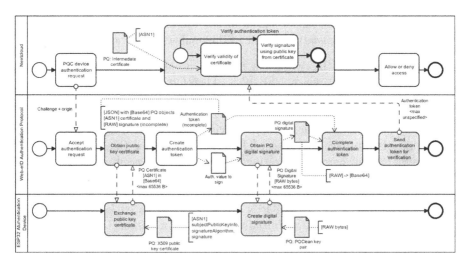

Fig. 2. Post-quantum data flow analysis

4.3   Authentication Device

Web-eID supports only smart cards using the Personal Computer/Smart Card (PC/SC) protocol stack. However, current cards lack the RAM and CPU capabilities to perform post-quantum digital signatures [18]. In [19], authors suggest using KEM algorithms to implement quantum-resistant banking protocols, but using KEM in our work would have required significant changes to the Web-eID authentication protocol. Lastly, [20] discusses implementations of PQ cryptography on constrained platforms, including smart cards. The authors conclude that there are no algorithms that can be run on off-the-shelf programmable smart cards, and one must use more powerful platforms.

Therefore, we decided to use an ESP32 system-on-chip microcontroller device as our authentication device, as they are sufficiently powerful and widely available low-cost products. We used two devices: *DFRobot FireBeetle 2* and the more powerful *LilyGO T-Display-S3* (for more technical details and benchmarks, see Sect. 5.2).

To make such a device Web-eID compatible, we developed a full-fledged firmware for the embedded device to imitate the functionality of the Estonian ID card. It receives custom APDU commands and sends the appropriate APDU responses after proper user PIN authorization. We used PlatformIO[16] with Arduino-ESP32 framework to enable Arduino features on the ESP32 platform.

Our authentication device does not use the PC/SC protocol stack to send data to the PC, but USB serial communication instead. To make this possible, we contributed with an application-wide abstraction layer in the Web-eID application to include USB serial devices. This layer allows developers to create custom serial devices and integrate them with modern authentication protocols.

The following list contains a subset of notable considerations and problems when developing an application for an ESP32 embedded device.

- *Device driver* – in this work, we consider using an authentication device connected to the PC via a USB port. Therefore, a USB-to-serial driver is required for the PC to recognize the device when connected. For *FireBeetle*, we used an installable *CH34X driver*. For *T3-Display-S3*, a device capability *USB CDC* (USB Communications Device Class), which is a common and recognizable interface, was used. The latter option has the benefit of being recognized in all current operating systems without needing to install any software in advance. However, there is a slight delay of 1–2 s after inserting the device.
- *Storage options* – to manage PIN states and generated key pairs, persistent file storage is essential. Initially, we opted for *LittleFS*, an open-source filesystem designed for embedded devices. Further investigation revealed that the ESP32 framework offers multiple storage API options for flash memory [21]. We decided to use *NVS*, a key-value flash storage with a maximum of 508KB data limitation, due to its faster write and read speeds, thus shortening authentication time.
- *Debugging* – to debug an ESP32 microcontroller, an external debugging probe must be connected to the device and PC. An alternative option is to print debug data to the serial buffer, but this interferes with the authentication protocol as it shares the serial buffer (PC expects pre-determined number of bytes in responses). To address this, we used a separate NVS namespace for logging and saving debug messages to the flash memory. After an operation, logs can be read from the serial buffer (and erased) on demand.
- *Serial communication on PC* – we initially used the *Boost::Asio*[17] C++ library to communicate with the PC device. However, to simplify the process (mainly using timeout and listing available ports features) and to reduce

---

[16] See https://platformio.org/.
[17] See https://www.boost.org/doc/libs/1_82_0/doc/html/boost_asio.html.

dependencies, we transitioned to the *QtSerialPort*[18] library, which is part of the Qt framework. For the Python application, we used *pyserial*[19].

- *Buffer size* – in the Arduino framework, `Serial.setRxBufferSize()` must be called before `Serial.begin()`, not after.
- *USB MODE* – we learned that in order for the device to work properly after reconnection during authentication,[20] `ARDUINO_USB_CDC_ON_BOOT` build flag must be on, and `ARDUINO_USB_MODE` must be off at the same time.

4.4   Post-quantum Implementations

In this section, we will provide details of our experience implementing post-quantum cryptography throughout the entire architecture, including low-level components.

General Remarks. For implementing key pair generation, digital signature, or verification with post-quantum algorithms, we used *PQClean* for the embedded device and *libOQS* for the rest of the codebase (see Sect. 2.1 for their descriptions). If an application already uses a cryptographic library such as OpenSSL, one approach is to search for a post-quantum version of it (or contribute one as open-source) – e.g. *OQS-OpenSSL* can be installed using the *libOQS* library. Alternatively, the application logic can be split into two branches: if classical algorithms are required, use the existing library; if post-quantum algorithms are needed, use raw implementation libraries like *libOQS*. We used both approaches in our authentication infrastructure.

PQ on Embedded Device. The biggest challenge when implementing post-quantum algorithms on embedded devices is memory management. As mentioned before, *PQClean* is the most suitable library in this situation, but it still needs to be adjusted.

On ESP32 platforms, all operations are managed by FreeRTOS [22], an operating kernel system for embedded devices. Therefore, even the `loop()` function runs as a task, with a predetermined 8KB stack in RAM. As stated in [16] and tested by us, 8KB is not sufficient for post-quantum algorithms.

To address this issue, we created a new FreeRTOS task with a larger stack allocation. Its purpose is to call a specified PQ function from the *PQClean* API and return the result. However, this approach is not consistent across multiple devices, as the upper memory limit for the stack allocation is not equal to the total free memory available (due to ESP32 having memory allocations for different purposes [23]). We also occasionally encountered errors stating that the task could not be created, even after checking for free memory.

---

[18] See https://doc.qt.io/qt-6/qtserialport-index.html.

[19] See https://github.com/pyserial/pyserial.

[20] More information about the issue can be found at https://esp32.com/viewtopic.php?f=19&t=33762.

Therefore, we allocated only 32MB of stack for these tasks and minimized memory allocation to the stack in the *PQClean* implementation, moving it to the heap memory. We changed large declarations in functions to use `malloc` and `free` functions. For even safer memory management, we chose to rewrite this code from C to C++ and use `std::unique_ptr` objects, which handle other objects' memory allocation for their lifetime.

Additionally, we converted all arrays to pointers in function signatures to prevent them from being copied to the stack when the function is called. This guarantees that every post-quantum operation has 32MB of memory for stack allocations and all algorithm-related objects are allocated dynamically on the heap, which prevents runtime errors.

PQ in Transit. Before implementing post-quantum algorithms on either side of the architecture, we checked that the increased (and variable in the case of Falcon) size of post-quantum data (such as public keys, digital signatures or certificates) would not break communication by sending mock data.

Web-eID transmits a custom authentication token in JSON format, consisting of a DER-encoded unverified public key certificate and a raw signature, both Base64 encoded. It uses multiple APIs, like the Browser Messaging, Native Messaging and HTTP API, to transfer the token between the components. These APIs have no significant size restrictions for Dilithium-5 or Falcon-1024 objects, so there was no need to make any codebase changes.

Algorithm identifiers are encoded in the ASN.1 structure of the unverified certificate and as a JSON Web Algorithm in the `algorithm` field of the Web-eID authentication token. During device personalization (generating key pairs, obtaining public keys, and creating client certificates), unofficial, *libOQS*-compatible OIDs (e.g. `1.3.6.1.4.1.2.267.7.8.7` for Dilithium-5) and drafted JSON Web Key identifiers (e.g. `CRYDI5` for Dilithium-5 + constant SHA512 for the hash function) are used.

PQ in Existing Architecture. In this section, we discuss the implementation of post-quantum cryptographic algorithms in the rest of our authentication architecture. We made changes to the following components.

- *Nextcloud Web-eID 2FA* – an installable Nextcloud application that allows using Web-eID authentication result as the second factor.[21] A switch to the PQC Web-eID AuthToken Validation Library for PHP was required (see below).
- *PQC Web-eID AuthToken Validation Library for PHP* – pre-quantum version of this library used both *OpenSSL* and *PHPSecLib*, so we adjusted both:
  - *OQS-OpenSSL* – the OpenQuantumSafe organization provides an *OpenSSL@1.1* fork and *OpenSSL@3* extension capable of post-quantum algorithms.[22] However, the current version of internal OpenSSL PHP

---

[21] See https://github.com/Muzosh/nextcloud_twofactor_webeid.

[22] See https://openquantumsafe.org/applications/tls.html.

extension only supports functions that do not require algorithm identification (e.g. `openssl_verify`, `openssl_sign`, not `openssl_pkey_new`). The reason for this is that DSA, DH, RSA and EC algorithms are hardcoded, and there is no way of specifying post-quantum algorithm identifiers from PHP source code.[23]

- *PQC-PHPSecLib* – we provide an open-source contribution in the form of preparation for post-quantum algorithms with *Dilithium-5* reference implementation. This uses either *OQS-OpenSSL* or our new PHP extension of C++ *libOQS* library created with *SWIG*. Before any function is run, `ASN1::loadOIDs` must be called with all new post-quantum algorithm object identifiers.

– *liboqs-php* and *liboqs-python* – OpenQuantumSafe offers several language wrappers for its *libOQS* library, but does not include a PHP wrapper. We created one using *SWIG*, an application that requires C++ interface for generating wrappers. We used this wrapper in our *PQC-PHPSecLib*. We also created a Python wrapper for our device personalization application (for creating post-quantum certificates and testing the device). *SWIG*-specific remapping was needed to transform PHP `string` and Python `bytearray` into C++ `uint8_t*` and vice versa.

– *PQC-Web-eID Application* – apart from the already mentioned new application-wide abstraction layer, an *ElectronicID* interface (required for each supported card/device) was implemented for our new authentication device. No post-quantum functions were required in this part, and data transit was described in Sect. 4.4.

– *Device Connector* – this console application allows administrators to initialize and issue our authentication devices, test Web-eID compatibility and post-quantum capabilities. It uses the *liboqs-python* library as it is written in Python.

5   Benchmarks

In this section, we present the results from our measurements and explain some of our choices based on these results.

5.1   Chosen Algorithms

Web-eID authentication protocol utilizes digital signature schemes, so we chose three post-quantum signature algorithms that NIST selected as finalists in 2022: *Dilithium*, *Falcon* and *Sphincs+* [24]. Out of these, we have chosen parameters that provide NIST security level 5.[24] In case of *Sphincs+* (which has multiple variants of level 5) we chose the most performant one.

---

[23] More about this issue at https://github.com/open-quantum-safe/openssl/issues/433.

[24] See   https://csrc.nist.gov/Projects/Post-Quantum-Cryptography/Post-Quantum-Cryptography-Standardization/Evaluation-Criteria/Security-(Evaluation-Criteria).

We measured the durations of key pair generation, digital signature creation, and digital signature verification of the post-quantum algorithms in the *libOQS* library on a dockerized version of Debian on an Apple M2 Pro chip. Table 1 shows the relevant object sizes for the three selected algorithms, and Table 2 displays the measurement results (averages from 30 retries).

Table 1. Object sizes of three selected algorithms

Algorithm	Public key size [B]	Private key size [B]	Signature size [B]
Dilithium-5	2952	4864	4595
Falcon-1024	1793	2305	1280
SPHINCS+-SHAKE256-256f-s	64	128	49856

Table 2. Performance measurement of three selected algorithms with PHPv8.1 interpreter in dockerized Debian on M2 Pro chip

Algorithm	Keypair gen. time [ms]	Sign. gen. time [ms]	Verif. time [ms]
Dilithium-5	1.314×10^{-7}	2.366×10^{-7}	1.134×10^{-7}
Falcon-1024	3.392×10^{-5}	7.658×10^{-6}	6.440×10^{-8}
SPHINCS+-SHAKE256-256f-s	4.926×10^{-6}	1.059×10^{-4}	2.541×10^{-6}

Sphincs+ is not suitable for embedded devices due to its large signatures. *Falcon* has smaller object sizes than *Dilithium*, but its signature operation takes 32 times longer. Thus, *Dilithium-5* was chosen as most suitable algorithm for our authentication infrastructure.

5.2 Digital Signature Creation Duration

Figure 3 illustrates the evolution of on-device signature creation during the development phase (the values shown are averages from 100 retries). Initially, we used the *DFRobot FireBeetle 2* device with an ESP32-E chip, 520KB of SRAM, and 32MB of storage without encrypting the content in the flash memory (blue column). To address the lack of Hardware Security module/Trusted Platform Module, we introduced data encryption (using quantum-safe AES256-OCB), with the symmetric key derived from the user PIN (green column, resulting in a longer duration). After evaluating storage options (discussed in Sect. 4.3), we moved some (grey column, leading to a significant decrease) or all (yellow column, slight decrease) stored data to NVS storage.

Switching to the *LilyGO T-Display-S3* device with an ESP32-S3 chip, 8MB of PSRAM, and 16MB of storage (red column), significantly decreased the digital signature creation time to 0.196 s. The reason is mostly higher computational power of the new ESP32 chip generation. For comparison, a *JavaCard*

SLJ52GCA150 (jTOP SLE78 Estonian ID card platform) achieved an ECDSA over P-382 elliptic curve signature creation in 0.262 s [17]. We also implemented the *Falcon-1024* algorithm (purple column) for demonstration purposes, which resulted in a significant increase in duration.

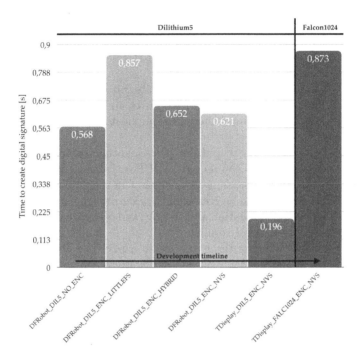

Fig. 3. Digital signature benchmark on ESP32 devices

5.3   User Experience Considerations

Our authentication infrastructure is in the proof-of-concept phase, so we can not provide exact evaluation of the whole authentication process. In our testing scenario, with a Nextcloud server running in a dockerized Debian on an Apple M2 Pro chip and a post-quantum enabled Web-eID, the user has to go through two more clicks and one PIN input. This is a lot more noticeable than the cryptographic operations running in the background. For a detailed view of the process from the administrator and user point of view, refer to chapters 4.1 and 4.2 in [17], which describe a similar authentication process with a smart card.

The USB CDC interface introduces a 1–2 s delay after device insertion. This delay is only noticeable during authentication if the device is inserted during the process. If inserted beforehand, the device is initialized in the background and ready when authentication starts.

6   Conclusions and Further Work

Post-quantum cryptography implementations impose several engineering problems, such as longer key/signature sizes and higher computational requirements. In this article, we discussed these problems, their possible solutions, and provided an example reference implementation in the form of post-quantum-enabled, modern, and open-source authentication infrastructure. We also developed an embedded client authentication device (with custom firmware and management console) and example server-side Nextcloud cloud storage using two-factor authentication.

Our work demonstrates the feasibility of integrating post-quantum cryptography into existing authentication infrastructures and provides a starting point for those interested in exploring the practical implications of post-quantum cryptography today.

For future work, we plan to publish post-quantum extensions of the used public repositories, such as Web-eID parts, *PHPSecLib*, and *liboqs-php* libraries. This step will probably require some development in the ASN.1 structures standardization. We would also like to create one Docker implementation of the whole infrastructure for easier installation and testing, and optimize the authentication device codebase for even faster results.

We also consider changing the hardware to a microcontroller with an integrated trusted execution environment and hardware secure module, so we do not have to encrypt stored data ourselves. Lastly, we plan to perform a full security analysis of this infrastructure and compare it with existing analyses.

Acknowledgments. Funded by the European Union under Grant Agreement No. 101087529. Views and opinions expressed are however those of the author(s) only and do not necessarily reflect those of the European Union or European Research Executive Agency. Neither the European Union nor the granting authority can be held responsible for them.

References

1. Preskill, J.: Quantum computing 40 years later. arXiv preprint arXiv:2106.10522 (2021). https://arxiv.org/abs/2106.10522
2. Shor, P.W.: Algorithms for quantum computation: discrete logarithms and factoring. In: 35th Annual Symposium on Foundations of Computer Science, Santa Fe, New Mexico, USA, 20–22 November 1994, pp. 124–134. IEEE Computer Society (1994). https://doi.org/10.1109/SFCS.1994.365700
3. Post-Quantum Cryptography. National Institute of Standards and Technology (2023). https://csrc.nist.gov/projects/post-quantum-cryptography
4. Schardong, F., et al.: Post-quantum electronic identity: adapting OpenID connect and OAuth 2.0 to the post-quantum era. In: Beresford, A.R., Patra, A., Bellini, E. (eds.) CANS 2022. LNCS, vol. 13641, pp. 371–390. Springer, Cham (2022). https://doi.org/10.1007/978-3-031-20974-1_20

5. López-González, P., et al.: A facial authentication system using postquantum-secure data generated on mobile devices. In: Proceedings of the 28th Annual International Conference on Mobile Computing and Networking. ACM (2022). https://doi.org/10.1145/3495243.3558761

6. Yao, J., Matusiewicz, K., Zimmer, V.: Post Quantum Design in SPDM for Device Authentication and Key Establishment. Cryptology ePrint Archive, Paper 2022/1049 (2022). https://doi.org/10.3390/cryptography6040048. https://eprint.iacr.org/2022/1049.pdf

7. Paul, S., Scheible, P., Wiemer, F.: Towards Post-Quantum Security for Cyber-Physical Systems: Integrating PQC into Industrial M2M Communication. Cryptology ePrint Archive, Paper 2021/1563.2021.https://doi.org/10.3233/JCS-210037. https://eprint.iacr.org/2021/1563.pdf

8. Stebila, D.: Key Format (2019). https://github.com/open-quantum-safe/liboqs/issues/507

9. Snetkov, N., Vakarjuk, J.: Integrating post-quantum cryptography to UXP. Technical report D-2-499. Cybernetica AS (2022). https://cyber.ee/uploads/PQC_UXP_report_8c97d91552.pdf

10. Jones, M.: JSON Web Algorithms (JWA). Technical report (2015). https://doi.org/10.17487/rfc7518

11. Ghinea, D., et al.: Hybrid Post-Quantum Signatures in Hardware Security Keys. Cryptology ePrint Archive, Paper 2022/1225 (2022). https://eprint.iacr.org/2022/1225.pdf

12. Sajimon, P.C., Jain, K., Krishnan, P.: Analysis of post-quantum cryptography for internet of things. In: 2022 6th International Conference on Intelligent Computing and Control Systems (ICICCS). IEEE (2022). https://doi.org/10.1109/iciccs53718.2022.9787987

13. Gonzalez, R., Wiggers, T.: KEMTLS vs post-quantum TLS: performance on embedded systems. In: Batina, L., Picek, S., Mondal, M. (eds.) SPACE 2022. LNCS, vol. 13783, pp. 99–117. Springer, Cham (2022). https://doi.org/10.1007/978-3-031-22829-2_6

14. Tasopoulos, G., et al.: Performance evaluation of post-quantum TLS 1.3 on resource-constrained embedded systems. In: Su, C., Gritzalis, D., Piuri, V. (eds.) ISPEC 2022. LNCS, vol. 13620, pp. 432–451. Springer, Cham (2022). https://doi.org/10.1007/978-3-031-21280-2_24

15. Raavi, M., et al.: QUIC protocol with post-quantum authentication. In: Susilo, W., Chen, X., Guo, F., Zhang, Y., Intan, R. (eds.) ISC 2022. LNCS, vol. 13640, pp. 84–91. Springer, Cham (2022). https://doi.org/10.1007/978-3-031-22390-7_6

16. Gonzalez, R., et al.: Verifying post-quantum signatures in 8 kB of RAM. In: Cheon, J.H., Tillich, J.P. (eds.) PQCrypto 2021. LNCS, vol. 12841, pp. 215–233. Springer, Cham (2021). https://doi.org/10.1007/978-3-030-81293-5_12

17. Muzikant, P.: Cloud Service Access Control using Smart Cards. MAthesis. Brno University of Technology (2022). http://hdl.handle.net/11012/208378

18. Greuet, A.: Smartcard and Post-Quantum Crypto (2021). https://csrc.nist.gov/Presentations/2021/smartcard-and-post-quantum-crypto

19. Bettale, L., De Oliveira, M., Dottax, E.: Post-quantum protocols for banking applications. In: Buhan, I., Schneider, T. (eds.) CARDIS 2022. LNCS, vol. 13820, pp. 271–289. Springer, Cham (2023). https://doi.org/10.1007/978-3-031-25319-5_14

20. Malina, L., et al.: Towards practical deployment of post-quantum cryptography on constrained platforms and hardware-accelerated platforms. In: Simion, E., Géraud-Stewart, R. (eds.) SecITC 2019. LNCS, vol. 12001, pp. 109–124. Springer, Cham (2020). https://doi.org/10.1007/978-3-030-41025-4_8

21. Storage API. Espressif Systems (Shanghai) Co., Ltd. (2023). https://docs.espressif.com/projects/esp-idf/en/latest/esp32/api-reference/storage/index.html
22. FreeRTOS (2023). https://www.freertos.org/
23. ESP32 Memory Types. Espressif Systems (Shanghai) Co., Ltd. (2023). https://docs.espressif.com/projects/esp-idf/en/latest/esp32/api-guides/memory-types.html
24. NIST Post-Quantum: Selected Algorithms 2022. National Institute of Standards and Technology (2022). https://csrc.nist.gov/Projects/post-quantum-cryptography/selected-algorithms-2022

SCORD: Shuffling Column-Oriented Relational Database to Enhance Security

Tieming Geng[1,2(✉)], Chin-Tser Huang[1], and Csilla Farkas[1]

[1] Department of Computer Science and Engineering, University of South Carolina, Columbia, SC 29208, USA
tgeng@email.sc.edu, huangct@cse.sc.edu, farkas@cec.sc.edu
[2] Department of Mathematics and Computer Science, Fayetteville State University, Fayetteville, NC 28301, USA
tgeng@uncfsu.edu

Abstract. Column-oriented database systems have drawn a lot of attention in recent years because of their performance advantages in terms of data querying and computation on columns. Since databases often contain sensitive and valuable information, protecting the confidentiality, integrity, and availability of the database is of utmost importance. In addition to encryption, shuffling can also be used to secure the database storage files. In this paper, we present a novel approach called SCORD to prevent the leakage of confidential data stored in the database management system by applying the shuffling technique on column-oriented databases. SCORD can protect column-oriented databases in both offline storage mode and online running mode. SCORD also bundles semantically or statistically associated attributes, such that the data is shuffled in a way that appears deceptively authentic and indistinguishable to potential attacks. We implement a prototype of SCORD and evaluate it using a set of real-world data. The experiment results demonstrate the effectiveness of our approach and show that the processing overhead is acceptable.

Keywords: Relational Database · Column-oriented · Columnar Storage · Cryptographic Shuffling · Attribute Association

1 Introduction

Cloud-based database systems are becoming widely used because of the benefits on scalability, continuity, and maintenance cost [3]. In contrast to establishing and maintaining the on-site data centers or database servers, cloud database service can provide the ability to quickly set up into production and effortlessly scale up based on the application resource requirement and business growth. Despite the benefits of cloud database service, one of the major obstacles in the way of completely migrating the database to the cloud is the security concern. In a report published by PricewaterhouseCoopers Audit [18], security concerns and fear of data loss are the top two barriers to the adoption of cloud database services. The main security concerns include incomplete control over data, data leakage, and insider threats which typically bring greater damage

© The Author(s), under exclusive license to Springer Nature Singapore Pte Ltd. 2024
G. Wang et al. (Eds.): UbiSec 2023, CCIS 2034, pp. 163–176, 2024.
https://doi.org/10.1007/978-981-97-1274-8_11

to the cloud database than the outsider security concerns because of the high privileges granted to the insiders. For example, in 2022, one vulnerability in T-Mobile's API was exploited, affecting 37 million customers with potential identity theft risks [7].

Currently, cryptographic encryption stands as one of the most widely adopted protection methods to address database attacks and data breaches. Various encryption techniques, such as transparent data encryption, token-based systems, and fully homomorphic encryption, have been employed for this purpose. In Transparent data encryption, the pages in the database are encrypted before being written to disk and decrypted when read into memory. This approach ensures that even if the database server is breached, the malicious attacker gains no valuable information. However, encryption in the database can reveal file importance, attracting attackers. Token-based systems like CryptDB [17] and searchable encryption [19] allow searching over encrypted data but face criticism from Grubbs et al. [10] for potential issues. It is worth noting that achieving semantic security [9] becomes challenging if even a single token value is known to attackers. Fully homomorphic encryption [16] enables algebraic operations on ciphertext without decryption but may have efficiency concerns due to large encryption keys in practical use [2].

In this paper, we introduce a novel approach called SCORD (Shuffled Column-Oriented Relational Database) which integrates a shuffling algorithm with a column-oriented storage approach to further enhance the security and efficiency of relational database management systems. SCORD leverages a collection of two-column association tables to record the disk locations of the actual data and their corresponding indexes. With the assistance of these association tables, SCORD can accomplish shuffling without physically relocating the data, resulting in significant savings in time and system resources.

Our contributions can be summarized as follows:

– Proposing SCORD, a novel approach that combines the shuffling algorithm and column-oriented storage in both the online and offline modes of the relational database management system.
– Presenting an efficient method for returning a deranged permutation sequence, enabling shuffling to be performed with minimal time consumption.
– Introducing the BAIT storage format, which significantly reduces the number of I/O operations required for relation columns shuffling and group shuffling.
– Conducting a thorough analysis of the security aspects and evaluating the performance of SCORD to demonstrate its feasibility and superiority.

The remainder of the paper is organized as follows. In Sect. 2, we discuss related work on database security and applications of shuffling. In Sect. 3, we provide an overview of our previous work on database storage shuffling and some other background knowledge. In Sect. 4, we introduce the details of SCORD which can improve the security of offline and online relational database management systems. In Sect. 5, we describe our prototype implementation and evaluate its performance. In Sect. 6, we analyze the security of our approach. Finally, we conclude in Sect. 7.

2   Related Work

Several studies have been conducted to enhance the database security by encrypting the data content. One type of at-rest encryption on the database called TDE (Transparent Database Encryption) has been applied in many popular relational database management systems such as Microsoft SQL Server and Oracle. Popa et al. [17] proposed to encrypt query processing by executing queries over encrypted data using a collection of efficient SQL-aware encryption schemes including order-preserving encryption and homomorphic encryption. [11] and [20] proposed searching in the encrypted data, which does not require data decryption on either the server side or the application side. However, some special keys must be offered to augment the searchable encryption.

3   Background Information and Previous Work

In this section, we provide an overview of some background knowledge and our previous work including the shuffling algorithm and attribute association discovery.

3.1   Column-Oriented Database

Column-oriented database is not a new technique. It can be traced back to a storage system called TAXIR focused on biology information retrieval in 1969 [6]. However, due to the hardware limitations and application scenarios of early databases, the mainstream OLTP (Online Transactional Processing) databases adopted row-oriented storage. Along with the emerging development of OLAP (Online Analytical Processing), column-oriented storage becomes prevalent again.

Data size in the storage of database becomes increasingly sensitive due to the cost of network bandwidth and storage media along with the business development. Thus data compression is critical in the database management system. Column-oriented database has an overwhelming advantage on the compression ratio comparing to the row-oriented database because the unit of storage is one column and all the data in this column is of the same data type. Since all compression algorithms can be applied on column-oriented databases, we will not discuss their details due to space constraint.

3.2   Previous Work

In our previous work [8], we introduced a robust shuffling algorithm with cryptographic strength. The primary objective of this algorithm was to shuffle the data values within each attribute of the database relation, thereby safeguarding against data confidentiality violations that may arise from compromise of the database storage disk.

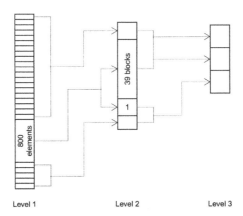

Fig. 1. Example of shuffling the blocks in three levels.

Shuffling Algorithm. In one relation, we will apply a secure shuffling based on a deranged permutation on each attribute. In our algorithm, we have the following arguments:

- l: the total number of tuples in the attribute. l could be divided into some equal-sized blocks, except that the size of the last one may be smaller.
- w: the number of tuples in one block. The default value of w is 20, and the number of tuples in the last block is $l \bmod w$. The number 20 was chosen based on a balance between the adequately large key space and a reasonable amount of overhead for handling the shuffling.
- $k^{[i]} : (k_0, k_1, ..., k_n)$: the shuffling sequence used to shift the tuples inside one block, which is based on a deranged permutation. The shuffling sequence specifies that the element currently at the position indicated by the value of k_j will be moved to position j after the shuffling. $k^{[i]}$ represents the shuffling sequence for level i (the conception of *level* will be introduced later in this section).

For example, one relation which contains 825 tuples (i.e., $l = 825$) will be divided into 42 blocks if the w is set as the default value 20. Since $l/20 = 41$ and $l \bmod 20 = 5$, therefore, there are 41 full blocks and one block with 5 tuples.

The shuffling will be conducted inside each block, in which all the tuples will be shifted based on one generated deranged permutation sequence. For example with the block (a, b, c) and shuffling sequence $(2, 0, 1)$, the element at position $k_0 = 2$, i.e., element c, will be moved to position 0, element at position $k_1 = 0$, i.e., element a, will be moved to position 1, and element at position $k_2 = 1$, i.e., element b, will be moved to position 2.

In order to increase the degree of diffusion and to hide the existence of shuffling, the entire shuffling may be performed on several levels. For the previous example of relation which contains 825 tuples, we will have 42 blocks at the first level. Since 42 is greater than the default value of w, another level of shuffling will be conducted. In this level, each block will be considered as the basic unit of shuffling, which means the tuples inside each block will not be shuffled individually while the position of the entire block may be changed. Based on the default value of w, these blocks will be divided into 3 blocks with 2 full blocks and one block whose size is 2. Figure 1 shows how the multi-level shuffling is performed.

For the factor of security, the shuffling sequence $k^{[i]}$ will be re-generated for each level i. We have one function $dp(w)$ to produce the permutation sequence which is used for shuffling. The function $dp(w)$ can be described as follows:

– Input: w which is the size of a block.
– Output: a set $k^{[i]} : (k_0, k_1, ..., k_n)$

Function $dp(w)$ works by first uniformly randomly generating a permutation sequence and checking if it is a deranged permutation; if so, return this deranged permutation, otherwise repeat the random generation until the generated permutation is a deranged one. Since a block of w elements will be treated as one single element in the next level, this exponential growth on multiple levels won't make i (the number of levels) very large. For instance, a relation with 3 million tuples can be managed with 5 levels because 20^5 is greater than 3 million.

Attribute Association. Some attributes of one tuple require extra care when performing shuffling to keep the deception from being exposed by semantic or statistical checking because those attributes are highly associated, such as zip code and U.S. cities. If these attributes are not shuffled synchronously, the hacker would be able to detect some mismatched combinations of data and then the existence of shuffling. Various techniques allow us to compute the association strength between individual variables, and each of them is contingent on the data type. When the attributes of interest are both categorical, the Pearson's chi-squared test (χ^2 test) is suitable for measuring the association [14]. When the attributes of interest are both quantitative, the correlation coefficient methods such as Pearson correlation coefficient (PCC) are suitable for discovering the association between them [14]. If one attribute is categorical and one attribute is quantitative, the analysis of variance (ANOVA) test is more suitable [14].

Considering the requirements of supporting online shuffling in addition to offline shuffling, we have identified the following research challenges in this work:

RC1: How can shuffling be performed while the database is running?
RC2: What measures can be taken to improve the efficiency of the shuffling algorithm?
RC3: Is there a more effective method for identifying if multiple columns need to be shuffled together?
RC4: How can we strike a balance between the security requirements and the performance requirements?

4   System Design

In this section, we present our proposed SCORD in detail from the perspective of data storage and how the shuffling is done. In our previous work, the objectives are to prevent the attacker from reconstructing the whole database by breaching the storage server even if he doesn't possess the data files and from retrieving the complete information about an individual or entity by tracing and assembling all the attributes of the same data tuple. However, the protection didn't cover the data inside memory, which means the protection of shuffling only covers the offline storage, but not the case when the database management is running on the server.

4.1 Threat Model

In the threat model, we make the following assumptions:

- *The database management system is trusted* [1]. We place our trust in the database management system to accurately carry out operations such as disk reading and writing, ensuring that no vulnerabilities are created for attackers to exploit.
- *The communications among the database management system clusters are trusted.* This aspect pertains to network security, and encryption during data transmission, such as SSL and IPSec, is extensively employed to safeguard communications. Consequently, our focus does not need to be directed towards protection against transmission attacks.
- *The hardware architectures or software systems where the database management system is located are vulnerable to compromise.* [1] Trusted database management systems commonly rely on the storage system offered by the underlying operating system. However, the vulnerability of the operating system creates a potential avenue for attackers to illicitly access the valuable information stored within the database.
- *The data in the database management system are beneficial from the attacker's perspective.* Network attacks can provide benefits to the attackers, which may include unauthorized access to valuable information, financial gain through theft or fraud, and competitive advantage through industrial espionage.

4.2 Deranged Permutation Generation

Similar to encryption, which relies on an encryption key, shuffling relies on a deranged permutation sequence. We propose a new design that can generate a deranged permutation in constant time, based on the work of Korsh and LaFollette [15]. Previously, our method involved randomly generating a permutation and then testing if it was deranged. However, as the tuple size w increases, the hit ratio (the probability of generating a deranged permutation) decreases due to the ratio R between the number of permutations N_p and the number of deranged permutations N_{dp}, where $R = N_{dp}/N_p$. Consequently, generating a deranged permutation becomes increasingly time-consuming. This enhancement significantly improves the efficiency of the shuffling algorithm itself and addresses the challenge RC2.

4.3   Data Storage

In disk-optimized database systems, data is accessed at the block level rather than through direct database engine control. Data files are treated as raw disks, with the OS mapping logical blocks to physical ones. Block sizes vary between systems, so one data file may contain multiple logical blocks, each with a block number. The pages in memory hold the content of blocks, and the so-called "buffer manager" is in charge of reading blocks into the buffer cache and writing pages back to disk blocks if some changes were made.

For this reason, the conception of page and block is sometimes used interchangeably to represent the basic unit of operations on data files, so we can say the data files are organized as a collection of pages, and each page is given a unique identifier. The most common layout scheme of a page is called a slotted page in which there are header, slot array, and values. The slot array maps slot_id to the value's starting position offset.

The main difference between row-oriented storage and column-oriented storage is how the data are organized in data files. In row-oriented storage, one tuple which consists of multiple attributes occupies one slot in the page file, so that the slot_id can be used for future addressing and each attribute can be traversed based on the attribute length predefined in relation scheme. In our design, the page files only store the values from one single attribute, and each value will be assigned one slot_id. Because of the fixed size of one page along with the growing number of tuples in the relation and the requirement of atomicity, the size of one page is usually a few kilobytes such as 4KB in SQLite and Oracle, thus one attribute may be stored in multiple pages. Given the page_id and slot_id, every value can be addressed.

For the purpose of improving security and preserving privacy, we apply the shuffling algorithm to attributes. As mentioned earlier, the attributes in one relation may be located on different pages due to the size limit, thus directly moving the attributes according to the permutation generated by the algorithm is extremely inefficient for the following reasons: 1) high diffusion feature and deranged permutation of our algorithm will move every attribute to another location, which requires a mass of I/O operations on data files, and 2) the newly inserted tuples need the shuffling to provide the security and privacy on those new tuples, and frequent insertions will hugely increase the time of reading and writing accesses.

Instead of directly moving the values themselves, our approach is inspired by the physical data model of MonetDB [12]. MonetDB represents relational data using Binary Association Tables (BATs) consisting of two columns. The right column stores the actual value, while the left column contains the object identifier (OID) of the corresponding tuple. In a relation R with m attributes, there are m BATs, and attribute values within the same tuple share the same OID. The OID values are generated in an ascending sequence during tuple insertion, indicating the explicit position of the tuple. In SCORD, we use the Binary Association Index Tables (BAITs) in the physical data model. As illustrated in Fig. 2 which depicts the architecture, the BAIT is positioned between the Index-

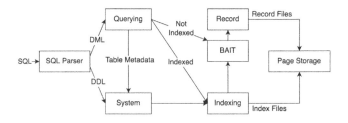

Fig. 2. System Architecture of SCORD with BAIT integrated.

ing module and Record module, responsible for managing querying indexes and unordered data records, respectively.

There are two main differences between MonetDB's BAT and our BAIT:

- In BAIT, the OID in the left column represents the iterator of either the indexing data structure or the record data structure. However, unlike the ascending sequence used in MonetDB, our design generates random and hashed OID values.
- The right column in BAIT does not store the actual data; instead, it holds the address of the storage location.

Left Column: The OID in the left column serves as the iterator for either the indexing data structure or the record data structure, depending on whether the column is indexed or not. To ensure the persistence of the iterator, each record or indexing iterator is assigned a unique identifier. To generate the OID, we employ a highly efficient hash algorithm called xxHash [4]. This algorithm operates at RAM speed limits, enabling fast processing. The value range of the random OID generator does not need to be excessively large to maintain optimal performance. To ensure the uniqueness of the OID, we concatenate the generated random number with the current timestamp. This concatenation is then passed through the xxHash algorithm, which guarantees both uniqueness and speed. The random number acts as a salt for the hash function, enhancing the security of the hash result and preventing attacks such as rainbow table attacks [21]. Since the hash result is not used for integrity verification, the randomness of the salt does not pose any issues for storage and reuse.

Right Column. We store in the right column only the concatenated address, represented as **page_id + slot_id**, rather than the actual value. This unified indexing approach significantly reduces the frequency of I/O operations by operating solely on the BAIT files, instead of reading and writing all the page files during the shuffling process. The BAITs can be efficiently utilized in memory, allowing for faster shuffling operations. Moreover, if the size of the BAIT files exceeds the available memory, cache replacement policies such as LRU (Least Recently Used) can be employed to manage memory usage effectively. This ensures optimal performance even when the BAIT files cannot be entirely held in memory.

4.4   Shuffling and Restoring

Based on the BAIT storage format, the entire shuffling on the relation doesn't have to touch the actual data files; only the left column of BAIT files will be changed. Comparing to the actual data, BAIT files are much smaller, so it is feasible and efficient to put BAIT files in memory during the running of the database management system. In an extreme case, every data insertion or update will trigger the full shuffling to guarantee the data security and privacy. Another extreme case is to execute the shuffling only before the shutdown of the database management system, which only provides the protection on offline storage. To balance the performance and security, a time interval can be set as the countdown to trigger the shuffling.

The efficiency of attribute statistical association bundle shuffling has significantly improved due to the adoption of column-oriented storage. In the computation of association strength, all values within a column are involved. However, when using a row-oriented storage scheme, this computation incurs a substantial amount of file I/O operations. In contrast, the column-oriented storage scheme benefits from a larger page size, such as the 1MB page size in Amazon Redshift. Consequently, measuring statistical strength can be achieved with just a few I/O requests, as the related columns are stored together. By leveraging the advantages of column-oriented storage, bundle shuffling processing can be accelerated.

Another essential algorithm in our design is the restoring algorithm for the sake of the transparency of shuffling. In restoring, the same shuffling parameter will be used but in the opposite direction – that is, the element at position j will be moved to the position indicated by the value of k_j.

5   Implementation and Performance Evaluation

In this section, we discuss the implementation and performance evaluation of SCORD. We first describe the parameter settings and datasets used in the implementation. Then, we discuss possible strategies to improve the security in the cloud environment. Last, we introduce the metrics used in the evaluation of our prototype and analyze the results.

5.1   Parameter Settings

It is necessary to stay with consistent shuffling parameters for the transparent restoring (i.e., unshuffling) of the data. For the shuffling of each relation, $\mathbb{K}$, as a three-layer structure, records the shuffling parameters as shown in Fig. 3. In the first layer, the shuffling parameters are represented as $\mathbb{K} : (K0, K1, ..., Kn)$ in which $K0$ means the shuffling parameters for the first attribute and Kn means the shuffling parameters for the last attribute. Coming to the next layer, same as described in Sect. 3, each $k^{[i]}$ indicates the shuffling parameters for each level. The sequence $(k_0, k_1, ..., k_n)$ stands for the shuffling parameters inside each block. Among these parameters, only the sequence of $(k_0, k_1, ..., k_n)$ is generated, and the sequence plays the role of leaf in the tree. Accordingly, the database engine randomly generates the shuffling sequence $(k_0, k_1, ..., k_n)$, and constructs all the shuffling sequences together.

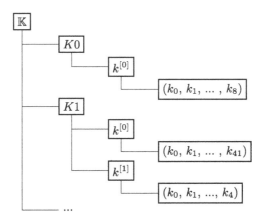

Fig. 3. General view of the shuffling parameter collection for one relation. $\mathbb{K}$ stands for root, next level contains the shuffling parameters of each attribute, then next level contains the shuffling parameters for each level.

5.2 Improve the Security

The randomly generated shuffling parameters can be encoded into a file and then encrypted by some symmetric encryption algorithm such as AES for one more layer of protection. Encoding algorithms can be chosen based on the preference for file size or encoding/decoding speed. After enabling the shuffling on the database engine, it is very important to protect the shuffling parameters. By migrating from single-cloud computing environment toward multi-clouds, the security can be improved [5].

The encryption key must be stored in a secure module external to the database, and many popular cloud service providers provide the service of Key Vault such as AWS Key Management Service.

5.3 Datasets and Implementation

We utilized a portion of the IMDB dataset for evaluating the performance of our proposed design. The dataset comprises alphanumeric unique identifiers of individuals, along with essential information. It was obtained from [13] and converted to SQL format.

Our implementation is developed in C++. Both the column-oriented storage scheme and row-oriented storage scheme are implemented for the purpose of comparison. The experimental environment is equipped with an Intel i7-10700 CPU and 32 GB of memory, running Debian 11. The shuffling parameters are stored in a separate machine functioning as the security key vault. Both the dataset server and key vault are connected to the same switch. Therefore, the time required for reading and storing the shuffling parameters in the actual product may vary depending on the connection between the database server and the key vault server.

5.4   Shuffling Overhead

To simplify the performance evaluation process, we have made the following assumptions: 1) The shuffling process is triggered based on the number of tuples that are inserted, deleted, or updated in the database; 2) All columns in the relation are indexed to optimize query performance. We evaluate the system performance using a collection of insertion and query statements denoted as $\mathbb{Q}$. The overall execution time without shuffling enabled is denoted as $T_{\text{OFF}}^{\mathbb{Q}}$, while the execution time with shuffling enabled is denoted as $T_{\text{ON}}^{\mathbb{Q}}$. To demonstrate the overhead of shuffling, we conducted evaluation tests using 50,000 and 100,000 statements for INSERT and SELECT operations. The average results of 10 rounds are shown in Table 1.

Table 1. Running Times When Shuffling is Disabled and Enabled.

Operation	# of Statements	$T_{\text{OFF}}^{\mathbb{Q}}$	$T_{\text{ON}}^{\mathbb{Q}}$	Difference
INSERT	50,000	5.46 s	5.98 s	0.52 s
INSERT	100,000	9.49 s	10.18 s	0.69 s
SELECT	50,000	281.45 ms	286.36 ms	4.91 ms
SELECT	100,000	376.29 ms	377.87 ms	1.58 ms

Based on the results, the following observations can be made: 1) The time consumed by the shuffling process is small compared to the overall execution time. It indicates that the shuffling operation has minimal impact on the system's performance. 2) For INSERT operations, the time taken for shuffling increases proportionally with the number of tuples being inserted. This demonstrates that the shuffling process scales well with the size of the dataset. 3) Enabling shuffling for SELECT operations does not significantly affect the execution time. This is because no additional steps are performed during the querying process for SELECT operations, resulting in minimal overhead. These results confirm the practicality and scalability of our design.

6   Security Analysis

In this section, we provide an analysis on the security of our proposed shuffling algorithm in terms of key space, and key sensitivity.

6.1 Key Space Analysis

In cryptography, one cryptosystem's key space means the set of all possible distinct keys based on key length. In our shuffling algorithm, the key space analysis is to show the range of all possible permutations of the shuffling parameters and to show the difficulty to successfully conduct the brute-force attack on our shuffling algorithm. Theoretically, the key space should be large enough to make the brute-force attack infeasible, and we can assess the key space from the following two perspectives: 1) arbitrary key space, and 2) global key space. Arbitrary key space stands for the key space of one single attribute's shuffling parameter. If the brute-force attack succeeds, the adversary can restore the original order of all tuples in this attribute. This restoring doesn't violate confidentiality (if the data are encrypted), integrity, and availability since the only difference is the order of those tuples. However, this may bring some concerns on the privacy preservation due to the revealing of data order. For example, in the relation *Salary* in which all attributes are ordered by ascending salary amount, shuffling on the attribute could remove the underlying relationship that Bob's salary is lower than Alice's because the *id* of Alice is bigger. As to the global key space, it indicates the maximum number of shuffling parameters to try for restoring the entire relation.

For one relation with m tuples and n attributes, the size of the global key space is at least $(!m)^n$ in combinatorics. The arbitrary key space for any attribute with m tuples would be $!m$ which is unfolded as

$$m! \sum_{i=0}^{m} \frac{(-1)^i}{i!} \tag{1}$$

From the above expression, we can see that the key space is highly dependent on the scale of relation. Because of the factorial in the global key size function, a small increase in the number of tuples will lead to huge growth. For instance, the key space of the relation with 5 tuples and 2 attributes is 1936, and when the number of tuples rises to 100 tuples and if there are 5 attributes, the size of the global key space dramatically grows to $3.18e + 24$. This key space is sufficiently large to protect the shuffling from brute-force attacks trying to guess the correct shuffling parameters.

6.2 Key Sensitivity Analysis

Good encryption should be sensitive to a very small change on the secret keys, therefore in our algorithm, we expect that any changes on the shuffling parameters would produce hugely different permutations. We continue to use the two concepts *coincidence* and *strong coincidence* defined in our previous work that one coincidence means there is one tuple in which any one or more attributes stay in the original position after shuffling (the case that the tuple alters the position in the first level of shuffling but goes back to the original position is included), and one *strong coincidence* means one shuffled tuple in which the origins of at least two attributes are identical one, in other words the correspondence between these attributes still exists after shuffling.

If the number of tuples is small enough to carry out the shuffling with one level, it is straightforward that there is no *coincidence* or *strong coincidence* in the shuffled data since the definition of deranged permutation requires that no element appears in its original position. However, multiple levels of shuffling could possibly move the tuple back to its original position theoretically. Thus, we conduct an experiment on five datasets containing different number of tuples: 5K, 10K, 50K, 100K, and 500K respectively, with the number of attributes set as 20 for all five cases. Each dataset will be shuffled for 1000 rounds with different randomly generated shuffling parameters and then each shuffled dataset will be compared to the original dataset for counting the number of *coincidence* and the number of *strong coincidence* accumulatively. Our result shows that for all datasets, both the number of *coincidence* and the number of *strong coincidence* are 0 in 1000 rounds of shuffling. Therefore, we can conclude that our shuffling algorithm is sensitive to the small changes on shuffling parameters.

7 Conclusion and Future Work

In this paper, we introduced SCORD, a novel approach which applies a shuffling algorithm on column-oriented databases to improve the security and efficiency of relational database management systems for both offline storage and online execution. Using SCORD, we can implement another type of protection on the database data in addition to data encryption, without modifying the original data. This makes the protection more deceptive so that some adversary tracking applications such as honeypot can be built on top of it. The prototype implementation, performance evaluation, and security analysis show strong security and high efficiency with small extra overhead in terms of time and system resources.

In our future work, we intend to develop and implement a distributed database management system that incorporates shuffling and column-oriented storage. This will enable the deployment of our solution across multiple nodes, enhancing scalability and performance.

References

1. Agrawal, R., Kiernan, J., Srikant, R., Xu, Y.: Order preserving encryption for numeric data. In: Proceedings of the 2004 ACM SIGMOD International Conference on Management of Data, pp. 563–574 (2004)
2. Alaya, B., Laouamer, L., Msilini, N.: Homomorphic encryption systems statement: trends and challenges. Comput. Sci. Rev. **36**, 100235 (2020)
3. Bello, S.A., et al.: Cloud computing in construction industry: use cases, benefits and challenges. Autom. Constr. **122**, 103441 (2021)
4. Cyan4973: Cyan4973/xxHash. https://github.com/Cyan4973/xxHash
5. Duncan, R.: A multi-cloud world requires a multi-cloud security approach. Comput. Fraud Secur. **2020**(5), 11–12 (2020)
6. Estabrook, G.F., Brill, R.C.: The theory of the taxir accessioner. Math. Biosci. **5**(3–4), 327–340 (1969)

7. Franceschi-Bicchierai, L.: T-mobile says hacker accessed personal data of 37 million customers. https://techcrunch.com/2023/01/19/t-mobile-data-breach/
8. Geng, T., Alsuwat, H., Huang, C.T., Farkas, C.: Securing relational database storage with attribute association aware shuffling. In: 2019 IEEE Conference on Dependable and Secure Computing (DSC), pp. 1–8. IEEE (2019)
9. Goldwasser, S., Micali, S.: Probabilistic encryption. J. Comput. Syst. Sci. **28**(2), 270–299 (1984)
10. Grubbs, P., Ristenpart, T., Shmatikov, V.: Why your encrypted database is not secure. In: Proceedings of the 16th Workshop on Hot Topics in Operating Systems, pp. 162–168 (2017)
11. Guan, Z., et al.: Cross-lingual multi-keyword rank search with semantic extension over encrypted data. Inf. Sci. **514**, 523–540 (2020)
12. Idreos, S., Groffen, F., Nes, N., Manegold, S., Mullender, S., Kersten, M.: Monetdb: two decades of research in column-oriented database. IEEE Data Eng. Bull. (2012)
13. IMDB: IMDB data files available for download. https://datasets.imdbws.com/
14. Jeong, D.H., Jeong, B.K., Leslie, N., Kamhoua, C., Ji, S.Y.: Designing a supervised feature selection technique for mixed attribute data analysis. Mach. Learn. Appl. **10**, 100431 (2022)
15. Korsh, J.F., LaFollette, P.S.: Constant time generation of derangements. Inf. Process. Lett. **90**(4), 181–186 (2004)
16. Marcolla, C., Sucasas, V., Manzano, M., Bassoli, R., Fitzek, F.H., Aaraj, N.: Survey on fully homomorphic encryption, theory, and applications. Proc. IEEE **110**(10), 1572–1609 (2022)
17. Popa, R.A., Redfield, C.M., Zeldovich, N., Balakrishnan, H.: Cryptdb: protecting confidentiality with encrypted query processing. In: Proceedings of the Twenty-Third ACM Symposium on Operating Systems Principles, pp. 85–100 (2011)
18. PWC: Cloud security report (2019)
19. Varri, U., Pasupuleti, S., Kadambari, K.: A scoping review of searchable encryption schemes in cloud computing: taxonomy, methods, and recent developments. J. Supercomput. **76**(4), 3013–3042 (2020)
20. Zheng, Y., Lu, R., Guan, Y., Shao, J., Zhu, H.: Achieving efficient and privacy-preserving exact set similarity search over encrypted data. IEEE Trans. Dependable Secure Comput. **19**(2), 1090–1103 (2020)
21. Zyuzin, V.D., Vdovenko, D.V., Bolshakov, V.N., Busenkov, A.A., Krivdin, A.D.: Attack on hash functions. EurAsian J. BioSciences **14**(1) (2020)

A SLAHP in the Face of DLL Search Order Hijacking

Antonin Verdier[✉], Romain Laborde, Mohamed Ali Kandi,
and Abdelmalek Benzekri

IRIT, Université de Toulouse, CNRS, Toulouse INP, UT3, Toulouse, France
{antonin.verdier,romain.laborde,Mohamed-Ali.Kandi,
abdelmalek.benzekri}@irit.fr

Abstract. DLL Search Order Hijacking (also known as DLL Hijacking or DLL planting) is a problem that is generally overlooked by software developers even though its existence has been known for over a decade. While Microsoft has designed and implemented mitigations to reduce the feasibility and the impact of DLL Search Order Hijacking, this issue is worth being brought back up due to the recent adoption of user-writable directories as potential, and sometimes default, software installation paths (in lieu of directories like "Program Files" which require administration privileges by default) in order to improve installation success rates. We conducted a study on 48 different software programs (Top software on Sourceforge across 4 different categories and the 4 major web browsers) and found that more than 88% of them were vulnerable to some form of DLL Search Order Hijacking. To alleviate this issue, we propose SLAHP, a novel way of preventing DLL Search Order Hijacking exploitation in the form of a proof-of-concept implementation that is both easy to integrate with new and existing products by software developers and users. It is invisible to end users while still allowing the usage of previously insecure installation locations. To further demonstrate the usability of our solution, we conducted performance tests and found that its impact is mostly negligible.

Keywords: DLL Search Order Hijacking · DLL Sideloading · Shared libraries · Security Policy · Advanced Persistent Threat

1 Introduction

The principle of DLL Search Order Hijacking (DSOH) is to confuse the Windows OS into loading a malicious DLL (Dynamic-Link Library) file instead of a genuine one by taking advantage of the way Windows locates DLL files. This attack enables attackers to hide malicious behaviour behind genuine applications by making trusted processes execute their code. While its existence has been known for over a decade [17,18] and is well documented by reputable sources [15], it still is regularly used by threat actors [3,6] as a mean to obtain persistence or

© The Author(s), under exclusive license to Springer Nature Singapore Pte Ltd. 2024
G. Wang et al. (Eds.): UbiSec 2023, CCIS 2034, pp. 177–190, 2024.
https://doi.org/10.1007/978-981-97-1274-8_12

to perform privilege escalation. Indeed, up to 20% of criminal and APT attacks in 2019 [2] used DSOH. In addition, as of 2021, no EDR was able to detect the attack mechanism itself [9]. Back in 2003, Microsoft added a mitigation that fixed most DSOH vulnerabilities, this mitigation was effective mainly because most software programs were installed in the C:\Program Files directory, which requires administrative privileges to be written into. However, this hypothesis does not hold anymore and the past decade has seen more and more software developers choosing different installation directories like AppData to facilitate the installation process. This directory, being located in the user directory, is writable by an unprivileged user. This enhances the user experience and the installation success rate. However, it also simplifies the task of attackers to place their malicious DLL in the targeted software installation directory. Furthermore, DSOH's underlying issue can also be exploited by attackers in order to gain initial access to a system: this is known as DLL Sideloading [11,16], which is sometimes considered to be a technique of its own. While DLL Sideloading isn't the main topic of this research, its similarity with DSOH makes it a secondary target.

In this article, we present SLAHP (for Shared Library Anti Hijack Protector), a solution against DSOH and similar techniques that is easy to integrate with new and already existing software as well as unnoticeable by end-users. These characteristics should facilitate the adoption of our solution by both developers and end-users, as well as allow advanced users to protect programs without any intervention from the original software developer. Our solution can be added as a static library during development or in the form of a custom launcher after compilation and/or distribution.

This paper is organised as follows. In Sect. 2, we explain how the way the Windows operating system performs DLL loading can be exploited by threat actors. Section 3 contains the results of a vulnerability survey we conducted on how widespread the issue of DSOH is. Then, we present our solution and evaluate its performance in concordance with our objectives. Next, we discuss related works before finally providing a summary of our contributions and discussing ideas to overcome our solution's limits in future works.

2   What Is DLL Search Order Hijacking?

In this section, we introduce the Windows DLL loading process exploitation and the current mitigations available.

2.1   Exploitation

DLLs are Windows shared libraries that can be referenced by name only. To accomplish this, the Windows OS employs a search order that specifies the list of directories it should sequentially inspect for libraries. It starts with the libraries listed in the KnownDLLs registry key, followed by the Application Installation directory, the System directories (e.g., C:\Windows\System32), the current working directory (CWD) and finally the directories listed in the PATH variable.

However, the simplicity of the DLL search order mechanism has its flaws. If we consider the hypothetical case where a threat actor is able to place an arbitrary file in an application's installation directory, the application could end up loading and executing malicious code against its will. This is because the Windows OS only looks at file names to locate DLLs. Thus, a malicious DLL file with the same name as the genuine system file could be loaded in lieu of the real one. This exploitation process is illustrated in Fig. 1.

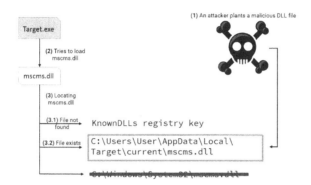

Fig. 1. Diagram of a search-order-hijacked DLL loading

However, such an attack requires two conditions: i) the threat actor must be able to write to the application's installation directory and ii) the malicious DLL must either be optional to the target program or be able to emulate the features of the usurped DLL, which is known as a proxy DLL. As mentioned earlier, the first condition is becoming more and more prevalent as applications seek out ease of installation by choosing directories that can be written to without administrative privileges as their installation location; while some software such as Google Chrome or Mozilla Firefox use these directories as a failsafe, more and more software — mostly observed amongst software using the Electron and Chromium Embedded Framework (CEF) — use these directories as their default installation location, sometimes without user consent. As for the second condition, it is only a matter of time and expertise for the threat actor to meet it.

2.2   Mitigations Proposed by the Windows OS

DllSearchMode. Windows 2000 SP3 [13] introduced an optional feature called `DllSearchMode` that moved the CWD further down the DLL search order (it was initially inspected before the system directories). This mitigation has been enabled by default since Windows XP SP2 in August 2004 and reduced the potential of DSOH exploitation, as software programs were generally installed in the `C:\Program Files` directory, which requires administrative privileges to write to.

PreferSystem32. As part of the 2017 Windows 10 Creators Update, Microsoft introduced a similar mitigation called `PreferSystem32`. This mitigation works by inverting the application installation directory and the system directories in the DLL search order. While this approach can prevent attacks such as the one described in Sect. 2.1, it also prevents by design a developer from loading a custom DLL that shares its name with a DLL present in the system directories. Surprisingly, the amount of documentation surrounding this mitigation is very poor and sometimes incorrect. Indeed, the Powershell documentation [21] describes the existence of a Powershell command that can be used to enable that mitigation on an executable, or system-wide. While that command exists, we found that an executable that is supposed to be protected is still vulnerable to the exploitation of DSOH vulnerabilities. The most complete piece of documentation we could find [4] is 4 sentences long. Nonetheless, we found out that the Mozilla Firefox browser uses `PreferSystem32` in order to protect itself from DSOH vulnerabilities. By reading Firefox's source code and experimenting with the OS-provided APIs, we observed that the only way we could make the mitigation work was by having a process acting as a launcher enable the mitigation, then start the program that we want to protect. In conclusion, `PreferSystem32` is just a partial mechanism to mitigate DSOH vulnerabilities. We believe that the complexity brought by its implementation is the main reason behind its observable absence in software development.

3   Survey of Software Currently Vulnerable to DLL Search Order Hijacking

In order to better understand how widedespread the issue of DSOH is, we developed a tool that allowed us to look for DSOH vulnerabilities in applications with as little human interaction as possible. We used a sample of 48 different programs, including programs from the top education, text editors and file-sharing software on Sourceforge, as well as the four major web browsers (Google Chrome, Mozilla Firefox, Microsoft Edge & Opera).

In order to detect DSOH vulnerabilities, our tool enumerates the dependencies of the program we are analysing and tries to usurp the name of each dependency, one by one. The detected vulnerabilities can be qualified as low-hanging, as our tool is not designed to mimic any of the features of the original DLLs. It only contains code that is executed on loading and creates a temporary file whose existence constitutes proof of successful exploitation.

We have observed that some programs refuse to start when some of their dependencies at start-up do not contain the expected DLL function exports; thus, the amount of vulnerable programs we have detected may be underestimated. Another consequence is that our tests induced apparent misbehaviour (e.g. black screen) from the programs we analysed. However, we do not believe that this would be a problem for an actual threat actor, as the creation of a malicious proxy DLL is a task that can be accomplished with open-source tools [12].

The results of the vulnerability tests we conducted are summarised in Table 1. We categorised the analyzed software according to their default installation directory. The motivation behind this partition is the fact that these installation directories largely represent the main difficulty of DSOH-based persistence attacks. Indeed, directories such as `C:\Program Files` can only be written to with administrative privileges making the task of a threat actor harder, while the `C:\%USERNAME%\AppData` directory can be written to by its owner, `%USERNAME%`. Portable applications were assigned their own category because the choice of their installation directory is up to the user. However, we can speculate that the users are more likely to install them in directories that do not require administrative privileges as it is the easiest solution.

Table 1. DSOH vulnerability survey results

Location	Vulnerable	Non-vulnerable	Total
AppData	15	3	18
Portable	6	1	7
Program Files	21	1	22
Total	42	5	47

We can see that most of the software we have tested is vulnerable to DSOH, regardless of the category. However, the programs installed into `Program Files` directory seem to exhibit the highest vulnerability proportion. It should be noted that the relatively small amount of programs we analyzed may not accurately represent the totality of computer software programs, and consequently our estimated total proportion of 89% vulnerable programs is only intended to highlight that this security issue is common for some of the most popular programs. Therefore, this justifies research in mitigating DSOH attacks.

We hypothesise that there are two reason explaining the amount of programs currently vulnerable to DSOH. We believe the first one is the general ignorance of its existence [19] by software developers and the lack of easily integrable mitigation mechanisms. The second possible reason is the nonchalant attitude adopted by some major software editors, such as Google [1] ignoring this security issue, arguing the fact that the exploitation of DSOH largely depends on a threat actor having had prior access to the targeted computer. Their reasoning is that Chrome cannot do anything against a threat actor having access to the computer. We know this rationale is not entirely correct, as Mozilla Firefox implements security features that are specifically designed to combat DSOH.

4 The Shared Library Anti Hijack Protector

4.1 General Principle

Our objective is to protect software programs against DSOH. Considering the problems of DSOH unawareness and lack of attention, we have tried to make our solution as easy to implement as possible to facilitate general adoption by developers. Furthermore, our solution is intended to be used by advanced users to protect vulnerable programs when the software editor is not interested in fixing vulnerabilities in its own software, for instance. The source code of SLAHP is available on Github[1].

Our solution is designed to filter DLL loading attempts based on a security policy. Thus, the first step consists of loading the security policy, either from a remote HTTP server or from a cached file. To prevent threat actors from tampering with the security policy configuration file, either by using man-in-the-middle network attacks or simply by modifying it during initial access, we provide the option of digitally signing it. Once the authenticity and integrity of the security policy has been verified, SLAHP will intercept every attempt to load a DLL, i.e. every absolute path from which Windows tries to load a DLL, and allow or deny it based on whether or not the DLL complies with the security policy. An overall framework is illustrated in Fig. 2.

We used the Microsoft Detours library [8] to intercept DLL loading attempts. SLAHP specifically hooks the `NtQueryAttributesFile` function, a general-purpose semi-documented function of the Windows API used to retrieve information about files; this function also allows the DLL loading system to determine whether or not a DLL file with the desired name exists at each location of the search order. While using this unspecialised function as a way to intercept DLL loading attempts is not ideal, it gives us the ability to pretend the file does not exist by modifying the return value of the function. This way, our solution "blocks" DLL loading attempts that do not conform to the defined security policy. This approach allows potentially under-attack programs to continue operating normally: if the DLL does not exist from the program's point of view, the rest of the search order is inspected until a compliant DLL is found and loaded.

When SLAHP denies the loading of a DLL, it can either automatically attempt to fetch a potentially newer security policy from the software developer's remote server or simply prompt the end-user for the action they want to take, while informing them of the potentially dangerous situation: they can ignore the issue, abort execution or try to update the security policy in case a DLL got updated to a version that was not allowed by the cached security policy. An important aspect of this choice is that none of the provided options can have a negative security impact. Hence, an inattentive or frustrated user cannot be used as a vector for acquiring higher attack capabilities.

Finally, SLAHP has been designed to be able to protect programs that employ a multi-process architecture; this is often the case with web browsers and software using the Electron Framework or the Chromium Embedded Framework. This is accomplished by using inter-process communication operating system features such as events, shared memory and mutexes.

---

[1] https://github.com/lacaulac/SLAHP.

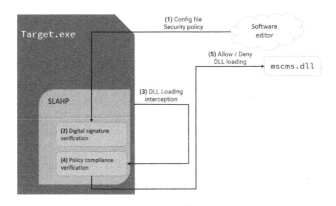

Fig. 2. Overall framework

4.2   Security Policy

The security policy for a given SLAHP-protected program is specified in a configuration file named `policy.cfg`. Its optional digital signature is contained by the `policy.cfg.sig` in base64 form. An example of such a configuration file is shown in Fig. 3. A configuration file is divided into two parts : the protection options and a list of allowed DLLs.

Every line of the allow-list defines a mapping between the name of an allowed DLL and one or more of its versions, each represented by a hash. In the example depicted in Fig. 3, two versions of `test_dll.dll` are allowed while only one version of `other_dll.dll` is permitted. By default any DLL not included in this list is denied.

In addition to the list of hashes of the allowed DLL, the current version of SLAHP provides three different protection options to change the default behavior to make it easier to write SLAHP configuration files. The first option is called `allowunspecified` and allows DLLs that are not explicitly listed in the list of allowed hashes to be accepted. In the case of Fig. 3, `test_dll.dll` and `other_dll.dll` should still match with the specified hashes. However, if the program requires `unspecified_dll.dll`, no constraint will apply to it. This option is interesting when the hash of a DLL is not known in advance which is the case for plugins or optional third-party dependencies.

The potential vulnerability introduced by enabling this option can be mitigated by using the `unspecifiedcantbeinlocaldirectory`, which prevents unknown DLLs to be loaded from the installation directory of the program, enforcing DLLs to be loaded only from files listed in the KnownDLLs registry key and files within the system directories, PATH directories and current working directory. Finally, the `signatureallowsbypass` configuration option can allow any DLL to be loaded regardless of the security policy as long as the DLL is signed using a valid code signing certificate. In the extreme case where an application and all of its dependencies are signed with a valid certificate, using this option would negate the need to define DLL hashes; however, this is far from the norm.

```
allowunspecified:yes
signatureallowsbypass:yes
unspecifiedcantbeinlocaldirectory:yes
test_dll.dll:[SHA-256],[SHA-256]
other_dll.dll:[SHA-256]
ENDCONFIG
```

```
InitProtector(L"SLAHP-UserAgent", L"soft-editor.net",
    L"/path/to/policy.cfg", useHttps, ignoreHttpsErrors,
    pubKey, useCache, useMultiProcess, hideFromUser);
```

Fig. 3. Example config file   **Fig. 4.** Calling InitProtector

4.3 Configuration Options

SLAHP also provides configuration options regarding how the security policy is obtained and the usage of certain specific behaviour options.

The first configuration options are the domain name and path to the security policy configuration file on the remote HTTP server and the desired user agent. Then, the developer/user can choose if they want SLAHP to communicate with the server using HTTPS and whether or not SLAHP should ignore HTTPS security errors (e.g. invalid X.509 chain of trust). If the security policy is signed, the issuer's public key must also be provided so that the integrity of the security policy configuration file can be verified. In order to avoid systematically relying on a remote server to obtain the security policy, which could lead to increased start-up delays as well as denial-of-service if the remote server can't be reached, the configuration file and its digital signature can optionally be stored locally.

Finally, the developer/user can also set whether or not the prompting for human decisions and the support for software using a multi-process architecture that are described in Sect. 4.1 should be enabled.

4.4 Integration Possibilities

SLAHP can integrate with new programs as a static library that can be added to the project during development (static integration) and with applications that are already compiled as a custom launcher (dynamic integration).

Static Integration. SLAHP is available as a static library (see Fig. 5) that can be added to any C/C++ project. Once this static library has been added to the project, SLAHP can be easily initialised by calling the `InitProtector` function, which takes as parameters the configuration options detailed in Sect. 4.3 as can be seen in Fig. 4. We recommend calling `InitProtector` as early as possible, as the filtering of DLL loading attempts only happens once SLAHP is initialised. If the developer is using the Microsoft Visual Studio compiler toolchain, using the delayed-loading [22] linking option wherever possible will help prevent DLLs from being loaded before SLAHP is initialised.

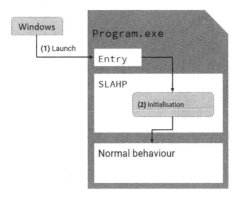

Fig. 5. Static library integration

Dynamic Integration. Our solution can also be used when the source code of the program is not available. We call this approach the dynamic integration, allowing virtually anyone to protect the software installed on their computer. This is also useful when the project is written in a language that does not provide any Foreign Function Interface that can work with our static library integration, or when SLAHP cannot be initialised before potentially vulnerable DLLs are loaded (e.g. packaged python software, Electron applications, etc.).

To accomplish this, the dynamic integration is separated in two components, as shown in Fig. 6. The first component is a SLAHP-protected launcher application that starts the target program in a suspended state (i.e. the program gets loaded into memory but no code execution takes place since all threads are suspended) and performs DLL Injection [20] on the target process, causing it to load the `ProtectorAgent`. Upon loading, the DLL will initialise SLAHP and resume the execution of the targeted process's thread(s).

We provide a secured launcher creator program whose task is to create a `Launcher.exe` & `ProtectorAgent.dll` file pair based on the configuration options described in Sect. 4.3. We decided to make the launcher creator work by patching the desired configuration options into pre-compiled binaries, making the presence of a compiler toolchain unnecessary to create a Launcher and a Protector Agent. This strategy makes our solution easier to use by non-developers.

A video demonstrating the dynamic integration of SLAHP with Microsoft Teams is available for watching[2].

4.5   Solution Evaluation

Security Analysis. Once it is initialised, SLAHP is able to successfully block any attempts of loading unauthorised DLLs. If we refer to the example described in Sect. 2.1, simply disallowing the loading of unspecified files in the security

---

[2] https://youtu.be/sb-lZN37tCg.

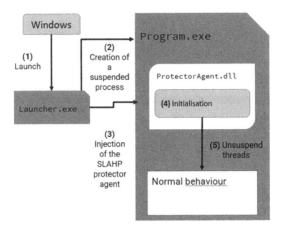

Fig. 6. Dynamic launcher-based integration

policy would mean the malicious file located in the installation folder does not comply with the policy. The DLL loading algorithm would thus ignore it and continue to inspect the next directories in the search order, where the genuine DLL should be found and loaded from.

As our solution aims at protecting software against DSOH attacks, we paid particular attention to minimise the attack surface of SLAHP. Since SLAHP depends on several libraries, we have built in security measures against DSOH. Firstly, the DLLs used by SLAHP are only loaded from system directories. We chose to trust the contents of these directories, because we are convinced that if an attacker were to gain the privileges to modify these directories, he would have access to much more advanced persistence capabilities. We also chose to load its dependencies using the delayed-loading [22] method to ensure the DLL origin restriction has been applied before any DLL can be loaded.

The integrity of the security policy is paramount, as its content dictates what DLLs can and cannot be loaded. An attacker may try to make SLAHP load an ineffective policy through Man-in-the-middle attacks when using HTTP(S) or by modifying the cached policy. However, our implementation provides an option to digitally sign the security policy and check its integrity before loading it.

Finally, regarding the integrity of SLAHP's code (i.e. the initialisation function or the launcher & protector agent library), our solution does not provide any protection against the modification of its compiled code by itself. Nonetheless, Code signature using Windows code sign certificates can overcome this issue.

Performance Evaluation. To assess the overall impact our solution can have on the performance of a protected software product, we considered the time taken by SLAHP to initialize and the overhead caused by the filtering of DLL loading attempts. For the initialisation time evaluation, we decided to consider only the cache-based loading, as retrieving a file from a remote server could introduce

Table 2. Performance impact - Startup time

	Unsigned security policy	Signed security policy
Time	1.01 ms	1.39 ms

Table 3. Performance impact - DLL load time

Policy situation	DLLs, by implicit dependencies	
	0	6
Unprotected (a)	0.16 ms	0.99 ms
Allow (hash-based) (b)	3.04 ms	3.4 ms
Disallow (hash-based) (c)	60.04 ms	59.32 ms
Allow (digital signature-based) (d)	11.88 ms	14.55 ms
Disallow (digital signature-based) (e)	67.58 ms	71.13 ms

delays through no fault of SLAHP. As detailed in Table 2, the average added delay is less than 2 ms, with little impact from verifying the digital signature of the security policy.

Regarding the evaluation of the efficiency of the DLL filtering mechanism, we decided to evaluate how fast DLLs were loaded in 5 different cases: (a) Without the protector, (b) Loading allowed if the DLL was compliant with the security policy because of its hash - no digital signature checks, (c) Loading blocked if the DLL was non-compliant with the security policy because of its hash - no digital signature checks, (d) Loading allowed if the DLL was compliant with the security policy because of its valid digital signature, but with an invalid hash, (e) Loading blocked if the DLL was non-compliant with the security policy because of both its hash and invalid digital signature.

An important aspect to consider in DLL loading is that any DLL can optionally depend on one or more DLL(s). In our performance tests, we only validate implicit (loaded before start) dependencies. Indeed, if a DLL needs to load other DLLs in order to complete its own loading, a higher number of dependencies will result in a longer overall load time. This is especially the case here, as each of these dependencies have to be verified by SLAHP; note that our tests always made the dependencies have a valid hash, so as not to skew the "block" results.

Table 3 shows the average load time for each of the 5 cases applied to two DLLs: one with no implicit dependencies and one with 6 implicit dependencies. Each test case was run 500 times for each DLL. Because the DLLs used to test the performance of our solution were written specifically for this task, they're only present in the installation directory of the performance test binary. Thus if a loading is blocked, looking for the file further down the search order will not yield any conclusive results but will still take a significant amount of time. This would generally not be the case when dealing with real-world DLLs, as most of the dependencies we've observed are already either in the application installation directory or in the system directories.

While the overhead introduced by our solution is proportionally significant, we can observe that during normal operation (i.e. no DLL gets blocked) the load time is always well under 50 ms, which would not be noticeable by the end-user.

5   Related Works

Min and Varadharajan [14] proposed a cross-verification mechanism which can be described as a bi-directional trust relationship between a caller and a callee (e.g. an executable and a DLL). The identity of a file is based on its digital signature, more precisely on the entity that signed the program. However, establishing mutual trust relationship at scale "may be hard", as per the author's own words.

Gates *et al.* [5] suggested adding an *installation mode* to Windows that requires a system reboot to be enabled. Only the binary files (e.g. .exe, .dll, etc.) that were created in the installation mode would be allowed to have their code executed. Nonetheless, it ultimately places the burden on users to avoid introducing malware on their computer. This is not a reasonable expectation, as social-engineering attacks are the easiest way for an APT to establish a foothold [10].

Wu and Yap [23] introduced the concept of "domains" for identifying binary files, with rules making domain-less binary files non-executable and to prevent files from different domains to tamper with each other. Their solution also employed an "install mode" mechanism that when enabled marked newly created files with the domain of the program that wrote them (as well as a special "temporary trusted" mode designed for software development and packed binary execution). The prerequisite for enabling the *install mode* is user authentication, with the same implications of potential social-engineering described before. However, correctly signed executables can be exempted which reduces the frequency of authentication, thus making users less tempted to authenticate without thinking about the implications.

Finally, Halim *et al.* [7] introduced a system-wide list of trusted software that covers all the file types containing executable code. This approach assigns identifiers to all binary files based on information such as their cryptographic hash, location, existing digital signature, etc. However, this system ultimately requires a qualified individual or entity to maintain the global allow list, which makes this approach incompatible with consumer use.

Conversely, our solution is easy to integrate, scalable thanks to per-program security policies (no administrator needed) and prevents social-engineering attacks, as user interactions cannot result in dangerous behaviour.

6   Conclusion and Future Work

We proposed SLAHP, a security solution against DLL Search Order Hijacking which can be easily and quickly integrated with both new and already existing software products. We conducted a survey on widely used programs that showed many of them are still vulnerable to DSOH. SLAHP provides Windows developers with a complete framework to protect their software products against DSOH. Additionally, they can continue choosing unsecure installation directories such as `AppData` to facilitate the installation process of their program without introducing new security issues. In addition, advanced users can also protect themselves should the editors of vulnerable software be indifferent. We assess the security as well as the performance, proving the feasibility of our solution.

There still are areas of our solution that could greatly benefit from further development and research. Indeed, we have observed that in certain cases, DLL loading attempts were made before SLAHP's initialisation which results in potential vulnerability; we believe the use of the `PreferSystem32` mitigation in SLAHP could solve this issue. As SLAHP is a proof-of-concept, some features are not currently as secure (e.g. IPC communications) or as configurable (i.e. No fine-grained configuration of `signatureallowsbypass`) as one would expect from a commercial software product.

In terms of long term research, we will extend the DLL Search Order Hijacking topic to low footprint attacks, in that they hide their malicious behaviour on infected systems behind the execution of trusted software, resulting in a very limited amount of indicators (e.g. dropped files). This is also the case of Living-off-the-Land (LotL) attacks, where threat actors abuse the features of trusted software components, chaining them together to accomplish their malicious activities without having to introduce new software components that could be subject to detection. In our ongoing research, we are delving deeper into the matter of LotL attacks and how we could detect them.

Acknowledgments. This work was partially supported by the European research projects H2020 CyberSec4Europe (GA 830929), LeaDS (GA 956562), Horizon Europe DUCA (GA 101086308), and CNRS EU-CHECK.

References

1. Chromium Docs - Chrome Security FAQ. https://chromium.googlesource.com/chromium/src/+/master/docs/security/faq.md
2. CrowdStrike: 2020 Global threat report (2020). https://go.crowdstrike.com/rs/281-OBQ-266/images/Report2020CrowdStrikeGlobalThreatReport.pdf
3. Faou, M.: Turla crutch: keeping the "back door" open (2020). https://www.welivesecurity.com/2020/12/02/turla-crutch-keeping-back-door-open/
4. Galvan, A., Nagaraju, S.S.: Triaging a DLL planting vulnerability | MSRC blog | microsoft security response center. https://msrc.microsoft.com/blog/2018/04/triaging-a-dll-planting-vulnerability/
5. Gates, C., Li, N., Chen, J., Proctor, R.: CodeShield: towards personalized application whitelisting. In: Proceedings of the 28th Annual Computer Security Applications Conference on - ACSAC 2012, p. 279. ACM Press, Orlando, Florida (2012)
6. Gatlan, S.: Realtek Fixes DLL Hijacking Flaw in HD Audio Driver for Windows (2020). https://www.bleepingcomputer.com/news/security/realtek-fixes-dll-hijacking-flaw-in-hd-audio-driver-for-windows/

7. Halim, F., Ramnath, R., Sufatrio, Wu, Y., Yap, R.H.C.: A lightweight binary authentication system for windows. In: Karabulut, Y., Mitchell, J., Herrmann, P., Jensen, C.D. (eds.) Trust Management II, vol. 263, pp. 295–310. Springer, Boston (2008). https://doi.org/10.1007/978-0-387-09428-1_19

8. Hunt, G., Brubacher, D.: Detours: Binary interception of win32 functions. In: Third USENIX Windows NT Symposium. p. 8. USENIX (1999). https://www.microsoft.com/en-us/research/publication/detours-binary-interception-of-win32-functions/

9. Karantzas, G., Patsakis, C.: An empirical assessment of endpoint detection and response systems against advanced persistent threats attack vectors. J. Cybersecur. Privacy **1**(3), 387–421 (2021)

10. Krombholz, K., Hobel, H., Huber, M., Weippl, E.: Advanced social engineering attacks. J. Inf. Secur. Appl. **22**, 113–122 (2015)

11. Lechtik, M., Rascagnères, P., Kayal, A.: LuminousMoth APT: Sweeping attacks for the chosen few. https://securelist.com/apt-luminousmoth/103332/

12. Malura, M.: Dll proxy generator. https://github.com/maluramichael/dll-proxy-generator. original-date: 2018-09-29T20:51:52Z

13. Microsoft: Windows 2000 security hardening guide: Security configuration. https://web.archive.org/web/20080323071041/https://www.microsoft.com/technet/security/prodtech/windows2000/win2khg/05sconfg.mspx#E6JBG

14. Min, B., Varadharajan, V.: Rethinking software component security: software component level integrity and cross verification. Comput. J. **59**(11), 1735–1748 (2016)

15. MITRE: Hijack Execution Flow: DLL Search Order Hijacking, Sub-technique T1574.001 - Enterprise | MITRE ATT&CK®. https://attack.mitre.org/techniques/T1574/001/

16. MITRE: Hijack Execution Flow: DLL Side-Loading, Sub-technique T1574.002 - Enterprise | MITRE ATT&CK®. https://attack.mitre.org/techniques/T1574/002/

17. National Vulnerability Database: NVD - CVE-2010-3129. https://nvd.nist.gov/vuln/detail/CVE-2010-3129

18. National Vulnerability Database: NVD - CVE-2010-3139. https://nvd.nist.gov/vuln/detail/CVE-2010-3139

19. Oliveira, D., Rosenthal, M., Morin, N., Yeh, K.C., Cappos, J., Zhuang, Y.: It's the psychology stupid: how heuristics explain software vulnerabilities and how priming can illuminate developer's blind spots. In: Proceedings of the 30th Annual Computer Security Applications Conference, pp. 296–305. ACM (2014)

20. Richter, J.: Load your 32 bit dll into another process's address space using injlib. Microsoft Syst. J. US Ed. 13–40 (1994)

21. Wheeler, S., Sherer, T.: Set-ProcessMitigation (ProcessMitigations). https://learn.microsoft.com/en-us/powershell/module/processmitigations/set-processmitigation

22. Whitney, T., et al.: Linker support for delay-loaded DLLs. https://learn.microsoft.com/en-us/cpp/build/reference/linker-support-for-delay-loaded-dlls

23. Wu, Y., Yap, R.H.C.: Simple and practical integrity models for binaries and files. In: Damsgaard Jensen, C., Marsh, S., Dimitrakos, T., Murayama, Y. (eds.) Trust Management IX. IFIPAICT, vol. 454, pp. 30–46. Springer, Cham (2015)

Poison Egg: Scrambling Federated Learning with Delayed Backdoor Attack

Masayoshi Tsutsui[✉], Tatsuya Kaneko, and Shinya Takamaeda-Yamazaki

Graduate School of Information Science and Technology, The University of Tokyo,
Bunkyo-ku, Tokyo 1138654, Japan
{tsutsui0344,tatsuya-kaneko,shinya}@is.s.u-tokyo.ac.jp

Abstract. Federated learning (FL) is a distributed machine learning method in which edge devices collaboratively train a global model without disclosing their private training data to others. Because many clients participate in FL, the global model is constantly exposed to the risk of attacks by malicious clients. In particular, backdoor attacks, which modify the global model to misclassify inputs with specific features, pose a significant threat. Feedback-based methods are regarded as effective defenses to achieve high robustness by monitoring the accuracy of the global model and rolling back its state if there is an abnormality. Against feedback-based methods, we propose Poison Egg, which is a delayed backdoor attack that scrambles the FL training process. Poison Egg exposes the vulnerability underlying the assumptions of feedback-based defense methods that model anomalies occur immediately after an attack. Poison Egg deceives feedback-based defenses by intentionally delaying the occurrence of anomalies. Through Poison Egg, we demonstrate the necessity of novel defense mechanisms against backdoor attacks in FL.

Keywords: Federated Learning · Deep Learning · Security · Backdoor Attacks · Model Poisoning

1 Introduction

Deep learning has achieved remarkable results in image recognition [13], natural language processing [18], and other domains [9,11,14]. With the evolution of hardware, low-power machine learning acceleration techniques (e.g., edge AI) have also become available. It is effective to utilize training samples obtained from edge devices to train such edge AIs. However, data collection from individual devices is undesirable in certain privacy-critical situations. Federated learning (FL) was proposed to address this problem. FL allows multiple edge device clients to train their models using their own training data and iteratively share and integrate the model parameters through the server. This method enables shared model training without directly accessing confidential client data. In particular, in cross-device settings with numerous clients, the server selects a subset of clients for each training round, thus rotating the clients. However, this setting carries the risk of model attacks by malicious clients.

G. Wang et al. (Eds.): UbiSec 2023, CCIS 2034, pp. 191–204, 2024.
https://doi.org/10.1007/978-981-97-1274-8_13

Backdoor attacks, specifically those that modify a model to misclassify inputs with specific features, are significant threats, and numerous corresponding defense methods have been studied [1–3,16]. Among these defense methods, the feedback-based approach, in which validation clients monitor the model's accuracy and roll back the model's state based on abnormality reports, is a robust defense mechanism that balances security and privacy preservation. However, feedback-based approaches assume that model anomalies occur immediately after an attack. Therefore, rolling back the model for only one round is considered sufficient to restore the model to its pre-attack state.

In this study, we challenge this assumption and propose Poison Egg, a novel backdoor attack method that introduces delays between attacks and the occurrence of model anomalies. Poison Egg bypasses existing feedback-based defenses and significantly scrambles the FL training process. Therefore, we introduce a new perspective for addressing backdoor attacks in FL.

2   Related Work

2.1   Federated Averaging

In the field of federated learning, Federated Averaging (FedAvg) [12] is a common approach.

First, all clients and the server keep the same models filled with the same initial parameters. Subsequently, partial clients are selected to participate in training, and the selected clients start updating the parameters using their local data. After updating the parameters several times, each client sends their gradients (the difference between the parameters before and after updating) to the server. The server averages the gradients and updates the global model with them. This new model is sent to newly selected clients, who start updating the parameters. A global model is developed by repeating this procedure as a training round. The left picture in Fig. 1 also depicts the overview of the FedAvg algorithm.

2.2   Backdoor Attack

Backdoor attacks [6] refer to intentional attacks on deep learning models, primarily where the model's parameters are maliciously modified to cause misclassification only for inputs with specific features. The typical steps involved in realizing this attack are as follows:

1. Prepare a backdoor dataset in which input images with specific features (triggers) are labeled with an incorrect target label that induces misclassification.
2. Train the model using mini-batches of mix-ups of the regular training dataset and backdoor dataset prepared in Step 1).

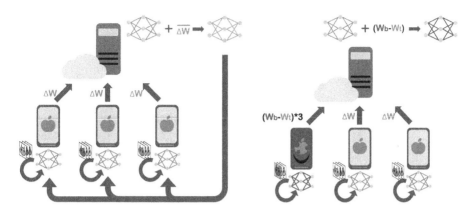

Fig. 1. The procedure overviews of FL (left) and backdoor attack in FL (right), where ΔW represents the updates of the model parameters. Backdoor attackers try to replace the global model with the contaminated model W_b.

Following these steps, a contaminated model that misclassifies only for inputs with triggers is built while maintaining main-task performance for clean inputs.

2.3 Backdoor Attack in FL

In the context of FL, the backdoor attacker is one of the clients and aims to transform the global model on the server into a contaminated model. One of the major methods for achieving this is model replacement [3]. The right picture in Fig. 1 shows an overview of this method. The specific steps involved are as follows:

1. Wait until the later training stages, when the parameter fluctuations have settled.
2. Perform trigger-mixed training, as described in Sect. 2.2, on the global model W_t loaded from the server, creating a contaminated model W_b.
3. Submit $N(W_b - W_t)$ as the model update to the server, where N represents the number of participating clients.

In the later training stages, the submitted parameter updates for each benign client are small, and their sum is close to zero. Therefore, including the attacker, the sum of the submitted updates from all clients can be approximated as $N(W_b - W_t)$. The server divides this value by the number of clients (taking the average) to update the global model. Therefore, the update procedure of the global model executed on the server is as follows.

$$\textbf{Premise}: \sum_{i=1}^{N-1} \Delta W_i \approx 0 \quad \text{(for each benign client } i)$$

$$W_{t+1} = W_t + \frac{1}{N}\sum_{i=1}^{N}\Delta W_i \tag{1}$$

$$= W_t + \frac{1}{N}(\sum_{i=1}^{N-1}\Delta W_i + N(W_b - W_t)) \tag{2}$$

$$\approx W_t + (W_b - W_t)(\because \textbf{Premise}) \tag{3}$$

$$= W_b \tag{4}$$

As a result, the attacker can transform the global model into an arbitrary one (W_b).

Backdoor attacks are particularly stealthy among the attacks on FL systems because FL principles prioritize preserving client privacy, making it impossible to directly verify whether each client is performing malicious training, as the content of their learning is not accessible. Thus, most defense methods against FL backdoor attacks adopt a non-intrusive approach, avoiding direct client intervention.

2.4   Defense Methods Against FL Backdoor Attacks

There are two main approaches for defending against backdoor attacks in FL. One approach is server-side anomaly detection on the model update submitted by clients [2,3,16]. The other is a feedback-based defense on the client side, where anomaly detection is performed based on the inference accuracy of the global model [1].

Server-Side Inspection Defenses. Server-side anomaly detection on model updates submitted by clients is a prevalent defense against backdoor attacks in FL. Techniques such as norm clipping, in which an update with large norms is scaled down before model aggregation in the server [3,16], and measuring the cosine distance between each client's update for anomaly detection [2] are used. Because these methods allow the server to scrutinize raw model updates, there is a risk of client information leakage.

Indeed, an attack method to reconstruct training data from model updates submitted by clients is proposed in [20]. The rough procedure is as follows. Firstly, the malicious server calculates dummy global model updates using random images and labels. Then, it calculates the difference between these dummy updates and the updates submitted by the client. Finally, updating the random images and labels to minimize this difference turns the images into the client's original ones. Such reconstruction attack is refined in subsequent research [19] and has also been applied not only to image classification but also to the field of natural language processing [4,7]. Thus, it is unfavorable to allow the server to see raw model updates from clients.

Feedback-Based Defenses. Feedback-based methods, which perform anomaly detection on the model's inference accuracy using clients are considered reliable defense approaches. One notable method, BAFFLE [1], operates under the assumption that backdoor attacks cause test accuracy fluctuations in the global model, even if there are no trigger data in the test dataset. BAFFLE is based on the setting in which each client maintains their private test data. The clients monitor the per-class accuracy changes in two types of misclassification rates: source-focused error (the rate at which data belonging to a specific class are misclassified into other classes) and target-focused error (the rate at which data belonging to other classes are misclassified into a specific class). BAFFLE uses Local Outlier Factor (LOF) [5] to determine whether the observed changes were anomalous. The clients that detect anomalies report them to the server. With a certain number of reports in a round, the server rolls back the global model state to the previous round and resumes training. Such feedback-based defenses are robust because they monitor the direct target of the attack, that is, changes in the inference accuracy of the global model. Furthermore, when combined with secure aggregation methods such as VerifyNet [17], in which clients can submit encrypted model updates while ensuring correct computation of the global model, it is possible to prevent the reconstruction of training data information from the updates.

3   Practical Feedback-Based Defense

When considering the practical implementation of FL, feedback-based defenses are preferable compared to server-side inspection defenses. This is because server-side inspections carry a critical risk of training data reconstruction from the model updates, which directly conflicts with FL's fundamental principle of ensuring privacy protection.

However, even in BAFFLE, the representative feedback-based defense method, there are some practical inconveniences, although not fatal, as listed below:

- Because BAFFLE uses LOF in anomaly detection, which relies on the "changes" in accuracy, significant accuracy improvement may also be regarded as an anomaly.
- It is difficult to set hyperparameters to minimize false negatives and false positives.

Furthermore, BAFFLE assumes that the test dataset contains no data with backdoor triggers. This assumption can be seen as one of BAFFLE's strengths since it can detect attacks even without the trigger data. However, this assumption seems unnatural because it implies that the attacker injects a backdoor into data that no one possesses. From the attacker's perspective, it should launch attacks on a trigger that appears in the data actually held by the clients. Furthermore, when considering what triggers would lead to the most severe attacks, it is likely a trigger that frequently appears in the data held by a few clients rather than many clients. Suppose the attacker selects trigger patterns associated with the data commonly held by many clients. In that case, there is a risk that the attack's impact will be limited because correctly labeled trigger data will frequently be mixed into the training process. In addition, it is natural to assume the existence of such triggers under non-i.i.d. data distribution in FL.

Given such inconveniences of BAFFLE and the attacker's motivation, we define another algorithm that follows the same feedback-based structure as BAFFLE but incorporates the following modifications to achieve practical simplicity and ease of implementation.

1. Validation clients measure the global model's per-class accuracy every round.
2. If any class's accuracy degradation from the previous round exceeds a certain threshold, the client reports it to the server.
3. If at least one report exists, the server rolls back the global model by one round and resumes training.

The intention behind the third modification, the strict criterion to perform a rollback, is to ensure the detection of attacks targeting triggers that frequently appear in data owned by a few clients. This algorithm achieves simplicity and robustness by restricting the range of triggers to be cautious and deliberately using a simple anomaly criterion. If we were to highlight one vulnerability of this approach, it would be the risk of false anomaly reports from malicious validation clients attempting to hinder the FL training process. However, if the same client repeatedly reports an anomaly, the server's suspicion will naturally fall on it. Therefore, the threat level of this vulnerability is negligible.

Henceforth, we refer to this algorithm as the Check & Rollback method.

4 Proposal

4.1 Assumption Underlying Feedback-Based Defenses

Feedback-based defenses, such as BAFFLE and Check & Rollback, are based on the assumption that the global model's accuracy shows anomalies immediately after the attack. Naturally, this assumption is reasonable. If an attacker submits harmful model updates and takes no action in subsequent rounds, the model's misclassification rate on the triggers will be at its highest immediately after the attack. Subsequently, it gradually decreases or remains stable, but it cannot increase beyond that point.

However, suppose this assumption is incorrect and that it is possible to introduce one or more rounds of delay between the attack and anomalies into the model's accuracy. In this case, attackers can evade the feedback-based defense and scramble the FL training process.

Specifically, the following phenomena can occur, as shown in Fig. 2:

– One-round rollback cannot bring the model back to its pre-attack state, and the anomaly reoccurs in subsequent rounds.

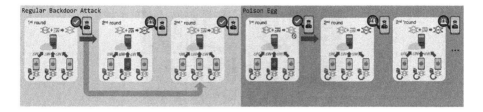

Fig. 2. How delayed backdoor attacks scramble FL compared to regular backdoor attacks.

– Validation clients with trigger data are led to submit reports repeatedly, raising suspicions from the server.

This study aimed to demonstrate that delayed backdoor attacks can be created by carefully manipulating model updates. These attacks introduce a new perspective on mitigating backdoor attacks in FL and emphasize the need for further research on FL backdoor defense.

4.2 Backdoor Revival

This study leverages an interesting phenomenon, "backdoor revival," as discussed in previous research on backdoor attacks in FL [3]. When an attack is launched, the global model's misclassification rate on triggers initially rises significantly, then drops sharply and gradually increases.

While the authors of [3] did not deeply analyze this phenomenon, they helped delay backdoor attacks if the phenomenon was reproducible. In particular, suppose that an attacker can predict the model parameters when the misclassification rate decreases significantly. If the attacker performs model replacement with the parameters at this point, they can create a phenomenon in which the misclassification rate is initially low and then spontaneously increases through the training rounds.

We conducted experiments under the following settings to investigate the reproducibility of this backdoor revival phenomenon. We performed FL using the CIFAR-10 [10] dataset, which consists of 50,000 RGB images for training and 10,000 images for testing, with a ResNet-18 [8] model. The training data were distributed equally among 100 clients, and 10 random clients participated in each round. The attacker's objective, which was the only malicious client among the 100 clients, was to cause the global model to misclassify car images with black and yellow striped backgrounds as an incorrect target class. While [3] also experimented with backdoors using green cars and cars with striped bodies, the black and yellow striped background yielded the most prominent revival tendency; therefore, we adopted this trigger in our experiments. We conducted experiments for all classes other than cars as misclassification targets.

The attack was performed after 1,000 rounds when the accuracy sufficiently converged. SGD was used as the optimizer for training. Benign clients used a

Fig. 3. The left four are trigger images in CIFAR-10, while the right four are created by Stable Diffusion.

learning rate of 0.1, while attackers used a learning rate of 0.025. The momentum and weight decay values were 0.9 and 0.0005, respectively. Benign clients trained for 2 epochs per round, while the attacker trained for 3. The batch size was set to 64. The attacker mixed seven images with triggers, each perturbed by Gaussian noise with a standard deviation of 0.05, in every mini-batch during training. In addition, in [3], the misclassification rate of the global model was measured using 1,000 randomly cropped and rotated versions of three trigger images in CIFAR-10. However, we deemed this evaluation unsuitable for explaining the generalizability of the phenomenon. Instead, we created 100 images with triggers using Stable Diffusion [15], as shown in Fig. 3, and measured the misclassification rate of the global model on these images. The left graph in Fig. 4 illustrates the ship-targeted backdoor results, which showed the backdoor revival most clearly among all target classes. The graph shows that the misclassification rate initially drops sharply after the 15th-round attack but then increases rapidly.

In the experiment conducted in [3], several rounds were required after the attack until the misclassification rate increased. In contrast, our experiment showed a rapid decrease and increase in the misclassification rate in one round. This discrepancy could be attributed to differences in the experimental settings, including the trigger data used for evaluation. Nonetheless, based on these results, we acknowledge the reproducibility of the backdoor revival phenomenon and aimed to use it to create delayed backdoor attacks.

4.3   Poison Egg

As mentioned in Sect. 4.2, the backdoor attack causes a sharp drop in the global model, followed by an increase in the misclassification rate. By predicting and replicating the global model parameters when this drop occurs, an attacker can create a scenario in which the misclassification rate is initially low and then increases automatically as illustrated in the right graph in Fig. 4. To establish how to predict these parameters, we review what happens to the global model after a backdoor attack step by step.

First, the global model parameters in the attack round are close to the contaminated ones that the attacker created at hand, as explained in Sect. 2.3. In the

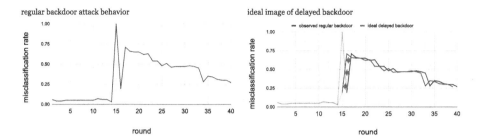

Fig. 4. The red lines in both graphs show the misclassification rate on 100 trigger images measured in the experiment. After the attack on the 15th round, the misclassification rate sharply drops once. At the attacking round, if the attacker could drive the global model parameters to be those at the sharp drop, the red line would shift left by one round; that is, the rate would behave like the blue line in the right graph to be an ideal delayed backdoor. (Color figure online)

next round, when the misclassification rate drops, the global model is updated based only on the submitted updates from benign clients, as the attacker does not participate in the round. To replicate these effects on the model within the capabilities of a single attacker, the most straightforward method would likely be as shown in Algorithm 1. The outline of the algorithm is as follows:

1. Train the local model with the training data containing the triggers.
2. Perform additional model training with clean training data that contain no trigger.
3. Perform model replacement on the global model with the model after Step 2).

Step 2) tries to replicate the effects of benign clients that the global model experiences one round after an attack. For simplicity, we assume that the amount of training data is the same as that of the benign clients in Steps 1) and 2).

We named this method Poison Egg, drawing an analogy to the scenario in which eggs hatch with a time delay.

5 Experiments

We conducted experiments to verify the behavior of Poison Egg.

5.1 Experimental Setup

We performed FL using the CIFAR-10 [10] dataset, which contains 50,000 RGB training images and 10,000 testing images, with a ResNet-18 [8] model. The training data were distributed equally among 100 clients, and 10 random clients participated in every round. The attacker's objective, which was the only malicious client among the 100 clients, was to cause the global model to misclassify automobile images with black and yellow striped backgrounds as ship class.

Algorithm 1. The procedure of Poison Egg performed by the attacker. The meaning of each variable is as follows. $\mathcal{L}$: classification loss, $\nabla\mathcal{L}$: gradients calculated from $\mathcal{L}$, W_t : global model parameters in t-th round, N : the number of clients selected in a round, E_{BD} : local epochs in backdoor train, η : learning rate, τ_{clean} : threshold of classification loss to stop clean training, D_{BD} : trigger images with target labels, D_{clean} : regular images with correct labels, D_{BD_test} : trigger images with target labels not used in training

---

procedure PoisonEggUpdate(W_t)
    $W_{backdoor} \leftarrow$ BACKDOOR_TRAIN(W_t, D_{BD}, D_{clean})
    $W_{egg} \leftarrow$ CLEAN_TRAIN($W_{backdoor}, D_{clean}, D_{BD\_test}$)
    return $N(W_{egg} - W_t)$
end procedure

function BACKDOOR_TRAIN(W, D_{BD}, D_{clean})
    $D_{mix} \leftarrow$ (mix D_{BD} and D_{clean})
    $\mathcal{B} \leftarrow$ (split D_{mix} into mini-batches)
    for epoch i from 1 to E_{BD} **do**
        for mini-batch $b \in \mathcal{B}$ **do**
            $W \leftarrow W - \eta_{BD}\nabla\mathcal{L}(W; b)$
        end for
    end for
    return W
end function

function CLEAN_TRAIN($W, D_{clean}, D_{BD\_test}$)
    $\mathcal{B} \leftarrow$ (split D_{clean} into mini-batches)
    while True **do**
        for mini-batch $b \in \mathcal{B}$ **do**
            $W \leftarrow W - \eta_{clean}\nabla\mathcal{L}(W; b)$
            $\mathcal{L}_{BD\_test} \leftarrow \mathcal{L}(W, D_{BD\_test})$
            if $\mathcal{L}_{BD\_test} \geq \tau_{clean}$ **then**
                return W
            end if
        end for
    end while
end function

The attack was performed after 1,000 rounds when the accuracy sufficiently converged. The test data were divided equally among 10 validation clients, with one client having all their automobile images replaced with 100 trigger images generated by Stable Diffusion. We also investigated the impact of applying the Check & Rollback method defined in Sect. 3 as a defense mechanism. We tested three different thresholds for per-class accuracy changes (0.1, 0.15, and 0.2) to examine the differences in their behavior. In addition, experiments were conducted to demonstrate the effectiveness of the Check & Rollback method when applied to a regular backdoor attack.

For benign clients, the hyperparameters were the same as those described in Sect. 4.2. For the attacker, hyperparameters used in training Step 1) described in Sect. 4.3 were the same as those described in Sect. 4.2. However, in the clean training Step 2), we used the following hyperparameters: SGD optimizer with a learning rate of 0.1, momentum of 0.9, weight decay of 0.0005, and batch size of 64. To decide when to stop updating the parameters in Step 2), the attacker utilized five trigger images that were not used in Step 1). Specifically, for every update with one mini-batch, the attacker calculated the loss of the model for these five images. If the loss exceeded 5.0, the attacker terminated the update process in Step 2).

5.2   Results

First, we verified whether Poison Egg could delay the backdoor by applying the defense method. The results are presented in Fig. 5, which compares the misclassification rate for the trigger between the regular backdoor attack and Poison Egg, both of which were conducted in the 15th round. It can be observed that the backdoor activation is indeed delayed by one round. Moreover, the misclassification rate decreased faster in the delayed backdoor attack than in the regular one.

Next, we compare the behavior of the misclassification rate when applying the Check & Rollback defense method (abnormality threshold of accuracy change is 0.2) to the regular backdoor attack and Poison Egg. The left graph in Fig. 6 illustrates a scenario of a regular backdoor attack. In this scenario, backdoor activation was detected immediately, causing the model to be rolled back and cleansed thoroughly. In contrast, in the Poison Egg scenario, as shown in the right graph in Fig. 6, the attacker successfully bypassed the defense method at the attacked round. The backdoor was activated one round later, causing a model rollback for that round owing to the defense method. However, because the attack occurred one round earlier, the state of the model could only be rolled back to that immediately after the attack. Consequently, a loop of backdoor activation and rollback occurs, leading to scrambling in the FL training process.

Finally, we examined the influence of different accuracy thresholds used in the Check & Rollback defense method on Poison Egg, as shown in Table 1. We tested three thresholds: 0.1, 0.15, and 0.2. For each value, we varied the random seed five times. We recorded the percentage of overlooked anomalies in the attacking round as the false negative rate and the percentage of rounds in which anomalies were detected before the attack as the false positive rate. A lower threshold leads to stricter anomaly detection.

When the threshold was set to 0.1, the Poison Egg was completely detected and cleansed during the attack round. However, a high false positive rate indicates that rollbacks occur frequently, even in rounds unrelated to the attack. Meanwhile, setting the threshold to 0.15 or higher reduces the false positive rate. However, it fails to reduce the false negative rate to zero, overlooking the Poison Egg at the attacking round. Consequently, the FL process is driven to confusion, as shown in Fig. 5.

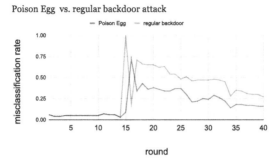

Fig. 5. Comparison between regular backdoor attack and Poison Egg. Both attacks occur in the 15th round, but Poison Egg shows a delay before the misprediction rate increases.

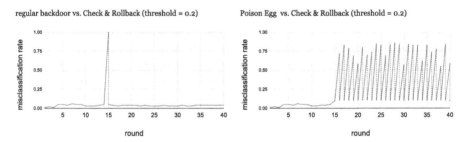

Fig. 6. Misclassification rate when applying Check & Rollback to the regular backdoor attack (left) and Poison Egg (right). The abnormality threshold of accuracy change is 0.2.

It is anticipated that fine-tuning the threshold may lower both the false positive and false negative rates. Nevertheless, it can be susceptible, depending on the dataset.

Furthermore, we emphasize that this attack method has room for refinement. Attackers possess only a few trigger images, the dataset size is only approximately twice that of the regular clients, and the hyperparameters require further research. Therefore, it is practically impossible to prevent Poison Egg by adjusting the accuracy threshold.

6   Discussion on Defense Mechanisms Against Poison Egg

An effective countermeasure against Poison Egg is to roll back two or more rounds in the Check & Rollback defense. However, this countermeasure assumes that the backdoor delay is limited to one round, as observed in the experiment. If we could find more than one round of delayed backdoor activation, the rollback rounds would need to be adjusted accordingly.

We believe that the number of delayed rounds depends heavily on the time required for the misclassification rate to decrease and recover in the regular back-

Table 1. Detection and false detection of Poison Egg based on different anomaly detection thresholds.

Threshold	False positive(%)	False negative(%)
0.1	**64.6**	**0.0**
0.15	**1.5**	**20.0**
0.2	**0**	**80.0**

door attack scenario. Therefore, if we identify the conditions for manipulating the number of rounds until backdoor revival, performing Poison Egg with an even greater delay would be possible. A previous study observed phenomena in which the backdoor required more than two rounds to revive [3].

7   Conclusion

Among the defense methods against backdoor attacks in FL, feedback-based defense methods are robust approaches that balance privacy protection and security. In this paper, we proposed Poison Egg, a delayed backdoor attack method that aims to expose the vulnerability underlying the assumption of feedback-based defense methods. called the Check & Rollback approach, which provides a more reasonable and effective defense strategy. Through experiments, we demonstrated that Poison Egg significantly scrambled the training process against the Check & Rollback approach, a practical feedback-based defense method.

Poison Egg pointed out the vulnerability in the common understanding of FL backdoor attacks; that is, the increase in misclassification rates triggered by attacks occurs immediately after the attacks. This highlights the necessity of introducing new perspectives to defend against backdoor attacks on FL.

Acknowledgments. This work was supported in part by JST CREST JPMJCR21D2.

References

1. Andreina, S., Marson, G.A., Möllering, H., Karame, G.: Baffle: backdoor detection via feedback-based federated learning. In: 2021 IEEE 41st International Conference on Distributed Computing Systems (ICDCS), pp. 852–863. IEEE (2021)
2. Awan, S., Luo, B., Li, F.: Contra: defending against poisoning attacks in federated learning. In: Bertino, E., Shulman, H., Waidner, M. (eds.) ESORICS 2021 Part I 26. LNCS, vol. 12972, pp. 455–475. Springer, Cham (2021). https://doi.org/10.1007/978-3-030-88418-5_22
3. Bagdasaryan, E., Veit, A., Hua, Y., Estrin, D., Shmatikov, V.: How to backdoor federated learning. In: International Conference on Artificial Intelligence and Statistics, pp. 2938–2948. PMLR (2020)
4. Balunović, M., Dimitrov, D.I., Jovanović, N., Vechev, M.: Lamp: extracting text from gradients with language model priors (2022)

5. Breunig, M.M., Kriegel, H.P., Ng, R.T., Sander, J.: Lof: identifying density-based local outliers. In: Proceedings of the 2000 ACM SIGMOD International Conference on Management of Data, pp. 93–104 (2000)
6. Chen, X., Liu, C., Li, B., Lu, K., Song, D.: Targeted backdoor attacks on deep learning systems using data poisoning. arXiv preprint arXiv:1712.05526 (2017)
7. Deng, J., et al.: Tag: gradient attack on transformer-based language models. arXiv preprint arXiv:2103.06819 (2021)
8. He, K., Zhang, X., Ren, S., Sun, J.: Deep residual learning for image recognition. In: Proceedings of the IEEE Conference on Computer Vision and Pattern Recognition, pp. 770–778 (2016)
9. Kamilaris, A., Prenafeta-Boldú, F.X.: Deep learning in agriculture: a survey. Comput. Electron. Agric. **147**, 70–90 (2018)
10. Krizhevsky, A., Hinton, G., et al.: Learning multiple layers of features from tiny images (2009)
11. Litjens, G., et al.: A survey on deep learning in medical image analysis. Med. Image Anal. **42**, 60–88 (2017)
12. McMahan, B., Moore, E., Ramage, D., Hampson, S., y Arcas, B.A.: Communication-efficient learning of deep networks from decentralized data. In: Artificial Intelligence and Statistics, pp. 1273–1282. PMLR (2017)
13. Milz, S., Arbeiter, G., Witt, C., Abdallah, B., Yogamani, S.: Visual slam for automated driving: exploring the applications of deep learning, pp. 247–257 (2018)
14. Min, S., Lee, B., Yoon, S.: Deep learning in bioinformatics. Brief. Bioinform. **18**(5), 851–869 (2017)
15. Rombach, R., Blattmann, A., Lorenz, D., Esser, P., Ommer, B.: High-resolution image synthesis with latent diffusion models. In: Proceedings of the IEEE/CVF Conference on Computer Vision and Pattern Recognition, pp. 10684–10695 (2022)
16. Sun, Z., Kairouz, P., Suresh, A.T., McMahan, H.B.: Can you really backdoor federated learning? arXiv preprint arXiv:1911.07963 (2019)
17. Xu, G., Li, H., Liu, S., Yang, K., Lin, X.: Verifynet: secure and verifiable federated learning. IEEE Trans. Inf. Forensics Secur. **15**, 911–926 (2020). https://doi.org/10.1109/TIFS.2019.2929409
18. Young, T., Hazarika, D., Poria, S., Cambria, E.: Recent trends in deep learning based natural language processing. IEEE Comput. Intell. Mag. **13**(3), 55–75 (2018)
19. Zhao, B., Mopuri, K.R., Bilen, H.: idlg: improved deep leakage from gradients. arXiv preprint arXiv:2001.02610 (2020)
20. Zhu, L., Liu, Z., Han, S.: Deep leakage from gradients. In: Advances in Neural Information Processing Systems, vol. 32 (2019)

Channel Spatio-Temporal Convolutional Network for Trajectory Prediction

Zhonghao Lu, Lina Xu, Ying Hu, Liping Sun, and Yonglong Luo[✉]

Ahnu Normal University, 189 Jiuhua South Road, Yijiang District, Wuhu City, China
ylluo@ustc.edu.cn

Abstract. Accurate and timely prediction of the future path of agents in the vicinity of an agent is the core of avoiding conflict in automated applications. The traditional method based on RNN model requires high computational cost in the process of prediction, especially for long series prediction. In order to obtain more efficient and accurate prediction trajectory, a channel spatio-temporal convolutional network framework, called CSTCN, is proposed in this paper. The framework models the spatial environment as a block of data input to the CSTCN and captures spatio-temporal interactions using an improved temporal convolutional network. Compared with the traditional model, the spatial and temporal modeling of the proposed model is calculated in each local time window so that it can be executed in parallel to obtain higher computational efficiency. Experimental results on 5 trajectory prediction benchmark datasets demonstrate that the proposed model is superior to other seven state-of-the-art models in both efficiency and accuracy.

Keywords: Channel attention · trajectory prediction · convolutional network

1 Introduction

Understanding human motion is essential for intelligent systems to coexist and interact with humans. In recent years, pedestrian trajectory prediction has received increasing attention in various application domains, such as autonomous driving vehicles [1], service robot navigation [2] and advanced surveillance systems [3]. In these applications, due to the interaction between pedestrians, agents must respond promptly and accurately to the environment to avoid collisions. Hence, agents should be equipped with ability of predicting the future path of their neighbors (neighboring pedestrian) efficiently and accurately.

Pedestrian trajectory prediction aims to model the temporal and spatial information of targets based on the positional and semantic attribute information during the past time, and then predicts a series of position coordinates of

This research was funded by the National Natural Science Foundation of China (Grant number 62272006), Natural Science Foundation of Anhui Province (Grant No. 2108085MF214) and the University Collaborative Innovation Project of Anhui Province (grant number GXXT-2022-049).

pedestrians in the future. However, the potential semantic information in the environment and the complex interactions among pedestrians make pedestrian trajectory prediction existing extremely challenges [4–6], especially for pedestrian trajectory prediction problem oriented to the interaction between pedestrians and complex environments. For example, people tend to take the ideal path that is convenient and comfortable [7], pedestrians in the back tend to follow the movement direction of pedestrians in front [8], and the performance of pedestrians walking in groups is different from that of pedestrians walking alone [9]. In addition, pedestrians will make behaviors that meet their own needs based on the current surrounding environment. For instance, if there are neighboring pedestrian in the direction of the destination in front of the pedestrian who block the forward path, the pedestrian will often choose to go around to the open area. At this time, it is imperative to avoid collision.

Due to the randomness, diversity and complexity of pedestrian trajectory prediction, the traditional polynomial fitting methods often fail to meet practical requirements. In recent years, data-driven approaches have gradually attracted extensive attention from scholars. Among them, recurrent neural networks (RNNs) have shown promise in capturing pedestrian behavior [8,10,11]. However, RNN models suffer from the problem of "gradient vanishing and explosion", as well as lower training and forecasting efficiency compared to convolutional neural networks (CNNs). In contrast, the time convolutional neural network (TCN) based on the improved CNN does not rely on the previous input and hidden state when processing sequence tasks [6]. Recent researches have used TCN to predict trajectory tasks and achieved satisfactory results [12,13]. However, none of these researches take into account the interaction between pedestrians and their surroundings.

Furthermore, Kitani et al. [9] have confirmed that knowledge based on static environment semantics is helpful to predict the trajectory of pedestrians in the future instant more accurately, compared with the model that ignores scene information. Subsequently, scene information was incorporated into the prediction process of some researches [14,15]. However, these researches often define the perception range of the main pedestrian as global when modeling the interaction between pedestrians and space, and do not consider the scenario in which pedestrians selectively pay attention to "key" information in a complex environment.

In this paper, a channel spatio-temporal convolutional network for pedestrian trajectory prediction method is proposed to consider pedestrian perception modeling and channel attention mechanism in complex environment. Among them, pedestrian perception modeling is used to generate multi-channel spatial feature data to assist modeling. Channel attention is used to simulate pedestrians' attention to multi-channel information at every moment.

2   Related Works

2.1   Pedestrian Trajectory Prediction Method Based on Deep Learning

Social long short-term memory networks (Social-LSTM) is one of the earliest deep models used for pedestrian trajectory prediction [11]. In order to improve the computational efficiency of the model, Gupta et al. [16] proposed a Social GAN model based on RNN. Xu et al. [17] designed a crowd interaction deep neural network framework (CIDNN), which introduces spatial correlation to represent the impact degree of other pedestrians on the pedestrians. Song et al. [14] also used cellular neural networks to generate multi-channel spatial features and used a deep LSTM model (Conv-LSTM) to predict trajectories. However, RNN-based models are susceptible to the "gradient vanishing and explosion" problem, which will affect the prediction accuracy and efficiency of the model.

In order to overcome the shortcomings, a trajectory prediction method based on CNNs was proposed in reference [18], and achieved good results in long sequence tasks. Nikhil et al. [12] proposed a fast CNN-based trajectory prediction model by mapping the fixed-length input trajectory to the complete trajectory in the future. Mohamed et al. [13] firstly carried out spatio-temporal convolution operations on the trajectory graph to obtain a compact representation of pedestrian trajectory history. Furthermore, Wang et al. [19] designed the GraphTCN prediction model and achieved satisfactory results, where spatial and temporal interaction is modeled using improved TCN. However, the above researches did not consider the typical scenario that pedestrians pay different attention to multi-channel information at different times.

2.2   Environmental Clues for Pedestrian Trajectory Prediction

Most clues used to predict a pedestrian's future state are related to the pedestrian himself. Earlier work mainly used the current position and velocity of the subject pedestrian as the input of the prediction model [20–22]. Considering additional semantic attributes of subject pedestrians can improve the quality of model prediction [15,23]. In order to further improve the accuracy, many researches have incorporated interactions between pedestrians into the investigation clues. Farina et al. [24] improved the traditional social force model by adding heading forces and torques. Ikeda et al. [25] modeled pedestrian routes as a series of decision points affected by the surrounding environment structure to obtain sub-goals of direction retrieval. However, the above methods are highly dependent on hand-crafted features and are designed to model interactions and physical constraints between pedestrians in certain scenarios. Therefore, its practicability is limited to some extent.

Deep learning is able to learn from rich data and automatically extract features to overcome the shortcomings. Shi et al. [26] used the spatio-temporal graph as input to score the spatial and temporal interaction generated by pedestrians. Song et al. [14] define the perception range of pedestrians as a certain area centered on themselves, and use grid maps to abstract the spatial features of pedestrians as multi-channel tensors. However, most pedestrian clues are global, and it is neglected that pedestrians should pay more attention to the neighboring pedestrians and the environment information in the observation range during movement.

2.3 Channel Attention

References [27] firstly proposed a visual attention mechanism to model the importance of features in image captioning tasks. Subsequently, a large number of methods began to use attention mechanisms to assist modeling. Wang et al. [28] proposed a residual attention network that uses a mixed attention mechanism based on down-sampling and up-sampling to better guide feature learning. Hu et al. [29] first proposed a squeeze-extent (SE) module, which can adaptively recalibrate the channel feature response through the interdependence between model channels. Based on this, Wang et al. [30] incorporated the self-attention mechanism into the Non-local Networks (NLNet) network to provide pairs of interactive information on video classification tasks. Shu et al. [31] simultaneously used self-attention LSTM and multi-scale convolutional jump LSTM to build a deep network architecture in a complementary form. The above achievements are useful, but do not extend the channel attention mechanism to the time dimension. In this paper, an improved SE module is introduced to simulate pedestrians' attention to information at different moments. To the best of our knowledge, this paper is the first time to apply channel learning technique to trajectory prediction.

3 Problem Description

Formally, trajectory prediction can be defined as follows: given N observed pedestrians in a scene with T_{obs} time step, the position of a single pedestrian i in each time step t is denoted as s_i^t, $i \in \{1, ..., N\}$, $t \in \{1, ..., T_{obs}\}$, and the multi-channel spatial information derived from the position information of pedestrian i and map data is represented by $\{p_i^1, ..., p_i^{obs}\}$. The objective of trajectory prediction is to predict all future positions of pedestrian i simultaneously, the future positions of pedestrian i is denoted as $\Gamma_i^{t'}$, $t' \in \{T_{obs+1}, ..., T_{pred}\}$, $pred$ refers to the last moment of prediction.

The goal of modeling is to train the model $F(\cdot)$ to effectively predict the future trajectory of the target pedestrian. The process can be formulated as follows:

$$\Gamma_i = \left(s_i^{obs+1}, ..., s_i^{pred}\right) = F\left(p_i^1, p_i^2, ..., p_i^{obs}, W^*\right) \tag{1}$$

where, W^* is the vector of all the parameters in the model.

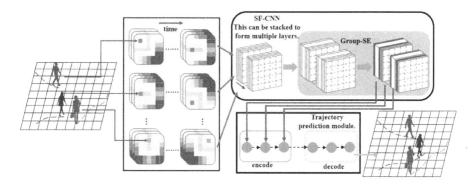

Fig. 1. The CSTCN Model

4   The CSTCN Model

4.1   Overall Framework

CSTCN consists of four key modules: data embedding module, Group-SE module, spatio-temporal feature convolution neural network and trajectory prediction module, as shown in Fig. 1. Firstly, the data embedding module is used to collect the multi-channel spatial feature information of each pedestrian. Secondly, the Group-SE module is used to recalibrate features to model the aggregated attention of pedestrians at each moment. Subsequently, SFCNN is a feedforward 3D convolutional network with gated activation units to use for capturing the most significant features. Finally, the trajectory prediction module is used to generate the future trajectory of the pedestrian.

4.2   Data Embedding

When constructing an end-to-end pedestrian motion decision network, a key problem is how to design well-represented input features. Studies have revealed that pedestrians can make movement decisions based on observations range of $d_x \times d_y$ around them [15].

The spatial region around the subject pedestrian of $d_x \times d_y$ is defined as the observation range (visual range) of pedestrians, and the spatial region where the subject pedestrian is the relative position center is defined as the perception range of pedestrians. Figure 2 simulates the visual range and perception range when pedestrian walking to the right. In this paper, the pedestrian's directions are divided into eight types according to a certain angle range and the corresponding observation range and perception range for each direction are shown in Fig. 3.

In order to reasonably represent the spatial characteristics of pedestrian multi-channel, this paper uses speed information, obstacle position information, neighbor position information and end point information as the attributes of data embedding. Among them, the location information of obstacles and neighbors is

Fig. 2. The perceptual range of pedestrians moving to the right

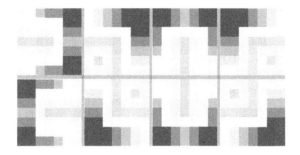

Fig. 3. The perceptual range during pedestrian movement.

directly perceived by pedestrians, if grid have obstacles or pedestrians, it is 1, otherwise it is 0; velocity information and terminal information are calculated from formula (2) and formula (3) respectively.

$$\begin{cases} v_{x_i}^t = \left(s_{x_i}^t - s_{x_i}^{t-1} \right) / \Delta T \\ v_{y_i}^t = \left(s_{y_i}^t - s_{y_i}^{t-1} \right) / \Delta T \end{cases} \tag{2}$$

$$\begin{cases} dis_{x_i}^t = \lambda \left(x_{end_i} - s_{x_i}^t \right) / W \\ dis_{y_i}^t = \lambda \left(y_{end_i} - s_{y_i}^t \right) / H \end{cases} \tag{3}$$

where, $s_{x_i}^t$ and $s_{y_i}^t$ represent the positions of X-axis and Y-axis for pedestrian i at time t, respectively; x_{end_i} and y_{end_i} represent the final horizontal and vertical coordinates of the pedestrian when they leave the scene, respectively. In addition, in order to prevent the lower sensitivity of the model caused by the closer the pedestrian is to the end point, the modified parameter λ is set.

4.3   Group-SE Module

Group-SE module is a spatio-temporal channel attention unit related to time series, which can improve the sensitivity of each time step information feature by explicitly simulating the interdependence between channels, thus extracting key features and suppressing useless features. For a given sequence of feature data $X \in \mathbb{R}^{c \times T_{obs} \times H \times W}$, it is first transposed to the time-related

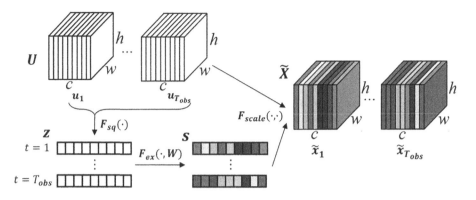

Fig. 4. the Group SE module

data $U \in \mathbb{R}^{T_{obs} \times c \times H \times W}$ through the data embedding module, where $u_t = [u_{t,1}, u_{t,2}, \ldots, u_{t,c}]$, $t = 1, 2, \ldots, c$. As shown in Fig. 4. This section adopts three stages to extract the key features of pedestrians, assuming that the information that pedestrians pay attention to is independent of each moments. It should be noted that each unit of the transform output U cannot take advantage of context information outside of that region; global spatial information is compressed into channel elements by using global average pools.

Compression phase: First, the global spatial information is compressed in the form of channel elements, which are represented by z, $z \in \mathbb{R}^{T_{obs} \times C}$. Here, z is generated by shrinking U in the spatial dimension $H \times W$, where H and W represent the length and height of the channels, respectively. Then, the k-th ($k = 1, 2, \ldots, c$) channel element of z at time step t is given by:

$$z_{t,k} = F_{sq}\left(u_{t,k}\right) = \frac{1}{H \times W} \sum_{i=1}^{H} \sum_{j=1}^{W} u_{t,k}\left(i, j\right) \tag{4}$$

Re-calibration phase: This part uses the information output from compression phase and adopts re-calibration operations to capture the dependencies between channels so as to extract the spatio-temporal node attention. A simple gating mechanism with S-type activation is chosen in this section:

$$s = F_{ex}\left(z, W\right) = \sigma\left(g\left(z, W\right)\right) = \sigma\left(W_2 \delta\left(W_1 z\right)\right) \tag{5}$$

where, δ represents the Tanh function, σ represents the Sigmoid function, $W_1 \in \mathbb{R}^{\frac{c}{r} \times C \times T_{obs}}$ denotes the parameters of the dimension reduction layer, and $W_2 \in \mathbb{R}^{T_{obs} \times C \times \frac{c}{r}}$ represents the parameters of the dimension increase layer. r is the reduction ratio, which controls the capacity and computational cost of the Group-SE module.

Output restoration phase: In order to emphasize the sensitivity of multi-channel data, the final output of the Group-SE module is obtained by re-adjust U, denoted as $\tilde{x}_t$, $\tilde{x}_t = [\tilde{x}_{t,1}, \tilde{x}_{t,2}, \ldots, \tilde{x}_{t,c}]$. Here, $\tilde{x}_{t,k}$ represents the output of the k-th channel at time t and the form is as follows:

$$\tilde{x}_{t,k} = F_{scale}\left(u_{t,k}, s_{t,k}\right) = s_{t,k} \cdot u_{t,k} \tag{6}$$

where, $F_{scale}\left(u_{t,c}, s_{t,c}\right)$ refers to the channel multiplication between the feature map $u_{t,c} \in \mathbb{R}^{H \times W}$ and the scalar $s_{t,c}$.

4.4 Spatiotemporal Feature Convolution Module

The function of Group-SE module is to calculate the sensitivity of multi-channel data and extract the spatio-temporal node attention. However, the objective of CSTCN is to predict the future motion trajectories of pedestrians, which is largely influenced by their historical trajectories and the surrounding environment. In this section, an improved temporal convolutional network (SF-CNN) is employed to capture spatio-temporal dynamic features. Figure 5 shows the improved SF-CNN structure diagram. SF-CNN is actually a simple sequence-to-sequence architecture. Among them, the lower convolutional layer focuses on local short-term interactions, while the higher layer uses a larger receptive field to capture long-term interactions. in addition, the output size of each layer convolution remains the same size as the input.

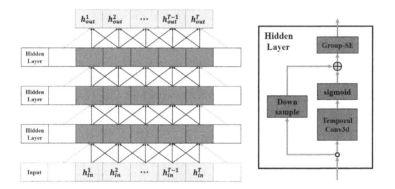

Fig. 5. The Structural diagram of SF-CNN

In each layer of SF-CNN, the gate activation units dynamically regulate the information flow using a non-linear function, as shown in formula (7).

$$H^{(l+1)} = G\left(\sigma\left(h^{(l)} * W_t^{(l)}\right)\right) \tag{7}$$

where, $W_t^{(l)}$ represents the learnable parameters of the l-th layer of SF-CNN, $H^{(l+1)}$ represents the output of the (l+1)-th layer of SF-CNN, $\sigma\left(\cdot\right)$ is the sigmoid function, and $G\left(\cdot\right)$ denotes the data transformation operation in the Group-SE module. In this framework, two hidden layers ($l = 2$) are employed to obtain the output of SF-CNN.

5   Experiments and Analysis

5.1   Datasets and Evaluation Metrics

ETH [32] dataset includes ETH and Hotel, and UCY [33] dataset includes UNIV, ZARA1 and ZARA2. In these datasets, pedestrians exhibit complex behaviors, including nonlinear trajectories, movement from different directions, walking together, unpredictable movements, collision avoidance, standing still, et al. The crowd density for a single scene in each environment varies from 0 to 51 pedestrians per frame. All datasets are recorded at 25 frames per second (FPS), with pedestrian trajectories extracted every 2.5 FPS. All models are trained using the leave-one-out method. Based on the observed result of 3.2 s (8 time steps), trajectories are generated for the next 4.8 s (12 time steps).

Two metrics are used to evaluate model performance: the Average Displacement Error (ADE) [17] defined in formula (8) and the Final Displacement Error (FDE) [11] defined in formula (9). Intuitively, ADE measures the average prediction performance along the trajectory, while the FDE considers only the prediction precision at the end points.

$$ADE = \frac{\sum_{i=1}^{N} \sum_{t_{obs}+1}^{t_{obs}+t_{pred}} \sqrt{\left(x_t^i - \hat{x}_t^i\right)^2 + \left(y_t^i - \hat{y}_t^i\right)^2}}{N * t_{pred}} \tag{8}$$

$$FDE = \frac{\sum_{i=1}^{N} \sqrt{\left(x_{t_{pred}}^i - \hat{x}_{t_{pred}}^i\right)^2 + \left(y_{t_{pred}}^i - \hat{y}_{t_{pred}}^i\right)^2}}{N} \tag{9}$$

5.2   Baselines

This section describes the baseline methods compared to the proposed CSTCN. All baseline methods follow the same training strategy. The baseline are as follow:

a) *Vanilla LSTM* (V-LSTM) [34]: This method employs the traditional LSTM-based autoencoder to generate the future trajectory.

b) *Social-LSTM* [11]: This method builds on top of LSTM and introduces a social pooling layer to capture the spatial interaction between pedestrians.

c) *CNN* [12]: This method uses CNN to predict the future trajectory sequences of pedestrians.

d) *DCLN* [16]: This method uses a convolutional network to extract the spatial features and employs deep LSTM to predict trajectories of pedestrians.

e) *Social-STGCNN* [13]: uses the graph convolutional network to calculate the mutual influence among pedestrians.

f) *Social-GAN* [16]: In this method, the generator and discriminator are based on LSTM, and an aggregation module is used to handle spatial interactions.

g) *SGCN* [26]: jointly models the movement trend of spatial interaction and trajectory and uses the time convolutional network to predict the future trajectory of pedestrians.

Table 1. ablation study of CSTCN

Data Embedding	modules			ADE	FDE
	Group-SE	SF-CNN	GRU		
non-use		✓	✓	0.52	0.79
	✓		✓	0.53	0.62
	✓	✓		0.47	0.73
	✓	✓	✓	0.38	0.55
use		✓	✓	0.53	0.88
	✓		✓	0.55	0.64
	✓	✓		0.42	0.62
	✓	✓	✓	**0.31**	**0.51**

5.3   Model Configuration

We train with SGD optimizer in 200 epochs with a learning rate of 0.001 for the first 100 epochs and then reduced to 0.0001 for the remaining 100 epochs to accelerate the convergence of the loss. The feature embedding kernel size is set to $1 \times 1 \times 1$. GRU is used to ensure that the decoder's output has the expected shape, and dropout (with a probability of 0.5) is also applied to prevent overfitting. And the loss function is logcosh, as shown in formula. Here, y_i represents the true value for the i-th training, and y_i^p represents the predicted value for the i-th training.

$$logcosh = \sum_{i=1}^{n} \log\left(cosh\left(y_i^p - y_i\right)\right) \tag{10}$$

5.4   Ablation Experiment

Ablation experiment on the ETH and UCY datasets is conducted to analyze the contribution of each module to the prediction performance. To validate the effectiveness of each module in pedestrian trajectory prediction, three variants are trained by considering different combinations of modules under the dynamic grasping algorithm. Table 1 shows the ablation experiment results of the three key modules and the dynamic grasping algorithm. Especially when Group-SE module is removed, the key information of pedestrians at every moment cannot be extracted, resulting in the failure to predict the future trajectory of pedestrians more accurately.

5.5   Prediction Result Analysis

This section compares the proposed CSTCN with baseline methods in terms of prediction error, model size, and inference speed. Since partial baseline methods can simultaneously predict multiple possible future trajectories for pedestrians, the optimal results of such baseline methods are selected for comparison for fairness.

Table 2. The average F1-Score, ACC and AUC values obtained PSO-EVFFS under three initialization strategies

Metrics	Sequences	CNN	LSTM	Social-LSTM	Social-STGCNN	Social-GAN	SGCN	DCLN	CSTCN
ADE	ETH	0.56	0.86	0.44	0.49	0.43	**0.32**	0.43	0.37
	hotel	1.04	1.09	0.50	0.64	0.76	0.63	0.50	**0.31**
	univ	0.57	0.65	0.43	0.44	0.62	0.37	0.38	**0.32**
	zara01	0.47	0.53	0.45	0.34	0.34	0.29	**0.25**	0.29
	zara02	0.44	0.42	0.38	0.30	0.36	0.25	**0.19**	0.26
	Average	0.62	0.70	0.45	0.44	0.50	0.37	0.35	**0.31**
FDE	ETH	2.41	2.47	0.72	1.11	0.83	1.03	0.77	**0.62**
	hotel	1.31	1.73	0.62	0.85	**0.50**	0.55	0.82	0.58
	univ	1.21	1.22	0.85	0.79	0.77	0.70	**0.63**	0.73
	zara01	0.81	0.88	0.63	0.53	0.57	0.53	0.45	**0.42**
	zara02	0.85	0.91	0.72	0.48	0.50	0.45	**0.32**	0.45
	Average	1.32	1.42	0.71	0.75	0.63	0.65	0.60	**0.56**

Comparison of Trajectory Prediction Results: Table 2 provides a comparison between the proposed CSTCN and different baseline methods in terms of ADE and FDE performance. In general, the proposed CSTCN outperforms the other seven baseline methods in terms of performance metrics for most datasets. For example, CSTCN has an ADE metric increase of 13.33% and 16.2% compared with DCLN and SGCN models, and an FDE metric increase of 19.04% and 6% compared with Social-GAN and DCLN models, respectively. It is verified that the CSTCN model exhibits excellent trajectory prediction performance.

Figure 6 shows the visualized results of the predicted trajectory. The red line represents the historical observation trajectory; the blue line represents the true trajectory; the green line represents the predicted trajectory of Conv-LSTM; the cyan line represents the predicted trajectory of SGCN, and the yellow line represents the predicted trajectory of CSTCN. This section selects four different scenarios for complex interactions, including: (a) pedestrian following and obstacle avoiding, (b) pedestrian standing and avoiding, (c) pedestrian counter-flowing, and (d) pedestrian avoiding. The visual results show that CSTCN can generate acceptable trajectories and is closer to the true trajectories compared to other baseline methods.

(a)   (b)   (c)

Fig. 6. Pedestrian path visualization

Inference Velocity and Model Capacity: Table 3 provides a comparison of different models in terms of reasoning speed and model capacity. In terms of reasoning speed, CSTCN achieves faster inference than most of the baseline methods, with an inference time of 0.0042 s per inference step. In terms of model capacity, both CSTCN and Social-STGCNN have much smaller model capacities than that of other baseline methods. Although Social-STGCNN achieves faster reasoning speed and smaller model capacity, it can be seen in combination with Table 4 that ADE and FDE values of Social-STGCNN are much worse than those of CSTCN for all 5 data sets.

Table 3. Number of parameters and inference time for different models

	Parameters count	Inference time
DCLN	2102k	0.167
Social-STGCNN	7.6kk	0.0027
Social-GAN	185.71k	0.0138
SGCN	84k	0.0104
CSTCN	20.46k	0.0042

6   Conclusion

This paper proposes a trajectory prediction method based on a channel spatio-temporal convolutional network (CSTCN) model. This method can model combined with the spatial information around pedestrians and historical information to predict the future trajectory of pedestrians. Firstly, spatio-temporal channel attention is employed for each moment of the historical trajectory. Then, the spatio-temporal features are extracted by using the time convolutional network, and the future trajectory is generated by the trajectory prediction module. Thus, the trajectory prediction model CSTCN based on the improved spatio-temporal convolutional network is obtained. Finally, the effectiveness and efficiency of the proposed CSTCN are verified by comparing with 6 advanced trajectory prediction methods on 2 public datasets. In the future, the model proposed in this paper should be extended to multiple object scenarios. Additionally, considering local static scene images as additional inputs to the model by introducing computer vision, and applying it to the proposed CSTCN, the prediction accuracy of the model will be further improved.

Acknowledgements. During the process of writing this paper, I would like to express my special gratitude to Ying Hu for her guidance and supervision, as well as for her understanding and tolerance. Thank you to Professor Yonglong Luo for providing guidance during the model design phase, and to the School of Computer Science and Technology at Anhui Normal University for providing me with a good learning environment.

References

1. Huang, Y., Du, J., Yang, Z., Zhou, Z., Zhang, L., Chen, H.: A survey on trajectory-prediction methods for autonomous driving. IEEE Trans. Intell. Veh. **7**(3), 652–674 (2022)
2. Li, J., Ma, H., Tomizuka, M.: Conditional generative neural system for probabilistic trajectory prediction. In: Proceedings of IEEE/RSJ International Conference Intelligent Robots and System, pp. 6150–6156 (2019)
3. Zhang, X., Yang, X., Zhang, W., et al.: Crowd emotion evaluation based on fuzzy inference of arousal and valence. Neurocomputing **445**, 194–205 (2021)
4. Rudenko, A., Palmieri, L., Herman, M., Kitani, K.M., Gavrila, D.M., Arras, K.O.: Human motion trajectory prediction: a survey. Int. J. Robot. Res. **39**(8), 895–935 (2020)
5. Ghorai, P., Eskandarian, A., Kim, Y.-K., Mehr, G.: State estimation and motion prediction of vehicles and vulnerable road users for cooperative autonomous driving: a survey. IEEE Trans. Intell. Transp. Syst. **23**(10), 16983–17002 (2022)
6. Korbmacher, R., Tordeux, A.: Review of pedestrian trajectory prediction methods: comparing deep learning and knowledge-based approaches. IEEE Trans. Intell. Transp. Syst. **23**(12), 24126–24144 (2022)
7. Lv, K., Yuan, L.: SKGACN: social knowledge-guided graph attention convolutional network for human trajectory prediction. IEEE Trans. Instrum. Meas. **72**, 1–11 (2023)
8. Yang, C., Pei, Z.: Long-short term spatio-temporal aggregation for trajectory prediction. IEEE Trans. Intell. Transp. Syst. **24**(4), 4114–4126 (2023)
9. Kitani, K.M., Ziebart, B.D., Bagnell, J.A., Hebert, M.: Activity forecasting. In: Fitzgibbon, A., Lazebnik, S., Perona, P., Sato, Y., Schmid, C. (eds.) ECCV 2012. LNCS, vol. 7575, pp. 201–214. Springer, Heidelberg (2012). https://doi.org/10.1007/978-3-642-33765-9_15
10. Xue, H., Huynh, D.Q., Reynolds, M.: SS-LSTM: a hierarchical LSTM model for pedestrian trajectory prediction. In: Proceedings of IEEE Winter Conference on Applications of Computer Vision (WACV), pp. 1186–1194 (2018)
11. Alahi, A., Goel, K., Ramanathan, V., Robicquet, A., Fei-Fei, L., Savarese, S.: Social LSTM: human trajectory prediction in crowded spaces. In: Proceedings of IEEE Conference on Computer Vision and Pattern Recognition (CVPR), pp. 961–971 (2016)
12. Nikhil, N., Tran Morris, B.: Convolutional neural network for trajectory prediction. In: Proceedings of the European Conference on Computer Vision (ECCV), pp. 186–196 (2018)
13. Mohamed, A., Qian, K., Elhoseiny, M., Claudel, C.: Social-STGCNN: a social spatio-temporal graph convolutional neural network for human trajectory prediction. InL Proceedings of IEEE Conference on Computer Vision and Pattern Recognition, pp. 14412–14420 (2020)
14. Song, X., et al.: Pedestrian trajectory prediction based on deep convolutional LSTM network. IEEE Trans. Intell. Transp. Syst. **22**(6), 3285–3302 (2021)
15. Bera, A., Randhavane, T., Manocha, D.: Aggressive, tense, or shy? Identifying personality traits from crowd videos. In: Proceedings of the International Conference on Artificial Intelligence (IJCAI), pp. 112–118 (2017)
16. Gupta, A., Johnson, J. Fei-Fei, L., Savarese, S., Alahi, A.: Social GAN: socially acceptable trajectories with generative adversarial networks. In: Proceedings of IEEE Conference on Computer Vision and Pattern Recognition, pp. 2255–2264 (2018)

17. Xu, Y., Piao, Z., Gao, S.: Encoding crowd interaction with deep neural network for pedestrian trajectory prediction. In: Proceedings of IEEE Conference on Computer Vision and Pattern Recognition, pp. 5275–5284 (2018)
18. Bai, S., Kolter, J.Z., Koltun, V.: An empirical evaluation of generic convolutional and recurrent networks for sequence modeling (2018). arXiv:1803.01271. [Online]. urlhttp://arxiv.org/abs/1803.01271
19. Wang, C., Cai, S., Tan, G.: GraphTCN: spatio-temporal interaction modeling for human trajectory prediction. In: Proceedings of IEEE Conference on Computer Vision and Pattern Recognition, pp. 3450–3459 (2021)
20. Ziebart, B.D., et al.: Planning-based prediction for pedestrians. In: Proceedings of the IEEE International Conference on Intelligent Robots and System (IROS), pp. 3931–3936 (2009)
21. Elfring, J., Van De Molengraft, R., Steinbuch, M.: Learning intentions for improved human motion prediction. Robot. Auton. Syst. 62(4), 591–602 (2014)
22. Møgelmose, A., Trivedi, M.M., Moeslund, T.B.: Trajectory analysis and prediction for improved pedestrian safety: integrated framework and evaluations. In: 2015 IEEE Intelligent Vehicles Symposium (IV), Seoul, Korea (South), pp. 330–335 (2015)
23. Helbing, D., Molnar, P.: Social force model for pedestrian dynamics. Phys. Rev. E 51(5), 4282 (1995)
24. Farina, F., Fontanelli, D., Garulli, A., Giannitrapani, A., Prattichizzo, D.: Walking ahead: the headed social force model. PLoS ONE, 12(1), e0169734 (2017)
25. Ikeda, T., Chigodo, Y., Rea, D., Zanlungo, F., Shiomi, M., Kanda, T.: Modeling and prediction of pedestrian behavior based on the sub-goal concept. Science and Systems. In: Proceedings of Robotics (2012)
26. Shi, L., et al.: SGCN: sparse graph convolution network for pedestrian trajectory prediction. In: Proceedings of IEEE Conference on Computer Vision and Pattern Recognition, pp. 8994–9003 (2021)
27. Xu, K., et al.: Show, attend and tell: neural image caption generation with visual attention. In: Proceedings of 31st International Conference on Machine Learning (ICML), pp. 2048–2057 (2015)
28. Wang, F., et al.: Residual attention network for image classification. In: Proceedings of IEEE Conference on Computer Vision and Pattern Recognition, pp. 6450–6458 (2017)
29. Hu, J., Li, S., Sun, G.: Squeeze-and-excitation networks. In: Proceedings of IEEE Conference on Computer Vision and Pattern Recognition, pp. 7132–7141 (2018)
30. Wang, X., Girshick, R., Gupta, A., He, K.: Non-local neural networks. In: Proceedings of IEEE Conference on Computer Vision Pattern Recognition, pp. 7794–7803 (2018)
31. Shu, X., Yang, J., Yan, R., Song, Y.: Expansion-squeeze-excitation fusion network for elderly activity recognition. IEEE Trans. Circuits Syst. Video Technol. 32(8), 5281–5292 (2022)
32. Pellegrini, S., Ess, A., Schindler, K., van Gool, L.: You'll never walk alone: Modeling social behavior for multi-target tracking. In: Proceedings of IEEE 12th International Conference on Computer Vision, pp. 261–268 (2009)
33. Lerner, A., Chrysanthou, Y., Lischinski, D.: Crowds by example. In: Computer Graphics Forum, vol. 26, no. 3, pp. 655–664. Blackwell Publishing Ltd, Oxford, U.K (2007)
34. Zhao, T., et al.: et al.: Multi-agent tensor fusion for contextual trajectory prediction. In: Proceedings of IEEE Conference on Computer Vision and Pattern Recognition, pp. 12126–12134 (2019)

Multi-NetDroid: Multi-layer Perceptron Neural Network for Android Malware Detection

Andri Rai(iD) and Eul Gyu Im$^{(\boxtimes)}$(iD)

Department of Computer and Software, Hanyang University, Seoul 04763, Korea
{andrirai,imeg}@hanyang.ac.kr

Abstract. Android malware detection has become a critical concern with the emergence of smartphones. Over the last few years, research has revealed a gradual improvement in the detection of malware from mobile operating systems through both static and dynamic analysis. Machine learning techniques are used to analyze various features and to train a larger dataset; to do this, a range of deep learning algorithms have been used previously. In this paper, we proposed a multi-layer perceptron (MLP) neural network for the Android malware detection method named as Multi-NetDroid. Training and evaluation of the proposed model have been done on publicly available datasets of the android applications. The data consist of features extracted from the manifest file (Intent, Permission), the dex file (API Call Signature), and command signatures existing within an APK file. The Multi-NetDroid model is built with four dense layers for training and classification of malware or benign applications and is evaluated as an improved classifier for Android malware detection. To evaluate our model performance we experimented with two separate datasets (Drebin-215 and Malgenome-15), and our model achieved 99.19% and 99.12% of accuracy. Furthermore, for the validation of our framework, we have also compared the results with different Machine Learning (ML) classifiers and found that our model Accuracy outperforms the classical ML methods.

Keywords: Android Malware · Malware Detection · Deep Learning · Multilayer Perceptron (MLP) · Machine Learning (ML) · Neural Network

1 Introduction

According to a Statista [1] report in 2021, the number of worldwide smartphone users was 1.54 billion, and the number has increased to 6 billion in the Statista February 2022 report. According to statistics of apps, over 2.59 million apps are available on the Google Play store. 96.7% of apps are free and 3.3% are paid apps, with approximately 111 billion downloads in 2021, as reported in the Statista March 2022 report [2]. With the rapid development of Android applications, the issue of malicious applications on mobile devices is also increasing.

G. Wang et al. (Eds.): UbiSec 2023, CCIS 2034, pp. 219–235, 2024.
https://doi.org/10.1007/978-981-97-1274-8_15

The problem of Android malware has become a concern for many users and companies. The Kaspersky 2021 mobile threat report [1] shows that 3.5 million malicious installation packages were discovered, resulting in 46.2 million attacks around the world. Furthermore, researchers also found that malware was used in 80% of the attacks, and attackers primarily targeted mobile banking services and mobile gaming credentials. For many years, Android malware detection issues have been a focus of research. Some researchers attempted to solve the problem of malware detection and classification on Android devices by distinguishing between benign and malicious apps. Android malware detection is a process to identify the malicious behaviors of an application using a machine learning model or a deep learning model. An Android malware detection process usually uses three analysis approaches: static analysis, dynamic analysis, and hybrid analysis. These malware detection analyses are performed without execution or while application execution.

Previously, researchers attempted to detect mobile malware through traditional methods based on signature-based features [4], which had the disadvantage of consuming more resources and of having a high false negative rate.

The machine learning (ML)-based approaches [5] are used to detect malicious Apps by building a model using extracted features from Apps. The development of a model is performed in three steps: first, extracting features from APK files; second, training a model based on those features; and last, classification and prediction of malicious and benign Apps. Although machine learning-based malware detection approaches are preferable, attaining high accuracy with larger and diverse datasets is challenging. Before a model is trained, ML-based techniques need manual experts to analyze and understand the Android malware feature extraction and selection.

Deep learning-based techniques are used to overcome the biases(weakness) of machine learning methods, such as SVM, RF, KNN, etc. [7,9]. Specific kinds of Android malware features, including basic blocks, API call, permissions, and raw opcodes, can be used to train a deep learning-based model. Some deep neural networks (DNNs) based on API call graph were proposed to detection Android malware. The API call graph samples are retrieved and evaluated using a method to create graph embedding characteristics through pseudo-dynamic analysis, which results in higher detection accuracy of malware. Researchers have also employed a Graphical Convolution Network (GCN) to learn the structural information and to detect the system call relationships by constricting the adjacency matrix of the benign and malware graphs [6]. However, much more research still has to be done on malicious behavior detection through various analysis techniques, such as dynamic and hybrid analysis.

This paper introduces and investigates a deep learning-based and static analysis-based multi-neural network model for Android malware detection. Our Multi-NetDroid framework is a classification model for Android malware detection that is trained on several dense layers. We conducted in-depth tests on our framework using datasets built by extracting features from two widely known malware sample collections, i.e. the Android Malgenome Project [3] and

DREBIN [8], prepared by Yerima and Sezer [9], to show the usefulness of the Multi-NetDroid technique. The contributions of this paper can be summed up as follows:

(1) We propose a classification strategy based on simple deep learning to detect Android malware.
(2) To show the effectiveness and feasibility of our proposed strategy, we experimented the proposed strategy with two separate datasets and presented the findings of experiments.
(3) In addition, we evaluate Multi-NetDroid's performance with a variety of well-known machine learning models.

The last of the paper is organized as follows: Sect. 2 presents related research on machine learning and deep learning techniques to detect Android malware, and Sect. 3 and Sect. 4 introduces our proposed system, i.e. the Multi-NetDroid framework. Section 5 presents experimental results and discussion. Finally, Sect. 6 provides the conclusion and directions for future research.

2   Related Work

In this section, the work on machine learning and deep learning-based methods to detect Android malware are briefly reviewed. To detect and categorize Android malware, a detection method trains a model with various properties extracted through static and dynamic analysis.

2.1   Static, Dynamic and Hybrid Malware Analysis

Prior literature has shown that the static analysis of Android application files with malicious patterns is carried out by extracting features like API calls, and static analysis is widely used in conventional approaches to detect malware. The primary purpose of static analysis is to extract features from APK files which contain AndroidManifestfiles.xml, smali files, and classes.dex files. The following features are typically included as static features [7,9,11–13]: permissions, API Calls, Function Call Graphs, Command Signature, and so on.

Dynamic analysis is used for behavior-based detection techniques that examine malicious programs' runtime features [32]. System calls, network data files, and memory changes are features extracted through dynamic analysis [9]. This approach provides additional information when examining the execution code by employing emulators and virtual runtime environments.

The extensive use of feature analysis is being used in the hybrid analysis by integrating dynamic and static features. In hybrid analysis, an app's various features are used to detect malware, which offers better performance utilization in terms of time, resources, and code coverage for malware detection [36].

2.2   Android Malware Detection Based on Machine Learning Techniques

This subsection includes a brief overview of the machine learning models and algorithms that are frequently employed to detect malware on Android devices. Several machine learning models were used in the Android malware detection research [14], each with its own implementation strategy. Li et al. [44] proposed the SIGPID model which is based on the extracted Android permissions using multiple levels of data pruning and they used SVM as a classifier. Some researchers also optimize the experimented scheme from the viewpoint of feature extraction, as Cai et al. [15] analyzed the feature weighting with joint optimization of weight mapping and evaluated classifiers such as kNN (k Nearest Neighbors), SVM, and LR (Logistic Regression), naming the model as JOWMDroid.

Additionally, Garg et al. [17] introduced a model based on network-based activity features that are selected by analyzing network traces and applying multiple machine learning detectors like kNN, Bayes, decision tree, Random Forest, and Logistic Regression for the data. Machine learning detectors can detect malware, but it is not possible to detect malicious Apps that are encrypted. Hasan et al. [19] proposed methodology based on model-driven event generation by analyzing dynamic behaviors through code monitoring, intents-utilizing information, and event production.

To identify malicious Apps using a hybrid malware analysis, Qaisar and Li [20] suggested a multi-model analysis based on case-based reasoning (CBR) and information fusion techniques. Furthermore, the MOCDroid model, proposed by Martin et al. [21], is an approach that combines clustering and multi-objective optimization to categorize malware using semantic features retrieved from the combination of third-party API calls which cannot be obfuscated.

2.3   Malware Detection with Deep Learning Techniques

To detect malware traits and to classify applications as benign or malicious, deep learning models are constructed from networks with several layers. These networks allow a model to be improved at each layer. Malicious applications are escalating more in terms of volume and complexity every year. To overcome this issue, Naway and Li [23] proposed a method that collects features from APK files using MobSF, then transformed and mapped all the features into a uniform joint vector. Xu et al. [24] employed a multilayer perceptron to analyze XML vectors and created a model, called as DeepRefiner, that employs Long Short Term Memory (LSTM) on the semantic structure of Android bytecode. Amin et al. [26] suggested a method for malware detection that involved vectorizing the opcodes after extracting the byte-codes from APK files to train the model on the BiLSTM network, and zero-day malware could be detected effectively using this approach.

Moreover, researchers use obfuscation features along with other features to detect malware using deep learning. Convolutional Neural Network (CNN) and Discriminative Adversarial Network (DAN) used in the DANdroid [27] model were created using obfuscation data to detect Android malware in both single-view and multi-view scenarios, and they used obfuscation features generated by DexProtector. Kim et al. [7] proposed a multimodal deep learning method to analyze the Android static features to detect Android malware, along with evaluating their model for obfuscated resilience on multiple malware datasets.

Researchers have also proposed to utilize visualization techniques to detect malware from benign apps and to train generated images with DL techniques. A Graph Convolution Network (GCN), which displays the graphical semantics of characteristics, can be used to classify malware families. The GCN-based AMal-Net [6] model was developed to learn and recognize the semantic and sequential patterns of Android malware automatically. The IndRNN is used to enhance the GCN network and to resolve the gradient and disappearance problems. Another study by Lu et al. [28] used a hybrid deep learning model with a DBN and GRU network to extract features and detect malware using both obfuscated and non-obfuscated datasets, albeit the computation time rose despite with small datasets.

3   Our Proposed Method

All the model selection, training, and evaluation in this paper adhere to the Deep Learning methodology. The overall design of our framework is depicted in Fig. 1. Our proposed framework which is named as Multi-NetDroid framework is built as a neural network classifier using four distinct types of features: intent, manifest permission, API call signature, and command signature. The framework performs key detection procedures, including features attribute standardization, neural network selection, and classification of unknown samples into benign or malicious classes. The description of the feature attributes and the essential steps of our framework are provided in the next subsection.

3.1   Feature Attributes

Yerima et al. [9] provide csv files of Android APK files by employing static analysis in order to get feature attributes. Each of these features in the csv files has unique characteristics that are significant for the analysis of Android malware obtained from APIs. Our model was built using these csv files, and our model's training aspects include the following feature attributes:

API Call Signature. The API call signature is obtained by the Classes and packages used in the app are provided through the APK decompilation process. Malware features that provide information about the actions performed by the application are frequently employed for API calls.

Manifest Permissions. To impose various restrictions on the Android process's ability to operate, the manifest permissions are deployed as an access control

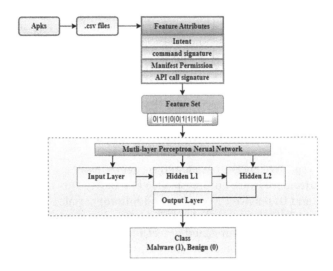

Fig. 1. Overview of the Multi-NetDroid Framework

mechanism for an Android system. The manifest file of an APK file which contains sensitive details about the application is typically where the permission features are set and restrained. These manifest permissions include features that safeguard the device and let an application interface with and access privacy-related data and components. Threats that misuse dangerous permissions, signature permission, and system permissions may be present in Android applications that can be analyzed statically.

Intents. The Android intent is a message sent by an App to communicate with other Apps or to invoke other Apps. The intent can be used to commence an activity, to broadcast an intent to any receiver components, and to begin a service as well as to establish a connection with a background service. Depending on the action required at the moment of the request, such as `android.intent.action.PACKAGE_RESTATED`, the intent features employed to launch the Android activities vary. The aspects of an Android application's activities and data are often contained in an intent.

Command Signature. An Android application may not operate without the command signature which is required to sign the Android label and activity class by setting some instructions. In the case of benign applications, the command signature certificate is the same as the permissions are declared, and the Android system gives the access without notifying the user for approval. Command signatures are used to sign the permissions that an application requests. However, the system resources can be accessed in the background by a malicious application with the same signature as the requested permission, which could be dangerous to the system's data.

3.2   Neural Network Selection and Classification

Understanding the network architecture that can reduce the error on the chosen instances of the dataset is critical in choosing the best deep learning model. Neural networks' model selection is influenced by the type of input and the number of neurons. The number of neurons for a model is primarily based on the network's under-fitting and over-fitting traits of the training data. A model must generate an adequate fit of the data and must have the appropriate degree of complexity. When it comes to input selection, a model's construction depends on a reduction in the number of input features which can help to reduce a model's computational overheads and complexity. In Sect. 4, we provide a brief description of our model building.

To determine if an application is benign or malicious, the classification process is carried out after selecting the appropriate neural network for our model. We have conducted multiple classification experiments by setting and adjusting the various parameters, such as an optimizer and activation functions, to achieve higher detection accuracy.

4   Multi-NetDroid Framework

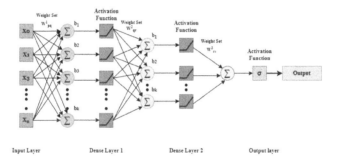

Fig. 2. Multi-Layer Perceptron Neural Network

Our framework's multi-layer perceptron neural network (MLP) [29] design is depicted in Fig. 2 for the detection of Android malware. A feed-forward artificial neural network is known as an MLP, and these models are created with a series of fully connected layers. Each successive layer is composed of a collection of non-linear functions that represent the weighted sum of all the outputs from the previous layer that are connected. In our architecture, we have used dense layers which are neural network layers in which every input and output node is coupled. The input layer of the network is the initial layer that accepts the feature vectors retrieved from the dataset. The MLP has three levels: one input layer, and two hidden or dense layers, and each layer is connected to the previous layer [45]. The last layer is an output layer for the classification of benign Apps and malware. The constraints utilized to create the neural network for malware detection using Drebin-215 and Malgenome-215 is described in Table 1.

In this network, every layer is completely interconnected, and the rectified linear units (ReLU) activation function is employed to set the weight values of nodes in the input and dense layers. The ReLU activation function preserves the important feature attributes when computing the gradient, allowing it to optimize the model. It also increases the weighted sum's correctness, which prevents neurons from being saturated. The final layer of the MLP is the output layer used for classification. We trained the output layer using a single neuron and the sigmoid activation function [30]. The sigmoid activation function performs better for models where we need to classify the output as binary classification that result into two classes either it is malicious or benign. The discussion of the outcomes from these frameworks are included in Sect. 5.

Table 1. The Constraints of Multi-layer Perceptron Neural Network for Malgenome-215

Network	Layers	Neurons	Params	Activation Function
First	Input	215	46440	ReLU
Second	Dense 1	100	21600	ReLU
Third	Dense 2	75	7575	ReLU
Last	Output	1	76	Sigmoid

4.1 Mathematical Definition of Methodology

This subsection explains a multi-layer perceptron neural network (MLP) [37] model's mathematical definition. Let $L = \{l1, l2, l3, l4\}$ be a layer for the described network, and the input vectors x_n which corresponds to the network, and z is the incoming hidden elements in layer $l1$, as well as w_n the weights, b as bias,y is the target output, x_n is the initial input and ϕ as a nonlinear activation function, respectively (ReLU is applied for hidden layers and sigmoid is applied for output layer), with these notations, the computation of the network can be expressed as:

$$y = \phi \left(\sum_n w_{in} * x_n + b_i \right) \tag{1}$$

$$z(h_i^{l1}) = \phi^{(1)} \left(\sum_n w_{in}^{l1} * x_n + b_i^{l1} \right) \tag{2}$$

$$z(h_i{}^{l2}) = \phi^{(2)} \left(\sum_n w_{in}{}^{l2} * h_n^{l1} + b_i{}^{l2} \right) \tag{3}$$

$$y' = \phi^{(3)} \left(\sum_n w_{in}{}^{l3} * h_n^{l2} + b_i{}^{l3} \right) \tag{4}$$

where, for the (1), (2) and (3), $\phi, \phi^{(1)}$, and $\phi^{(2)}$ is $max(0, z(h_i^l))$

and for the output in (4) $\phi^{(3)}$ is $\frac{1}{(1+e^x)}$.

During the model training, the loss function is an important component. By assessing how well the model fits the data distribution, we can select a suitable loss function for the model. The cross-entropy loss function for binary classification that is utilized in this model is defined as follows:

$$L = -(y \log(d) + (1 - y) \log(1 - d)) \tag{5}$$

where: L is the loss function $L(f(x_n), y_n)$, d is the predicted probability, and y is the indicator for $\{y' \geq 0.5, y = 1$ and $y' < 0.5, y = 0$

$$y = \begin{cases} 1, & \text{if } y' \geq 0.5 \\ 0, & \text{if } y' < 0.5 \end{cases}$$

4.2   Dataset Description

The experiments to evaluate the Multi-NetDroid were conducted using two datasets from two collections of Android app samples provided in [9]. We have listed each dataset's specifics in Table 2. The initial Drebin-215 contains 215 feature attributes derived from 15036 app samples of which 9476 were malware samples and 5560 were benign samples from the Drebin project [10]. The second dataset, Malgenome-215, was obtained from 3799 app samples of which 1260 were malware samples and 2539 were benign samples from the Android malware genome project [3].

Additionally, we have visualized the dataset features randomly selected by using the Principle Component Analysis (PCA) for both datasets, as shown in Fig. 3. The x-axis displays the features of the datasets and the y-axis displays the class of benign and malware samples. The 3D visualization of dataset features are uploaded on the GitHub repository [31].

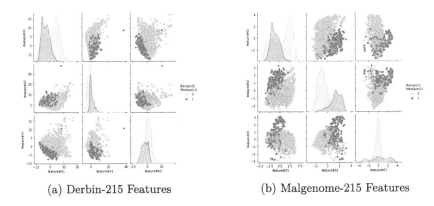

(a) Derbin-215 Features   (b) Malgenome-215 Features

Fig. 3. Datasets Feature Visualization

Table 2. Dataset Details for Evaluation

Dataset	Samples	Benign	Malware	Features
Drebin-215	15036	9476	5560	215
Mlagenome-215	3799	2539	1260	215

5 Experimental Results and Discussion

This section presents and discusses experiments performed to evaluate the Multi-NetDroid system. We implemented and evaluated our approach using the open source Google Colaboratory platform [35]. We used a variety of evaluation criteria and compared our findings to those of the previous researchers. To assess and validate our methodology further, we have also compared the results of our model to the outcomes of several machine learning algorithms. The experimental parameters and findings of our method are more thoroughly discussed and summarized in the following subsections.In addition to the comparative code for machine learning methods, the code for the Multi-NetDroid system implementation's findings for the Drebin and Malgenome datasets are uploaded to the GitHub repository [31].

5.1 Experimental Setup

To experiment our suggested framework, we used a Windows 10 workstation with an Intel Core i5- 7400 CPU and 32 GB of RAM. The framework's modules were developed in Python, and the majority of the work was done on Google Colab [35] which offers runtime GPU usage optimizations. The Keras library [25], Scikit Learn [22], and Tensorflow [18] is used to create the multi-layer perceptron neural network modeling in order to take advantage of the development of other machine learning methods with visualizations. We have also used libraries like PyCuda [42] and PyTorch [16] for a few algorithms.

5.2   Multi-NetDroid Performance for Drebin-215

In order to assess Multi-NetDroid on the Drebin-215 dataset, we divided the dataset into three sets: for training, validation and testing the model. The dataset was split by using the train_test_split function in Python with a ratio of 60–30-10% for training, validation and testing. After splitting the dataset, we did the component analysis of the dataset to understand the variance of feature classes, as shown in Fig. 3. The NumPy function was used to reshape the dimension of the dataset for training the model, converting the 2D dimension array to a 1D array with reshape $(-1,1)$.

As described in Sect. 4, we built our model using the sigmoid activation function in the output layer for classification and the ReLU activation function in the inner layers. We used the RMSProp with a (0.001) learning rate and set the loss function as binary cross-entropy. Our model attained an training accuracy of 99.87% and a validation accuracy of 99.19% for classifying the benign and malicious classes with a training loss of 0.005 and a Val-loss of 0.08 on training the model with 15 epochs. The testing of our model with Drebin-215 dataset is done on 10% of untrained data and achieved the testing accuracy of 98.23 with loss of 0.22.

Furthermore, we have also tried other optimizers like Adam with a (0.001) learning rate to check whether there will be any more improvement in the the model's accuracy, but we have found that the accuracy is decreased to 98.43%. Other than this, we have also changed the learning rate to (0.02), but the accuracy showed more of a fall for the classification. Table 3 shows the performance evaluation based on accuracy, precision, recall, and F1-score for both the training and validation of our model. We also constructed the accuracy and loss graphs in Fig. 4 and Fig. 5 as additional evidence.

Table 3. Performance Results of Multi-NetDroid on Drebin-215 and Malgenome-215

Dataset	Accuracy	Precision	Recall	F1-Score
Drebin-215	99.19	99.29	98.40	98.84
Mlagenome-215	99.12	100	97.29	98.63

5.3   Multi-NetDroid Performance for Malgenome-215

This section presented the evaluation of Multi-NetDroid on the Malgenome-215 dataset. The dataset is divided in 60-30-10 split between training, validation, and testing using Python's train_test_split function. The model training process was the same as what we used for the Drebin-215 dataset.

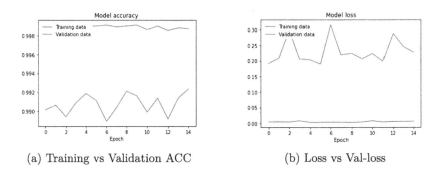

(a) Training vs Validation ACC   (b) Loss vs Val-loss

Fig. 4. Multi-NetDroid accuracy and loss results on Drebin-215

As shown in Table 1 in Sect. 4, we constructed our model for this dataset using different parameters while using the same sigmoid activation function for classification in the output layer and the ReLU activation function in the inner layers and used the RMSProp with a (0.001) learning rate, with binary cross-entropy as the loss function. In categorizing benign and malicious classes, our model achieved a training accuracy of 100% and a validation accuracy of 99.12% with a training loss of 2.2008e-09 and a Val-loss of 0.22 when trained on 15 epochs. The testing of model with Malgenome-215 is done on the 10% of untrained data and achieved the testing accuracy of 99.01 with loss of 0.28. For both the training and validation of our model, Table 3 displays the performance evaluation based on accuracy, precision, recall, and F1 score. As additional proof, we also provided the accuracy and loss graphs in Fig. 5.

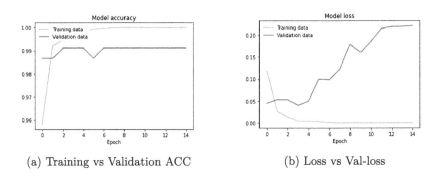

(a) Training vs Validation ACC   (b) Loss vs Val-loss

Fig. 5. Multi-NetDroid accuracy and loss results on Malgenome-215

5.4 Further Comparison of Model with Different Machine Learning Classifiers

This section shows the findings from tests conducted to see if the Multi-NetDroid model can compete with more established machine learning classifiers. Our objective is to determine whether applying machine learning classifiers can increase accuracy or not. On the datasets for Malgenome-215 and Drebin-215, we evaluated our model and compared our results with other those of machine learning algorithms. We have compared our results using the following machine learning classifiers: logistic regression, decision tree, linear discriminant analysis, KNN, Gaussian NB, and SVM. Tables 4 and 5 demonstrate how well our framework performs in comparison to cutting-edge detection systems using various machine learning algorithms.

Table 4. Comparison of Machine Learning Algorithms on Drebin-215

Models	Accuracy	Precision	Recall	F1-Score
LR	97.58	97.13	94.80	95.93
LDA	96.70	95.69	91.73	93.62
KNN	97.83	96.27	93.40	94.79
CART	97.58	92.42	95.54	93.69
NB	70.66	53.55	98.32	69.33
SVM	98.17	98.25	94.70	96.43
Proposed	**99.19**	**99.29**	**98.40**	**98.84**

Table 5. Comparison of Machine Learning Algorithms on Malgenome-215

Models	Accuracy	Precision	Recall	F1-Score
LR	99.01	97.39	96.26	96.81
LDA	98.51	92.06	91.80	91.84
KNN	98.05	96.25	89.55	92.67
CART	98.25	92.14	92.89	92.21
NB	69.56	59.61	95.15	73.17
SVM	98.94	98.41	91.06	94.53
Proposed	**99.12**	**100**	**97.29**	**98.63**

5.5 Comparison with Existing Deep Learning Methods

We investigated the deep learning methodologies that have previously been proposed for Android malware detection methods in order to demonstrate the performance of our framework in comparison with elaborated detection systems. The findings of the investigation are showed in Table 6. The malware samples from the Drebin Project, Malgenome Project and static analysis are used in numerous existing researches. Since these two datasets were used in the malware detection, we have included the performance results in the table. The results of previously described experiments accuracy, precision, recall, and F1-score values are included for comparison.

Table 6. Comparison of Multi-NetDroid with Existing Deep Learning Methods

Models	Accuracy	Precision	Recall	F1-Score
Ours(Malgenome-215)	**99.12**	**100**	**97.29**	**98.63**
Ours(Drebin-215)	**99.19**	**99.29**	**98.40**	**98.84**
Millar et al. [27]	97.30	96.50	98.10	97.30
Zhang et al. [14]	97.40	96.60	98.30	97.40
Tang et al. [32]	96.35	N/A	N/A	N/A
Li et al. [44]	97.16	96.00	95.23	96.08
Vu et al. [33]	94.33	91.00	92.00	92.00
Elayan et al. [34]	98.20	96.90	99.20	98.00
Kim et al. [7]	98.00	98.00	99.00	99.00
Zhang et al. [36]	96.70	97.60	97.21	96.10
Pekta et al. [38]	98.86	98.84	98.47	98.65
Yerima et al. [9]	N/A	N/A	N/A	98.72
Chen et al. [39]	99.10	N/A	N/A	N/A
Gao et al. [40]	98.99	98.90	98.30	98.60
Wu et al. [41]	99.00	98.20	99.80	99.00
Kinkead et al. [43]	98.00	98.00	98.00	97.00
Naway et al. [23]	95.31	95.35	95.31	95.31

5.6 Limitations and Future Work

Our framework still has constraints for creating the dynamic analysis-based detection results, despite the experiment results demonstrating that our model is effective against static analysis-based methods. As the Mutil-NetDroid can be extended to malware multi-class classification in future research, there is still room for improvement. Using dynamic analysis, this approach can easily be expanded to detect Android malware on larger datasets. In account of this, future work includes to investigate the suitability of Multi-NetDroid in identifying the malware families.

6   Conclusion

In this paper, we suggested a novel Multi-NetDroid, a new method to detect Android malware, based on static analysis and multi-layer perceptron neural networks. Using two different datasets, we empirically assessed Multi-NetDroid, and the results show how well the model works to enhance detection performance on the Malgenome-215 and Drebin-215 datasets. We contrasted the outcomes of our investigations and demonstrated that Multi-NetDroid Accuracy, Precision, Recall, and F1-Score performed better than traditional ML approaches. Future research will address the other Android malware detection limitations and expand the method's utilization effectiveness for dynamic and hybrid analysis.

Acknowledgements. This work was supported by National Research Foundation (NRF) grant (No. NRF-2021R1F1A1061362) funded by the Korea government (MSIT), and Institute of Information & communications Technology Planning & Evaluation (IITP) grant funded by the Korea government(MSIT) (No. 2021-0-00590).

References

1. Statista, "Accesed: online," 2021
2. Statista, "Accesed: online," 2022
3. Zhou, Y., Jiang, X.: Dissecting android malware: characterization and evolution. In: 2012 IEEE Symposium on Security and Privacy, pp. 95-109 (2012)
4. Payer, S., Garrett, F., Yu, K., Richard Harang, E.: Characterization of extremely lightweight intrusion detection (ELIDe) power utilization by varying N-gram and hash length. Army Research Lab Adelphi MD Computational and Information Science Directorate (2015)
5. Liu, K., Xu, S., Xu, G., Zhang, M., Sun, D., Liu, H.: A review of android malware detection approaches based on machine learning. IEEE Access **8**, 124579–124607 (2020)
6. Pei, X., Yu, L., Tian, S.: AMalNet: a deep learning framework based on graph convolutional networks for malware detection. Comput. Secur. **93**, 101792 (2020)
7. Kim, T., Kang, B., Rho, M., Sezer, S., Im, E.G.: A multimodal deep learning method for android malware detection using various features. IEEE Trans. Inf. Forensics Secur. **14**(3), 773–788 (2018)
8. Arp, D., Spreitzenbarth, M., Hubner, M., Gascon, H., Rieck, K., Siemens, C.E.R.T.: Drebin: effective and explainable detection of android malware in your pocket. In: Ndss, vol. 14, pp. 23–26 (2014)
9. Yerima, S.Y., Sezer, S.: Droidfusion: a novel multilevel classifier fusion approach for android malware detection. IEEE Trans. Cybern. **49**(2), 453–466 (2019)
10. Abdulla, S., Altaher, A.: Intelligent approach for android malware detection. KSII Trans. Internet Inf. Syst. **9**(8) 2015
11. Qamar, A., Karim, A., Chang, V.: Mobile malware attacks: review, taxonomy and future directions. Futur. Gener. Comput. Syst. **97**, 887–909 (2019)
12. Tam, K., Feizollah, A., Anuar, N.B., Salleh, R., Cavallaro, L.: The evolution of android malware and android analysis techniques. ACM Comput. Surv. (CSUR) **49**(4), 1–41 (2017)
13. McGiff, J., Hatcher, W.G., Nguyen, J., Yu, W., Blasch, E., Lu, C.: Towards multi-modal learning for android malware detection. In: 2019 International Conference on Computing, Networking and Communications (ICNC), pp. 432–436. IEEE (2019)
14. Zhang, P., Cheng, S., Lou, S., Jiang, F.: A novel Android malware detection approach using operand sequences. In: 2018 Third International Conference on Security of Smart Cities, Industrial Control System and Communications (SSIC), pp. 1–5. IEEE (2018)
15. Cai, L., Li, Y., Xiong, Z.: JOWMDroid: android malware detection based on feature weighting with joint optimization of weight-mapping and classifier parameters. Comput. Secur. **100**, 102086 (2021)
16. PyTorch. 2022. Accesed: Online
17. Garg, S., Peddoju, S.K., Sarje, A.K.: Network-based detection of Android malicious apps. Int. J. Inf. Secur. **16**, 385–400 (2017)
18. Tensorflow. 2022. Accesed: Online

19. Hasan, H., Ladani, B.T., Zamani, B.: MEGDroid: a model-driven event generation framework for dynamic android malware analysis. Inf. Softw. Technol. **135**, 106569 (2021)
20. Qaisar, Z.H., Li, R.: Multimodal information fusion for android malware detection using lazy learning. Multimedia Tools Appl. **81**, 1–15 (2022)
21. Martín, A., Menéndez, H.D., Camacho, D.: MOCDroid: multi-objective evolutionary classifier for android malware detection. Soft. Comput. **21**, 7405–7415 (2017)
22. Scikit-Learn. 2022. Accesed
23. Naway, A., Li, Y.: Using deep neural network for Android malware detection. arXiv preprint arXiv:1904.00736 (2019)
24. Xu, K., Li, Y., Deng, R.H., Chen, K.: Deeprefiner: multi-layer android malware detection system applying deep neural networks. In: 2018 IEEE European Symposium on Security and Privacy (EuroS and P), pp. 473–487. IEEE (2018)
25. Keras. 2022. Accesed: Online
26. Amin, M., Tanveer, T.A., Tehseen, M., Khan, M., Khan, F.A., Anwar, S.: Static malware detection and attribution in android byte-code through an end-to-end deep system. Futur. Gener. Comput. Syst. **102**, 112–126 (2020)
27. Millar, S., McLaughlin, N., Martinez del Rincon, J., Miller, P., Zhao, Z.: DANdroid: a multi-view discriminative adversarial network for obfuscated Android malware detection. In: Proceedings of the Tenth ACM Conference on Data and Application Security and Privacy, pp. 353–364 (2020)
28. Lu, T., Du, Y., Ouyang, L., Chen, Q., Wang, X.: Android malware detection based on a hybrid deep learning model. Secur. Commun. Netw. **2020**, 1–11 (2020)
29. MLP. 2022. Accesed: Online
30. Wanto, A., Windarto, A.P., Hartama, D., Parlina, I.: Use of binary sigmoid function and linear identity in artificial neural networks for forecasting population density. IJISTECH Int. J. Inf. Syst. Technol. **1**(1), 43–54 (2017)
31. GIT. 2022. Accesed: Online
32. Tang, J., Li, R., Jiang, Y., Gu, X., Li, Y.: Android malware obfuscation variants detection method based on multi-granularity opcode features. Futur. Gener. Comput. Syst. **129**, 141–151 (2022)
33. Vu, L.N., Jung, S.: AdMat: a CNN-on-matrix approach to android malware detection and classification. IEEE Access **9**, 39680–39694 (2021)
34. Elayan, O.N., Mustafa, A.M.: Android malware detection using deep learning. Procedia Comput. Sci. **184**, 847–852 (2021)
35. Google Colaboratory. 2022. Accesed: Online
36. Zhang, N., Tan, Y.A., Yang, C., Li, Y.: Deep learning feature exploration for android malware detection. Appl. Soft Comput. **102**, 107069 (2021)
37. Grosse. 2018. Accesed: Online
38. Pektaş, A., Acarman, T.: Deep learning for effective android malware detection using API call graph embeddings. Soft. Comput. **24**, 1027–1043 (2020)
39. Chen, T., Mao, Q., Lv, M., Cheng, H., Li, Y.: Droidvecdeep: android malware detection based on word2vec and deep belief network. KSII Trans. Internet Inf. Syst. (TIIS) **13**(4), 2180–2197 (2019)
40. Gao, H., Cheng, S., Zhang, W.: GDroid: android malware detection and classification with graph convolutional network. Comput. Secur. **106**, 102264 (2021)
41. Wu, Q., Li, M., Zhu, X., Liu, B.: Mviidroid: a multiple view information integration approach for android malware detection and family identification. IEEE Multimedia **27**(4), 48–57 (2020)
42. PyCUDA. 2022. Accesed: Online

43. Kinkead, M., Millar, S., McLaughlin, N., O'Kane, P.: Towards explainable CNNs for android malware detection. Procedia Computer Science **184**, 959–965 (2021)
44. Li, W., Wang, Z., Cai, J., Cheng, S.: An android malware detection approach using weight-adjusted deep learning. In 2018 International Conference on Computing, Networking and Communications (ICNC), pp. 437–441. IEEE (2018)
45. Liu, H., Dai, Z., So, D., Le, Q.V.: Pay attention to mlps. Adv. Neural. Inf. Process. Syst. **34**, 9204–9215 (2021)

SmartBuoy: A Machine Learning-Based Detection Method for Interest Flooding Attacks in VNDN

Yuwei Xu[1,2,3]([✉]), Tiantian Zhang[1,3], Junyu Zeng[1,3], Rongrong Wang[1,3], Kehui Song[4], and Jingdong Xu[4]

[1] School of Cyber Science and Engineering, Southeast University, Nanjing 211102, China
{xuyw,zhangtiantian,zengjunyu,wangrr}@seu.edu.cn
[2] Purple Mountain Laboratories for Network and Communication Security, Nanjing 211102, China
[3] Engineering Research Center of Blockchain Application, Supervision and Management, Nanjing 211102, China
[4] College of Computer Science, Nankai University, Tianjin 300071, China
{songkehui,xujd}@nankai.edu.cn

Abstract. Due to the advantages of multi-source, multi-path, and in-network caching, Named Data Networking (NDN) can improve the efficiency of data exchange in Vehicular Ad-hoc NETworks (VANETs). As Vehicular Named Data Networking (VNDN) has become a new paradigm for connected vehicles, it also introduces a new security issue. Since VNDN follows the 'request-response' communication mode, malicious nodes can flood many interest packets to occupy resources, block the network, and damage intelligent transportation applications. Therefore, fast detection of Interest Flooding Attacks (IFA) is an urgent problem in VNDN. Some researchers have transplanted the IFA detection methods in NDN to VNDN, but there are still defects such as single detection category, low accuracy rate, and high overhead. Aiming at the above defects, an IFA detection method based on machine learning is proposed and named SmartBuoy. The contribution of our work lies in the following three points. Firstly, we present an IFA traffic generation method based on three simulation tools and construct a fine-grained dataset by building a dynamic directional interface model (DDIM). Secondly, by analyzing the traffic through directional interfaces, we propose 22 new features for IFA detection. Finally, we design a Two-Stage Two-Dimension feature selection algorithm (TSTD) to construct the optimal feature subset for a selected classifier with a specified number of features. We have verified the effectiveness of SmartBuoy through experiments. The results show that: (1) Compared with the rule-based methods, SmartBuoy can obtain a higher detection accuracy. (2) The new features designed according to DDIM can improve the performance of classifiers. (3) TSTD can help classifiers achieve higher accuracy than the other two classical algorithms with a specified number of features.

Keywords: Interest Flooding Attacks (IFA) · Vehicular Named Data Networking (VNDN) · Machine Learning · Feature Selection

© The Author(s), under exclusive license to Springer Nature Singapore Pte Ltd. 2024
G. Wang et al. (Eds.): UbiSec 2023, CCIS 2034, pp. 236–252, 2024.
https://doi.org/10.1007/978-981-97-1274-8_16

1   Introduction

Due to rapid topology changes and frequent link disconnections, efficient data transmission has been a formidable challenge in Vehicular Ad-hoc NETworks (VANETs). As a future-oriented network paradigm, Named Data Networking (NDN) [16] has the advantages of multi-source, multi-path, and in-network cache. In recent years, researchers began to apply NDN to VANETs [7] to speed up data transmission between vehicles and proposed the concept of Vehicular Named Data Networking (VNDN).

As VNDN has become a research hotspot in academia and industry, a crucial security issue has emerged and received widespread attention. Since VNDN follows the 'request-response' communication mode, malicious vehicle nodes can launch Interest Flooding Attacks (IFA) [5] by broadcasting many interest packets requesting data. Compared with the IFA in the wired networks, the impact of IFA targeting VNDN is more serious. Due to the limited resources of wireless channels and vehicle nodes, the excessive consumption caused by IFA can destroy the transmission of named data [14], lead to the collapse of related applications [13], and even cause road traffic accidents [12]. Therefore, detecting IFA through network traffic has become an urgent problem in current VNDN researches.

Some researchers have transplanted the detection methods proposed for wired networks into VNDN and achieved some results. However, previous studies still have three shortcomings. (1) Since it is difficult to capture traffic data in real traffic scenarios, most previous studies only involve one type of IFA, and none release public data sets. (2) As vehicles do not have fixed interfaces like wired network devices, the granularity of IFA detection is low. (3) Machine learning-based detection methods rely on valuable features. Due to the limited resources of vehicle nodes, it is necessary to design a feature selection algorithm that can construct an optimal feature subset for a specified classifier under the premise of setting the number of features.

Aiming at the shortcomings of previous studies, we propose SmartBuoy, a machine learning-based IFA detection method. It can detect IFA in VNDN as efficiently as a buoy to warn of floods. The main contribution of our work contains the following four points.

- To obtain high-quality IFA flow data, we propose a traffic flow collection method based on simulation experiments. Through it, we construct a rich dataset that covers three types of traffic scenarios and contains two different kinds of IFA. (In Subsect. 3.1).
- To solve the problem of low detection granularity, we design a dynamic directional interface model (DDIM). By mapping the traffic flows to the directional interfaces, we propose 22 new features to make up for the disadvantages brought by wireless broadcasting and realize interface-level IFA detection. (In Subsect. 3.2).
- To efficiently perform machine learning-based detection on vehicles, we design a Two-Stage Two-Dimension feature selection algorithm (TSTD). In the filtering stage, TSTD can reduce the error of feature redundancy calculation by

adjusting the feature weight. In the packaging stage, it can quickly construct the optimal feature subset for different classifiers by introducing the feature ranking of Chi-Square (CS). (In Sect. 4).

- To verify the effectiveness of SmartBuoy, we have conducted comparative experiments. The results show that SmartBuoy improves the accuracy of IFA detection compared with the rule-based methods. Besides, the feature set proposed on DDIM helps most classifiers obtain better classification results than previous feature sets. Finally, TSTD helps most classifiers achieve higher accuracy than two classic feature selection algorithms. (In Sect. 5).

2   Related Work

2.1   IFA in VNDN

In VNDN, malicious nodes send a large number of interest packets to launch IFA in a very short time, occupying network resources and affecting the surrounding nodes. IFA can be divided into two types according to different attack generation processes [9], as shown in Fig. 1. In type A, the attacker V_1 firstly generates random strings as the names of the interest packets, for example, '/sfjnjbu/dhfbj/sadhjhf', and secondly broadcasts the interest packets with same names at a high frequency. In type B, the attacker V_1 firstly extracts name prefix from the existing interests packets by sniffing other nodes V_2 and V_3, secondly concatenates the name prefix with randomly generated suffixes, such as '/Nanjing/Yuhua/RoadX/stfdtgt', and finally broadcasts the interest packets. According to the process of IFA, the two types have different ways of generating names. The names of interest packets sent by type A are randomly generated, and the names of interest packets sent by the second type are obtained by sniffing other nodes. Compared with type A, the names of interest packets sent by type B are similar to the names of normal interest packets and type B has stronger anti-detection ability.

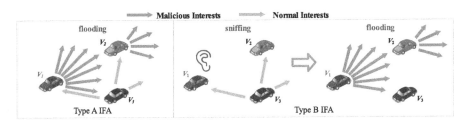

Fig. 1. Two types of IFA in VNDN

2.2   IFA Detection Methods

With the emergence of IFA in NDN, researchers begin to study the detection methods of IFA. As shown in Table 1, we have sorted out, summarized and listed related work in recent years. From the related work, it can be seen that the data to be detected are obtained through simulation.

Table 1. Studies on IFA detection in VNDN.

No.	Paper	Application scenarios	Data source	Detection granularity	Feature Numbers	Feature sets	Feature selection	Detection model	classifier
1	[2]	NDN	simulated	interface-based	1	△	×	Rule-based	/
2	[3]	NDN	simulated	interface-based	2	△ + □	×	Rule-based	/
3	[6]	NDN	simulated	node-based	1	▽	×	Rule-based	/
4	[17]	NDN	simulated	interface-based	2	△	×	ML-based	Hidden Markov Model
5	[19]	NDN	simulated	node-based	3	△ + ▽ + □	×	ML-based	SVM
6	[9]	NDN	simulated	interface-based	12	△ + □	✓	ML-based	4 types of ML classifiers
7	[15]	NDN	simulated	node-based	4	△ + □	×	ML-based	Isolation Forest
8	[1]	VNDN	simulated	node-based	5	△	×	Rule-based	/
9	[11]	VNDN	simulated	node-based	2	△	×	Rule-based	/
10	[4]	NDN	simulated	node-based	1	△	×	Rule-based	/
11	[18]	NDN	simulated	node-based	4	△+ □	×	ML-based	LSTM
12	SmartBuoy	VNDN	simulated	interface-based	12	△ + ▽ + □	✓	ML-based	6 typical ML classifiers

△ represents basic features, ▽ represents statistical features, and □ represents PIT related features, as shown in Table 4, 5 and 6.

Rule-Based Methods. Early researchers build a set of rules to detect IFA by analyzing the correlation features of named data. In [2], a detection method based on the satisfaction rate of interest packets is proposed. If the rate is greater than the preset threshold, IFA is detected. Besides the satisfaction rate of interest packets, the authors of [3] also extract the feature of PIT occupancy size. If both exceed the preset thresholds, it detects IFA. Since interest packets names in IFA are randomly generated, the name distribution of it is different from that in normal times. In [6], the authors calculate entropy based on the name distribution of interest packets and set thresholds for the features. In [4], the authors use interest name prefix to detect IFA. Unlike previous methods, it detects IFA based on the content provider rather than the router, which is a lightweight and effective method. In [1], the authors propose a feature named priority, which is calculated by five features, such as satisfaction rate of interest packets and satisfaction delay of interest packets. IFA is detected if the priority is below the preset threshold. The authors of [11] regularly check the number of interest packets sent by the vehicles. If the number exceeds the threshold, the vehicles are considered suspicious. If the satisfaction rate is low, IFA is detected. It is important and difficult to set thresholds according to the feature distribution. On the one hand, the setting of thresholds relies heavily on expert experience. On the other hand, when the same rules are applied to new network scenarios, the corresponding thresholds need to be updated.

Machine Learning-Based Methods. To overcome the shortcomings of rule-based methods, researchers try to detect IFA by machine learning-based methods. In [17], a mechanism based on Hidden Markov Model is proposed to detect IFA. This method builds a Hidden Markov Model based on the statistical characteristics of normal named data to detect the attack state. The authors of [19] select the satisfaction rate of interest packets, the occupancy rate of PIT and the entropy of interest packets names as features, and make detection by SVM. In [15], the authors extract four new features based on interest name prefixes and realize IFA detection by building an isolated forest model. The authors of [9] extract 12 features and select features based on Information Gain to construct an optimal subset and the results show that the method is effective. In [18], the authors extract four common features and combine LSTM and attention mechanism to detect IFA.

Although researchers have carried out researches on machine learning-based methods, there are still three shortcomings in these researches. (1) The type of IFA involved in the these methods is single and there is no public dataset. (2) The detection granularity is rough. (3) There is lack of extracting valuable features based on in-depth analysis of IFA in VNDN. Therefore, we propose a traffic flow collection method based on simulation experiments and a detection method named SmartBuoy to make up for the above deficiencies.

3   Traffic Collection and Processing

In this section, we propose a traffic flow collection method based on simulation experiments. Firstly, traffic is collected based on simulation tools, which is mainly divided into three steps: constructing scene, generating traffic and collecting traffic. Then a DDIM is proposed to prepare for partitioning samples. Finally, samples are processed using scripts.

3.1   Traffic Collection

Scenario Construction. This work is divided into 3 steps: generating maps, constructing roads and arranging traffic flows. We firstly generate three different maps by simulation tools SUMO [8] and OpenStreetMap which include a highway, a Manhattan model and a real street. Secondly roads are constructed on the map. Finally, traffic flows are arranged on the road. In the simulation, all the vehicles can perform basic operations such as accelerating, decelerating and turning, as well as obeying traffic rules before and after traffic lights. The parameters related to traffic scenarios are shown in Table 2.

Table 2. Simulation parameters related to traffic scenarios.

Parameter	Value		
	Highway	Manhattan	Real streets
Scenario area	$8 \times 0.02\,\mathrm{km}^2$	$2 \times 2\,\mathrm{km}^2$	$2 \times 2\,\mathrm{km}^2$
Number of vehicles	50	80	50
Number of consumers	5	4	5
Number of attackers	5	4	5
Number of traffic flows	1	4	5
Vehicle speed limit	72 km/h	72 km/h	36 km/h
Vehicle distance	50~100 m	100~200 m	10 m
Normal Interest packets rate	10 pps	10 pps	10 pps
Attack Interest packets rate	100 pps	100 pps	100 pps

Traffic Generation. We generate two types of traffic by ndnSIM [10] based on NS-3, the first one is normal traffic and the second one is IFA traffic. We firstly select random consumers and set them to send interest packets at a fixed frequency to request data. Each vehicle can then act as a relay node to forward interest packets and data packets. When interest packets finally reach the nearest RSUs, the RSUs satisfy interest packets and reply the corresponding data. The above process generates normal traffic. The consumers normally send interest packets while the attackers send interest packets 10 times more often than normal consumers to launch IFA. The above process generates IFA traffic. Simulation parameters related to named data transmission are shown in Table 3.

Table 3. Simulation parameters related to named data transferring.

Parameter	Value
Antenna type	Omnidirectional
Propagation Model	3LogDistance&Nakagami
Interest lifetime	2 s
PIT size	100 entries
PIT lifetime	2 s
PIT Replacement policy	Least recently used
CS size	100 entires
CS Replacement policy	Least recently used
Transmission range	500 m

Traffic Collection. We randomly select vehicle nodes to collect traffic. The built-in function of ndnSIM simulator is used to trace the simulation results and generate data files. To get more information, we print out the running logs and use it. In addition, the source codes are modified to configure the data we need.

We preliminarily analyze the collected data to verify its validity. Figure 2 is drawn by calculating the interest satisfaction ratios in all scenarios. Under no attack, the interest satisfaction ratios of the three traffic scenarios are consistently above 90%. When IFA occurs, the ratios of three traffic scenarios drop significantly, to less than 80% or even lower.

3.2 Data Processing

Dynamic Directional Interface Model. A Dynamic Direction Interface Model (DDIM) is proposed to realize more fine-grained IFA detection. As shown in Fig. 3, we set the vehicle's driving direction as a reference for interface division. In DDIM, the vehicle-centric area is divided into four parts. Each part is mapped to one directional interface. In Fig. 3, the forward interface (*F-INF*) covers the 90-degree area in front of the vehicle. Opposite to *F-INF*, the backward interface (*B-INF*) covers the 90-degree area behind the vehicle. Besides, the left interface (*L-INF*) and the right interface (*R-INF*) are corresponding to the 90-degree areas on both sides of the vehicle. Different from the fixed interfaces, the interfaces of DDIM can rotate with the change of driving direction. Subsequent operations are based on DDIM including constructing training and testing samples and extracting features.

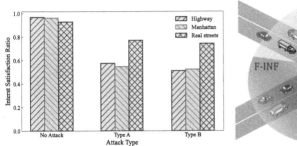

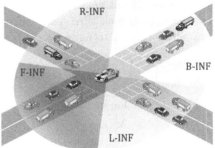

Fig. 2. Comparison of interest satisfaction ratios

Fig. 3. Dynamic directional interface model

Data Processing. After data collection, samples are processed and then fed into the classifier for model training. The process is divided into four steps: generating samples, filtering, labeling and undersampling. We firstly divide samples based on the DDIM, and construct training and testing sets according to our new definition of samples. In SmartBuoy, a sample is defined as the traffic passing through interface i of node n in the interval ΔT. Secondly each sample is labeled by using scripts according to the log files generated during the simulation. In the filtering step, the empty samples with no transmission information from training and testing sets are filtered out. Finally, to ensure the best performance of the classifier, we undersample training and testing sets to balance samples. For the two types of IFA, 5000 samples are randomly selected from qualified candidates in each scenario. Besides, 10,000 normal samples are randomly selected from qualified candidates in each scenario. Therefore, we build a dataset containing 90,000 samples and covering three types of traffic scenarios and two types of IFA.

4   Feature Optimization

In this section, we first propose an IFA detection framework by defining two classification tasks, then analyze the characteristics of IFA in VNDN and extract 22 features and finally design a Two-Stage Two-Dimension feature selection algorithm (TSTD) to construct the optimal feature subset.

4.1   IFA Detection Framework

According to the definition of sample mentioned in Sect. 3.2, we construct an IFA detection framework. In our framework, the training set containing m samples is denoted as $\mathbb{X} = \{s_1, s_2, ..., s_m\}$, and the testing set containing n samples is denoted as $\mathbb{Y} = \{s_{(m+1)}, s_{(m+2)}, ..., s_{(m+n)}\}$. Two label sets are defined for different tasks where $\mathbb{L}_1 = \{0, 1, 2\}$ denotes the type of samples which include normal samples, warning samples and IFA samples and $\mathbb{L}_2 = \{1, 2\}$ denotes the type of IFA. Assume that $\mathbb{F}$ is defined as a complete set containing all features. For a given task, k features are selected from $\mathbb{F}$ to construct a classifier-oriented optimal subset $\mathbb{C} = \{c_i | i = 1, ..., k, c_i \in \mathbb{F}\}$. For all samples, features are calculated differently according to $\mathbb{C}$ which are used as input of classification. IFA detection is mainly divided into two steps. (1) We use the $\mathbb{X}$ value on $\mathbb{C}$ to construct the feature matrix C^X, and use the $\mathbb{X}$ value on $\mathbb{L}_1$ and $\mathbb{L}_2$ to construct two column vectors L_1^X and L_2^X. Then use C^X, L_1^X, L_2^X as input to train a classifier. (2) We construct a feature matrix C^Y for $\mathbb{Y}$ and input it into the trained classifier to get results. The result of $\mathbb{Y}$ on $\mathbb{L}_1$, $\mathbb{L}_2$ are two column vectors L_1^Y and L_2^Y. The definitions of C^X, L_1^X and L_2^X are shown in Eq. 1 and 2. C^Y, L_1^Y and L_2^Y are defined similarly to them. In Eq. 1, C^X is an $m \times k$ matrix. Each row represents a sample, each column represents the calculation results of m samples for a feature, and v_{ij} represents the j-th feature of the i-th sample. In Eq. 2, L_1^X and L_2^X are column vectors containing m elements, which together constitute the label matrix L^X of all samples on $\mathbb{X}$.

$$C^X = \begin{bmatrix} v_{11} & v_{12} & \cdots & v_{1k} \\ v_{21} & v_{22} & \cdots & v_{2k} \\ \vdots & \vdots & \vdots & \vdots \\ v_{m1} & v_{m2} & \cdots & v_{mk} \end{bmatrix} \tag{1}$$

$$L^X = \begin{bmatrix} L_1^X & L_2^X \end{bmatrix} = \begin{bmatrix} l_{11} & l_{12} \\ l_{21} & l_{22} \\ \vdots & \vdots \\ l_{m1} & l_{m2} \end{bmatrix} \tag{2}$$

Based on the IFA definitions, we propose two basic classification tasks. As shown in Fig. 4. The task T1 is designed for basic classification including normal samples, warning samples and IFA samples. In addition, the task T2 is used for fine-grained classification of which type of IFA. According to the above definition, we give the accurate definition of two tasks by the formal method.

T1: Using C^X and L_1^X as inputs, train the model with the given classifier. Using C^Y as input, identify whether each sample in $\mathbb{Y}$ is an IFA sample, and output L_1^Y.

T2: Using $C^{\tilde{X}}$ and $L_2^{\tilde{X}}$ as inputs, train the model with the given classifier. Using $C^{\tilde{Y}}$ as input, identify whether each sample in $\tilde{\mathbb{Y}}$ belongs to type A or type B, and output $L_1^{\tilde{Y}}$.

Based on the framework, we extract the features and propose the TSTD to construct optimal feature subsets on a given classifier for different identification tasks.

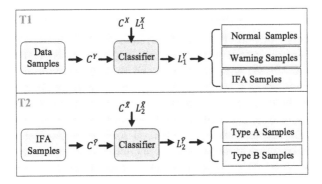

Fig. 4. IFA detection framework

4.2   Feature Extraction

To accurately describe the characteristics of IFA traffic, we design 22 features covering three categories referring to [19]. The basic ideas for each category are described below and all features are listed in Table 4, 5 and 6.

Table 4. Basic features.

Features	Meanings
InInterests	The number of arrival interests packets
InSatisfiedInterests	The number of satisfied interest packets

Table 5. Statistical features.

Features	Meanings
MinIntervalInInterests	Minimum of interest packets' arrival intervals
MaxIntervalInInterests	Maximum of interest packets' arrival intervals
AvgIntervalInInterests	Mean of interest packets' arrival intervals
StdIntervalInInterests	Standard deviation of interest packets' arrival intervals
MinIntervalInSatisfiedInterests	Minimum of interest packets' satisfied intervals
MaxIntervalInSatisfiedInterests	Maximum of interest packets' satisfied intervals
AvgIntervalInSatisfiedInterests	Mean of interest packets' satisfied intervals
StdIntervalInSatisfiedInterests	Standard deviation of interest packets' satisfied intervals
MinLenInInterestsNames	Minimum length of arrival interests packets' names
MaxLenInInterestsNames	Maximum length of arrival interests packets' names
AvgLenInInterestsNames	Mean length of arrival interests packets' names
StdLenInInterestsNames	Standard deviation of arrival interests packets' names
InInterestsNamesEntropy	The entropy of arrival interests packets' names

- These two basic features including 'InInterests' and 'InSatisfiedInterests' are designed for describing intuitive performance about the traffic passing through interface i of node n in ΔT. These two features can be obtained directly during the simulation.
- 13 statistical features describe the statistics of the traffic passing through interface i of node n in ΔT including three measures, the length of the interest packet names, the interest packet arrival interval and the interest packet satisfied interval. We calculate its maximum, minimum, mean and standard deviation for each measure. In addition, statistical features include the entropy value of the interest packet name prefixes.
- 7 PIT features represent statistical results related to PIT in interface i of node n in ΔT, such as 'PITNewEntries' and 'PITExpiredEntries'.

Table 6. PIT features.

Features	Meanings
PITNewEntries	The number of PIT new entries
PITMatchInterests	The number of arrival interest packets matching with entries
PITNewEntriesandInterestsRatio	The ratio of PIT new entries to arrival interest packets
PITReplaceEntries	The number of PIT replaced entries
PITExpiredEntries	The number of PIT expired entries
PITChangedEntries	The number of PIT changed entries
PITChangedEntriesProportion	The change of ratio of PIT new entries to PIT entries

4.3   Feature Selection

To ensure relatively high detection performance on vehicle nodes with limited resource, it is necessary to apply the feature selection algorithm to construct the optimal feature subset for specific classification tasks and classifiers. In this section, we propose a Two-Stage Two-Dimension feature selection algorithm (TSTD) considering both the correlation between labels and features and the redundancy between features.

TSTD is divided into two stages as shown in Algorithm 1. In the first stage, we use two classical algorithm mRMR and Chi-Square (CS) to get two ranking lists from two different dimensions. The CS algorithm mainly evaluates the correlation between features and labels. The mRMR algorithm not only considers the correlation between features and labels, but also eliminates the redundancy between features. However, the mRMR algorithm suffers from inaccuracy when calculating redundancy.

As shown in Fig. 5, f_1 represents the feature in the feature subset, f_2 represents the feature to be evaluated, and l is the class label. We define r_5 as the part where f_1, f_2 and l intersect, r_2+r_5 as the part where f_1 and f_2 intersect, r_4+r_5 as the part where f_1 and l intersect, r_5+r_6 as the part where f_2 and l intersect.

Algorithm 1: TSTD (Two-Stage Two-Dimension feature selection algorithm)

---

input : $\mathbb{F}$: full set of features; $\mathbb{P}$: set of samples; N: limit of feature number; c: selected classifier; s: size of sublist;

output: $\overline{\mathbb{C}}$: optimal subset of features when N and c are specified; $\overline{A}$: accuracy with feature set $\overline{\mathbb{C}}$;

1 **Stage 1: The Filter part**
2 $list_1 \leftarrow$ ***improved mRMR***$(\mathbb{F})$;
3 $list_2 \leftarrow$ ***chi_square***$(\mathbb{F})$;
4 $\mathbb{S}_1 \leftarrow$ ***div_sublists***$(list_1, s)$;
5 $\mathbb{S}_2 \leftarrow$ ***div_sublists***$(list_2, s)$;
6 **Stage 2: The Wrapper part**
7 **for** $i \leftarrow 1$ **to** $\lceil size(\mathbb{F})/s \rceil$ **do**
8 $\quad$ $sl[0] \leftarrow$ ***get_sublist_by_no***$(\mathbb{S}_1, i)$;
9 $\quad$ $sl[1] \leftarrow$ ***get_sublist_by_no***$(\mathbb{S}_2, i)$;
10 $\quad$ $acc[0] \leftarrow$ ***get_acc_by_clf***$(\mathbb{P}, sl[0], c)$;
11 $\quad$ $acc[1] \leftarrow$ ***get_acc_by_clf***$(\mathbb{P}, sl[1], c)$;
12 $\quad$ **if** $acc[0] \geq acc[1]$ **then**
13 $\quad\quad$ $r_1 \leftarrow$ ***Search***$(\overline{\mathbb{C}}, \overline{A}, sl[0])$;
14 $\quad\quad$ **if** $r_1 == 0$ **then** break;
15 $\quad\quad$ $r_2 \leftarrow$ ***Search***$(\overline{\mathbb{C}}, \overline{A}, sl[1])$;
16 $\quad\quad$ **if** $r_2 == 0$ **then** break;
17 $\quad$ **else**
18 $\quad\quad$ $r_1 \leftarrow$ ***Search***$(\overline{\mathbb{C}}, \overline{A}, sl[1])$;
19 $\quad\quad$ **if** $r_1 == 0$ **then** break;
20 $\quad\quad$ $r_2 \leftarrow$ ***Search***$(\overline{\mathbb{C}}, \overline{A}, sl[0])$;
21 $\quad\quad$ **if** $r_2 == 0$ **then** break;
22 $\quad$ $\mathbb{C}, A \leftarrow$ ***Backtrack***$(\mathbb{C}, A)$;
23 **return** $\overline{\mathbb{C}}, \overline{A}$;
24 **Function** *Search* $(\overline{\mathbb{C}}, \overline{A}, list)$:
25 $\quad$ **for** $j \leftarrow 1$ **to** $size(list)$ **do**
26 $\quad\quad$ **if** $list[j] \notin \overline{\mathbb{C}}$ **then**
27 $\quad\quad\quad$ $\mathbb{C}' \leftarrow \overline{\mathbb{C}} + list[j]$;
28 $\quad\quad\quad$ $acc' \leftarrow$ ***get_acc_by_clf***$(\mathbb{P}, \mathbb{C}', c)$;
29 $\quad\quad\quad$ **if** $acc' > \overline{A}$ **then**
30 $\quad\quad\quad\quad$ $\overline{\mathbb{C}} \leftarrow \mathbb{C}'$;
31 $\quad\quad\quad\quad$ $\overline{A} \leftarrow acc'$;
32 $\quad\quad\quad\quad$ **if** $size(\overline{\mathbb{C}}) \geq N$ **then**
33 $\quad\quad\quad\quad\quad$ **return** 0;
34 $\quad$ **return** 1;
35 **Function** *Backtrack* $(\overline{\mathbb{C}}, \overline{A}, list)$:
36 $\quad$ **for** $j \leftarrow 1$ **to** $size(list)$ **do**
37 $\quad\quad$ $\mathbb{C}' \leftarrow \overline{\mathbb{C}} - list[j]$;
38 $\quad\quad$ $acc' \leftarrow$ ***get_acc_by_clf***$(\mathbb{P}, \mathbb{C}', c)$;
39 $\quad\quad$ **if** $acc' > \overline{A}$ **then**
40 $\quad\quad\quad$ $\overline{\mathbb{C}} \leftarrow \mathbb{C}'$;
41 $\quad\quad\quad$ $\overline{A} \leftarrow acc'$;
42 $\quad$ **return** $\overline{\mathbb{C}}, \overline{A}$;

According to the mRMR algorithm, it is assumed that there is a feature subset S, and features are selected by maximizing Eq. 3.

$$\max \left\{ \frac{F(i,h)}{\frac{1}{|S|} \sum_{j \in S} |F(i,j)|} \right\} \tag{3}$$

i represents the feature being evaluated, j represents the existing feature in the feature subset, h represents the label, $F(i,h)$ represents the correlation degree between feature i and label h, and $F(i,j)$ represents the redundancy degree between feature i and other feature j in the feature subset, $F(j,h)$ represents the correlation between feature j and label h.

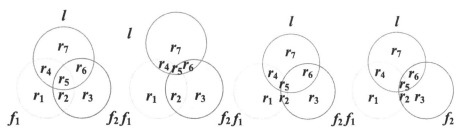

(a) f_1, f_2 and l inter-(b) If the intersection(c) If the intersec-(d) If the intersection
sect   of f_1 and l decreases,tion of f_1 and f_2 de-of f_2 and l decreases,
                            r_5 decreases   creases, r_5 decreases3r_5 decreases

Fig. 5. The influencing factors of redundancy

The redundancy calculated based on the above Eq. 3 is $r_2 + r_5$ but the actual redundancy is r_5. Therefore, the calculated redundancy is greater than the actual redundancy. To calculate redundancy more accurately, we design a redundancy factor. The redundancy factor is related to r_5. r_5 is correlated with three parts, the part where f_1 and f_2 intersect, the part where f_2 and l intersect, and the part where f_1 and l intersect, as shown in Fig. 5b, Fig. 5c, Fig. 5d.

Therefore, with the above ideas we calculate the redundancy by adding a redundancy factor, as shown in the following Eq. 4:

$$\alpha_{ij} = \frac{F(i,j) + F(i,h) + F(j,h)}{3 \times F(i,j)} \tag{4}$$

The mRMR algorithm is modified by redefining the calculation of the redundancy factor to obtain a new algorithm. So Eq. 3 is updated to Eq. 5 as follows:

$$\max \left\{ \frac{F(i,h)}{\frac{1}{\left|\sum_{j \in S} \alpha_{ij}\right|} \sum_{j \in S} |\alpha_{ij} \times F(i,j)|} \right\} \tag{5}$$

In the second stage, we use a wrapper process to construct the optimal subset. We obtain two ranking lists S_1 and S_2 from the filter stage. Firstly, we put the features of two sublists of S_1 and S_2 into the same classifier to compare the accuracy in each round of feature selection. The sublist with high accuracy is the first candidate set, and the other sublist is the second candidate set. When the accuracy is equal, the sublist corresponding to the improved mRMR algorithm is the first candidate set. Secondly, we select one feature from the candidate set each time. If its addition can improve the accuracy of the optimal subset, it is added to the optimal subset. Otherwise, it is dropped. Thirdly, a feature is removed from the candidate feature set one at a time. If the deleted subset improves the accuracy of the optimal subset, it is retained as the optimal subset. And the highest classification accuracy and corresponding optimal subsets are recorded. Finally, the greedy search stops until one of the following three conditions is met. (1) The number of the optimal subset reaches the initial set value N. (2) All features in S_1 and S_2 have been tested.

5   Experiments and Analysis

5.1   Experiment Settings

To verify the universality of SmartBuoy, we use six kinds of the most general classifiers, which are K-Nearest Neighbor (KNN), Support Vector Machine (SVM), Naive Bayes (NB), Random Forest (RF), XGBoost (XGB) and Multilayer Perceptron (MLP). The evaluation metric used in this paper is accuracy, which represents the proportion of correctly classified samples in the total samples. Each experiment is repeated 10 times for a more objective comparison and we calculate their the mean and standard deviation.

5.2   Results Analysis

Table 7. Performance comparison between SmartBuoy and two rule-based methods.

Methods	Accuracy(%)	Threshold value 1	Threshold value 2
[3]	50.991	1.6/120	2/120
[2]	36.388	0.6	0.1
KNN	98.673	\	\
SVM	98.674	\	\
NB	97.015	\	\
RF	99.288	\	\
XGB	99.363	\	\
MLP	98.975	\	\

Comparison with Two Rule-Based Methods. We compare TSTD with two rule-based methods in [3] and [2]. The detection method proposed in [3] uses two parameters, the size of PIT and the ratio of the number of interest packets received to the number of packets forwarded from an interface. In [2], only the satisfaction rate of interest packets is considered. The classification accuracy of all methods for T1 are shown in Table 7. The thresholds in the table are calculated according to the methods given in [3] and [2]. The accuracy of SmartBuoy is much higher than these two rule-based methods. The rule-based methods can only detect whether there is IFA, but cannot handle with complex attack detection. Therefore, it is difficult for these two methods to achieve high accuracy on multi-classification tasks T1. Among all classifiers, XGBoost classifier has the highest detection accuracy because it can reduce the risk of overfitting and improve model accuracy by using an ensemble learning approach.

Comparison Between the Optimal Feature Subsets Calculated by TSTD and Other Feature Sets. To verify the effect of TSTD, we conduct comparative experiments among the feature set in [9, 15, 19], the full set and the optimal feature subsets calculated by TSTD. Table 8 shows the IFA classification accuracy by using different feature sets under 6 classifiers. Since the features in [19] are mainly related to the basic information and statistics of traffic which classify T2 well, the feature set has a low classification accuracy for T1 and a high classification accuracy for T2. The feature set in [15] and [9] has a high classification accuracy for T1 while has a low classification accuracy for T2 because they contain some features related to PIT which are beneficial to improving the performance of classification for T1. The classification accuracy of TSTD for T1 and T2 are all very high, and the method can keep the accuracy of all classifiers above 90%. In addition, the classification performance of TSTD is also higher than the full set. Therefore, for different tasks and classifiers, the performance of TSTD is excellent and stable.

Table 8. Performance comparison between the optimal feature subsets calculated by TSTD and other feature sets.

Methods	Tasks	Accuracy(%)				
		[19]	[15]	[9]	Full set	TSTD
KNN	T1	84.634	94.220	98.333	92.730	**98.673(7)**
	T2	98.858	78.858	88.525	98.367	**99.691(12)**
SVM	T1	78.493	94.425	97.940	94.617	**98.674(8)**
	T2	98.658	78.058	86.925	98.943	**99.833(10)**
NB	T1	70.781	80.075	95.727	96.030	**97.015(9)**
	T2	90.565	77.220	85.691	**91.628**	90.833(7)
RF	T1	85.845	95.022	98.512	98.988	**99.288(12)**
	T2	98.966	79.595	91.587	99.855	**99.918(11)**
XGB	T1	85.533	95.304	98.516	99.164	**99.363(14)**
	T2	98.900	80.429	91.670	99.935	**99.946(13)**
MLP	T1	80.025	94.654	97.852	97.950	**98.975(9)**
	T2	98.712	78.000	86.583	99.585	**99.811(12)**

Table 9. Performance comparison between TSTD and other feature selection algorithms ($N=10$).

Methods	Tasks	Accuracy(%)		
		CS	mRMR	TSTD
KNN	T1	94.059	86.399	**98.673(7)**
	T2	**97.980**	95.670	97.142
SVM	T1	94.871	81.923	**98.674(8)**
	T2	96.677	92.655	**98.038**
NB	T1	96.041	51.691	**97.015(9)**
	T2	89.840	80.977	**90.833(7)**
RF	T1	98.400	94.041	**98.865**
	T2	99.192	98.255	**99.436**
XGBoost	T1	98.405	93.962	**99.177**
	T2	99.293	98.472	**99.576**
MLP	T1	97.502	84.979	**98.975(9)**
	T2	96.603	92.258	**98.678**

Comparison Between TSTD and Other Feature Selection Algorithms.
We compare TSTD with two classical algorithms, CS and mRMR for a specific number of features and under the same classifier. In the experiment, the specific maximum number of features N is set to 10 and 15. The classification accuracy of three feature selection algorithms is shown in Table 9 and 10. Since TSTD has a wrapper stage for specific tasks and classifiers, it can achieve a higher classification accuracy than CS and mRMR regardless of N is 10 or 15. In addition, the number of features used by TSTD does not reach the maximum requirement but TSTD achieves the highest classification accuracy for specific tasks and classifiers because we consider both the correlation between labels and features and the redundancy between features.

Table 10. Performance comparison between TSTD and other feature selection algorithms (N=15).

Methods	Tasks	Accuracy(%)		
		CS	mRMR	TSTD
KNN	T1	92.735	92.392	**98.673(7)**
	T2	98.767	95.712	**99.691(12)**
SVM	T1	94.761	81.837	**98.674(8)**
	T2	97.623	92.473	**99.833(10)**
NB	T1	95.718	64.070	**97.015(9)**
	T2	90.587	90.620	**90.833(7)**
RF	T1	98.473	98.085	**99.288(12)**
	T2	99.468	98.390	**99.918(11)**
XGB	T1	98.445	98.309	**99.363(14)**
	T2	99.510	98.490	**99.946(13)**
MLP	T1	97.669	96.954	**98.975(9)**
	T2	97.293	92.567	**99.811(12)**

6   Conclusion

We propose a detection method named SmartBuoy based on machine learning to identify IFA in VNDN. Firstly, we design an IFA traffic collection method based on three simulation tools, and build a fine-grained dataset by DDIM. Secondly, we analyze the named data traffic on the directed interface and present 22 new IFA detection features. Finally, we design a feature selection algorithm named TSTD to construct an optimal feature subset for selected classifiers with specified numbers of features. To verify the effectiveness of SmartBuoy, we conduct comparative experiments. The results show that SmartBuoy improves the accuracy of IFA detection compared with two rule-based methods. And the feature set proposed according to DDIM helps most classifiers achieve better classification results than previous feature sets. Besides, TSTD helps most classifiers obtain higher accuracy than two classic feature selection algorithms.

Acknowledgments. This work was supported in part by the National Natural Science Foundation of China under Grant 61702288, and in part by the Fundamental Research Funds for the Central Universities under Grant 2242023K30034.

References

1. Abdullah, M., Raza, I., Zia, T., Hussain, S.A.: Interest flooding attack mitigation in a vehicular named data network. IET Intell. Transp. Syst. **15**(4), 525–537 (2021)
2. Afanasyev, A., Mahadevan, P., Moiseenko, I., Uzun, E., Zhang, L.: Interest flooding attack and countermeasures in named data networking. In: 2013 IFIP Networking Conference, pp. 1–9. IEEE (2013)

3. Compagno, A., Conti, M., Gasti, P., Tsudik, G.: Poseidon: mitigating interest flooding DDOS attacks in named data networking. In: 38th Annual IEEE Conference on Local Computer Networks, pp. 630–638. IEEE (2013)

4. Dong, J., Wang, K., Quan, W., Yin, H.: Interestfence: simple but efficient way to counter interest flooding attack. Comput. Secur. **88**, 101628 (2020)

5. Fang, C., Yao, H., Wang, Z., Wu, W., Jin, X., Yu, F.R.: A survey of mobile information-centric networking: research issues and challenges. IEEE Commun. Surv. Tutor. **20**(3), 2353–2371 (2018)

6. Hou, R., et al.: Theil-based countermeasure against interest flooding attacks for named data networks. IEEE Netw. **33**(3), 116–121 (2019)

7. Khelifi, H., et al.: Named data networking in vehicular ad hoc networks: state-of-the-art and challenges. IEEE Commun. Surv. Tutor. **22**(1), 320–351 (2019)

8. Krajzewicz, D., Erdmann, J., Behrisch, M., Bieker, L.: Recent development and applications of sumo-simulation of urban mobility. Int. J. Adv. Syst. Meas. **5**(3&4) (2012)

9. Kumar, N., Singh, A.K., Srivastava, S.: Feature selection for interest flooding attack in named data networking. Int. J. Comput. Appl. **43**(6), 537–546 (2021)

10. Mastorakis, S., Afanasyev, A., Zhang, L.: On the evolution of ndnSIM: an open-source simulator for NDN experimentation. ACM SIGCOMM Comput. Commun. Rev. **47**(3), 19–33 (2017)

11. Rabari, J., Kumar, A.R.P.: FIFA: fighting against interest flooding attack in NDN-based VANET. In: 2021 International Wireless Communications and Mobile Computing (IWCMC), pp. 1539–1544. IEEE (2021)

12. Wang, R., Xu, Z., Zhao, X., Hu, J.: V2V-based method for the detection of road traffic congestion. IET Intell. Transp. Syst. **13**(5), 880–885 (2019)

13. Wang, X., Li, Y.: Vehicular named data networking framework. IEEE Trans. Intell. Transp. Syst. **21**(11), 4705–4714 (2020). https://doi.org/10.1109/TITS.2019.2945784

14. Wu, W., et al.: A survey of intrusion detection for in-vehicle networks. IEEE Trans. Intell. Transp. Syst. **21**(3), 919–933 (2020). https://doi.org/10.1109/TITS.2019.2908074

15. Xing, G., et al.: Isolation forest-based mechanism to defend against interest flooding attacks in named data networking. IEEE Commun. Mag. **59**(3), 98–103 (2021)

16. Zhang, L., et al.: Named data networking. ACM SIGCOMM Comput. Commun. Rev. **44**(3), 66–73 (2014)

17. Zhang, X., Li, R.: An ARI-HMM based interest flooding attack countermeasure in NDN. In: 2019 IEEE 23rd International Conference on Computer Supported Cooperative Work in Design (CSCWD), pp. 10–15. IEEE (2019)

18. Zhang, X., Li, R., Hou, W.: Attention-based LSTM model for IFA detection in named data networking. Secur. Commun. Netw. **2022** (2022)

19. Zhi, T., Liu, Y., Wang, J., Zhang, H.: Resist interest flooding attacks via entropy-SVM and Jensen-Shannon divergence in information-centric networking. IEEE Syst. J. **14**(2), 1776–1787 (2019)

Cyberspace Privacy

Loft: An Architecture for Lifetime Management of Privacy Data in Service Cooperation

Cong Zha[1], Zhenan Xu[1], Ju Xing[2], and Hao Yin[1(✉)]

[1] Beijing National Research Center for Information Science and Technology,
Tsinghua University, Beijing 100084, China
{chac16,xzn20}@mails.tsinghua.edu.cn, h-yin@mail.tsinghua.edu.cn
[2] Suzhou Think-Land Technology Co., Ltd., Suzhou 201701, China

Abstract. With the fast development of information technology, more and more computation applications are served in the cloud and cooperate together to provide computation services for end-users. However, the lack of inspection on the use and circulation of users' private data makes security a big concern blocking the circulation and sharing of the data. Once a user handles her private data, she loses control of it. Thus, the data's right to be forgotten is hard to be enforced. From the aspect of data's lifetime management, this paper proposes an architecture named Loft to take care of the lifespan of private data in multi-service cooperation. Loft is designed with the serverless computing architecture to conform with nowadays popular cloud computing scenarios. Loft gives a fine-grained definition for the lifetime of private data and promotes corresponding policy negotiation based on blockchain technologies. Besides, through careful system design, Loft decouples the management of lifetime management from the service itself and makes it a fundamental capability of cloud computing infrastructure. The experiment shows that the extra overhead incurred by Loft is low: its impacts on the latency and throughput of chosen computing services are typically bounded with 15.6% and 5.3% and are no more than 20.5% and 7.6%.

Keywords: Blockchain · Private data · Service cooperation · lifetime management · serverless computing

1 Introduction

With the rapid advancement of information technology, data is gradually becoming an essential element of production, serving various aspects of human societal life. In the process of utilizing and sharing this data, security issues have emerged as significant constraints hindering the realization of its full value. This problem is mainly manifested in two areas:

First, the data itself is easily stolen. The electronic nature of data makes it more susceptible to replication in digital space. Current applications, such as

© The Author(s), under exclusive license to Springer Nature Singapore Pte Ltd. 2024
G. Wang et al. (Eds.): UbiSec 2023, CCIS 2034, pp. 255–273, 2024.
https://doi.org/10.1007/978-981-97-1274-8_17

those in healthcare, finance, and government, provide convenient online data services, compelling users to share their data with application interfaces to obtain corresponding services. When privacy data shared online cannot be timely erased, the risk of data loss escalates substantially. Online data service security risks and unregulated data usage further exacerbate the risk of data theft. Additionally, the reliance on third parties, such as cloud providers, for data service deployment complicates coordination with users in data security protection, leading to high costs and difficulties in preventing data leakage.

Second, the flow of data lacks supervision. The vertical and specialized development of data services leads to diverse offerings, allowing different data service providers to enhance their overall service capabilities by connecting services. For example, in the industrial internet platform, one-stop service for customer data is achieved by organizing connections with different SaaS providers. This connection between data services leads to user data flow across various service domains, lacking end-to-end supervision. It makes data existence and usage highly opaque to users and increases the probability of data loss.

An essential measure to combat user data loss is to manage the data's lifecycle [1,2], minimizing data retention in unnecessary circumstances to mitigate the risk of data leakage. Some social applications, such as Snapchat, have introduced a "self-destruct" feature (e.g., images have a 10-second lifespan in the Snapchat app) to prevent privacy data loss. Blockchain technology, a decentralized trust ledger technology, is inherently suited for service collaboration and can be used for negotiation and proof-of-use in data usage behavior. Combining these two aspects can ensure the security of data elements in shared applications.

Simultaneously, the technical form of online data services continues to evolve. With the rise of serverless computing technology [3,4], responding to service providers' demands to reduce operational costs and cloud providers' needs for fine-grained cloud resource operation, it has become a critical form of cloud computing technology. In serverless computing, data service developers only focus on the logic of data computation, leaving the software and hardware infrastructure to cloud providers. This paradigm has the characteristic of "Function as a Service": the computation function is light and well-defined, leading to more refined collaboration between services. Therefore, how to manage user data during this intricate cooperation becomes a significant issue, especially today when data is increasingly being treated as an asset. This management is economically significant as well as policy-oriented. Previous research has shown that the close coupling of data and applications often leads to poor scalability and high cost in privacy data lifecycle management. This problem is exacerbated in dynamically open computing service collaboration, where trustworthy mechanisms for supervising privacy data usage are lacking. Some typical online data services, such as disease inference, photo beautification, and bill processing, involve in-memory computing (e.g., processing input data through relatively fixed preset models) without involving much external storage I/O. When deployed in a serverless computing architecture, these applications require higher performance and more efficient management of privacy data lifecycle.

In the context mentioned above, this paper introduces a rule-driven data lifecycle management framework called Loft, combining blockchain technology. This framework manages data lifecycle based on a quota system and explicitly separates data lifecycle management from the application. Further, it defines end-to-end privacy data lifecycle policies in a multi-service collaboration process on the chain and integrates it with system design in a serverless architecture, making privacy data lifecycle management a fundamental universal capability provided by cloud computing infrastructure.

The main contributions of this paper are:

(1) We proposed a method to define the lifecycle model of privacy data in computing services and express it in temporal terms.
(2) We proposed a framework for managing the privacy data lifecycle in a multi-service collaboration process in a serverless scenario.
(3) We implemented the proposed framework, combined with the open-source system Openfaas, and an evaluation of its performance. Experimental results show that the additional overhead introduced by the framework to the computing service operation is minimal, with additional delay and throughput costs generally not exceeding 15.6% and 5.3%, and at most not surpassing 20.5% and 7.6%.

2   Related Work

2.1   Data Erasing

The existing research on data erasing can be categorized into two main types: The first type equates data erasing with key management issues. This line of investigation posits that once the encryption key for the data has been eradicated, the data becomes irrecoverable, effectively rendering it as deleted. The project Vanish [5] scatters the encryption keys of the data throughout a P2P system using a secretive sharing method, capitalizing on the P2P system's inherent data object expiration mechanism to demolish the fragments of the key, thereby eradicating the data. Conversely, FADE [6] encrypts the file's decryption key with a control key corresponding to the file access policy. When the access policy is revoked, the corresponding control key is also eliminated, rendering the decryption key unrecoverable. Literature [7] expands on FADE to accommodate the deletion of files under multi-version file management. Literature [8] employs Trusted Platform Module (TPM) for the management of encryption data keys, verifying key deletion within TPM through a designed verification protocol.

The second category of research focuses on the elimination of the data itself, mainly dividing into application-oriented data erasing and storage system-oriented data erasing. This type of deletion research aims to mitigate the risks stemming from the lingering presence of the data. Application-oriented data erasing emphasizes the cleansing of sensitive information during the application's execution process, warding off potential data leakage caused by certain memory attacks [9–11]. Various studies [12,13] formally outline the strategies for data erasing from the perspective of programming languages, Literature [14] enhance multi-layer software stack memory recovery interfaces with zeroing operations to ensure genuine data erasing. Literature [15] furnish isolated channels between peripherals and applications for sensitive information, and execute memory erasure upon the completion of calculations. Swipe [16] identifies when private data will no longer be used through static information flow analysis and incorporates data cleaning procedures to obliterate the private information. Literature [17] suggests utilizing the reconstruction of application computational states to obscure the traces of private data operations, thereby achieving the effect of data being forgotten. Storage system-oriented data erasing primarily targets persistent storage mediums, and their non-volatile characteristics necessitate the explicit eradication of residing private information. Literature [18] introduces DNEFS, a filesystem based on flash storage medium, utilizing software approaches to dynamically encrypt and decrypt data blocks within the filesystem to regulate their visibility. This system inhibits access to deleted files by obstructing key acquisition. Evanesco [19] introduces a lock mechanism in 3D NAND flash to isolate access to deleted data at a fine granularity, reducing the performance overhead of file deletion.

2.2   Blockchain

Blockchain technology, renowned for its decentralized trust-building mechanism, is extensively utilized in multi-party collaborative environments for evidence preservation regarding relevant policies. The typical applications can be clustered into the following categories:

Blockchain-Based Authorization Systems. Enigma [20] combines Distributed Hash Table (DHT) and multi-party secure computation technology to forge a data authorization system tailored for mobile applications. Literature [21,22] provide evidence of authorization policies for collaboration between multi-cloud environments, employing trusted computing techniques to ensure policy implementation. Literature [23,24] targets the Internet of Things (IoT) environment, leveraging blockchain to control user data sharing across devices. Systems like Medrec [25] and Ancile [26] architect personal medical data utilization authorization structures founded on blockchain.

Blockchain-Based Identity Verification Systems. Literature [27] utilizes smart contracts to effectuate device identity verification within the IoT framework. Literature [28] employs a hybrid chain deployment method to consummate varying levels of identity verification under disparate IoT contexts. Homechain [29] amalgamates blockchain with group signature technology to construct an identity authentication system for devices in a smart home environment. Block-CAM [30] formulates a cross-domain authentication model based on blockchain.

Blockchain-Based Routing Systems. BGPcoin [31] and RouteChain [32] capitalize on blockchain for the design of routing mechanisms, effectively countering BGP prefix hijacking attacks. Literature [33] erects infrastructure in wide-area networks supporting BGP and DNS using blockchain. Literature [34] integrates blockchain to render redundancy in DNS record resolution.

3   Privacy Data Lifecycle Model

Figure 1 illustrates Loft's methodology for defining the lifecycle of private data and its dimensional representation. In terms of defining the lifecycle of private data, Loft references traditional methods, defining the lifecycle by delineating when private data is "no longer required" from an information processing perspective. For the dimensional representation of the private data lifecycle, Loft estimates the lifecycle in the time domain, facilitating the computational infrastructure in decoupling data from computation for private data lifecycle management.

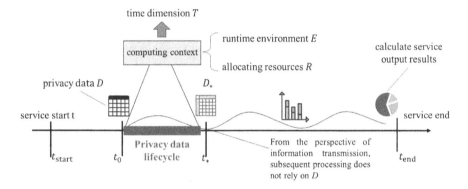

Fig. 1. Definition of Loft architecture privacy data lifecycle.

3.1   Definition of Privacy Data Lifecycle

Definition 1: Privacy Data Lifecycle. For a given set of privacy data D, and a computational service S, utilizing it, let the timeline t correspond to the computational process of S. The moment t_0 signifies when the privacy data begins its utilization. When this privacy data undergoes computation to become D^*, all subsequent computations of S are independent of D itself. At this juncture, the privacy data D is considered to have reached the end of its lifecycle. The period $T = t^* - t_0$ is termed the lifecycle of privacy data D within the computational service S. The program path P, correlating D to D^*, is recognized as the strongly related computational path of privacy data D within the computational service S.

The determination of a privacy data's strongly related computational path (i.e., the selection of D^*) establishes the relative length of the privacy data's lifecycle within the computational service, and influences the temporal prediction of this lifecycle. In practice, the choice of D^* is often made by the computational service provider based on the utilization of the privacy data.

3.2   Metrics for Privacy Data Lifecycle

Estimating the lifecycle of privacy data temporally is fundamentally an evaluation of the strongly related computational path's duration. Given the intricacies of modern processors and operating systems, it's infeasible to deduce the execution time of a program through theoretical models, hence it's usually determined through measurement methods. In existing research, estimations of program runtime often derive from statistical inferences of measurement results. For instance, in studies related to the Worst Case Execution Time (WCET [35]), the program's maximum runtime is frequently ascertained by fitting the kernel density function of the measurement results using an extreme value distribution model [36]. Similarly, Loft utilizes measurement methodologies to estimate the runtime of the privacy data's strongly related computational path, using it as a representation of the privacy data's lifecycle within the computational service.

Moreover, the maturation of computational virtualization technologies has refined the partitioning and scheduling of computational resources within the cloud, resulting in more stable metrics for the lifecycle of privacy data temporally. Combining features of serverless computing environments and in-memory computation, this study models the lifecycle of privacy data within computational services as follows:

Assuming the privacy data input to the computational service is D, with its strongly related computational path being ν. The logical core constraints of the computational service are n (encompassing core count and usage proportion, etc.), memory constraints are m, scheduling method is l, and the overall computational environment's load is V, the lifecycle modeling of privacy data is:

$$T = \Theta(D, \nu, n, m, l) + \gamma(V) \tag{1}$$

In this study, it's assumed all computational hardware possesses homogenous capabilities, thus discussions center around software-based computational resources without delving into the hardware's capabilities. The Θ term signifies the ideal runtime of the computational logic corresponding to the lifecycle of privacy data under stipulated computational resource conditions; the γ term represents the lifecycle measurement offset due to resource contention. The impact of resource contention is hard to articulate using intuitive external resource conditions. This formula employs the degree of load as a surrogate for resource contention magnitude, typically a higher load results in a greater offset from contention.

Within serverless architectures focusing on in-memory computational services, the primary contended resources are the CPU and memory.

To elucidate the temporal statistical characteristics of the privacy data lifecycle within in-memory computational services, this study utilizes the computational service QR (a QR code generation service, with the load details available in the system evaluation section). This examines the lifecycle of its input privacy data under varying environmental loads. In terms of load formation, this study continuously accesses a 6MB matrix, looping through each element for incremental operations to saturate computational and memory access volumes. Concurrent thread count adjusts the degree of load. For temporal measurements, the RTDSCP instruction records the runtime of the corresponding computational logic for privacy data, reflecting wall clock time. During measurements, server features like dynamic frequency and voltage scaling are disabled, as is Turbo Boost. The QR service runs as a Docker container, with a single core, CPU share set to 10, and memory capped at 1 GB.

3.3   Highlighting the Application Ecosystem of Private Data Lifecycle Management

Under the aforementioned model of private data lifecycle, the development and deployment of computational services diverge slightly from conventional methods.

Service providers/developers are entrusted with the development of computational services. Upon completion, they relay a chosen computation pathway tau (in source code or bytecode format) that's robustly linked to private data, to the entity responsible for estimating the private data's lifecycle. Given that tau typically encompasses only a fraction of the entire computational service software space, sharing this segment does not unveil the entirety of the computational service. This ensures a degree of protection for computational services that possess asset-like attributes.

Cloud service providers furnish the deployment environment for the computational services. Before deployment, these providers relay both the resource allocation R designated for the computational service and the load conditions V to the entity gauging the lifecycle of private data.

Private data owners supply their data during the actual operation of the computational service. They retrieve an estimation of the lifecycle, predicated on the specifications of their private data $\|D\|$, from the estimation entity. Leveraging this forecast, they engage in formulating strategies for the lifecycle of private data in a collaborative multi-service setting.

Lifecycle estimator proffers estimations based on provided values of tau, $\|D\|$, R, and E. This forecasting body can often be synonymous with the cloud service provider. In such instances, estimations pertaining to the private data lifecycle can be gleaned from pertinent measurements of tau in the actual deployment environment. When they are distinct entities, the lifecycle estimations can be ascertained through measurements of *tau* in a simulated cloud computing environment. Deliberations on simulation methodologies are beyond the purview of this document.

4   System Design

4.1   System Overview

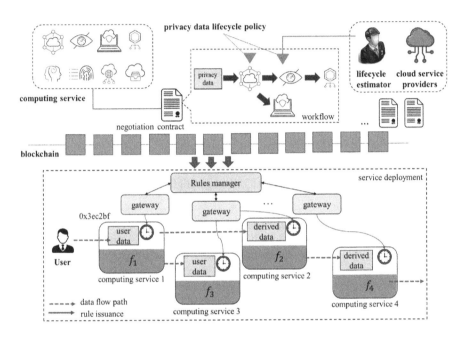

Fig. 2. Loft lifecycle management system architecture.

Figure 2 presents the system architecture of the Loft lifecycle management framework.

Loft, constructed on blockchain technology, is proposed for end-to-end lifecycle management of private data throughout a multi-service collaboration process. Its on-chain component oversees the negotiation of private data lifecycle policies during collaboration (refer to Sect. 4.2), while the off-chain component manages the implementation of these policies in a serverless computing framework.

The on-chain portion primarily comprises collaborative negotiation smart contracts. These contracts not only facilitate the negotiation of collaborative workflows but also establish lifecycle policies for private data within these workflows. During the negotiation, computational services affirm connections to their upstream counterparts and designate downstream services. When stipulating the lifecycle policies for private data, each computational service relies on cloud service providers and the private data lifecycle estimation entity to delineate the lifecycle of private data passed on to its downstream services. A more detailed exposition of this procedure can be found in Sect. 4.2.

The off-chain segment predominantly consists of serverless computing gateways, serverless computing runtime, policy managers, and data applications. Data applications interact through service identifiers. The serverless computing gateway facilitates data service request forwarding and adjusts the number of service instances based on load conditions. Policy managers synchronize with blockchain-attested policies and disseminate hot policies to stored gateways. Within Loft, gateways manage the issuance of private data lifecycle policies. They encode specific private data policies into data service requests based on user data input identifiers in the computational flow. The serverless computing runtime primarily invokes specific data service applications based on data service requests and manages the private data lifecycle as encoded within the services. By default, the runtime isolates private data prior to data service operation. Data services explicitly request permission to utilize private data.

4.2   Blockchain-Based Multi-service Collaboration Negotiation

During on-chain negotiations, the initiator of the service collaboration (usually the topmost computational service in the collaboration) crafts a collaboration contract and specifies the required downstream computational services. Each collaborating computational service not only confirms specifications from its upstream counterpart in the contract but also provides a cryptographic digest 'h' of its resource allocation information at the cloud provider, designates required downstream computational services, and defines the private data specifications $\|D\|$ they output. This private data might either be user-input original data or derived data pertinent to users generated after processing.

In Loft, the approach to stipulating private data lifecycle policies is end-to-end - the upstream computational service i sets the lifecycle policy $p_{i}j$ for its output private data in the downstream computational service j. As service i establishes $p_{i}j$, the private data lifecycle estimation entity offers a time-dimension reference: 1) The estimation entity first procures the resource allocation information R corresponding to the service j from its cloud provider, verifying its computational summary, while also obtaining load intensity data V. 2) Combining data specifications $\|D\|$ from service i with R, V, and information about j, the estimation entity provides a time-dimension estimation for private data within service j. This policy $p_{i}j$ specifically manifests as:

$$p_{ij} = (T_1, T_2, ..., T_q) \mid \lambda \qquad (2)$$

where the lifecycle of private data is represented as a finite series of time allotments, and q is termed the allotment count.

The workflow's private data lifecycle policy $P = p_{i}j$ embodies a collection of discrete computational stage private data lifecycle policies, correlating with data genuinely processed and transferred within that workflow. In Loft, this policy is identified by user data input at the workflow's source. This identifier accompanies the computational process, transferring between service domains, enabling Loft to assign relevant policies to each computational phase of the workflow. Since the same collaborative workflow caters to different user data inputs, inputs of similar specifications generally correspond to the same workflow private data lifecycle policy. To enhance management efficiency and scalability, Loft maintains identifiers of inputs with the same private data lifecycle policy under a singular identifier prefix. Thus, the maintenance and retrieval of private data lifecycle policies in the workflow can be achieved through this prefix. During private data lifecycle policy negotiations, every downstream computational service j must affirm $p_i j$ until all policies are confirmed. Ultimately, the data provider at the workflow's source confirms $P = p_i j$ and finalizes the binding of input data identifiers with policies. The entire negotiation logic for collaboration and the establishment of private data lifecycle policies are recorded on the blockchain.

4.3 Privacy Data Control in Serverless Computing Architecture

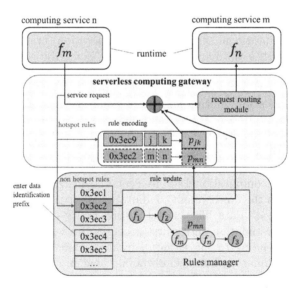

Fig. 3. Loft gateway architecture.

Gateway. Fig. 3 elucidates the operational mechanics of the Loft gateway. It reveals that user-input data identifiers, along with private data, circulate amongst computational services, signifying the workflow granularity of the private data lifecycle policy. The gateway pinpoints the privacy data lifecycle policy associated with a specific computational phase in the policy manager by discerning the prefix of the input data identifier and the identifiers of the upstream and downstream service requests. Upon acquiring the private data lifecycle policy, the gateway encodes this policy directly into the service request, which, in turn, along with the private data, is forwarded to the target service. To optimize the efficiency of policy retrieval, Loft caches frequently encountered policies at the computational phase granularity in the gateway.

This use of "Sticky policy" mainly correlates with the inherent characteristics of serverless computing architectures: services manifest as loosely coupled entities, interconnected typically using stateless protocols (like HTTP). Cooperation between services lacks the maintenance of a global state. Furthermore, the scaling of service units in this architecture is highly dynamic, allowing "Sticky policy" to remain unaffected by dynamic scaling of computational services. In Loft, service requests employ the HTTP protocol, encapsulating both the user-input data identifier and the superimposed private data lifecycle policy in the HTTP header.

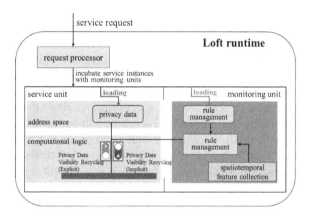

Fig. 4. Loft runtime composition.

Computational Runtime. Fig. 4 portrays the composition of Loft's computational runtime. Upon receiving a service request, within the same process space, Loft launches both a computational service instance and a monitoring unit. The latter predominantly manages the lifecycle of private data within the computational service. To stave off malicious computational services, Loft employs page isolation techniques, ensuring that the computational service cannot access the memory space of the monitor. The monitoring unit chiefly consists of a policy management module and a policy enforcement module. The former retrieves the private data lifecycle policy from the service request, validating the use of private data based on these policies. In contrast, the latter reclaims the visibility of private data to the computational service in line with the respective policies during its use. The enforcement module discerns the specifications of the private data and autonomously chooses an appropriate visibility reclamation mechanism, capturing the temporal characteristics of private data through a high-precision timing unit.

When initializing the computational service, the private data from the service request is stationed in a fixed memory space, using predetermined isolation mechanisms to prevent direct access by the service logic. Should the computational service need to access this private data, it leverages the application interface provided by Loft to request its use. The policy management module verifies whether this request aligns with the pertinent policies. In case of a conflict between the application and the policy, the runtime terminates the computational service, flagging an alert. Conversely, if congruent, the policy management module grants the computational service the right to use the private data, notifying the policy enforcement module to manage the data's lifecycle accordingly.

As for the methods to reclaim memory data visibility, they typically encompass: 1) Memory Isolation - typically relying on both hardware and software methods to sequester memory space, rendering it inaccessible to target programs. 2) Memory Erasure - employing software instructions to zero out designated memory regions. 3) Memory Encoding - encoding memory objects to facilitate their restoration when needed. This document selected representative methods of these categories to gauge their performance in practice. For memory isolation, the research utilizes the hardware-specific Intel-MPK isolation mechanism; for memory erasure, it employs the software instruction 'memset'; and for memory encoding, it harnesses AES stream encryption, taking advantage of Intel's high-performance encryption library IPP-crypto. Throughout the measurement process, the server's dynamic frequency and voltage scaling features were disabled, and the chip's turbo boost technology was also deactivated. The overhead data for each mechanism was averaged from 100 experimental measurements.

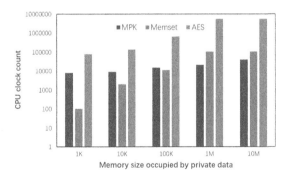

Fig. 5. Performance overhead of privacy data visibility recycling mechanism.

Figure 5 reveals the relationship between the overhead of these three visibility control mechanisms and data size. It's evident that, despite support from modern processor optimization instructions, employing encryption algorithms for memory object visibility control incurs substantial overhead, orders of magnitude higher than the other two methods. For smaller sets of private data, the overhead of memset is minimal, but this rapidly escalates with growing data volume. Intel-MPK's memory isolation, being page-granularity-based, introduces a comparatively slower-growing overhead with increased data volume. However, owing to its involvement in high-overhead system calls [37], it still imposes significant overheads for smaller private data sets. Consequently, Loft employs the following mechanism to control the visibility of private data to services:

$$\tau = \begin{cases} MPK & size(D) > 150KB \; or \; m > 1 \\ memset & size(D) < 150KB \end{cases} \tag{3}$$

Here, $size(D)$ denotes the size of the private data, and q represents the quota number corresponding to the private data.

5   System Evaluation

5.1   System Implementation

Loft's on-chain segment is prototyped using fabric (release-2.1), with the contract logic for collaborative workflow and privacy data lifecycle policy negotiation detailed in the appendix. The off-chain segment of Loft is built upon Openfaas (release-0.20.7). Modifications were made to Openfaas's gateway service request forwarding section, incorporating the lifecycle policy management unit. The caching for hot policies is implemented using go's concurrent cache library, ristretto. Furthermore, Loft has adjusted Openfaas's watchdog module to support runtime alerts and privacy data lifecycle policy configuration.

For the enforcement of privacy data lifecycles based on temporal and spatial features, Loft constructed respective serverless computing runtime environments. Under the temporal feature-based privacy data lifecycle model, the serverless computing function's development language is C++. Loft's monitor and application program share the same process space, and the time measurement collection within the monitor utilizes the Linux operating system's High-Resolution Timer (HRT). With a time measurement precision down to nanoseconds, HRT offers stable time metrics in low-latency applications. The visibility revocation mechanisms for privacy data in this runtime environment adopt Intel MPK and GUNC's memset function.

All experiments were carried out on an R730 server. This server is equipped with an Intel Xeon Silver 4210R chip (10 cores, single-core frequency at 2.4 GHz, 13.75MiB cache) and 64GiB of memory. The server's dynamic frequency and voltage scaling features were deactivated, as was the Turbo Boost feature of the chip. The server runs on the Ubuntu 16.04 server edition, and for synthetic workloads, the GCC compiler version used was 5.4.0.

5.2   Workload Overview

To evaluate the performance of the Loft framework, this study constructed a series of computational services based on real-world applications and synthetic workloads for experimental measurements. The overview of these computational services is depicted in Table 1. They aptly represent commonly observed computational service types in actual scenarios and exhibit diverse input privacy data types (ranging from reports and images to numerical data). Furthermore, under the serverless computing framework, given that computational service instances can dynamically scale, the processing capability for privacy data typically depends on the concurrency level of computational units. Loft can revoke visibility for privacy data in each computational unit, thus it flexibly adapts to diverse volumes of privacy data processing needs. The privacy data lifecycle in each computational service is set to the 90th percentile of kernel density estimates from 1,000 measurements.

Table 1. Experimental load.

Service	Load details	Proportion of private data related paths (LoC)	Privacy data size
QR	QR code generation	57%	1KB
IP1	Image processing	40%	33.9KB/305KB
IP2	Image processing	40%	33.9KB/305KB
Bill	Billing statistics	51%	163KB
Diet	Dietary guidelines	23%	7B
SP	Sequence prediction	54%	96B
Workflow1 (IP1->IP2)	Workflow	/	/
Workflow1 (Bill->SP->QR)	Workflow	/	/

Workflows are built upon individual computational services. In this section, different sizes of privacy data inputs for image-based computational services are provided to measure the impact of Loft's various visibility revocation mechanisms on the performance of computational services.

5.3   System Assessment

Table 2 presents the data associated with the aforementioned services under static deployment. It is evident from the table that the integration of Loft has minimal impact on the compilation time of the computing services. However, it does exert some influence on the size of the binary files compiled from certain computing services. This influence predominantly stems from Loft's runtime.

Table 2. Static deployment data.

Service	Compilation time (native)/s	Compilation time (Loft)/s	Compilation size (native)/KB	Compilation size (Loft)/KB
QR	1.71	1.71(0.0%)	68.3	69.8(2.2%)
IP1	1.38	1.45(5.0%)	49	61(24.5%)
IP2	1.38	1.44(4.3%)	49	61(24.5%)
Bill	1.15	1.16(0.8%)	18.8	34.8(85.1%)
Diet	1.16	1.16(0.0%)	17.9	34.1(90.5%)
SP	1.02	1.06(3.9%)	17.9	34.1(90.5%)

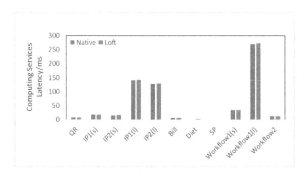

Fig. 6. Comparison of computing service latency between Loft and Openfaas frameworks.

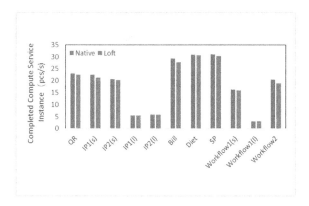

Fig. 7. Comparison of computing service throughput between Loft and Openfaas frameworks.

Figure 6 and Fig. 7 depict the comparative delay and throughput of computing services under the Loft framework versus the native Openfaas framework, respectively. The delay measurement results represent the average of 1,000 individual runs of the computing services, while the throughput measurement represents instances of computing services completed per second when distributing 500 sets of computing tasks simultaneously. Image-based applications (IP1, IP2, and Workflow1) utilized varying sizes of private data input to test the different visibility recovery mechanisms during Loft's runtime.

The results indicate that Loft has a relatively minor impact on the delay and throughput of the computing services. In terms of delay overhead, the services experiencing the most significant increase are "diet" (by 20.5%), "SP" (by 15.6%), and "Workflow2" (by 10.1%). This is primarily because these services inherently have extremely short running times, and the context switching introduced by Loft's runtime lifecycle executor becomes a significant factor in the overall delay. The delay increase for the remaining computing services is less than 2%. Regarding throughput overhead, the impact caused by Loft is even more negligible. The most substantial throughput reduction is observed in "Workflow2" (by 7.6%), while the rest see reductions of less than 5.3%, which is largely attributed to the lightweight monitoring unit of Loft.

6   Discuss

Under the proposed framework for private data lifecycle management, once the lifecycle constraints of private data are surpassed, the data becomes inaccessible to applications. This rigid cut-off approach demands a high level of accuracy in predicting the lifecycle of private data. In a practical production environment, these predictions are highly dynamic, fluctuating with changes in the computational infrastructure's workload. The pursuit of accurate and timely predictions becomes the focal point for future work in this paper.

Furthermore, it's conceivable that the execution path of certain private data might not be statically predicted in advance. In such instances, it becomes imperative to estimate time based on all potential paths closely related to private data. When utilizing private data, the determination of its lifecycle constraints relies on the contextual information of the computing service, such as branch conditions.

7   Conclusion

Addressing the challenges of governing private data during its computation and transmission processes, due to the close coupling of applications and data, this paper presents the Loft system architecture. This architecture, crafted with blockchain technology, is designed for collaborative multi-service scenarios focused on private data lifecycle management. Initially, by analyzing the characteristics of computation paths related to private data, a time-based private data lifecycle model is introduced, establishing foundational rules for fine-grained management. Subsequently, leveraging blockchain technology, an end-to-end mechanism is proposed for the lifecycle management of private data in multi-service collaborative scenarios, ensuring data privacy during transitions. Ultimately, pivotal components are designed under the serverless computing architecture, ensuring that private data lifecycle management seamlessly integrates into cloud computing capabilities. Through empirical evaluation of the prototype system, the results underscore that the proposed system introduces a minimal operational overhead while effectively governing the lifecycle of private data.

Acknowledgements. This work has received funding from National Key Research and Development Program of China (Grant No.2022YFB2702801) and National Natural Science Foundation of China (Grant No.92067206, No.61972222).

References

1. Schnitzler, T., Mirza, M.S., Dürmuth, M., Pöpper, C.: SOK: managing longitudinal privacy of publicly shared personal online data. Proc. Priv. Enhanc. Technol. **2021**(1), 229–249 (2021)
2. Schnitzler, T., Utz, C., Farke, F.M., Pöpper, C., Dürmuth, M.: User perception and expectations on deleting instant messages–or–what happens if i press this button? Regulation (GDPR) **4**, 5 (2018)
3. Jonas, E., et al.: Cloud programming simplified: a Berkeley view on serverless computing. arXiv preprint arXiv:1902.03383 (2019)
4. Shahrad, M., Balkind, J., Wentzlaff, D.: Architectural implications of function-as-a-service computing. In: Proceedings of the 52nd Annual IEEE/ACM International Symposium on Microarchitecture, pp. 1063–1075 (2019)
5. Geambasu, R., Kohno, T., Levy, A.A., Levy, H.M.: Vanish: increasing data privacy with self-destructing data. In: USENIX Security Symposium, vol. 316, pp. 10–5555 (2009)
6. Tang, Y., Lee, P.P., Lui, J.C., Perlman, R.: FADE: secure overlay cloud storage with file assured deletion. In: Jajodia, S., Zhou, J. (eds.) Security and Privacy in Communication Networks. SecureComm 2010. LNICST, Social Informatics and Telecommunications Engineering, vol. 50, pp. 380–397. Springer, Berlin, Heidelberg (2010). https://doi.org/10.1007/978-3-642-16161-2_22
7. Rahumed, A., Chen, H.C., Tang, Y., Lee, P.P., Lui, J.C.: A secure cloud backup system with assured deletion and version control. In: 2011 40th International Conference on Parallel Processing Workshops, pp. 160–167. IEEE (2011)
8. Hao, F., Clarke, D., Zorzo, A.F.: Deleting secret data with public verifiability. IEEE Trans. Dependable Secure Comput. **13**(6), 617–629 (2015)
9. Halderman, J.A., et al.: Lest we remember: cold-boot attacks on encryption keys. Commun. ACM **52**(5), 91–98 (2009)
10. Müller, T., Dewald, A., Freiling, F.C.: AESSE: a cold-boot resistant implementation of AES. In: Proceedings of the Third European Workshop on System Security, pp. 42–47 (2010)
11. Zhao, L., Mannan, M.: Hypnoguard: protecting secrets across sleep-wake cycles. In: Proceedings of the 2016 ACM SIGSAC Conference on Computer and Communications Security, pp. 945–957 (2016)
12. Chong, S., Myers, A.C.: Language-based information erasure. In: 18th IEEE Computer Security Foundations Workshop (CSFW'05), pp. 241–254. IEEE (2005)
13. Gollamudi, A., Chong, S.: Automatic enforcement of expressive security policies using enclaves. In: Proceedings of the 2016 ACM SIGPLAN International Conference on Object-Oriented Programming, Systems, Languages, and Applications, pp. 494–513 (2016)

14. Chow, J., Pfaff, B., Garfinkel, T., Rosenblum, M.: Shredding your garbage: reducing data lifetime through secure deallocation. In: USENIX Security Symposium, p. 22 (2005)

15. Dunn, A.M., et al.: Eternal sunshine of the spotless machine: protecting privacy with ephemeral channels. In: 10th USENIX Symposium on Operating Systems Design and Implementation (OSDI 12), pp. 61–75 (2012)

16. Gondi, K., Bisht, P., Venkatachari, P., Sistla, A.P., Venkatakrishnan, V.: Swipe: eager erasure of sensitive data in large scale systems software. In: Proceedings of the second ACM conference on Data and Application Security and Privacy, pp. 295–306 (2012)

17. Kannan, J., Chun, B.G.: Making programs forget: enforcing lifetime for sensitive data. In: 13th Workshop on Hot Topics in Operating Systems (HotOS XIII) (2011)

18. Reardon, J., Capkun, S., Basin, D.: Data node encrypted file system: efficient secure deletion for flash memory. In: 21st USENIX Security Symposium (USENIX Security 12), pp. 333–348 (2012)

19. Kim, M., et al.: Evanesco: architectural support for efficient data sanitization in modern flash-based storage systems. In: Proceedings of the Twenty-Fifth International Conference on Architectural Support for Programming Languages and Operating Systems, pp. 1311–1326 (2020)

20. Zyskind, G., Nathan, O., et al.: Decentralizing privacy: using blockchain to protect personal data. In: 2015 IEEE Security and Privacy Workshops, pp. 180–184. IEEE (2015)

21. Alansari, S., Paci, F., Margheri, A., Sassone, V.: Privacy-preserving access control in cloud federations. In: 2017 IEEE 10th International Conference on Cloud Computing (CLOUD), pp. 757–760. IEEE (2017)

22. Alansari, S., Paci, F., Sassone, V.: A distributed access control system for cloud federations. In: 2017 IEEE 37th International Conference on Distributed Computing Systems (ICDCS), pp. 2131–2136. IEEE (2017)

23. Dukkipati, C., Zhang, Y., Cheng, L.C.: Decentralized, blockchain based access control framework for the heterogeneous internet of things. In: Proceedings of the Third ACM Workshop on Attribute-Based Access Control, pp. 61–69 (2018)

24. Pinno, O.J.A., Gregio, A.R.A., De Bona, L.C.: Controlchain: blockchain as a central enabler for access control authorizations in the IoT. In: GLOBECOM 2017–2017 IEEE Global Communications Conference, pp. 1–6. IEEE (2017)

25. Azaria, A., Ekblaw, A., Vieira, T., Lippman, A.: Medrec: using blockchain for medical data access and permission management. In: 2016 2nd International Conference on Open and Big Data (OBD), pp. 25–30. IEEE (2016)

26. Dagher, G.G., Mohler, J., Milojkovic, M., Marella, P.B.: Ancile: privacy-preserving framework for access control and interoperability of electronic health records using blockchain technology. Sustain. Urban Areas **39**, 283–297 (2018)

27. Hammi, M.T., Hammi, B., Bellot, P., Serhrouchni, A.: Bubbles of trust: a decentralized blockchain-based authentication system for IoT. Comput. Secur. **78**, 126–142 (2018)

28. Cui, Z., et al.: A hybrid blockchain-based identity authentication scheme for multi-WSN. IEEE Trans. Serv. Comput. **13**(2), 241–251 (2020)

29. Lin, C., He, D., Kumar, N., Huang, X., Vijayakumar, P., Choo, K.K.R.: Homechain: a blockchain-based secure mutual authentication system for smart homes. IEEE Internet Things J. **7**(2), 818–829 (2019)

30. Wang, W., Hu, N., Liu, X.: Blockcam: a blockchain-based cross-domain authentication model. In: 2018 IEEE Third International Conference on Data Science in Cyberspace (DSC), pp. 896–901. IEEE (2018)

31. Xing, Q., Wang, B., Wang, X.: Bgpcoin: blockchain-based internet number resource authority and BGP security solution. Symmetry **10**(9), 408 (2018)
32. Saad, M., Anwar, A., Ahmad, A., Alasmary, H., Yuksel, M., Mohaisen, D.: Routechain: towards blockchain-based secure and efficient BGP routing. Comput. Netw. **217**, 109362 (2022)
33. Hari, A., Lakshman, T.: The internet blockchain: a distributed, tamper-resistant transaction framework for the internet. In: Proceedings of the 15th ACM Workshop on Hot Topics in Networks, pp. 204–210 (2016)
34. Liu, J., Li, B., Chen, L., Hou, M., Xiang, F., Wang, P.: A data storage method based on blockchain for decentralization DNS. In: 2018 IEEE Third International Conference on Data Science in Cyberspace (DSC), pp. 189–196. IEEE (2018)
35. Edgar, S., Burns, A.: Statistical analysis of WCET for scheduling. In: Proceedings 22nd IEEE Real-Time Systems Symposium (RTSS 2001)(Cat. No. 01PR1420), pp. 215–224. IEEE (2001)
36. Gil, S.J., Bate, I., Lima, G., Santinelli, L., Gogonel, A., Cucu-Grosjean, L.: Open challenges for probabilistic measurement-based worst-case execution time. IEEE Embed. Syst. Lett. **9**(3), 69–72 (2017)
37. Park, S., Lee, S., Xu, W., Moon, H., Kim, T.: Libmpk: software abstraction for intel memory protection keys (intel {MPK}). In: 2019 USENIX Annual Technical Conference (USENIX ATC 19), pp. 241–254 (2019)

Privacy-Preserving Blockchain-Based Traceability System with Decentralized Ciphertext-Policy Attribute-Based Encryption

Tsz Ho Pun[1(✉)], Yi Jun He[1], and Siu Ming Yiu[2]

[1] Logistics and Supply Chain MultiTech R&D Centre,
Pokfulam, Hong Kong
{thpun,ahe}@lscm.hk
[2] Department of Computer Science, The University of Hong Kong,
Pokfulam, Hong Kong
smyiu@cs.hku.hk

Abstract. Traceability, being the ability to access information of an item throughout its lifecycle, plays an important part in current supply chain, facilitating prompt response in case of incidents. In recent years, blockchain-based traceability systems are proposed to address the multi-party data exchange issue with the emerging technology while achieving external traceability. To tackle the privacy issues that arose in blockchain-based traceability system, we propose and implement an architecture of privacy-preserving blockchain-based traceability system. We propose a statically-secure decentralized ciphertext-policy attribute-based encryption (DCP-ABE) scheme with delegation and hidden access policy, which is integrated together with zero-knowledge succinct non-interactive arguments of knowledge (zk-SNARK) into the proposed system. The proposed system is implemented with Quorum, InterPlanetary File System (IPFS), Dgraph and hierarchical deterministic key generation. These components and cryptographic algorithms help the implemented system achieve data confidentiality and improve the identity anonymity, which are important to safeguard trade secrets. A case study of product recall, in collaboration with a company in Hong Kong, is also conducted to demonstrate how the implemented system can assist.

Keywords: Attribute-based encryption · Decentralized · Hidden access policy · Blockchain-based traceability system

1 Introduction

Traceability, defined as the ability to access information of a traced item throughout its lifecycle [24], is important to today's supply chain. In case of product recall, if traceability is achieved, investigators can gather all related information

G. Wang et al. (Eds.): UbiSec 2023, CCIS 2034, pp. 274–288, 2024.
https://doi.org/10.1007/978-981-97-1274-8_18

throughout the product lifecycle easily. This improves the process and helps in quick response to the situation.

To achieve traceability, electronic systems, namely traceability systems, are designed and built. In recent years, development of traceability systems endeavors to address the issue of information sharing across multiple parties with blockchain technology, which are known to provide decentralization, immutability and trustlessness [12,30]. While blockchain-based solutions seem perfect for traceability systems, privacy issues arise. Information shared in such system, for instance, product manufacturer and quantities, can be confidential. To restrict access of such information in the system, privacy-preserving techniques are required to ensure only authorized users can access these restricted data.

There are several goals for applying the privacy-preserving techniques to secure the trade secret:

Data Confidentiality. The content of traceability records is possibly sensitive and part of trade secrets. Traditional systems address this with access control of data by central authority [7]. However, central authority does not exist in a decentralized solution like blockchain. Alternative measure to protect data confidentiality in blockchain-based traceability system is needed.

Data Verifiability. To leverage the trustlessness of blockchain on integrity of traceability records, the records should be verifiable during consensus, while protecting confidentiality of records and thus trade secrets.

Identity Anonymity. Identities in the blockchain-based traceability system can also leak trade secrets. In blockchain-based systems, traceability records are submitted as blockchain transactions which come with senders and recipients being blockchain accounts [22]. These transactional identities are often linked with some real-world identities. Though blockchain accounts are designed to be anonymous, research has showed that such anonymity can be broken by analyzing the transaction history [13,14]. To safeguard the trade secret in terms of identity, the system should not provide excess information to link up multiple blockchain identities for unveiling the actual identity.

In this paper, we propose a DCP-ABE with delegation and hidden access policy. The proposed scheme is constructed under bilinear maps and supports monotonic access structure. We also propose a design of blockchain-based traceability system which integrates the proposed encryption scheme together with hierarchical deterministic key generation and zero-knowledge proof to address the trade secret leakage problem, and have such design implemented.

The rest of the paper is organized as follows. In Sect. 2, the design of the proposed privacy-preserving blockchain-based traceability system is presented. Section 3 describes the preliminaries which are useful for the proposed DCP-ABE scheme and the proposed blockchain-based traceability system. We present the proposed DCP-ABE scheme in Sect. 4. In Sect. 5, the implementation of the proposed blockchain-based traceability system is described and a case study of product recall is conducted to showcase how the proposed blockchain-based traceability system can facilitate. In Sect. 6, the related works are described and compared with our work, followed by limitation and conclusion in Sect. 7.

2 Privacy-Preserving Blockchain-Based Traceability System

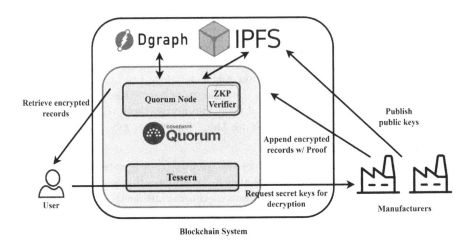

Fig. 1. System Architecture

Here explains the entities and interactions in the proposed blockchain-based traceability system, as depicted in Fig. 1.

Blockchain System. The blockchain system stores encrypted traceability records and their relationships in a graph form. Each record represents a traceable item in the supply chain and is assigned a unique identifier by the manufacturer. Additionally, the blockchain system serves as the keyserver for entities to distribute public keys.

Users. Users retrieve traceability records from the blockchain system and view them by requesting decryption keys from manufacturers.

Manufacturers. Manufacturers are a subset of users with additional capabilities. They manufacture traceable items and upload corresponding traceability records to the system. Each manufacturer is independent and generates key pairs to encrypt the records. They also respond to requests for secret keys.

The following cryptographic primitives are utilized in the proposed system to meet the goals.

Proposed DCP-ABE. The proposed scheme encrypts all traceability records in the system. Only users with authorized sets of attributes can decrypt the ciphertexts. Delegation provides an alternative method for users to obtain the authorized attribute sets without directly requesting them from attribute authorities. The hidden access structure ensures that the access policy does not reveal information that could allow adversaries to relate ciphertexts, thereby helping to achieve identity anonymity.

Hierarchical Deterministic Key Generation. As suggested in [22], users send transactions using *fresh* blockchain accounts. This practice makes it more challenging to analyze transaction history and link transactional identities. To achieve scalable and easy key management, each user utilizes a hierarchical deterministic wallet (HD wallet) [29]. One-time accounts are generated in a hierarchical and deterministic manner from the HD wallet. By the property of HD key generation, the computational infeasibility of relating one-time accounts ensures anonymity and prevents the disclosure of user identities.

zk-SNARK. zk-SNARK [4] verifies traceability records from users. Each traceable item has an embedded secret code. Users such as manufacturers and distributors generate a zero-knowledge proof (ZKP) using zk-SNARK prover program and the code to add a traceability record. The traceability record and the ZKP are submitted to the blockchain. The on-chain verifier verifies the ZKP, and only traceability records with verified proofs are added. This ensures data verifiability without leaking the secret code.

3 Preliminaries

In this section, the key preliminaries for the proposed DCP-ABE are introduced. The definitions of bilinear maps, access structures, linear secret sharing schemes and q-Decisional Parallel Bilinear Diffie-Hellman Exponent 2 Assumption (q-DPBDHE2), on which the proposed DCP-ABE is grounded, follow those in [15,26] and are omitted here due to lack of space.

3.1 One-Way Anonymous Key Agreement [9]

Suppose there is a private key issuance authority with s being master secret key in the cryptosystem. There is also a strong collision-resistant hash function $H : \{0,1\}^* \to \mathbb{G}$. Alice and Bob are clients of this authority, having identity and private key $\mathrm{ID}_A, d_A = Q_A{}^s = H(\mathrm{ID}_A)^s$ and $\mathrm{ID}_B, d_B = Q_B{}^s = H(\mathrm{ID}_B)^s$ respectively. Alice wants to remain anonymous to Bob during the key agreement process. The protocol proceeds as follows:

1. Alice computes $Q_B = H(\mathrm{ID}_B)$, and then chooses a random integer $r_A \leftarrow_\$ \mathbb{Z}_p^*$ to generate $P_A = Q_A{}^{r_A}$. Alice also computes the session key $K_{AB} = e(d_A{}^{r_A}, Q_B) = e(Q_A, Q_B)^{s r_A}$. Finally, Alice sends P_A to Bob.
2. Bob computes the session key $K_{AB} = e(P_A, d_B) = e(Q_A, Q_B)^{s r_A}$.

Note that in the end of step 1, Alice and Bob have already come up with on a shared session key which Alice can use it to encrypt some messages to Bob.

A one-way anonymous key agreement protocol has the following security requirements to which may be relevant:

Theorem 1 (Session Key Secrecy of One-way Anonymous Key Agreement [9]). *It is infeasible for anyone other than the two participants or the private key issuance authority to determine a session key generated during a protocol run.*

3.2   DCP-ABE with Delegation and Hidden Access Policy

This section describes the algorithms constituting the DCP-ABE with delegation and hidden access policy, and defines the correctness and security model of captioned scheme. A DCP-ABE with delegation and hidden access policy consists of the following PPT algorithms:

GlobalSetup(1^κ) $\to$ GP The global setup algorithm is run once during system initialization, taking as input the implicit security parameter 1^κ and outputting the global public parameters GP.

AuthSetup(GP, θ) $\to$ {PK$_\theta$, SK$_\theta$} The attribute authority setup algorithm is run by each attribute authority during its initialization stage, taking as input GP and authority identity θ, and outputting the authority key pair {PK$_\theta$, SK$_\theta$}.

AttrPublicKeyGen(GP, SK$_\theta$, u) $\to$ APK$_u$ The attribute public key generation algorithm is run by each attribute authority, taking as input GP, secret key of attribute authority SK$_\theta$, and attribute u where $u \in \mathcal{U}_\theta$, and outputting the attribute public key APK$_{F(u)}$.

KeyGen(GP, SK$_\theta$, GID, $\mathcal{U}_{\mathrm{GID},\theta}$) $\to$ SK$_{\mathrm{GID},\mathcal{U}_{\mathrm{GID},\theta}}$ The key generation algorithm is run by each attribute authority, taking as input GP, SK$_\theta$, user's global identifier GID, and set of attributes $\mathcal{U}_{\mathrm{GID},\theta}$ entitled to user identifier GID and managed by authority θ. It outputs a set of user secret keys SK$_{\mathrm{GID},\mathcal{U}_{\mathrm{GID},\theta}}$ for user identity GID entitled with attribute set $\mathcal{U}_{\mathrm{GID},\theta}$.

Delegate(GP, {SK$_{\mathrm{GID},\mathcal{U}_{\mathrm{GID},\theta}}$}, GID$'$, $\mathcal{U}_{\mathrm{GID}'}$) $\to$ $\widetilde{\mathrm{SK}}_{\mathrm{GID}',\mathcal{U}_{\mathrm{GID}'}}$ The delegate algorithm is run by holders of attribute secret keys. It takes as input the global parameters GP, set of secret keys {SK$_{\mathrm{GID},\mathcal{U}_{\mathrm{GID},\theta}}$} owned by user identifier GID from all available attribute authorities following the same delegation path, delegatee identifier GID$'$, and set of attributes $\mathcal{U}_{\mathrm{GID}'}$ entitled to delegatee identifier GID$'$. It outputs a set of user secret keys $\widetilde{\mathrm{SK}}_{\mathrm{GID}',\mathcal{U}_{\mathrm{GID}'}}$ for the set of delegated attributes.

Encrypt(GP, M, $\mathbb{A}$, {APK$_{F(u)}$}) $\to$ CT The encryption algorithm takes as inputs GP, message M, an access policy $\mathbb{A}$ and a set of attribute public keys {APK$_{F(u)}$} of the relevant attributes, outputting the ciphertext CT.

Decrypt(GP, CT, {SK$_{\mathrm{GID},F(u)}$}) $\to$ ($M/\perp$) The decryption algorithm can be run by any type of users in the system. The algorithm takes as input the global parameter GP, ciphertext CT, and the set of secret keys {SK$_{\mathrm{GID},F(u)}$} entitled to user identifier GID which shares the same delegation path. If the attributes of the user GID satisfy the access policy $\mathbb{A}$ and the corresponding attribute secret keys share the same delegation path, it outputs M. Otherwise, it outputs $\perp$.

Definition 1. *A DCP-ABE scheme with delegation and hidden access policy is correct if for any* GP *generated by* GlobalSetup(1^κ), *for any set of keypairs* {PK$_\theta$, SK$_\theta$} *generated by* AuthSetup(GP, θ), *for any set of attribute public keys* {APK$_{F(u)}$} *generated by* AttrPublicKeyGen(GP, SK$_\theta$, u), *for any* CT *generated by* Encrypt(GP, M, $\mathbb{A}$, {APK$_{F(u)}$}) *using attribute public keys of relevant attributes on any message M and access structure $\mathbb{A}$, for any set of secret keys*

$\{\mathrm{SK}_{\mathrm{GID},F(u)}\}$ *generated by* $\mathsf{KeyGen}(\mathrm{GP},\mathrm{SK}_\theta,\mathrm{GID},\mathcal{U}_{\mathrm{GID},\theta})$ *using secret keys of relevant attribute authorities for a user* GID, *it is true under all of the followings:*

1. $\mathsf{Decrypt}(\mathrm{GP},\mathrm{CT},\{\mathrm{SK}_{\mathrm{GID},F(u)}\}_{u\in\mathcal{U}_{\mathrm{GID}}}) = M$ *iff* $\mathcal{U}_{\mathrm{GID},\theta}$ *satisfies* $\mathbb{A}$

2. *For any set of delegated secret keys* $\{\widetilde{\mathrm{SK}}_{\mathrm{GID}',F(u)}\}$ *generated from* $\mathsf{Delegate}(\mathrm{GP},\{\mathrm{SK}_{\mathrm{GID},\mathcal{U}_{\mathrm{GID}}}\},\mathrm{GID}',\mathcal{U}_{\mathrm{GID}'})$ *using the secret key of user* GID *for a delegate* GID', $\mathsf{Decrypt}(\mathrm{GP},\mathrm{CT},\{\widetilde{\mathrm{SK}}_{\mathrm{GID}',F(u)}\}) = M$ *iff* $\mathcal{U}_{\mathrm{GID}',\theta}$ *satisfies* $\mathbb{A}$, $\mathcal{U}_{\mathrm{GID}'} \subseteq \mathcal{U}_{\mathrm{GID}}$, *and the satisfying set of delegated secret keys* $\{\widetilde{\mathrm{SK}}_{\mathrm{GID}',F(u)}\}$ *is generated from the same sequence of calls on* $\mathsf{Delegate}(\mathrm{GP},\{\mathrm{SK}_{\mathrm{GID},\mathcal{U}_{\mathrm{GID}}}\},\mathrm{GID}',\mathcal{U}_{\mathrm{GID}'})$.

Here gives the security model of the DCP-ABE with delegation and hidden access policy, which defines the static security game between a challenger and an attacker. In a static security game, all queries done by the attacker are sent to the challenger immediately after seeing the global public parameters, and the attacker is allowed to corrupt a certain set of authorities, which are chosen by the attacker after seeing the global parameters and the set remains the same until the game ends [26].

The game consists of the following phases:

Global Setup. The challenger runs $\mathsf{GlobalSetup}(1^\kappa) \to \mathrm{GP}$ to obtain the global parameter GP, and gives GP to the attacker.

Attacker's Queries. The attacker chooses the set of corrupting attribute authorities $\mathcal{C}_\Theta \subset \mathcal{U}_\Theta$, meaning that the rest of attribute authorities $\mathcal{N}_\Theta = \mathcal{U}_\Theta \setminus \mathcal{C}_\Theta$ remains uncorrupted. Then the attacker responds with:

  – Set of corrupted authorities $\mathcal{C}_\Theta$, the corresponding authority public keys $\{\mathrm{PK}_\theta\}_{\theta\in\mathcal{C}_\Theta}$ and the corresponding attribute public keys $\{\mathrm{APK}_u\}_{u\in\mathcal{U}_\theta,\theta\in\mathcal{C}_\Theta}$, which the attacker can generate them in a malicious way as long as they match the type defined in the scheme.
  – Set of non-corrupted authorities $\mathcal{N}_\Theta$ for which the attacker queries the authority public keys.
  – Set of attributes $\mathcal{L}_u$ as input for attribute public key query where the requested attributes are not from any corrupted attribute authorities.
  – A sequence of inputs $\mathcal{Q} = \{(\mathrm{GID}_i, S_i)\}_{i=1}^m$ for the secret key queries, where the global identities GID_i are distinct, requested sets of attributes $S_i \subset \mathcal{U}$ and the requested attributes are not from any of the corrupted attribute authorities.
  – A sequence of inputs $\tilde{\mathcal{Q}} = \left\{(\{\mathrm{SK}_{\mathrm{GID},S_i}\}_{i=1}^m, \mathrm{GID}', \tilde{S}_j)\right\}_{j=1}^m$ for key delegation queries, where $\{\mathrm{SK}_{\mathrm{GID},S_i}\}$ denotes the set of secret key obtained by the attacker from the secret key queries, the global identities of delegatee GID' are distinct, and the delegated attributes are not from any of the corrupted attribute authorities.
  – Two messages M_0, M_1 of equal length, and a challenge access structure $\mathbb{A}$, where none of the challenge access structure can be satisfied

by the union of any attribute set appeared in secret key queries and all attributes issued by the corrupted attribute authorities. This prevents the attacker from trivially winning the game by decrypting the challenge ciphertext with secret keys issued in secret key queries together with the keys from the corrupted authorities.

Challenger's Replies. The challenger flips a random bit $b \leftarrow_\$ \{0,1\}$ and replies with:

- Public key of attribute authorities $\mathrm{PK}_\theta \leftarrow \mathsf{AuthSetup}(\mathrm{GP}, \theta)$ for all $\theta \in \mathcal{N}_\Theta$
- Attribute public keys $\mathrm{APK}_{F(u)} \leftarrow \mathsf{AttrPublicKeyGen}(\mathrm{GP}, \mathrm{SK}_\theta, u)$ for all $u \in \mathcal{L}_u$.
- Secret keys $\mathrm{SK}_{\mathrm{GID}, S_i} \leftarrow \mathsf{KeyGen}(\mathrm{GP}, \mathrm{SK}_{T(S_i)}, \mathrm{GID}, S_i)$ for all $i \in [m]$.
- Delegated keys $\widetilde{\mathrm{SK}}_{\mathrm{GID}', \tilde{S}_j} \leftarrow \mathsf{Delegate}(\mathrm{GP}, \{\mathrm{SK}_{\mathrm{GID}, S_i}\}, \mathrm{GID}', \tilde{S}_j)$ for all $i, j \in [m]$.
- The challenge ciphertext $\mathrm{CT}^* \leftarrow \mathsf{Encrypt}(\mathrm{GP}, M_b, \mathbb{A}, \{\mathrm{APK}_{F(u)}\})$ where $\{\mathrm{APK}_{F(u)}\}$ is the set of attribute public keys of all relevant attributes.

Guess. The attacker outputs a guess b' of b.

The attacker wins if $b' = b$. The advantage of the attacker in winning this game is defined as $\Pr[b' = b] - \frac{1}{2}$.

Definition 2. *The scheme is non-adaptively secure in the random oracle model if all PPT attackers have at most a negligible advantage in this security game.*

4   Our Scheme

4.1   Construction

The proposed DCP-ABE with delegation and hidden policy is extended from [26] to support delegation with hidden access policy. To support delegation, we re-use the technique in [26] to map global identities into group elements, and the re-randomization technique in [3]. To avoid linkability among access structures, one-way anonymous key agreement is used to hide the access structure such that only users entitled with attributes can learn that those attributes are part of the access policy. Algorithms of the proposed scheme are as follows:

$\mathsf{GlobalSetup}(1^\kappa) \to \mathrm{GP}$: The global setup algorithm chooses a bilinear map $e : \mathbb{G} \times \mathbb{G} \to \mathbb{G}_T$, where $\mathbb{G}$ and $\mathbb{G}_T$ are two multiplicative cyclic groups of prime order p, with g as a generator of $\mathbb{G}$. $\mathcal{U}$ and $\mathcal{U}_\Theta$ denote the set of attributes and attribute authorities respectively. Four cryptographic hash functions $H_\mathbb{G}$, $H_\mathbb{Z}$, F and $F_\mathbb{Z}$ are modelled as random oracles. $H_\mathbb{G} : \{0,1\}^* \to \mathbb{G}$ and $H_\mathbb{Z} : \{0,1\}^* \to \mathbb{Z}_p$ map user identifier GID to elements of $\mathbb{G}$ and $\mathbb{Z}$ respectively. Function $F : \{0,1\}^* \to \mathbb{G}$ and $F_\mathbb{Z} : \{0,1\}^* \to \mathbb{Z}_p$ map arbitrary string to elements of $\mathbb{G}$ and $\mathbb{Z}_p$ respectively. The algorithm outputs global parameters $\mathrm{GP} = \{\mathbb{G}, \mathbb{G}_T, p, g, e, \mathcal{U}, \mathcal{U}_\Theta, H_\mathbb{G}, H_\mathbb{Z}, F, F_\mathbb{Z}\}$.

AuthSetup(GP, θ) $\rightarrow$ {PK$_\theta$, SK$_\theta$}: This authority setup algorithm chooses four random exponents $\alpha_\theta, \beta_\theta, y_\theta, z_\theta \leftarrow_\$ \mathbb{Z}_p$. It returns public key PK$_\theta$ = {$e(g,g)^{\alpha_\theta}, g^{y_\theta}, g^{z_\theta}$}, and secret key SK$_\theta$ = {$\alpha_\theta, \beta_\theta, y_\theta, z_\theta$}.

AttrPublicKeyGen(GP, SK$_\theta$, u) $\rightarrow$ {APK$_{F(u)}$}: This attribute public key generation algorithm first chooses a random $k_u \leftarrow_\$ \mathbb{Z}_p$, computes $Q_u = g^{F_\mathbb{Z}(u||\beta_\theta)}$, and returns APK$_{F(u)}$ = {$e(F(u),g)^{\alpha_\theta k_u}, g^{y_\theta k_u}, g^{z_\theta k_u}, g^{k_u}, F(u)^{k_u}, Q_u$}.

KeyGen(GP, SK$_\theta$, GID, $\mathcal{U}_{\text{GID},\theta}$) $\rightarrow$ SK$_{\text{GID},\mathcal{U}_{\text{GID},\theta}}$: For each attribute $u \in \mathcal{U}_{\text{GID},\theta}$, the algorithm first chooses a random $t_u \leftarrow_\$ \mathbb{Z}_p$, computes:

$$K_{\text{GID},F(u),1} = F(u)^\alpha H_\mathbb{G}(\text{GID})^{y_\theta} F(u)^{t_u} g^{z_\theta \cdot 0}$$

$$K_{\text{GID},F(u),2} = g^{t_u}, K_{\text{GID},F(u),3} = g^{z_\theta}, K_{\text{GID},F(u),4} = g^0,$$

$$K_{\text{GID},F(u),5} = F(u)^{F_\mathbb{Z}(u||\beta_\theta)}, \text{src}_{\text{GID},F(u)} = H_\mathbb{G}(\text{GID})$$

Finally, the algorithm outputs SK$_{\text{GID},\mathcal{U}_{\text{GID},\theta}}$ = {$K_{\text{GID},F(u),1}, K_{\text{GID},F(u),2}, K_{\text{GID},F(u),3}, K_{\text{GID},F(u),4}, K_{\text{GID},F(u),5}, \text{src}_{\text{GID},F(u)}$}$_{u \in \mathcal{U}_{\text{GID},\theta}}$

Delegate(GP, {SK$_{\text{GID},\mathcal{U}_{\text{GID},\theta}}$}, GID$'$, $\mathcal{U}_{\text{GID}'}$) $\rightarrow$ $\widetilde{\text{SK}}_{\text{GID}',\mathcal{U}_{\text{GID}'}}$: The algorithm first chooses a random $r \leftarrow_\$ \mathbb{Z}_p$. Then for each attribute $u \in \mathcal{U}_{\text{GID}'}$, it chooses a random $r_u \leftarrow_\$ \mathbb{Z}_p$ and computes:

$$\tilde{K}_{\text{GID}',F(u),1} = K_{\text{GID},F(u),1} \cdot F(u)^{r_u} \cdot K_{\text{GID},F(u),3}^{H_\mathbb{Z}(\text{GID}')r}$$

$$\tilde{K}_{\text{GID}',F(u),2} = K_{\text{GID},F(u),2} \cdot g^{r_u}, \tilde{K}_{\text{GID}',F(u),3} = K_{\text{GID},F(u),3},$$

$$\tilde{K}_{\text{GID}',F(u),4} = K_{\text{GID},F(u),4} \cdot g^{H_\mathbb{Z}(\text{GID}')r}$$

$$\tilde{K}_{\text{GID}',F(u),5} = K_{\text{GID},F(u),5}, \text{src}_{\text{GID}',F(u)} = \text{src}_{\text{GID},F(u)}$$

Finally, the algorithm outputs $\widetilde{\text{SK}}_{\text{GID}',\mathcal{U}_{\text{GID}'}}$ = {$\tilde{K}_{\text{GID}',F(u),1}, \tilde{K}_{\text{GID}',F(u),2}, \tilde{K}_{\text{GID}',F(u),3}, \tilde{K}_{\text{GID}',F(u),4}, \tilde{K}_{\text{GID}',F(u),5}, \text{src}_{\text{GID}',F(u)}$}$_{u \in \mathcal{U}_{\text{GID}'}}$

Encrypt(GP, M, (A,δ), {APK$_{F(u)}$}) $\rightarrow$ CT: Denote access policy as (A,δ) with $A \in \mathbb{Z}_p^{l \times n}$, constructed with masked attributes $F(u)$. δ is a function that maps a row in A to a masked attribute, i.e. $\delta(x) = F(u)$. The algorithm first chooses a random $a \leftarrow_\$ \mathbb{Z}_p$. And then, for each masked attribute $F(u_i)$ in access policy A, it computes $f_{u_i} = e(Q_{u_i}{}^a, F(u_i)) = e(g, F(u_i))^{a F_\mathbb{Z}(u_i||\beta_\theta)}$. After that, access policy A is converted to A' by replacing attribute $F(u_i)$ with f_{u_i}, and δ' is a function that maps a row in A' to the hidden attribute f_u. The algorithm also computes $h_0 = g^a$.

Following the construction of (A', δ'), the algorithm chooses three random vectors $\boldsymbol{v} = (s, v_2, ..., v_n)^\mathsf{T}$, $\boldsymbol{w} = (0, w_2, ..., w_n)^\mathsf{T}$ and $\boldsymbol{w'} = (0, w'_2, ..., w'_n)^\mathsf{T}$, where $s, v_2, ..., v_n, w_2, ..., w_n, w'_2, ..., w'_n \leftarrow_\$ \mathbb{Z}_p$. Denote $\lambda_x = \langle \boldsymbol{A}_x, \boldsymbol{v} \rangle$, $\omega_x = \langle \boldsymbol{A}_x, \boldsymbol{w} \rangle$ and $\omega'_x = \langle \boldsymbol{A}_x, \boldsymbol{w'} \rangle$, where $\boldsymbol{A}_x$ is the x-th row of A.

The algorithm computes $C_0 = M \cdot e(g,g)^s$. Then for each row x of A', it chooses a random $t_x \leftarrow_{\$} \mathbb{Z}_p$ and computes:

$$C_{1,x} = e(g,g)^{\lambda_x}(\text{APK}_{\delta'(x),1})^{t_x} = e(g,g)^{\lambda_x}e(F(u),g)^{\alpha_\theta kt_x},$$

$$C_{2,x} = (\text{APK}_{\delta'(x),4})^{-t_x} = g^{-kt_x}, C_{3,x} = (\text{APK}_{\delta'(x),2})^{t_x}g^{\omega_x} = g^{y_\theta kt_x}g^{\omega_x},$$

$$C_{4,x} = (\text{APK}_{\delta'(x),5})^{t_x} = F(u)^{kt_x}, C_{5,x} = (\text{APK}_{\delta'(x),3})^{t_x}g^{\omega'_x} = g^{z_\theta kt_x}g^{\omega'_x}$$

Finally, the algorithm outputs $CT = \{(A',\delta'),C_0,\{C_{1,x},C_{2,x},C_{3,x},C_{4,x}, C_{5,x}\}_{x\in[l]},h_0\}$

Decrypt$(GP,CT,\{\text{SK}_{\text{GID},F(u)}\}) \rightarrow (M/\perp)$: The algorithm starts with computing $f'_u = e(h_0,K_{GID,F(u),5}) = e(g,F(u))^{aF_{\mathbb{Z}}(u||\beta_\theta)}$ for each attribute secret key in $\{\text{SK}_{\text{GID},F(u)}\}$ held by user.

If the decryptor has the secret keys $\{\text{SK}_{\text{GID},F(u)}\}$ for a subset of rows A'_x in A' such that $(1,0,...,0)$ is in the span of these rows, then it computes constants $c_x \in \mathbb{Z}_p$ such that $\sum_x c_x A'_x = (1,0,...,0)$. After that, for each such row x, the algorithm computes:

$$C_{1,x} \cdot e(K_{\text{GID},\delta'(x),1},C_{2,x}) \cdot e(\text{src}_{\text{GID},\delta'(x)},C_{3,x}) \cdot e(K_{\text{GID},\delta'(x),2},C_{4,x})$$
$$\cdot e(K_{\text{GID},\delta'(x),4},C_{5,x}) = e(g,g)^{\lambda_x}e(H_{\mathbb{G}}(\text{GID}),g)^{\omega_x}e(g^{\sum H_{\mathbb{Z}}(\text{GID}_i)r_i},g)^{\omega'_x}$$

Following that, the algorithm computes:

$$\prod_x(e(g,g)^{\lambda_x}e(H_{\mathbb{G}}(\text{GID}),g)^{\omega_x}e(g^{\sum H_{\mathbb{Z}}(\text{GID}_i)r_i},g)^{\omega'_x})^{c_x} = e(g,g)^s$$

Finally, the algorithm outputs message $M = C_0/e(g,g)^s$. If the decryptor does not have the secret keys to satisfy the above condition, the algorithm returns $\perp$.

4.2   Security Proof

In addition to [26], the security proof has the query of delegate keys and attribute public keys added. The challenger in this security proof has the functions of attribute public key generation and delegate key generation, and the hidden access structure encoding phase in encryption function added. The idea of proof is to have a PPT adversary who has a non-negligible advantage in non-adaptively breaking the security game defined in 3.2 such that we can construct a simulator in non-adaptively breaking the q-DPBDHE2 assumption. Due to lack of space, the security proof is omitted here.

Theorem 2. *If the q-DPBDHE2 assumption holds, then all PPT adversaries have at most a negligible advantage in statically breaking this scheme in the random oracle model.*

5   Implementation

5.1   Overview

We implemented a proof-of-concept blockchain-based traceability system using the architecture shown in Fig. 1. The system was built on ConsenSys Quorum [21], a private and permissioned blockchain based on Ethereum [28]. Quorum supports private transactions through its private transaction manager Tessera, ensuring secure communication between users and manufacturers without introducing additional components.

In addition, we integrated a private IPFS [2] network as an off-chain storage solution for encrypted traceability records and attribute public keys. IPFS is a distributed file system that allows for high availability and efficient storage of application data, reducing the burden on the blockchain [2].

To optimize query performance, we integrated Dgraph [8], a graph database solution, to cache and speed up traceability graph traversal. The traceability graph was primarily stored in smart contracts as adjacency lists, but using Dgraph as a mirror of the graph improved system efficiency and performance.

The implemented system consisted of a 7-node private network, with each node running Quorum, Tessera, and IPFS nodes. Smart contract was written in Solidity 0.8.0. The ZKP proving circuit and verifier was developed with ZoKrates [6] 0.7.12. The proposed DCP-ABE scheme was implemented using Charm [1] 0.50 with PBC [18] as the pairing library.

5.2   Case Study on Product Recall

A case study on product recall, in collaboration with a company in Hong Kong, in food supply chain was conducted on the implemented blockchain-based traceability system. The study involved seven users representing different parties in the chain.

To simplify the workflow, we assumed each item had authentication secret generated by the manufacturer, which was used in ZKP for linking up relationships of items. The ZKP is to prove the knowledge of the preimage given hash of authentication secret of the parent item in order to link up a parent-child relationship of an item. It was assumed that the authentication secret was distributed securely to buyers of the item.

Users registered newly produced items by generating a unique identifier and authentication secret, and the information was recorded in the system. To establish relationships between traceability records, a zero-knowledge proof (ZKP) on the authentication code of ingredient items was required. Once verified, the relationships were recorded in the traceability graph smart contract.

For product recall, each traceable item's unique identifier was mapped to a descriptive attribute name in the proposed DCP-ABE scheme. The access policy of each traceability record was defined as an OR policy of all ancestor identifiers, allowing authorized users to view the records.

In the case study, traceability records for an Angus cheeseburger were created including its ingredients. That is Angus burger, sesame seed bun and American cheese. The cheeseburger, burger and the bun were produced by the same food processing company, and thus their traceability records were viewable in the manufacturer's view, as shown in Figure 2a. Figure 2b shows the view of the manufacturer of fresh cow milk, who was the dairy farm supplying raw material for American cheese. It visualized all downstream products made of its fresh cow milk. If the dairy farm figured out that batch of fresh cow milk was spoiled due to poor temperature control, this view as shown in Fig. 2b allowed for quick identification of affected products in the event of a recall, enabling appropriate actions to be taken.

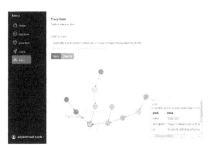
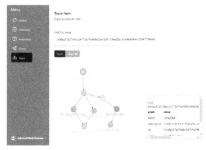

(a) Angus cheeseburger from viewpoint of the food processing company

(b) Fresh cow milk from viewpoint of the dairy farm

Fig. 2. Traversal of traceable items from different viewpoints

The DCP-ABE scheme ensured data confidentiality, as unauthorized users could only see the relationships in the traceability graph, not the plaintext records. Data verifiability was achieved through the applied ZKP, ensuring that recorded relationships in the traceability graph were backed by verified proofs. Identity anonymity was protected by the proposed DCP-ABE scheme, which hid the identity of the attribute authority through hidden access structures. Moreover, by using HD key generation, each transaction is sent by a different blockchain address. This also made the deanonymization through transaction history graph hard.

6 Related Works

6.1 Attribute-Based Encryption

Bethencourt, Sahai and Waters [3] introduced CP-ABE, associating private keys with attributes and ciphertexts with access structures. This is also among the first ABE schemes providing Delegate function, allowing third-party access on behalf of delegator.

Lewko and Waters [10] introduced Decentralized ABE (DABE) as a subset of Multi-Authority ABE (MA-ABE). Unlike MA-ABE proposed by Chase [5], DABE eliminates the need for a master secret key and global coordination during setup. They also introduced an algorithm for converting Boolean formulas of AND and OR gates into an equivalent linear secret sharing scheme. This method is widely adopted [16,17,26].

To address anonymity concerns in ABE schemes for cloud storage, techniques of policy hiding were proposed [11,23,25]. In particular, Zhong et al. [32] proposed a CP-ABE scheme with user revocation and policy-hiding by applying one-way anonymous key agreement [9] to Lewko and Waters scheme [10].

Our proposed scheme is based on RW15 [26] and thus shares similar properties. In addition, our scheme supports delegation and generation of attribute public keys while achieving policy-hiding. Such generation function removes the need of sharing the descriptive attribute names to others for attribute public key generation and maintains the property of identity anonymity (Table 1).

Table 1. Comparison of characteristics with related ABE literature.

Scheme	Security	Multi-Authority	Decentralization	Delegation	Policy-hiding
BSW07 [3]	Non-adaptive	No	No	Yes	No
LW11 [10]	Adaptive	Yes	Yes	No	No
RW15 [26]	Non-adaptive	Yes	Yes	No	No
PYS15 [25]	Non-adaptive	No	No	No	Yes
ZZXC18 [32]	Adaptive	Yes	Yes	No	Yes
Our Work	Non-adaptive	Yes	Yes	Yes	Yes

6.2   Blockchain-Based Traceability System

Recent works on blockchain-based traceability systems leverage different cryptographic primitives to address different requirements of such systems.

Mitani and Otsuka [20] proposed a dual-blockchain traceability system using interactive zero-knowledge proof and homomorphic encryption in order to prove the traceability of certain item in one blockchain to the counterpart blockchain without unneeded information leakage.

Zhao, Cui and Xu [31] integrated DCP-ABE [10] with Hyperledger Fabric for access control in a medical data traceability system. Moreover, they applied reversible data desensitization and encryption protect personal privacy [31].

Maouchi, Ersoy and Erkin [19] introduced the PASTA protocol for anonymity in a blockchain-based traceability system. They used Schnorr signature, ring signature and modified stealth address to achieves anonymity and applied Elliptic Curve Integrated Encryption Scheme [27] for data confidentiality.

7 Limitation and Conclusion

One limitation of our work is that expensive pairing operations during decryption are proportional to the number of utilized attributes, causing a drop in system performance when searching for attributes satisfying the hidden access policy. One research direction to improve such situation is to consider ABE schemes with fast decryption while satisfying the same set of requirements. Future research should also consider quantum attack resistance in the blockchain-based traceability system, involving lattice-based ABE and quantum-resistant alternatives of zk-SNARK, since the utilized security assumptions may not hold under quantum computing.

In this paper, we proposed a privacy-preserving blockchain-based traceability system and a DCP-ABE scheme with delegation and hidden access policy to prevent trade secret leakage in data and identities. Delegate algorithm offers an alternative for requesting decryption keys, while hidden access policy ensures no identity information leaks through access structures. The PoC system was implemented on Quorum and integrated with IPFS and Dgraph to improve performance. A product recall case study demonstrated the efficient identification of affected downstream manufacturers.

Acknowledgments. This work is supported by Logistics and Supply Chain Multi-Tech R&D Centre and funded by the Innovation and Technology Fund of the Hong Kong Special Administrative Region under project ITP/026/21LP.

References

1. Akinyele, J.A., et al.: Charm: a framework for rapidly prototyping cryptosystems. J. Cryptogr. Eng. **3**(2), 111–128 (2013)
2. Benet, J.: IPFS-content addressed, versioned, p2p file system. arXiv preprint arXiv:1407.3561 (2014)
3. Bethencourt, J., Sahai, A., Waters, B.: Ciphertext-policy attribute-based encryption. In: 2007 IEEE Symposium on Security and Privacy (SP'07), pp. 321–334. IEEE (2007)
4. Bitansky, N., Canetti, R., Chiesa, A., Tromer, E.: From extractable collision resistance to succinct non-interactive arguments of knowledge, and back again. Cryptology ePrint Archive, Paper 2011/443 (2011). https://eprint.iacr.org/2011/443
5. Chase, M.: Multi-authority attribute based encryption. In: Vadhan, S.P. (eds.) Theory of Cryptography. TCC 2007. LNCS, vol. 4392, pp. 515–534. Springer, Berlin, Heidelberg (2007). https://doi.org/10.1007/978-3-540-70936-7_28
6. Eberhardt, J., Tai, S.: Zokrates-scalable privacy-preserving off-chain computations. In: 2018 IEEE International Conference on Internet of Things (iThings) and IEEE Green Computing and Communications (GreenCom) and IEEE Cyber, Physical and Social Computing (CPSCom) and IEEE Smart Data (SmartData), pp. 1084–1091. IEEE (2018)
7. Greene, J.L.: Animal identification and traceability: overview and issues. Library of Congress, Congressional Research Service Washington, DC, USA (2010)
8. Jain, M.: Dgraph: synchronously replicated, transactional and distributed graph database. birth (2005)

9. Kate, A., Zaverucha, G., Goldberg, I.: Pairing-based onion routing. In: Borisov, N., Golle, P. (eds.) Privacy Enhancing Technologies. PET 2007. LNCS, vol. 4776, pp. 95–112. Springer, Berlin, Heidelberg (2007). https://doi.org/10.1007/978-3-540-75551-7_7

10. Lewko, A., Waters, B.: Decentralizing attribute-based encryption. In: Paterson, K.G. (eds.) Advances in Cryptology – EUROCRYPT 2011. EUROCRYPT 2011. LNCS, vol. 6632, pp. 568–588. Springer, Berlin, Heidelberg (2011). https://doi.org/10.1007/978-3-642-20465-4_31

11. Li, X., Gu, D., Ren, Y., Ding, N., Yuan, K.: Efficient ciphertext-policy attribute based encryption with hidden policy. In: Xiang, Y., Pathan, M., Tao, X., Wang, H. (eds.) Internet and Distributed Computing Systems. IDCS 2012. LNCS, vol. 7646, pp. 146–159. Springer, Berlin, Heidelberg (2012). https://doi.org/10.1007/978-3-642-34883-9_12

12. Liang, S., Li, M., Li, W.: Research on traceability algorithm of logistics service transaction based on blockchain. In: 2019 18th International Symposium on Distributed Computing and Applications for Business Engineering and Science (DCABES), pp. 186–189. IEEE (2019)

13. Liao, K., Zhao, Z., Doupé, A., Ahn, G.J.: Behind closed doors: measurement and analysis of cryptolocker ransoms in bitcoin. In: 2016 APWG Symposium on Electronic Crime Research (eCrime), pp. 1–13. IEEE (2016)

14. Lin, Y.J., Wu, P.W., Hsu, C.H., Tu, I.P., Liao, S.W.: An evaluation of bitcoin address classification based on transaction history summarization. In: 2019 IEEE International Conference on Blockchain and Cryptocurrency (ICBC), pp. 302–310. IEEE (2019)

15. Liu, Z., Jiang, Z.L., Wang, X., Wu, Y., Yiu, S.M.: Multi-authority ciphertext policy attribute-based encryption scheme on ideal lattices. In: 2018 IEEE International Conference on Parallel & Distributed Processing with Applications, Ubiquitous Computing & Communications, Big Data & Cloud Computing, Social Computing & Networking, Sustainable Computing & Communications (ISPA/IUCC/BDCloud/SocialCom/SustainCom), pp. 1003–1008. IEEE (2018)

16. Liu, Z., Jiang, Z.L., Wang, X., Yiu, S.M.: Practical attribute-based encryption: outsourcing decryption, attribute revocation and policy updating. J. Netw. Comput. Appl. **108**, 112–123 (2018)

17. Liu, Z., Cao, Z., Huang, Q., Wong, D.S., Yuen, T.H.: Fully secure multi-authority ciphertext-policy attribute-based encryption without random oracles. In: Atluri, V., Diaz, C. (eds.) Computer Security – ESORICS 2011. ESORICS 2011. LNCS, vol. 6879, pp. 278–297. Springer, Berlin, Heidelberg (2011). https://doi.org/10.1007/978-3-642-23822-2_16

18. Lynn, B.: The pairing-based cryptography (pbc) library (2010)

19. Maouchi, M.E., Ersoy, O., Erkin, Z.: Decouples: a decentralized, unlinkable and privacy-preserving traceability system for the supply chain. In: Proceedings of the 34th ACM/SIGAPP Symposium on Applied Computing, pp. 364–373 (2019)

20. Mitani, T., Otsuka, A.: Traceability in permissioned blockchain. IEEE Access **8**, 21573–21588 (2020)

21. Morgan, J.: Quorum Whitepaper. JP Morgan Chase, New York (2016)

22. Nakamoto, S.: Bitcoin: a peer-to-peer electronic cash system. Decent. Bus. Rev. 21260 (2008)

23. Nishide, T., Yoneyama, K., Ohta, K.: Attribute-based encryption with partially hidden encryptor-specified access structures. In: Bellovin, S.M., Gennaro, R., Keromytis, A., Yung, M. (eds.) Applied Cryptography and Network Security.

ACNS 2008. LNCS, vol. 5037, pp. 111–129. Springer, Berlin, Heidelberg (2008). https://doi.org/10.1007/978-3-540-68914-0_7

24. Olsen, P., Borit, M.: How to define traceability. Trends Food Sci. Technol.**29**(2), 142–150 (2013). https://doi.org/10.1016/j.tifs.2012.10.003, https://www.sciencedirect.com/science/article/pii/S0924224412002117

25. Phuong, T.V.X., Yang, G., Susilo, W.: Hidden ciphertext policy attribute-based encryption under standard assumptions. IEEE Trans. Inf. Forensics Secur. **11**(1), 35–45 (2015)

26. Rouselakis, Y., Waters, B.: Efficient statically-secure large-universe multi-authority attribute-based encryption. Cryptology ePrint Archive, Paper 2015/016 (2015). https://eprint.iacr.org/2015/016

27. Shoup, V.: A proposal for an ISO standard for public key encryption. Cryptology ePrint Archive, Paper 2001/112 (2001). https://eprint.iacr.org/2001/112

28. Wood, G., et al.: Ethereum: a secure decentralised generalised transaction ledger. Ethereum Proj. Yellow Pap. **151**(2014), 1–32 (2014)

29. Wuille, P.: Bip32: hierarchical deterministic wallets (2012). https://github.com/genjix/bips/blob/master/bip-0032.md

30. Xu, X., Lu, Q., Liu, Y., Zhu, L., Yao, H., Vasilakos, A.V.: Designing blockchain-based applications a case study for imported product traceability. Futur. Gener. Comput. Syst. **92**, 399–406 (2019)

31. Zhao, Y., Cui, B., Xu, J.: A privacy-preserving medical data traceability system based on attribute-based encryption on blockchain. In: Lu, W., Zhang, Y., Wen, W., Yan, H., Li, C. (eds.) Cyber Security. CNCERT 2021. CCIS, vol. 1506, pp. 27–36. Springer, Singapore (2022). https://doi.org/10.1007/978-981-16-9229-1_2

32. Zhong, H., Zhu, W., Xu, Y., Cui, J.: Multi-authority attribute-based encryption access control scheme with policy hidden for cloud storage. Soft. Comput. **22**(1), 243–251 (2018)

A Probability Mapping-Based Privacy Preservation Method for Social Networks

Qingru Li[1] , Yahong Wang[1] , Fangwei Wang[1(✉)] , Zhiyuan Tan[2] ,
and Changguang Wang[1(✉)]

[1] College of Computer and Cyberspace Security, Hebei Normal University,
Shijiazhuang 050024, China
{fw_wang,wangcg}@hebtu.edu.cn

[2] School of Computing, Engineering and the Built Environment, Edinburgh Napier University,
Edinburgh EH10 5DT, UK

Abstract. The mining and analysis of social networks can bring significant economic and social benefits. However, it also poses a risk of privacy leakages. Differential privacy is a de facto standard to prevent such leaks, but it suffers from the high sensitivity of query functions. Although projection is a technique that can reduce this sensitivity, existing methods still struggle to maintain a satisfactory level of sensitivity in query functions. This results in lower data utility and an inevitable risk of privacy leakage. To prevent the disclosure of user privacy, we need to significantly reduce the sensitivity of the query functions and minimize the error of the projected values with respect to the original values. To address this issue, we first explore the influence of mapping and projection on reducing the sensitivity of query functions. We then propose a Probability Mapping (PM) algorithm, based on multi-armed bandit, which however tends to generate mapped graphs with a wide range of degrees and containing considerable nodes with high degrees. Thus, we develop a new Probability Projection (PP) algorithm to overcome these weaknesses. Finally, we propose four histogram publishing algorithms built upon PM and PP, namely PMTC, PPTC, PMCTC and PPCTC. Extensive experimental results on three different sized datasets show that PM and PP not only retain more edge information and reduce the error but also improve the data availability.

Keywords: Differential Privacy · Multi-Armed Bandit · Mapping · Projection · Histogram · Social Networks

1 Introduction

The amount of data shared on social networks has increased significantly and contains a lot of personal information and social connections. This sharing has led to a significant breach of privacy. For instance, in March 2020, some data sets from Sina Weibo were stolen by attackers, which resulted in the exposure of information belonging to 538 million Weibo users. Similarly, in June 2021, LinkedIn was hacked, and data of approximate 500 million users were stolen. As a result, researchers are now focusing on the issue of privacy protection for social networks, and the development of social networks with privacy protection features is a current research priority.

Nowadays, there are various techniques available to safeguard data privacy. Some of these include K-anonymity [1], L-diversity [2], t-closeness [3], and m-invariance [4]. While these methods can effectively prevent the disclosure of user information, they may not be able to protect against background knowledge attacks. However, the differential privacy mechanism has a solid mathematical foundation and is capable of defending against such attacks. As a result, this mechanism is commonly employed in the release of private data on social media platforms [5].

When publishing differential privacy data, it can be difficult to balance query function sensitivity and data availability. To reduce query function sensitivity, projection is a common technique that maps an original graph to a graph with nodes having a maximum degree of θ. However, current projection methods may compromise privacy or lose original information. To address these issues, we introduce a new projection method, Probability Projection (PP), that limits edge increase through probability and node degree thresholds. Our proposed method provides better privacy protection with less information loss. Overall, our contributions include developing a novel projection method that enhances privacy and preserves data integrity.

This paper is structured as follows. Section 2 reviews related research on differential privacy algorithms. Section 3 provides definitions and explanations of social networks, differential privacy, and the multi-armed bandit. Section 4 introduces the Probability Selection Algorithm Based on Multi-Armed Bandit (PSMAB), Probability Mapping (PM), PP, and four histogram publishing methods based on PM and PP. Section 5 conducts experimental verification analysis and measures the data utility of the proposed algorithms. Section 6 summarizes the paper.

2 Related Work

Data publishing using differential privacy [6] involves adding random noise to real datasets. This approach can be divided into two categories: edge differential privacy and node differential privacy. Edge differential privacy is where the two graphs are adjacent only if they differ on a single edge. On the other hand, node differential privacy is where deleting a node and all its connected edges in a graph results in a new graph that is adjacent to the original graph.

2.1 Edge Differential Privacy

To the problem of losing original information and weak privacy protection in edge differential privacy, Lv et al. [7] developed an edge removal projection algorithm based on the Triangle-count Sort Edge Removal (TSER) algorithm. This algorithm preserves more triangles in the original graph and enhances the availability of data. Zhou et al. [8] also proposed a model for generating social networks called the structure-attribute social network model. This model introduces uncertainty graphs into network partitions. However, it has high time complexity and low data validity. Huang et al. [9] proposed the Privacy-preserving approach Based on Clustering and Noise (PBCN). This approach makes the published graph resistant to degree and graph structure attacks while maintaining high execution efficiency. Gao et al. [10] proposed a differential private graph model that combines sequences dK-1, dK-2, and dK-3 and adds three levels of rewiring algorithms. This model preserves the original graph structure information to a greater extent.

However, edge differential privacy is vulnerable to attacks that involve re-identifying nodes in anonymized graph data. Besides, it is designed to protect the relationship between two entities, which is represented in the form of an edge, from being disclosed, but in social networks, a node and its associated edges represent all of a person's data, whereas an edge cannot represent all of a person's data.

2.2 Node Differential Privacy

On contrast, node differential privacy offers a greater level of privacy protection compared to edge differential privacy. In order to address the issue of large errors in algorithm under node differential privacy, several methods have been proposed. Day et al. [11] introduced π_θ, which involves adding edges while ensuring that the degree of the two connected nodes does not exceed the node degree threshold. This helps reduce errors in fitting the true degree distribution. Meanwhile, Zhang et al. [12] proposed a Sequential Edge Removal (SER) algorithm to decrease the global sensitivity of histogram publication. However, both π_θ and SER suffer from uncertainty in edge ordering, which limits their ability to preserve edge information to the fullest extent.

Liu et al. [13] put forth two algorithms for releasing the intensity distribution and analyzed the impact of projection on node intensity histograms through introspection. Ding et al. [14] suggested the Best Adaptation (BA) strategy, which involves removing the connection edge of a node that has the largest number of triangles adjacent to it. However, while this method improves data availability, it also reduces privacy protection effects. Prasad et al. [15] introduced FlowGraph (FG), which constructs a weighted graph by creating new nodes between a source node v and a sink node u. It then calculates the maximum flow from v to u, removes v from the maximum flow graph, and constructs the degree distribution. By combining the Lipschitz extension and the generalized exponential mechanism, FG greatly published a degree distribution that approximates the original graph and is more accurate than previous algorithms.

However, current node differential privacy methods often suffer from issues such as loss of original information and significant errors before and after projection. To address these challenges, this paper aims to minimize errors and preserve more of the original data while enhancing data availability and ensuring privacy protection.

3 Preliminaries

This section introduces the preliminaries to our proposed probability mapping-based privacy preservation method. They include social network graphs and differential privacy.

3.1 Social Network Graph

A social network can be represented by a graph, which is defined as $G = (V, E)$. In this graph, $V = \{v_1, v_2, \ldots, v_n\}$ represents a set of users, and $E = \{e_1, e_2, \ldots, e_m\}$ represents a set of relationships between users.

3.2 Differential Privacy

Differential privacy is a technique that allows for sharing information about a group of individuals, while protecting their personal privacy by obscuring their data. The following are the key concepts in contemporary differential privacy.

ε-**Differential Privacy [6].** A random algorithm $M : D \rightarrow M(D)$ satisfies ε- Differential Privacy if any two neighboring datasets D and D' maintains the following relationship.

$$P_r[M(D) \in S] \le e^{\varepsilon} \cdot P_r[M(D') \in S], \tag{1}$$

where the probability P_r is controlled by the randomness of the algorithm M, $S \in Range(D)$ and ε is a parameter for privacy level.

Global Sensitivity [16]. For any function f, given two adjacent datasets D and D' that differ at most one record, the global sensitivity of f is defined as:

$$\Delta f = \|f(D) - f(D')\|_1, \tag{2}$$

where $\|f(D) - f(D')\|_1$ is the $L1$ normal form. The higher global sensitivity is, the less data is available and more noise is added.

Laplace Mechanism. Given a dataset D, there exists a function $f : D \rightarrow R$ with sensitivity Δf. If the mechanism M satisfies ε -Differential Privacy, its output satisfies:

$$M(D) = f(D) + Lap\left(\frac{\Delta f}{\varepsilon}\right), \tag{3}$$

where $Lap\left(\frac{\Delta f}{\varepsilon}\right)$ is a random noise following the Laplacian distribution.

3.3 Multi-armed Bandit

The multi-armed bandit model has n arms. Each pull of the arm α results in a reward. The reward of each arm follows the same function r. The goal of the multi-armed bandit model is to find the arm with the most appropriate reward after t iterations.

We define the reward function r for each arm as follows:

$$r = \alpha \times L + \beta \times p + \gamma \times \Delta f, \tag{4}$$

where L represents the error of the histogram, p represents the utility of the probability, Δf represents the privacy loss, and α, β, and γ are the weight. The errors obtained by each probability are set as the reward function of each arm.

4 Proposed Method

Our Probability Mapping (PM) and Probability Projection (PP) algorithms are built upon the Probability Selection Algorithm Based on Multi-Armed Bandit (PSMAB). They only differ in the node degree threshold that restricts the addition of edges. See Sects. 4.1, 4.2 and 4.3 for the details of PSMAB, PM and PP algorithms.

The process flowchart for safeguarding social network privacy through PM or PP is illustrated in Fig. 1. We start by inputting a social network G and a node degree threshold θ. Then, we select probability p based on PSMAB. Finally, we obtain four triangle count histograms: PM-based Triangle Counting (PMTC), PP-based Triangle Counting (PPTC), PM-based Cumulative Triangle Count (PMCTC), and PP-based Cumulative Triangle Count (PPCTC) histograms, through processing by PM or PP.

Fig. 1. Flowchart of publishing algorithm of triangle count histogram in social networks based on PM or PP.

4.1 The Probability Selection Algorithm Based on Multi-armed Bandit

A probability selection algorithm based on multi-armed bandit (PSMAB) is a method for selecting an action from a group of options that have uncertain rewards. The algorithm aims to balance the exploration of new actions that may provide greater rewards with exploiting the best known action. We came up with PSMAB inspired by [17]. The process flowchart of PSMAB is shown in Fig. 2, where r_i denotes the reward of arm i, and L_{p_i} and L_i denote the probability error and total error corresponding to r_i, respectively.

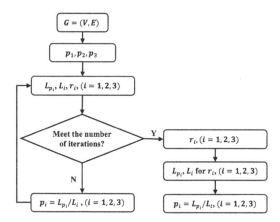

Fig. 2. Flowchart of PSMAB.

PSMAB first initializes the reward, probability, and reward function of each arm. In each iteration, PSMAB starts with the comparison between the generated random number r and an initial parameter lr. If r is less than lr, PSMAB randomly selects an arm and then updates its reward. If r is greater than lr, PSMAB selects the arm with the largest reward and updates its reward. Then, the probability error L_p and total error L for each arm are calculated based on the reward and probability of the three arms, respectively. The ratio of L_p to L for each arm is then obtained using Eq. (5).

$$p = L_p/L, \tag{5}$$

where L_p is the probability error, and L is the total error caused by the probability, noise, and node degree threshold. p is the new probability for each arm. The three arms with the latest probabilities are carried into the next iteration. Then, p, L_p, and L of each arm are recalculated. To account for the randomness of probabilities, this process is repeated 10 iterations. Once complete, the probability with the medium value r_i is selected as the proper probability. This is due to the fact that when there is a larger error, fewer edges are retained, resulting in decreased data utility. Conversely, when there is a smaller error, more original data must be retained, which can lead to a weaker privacy protection effect.

4.2 Probability Mapping Algorithm

This section proposes a novel edge addition algorithm, named Probability Mapping (PM) that is built upon PSMAB. In the PM algorithm, the first step involves creating a new graph G' by mapping all the nodes in the original graph G. However, no edges are added at this stage. Next, PM traverses through the edge set of the original graph and generates a random number ra. ra is then compared with the probability p chosen by PSMAB. If ra is less than p, the edge $e = (u, v)$ is added, and the degrees of the nodes at each end of the edge are incremented by one. On the other hand, if ra is greater than or equal to p, no edge is added. Once the traversal is complete, the new mapped graph $G' = (V, E')$ is generated. The pseudocode of PM is shown in Algorithm 1.

Algorithm 1: PM Algorithm.

Input: An original social network $G = (V, E)$, probability p, and an edge ordering $\Lambda = <e_1, e_2, ..., e_n>$.
Output: A mapped graph $G' = (V, E')$.
1:   $d(v) \leftarrow 0$ for each $v \in V$, $E' \leftarrow \phi$
2:   for $e = (u, v) \in \Lambda$ do
3:     if random number $ra < p$
4:       $E' \leftarrow E' \cup \{e\}$
5:       $d(u) \leftarrow d(u) + 1$; $d(v) \leftarrow d(v) + 1$
6:     end if
7:   end for
8:   return $G' = (V, E')$

4.3 Probability Projection Algorithm

There are several nodes in the mapped graph with large degrees, and the range of degree values is also quite broad. This can result in increased errors in the histogram. To address this issue, we introduce the Probability Projection (PP) algorithm, which is an enhancement of the PM algorithm. PM and PP follow the same principles, with the difference being that PP imposes a stricter condition by adding a node degree threshold for adding edges. The pseudocode for PP is shown in Algorithm 2. Compared to the existing methods of π_θ [11] and FG [15], PP can reduce the sensitivity of query functions, minimize the error between the original and projected data, and preserve more original information. This reduces the risk of user privacy breaches.

The total time complexity of both Algorithm 1 and Algorithm 2 is $O(|E|)$, as the majority of time is consumed in the process of traversing the edges. The total space complexity of both algorithms is $O(|E| + |V|)$ because they both need to create new memory to save nodes and edges during the process of constructing a mapping graph and a projection graph.

Algorithm 2: PP Algorithm.

Input: An original social network $G = (V, E)$, probability p, node degree threshold θ and an edge ordering $\Lambda = < e_1, e_2, ..., e_n >$.
Output: A projected graph $G'' = (V, E'')$.
   1:   $d(v) \leftarrow 0$ for each $v \in V$, $E'' \leftarrow \phi$
   2:   for $e = (u, v) \in \Lambda$ do
   3:      if $d(u) < \theta$ & $d(v) < \theta$ then
   4:         if random number $ra < p$
   5:            $E'' \leftarrow E'' \cup \{e\}$
   6:            $d(u) \leftarrow d(u) + 1$; $d(v) \leftarrow d(v) + 1$
   7:         end if
   8:      end if
   9:   end for
  10:   return $G'' = (V, E'')$

4.4 Publishing Algorithm for Triangle Counting Histogram

For counting triangles in social networks, we create two types of histograms: PM-based Triangle Counting histogram (PMTC) and PP-based Triangle Counting histogram (PPTC).

The process of generating PMTC involves generating a probability from PSMAB, creating a mapped graph G' from PM and generating a histogram of the corresponding triangle count. To make the histogram publishable, we add noise to each bucket. This results in a histogram that can be used to count triangles in social networks. The process of generating PPTC is similar to that of PMTC.

Theorem 1. Given two adjacent graphs G and G' that only differ by one node, the following equation holds:

$$\Delta_{PMTC} = \left\| PMTC(G) - PMTC(G') \right\|_1 < 4p + 1.$$

Proof: Suppose the graphs $G = (V, E)$ and $G' = (V, E')$ differ by only one node v'. We refer to the set of all triangles that exists solely in G' as T, and the number of triangles in this set as m. All triangles in the set T have a common node v' at least. Removing the node v' from the graph G' effectively removes all triangles from the set T. Every triangle in T change the triangle count result of the other two nodes, both nodes have a difference of 1. Because each bucket in the triangle count histogram result represents the number of nodes corresponding to the number of triangles.

In the worst-case scenario, all triangles in the set T have only one common node v', which means that the number of nodes influenced by triangles in the set T is at most 2 m. Every node under the influence of the set T will cause a difference of at most 2 in the histogram. The difference, caused by the removal of the node v', in the histogram is 1. Therefore, the difference between the graphs $G = (V, E)$ and $G' = (V, E')$ is $4m + 1$.

In PMTC, the number (i.e., m) of the triangles in the set T is determined by the ratio of the probability p to the value range of a random number. As a random number range between 0 and 1, the ratio between p and the random number also falls in the range of [0,1]. Thus, Δ_{PMTC} is always less than $4p + 1$.

Theorem 2. Given two adjacent graphs G and G' that only differ by one node, the following equation holds:

$$\Delta_{PPTC} = \left\| PPTC(G) - PPTC(G') \right\|_1 < 4p\theta + 1.$$

Proof: The proof procedure is similar to Theorem 1. The difference is that a node degree threshold θ is set in PPTC to limit the addition of edges, and the difference caused in the histogram is $4p\theta + 1$ at most.

4.5 Publishing Algorithm for Cumulative Triangle Counting Histogram

To minimize noise-caused errors, this section proposes two enhanced publishing algorithms: PM-based Cumulative Triangle Count histogram (PMCTC) and PP-based Cumulative Triangle Count histogram (PPCTC).

Theorem 3. Given two adjacent graphs G and G' that only differ by one node, the following equation holds:

$$\Delta_{PMCTC} = \left\| PMCTC(G) - PMCTC(G') \right\|_1 < 2p + 1.$$

Proof: Using the notations in Theorem 1. Suppose the node v' connects to m triangles, then removing it from G' will cause a shift in all the bins of the cumulative histogram by 1. The maximum number of nodes affected by deleting the node v' is 2 m. In the cumulative histogram, the difference of histogram caused by every 2 m nodes is 1, which means that the total difference between the graphs $G = (V, E)$ and $G' = (V, E')$ in the cumulative histogram is $2m + 1$.

In PMCTC, the probability p is used to decide whether to add or delete an edge. The value of m is determined by the ratio of p to the value range of a random number. As the random numbers range between 0 and 1, the ratio between p and the random number also falls in the range of [0,1]. This means that Δ_{PMCTC} is always less than $2p + 1$.

Theorem 4. Given two adjacent graphs G and G' that only differ by one node, the following equation holds:

$$\Delta_{PPCTC} = \left\| PPCTC(G) - PPCTC(G') \right\|_1 < 2p\theta + 1.$$

Proof: The proof procedure is similar to Theorem 2 and Theorem 3, and the difference caused by PPCTC is $2p\theta + 1$ at most.

The probability p takes a value ranging from $[0, 1]$. Taking the probability value into Theorems 1–4 shows that the algorithms proposed in this paper reduce the sensitivity of the query functions compared with π_θ [11] and FG [15]. The sensitivity of π_θ [11] is $2\theta + 1$, and the sensitivity of FG [15] is 6θ.

5 Experimental Results and Analysis

5.1 Datasets

Three real-world datasets from [18], as shown in Table 1, were used in our experiments. Tri_Num is the number of node triangles in the dataset, and Max_degree is the maximum degree of nodes in the dataset. Each network dataset was pre-processed and converted into an undirected graph.

Table 1. Information of the datasets.

Graph	$|V|$	$|E|$	Tri_Num	Max_degree
Facebook	4,039	88,234	1,612,010	1,045
Email-Enron	36,692	183,831	727,044	1,383
Twitter	75,879	1,768,149	1,768,149	81,306

The initial range of probability for PSMAB is set to $[0, 1]$. However, when the probability ranges from $[0,0.5]$, it retains little of the original graph information, which significantly affects the availability of data. On the other hand, when the probability is $[0.9,1]$, too much original graph information is retained, resulting in too much noise. To balance between the availability of data and retaining original graph information, the multi-armed bandit model has three arms that correspond to different probabilities: $p = 0.6$, $p = 0.7$, and $p = 0.8$. The selection of the specific probability is performed by iterations based on PSMAB depicted in Fig. 2.

5.2 Performance Indicators

L1 error, *edge retention rate*, and *KS distance* are used to evaluate the experimental results, and their definitions are as follows:

- **L1error**: The *L1 error* shows the difference between the two histograms obtained before and after PM or PP algorithm. The *L1 error* is defined in Eq. (6):

$$L = \sum\nolimits_{i=1}^{n} |f(x_i)' - f(x_i)|, \tag{6}$$

  where $f(x_i)'$ represents the frequency of each degree value after any one of the four algorithms is processed in this paper, and $f(x_i)$ represents the frequency of each degree value in the original social network graph.
- **Edge retention rate**: It can be expressed as $(|E'|/|E|)$, where E' represents the edge in the graph after projection, and E represents the edge in the original graph.
- **KSdistance**: The smaller the *KSdistance*, the more similar the histogram after noise is added to the original histogram, and the higher the data availability. The *KSdistance* is defined in Eq. (7):

$$K = max|f(x)' - f(x)|, \tag{7}$$

  where $f(x)'$ represents the histogram data distribution after adding noise, and $f(x)$ represents the histogram data distribution of the original social network.

5.3   Experimental Results and Analysis

The Effect of Error on Probability Selection.   We explored the effect of total error on probability in PSMAB by setting a node degree threshold of $\theta = 128$. Considering the randomness of the probability and Laplacian noise, the averaged results shown in Fig. 3 were obtained from 100 trials.

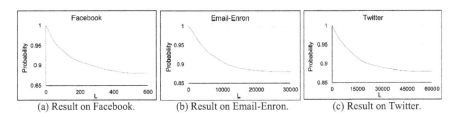

(a) Result on Facebook.   (b) Result on Email-Enron.   (c) Result on Twitter.

Fig. 3.   The effect of different errors on probability selection.

It can be seen from Fig. 3 that the probability tends to stabilize at a constant value of 0.88 as the error increases across the three datasets. The reason behind this phenomenon can be attributed to the fact that PSMAB algorithm restricts the addition of edges based on probability and node degree threshold, while ignoring the dataset size. PSMAB takes into account the balance between preserving privacy and maximizing data utility, hence it retains more data information while minimizing the error rate.

Comparison Between PM and PP.   We conducted a study to compare PM and PP by setting a node degree threshold of $\theta = 128$. We compared the *L1 errors* and the *edge retention rates* $(|E'|/|E|)$ of PM and PP against the various probabilities, respectively across three datasets. The averaged results shown in Fig. 4 were obtained from 100 trials.

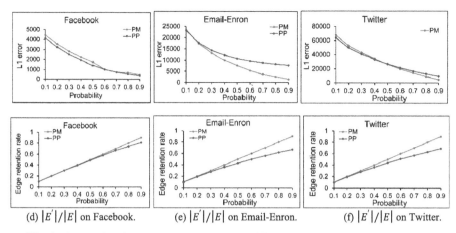

(d) $|E'|/|E|$ on Facebook.   (e) $|E'|/|E|$ on Email-Enron.   (f) $|E'|/|E|$ on Twitter.

Fig. 4. Comparison between PM and PP under different probabilities across 3 datasets.

As can be seen in Fig. 4, the $L1$ *errors* of both PM and PP show a decreasing trend as the probability increases, while the $|E'|/|E|$ show an increasing trend. PP has a smaller $L1$ *error* than PM on smaller datasets (e.g., Facebook) and a higher $L1$ *error* on larger datasets (e.g., Email-Enron and Twitter). However, the $|E'|/|E|$ of PM is higher than that of the PP on any dataset. Because PP has stricter restrictions on adding edges compared with PM, and the relationship between nodes and edges is more intensive in a large social network, deleting edges is more likely to lead to a larger $L1$ *error*.

In summary, PM is more suitable for large datasets with complex relationships, while PP is more suitable for small datasets with simpler relationships.

Comparison with Other Projection Algorithms. Comparing PP with π_θ [11] and FG [15], two metrics (i.e., the $L1$ *error* of the node degree histogram and the $|E'|/|E|$ before and after projection) are used. In this experiment, a node degree threshold of $\theta = 128$ was set. Considering the randomness of the probability and Laplacian noise, the averaged results shown in Tables 2 and 3 were obtained from 100 trials.

Table 2. Comparison of $L1$ *error* of our methods with other projection methods.

Dataset	FG	π_θ	PP
Facebook	1092	801	611
Email-Enron	13602	12577	7126
Twitter	17116	15293	12623

Table 3. Comparison of the edge retention rate of our methods with other projection methods.

Dataset	FG	π_θ	PP
Facebook	0.90	0.88	0.86
Email-Enron	0.75	0.74	0.71
Twitter	0.77	0.74	0.74

The experimental results in Table 2 show that PP has a smaller $L1$ *error* than the other three methods, which implies that the error caused by PP is smaller and a better distribution shape is maintained. Moreover, based on Theorems 2 and 4, it can be inferred that PP reduces the sensitivity of the query function, which reduces the risk of user privacy leakages. The stricter the conditions for adding edges, the lower the edge retention rate, but the more edge information is retained. Our purpose is to reduce the sensitivity of the query function and the error before and after projection while ensuring that more edge information is retained.

In conclusion, PP not only significantly reduces the $L1$ *error* of the degree histogram and the sensitivity of the query function on each dataset, but also retains more edge information, effectively mitigating the risk of user privacy leakage.

Comparison of Triangle Retention Numbers. This section compares the numbers of triangles retained by PMTC and PPTC with that of π_θ [11]. On different datasets, we set different node degree thresholds. Considering the randomness of the probability, the averaged results shown in Fig. 5 were obtained from 100 trials.

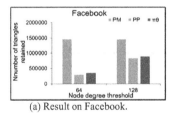 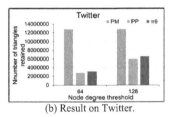

(a) Result on Facebook.   (b) Result on Twitter.

Fig. 5. Comparison of number of triangles retained.

It can be seen from Fig. 5 that PM retains more triangles than other algorithms. Besides, the number of triangles retained by PP and π_θ is increasing as the node degree threshold increases. Because in PM, the probability is the basis for adding edges, and the node degree threshold does not affect the results of PM, while the results of other algorithms are affected by the node degree threshold. The larger the node degree threshold, the more edges are added. In addition, the number of triangles retained by PP is less than that of π_θ. An explanation is that PP is limited by probability and node degree threshold, while π_θ is limited only by node degree threshold.

Comparison with Other Publishing Algorithms. PMTC, PPTC, PMCTC, and PPCTC are compared with TSER [7] and BA [14] on the Facebook and Twitter datasets. The results are shown in Fig. 6.

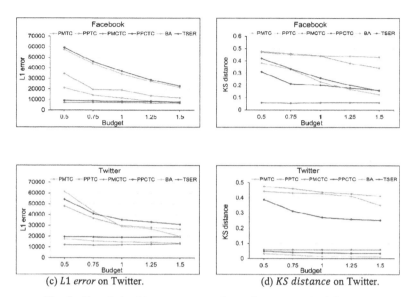

(c) *L1 error* on Twitter.   (d) *KS distance* on Twitter.

Fig. 6. Cumulative histogram comparison of *L1error* and *KSdistance*.

Figure 6 shows that the *L1 error* of the four algorithms proposed is better than BA and TSER. As the privacy budget increases, the *L1 error* of the four methods shows a decreasing trend. Due to the randomness of probability, the *KSdistance* generated by the four algorithms may produce the same result under different privacy budgets. As the privacy budget increases, the added noise decreases, the data availability increases and more original graph information is preserved. It can be seen from Fig. 6 on the smaller dataset (Facebook) that the *KSdistance* of PPCTC is slightly higher than BA when the budget is greater than 1.25. Because BA retains more edges while maintaining a data distribution more similar to the original social network. However, PPCTC does not take into account the number of node triangles connected to the edges in the process of adding the edges. While on the larger dataset (Twitter), the *KSdistance* of PPCTC and PMCTC is higher than BA and TSER. Because in PPCTC and PMCTC, the probability is used as a constraint for adding edges, and the probability is random. In addition, the *L1 error* and *KSdistance* of PPCTC are higher than PMCTC on any dataset. Because PPCTC has stricter restrictions on adding edges.

Comparing PMTC, PPTC, PMCTC and PPCTC, Fig. 6 shows that the *L1 error* and *KSdistance* of PMTC and PPTC are higher than PMCTC and PPCTC. Because from Theorems 1–4 the sensitivity of PMTC and PPTC is higher than that of PMCTC and PPCTC, leading to the addition of more noise and a larger error in the histogram.

6 Conclusions

In this paper, we have presented the probability selection technology based on PSMAB. We have also developed PM and PP to anonymize triangles in large social networks using node differential privacy. Based on PM and PP, we have built four methods for displaying triangles. These include the PMTC and PPTC histogram publishing algorithms, as well as the cumulative PMCTC and PPCTC histogram publishing algorithms. Extensive experiments were conducted to validate the probability effects of PM and PP. The experimental results show PP algorithm achieves a smaller $L1error$ rate than those of the existing algorithms. Furthermore, PMCTC and PPCTC have higher data usage and lower global sensitivity than other algorithms. However, it should be noted that our research focuses on data from static social networks. In real-world scenarios, social networks change dynamically in real time. Consequently, the application of these algorithms to dynamic social networks is a key field of future research.

Acknowledgement. This research was funded by NSFC under Grant 61572170, Natural Science Foundation of Hebei Province under Grant F2021205004, Science Foundation of Returned Overseas of Hebei Province Under Grant C2020342, and Key Science Foundation of Hebei Education Department under Grant ZD2021062.

References

1. Sweeney, L.: K-anonymity: a model for protecting privacy. Int. J. Uncertain. Fuzziness Knowl.-Based Syst. **10**(05), 557–570 (2002). https://doi.org/10.1142/S0218488502001648
2. Machanavajjhala, A., Gehrke, J., Kifer, D., Muthuramakrishnan, V.: L-diversity: privacy beyond k-anonymity. ACM Trans. Knowl. Discov. Data (TKDD) **1**(1), 1–52 (2007). https://doi.org/10.1145/1217299.1217302
3. Li, N., Li, T., Venkatasubramanian, S.: T-Closeness: privacy beyond k-anonymity and l-diversity. In: 2007 IEEE 23rd International Conference on Data Engineering, pp. 106–115 (2006)
4. Xiao, X., Tao, Y.: M-invariance: towards privacy preserving re-publication of dynamic datasets. In: Proceedings of the 2007 ACM SIGMOD International Conference on Management of Data, pp. 689–700 (2007)
5. Jiang, H., Pei, J., Yu, D., Yu, J., Gong, B., Cheng, X.: Applications of differential privacy in social network analysis: a survey. IEEE Trans. Knowl. Data Eng. **35**(1), 108–127 (2021). https://doi.org/10.1109/TKDE.2021.3073062
6. Dwork, C.: Differential privacy. In: Bugliesi, M., Preneel, B., Sassone, V., Wegener, I. (eds.) Automata, Languages and Programming. ICALP 2006. LNCS, vol. 4052, pp. 1–12. Springer, Berlin, Heidelberg (2006). https://doi.org/10.1007/11787006_1
7. Lv, T., Li, H., Tang, Z., Fu, F., Cao, J., Zhang, J.: Publishing triangle counting histogram in social networks based on differential privacy. Secur. Commun. Netw. **2021**, 1–16 (2021). https://doi.org/10.1155/2021/7206179
8. Zhou, N., Long, S., Liu, H.: Structure-attribute social network graph data publishing satisfying differential privacy. Symmetry **14**(12), 2531–2541 (2022)
9. Huang, H., Zhang, D., Xiao, F., Wang, K., Gu, J., Wang, R.: Privacy-preserving approach PBCN in social network with differential privacy. IEEE Trans. Netw. Serv. Manag. **17**(2), 931–945 (2020). https://doi.org/10.1109/TNSM.2020.2982555

10. Gao, T., Li, F.: Protecting social network with differential privacy under novel graph model. IEEE Access **8**(23), 185276–185289 (2020)
11. Day, W.Y., Li, N., Min, L.: Publishing graph degree distribution with node differential privacy. In: Proceedings of the 2016 International Conference on Management of Data, pp. 123–138 (2016)
12. Zhang, Y., Wei, J., Li, J.: Graph degree histogram publication method with node-differential privacy. J. Comput. Res. Dev. **56**(3), 508–520 (2019). https://doi.org/10.7544/issn1000-1239. 2019.20170886
13. Liu, G., Ma, X., Li, W.: Publishing node strength distribution with node differential privacy. IEEE Access **8**(23), 217642–217650 (2020)
14. Ding, X., et al.: Differential private triangle counting in large graphs. IEEE Trans. Knowl. Data Eng. **34**(11), 5278–5292 (2021). https://doi.org/10.1109/TKDE.2021.3052827
15. Sofya, R., Adam, S.: Efficient Lipschitz extensions for high-dimensional graph statistics and node private degree distributions (2015). arXiv preprint arXiv:1504.07912
16. Wu, X., Zhang, Y., Shi, M., Li, P., Li, R., Xiong, N.: An adaptive federated learning scheme with differential privacy preserving. Futur. Gener. Comput. Syst. **127**(1), 362–372 (2022). https://doi.org/10.1016/j.future.2021.09.015
17. Odeyomi, O.T.: Differential privacy in social networks using multi-armed bandit. IEEE Access **8**, 11817–11829 (2022)
18. Jure, L., Andrej, K.: June 2014. http://snap.stanford.edu/data

TruFaaS - Trust Verification Framework for FaaS

Avishka Shamendra, Binoy Peries, Gayangi Seneviratne[✉],
and Sunimal Rathnayake

Department of Computer Science and Engineering, University of Moratuwa,
Moratuwa 10400, Sri Lanka
{avishkas.18,binoy.18,gayangi.18,sunimal}@cse.mrt.ac.lk

Abstract. As the Function as a Service (FaaS) model on cloud grows increasingly popular, more mission critical applications have begun to adopt it as a development paradigm. It is essential for such applications to trust its component functions, as they heavily rely on the functions performing as intended. While FaaS platform security is well-researched, there has been little attempt to address the issue of trust, which pertains to ensuring that function invokers use the original function deployed by the provider. To address trust concerns in FaaS, we present *TruFaaS*, a novel trust verification framework for FaaS which enables function invokers to verify the trust of functions deployed on a FaaS platform. We present a generic framework architecture which can be incorporated into any open source FaaS platform. The framework performs trust calculation, storage and verification. The trust verification mechanism can detect unauthorized modification of a function. *TruFaaS* also has a trust protocol to communicate trust of functions to function invokers. We implement *TruFaaS* on the open source FaaS platform Fission to demonstrate its effectiveness practically. Our implementation performs with <4% overhead for function deployment and <20% for function invocation.

Keywords: Function-as-a-Service · Serverless Computing · Trusted Computing · Trust Verification · Trusted Execution

1 Introduction

Serverless computing is a cloud-native development model that allows developers to build and run applications without having to manage servers, allowing them to focus only on the application logic. Function as a Service (FaaS) has emerged as a prominent service delivery model in serverless computing, and is widely regarded as the most prevailing type of serverless computing [7], resulting in the terms FaaS and serverless often being used interchangeably.

In addition to proprietary FaaS offerings like AWS Lambda, Azure Functions and Google Cloud Functions, open-source FaaS platforms like OpenWhisk [3], OpenFaaS [23] and Fission [13] are also becoming increasingly popular. These open-source platforms enable organizations to host their own FaaS platforms even privately, broadening traditional FaaS use cases.

G. Wang et al. (Eds.): UbiSec 2023, CCIS 2034, pp. 304–318, 2024.
https://doi.org/10.1007/978-981-97-1274-8_20

A growing number of applications including mission critical software have begun to adapt FaaS as the development paradigm. For example, serverless functions are used to build cost effective and scalable systems for the Optical Character Recognition (OCR) processing of spacesuit safety and test documentation at NASA [5]. Another example is HiveMind [16], a central control platform for unmanned aerial vehicles (UAVs) that uses serverless computing to perform resource intensive tasks. In such mission critical applications, the application should be able to trust the functions it uses to guarantee the intended behavior. If an attacker can manipulate the stored function source code, they can cause the function to execute a malicious code that could potentially disrupt the entire application, leading to catastrophic outcomes. Moreover, any modification, even a minor change, to any attribute essential to the function's execution such as timeouts, resource allocations, or concurrency, may cause the typical workflows to diverge from their intended behavior, affecting the application's availability and performance.

As with any cloud technology, security and trust are crucial aspects of FaaS which cannot be ignored. While security of FaaS has been addressed in research [8,10,24], comparatively little work has been done to address trust in FaaS. At the time of writing, no FaaS platform addresses and communicates the trust of a function to function invokers, which is the primary motivation behind TruFaaS.

In this paper, trust in FaaS is defined as the ability of the function invoker to feel confident that the function they intend to use is the exact same function that the provider originally deployed. To address trust in FaaS platforms, we consider the following research questions.

1. What attributes can be used to generate a function's trust measurement?
2. How and when should the trust of a deployed function be verified?
3. How can the trust of a function be communicated to a function invoker?

Addressing these research questions, we present *TruFaaS*, a trust verification framework for FaaS which allows the trust verification of functions in a FaaS environment. *TruFaaS* is platform agnostic and can be integrated with any FaaS platform with minor modifications. *TruFaaS* has currently been implemented and tested on top of Fission, an open source serverless platform to demonstrate its effectiveness. This paper makes the following contributions;

1. A trust verification framework architecture for FaaS which allows function invokers to verify the trust of functions.
2. A protocol to communicate the trust of a function to a function invoker.
3. *TruFaaS* implementation on an open-source FaaS platform, Fission, and its usage demonstration.
4. Performance evaluation of the framework compared to vanilla Fission.

2 Related Work

2.1 Trust and Trusted Computing

Hardware Trust. C. Mitchell [21] defines a trusted system as a system that an entity can reasonably rely on to operate as expected. Trusted computing was initially designed for computer systems using hardware based approaches. The security of the system is derived from a root of trust (RoT), which is a source that can always be trusted within a cryptographic system. The TPM is a tamper-resistant hardware chip that acts as the RoT for a platform. Trust in a platform begins from a physical RoT like the TPM, and extends through the Operating System up to the application level [22].

Trust in Cloud. Since the TPM was not designed for use in virtual environments, it cannot be natively used in cloud computing which is based on virtualization. Therefore TPMs were extended to be used by VMs and resulted in vTPMs [27]. Ren et al. [25] proposes a two-phase trusted cloud framework that allows the configuration and remote attestation of VMs by tenants. However, this framework is applied to VMs, and has not been extended up to the level of FaaS. Several researches have been conducted to establish trust at the level of containers. Y. Guo *et al.* propose a *Digital Signature Algorithm* to build trust between users and their containers [14]. The developers can generate a signature list to authorize programs which can run in their container. Similarly, Docker Content Trust (DCT) [12] enables users to use digital signatures for images exchanged between them and remote Docker registries. This digital signature is to check the integrity of the images. Although trust in containers has been addressed as explained above, it requires several changes before the same concepts can be applied in the context of FaaS.

Trust in FaaS. AWS uses code signing [6] enables users to ensure the integrity of their AWS Lambda function code. Users can verify that the code running within their Lambda functions has not been modified since signing and that it originates from a trusted publisher. This approach checks whether the publisher is trusted, and only checks whether the code package has been altered before deployment. In contrast, instead of relying solely on the source code, *TruFaaS* considers various function attributes for trust calculation, going beyond code integrity. Furthermore, implementing code signing imposes an additional burden on the deployer and shifts responsibility to the invoker, which contrasts with the proposed approach in this paper.

Trust Quantification. Trust verification in a system requires trust to be quantifiably measured in some way. J. Szefer extends the hardware based trust calculation concept [25] to services running on VMs [26]. In *TruFaaS*, a similar hashing approach is used to quantify trust.

2.2   Security in FaaS

Security Vulnerabilities in FaaS. X. Li *et al.* [19] has divided security threats on serverless into five categories based on from where they are launched, which includes vertical attacks on serverless infrastructures from malicious tenants such as container escape attacks and function injection attacks. Adversaries may perform code changes in platforms where the function code is stored in a database by gaining access to the database. For example, in OpenWhisk, the function code is stored directly in CouchDB. Further, Fission allows the function provider to give a URL pointing to the source code, which will be accessed each time the function is invoked. P. Datta *et al.* [11] investigate attacks that exploit both serverless specific and more traditional vulnerabilities. However, they primarily focus on attacks that target data exfiltration and do not consider integrity attacks.

Secure Serverless Architectures. Researches have proposed serverless architectures such as VALVE [10] and SCIFFS [24], which introduce labeling mechanisms to secure communication between functions and to prevent sensitive data exposure in third-party security analytics platforms, respectively. S. Brenner *et al.* [8] propose a generic architecture for secure FaaS platforms using Intel SGX. It primarily focuses on securing FaaS by ensuring the network communication's confidentiality, integrity and protection of data and execution state of the function. Intel SGX is also used by F. Alder *et al.* [2] to develop an architecture that ensures the integrity of function inputs and outputs. Although a fair amount of research has been dedicated to FaaS, most research revolves around the topic of security and not trust. Therefore, a proper mechanism is required to detect whether a function has been compromised after an attack, and whether the function and the service provided by the function can be trusted anymore.

3   TruFaaS Design

3.1   Overview

As illustrated in Fig. 1, *TruFaaS* contains two components: the *internal component* which resides within the FaaS platform, and the *external component*, which is outside of the FaaS platform. A *trust protocol* is implemented to communicate the trust verification outcome to the invoker.

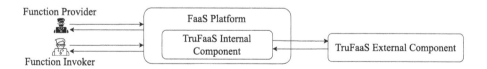

Fig. 1. Main entities in the *TruFaaS* architecture.

Fig. 2 is a more comprehensive diagram of the *TruFaaS* architecture and has been further described in the following sections.

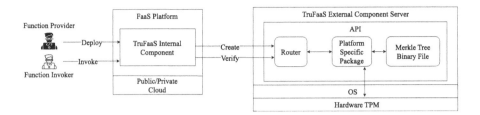

Fig. 2. Detailed *TruFaaS* architecture.

3.2   Design Considerations and Assumptions

– We assume that the organization/individual that hosts the FaaS platform also deploys the functions.
– Since FaaS platforms store function source code and attributes in some form of storage, we assume that it is the most vulnerable place that an attacker can manipulate.
– The communication between the function invoker and the platform, as well as between the platform and the external component is assumed to be conducted via secure connection such as HTTPS.
– The *TruFaaS* external component is assumed to have access to the TPM of it's hosting device.
– We assume that the deployer ensures the security of the external component.

3.3   TruFaaS Internal Component

TruFaaS internal component extracts the required function information from the FaaS platform and sends it to the external *TruFaaS* component for trust calculation and verification. *Function information* refers to the function source code and all other attributes required to run the function, such as scaling factors, timeouts, and resource allocations. The internal component is utilized in both the function deployment flow and invocation flow. In the deployment flow, it intercepts the deployment request, extracts the function information needed for trust calculation, and forwards it to the external *TruFaaS* component for trust calculation and storage. Similarly, during the invocation flow, it intercepts the invocation request, and sends the function information necessary to verify the trust of the function to the external *TruFaaS* component. When sending function information, the source code is included as a hash to avoid sending bulky files to the external component, minimizing latency.

3.4   TruFaaS External Component

TruFaaS external component is responsible for conducting trust-related calculations, storage, and verifications, ultimately being presented as an API. It operates independent of the FaaS platform and can be set up to connect to various

FaaS platforms. The external component is utilized during both function deployment and invocation flows. In function deployment, the internal component sends function information to this component, which will then calculate the trust value and store it. During the invocation flow, the internal component will again send the function information to this component, which recalculates the trust value and verifies the trust of the function by comparing it with the stored trust value. The *TruFaaS* external component must be hosted on a secure, dedicated server by the same deployer who deploys the modified FaaS platform containing the internal component.

3.5   Trust Calculation, Storage and Verification

In *TruFaaS*, trust is quantified by means of a hashing mechanism that employs the SHA-256 hashing algorithm. Upon function deployment, the relevant function information is received from the internal component and hashed. The resulting hash values are then stored in a Merkle tree data structure [1,20], which is built using the hash values of each function as the tree's leaves as shown in Fig. 3. The generated root hash is stored in a TPM register of the device hosting the external component. Storing the Merkle root in the TPM keeps it secure and prevents it from being accessed by unauthorized parties. To prevent the loss of the tree structure in case of application failure, the Merkle tree is stored as a binary file.

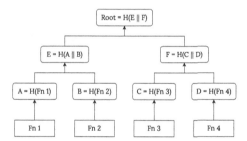

Fig. 3. Visualization of a Merkle tree generated using functions.

When a function is invoked, trust verification is initiated by comparing the Merkle root in the binary file to the Merkle root stored in the TPM. If they don't match, verification fails. If verification is successful, function information received from the internal component is hashed. The Merkle tree is searched for a leaf with the same hash value as the one calculated. If not found, trust verification fails. If a leaf with the same hash value is found, the verification process progresses up the tree. At each level of the tree, the node and its sibling is used to calculate the parent hash value, which is cross-checked with the parent hash initially saved. If the hash values match, the verification process moves on to the next level. If not, the verification fails. This process is repeated until the root hash is reached. Finally, the calculated root hash is cross-checked with the root value that was initially stored.

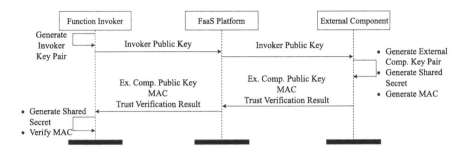

Fig. 4. Sequence of interactions involved in the trust protocol between the function invoker, FaaS platform and the *TruFaaS* external component.

3.6 Trust Protocol

The primary objective of the trust protocol to give an additional layer of confidence at the application level to the invoker, ensuring that the trust verification result has not been altered since it was sent from the external component.

The protocol is built on top of HTTPS and uses Hash based Message Authentication Code (HMAC) [18] to ensure that the trust verification result from the *TruFaaS* external component is unchanged until it is received by the function invoker. Elliptic Curve Diffie-Hellman (ECDH) Key Exchange [15] is used to generate the private and public keys between the function invoker and the *TruFaaS* external component. These keys are used to generate a shared secret and generate the aforementioned MAC.

The following are the steps involved in the trust protocol.

1. The function invoker generates their private key and public key. The public key is sent to the FaaS platform as a header in the function invocation request.
2. The *TruFaaS* internal component extracts the function invoker's public key from the request header and adds it as a header to the trust verification request sent to the *TruFaaS* external component.
3. The external component generates its private key and public key, and extracts the function invoker's public key from the received trust verification request.
4. The external component generates the shared secret key using its private key and the function invoker's public key.
5. After the external component verifies trust of the function, it generates the MAC using the shared secret key and the resulting success or failure of trust.
6. The trust verification result, the MAC and the external component's public key are added as headers in the response sent back to the platform from the external component.
7. Based on the trust verification results, the function will either be invoked or a relevant error will be generated. The headers received from the external component (the trust verification result, the MAC and the external component's public key) will be added unchanged to the response to be sent to the function invoker.

Fig. 5. Overview of the function deployment flow in Fission.

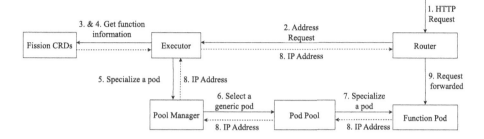

Fig. 6. Overview of the function invocation flow in Fission.

8. The function invoker receives the response sent by the *TruFaaS* internal component. The shared key is generated using the function invoker's private key and the external component's public key received in the response. The MAC is generated using the trust verification result received in the header and the shared key. This generated MAC is compared to the MAC received in the response header. If the values match, the trust value included in the header is the value originally sent by the external *TruFaaS* component.

3.7 Summary

In summary, upon a function deployment request, the function provider provides the source code and the necessary attributes required to run a function. When this information is sent to the FaaS platform, the internal component intercepts the flow and forwards the information to the external component, where the trust value is calculated and stored.

Upon a function invocation request, the platform retrieves the function information from storage to run the function in a container. The internal component intercepts the flow and sends the function information to the external component for trust verification. The external component verifies the trust and sends the result back to the platform. Based on the trust verification result, the internal component decides whether or not to allow the platform to proceed with the function invocation. If the trust verification is successful, the platform is allowed to continue with the function invocation flow. Otherwise, a verification failure error is generated and function invocation is stopped. The final response is sent to the function invoker, with the response body being either the function invocation results or the trust verification failure error, along with the trust protocol headers.

4 TruFaaS Implementation

TruFaaS is implemented on Fission. For the PoC implementation, we used Fission version 1.17. Go 1.19 was used to develop both the *TruFaaS* internal and external components.

4.1 Fission Background

Fission is a lightweight framework for serverless functions on Kubernetes and is typically deployed on a dedicated Kubernetes cluster by an individual/organization. This same entity provides the functions deployed on the platform, which can then be accessed through the function service addresses. It consists of multiple components and several workflows, of which only the function deployment and invocation flows are relevant to this implementation.

The fission-cli (as shown in the Fig. 5) can be used to connect to Fission to deploy the source code as a function. The relevant function information will be stored in a Fission Custom Resource Definition (CRD). The source code will be stored in the storage service if it is larger than 256 kB, and in the Fission CRD otherwise.

As shown in Fig. 6, invocation starts when an HTTP request is sent to the router, and ends when the request is serviced by the function pod. This process involves pod specialization, where a container is picked from a pool of language specific containers and the function is injected. Once specialized, the pod's IP address is returned to the router, which then forwards the HTTP request to that IP address.

4.2 TruFaaS Internal Component

The internal component was implemented as a Go package called *trufaas* within the vanilla Fission codebase. The process of function deployment and invocation was modified to extract the necessary information. This involved defining a new Go struct, *FunctionMetaData*, which is populated with the required values and then sent to the external component during both workflows. The workflow for function deployment was modified at the *Controller* of Fission to accommodate *TruFaaS*, while the workflow for function invocation was intercepted at the *Fetcher* to verify the trust of the function being invoked.

4.3 TruFaaS External Component

The external component of *TruFaaS* was developed as a Go REST API, which can be configured based on the FaaS platform it will connect with via a configuration file. This is decided at API deployment using the configuration file.

Only routes that belong to the specified FaaS platform will be initialized. It is important to note that you need to have an instance of the API per FaaS platform instance. For this PoC, two API endpoints were implemented - one for the FaaS platform to send functions to create trust values, and another for the FaaS platform to verify the trust of a function.

Merkle Tree Implementation. The Merkle tree data structure was implemented as a separate Go package named *merkle_ tree*. The implementation process referred to [9]. The Merkle root is saved in a secure register in the TPM and the Merkle tree structure is saved in a Go binary file upon creation and after any subsequent updates to the Merkle tree.

TPM Access. The implementation utilized the *go-tpm* and *go-tpm-tools* libraries, which are Google Open Source libraries that provide Go interfaces to connect with the TPM. The Merkle root is stored in the TPM by extending it into a Platform Configuration Register(PCR) [4]. In the PCR extension process, the new value is the hash of its old value, concatenated with the value that was extended. In this implementation, the value that is extended into the PCR is the Merkle root, as shown by the following operation

$$pcrNew = H(pcrOld \mathbin{\|} merkleRoot)$$

This operation is used to cross check whether the root hash stored in the binary file is the same as the value stored in the TPM to complete trust verification.

4.4   Trust Protocol Implementation

For the trust protocol, a Go package named *trust-protocol* was implemented in the external component codebase. This package is responsible for key generation and setting necessary headers. *ecdsa* and *hmac* Go pacakages were used for Diffie-Hellman key generation and MAC related operations, respectively.

5   Evaluation

5.1   Attack Scenario

Since serverless infrastructures rely heavily on shared resources, they become vulnerable to vertical attacks from malicious tenants like Function Injection Attacks and Container Escape Attacks as described below.

– *Function Injection Attack*: This attack involves the injection of malicious code into a function by an attacker. The function then executes this modified code within the FaaS platform and therefore potentially accesses and modifies function source code and attributes that belong to other tenants.

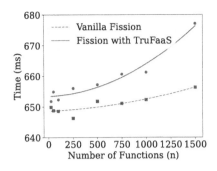
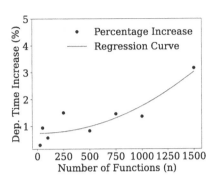

Fig. 7. Average function deployment time against number of deployed functions.

Fig. 8. Percentage increase of function deployment time against number of deployed functions.

- *Container Escape Attack*: This attack involves a malicious tenant exploiting a vulnerability in the container runtime to gain unauthorized access to the host machine, and accesses or modifies function source code and attributes that belong to other tenants.

In the context of Fission, during function deployment, the function information that is provided to the platform is stored in Fission CRDs and/or the storage service [13]. An attacker executing a vertical attack could gain access to these locations and change the stored function information. In vanilla Fission, there is no way for the function invoker to detect that such a modification has occurred. As a result, function invokers may unknowingly invoke a function that deviates from the original function deployed by the function provider.

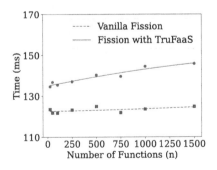
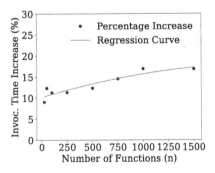

Fig. 9. Average function invocation time against number of deployed functions.

Fig. 10. Percentage increase of function invocation time against number of deployed functions.

With *TruFaaS*, such attacks can be detected. Prior to container specialization, the function information retrieved from the storage service and/or the

Fission CRDs is sent to the *TruFaaS* external component for trust verification. At the external component, if the function information is found to be altered, the trust verification fails and the result is conveyed to the internal component to stop the function invocation from proceeding. The trust verification failure will then be returned to the function invoker. If no alteration of the function information is found, the function invocation will proceed as normal and the function invocation results and trust verification value will be returned to the invoker. Moreover, by utilizing the trust protocol, function invokers can increase their confidence in the trust verification outcome as the protocol lets them confirm that the trust value hasn't been altered during the interaction between the external platform and the function invoker as any alterations to the trust verification values would cause a mismatch of the MAC tags at the function invoker's end.

5.2   Performance Evaluation

Experimental Setup. To quantify the performance overhead due to changes to vanilla fission and due to the use of Merkel tree for trust calculation, a set of *n-1* functions was initially deployed on the FaaS platform for predetermined values of n. Subsequently, the deployment and invocation times for the nth function were separately recorded multiple times and then averaged. This was done for both the vanilla and modified versions of Fission using a JavaScript function that generates the first hundred prime numbers.

The experiments were conducted on a machine with 6-core Intel(R) Core(TM) i7-8750H CPU @ 2.20 GHz and 8 GB of memory, running 64-bit Ubuntu 22.04 LTS. A KinD v0.18.0 [17] cluster was created using the Docker runtime v20.10.16. Both vanilla Fission and the modified Fission were deployed onto the KinD cluster. When testing the modified version, the external component was hosted on the same machine to eliminate the effects of the network latency on the experimental results.

5.3   Experimental Results

In this section, we describe the results of the above experiments.

- *Function Deployment Overhead* - Fig. 7 shows the average time (in milliseconds) taken for function deployment for both the vanilla and modified versions of Fission as the number of functions deployed to the FaaS platform was increased. The regression curve fitted for the percentage function deployment time increase is depicted in 8. It can be observed that the deployment time overhead increases as the number of functions deployed increases. This can be attributed to the use of the Merkle tree for trust storage. As the number of functions deployed increases, the time taken for trust value insertion increases. However, the increase in overhead observed in the graph is below 4% in the range tested, and the overheads are in the order of a few milliseconds.

– *Function Invocation Overhead* - Fig. 9 shows the average time (in milliseconds) taken for function invocation for both the vanilla and modified versions of Fission as the number of functions deployed to the FaaS platform was increased. The regression curve fitted for the percentage function invocation time increase is depicted in 10. It can be observed that the invocation time overhead initially increases, then will level off at a constant value. The performance overhead is in the range of 10% to 20%, and can be mainly attributed to the time taken for Merkle tree traversal during the trust verification process, and the trust protocol.

These overheads should be considered in the context of the benefits that *TruFaaS* can provide for certain types of applications. In these cases, the small performance loss associated with using the modified version of Fission can be a reasonable trade-off for achieving higher levels of trust.

6   Conclusion

In this paper, we introduce *TruFaaS*, a trust verification framework for FaaS which addresses the issue of trust that has not been comprehensively addressed. *TruFaaS* can be integrated with open source FaaS platforms and comprises two components: the internal component, which resides within the FaaS platform, and the external component, located outside of the FaaS platform. The internal component is responsible for function information extraction, while the external component is responsible for trust calculation, storage, and verification. Additionally, we designed a trust protocol to communicate the trust of functions to function invokers. In this paper, we present how *TruFaaS* can detect any unauthorized modifications made to the function source code and related attributes. We implemented the framework on Fission to demonstrate its effectiveness in practice. The version of Fission with *TruFaaS* incurred a performance overhead of less than 4% (in the range tested) during function deployment compared to vanilla Fission, and the function invocation overhead was below 20%.

7   Limitations and Future Work

A limitation of the current *TruFaaS* architecture is its focus on function information manipulation, which assumes that the most vulnerable point of attack lies in static storage. Future work could expand the architecture scope to include other potential vulnerabilities like function runtime manipulation.

Additionally, in this paper, based on the definition of trust, we specifically focus on determining whether the function supplied by the function provider has undergone any unauthorized modifications prior to its execution. We do not take into account whether the invoker can trust the function that is initially provided by the provider.

Although we consider function source code and attributes for trust calculation, we do not account for the data used by functions from external sources during execution. Manipulation of this data could also lead to the function being compromised without altering the function source code and attributes. This aspect's effect on trust could be addressed in future research.

References

1. Mykletun et al., E.: Providing authentication and integrity in outsourced databases using merkle hash trees. UCI-SCONCE Technical report (2003)
2. Alder, F., et al.: S-FAAS: trustworthy and accountable function-as-a-service using intel SGX. In: 2019 ACM SIGSAC Conference, pp. 185–199. ACM (2019)
3. Apache: Apache openwhisk is a serverless, open source cloud platform
4. Arthur, W., Challener, D., Goldman, K.: Platform Configuration Registers, pp. 151–161 (2015)
5. AWS: Serverless optical character recognition in support of nasa astronaut safety, February 2018. https://aws.amazon.com/blogs/publicsector/serverless-optical-character-recognition-in-support-of-nasa-astronaut-safety/
6. AWS: Configuring code signing for AWS lambda (2022)
7. Baldini, I.E.A.: serverless computing: current trends and open problems, pp. 1–20 (2017). https://doi.org/10.1007/978-981-10-5026-8_1
8. Brenner, S., Kapitza, R.: Trust more, serverless. In: Proceedings of the 12th SYSTOR, pp. 33–43. ACM (2019). https://doi.org/10.1145/3319647.3325825
9. CBERGOON: a merkle tree implementation written in go (2023). https://github.com/cbergoon/merkletree
10. Datta, P.E.A.: Valve: securing function workflows on serverless computing platforms (2020). https://doi.org/10.1145/3366423.3380173
11. Datta, P.E.A.: Alastor: reconstructing the provenance of serverless intrusions. In: USENIX Security Symposium (2022). https://api.semanticscholar.org/CorpusID:247314788
12. Docker: Content trust in docker (2022). https://docs.docker.com/engine/security/trust/
13. Fission: Fission (2023). https://fission.io/
14. Guo, Y.E.A.: Building trust in container environment. In: 2019 18th IEEE TrustCom/BigDataSE, pp. 1–9. IEEE (2019). https://doi.org/10.1109/TrustCom/BigDataSE.2019.00011
15. Haakegaard, R., Lang, J.: The elliptic curve diffie-hellman (ecdh) (2015). http://koclab.cs.ucsb.edu/teaching/ecc/project/2015Projects/Haakegaard+Lang.pdf
16. Hu, J., et al.: Hivemind: a scalable and serverless coordination control platform for UAV swarms. arXiv preprint arXiv:2002.01419 (2020)
17. KinD: Kind (2022). https://kind.sigs.k8s.io/
18. Krawczyk, H., Bellare, M., Canetti, R.: RFC2104: HMAC: keyed-hashing for message authentication (1997)
19. Li, X., Leng, X., Chen, Y.: Securing serverless computing: challenges, solutions, and opportunities. IEEE Netw. (2022). https://doi.org/10.1109/MNET.005.2100335
20. Merkle, R.C.: A digital signature based on a conventional encryption function. In: Pomerance, C. (eds.) Advances in Cryptology – CRYPTO '87. CRYPTO 1987. LNCS, vol. 293, pp. 369–378. Springer, Berlin, Heidelberg (1988). https://doi.org/10.1007/3-540-48184-2_32
21. Mitchell, C.: Trusted Computing. IET (2005)

22. Mohamed, F., Hemayed, E.: Trusted cloud computing architectures for IAAS. Comput. Secur. **82** (2019). https://doi.org/10.1016/j.cose.2018.12.014
23. OpenFaaS: Openfaas - serverless functions made simple (2023)
24. Polinsky, I., Datta, P., Bates, A., Enck, W.: Sciffs: enabling secure third-party security analytics using serverless computing, pp. 175–186. Association for Computing Machinery (2021). https://doi.org/10.1145/3450569.3463567
25. Ren, J.E.A.: Tenants attested trusted cloud service. In: 2016 IEEE 9th CLOUD (2016). https://doi.org/10.1109/CLOUD.2016.0085
26. Szefer, J.: Principles of Secure Processor Architecture Design, vol. 13 (2018)
27. Wan, X.E.A.: Building trust into cloud computing using virtualization of TPM. In: 2012 MINES, pp. 59–63 (2012). https://doi.org/10.1109/MINES.2012.82

Detection of Cyberbullying in Social Media Texts Using Explainable Artificial Intelligence

Mohammad Rafsun Islam, Ahmed Saleh Bataineh$^{(\boxtimes)}$,
and Mohammad Zulkernine

School of Computing, Queen's University, Kingston K7L 2N8, Canada
{20mri,ahmed.bataineh,mz}@queensu.ca

Abstract. The widespread use of social media has opened the door to new forms of harassment and abuse, such as cyberbullying, that have a serious impact on individuals' psychological health. Therefore, research communities have recently developed detection approaches using Natural Language Processing (NLP) combined with machine learning algorithms to identify instances of cyberbullying in social media texts. However, they are unable to determine the type of cyberbullying and the reasons why victims may be targeted. This paper develops a novel detection approach that can identify the type of cyberbullying based on characteristics such as gender, religion, age, and ethnicity, even if the original records in the training dataset do not include such information or features. This paper has accomplished this objective by utilizing Explainable Artificial Intelligence (XAI) technology alongside machine learning models to justify and explain the classification of text as cyberbullying. Technically speaking, XAI technology enables machine learning models to capture and highlight the most influential words that affect the decision to classify a text as cyberbullying. Those influential words are utilized to re-label and update the training data. The machine learning models are then re-trained using the updated data. To evaluate the performance of the proposed approach, a simulation experiment has been conducted on a large dataset containing texts from Twitter. Simulation results show that XAI technology provides convincing explanations for classifying a text as cyberbullying. It also enables machine learning models to identify various types of cyberbullying and enhances their performance in terms of classification accuracy.

Keywords: Cyberbullying · Explainable Artificial Intelligence (XAI) · Local Interpretable Model-Agnostic Explanations (LIME) · Natural Language Processing (NLP)

1 Introduction

Social media has become an integral part of modern life, transforming the way we consume news, express ourselves, do business, and entertain ourselves. However, this widespread use of social media has also given rise to new forms of

© The Author(s), under exclusive license to Springer Nature Singapore Pte Ltd. 2024
G. Wang et al. (Eds.): UbiSec 2023, CCIS 2034, pp. 319–334, 2024.
https://doi.org/10.1007/978-981-97-1274-8_21

harassment and abuse that significantly affect mental health, such as cyberbullying. Cyberbullying is a form of online harassment that happens through various offensive acts, including sending vulgar messages, posting inappropriate and hurtful comments, propagating online rumors, posting inappropriate images and videos, and cyberstalking [2, 27]. With the increasing use of social media and other online platforms, cyberbullying has become a pervasive issue that affects people of all ages, especially children and teenagers. The effects of cyberbullying can be devastating, leading to psychological distress, social isolation, and even suicide. Studies [4, 14] indicate that cyberbullying affects over 60% of US and 35% of Canadian teenagers. The Pew Research Center found that 59% of US adolescents who are victims of cyberbullying show at least one symptom of stress, embarrassment, isolation, and aggression [4]. According to a study published by US News [21], 7.6% of US children who experience cyberbullying consider suicide. As a result, cyberbullying has become a serious problem that requires urgent attention.

The computer science research community is paying attention to developing detection approaches that can identify instances of cyberbullying in text posted on social media platforms such as comments and posts. Mainly, Natural Language Processing (NLP), along with other machine learning algorithms, is utilized to learn, analyze, understand, and identify patterns of harassing or abusive behavior in social media texts. However, the current capabilities of these approaches are limited to classifying social media texts into two categories: cyberbullying and non-cyberbullying, which we refer to in this paper as "binary classification". Specifically, binary classification is unable to determine the type of cyberbullying and the reasons why victims of cyberbullying may be targeted based on certain characteristics, such as gender, religion, age, and ethnicity. Such information are needed by both psychologists and social media platforms to appropriately assist the victims and build proactive strategies that may help prevent cyberbullying attacks from occurring in advance. For instance, social media platforms can leverage such information to prevent bullies who engage in abusive behavior against a certain race from seeing posts made by individuals belonging to that race. Furthermore, these approaches are unable to provide justifications and explanations for their decisions to classify a text as cyberbullying or not. Such information can assist programmers in diagnosing their learning models and identifying underlying technical errors to improve model performance. In addition, the performance of these approaches in terms of classification accuracy is sometimes unsatisfactory, with relatively low accuracy.

The paper focuses on developing a novel approach for cyberbullying detection that has three main contributions. Firstly, the proposed approach identifies the type of cyberbullying by utilizing characteristics such as gender, religion, age, and ethnicity. This approach is referred to as "Multiclass classification" in the paper, which is a substantial advancement compared to existing methods that only classify cyberbullying into binary categories. This approach provides a more comprehensive understanding of cyberbullying and can lead to better prevention and intervention strategies. Secondly, the proposed approach not only classifies a text as a particular type of cyberbullying but also provides justification for the classification decision. Specifically, the approach highlights the most influential factors contributing to the classification decision. This feature is essential because it allows for a better understanding and interpretation of the results, which can help improve the model's performance. The justification can also assist in explaining the classification outcome to stakeholders such as educators, parents, and law enforcement officials, enabling them to take appropriate action. Lastly, the approach improves the overall classification accuracy.

Those contributions are accomplished through the application of Explainable Artificial Intelligence (XAI) technology, which assists in identifying the most relevant features for the classification process. Specifically, we have gone beyond the traditional use of XAI by solely obtaining explanations. Instead, we have utilized these explanations to provide feedback into the training dataset, following which the machine learning models are retrained on the updated dataset. This idea allows us to automatically detect and identify the type of cyberbullying based on characteristics such as religion, gender, ethnicity, and age, even if the original records in the training dataset do not include such information or features. In our approach, the original records are limited to two classes: cyberbullying and non-cyberbullying. This idea also significantly improves the performance of the machine learning models in terms of classification accuracy.

The paper is structured and organized as follows. Section 2 provides a literature review of ongoing research on detecting cyberbullying in social media texts. In Sect. 3, we present our proposed approach to identifying the type of cyberbullying. In Sect. 4, we discuss the simulation results of the proposed approach. Finally, Sect. 5 concludes the paper and suggests future directions.

2   Related Work

The current state of cyberbullying detection solutions predominantly relies on NLP and machine learning technologies, owing to their high efficiency in identifying instances of cyberbullying in social media texts. For instance, the research proposals [12,22,32] employed sentiment analysis from NLP technology to distinguish the emotions expressed in the posts of victims and bullies. They found that cyberbullying posts have significantly higher negative sentiment scores than other posts. Additionally, research studies, such as [15,24,30], use the Term Frequency-Inverse Document Frequency (TF-IDF) techniques from NLP technology to identify and rank key offensive words by importance. They found that most offensive words are ethnic slurs for different races of people, and offensive words usually appear at the beginning or end of texts.

Multiple proposals, such as [10,16,20], utilized the Gradient Boosting model to identify cyberbullying instances. Their experiments found that the Gradient Boosting model achieves high accuracy while minimizing false positives and negatives. Random Forest Classifier (RFC) has also been widely used to develop predictive models for identifying instances of cyberbullying in text. For instance, the research proposals [2,6,23] utilized the RFC model to develop automated cyberbullying detection models. Their experiments show that the RFC consistently demonstrates promising results in detecting instances of cyberbullying on social media. This can be attributed to its effective handling of both numerical and categorical features. Several proposals have used Support Vector Machine (SVM) models to detect and identify cyberbullying in social media texts. For example, the research proposals [7,24,26] used SVM to distinguish between cyberbullying and non-cyberbullying instances in social media texts. Typically, offensive words were labeled with negative values, while non-offensive words were labeled with positive values. The labeled data was then used to train the SVM model to distinguish between both classes. Their simulation results show that SVM can effectively distinguish between cyberbullying and noncyberbullying texts, even in the presence of noisy or overlapping data. Multiple research proposals, such as [1,3,5,13], have employed Long Short-Term Memory (LSTM) for detecting cyberbullying in texts. Their experiments demonstrate that LSTM achieves the highest accuracy in predicting instances of cyberbullying. This can be attributed to its ability to effectively track and retain important information in long sequences of text. Specifically, LSTM successfully models the relationships between words and phrases, enabling it to detect patterns that indicate cyberbullying.

The literature review reveals three limitations of current proposals for identifying cyberbullying. Firstly, these approaches are primarily limited to a binary classification of text as cyberbullying or non-cyberbullying. They are unable to determine specific types of cyberbullying or the underlying reasons why certain individuals may be targeted. This is due to the use of supervised learning algorithms that require labeled data for training. Mainly, if the labeled data only contains information about whether a text is cyberbullying or not, then the model will only be able to make binary classifications. Secondly, these approaches rely on black-box machine learning models that do not provide explanations for their predictions. This lack of transparency makes it difficult for end-users to understand and interpret the reports generated by these models. Finally, the classification accuracy of these approaches is sometimes unsatisfactory.

To address these limitations, this paper proposes the use of XAI technology in conjunction with machine learning models. XAI provides justifications and explanations that facilitate understanding of the decision-making process. In terms of technical contributions, the machine learning models are fed by the explanations generated by XAI to detect and identify different types of cyberbullying. To the best of our knowledge, this is the first work that leverages XAI capabilities to detect and identify various types of cyberbullying in a social media text.

3   Cyberbullying Text Detection Methodology

This section describes the proposed approach to detecting instances of cyberbullying in texts. This approach, as shown in Fig. 1, is built into three layers: Text Pre-processing, Text Training, and Decision Explanation. In the layer of Texts Pre-processing, Natural Language Processing (NLP) technology is utilized

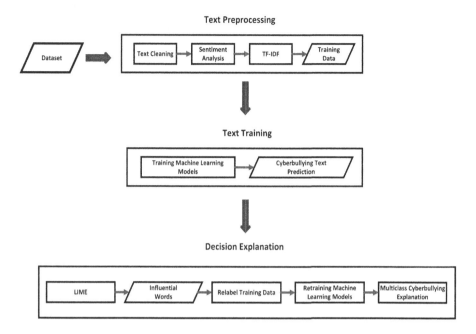

Fig. 1. Overview of Cyberbullying Detection Model

to prepare the data (social media texts) for the training process. In the second layer, Text Training, four different machine learning models are trained on the data generated by the first layer (Text Pre-Processing). Those models work in parallel and independently in the sense that they are not sharing inputs and outputs with each other. In the third layer, Decision Explanation, LIME (Local Interpretable Model-agnostic Explanations) from XAI technology is utilized to justify the decisions taken by the four machine learning models in the second layer. The training dataset generated by the first layer is then re-labeled by the explanations generated by the third layer. Specifically, if it contains cyberbullying, each text (a record) in the updated training dataset is re-labeled by one of the following classes: gender, religion, age, and ethnicity. We then retrain the machine learning models for multiclass cyberbullying predictions. Finally, we utilize LIME to generate explanations for the multiclass cyberbullying predictions.

3.1   Dataset

The study relies on a publicly accessible dataset published on Kaggle [17]. The dataset comprises a total of 47,000 plain-text tweets and is structured into two columns: the first column, labeled "tweet text" contains plain-text tweets from diverse Twitter accounts, while the second column, labeled "cyberbullying type" distinguishes between cyberbullying and noncyberbullying tweets.

3.2   Text Pre-processing Layer

The text pre-processing layer uses three Natural Language Processing (NLP) techniques: text cleaning, sentiment analysis, and Term Frequency-Inverse Document Frequency (TF-IDF). Text cleaning is used to remove noise, such as special characters, punctuation, and stopwords, from all the texts in the dataset. Those text noises hinder machine learning models from analyzing the data smoothly and recognizing human writing patterns, thereby impacting the accuracy of the machine learning process [15].

Sentiment analysis is used to evaluate the emotional tone of a text. This tool assigns a sentiment score to each word in a text by consulting a lexicon-based dictionary and its corresponding score for the given word [19]. For example, the word 'stupid' has a sentiment score of -1 in the lexicon-based dictionary. The tool calculates the overall sentiment score for each text in the dataset by aggregating the sentiment scores of all the words present in the text. The sentiment score for a text takes a value in the range of $[-1, 1]$, where a value of -1 indicates an extreme case of negative sentiment and a value of 1 indicates an extreme case of positive sentiment.

Term Frequency-Inverse Document Frequency (TF-IDF), one of NLP's tools, is utilized to evaluate the weights of texts' words in the dataset [31]. Specifically, Term Frequency (TF) score indicates the number of times a word appears in a text, while the IDF score of a word measure how common or rare a word is across all the texts in the dataset [31]. These NLP techniques are implemented in our research to produce training data, which the machine learning models use to predict cyberbullying texts.

3.3   Text Training Layer

Four machine learning models, Random Forest, Gradient Boosting, SVM, and LSTM, are used to predict cyberbullying texts based on the TF-IDF and sentiment scores of each text in the dataset. We selected the above models because of their ability to handle noisy and large amounts of data and the complex relationships among input features, such as the relationship between sentiment and TF-IDF scores [20]. As a result, they are more reliable and accurate for detecting cyberbullying text. The key idea is to represent the text in a numerical form that captures each text's sentiment and TF-IDF scores. Then machine learning models use this information to predict whether a text is cyberbullying or noncyberbullying [9,11,20,23,28].

3.4   Decision Explanation Layer

In this layer, the LIME algorithm from XAI technology is utilized to explain and justify the decisions taken by the four machine learning models in the second layer. First, LIME generates explanations of cyberbullying predictions, including the weights for influential words in a cyberbullying text. Next, these influential words are utilized to re-label the cyberbullying texts in the dataset based on

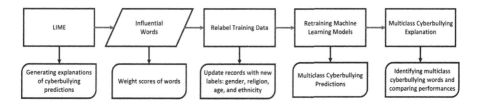

Fig. 2. Decision Explanation Layer

the following classifications: gender, religion, age, and ethnicity. The machine learning models are then re-trained to predict multiclass cyberbullying texts. Finally, LIME is employed to generate explanations of multiclass cyberbullying texts to show the important words. Figure 2 graphically illustrates the Decision Explanation Layer.

LIME. A common algorithm in (XAI) is LIME (Local Interpretable Model-agnostic Explanations), which aims to provide explanations that humans understand for the predictions made by a machine learning model [18,25]. The LIME works as follows.

1. **Producing perturbed texts:** When given a text containing cyberbullying content as input, LIME produces perturbed texts by randomly removing some words from the input text [25]. Taking the cyberbullying text "You loser clearly I hate you" as an example, LIME generates perturbed texts like "You loser I hate you" and "You clearly I hate you". In the first perturbed version, 'clearly' is randomly removed, while in the second, 'loser' is randomly removed. This step is repeated multiple times to create all possible perturbed texts.
2. **Calculating words' weight:** LIME calculates the weight of words by measuring the difference between their TF-IDF scores in perturbed texts and their TF-IDF scores in the original text.
3. **Generating explanations:** LIME selects the most influential words with the highest weights. For example, in the text "You loser clearly I hate you", the words 'loser' and 'hate' have the highest weights. These words significantly contribute to the decision of the machine learning model to classify the text as cyberbullying. The words, along with their weights, are then included in a report as explanations for the decision made by the machine learning model.
4. **Training perturbed texts:** The perturbed texts serve as inputs for the four machine learning models in the second layer, which determine whether the perturbed texts constitute cyberbullying [25]. For instance, the perturbed text "You loser I hate you" is fed into the RFC model in the second layer and subsequently classified as cyberbullying. LIME creates new interpretable linear models and trains them on the perturbed texts. Afterward, LIME compares the accuracy score of the interpretable linear models with the accuracy score of the machine learning models in the second layer.

5. **Generating report:** LIME generates a report that includes the reliability score, the prediction probability of a text being cyberbullying or noncyberbullying, and the most influential words with their weight scores.

Multiclass Cyberbullying Detection: In this stage, the explanations for binary classification are fed back into the training dataset to re-label the texts (records) based on one of the following categories: gender, religion, age, or ethnicity. The machine learning models are then re-trained on the updated dataset to perform multiclass classification. This step enables the machine learning models to identify the type of cyberbullying, such as gender-based, religion-based, age-based, or ethnicity-based. The following steps are used in this research to detect multiclass cyberbullying texts:

1. **Multiclass cyberbullying word list:** We compile and utilize standard libraries, including Urban Dictionary, Wiktionary, Wikipedia, and GitHub [8, 29], to retrieve and match the most common words associated with different types of cyberbullying.
2. **Generating influential cyberbullying words:** LIME technology is utilized to generate the most influential words, along with their weights, that affect the classification of a text as cyberbullying.
3. **Matching words and classifying cyberbullying texts:** The first three most influential words with the highest weight scores are selected and matched with the word list generated in step 1. As an example, let us consider the text "I am not sexist, I hate those women who accuse me of sexism" as an instance of cyberbullying. LIME identifies the words 'sexist', 'sexism', and 'women' as the most influential, with weight scores of 0.26, 0.23, and 0.29, respectively. By exploring the word lists generated in Step 1, these words are matched to the category of gender-based cyberbullying. Therefore, the text is re-labeled as a gender-based cyberbullying in the training dataset.
4. **Re-training machine learning models:** The updated data is used to re-train the machine learning models for performing multiclass classification.
5. **Evaluating performance:** LIME is used to explain and justify the multiclass classifications, which helps to evaluate the accuracy and reliability of the machine learning models.

4   Evaluation Results

This section discusses the comparative evaluation results of binary and multiclass cyberbullying texts to evaluate the performance of the proposed approach. Mainly, we evaluate the performance of the proposed approach according to the following four metrics: accuracy, recall, precision, and F- score [15,20].

4.1   Binary vs Multiclass Performance

Table 1 presents the performance of the machine learning models used in the binary classification task. As shown in the table, the LSTM model achieves the

Table 1. Binary Cyberbullying Prediction Results

Model	Accuracy	Precision	Recall	F-Score
LSTM	92%	93%	92%	92%
SVM	90.67%	91%	91%	91%
Random Forest	86.84%	87%	85%	86%
Gradient Boosting	85.71%	86%	86%	86%

Table 2. Multiclass Cyberbullying Prediction Results

Model	Avg Accuracy	Avg Precision	Avg Recall	Avg F-Score
LSTM	97.5%	98%	99%	97%
SVM	95.25%	96%	96%	96%
Random Forest	95%	94%	96%	96%
Gradient Boosting	94.75%	95%	95%	95%

highest accuracy, precision, recall, and F-Scores. Specifically, the accuracy score is 92%, and the precision score is 93%, while the recall and F-score are both 92%. The SVM and RFC models achieve the second and third highest performance, respectively. On the other hand, the Gradient Boosting model achieves the lowest performance, with an accuracy of 85.71%, and precision, recall, and F-Score results of 86%.

The results of the multiclass classification for cyberbullying texts are shown in Table 2. As can be seen from the table, all models exhibit better performance in terms of accuracy, precision, recall, and F-score compared to the binary classification case (see Table 1). For example, the Random Forest model shows a significant improvement in accuracy from 86.85% to 95%, precision from 87% to 94%, recall from 85% to 96%, and F-score from 86% to 96%.

4.2 Explanation of Multiclass Classification

In this section, we demonstrate the explanations generated by LIME when the machine learning models perform multiclass classification on text data that includes instances of cyberbullying.

Gender-Based Cyberbullying. In this section, we aim to compare the explanations behind the decisions taken by the machine learning models when they are used to detect gender-based cyberbullying. To accomplish this, we generate the explanations for the following tweet: "Females and guys. @AwkwardEP I'm not sexist but a lot of females lack true logic sometimes. A lot of guys are just dumb though". Once this text is processed, it is transformed into "females guy sexist lot females lack true logic sometimes lot guy dumb though".

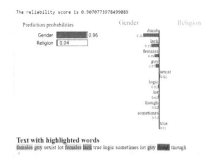

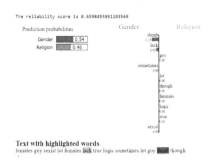

Fig. 3. Gender-Based Cyberbullying Explanation with Random Forest

Fig. 4. Gender-Based Cyberbullying Explanation with Gradient Boosting

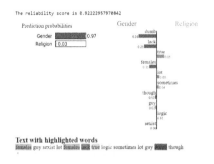

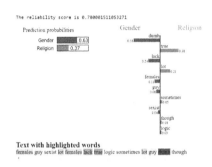

Fig. 5. Gender-Based Cyberbullying Explanation with SVM

Fig. 6. Gender-Based Cyberbullying Explanation with LSTM

The explanations for RFC, Gradient Boosting, SVM, and LSTM are graphically presented in Figs. 3, 4, 5, and 6 respectively. As illustrated in these figures, the machine learning models have arrived at a consensus that the input text is indicative of gender-based cyberbullying with different levels of confidence, as indicated by their respective prediction probabilities. For instance, as shown in Fig. 5, the SVM model shows the highest level of confidence with a prediction probability of 97% that the input text is gender-based cyberbullying. In contrast, as shown in Fig. 4, the Gradient Boosting model achieves the lowest confidence level among the models, predicting with a probability of only 54% that the input text is gender-based cyberbullying.

Using XAI, these machine learning models exhibit similar justifications for their decision-making. For example, the words 'females' and 'guy' are highlighted by RFC, SVM, and LSTM models as influential words affecting the classification of input text as gender-based cyberbullying. In Fig. 6, for instance, the word 'females' has a weight of 0.11, followed by 'guy' at 0.08. These words have similar weights across those machine learning models (RFC, SVM, LSTM), as illustrated in Figs. 3, 5, and 6.

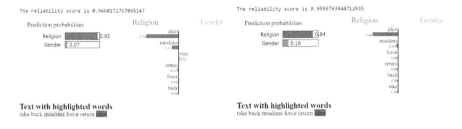

Fig. 7. Religion-Based Cyberbullying Explanation with Random Forest

Fig. 8. Religion-Based Cyberbullying Explanation with Gradient Boosting

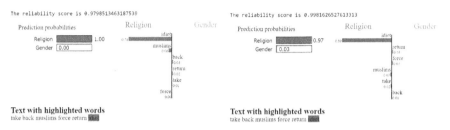

Fig. 9. Religion-Based Cyberbullying Explanation with SVM

Fig. 10. Religion-Based Cyberbullying Explanation with LSTM

On the other hand, the words 'females' and 'guy' cause the Gradient Boosting model to misclassify the input text as religion-based cyberbullying with a relatively high prediction probability of 0.46. This explains why, as shown in Fig. 4, the Gradient Boosting model has the lowest reliability score (0.65) among the models. It is noted that the input text is misclassified as religion-based cyberbullying by machine learning models at varying levels of confidence. This can be attributed to the large number of records in the training dataset that include certain words ("females". "guy", "sexist") and are labeled as religion-based cyberbullying. In fact, religions often discuss sexual relationships and women's rights, and individuals may use these issues to attack religions on social media platforms, resulting in religion-based cyberbullying.

Religion-Based Cyberbullying. In this section, our goal is to compare the explanations for the decisions made by machine learning models when detecting religion-based cyberbullying. To achieve this, we generate an explanation for the following Twitter text: "No, we took it back from Muslims by force. Then what returning you idiot?" After preprocessing, the text is transformed into "take back Muslims force return idiot".

The explanations for RFC, Gradient Boosting, SVM, and LSTM are presented graphically in Figs. 7, 8, 9, and 10, respectively. As shown in these figures, the machine learning models have arrived at a consensus that the input text indicates religion-based cyberbullying with a high level of confidence, as indicated by their respective prediction probabilities. For example, Fig. 9 shows that the SVM model exhibits the highest level of confidence, with a prediction probability of 100% that the input text is religion-based cyberbullying. In contrast, Fig. 8 shows that the Gradient Boosting model exhibits the lowest level of confidence among the models, predicting with a probability of only 84% that the input text is religion-based cyberbullying.

All models highlight the words 'idiot' and 'Muslims' as the most influential words affecting the classification of input text as religion-based cyberbullying. Moreover, all machine learning models achieve high-reliability scores, as their justifications are highly consistent with the decision that the input text is religion-based cyberbullying. It is worth noting that the input text may be misclassified as gender-based cyberbullying by machine learning models, albeit at very low levels of confidence. For instance, as shown in Fig. 8, the Gradient Boosting model suggests that the input text may be gender-based cyberbullying with a probability of 0.16. This can be attributed to the high number of shared words between religion-based and gender-based cyberbullying in the training dataset, as discussed previously.

Age-Based Cyberbullying. In this section, our goal is to compare the explanations for the decisions made by machine learning models when detecting age-based cyberbullying. To achieve this, we generate an explanation for the following Twitter text: "Lhdab @ this child here...do ya homework jerk, u new 2d play ground, I'm a school yard bully u new kid". After preprocessing, the text is transformed into "lhdab child ya homework jerk u new play grind school yard bully u new kid".

The graphical explanations for the RFC, Gradient Boosting, SVM, and LSTM models are presented in Figs. 11, 12, 13, and 14, respectively. These figures demonstrate that the machine learning models have arrived at a consensus that the input text indicates age-based cyberbullying with a high level of confidence, as indicated by their respective prediction probabilities. For example, Figs. 13 and 14 show that the SVM and LSTM models exhibit the highest level of confidence, predicting with a probability of 100% that the input text is age-based cyberbullying. In contrast, Fig. 12 shows that the Gradient Boosting model exhibits the lowest level of confidence among the models, predicting with a probability of only 73% that the input text is age-based cyberbullying.

RFC, SVM, and LSTM models highlight the words 'child' and 'homework' as influential words that affect the classification of input text as age-based cyberbullying. On the other hand, the use of certain words like 'school', 'kid', and 'child' in the text causes the Gradient Boosting model to misclassify the input as ethnicity-based cyberbullying with a relatively high prediction probability of 0.27, as shown in Fig. 12. This may explain why the Gradient Boosting model has the lowest reliability score (0.75) compared to the other models.

It is important to note that machine learning models may misclassify input text as ethnicity-based cyberbullying with varying levels of confidence. This is likely due to the large number of records in the training dataset that contain these words and are labeled as ethnicity-based cyberbullying. It is worth noting

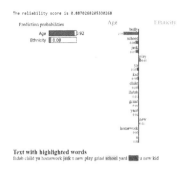

Fig. 11. Age-Based Cyberbullying Explanation with Random Forest

Fig. 12. Age-Based Cyberbullying Explanation with Gradient Boosting

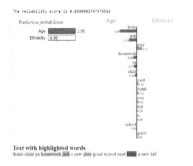

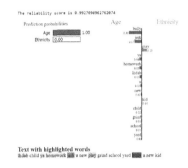

Fig. 13. Age-Based Cyberbullying Explanation with SVM

Fig. 14. Age-Based Cyberbullying Explanation with LSTM

that most cyberbullying among teenagers in schools is related to ethnicity, so words like 'school' and 'kid' frequently appear in ethnicity-based cyberbullying.

Ethnicity-Based Cyberbullying. The aim of this section is to compare the explanations provided by the machine learning models when detecting ethnicity-based cyberbullying. To achieve this, we analyze the decision-making process of each model using the following Twitter text: "For example: racism ain't the same as 'speciesism'. Why are you comparing colored people to cows, homie?". After preprocessing the text, we transform it into "example racism speciesism u compare color people cow homie".

The graphical explanations for the RFC, Gradient Boosting, SVM, and LSTM models are presented in Figs. 15, 16, 17, and 18, respectively. These figures demonstrate that the machine learning models have arrived at a consensus that the input text indicates ethnicity-based cyberbullying with a high level of confidence, as indicated by their respective prediction probabilities. For example, Fig. 18 shows that the LSTM model exhibits the highest level of confidence, predicting with a probability of 100% that the input text is ethnicity-based cyber-

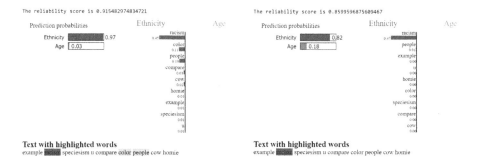

Fig. 15. Ethnicity-Based Cyberbullying Explanation with Random Forest

Fig. 16. Ethnicity-Based Cyberbullying Explanation with Gradient Boosting

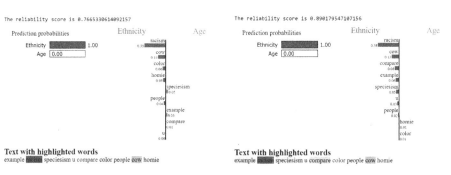

Fig. 17. Ethnicity-Based Cyberbullying Explanation with SVM

Fig. 18. Ethnicity-Based Cyberbullying Explanation with LSTM

bullying. In contrast, Fig. 16 shows that the Gradient Boosting model exhibits the lowest level of confidence among the models, predicting with a probability of only 82% that the input text is ethnicity-based cyberbullying. All the machine learning models identify the words 'racism', 'people', and 'color' as significant terms that affect the classification of input text as ethnicity-based cyberbullying.

5   Conclusion

This paper addresses the challenge of identifying instances of cyberbullying in social media texts. The problem is approached from three perspectives: 1) How can current research be improved to identify the type of cyberbullying based on characteristics such as religion, gender, age, and ethnicity, given a dataset that provides limited information for classifying texts as cyberbullying or non-cyberbullying? 2) How can current research be improved to enable end-users to easily understand the decisions made by machine learning models, including why victims are attacked by bullies? 3) How can current research be improved to increase the performance of machine learning models, specifically in terms of accuracy?

This paper demonstrates that the use of XAI technology in conjunction with machine learning models can address those raised issues. The simulation results demonstrate the efficiency of XAI technology in identifying different types of cyberbullying text. Additionally, the simulation results show that XAI technology also significantly enhances the performance of the machine learning models. In future work, we will investigate the capabilities of other XAI algorithms such as SHAP in detecting cyberbullying in texts. We are also interested in applying the proposed approach to detect and identify cyberbullying in images and videos.

References

1. Agrawal, S., Awekar, A.: Deep learning for detecting cyberbullying across multiple social media platforms. In: Advances in Information Retrieval, pp. 141–153 (2018)
2. Al-Garadi, M.A., Varathan, K.D., Ravana, S.D.: Cybercrime detection in online communications: the experimental case of cyberbullying detection in the Twitter network. Comput. Hum. Behav. **63**, 433–442 (2016)
3. Al-Hassan, A., Al-Dossari, H.: Detection of hate speech in Arabic tweets using deep learning. Multimed. Syst. **28**, 1963–1974 (2021)
4. Anderson, M.: A majority of teens have experienced some form of cyberbullying (2018). https://www.pewresearch.org/internet/2018/09/27/a-majority-of-teens-have-experienced-some-form-of-cyberbullying/
5. Balakrishna, S., Gopi, Y., Solanki, V.K.: Comparative analysis on deep neural network models for detection of cyberbullying on social media. Ingeniería Solidaria **18**(1), 1–33 (2022)
6. Balakrishnan, V., Khan, S., Arabnia, H.R.: Improving cyberbullying detection using Twitter users' psychological features and machine learning. Comput. Secur. **90**, 101710 (2020)
7. Bhagya, J., Deepthi, P.S.: Cyberbullying detection on social media using SVM. In: Inventive Systems and Control, pp. 17–27 (2021)
8. Bierner, M.: Urban-dictionary-word-list. https://github.com/mattbierner/urban-dictionary-word-list. Accessed 11 Mar 2023
9. Breiman, L.: Random forests. Mach. Learn. **45**(1), 5–32 (2001)
10. Chatzakou, D., Kourtellis, N., Blackburn, J., De Cristofaro, E., Stringhini, G., Vakali, A.: Mean birds: detecting aggression and bullying on Twitter. In: Proceedings of ACM on Web Science Conference, pp. 13–22 (2017)
11. Cristianini, N., Ricci, E.: Support Vector Machines. Springer, Heidelberg (2008)
12. Dani, H., Li, J., Liu, H.: Sentiment informed cyberbullying detection in social media. In: Ceci, M., Hollmén, J., Todorovski, L., Vens, C., Džeroski, S. (eds.) ECML PKDD 2017. LNCS (LNAI), vol. 10534, pp. 52–67. Springer, Cham (2017). https://doi.org/10.1007/978-3-319-71249-9_4
13. Dass, A., Daniel, D.K.: Cyberbullying detection on social networks using LSTM model. In: (ICISTSD), pp. 293–296 (2022)
14. Dojchinovska, A.: Cyberbullying statistics Canada infographics (2022). https://reviewlution.ca/resources/cyberbullying-statistics-canada/
15. Kadamgode, S., Shi, W., Corriveau, J.P.: Cyberbullying detection using ensemble method. In: International Conference on Data Science and Machine Learning, vol. 12, pp. 75–94 (2022)

16. Kurniawanda, M.R., Tobing, F.A.: Analysis sentiment cyberbullying in Instagram comments with XGBoost method. Int. J. New Media Technol. **9**(1), 28–34 (2022)
17. Maranhão, A.: Cyberbullying dataset (2022). https://www.kaggle.com/datasets/andrewmvd/cyberbullying-classification
18. Mardaoui, D., Garreau, D.: An analysis of lime for text data. In: International Conference on Artificial Intelligence and Statistics, pp. 3493–3501 (2021)
19. Muhammad, A., Dahiru, A.: Lexicon-based sentiment analysis of web discussion posts using SentiWordNet. J. Comput. Sci. Appl. **26**(2), 1 (2020)
20. Muneer, A., Fati, S.M.: A comparative analysis of machine learning techniques for cyberbullying detection on Twitter. Future Internet **12**(11) (2020)
21. Murez, C.: More cyberbullying, more suicidal thoughts among teens: study (2022). https://www.usnews.com/news/health-news/articles/2022-06-28/more-cyberbullying-more-suicidal-thoughts-among-teens-study
22. Nahar, V., Al-Maskari, S., Li, X., Pang, C.: Semi-supervised learning for cyberbullying detection in social networks. In: Databases Theory and Application, pp. 160–171 (2014)
23. Novalita, N., Herdiani, A., Lukmana, I., Puspandari, D.: Cyberbullying identification on Twitter using random forest classifier. In: Journal of Physics: Conference Series, vol. 1192, no. 1, p. 012029 (2019)
24. Purnamasari, N.M.G.D., Fauzi, M.A., Indriati, I., Dewi, L.S.: Cyberbullying identification in Twitter using support vector machine and information gain based feature selection. Indonesian J. Electr. Eng. Comput. Sci. **18**, 1494–1500 (2020)
25. Ribeiro, M.T., Singh, S., Guestrin, C.: "Why should I trust you?" Explaining the predictions of any classifier. In: International Conference on Knowledge Discovery and Data Mining, pp. 1135–1144 (2016)
26. Sharma, H.K., Kshitiz, K., Shailendra: NLP and machine learning techniques for detecting insulting comments on social networking platforms. In: ICACCE, pp. 265–272 (2018)
27. Van Bruwaene, D., Huang, Q., Inkpen, D.: A multi-platform dataset for detecting cyberbullying in social media. Lang. Resour. Eval. **54**(4), 851–874 (2020)
28. Wang, S., Zhou, W., Jiang, C.: A survey of word embeddings based on deep learning. Computing **102**(3), 717–740 (2019)
29. Wikitionary-ethnic: English ethnic slurs. https://en.wiktionary.org/wiki/Category:English_ethnic_slurs. Accessed 11 Mar 2023
30. Wu, J., Wen, M., Lu, R., Li, B., Li, J.: Toward efficient and effective bullying detection in online social network. Peer-to-Peer Netw. Appl. **13**(5), 1567–1576 (2020)
31. Xiang, L.: Application of an improved TF-IDF method in literary text classification. Adv. Multimed. **2022**, 10 (2022)
32. Xu, J.M., Jun, K.S., Zhu, X., Bellmore, A.: Learning from bullying traces in social media. In: Conference of the North American Chapter of the Association for Computational Linguistics: Human Language Technologies, pp. 656–666 (2012)

Privacy Preserving Elder Fall Detection Using Deep Learning

Faseeh Iftikhar[1], Muhammad Faizan Khan[1,2] (ID), Guojun Wang[2(✉)] (ID), and Fazli Wahid[1]

[1] Department of Information Technology, The University of Haripur, Haripur 22620, Pakistan
[2] School of Computer Science and Cyber Engineering, Guangzhou University, Guangzhou 510006, China
`csgjwang@gzhu.edu.cn`

Abstract. Falls are among the most challenging issues for the elderly community because these indicate frailty and chronic health impairment in senior citizens. As the rate of unexpected falls in elderly people continues to increase, accurate identification is needed to address this problem. Diverse approaches, such as sensors and fusion, were introduced to determine the problem. However, these methods are not able to preserve the privacy of the elderly. Our proposed article identifies the elderly's fall detection by their activities and gestures. We aim to create our Fall/N. Fall dataset (pictures, videos) using cameras in various indoor settings and then employ that dataset for image processing, such as grayscale, resizing, and denoising. After that, we use the Convolutional Neural network (CNN) to train and test classified fall videos or pictures. This model extracts particular features and reduces the number of parameters of classified data. We use the background subtraction technique to generate a foreground mask on the entire fall data for privacy preservation. The proposed system provides an accurate privacy preservation solution in elder fall detection.

Keywords: Fall Detection · Elderly People · Privacy Preservation · Deep Learning · Convolutional Neural Network (CNN)

1 Introduction

Fall among the elderly is highly destructive and devastating, the leading cause of life-threatening injuries. Fall indicates debility, stillness, and acute and immortal health disability in elderly persons. In 2019, the United Nations (UN) predicted a report that by 2050 [1], most countries can experience the fastest growth of the elderly population. According to the World Health Organization (WHO) [2], the fall frequency of elderly people is increasing by 30% to 50% worldwide approximately. Fall detection is a challenging problem for elders; therefore, it is essential to have various fall detection methodologies or techniques [3].

© The Author(s), under exclusive license to Springer Nature Singapore Pte Ltd. 2024
G. Wang et al. (Eds.): UbiSec 2023, CCIS 2034, pp. 335–347, 2024.
https://doi.org/10.1007/978-981-97-1274-8_22

Normally, the fall detection system works on the elder's body motion and gestures. The falling pattern in elderly people often exhibits specific characteristics. In cases of neurological disorders, there is a distinct pattern associated with falls that need to be addressed. A fall detection system preserves life by giving quick responses to future emergencies [4]. Several research approaches were proposed for fall detection systems: wearable, ambient, and vision-based sensors. First, wearables are intelligent digital devices that identify fall detection by implanted sensors like (watches or belts) [5]. The limitations of wearables are that they are challenging to wear all day, can cause enormous discomfort, or can cause older people to forget to wear them daily, resulting in a decreased ability to detect falls. Second, the ambient-based uses multiple sensors [6] like RFID, microphones, passive infrared, and ultrasonic for fall detection. These are installed in elderly living environments to monitor daily activity. This method is challenging to maintain and also costly. Moreover, this gives a high risk of false fall alertness. Vision-based fall detection is another eminent method [7]. It uses the image captured by the camera to determine the presence and orientation. Vision-based fall detection system has privacy violations among challenges due to capturing personal appearance and daily information.

It is evident that various techniques have been studied in fall detection systems till now, but privacy preservation has been the primary concern in all cases [8]. After solving the fall detection techniques, there is a dire need to pay more attention to preserving elder privacy. Authors of [9] worked on video surveillance to monitor elder fall detection using visual shielding multi-layer compressed sensing to ensure the elder's privacy. They have used low rank and decomposing theory to subtract background noise or information. As the compression layer increases, the quality of capture data resolution decreases, which causes low resolution of the optical frame that makes it difficult to analyze the accuracy of the elder falls. Moreover, the number of compressed layers increased in the experiments; the face became hazier. The processed dataset can preserve privacy and secure background noise, but there is a loss of information that can cause difficulty detecting falls or a high rate of false alarms. Furthermore, the limitation of this study is that they capture images with only a single camera, which cannot give an accurate result. They focus on the person's privacy by creating a skeleton, and background extraction is not removed. These deficiencies give us room to investigate the privacy problem further.

The research gap motivates us to work on the deficiencies and enhance privacy preservation. To study these challenges, we use cameras to improve the vision-based approach for the time being through predefined objectives. Firstly, when an elderly person falls, the face and body parts are hidden by the skeleton. We detect falls by their movement and body gestures. Secondly, we must secure the elderly person's background privacy by extracting the information. In summary, the contributions of the paper are as follows:

- We use cameras and indoor setups to develop our dataset in the form of images and videos to detect Fall/N. Fall of the older person and refine this dataset for image processing into grayscale, resizing, and denoising to ensure privacy.

- We employ the deep learning model Convolutional Neural network (CNN) for dataset training and testing, which extracts the particular features of the elderly fall detection data. We acquired both datasets, trained the images successfully, and then trained the dynamic frame videos.
- We use the background subtraction technique to remove background information for elderly fall data to make it secure from third-party access. Background subtraction is the background portion of an image that can be subtracted or eliminated. This method helps older people to secure their private information.

The remainder of this paper is as follows: We discuss related work in Sect. 2. We briefly present the methodology in Sect. 3, and simulation methods and results have been provided in Sects. 4.1 and 4.2. After that, we discuss the performance in Sect. 5. Finally, we mention the conclusions and future work in Sect. 6.

2   Related Work

This section discusses the recent research on wearable sensors, ambient sensors, vision sensors, and privacy preservation.

In a wearable device, sensors can detect the movement of the human body using accelerometers, gyroscopes, glucose meters, pressure sensors, ECGs, EEGs, and electromyograms [10]. Wearable devices use embedded sensors to detect fall behaviors, for example, smart watches, belts, etc. Despite not being sensitive to the environment, these wearable devices are uncomfortable for elderly people, and many forget to wear them. As a result, the ability to detect falls is diminished. The privacy of the older person can be compromised if these wearable devices are lost.

In ambient sensing systems, multiple ambient devices are used in the living area environment. Ambient-based approaches use ground pressure sensors, passive infrared sensors, and microphones [11] to obtain the daily movement and gestures of the elderly person. However, if one of the sensors gets damaged, then as a result, fall signals would be lost. Moreover, the elderly person's privacy is also violated by simultaneous microphone recordings of their daily activities. For vision-based methods, [12–14] capture images with a camera, process the images and recognize patterns to detect falls. There is a small amount of interference, but cameras can record daily routines, which could jeopardize the elderly's privacy. This fall detection method is mainly concerned with privacy preservation, and elderly people are highly conscious of their privacy.

Although recent advances in technologies enabled researchers to develop the elderly fall detection system, these technological advancements also have high risks of violation or privacy threats in a person's life. The new competency of such approaches allows them to collect and index a massive amount of private information about each individual. According to the authors of [15], visual privacy protection differentiates personal identity and personal information, which must be kept confidential. Video can convey an enormous amount of data that should stay private. Currently, vision-based approaches use methods for privacy-preserving as follows: 1) Face is obscured [16], meaning the face is only masked in the person's video without impacting the subject's physical features. This method is insufficient for privacy protection because indoor setup contains many more important things or a person is in his private space. 2) Encode the images and videos [17]. It is a privacy-preserving technique in which the imported information is protected from unauthorized access. But by destroying valuable information, identification is more complicated. The problem is that encoded data, once the key is leaked, can be reconstructed easily. 3) Reduce the resolution of images and videos [18]. Splitting 3-dimensional (3D) video sequences recorded by stationary cameras generate recordings with extremely low resolutions [19]. A computer vision system that shows the capabilities of the classifier for handling low video in addition to the computer vision features [20]. By employing this technique, personal privacy may be preserved while data usage is minimized.

In this related work, different techniques are effective in respecting the privacy of the elderly to certain extent; however, there are still certain drawbacks, which need to be addressed. Therefore, this paper considers aforementioned drawbacks of the privacy preserved fall detection in elderly people using deep learning.

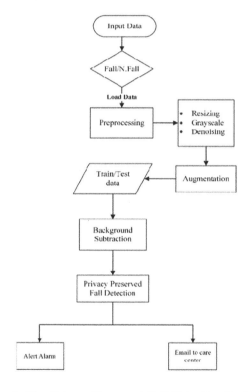

Fig. 1. The Privacy Preserved Fall Detection System

3 System Model

To build an elderly fall detection system, we need to solve two significant problems: Activity Classification and changing poses sequentially. The daily activities of elderly are quite similar and change in poses can detect falls. In our research, we create such a mechanism that preserves the privacy of the older person's fall detection from the disclosure and third-person access. We implement cameras in an indoor environment to detect elders' daily movement of Fall/N.Fall. Thereafter, we perform image processing on the dataset by converting it to grayscale, resizing, and denoising. Since, Convolutional Neural Network (CNN) is a deep learning model that processes information such as images and videos, so, we train and test elder fall detection data in the CNN model, which is used to extract specific features of the data and identify Fall and N.Fall. To preserve the privacy of the elderly person from the third party, we apply background subtraction on the train data (images, videos) to create a mask on the entire elder fall data, hide background information (lockers, wallets, etc.), and also personal privacy. Figure 1 shows the conceptual block diagram of our research methodology.

3.1 Image Pre-processing

Image pre-processing is one of the essential tasks, which refers to the process taken on image data conducted at the most basic level of abstraction [23]. The purpose of pre-processing is to enhance the quality, which will be helpful during further analyses and improve the image data by removing undesired distortions. Image pre-processing is the operation that is performed on the most basic level of the image.

The four types of image pre-processing are as follows:

- Pixel brightness transformation
- Geometric transformation
- Image filtering
- Image Restauration

In this study, we use image pre-processing to raise the quality and enhance the feature of the image for precise fall detection. To remove the distortion, we apply a pre-processing image approach when the data is noisy, has missing values, or has erroneous values that might lead to false fall detection. Moreover, image pre-processing can speed up model inference and reduce training time. When the input images are enormous, reducing their size will significantly speed up model training time without affecting model performance. Pre-processing is necessary for accurate elder fall detection.

Image pre-processing techniques use significant redundancy in data. Suppose a deformed pixel can be located in the image. In that case, it can typically be restored as the average value of nearby pixels since neighborhood pixels in actual images that relate to the same object have essentially the same or equivalent intensity values.

3.2   Resizing

Image resizing is also known as image scaling. Image resizing is required when we maximize or minimize the total amount of pixels of the image [23]. Scaling is used as a limited pre-processing in multi-stage image processing chains that operate on features of a specific scale to modify the visual look of an image and to change the amount of information contained in a scene representation.

If the elderly fall image has the wrong size or is pixelated, it affects the elder's fall detection method and may cause false fall detection. Since we can not take the risk of false alarms in privacy preservation, we employ image resizing techniques.

3.3   Grayscale

In grayscale, gray levels represent the interval amount of quantization [23]. 8-bit storage is the most popular type of storage. There are 256 gray levels in an 8-bit grayscale image, and each pixel's intensity can range from 0 to 255, with 0 being black and 255 being white.

1-bit storage is another frequently used storage technique. There are two shades of grey, where 0 represents black, and 1 illustrates white. The ultimate focus of grayscale transformation is to decrease or increase the original fall image's grayscale range so that the contrast between the background and the target of the fall detection of the elder person (in this case, a pavement crack) may be changed.

The grayscale range of the entire image can be increased with a linear function. However, it also improves the noise in the appearance in addition to the image's crack information.

3.4   Denoising

The denoise node is a powerful tool for effective noise suppression or grain from video [23]. It employs spatial or temporal filtering to reduce noise without sacrificing image quality. In other words, we must reconstruct the original image by removing noise.

In the elder fall detection system, the noise image has obscure information, and that image gives undesirable fall detection. We remove noise from the image to get accurate fall detection of elderly people. Image denoising may be conceptualized mathematically as follows:

$$z = y + w \tag{1}$$

Let z represent the identified noisy image, y unidentified clean image, and w indicate the standard deviation.

3.5   Augmentation

The data augmentation phase aims to improve the classification model artificially without adding labeling costs. Image augmentation uses various processing methods, including random rotation, shifts, shear, and flips, among others, to produce training images artificially. Through various processing techniques or combinations of multiple processing, like flip, rotations, shifting, etc., image augmentation generates different fall detection train images, which helps in accurate fall results [21].

3.6 Convolutional Neural Network

The CNN comprises an input layer, an output layer, and a hidden layer for analyzing and classifying images. The hidden layers consist of convolutional layers, ReLU layers, pooling layers, and fully connected layers; these all have significant impacts [22].

Image Classification in CNN. We input the elder fall image into the convolutional layer as shown in Fig. 2. The elder fall detection data has been in colored data, which is converted into a 3D array with layers of blue, green, and red with color values ranging from 0 to 255.

Matrix interpretation is begun then; a smaller image is chosen, which is called a "filter" (or kernel). A filter's depth matches the input's depth. A convolution filter movement is then added to the input image, shifting it by 1 unit forward. The values are then multiplied by the importance of the original image. One number is produced by adding all of the multiplied numbers together. Repetition of the process, the whole idea, and the smaller matrix than the initial input image are obtained.

The feature map of an activation map is the final array. An image can be convoluted by using several filters to perform tasks such as edge recognition, sharpening, and blurring. All required is the specification of elements like filter size, filter count, and network design. This activity is comparable to recognizing an image's primary colors and edges. To classify and identify the features of the image. Therefore, distinguishing motions like lying on the ground for an extended period or being recognized is necessary to categorize the image and identify the activity that, for example, makes it say fall or not fall. The non-linear and pooling layers enter the idea here.

The activation function is used for the feature maps in the non-linear layer (ReLU), which comes after the convolution layer, to boost the non-linearity of the images. The ReLU layer improves the correctness of the picture by eliminating any negative values. ReLU is the most often used operation, even if others, such as tanh or sigmoid, since it can instruct the network much more quickly. This step is to make many images of the same item to guarantee that the network can always recognize that image, regardless of its size or location. In particular, in the image of the older person falling, the network must determine whether the person is falling or not and whether they are moving. Image flexibility is required, and the pooling layer fills that role.

Pooling layers use the picture's dimensions (height and width) to gradually shrink the size of the original image, enabling the detection and identification of any falls or not falls in the picture, no matter where they may be found. Pooling also aids in preventing "overfitting", which occurs when there is insufficient data and no room for more. The image is split into several non-overlapping sections in max pooling, possibly the most typical instance of pooling. The main goal of max pooling is to figure out the maximum value in each region so that any superfluous information is eliminated and the picture is compressed. The imperfections in the image are also taken into consideration by this process.

The fully connected layer, which incorporates much information, makes greater accuracy in classifying images. At this point, the gradient of the error function concerning the weight of the neural network is determined to maximize performance, and the consequences and image detectors are changed periodically.

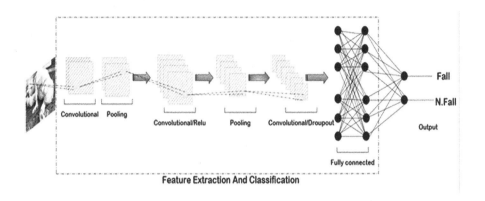

Fig. 2. Fall/N. Fall Dataset Classification in CNN

3.7 Background Subtraction

Background Subtraction (BS) is the technique used to create the mask in the foreground (specifically, a binary picture including the pixels of moving objects in the scene) using the camera. It performs the background subtraction between the original image and the background information [24]. We use the OpenCV library in BS to detect elderly privacy-preserved fall detection by removing all the background information. The background is estimated in this method based on the Original N frames. The foreground is constructed by subtracting the background from the current frame. BS has two significant steps, which are:

1. Background Initialization
2. Background Update

The initial background model is computed in the first step, and in the second step, that model is updated to account for any changes to the scene.

4   Simulation Results

Below, we discuss the experiment simulation methods and results.

4.1   Simulation Method

This privacy-preserved fall detection method has been implemented using Windows 10 Pro with Intel core i5-8250U 8GB RAM, and we use Python language in Jupiter Notebook to test data for elderly fall detection.

In our experiment method, we placed cameras in the indoor environment to detect the elderly daily movements and gestures like walking, sitting, and falling. We collected the dataset on the base of the daily activities of older people. The dataset is in the form of videos and images, and then we train and test around 2000 of that data to detect the Fall and N. fall of the older person.

(a) Original Frame

(b) Background Subtracted Frame

Fig. 3. Figure (a) shows the original image of the fall, and frame (b) shows the background subtracted fall detection result

4.2   Simulation Results

It can be observed from the simulation results that we used the background subtraction method to remove noise from their background data, creating a white blur mask on the elder's body to maintain its confidentiality. Sub-figs. 3a show the original image of the fall, and 3b show the background subtracted fall detection result, respectively. The background subtraction results give us a high accuracy for preserving the older person's privacy. We maintain the elderly body's privacy by removing the background.

Furthermore, we do perform an accuracy test of our proposed method as shown in Fig. 4. The accuracy line of the graph is steady. The accuracy x-axis shows the iteration step, and the y-axis shows the prediction. The steady black line indicates the training set accuracy, and the red line shows the Validation (Val) accuracy of the training dataset. The accuracy of testing data gives the best results for elderly fall detection. There is no overfitting or underfitting in the graph. It provides 99% accurate fall results. When the training process starts, the accuracy of the training data set is steady.

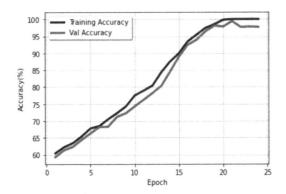

Fig. 4. Model Accuracy Curve

5   Performance Analysis

Many researchers studied the elderly person's fall detection system with different devices or techniques. The studies [7,8] used visual shielding senses and embedded private information to secure the person's information. Image or video compression causes low resolution; therefore, we are unable to detect the fall, and once the embedded video key gets leaked, the privacy is not secure. On the contrary, in our elderly fall detection system, privacy is protected from unauthorized access by subtracting background information, and it also prevents personal privacy.

According to the study, [19], by using V2V-PostNet, the body skeleton is detected, the joints of the structure are first characterized in the Riemannian manifold and time-parameterized trajectories are generated using semidefinite matrices of fixed-rank 2. The rotations are warped in time, producing a measure of their (dis-)similarity. Lastly, a pairwise proximity function, SVM is used to divide them into fall and non-fall categories, adding the (dis-)similarity measure into the kernel function. This paper has limitations; it only preserves the person's body privacy and background information is not emphasized. Fall is not detected in the dark environment, and cannot detect multiple people are falling. In our research, both the persons and background information are analyzed to protect their privacy, and our fall detection system can detect numerous persons even in a dark environment.

Limitations

Although, this study preserves the privacy of elderly people using background subtraction information, still there are certain limitations of our work. Current Fall/N.Fall dataset only considers elderly people, but employed methods will also detect normal falls as well. As of now, we have assumed that only elderly people will be using this system. Moreover, we did not consider pose estimation in this study, which will be more fruitful in distinguishing between young and elderly. As far as accuracy of the results is concerned, it's 99% because we have only considered elderly people with specific needs with either fall or not fall condition. Since, our main objective in this was to preserve background and personal privacy while detecting falls, so accuracy is quite high. However, when we will use pose estimation techniques with hybrid dataset of old and young, accuracy curve will be somehow low. Anyhow, this study has due importance because elderly people are normally alone at home and are very seldom willing to use wearable. Moreover, if they are asked to be monitored through onsite cameras, they refuse to do so as no-one wants to record his/her fall. Furthermore, house privacy is also preferred because if fall monitoring is compromised, any burglar may enter the house. Therefore, even background removal can encourage elderly to get their activities monitored is well-deserved contribution.

6   Conclusion

In this paper, we studied the activities and gestures of elders used to detect falls. A dataset of Fall/N. Fall has been constructed. In different indoor settings, cameras can detect falls and use that dataset for image processing like Grayscale, Resizing, and Denoising. The Convolutional Neural Network (CNN) model extracts specific characteristics, minimizes the number of parameters of classified data, and is used to train/test classified fall videos or images. We used the OpenCV library in background subtraction to detect elderly privacy-preserved fall detection by removing all the background information. In the future, we aim to apply pose estimation on Background Subtracted elder fall data. Moreover, we envision using Person Pose Estimation techniques for elder fall detection, which primarily find essential features in the image and video frames and connect them to construct a crude human skeleton.

Acknowledgments. This work was supported in part by the National Key Research and Development Program of China (2020YFB1005804), and in part by the National Natural Science Foundation of China under Grant 62372121.

References

1. Lai, N.M.S.: World population ageing (2019). https://digitallibrary.un.org/record/3846855
2. Step Safely: Strategies for preventing and managing falls across the life-course. https://www.who.int/publications/i/item/978924002191-4
3. Wang, X., Ellul, J., Azzopardi, G.: Elderly fall detection systems: a literature survey. Front. Robot. AI **7**, 71 (2020)
4. Chelli, A., Patzold, M.: A machine learning approach for fall detection and daily living activity recognition. IEEE Access **7**, 38670–38687 (2019). https://doi.org/10.1109/ACCESS.2019.2906693

5. Makma, J., Thanapatay, D., Isshiki, T., Chinrungrueng, J., Thiemjarus, S.: Toward accurate fall detection with a combined use of wearable and ambient sensors. In: 7th International Conference on Digital Arts, Media and Technology, DAMT 2022 and 5th ECTI Northern Section Conference on Electrical, Electronics, Computer and Telecommunications Engineering, NCON 2022, pp. 298–301 (2022). https://doi.org/10.1109/ECTIDAMTNCON53731.2022.9720383

6. Al-Okby, M.F.R., Al-Barrak, S.S.: New approach for fall detection system using embedded technology. In: Proceedings of IEEE 24th International Conference on Intelligent Engineering Systems, INES 2020, pp. 209–213 (2020). https://doi.org/10.1109/INES49302.2020.9147170

7. Chen, G., Duan, X.: Vision-based elderly fall detection algorithm for mobile robot. In: 2021 IEEE 4th International Conference on Electronics Technology, ICET 2021, pp. 1197–1202 (2021). https://doi.org/10.1109/ICET51757.2021.9450950

8. Liu, J., Xia, Y., Tang, Z.: Privacy-preserving video fall detection using visual shielding information. Vis. Comput. **37**(2), 359–370 (2021). https://doi.org/10.1007/s00371-020-01804-w

9. Liu, J., Tan, R., Han, G., Sun, N., Kwong, S.: Privacy-preserving in-home fall detection using visual shielding sensing and private information-embedding. IEEE Trans. Multimed. **23**, 3684–3699 (2021). https://doi.org/10.1109/TMM.2020.3029904

10. Kerdjidj, O., Ramzan, N., Ghanem, K., Amira, A., Chouireb, F.: Fall detection and human activity classification using wearable sensors and compressed sensing. J. Ambient. Intell. Humaniz. Comput. **11**(1), 349–361 (2020). https://doi.org/10.1007/s12652-019-01214-4

11. Toward Accurate Fall Detection with a Combined Use of Wearable and Ambient Sensors | IEEE Conference Publication | IEEE Xplore. https://ieeexplore.ieee.org/document/9720383

12. Harrou, F., Zerrouki, N., Sun, Y., Houacine, A.: An integrated vision-based approach for efficient human fall detection in a home environment. IEEE Access **7**, 114966–114974 (2019). https://doi.org/10.1109/ACCESS.2019.2936320

13. Tsai, T.-H., Hsu, C.-W., Wan, W.-C.: Live demonstration: vision-based real-time fall detection system on embedded system. In: 2020 IEEE International Symposium on Circuits and Systems (ISCAS) (2020). https://ieeexplore.ieee.org/document/9181262/

14. Chen, Y., Kong, X., Chen, L., Meng, L., Tomiyama, H.: A dynamic height analysis on vision based fall detection system. In: 2019 International Conference on Advanced Mechatronic Systems (ICAMechS) (2019). https://ieeexplore.ieee.org/document/8861676/

15. Asif, U., et al.: Privacy preserving human fall detection using video data. Proc. Mach. Learn. Res. **XX**, 1–12 (2019). http://proceedings.mlr.press/v116/asif20a.html

16. Vičič, J., Burnard, M.D., Tošić, A.: Privacy preserving indoor location and fall detection system. In: 22nd International Multiconference Information Society (2019)

17. Arulselvi, G., Poornima, D., Anand, S.J.: Privacy preserving elderly fall detection using kinetic depth images based on deep convolutional neural networks (2020)

18. Oumaima, G., Hamd, A.A., Youness, T., Rachid, O.H.T., Omar, B.: Vision-based fall detection and prevention for the elderly people: a review & ongoing research. In: 2021 Fifth International Conference on Intelligent Computing in Data Sciences (ICDS) (2021). https://ieeexplore.ieee.org/document/9626736/

19. Bhatlawande, S., Khapre, D., Kinge, M., Khairnar, T.: Vision based assistive system for fall detection. In: 2022 2nd International Conference on Intelligent Technologies (CONIT) (2022). https://ieeexplore.ieee.org/document/9847697/

20. Alaoui, A.Y., Tabii, Y., Thami, R.O.H., Daoudi, M., Berretti, S., Pala, P.: Fall detection of elderly people using the manifold of positive semidefinite matrices. J. Imaging **7**(7) (2021). https://doi.org/10.3390/jimaging7070109

21. Xu, M., Yoon, S., Fuentes, A., Yang, J., Park, D.S.: Style-consistent image translation: a novel data augmentation paradigm to improve plant disease recognition. Front. Plant Sci. **12**, 3361 (2022)

22. Sun, Y., Xue, B., Zhang, M., Yen, G.G.: Evolving deep convolutional neural networks for image classification. IEEE Trans. Evol. Comput. **24**(2), 394–407 (2019)

23. Gayathri Devi, T., Neelamegam, P., Sudha, S.: Image processing system for automatic segmentation and yield prediction of fruits using open CV. In: International Conference on Current Trends in Computer, Electrical, Electronics and Communication (CTCEEC), Mysore, India, pp. 758–762 (2017)

24. Tirpude, P., Girhepunje, P., Sahu, S., Zilpe, S., Ragite, H.: Real time object detection using OpenCV-Python. Int. Res. J. Modernization Eng. Technol. Sci. **4**(5), 1–6 (2022)

Research on Authorization Model of Attribute Access Control Based on Knowledge Graph

Li Ma, Qidi Lao, Wenyin Yang(✉), Zexian Yang, Dong Yuan,
and Zhaoxiong Bu

Foshan University, Foshan 528000, China
cswyyang@fosu.edu.cn

Abstract. Knowledge graph is an extended graphical data structure tool that can store interrelated data and visually display the relationships between different objects in large systems. It is widely used in various fields. This paper proposes an attribute-based knowledge graph authorization policy model. This model presents the access control authorization policy between users and resources, and can intuitively display the authorization relationships between various types of nodes, making it easier to understand and implement access control policies. Compared with the traditional text access control policy presentation form, the knowledge graph authorization model presentation form proposed in this article is more intuitive and easy to understand and has strong operability. Finally, this article implemented the knowledge graph authorization strategy model on the NEO4J platform, using Cypher statements to implement the graph traversal algorithm to effectively evaluate the accuracy of the authorization strategy. This experiment implements the access control knowledge graph on the NEO4J platform and combines Cypher statements to search and match access control policies more finely.

Keywords: Access control · Neo4j · Cypher query language · Knowledge graph · Authorization policy

1 Introduction

With the widespread application of information systems and digital devices, enterprises and organizations have accumulated a large amount of valuable or sensitive data locally or in the cloud [1–3]. Once this data is leaked or used maliciously, it will cause serious economic losses or pose a major threat to user privacy [4–6]. Therefore, protecting sensitive information has become an important task for enterprises and organizations to protect customers and attract users [7, 8]. In this context, access control is widely recognized as the first line of defence, and its purpose is to ensure that only authorized users can access sensitive data to prevent data leakage.

Attribute-Based Access Control (ABAC) [9] is a method of determining access permissions to resources through the attributes of users, resources, or environment parameters in access requests. The ABAC model has the ability to implement complex access control policies that can involve any combination of attributes and static, dynamic, and

G. Wang et al. (Eds.): UbiSec 2023, CCIS 2034, pp. 348–359, 2024.
https://doi.org/10.1007/978-981-97-1274-8_23

relationship-based values. Compared with the currently widely used role-based access control (RBAC), ABAC can achieve more granular and flexible access control. The U.S. federal government [9] has identified ABAC as the recommended access control model, and so far, 70% of enterprises around the world have adopted ABAC as the main mechanism to protect their critical information assets.

Although Attribute-Based Access Control (ABAC) features highly fine-grained, flexible access policies, implementing ABAC is a challenging task as setting up, deploying, and handling ABAC at runtime requires more time and effort. Furthermore, as the flexibility and complexity of the policy increases, so does the average processing time. Therefore, this paper aims to study an access control authorization policy graph model that can present the access control authorization policy between users and resources and show the relationship between various nodes, making it easier to understand and implement access control policies. The management and maintenance of real-time changing policies can be simplified during policy use. The graph model in this article uses user attributes and resource attributes to construct the corresponding access control knowledge graph, in which subjects, objects and the relationships between them are represented by corresponding graph nodes and edges. Authorization policies can be viewed as a subgraph of the entire knowledge graph, which allows the access management system to make policy decisions based on complete and efficient graph traversal algorithms. To implement the authorization policy graph model, this article uses the Neo4j graph database as a platform to avoid the problems caused by dealing with traditional relational databases and their inherent JOIN operations.

2 Relate Work

Attribute-based access control policy model is a hot research topic among current scholars. Wang et al. [11] proposed a logic-based ABAC framework that utilizes logic rules to define and execute access control policies. Zhang et al. [12] proposed attribute-enhanced access matrix as an ABAC implementation model, which allows attributes to be associated with entries of the access matrix to achieve more fine-grained access control. Rubio Medrano et al. [13] proposed a method to implement ABAC using security tokens. Ferraolo et al. [14] formally proposed the concept of ABAC's "strategy machine". Jahid et al. [15] developed an ABAC implementation called MyABDAC, relying on relational database capacity and the XACML policy language. Li [16] proposed an ontology-based model OABACM, which combines the basic concepts and properties of common ABAC models. Santiago et al. [17] and more recently Jin and Kaja [18] studied the idea of using graph implementations for ABAC. These research efforts explore the potential of using graph data structures and graph traversal algorithms to represent and decide on access control policies. In particular, Hadi and Derek [19] proposed a method of using the Neo4j graph database platform to implement the ABAC graph model; You [20] proposed an algorithm for constructing an access control knowledge graph from user attributes and resource attributes. Furthermore, based on the constructed knowledge graph. Although these research works have similarities in ABAC implementation, the methods of implementing the policy graph model in [17–20] are different, and therefore cannot provide a general graph traversal algorithm to support policy decision-making. In future research, graph-based implementation methods can be further explored to improve the efficiency and scalability of ABAC and provide better support for strategic decision-making.

3 Access Control Policy Authorization Model

In the notation of Attribute Based Access Control (ABAC), an access control policy is defined as an "allow" or "deny" decision on a set of conditional predicates (or conditions for short) to restrict access to protected objects. An access request consists of a subject, an action, and an object.

In a simplified expression, the access policy can be expressed as (allow/deny: condition): allow/deny the subject who meets the rule condition to perform the specified operation on the object. Each condition involves subjects, objects, actions, and the relationships between them. Examples of conditional clauses include:

Subject: Employee with job ID "42204".
Object: Resource file with file ID "8978".
Action: The operation requested by the subject to be performed on the object.
Relationship: The access control relationship between the subject and the object.

In the access control policy authorization model proposed in this article, the model includes the access control authorization relationship between the user subject and the resource object. Users, resource attributes, and the access control relationships between them are represented in the form of triples composed of knowledge graphs, that is subject-relationship->object.

In addition to subject, object and relationship, there are different attributes between each subject and object. In the access control policy authorization model, each attribute is attributed to the subject, object or relationship to represent the characteristics they originally had. These attributes can be associated with subjects, objects, or relationships to better control access to document resources. For example, user attributes can include the user's ID number, department and group, etc. A certain policy only allows users in a specific department to read and write specific resources.

Additionally, in this access control policy authorization model, three operational attributes are part of the access control relationship:

(1) Read operation: Allows users to read the contents of a file or view the file list in the directory.
(2) Write operation: Allows users to modify the contents of files or create or delete files in the directory.
(3) Execute: Allows users to run files as programs or enter directories.

The access control policy authorization model can also support graph traversal algorithms for policy decisions. Each access control policy in this model can be viewed as a set of paths. In other words, specific access control policies can be represented as a "policy subgraph" on the knowledge graph. By using the graph traversal algorithm, access requests and access policies can be effectively matched, and access control decisions can be made according to the conditions defined in the policies.

4 Knowledge Graph Construction Algorithm

This section will introduce in detail the construction algorithm of the access control knowledge graph, which aims to construct a knowledge graph based on the given user information, access resource information and the access control relationship between the two.

The knowledge graph is composed of different nodes and the relationships between them. Each node has its type label, and the relationship nodes also have their type label. Nodes and relationships can have various attributes and attribute values of their own. To build an access control knowledge graph one must extract all user information (access subject), resource information (access object) and the relationships between them to form a knowledge graph.

4.1 Classification of Attributes

This research focuses on building an access control knowledge graph that can reflect the relationship between users and resources. This kind of graph effectively provides a comprehensive view of user access rights and resource allocation. To achieve this goal, experiments first need to conduct an in-depth analysis and classification of the attributes of users and resources to ensure that the most representative and practical node types can be constructed.

During the analysis of the data, it was found that user ID and resource ID are key attributes of user-type nodes and resource-type nodes because they can uniquely identify each user and resource. Therefore, these two attributes are defined as required attributes, which means that each user node or resource node must have a user ID or resource ID associated with it.

However, there are other attributes besides the two mentioned above, and the number of unique values for these attributes can vary greatly. To deal with this problem, the experiment defined a threshold value −300. The selection of this threshold is based on a preliminary analysis of the data set. It is found that the number of unique values for most attributes is much lower than this value, and only a few attribute values are higher than this value, so a value of 300 is used as the threshold for differentiation. Therefore, if the number of unique values for an attribute is greater than or equal to this threshold, then the attribute has sufficient complexity to be treated as an independent node attribute. For example, if the "Manager" property has more than 300 unique values, then a separate node type will be created for "Manager". Conversely, if the number of unique values for an attribute is less than this threshold, the attribute may not be complex enough to be a standalone node. In this case, the experiment will define this attribute as other attribute and attribute it to the existing node type. For example, if the "PERSON_COMPANY" attribute has only 34 unique values, then it will belong to the "User" node type, as shown in Table 1.

In this way, various attributes can be effectively classified and managed, ensuring that the knowledge graph constructed through experiments is both representative and easy to understand and use.

Table 1. Attribute classification

attribute category	Analyzing conditions
required attribute	The ID of the user The ID of the resource
node attribute	greater than or equal to 300
other attribute	less than 300

4.2 Access Control Knowledge Graph Composition Algorithm

Algorithm 1 will use the data attributes analyzed in Sect. 4.1 and the relationship between data to construct an access control knowledge graph. Some execution statements of the pseudocode in Algorithm 1 are written in Cypher query language, which is the graph query language of the Neo4j graph database. The composition algorithm mainly includes two steps. The first step is the construction of knowledge graph nodes, and the second step is the construction of relationships. Algorithm 1 describes the construction process of the access control knowledge graph in detail.

The first step in Algorithm 1 is the construction of access control knowledge graph nodes, which is specifically implemented in lines 2–11 of the pseudocode. In line 4, the algorithm creates a node labelled *Resource* according to the ID number of the resource in the dataset, and the ID number of the resource is used as the attribute of the resource node. In line 6, the algorithm creates a node labelled *User* type based on the user attributes in the dataset. Among the user attributes, each user node is identified by its unique user ID attribute. In addition to the ID attribute, other user attributes are also added to the User type node. In lines 8–10, create nodes that belong to the node attribute type defined in Sect. 4.1. Because the unique number is greater than or equal to the threshold of 300, three types of nodes, *manager*, *title*, and *department*, can be constructed after data analysis.

The second step in Algorithm 1 is the construction of relationships in the access control knowledge graph, which is specifically implemented in lines 14–29 of the pseudocode. In lines 15–17, this algorithm creates a relationship named *access_control* type for the *User* node and *Resource* node. Each *Resource* node and *User* node are identified by their unique ID numbers, and the attributes of the *access_control* relationship between them are also the same. And added to the relationship. In lines 18–29, the algorithm builds *has_manager*, *has_title* and *has_department* relationships between the *User* node and the three types of nodes: *manager*, *title* and *department* respectively.

After the above two steps, an access control knowledge graph for a graphical representation of access control policies is established.

Algorithm 1: Construction Algorithm of Access Control Knowledge
Graph

   Data: access control dataset
   Result: access control knowledge graph
1 Step1:create graph node with properties;
2 **while** *node attributes are in the dataset* **do**
3   //create resource nodes;
4   CREATE Resource node with properties: RESOURCE_ID ;
5   //create people nodes;
6   CREATE User node with properties: PERSON_ROLLUP_1;
      PERSON_ROLLUP_2; PERSON_ROLLUP_3;
      PERSON_COMPANY; PERSON_ID; PERSON_JOB_CODE;
      PERSON_JOB_FAMILY; PERSON_LOCATION ;
7   //create nodes with the number of attributes greater than or equal
      to the threshold of 300;
8   CREATE manager node with MGR_ID ;//create manager nodes
9   CREATE title node with PERSON_TITLE;//create title nodes
10   CREATE department node with PERSON_DEPTNAME ;//create
      department nodes
11 **end**
12 Step2:create graph relationships with properties;
13 **while** *relationships are in the dataset* **do**
14   //Create a relationship between resource nodes and User nodes;
15   from =MATCH("User", { PERSON_ID });
16   to=MATCH("Resource",{RESOURCE_ID});
17   MERGE(from)-[r:access_control
      {ACTION;EXECUTE;READ;WRITE}]->(to);
18   //Create a relationship between the User node and the manager
      node;
19   from =MATCH("User", { PERSON_ID });
20   to=MATCH("manager",{MGR_ID});
21   MERGE(from)-[r:has_manager]->(to);
22   //Create a relationship between the User node and the title node;
23   from =MATCH("User", { PERSON_ID});
24   to=MATCH("title",{PERSON_TITLE});
25   MERGE(from)-[r:has_title]->(to);
26   //Create a relationship between the User node and the department
      node;
27   from =MATCH("User", {PERSON_ID});
28   to=MATCH("department",{PERSON_DEPTNAME});
29   MERGE(from)-[r:has_department]->(to);
30 **end**

---

5   Implementation of the Access Control Authorization Knowledge Graph Model

This section will introduce the access control data set used in the experiment. On this data set, this experiment uses the Cypher statement of Algorithm 1 to construct the corresponding access control knowledge graph and shows each construction step in detail, and then it will show its usage examples on this access control knowledge graph.

This experiment is carried out on an open source real Amazon employee access dataset Amazon Access Samples Data Set. The dataset contains a file listing all user and resource attributes, as well as a file of access control requests and corresponding permission records. Because the users and resource attributes in the data set and the access control records between them are scattered and there are many repeated access control records, this experiment processed the two files into a triplet form of access control suitable for the composition of the neo4j knowledge graph. Strategy, and deduplicated it. Because in the original data set, only the results of the access request exist and the specific operations of the access request are missing, this experiment completes the specific operations of access control and adds three access operations to it, namely read and write. And perform operations.

Table 2 lists the basic information of the processed data set. As shown in Table 2, there are 4253 unique users and 861 unique resources. The attribute values in the data set have their basic information listed in Table 2, and there are 28843 corresponding access control policies. In "Attribute Type", this experiment uses the attribute type defined in Sect. 4.1 to classify each attribute. The attribute information will be used for the construction of a knowledge graph, as described in Sect. 5.1.

Table 2. Dataset information

Subject	Attribute name	The number of the attribute	Attribute type	Description
User	PERSON_ID	4253	Required Attribute	The ID of the user
	PERSON_BUSINESS_TITLE	1326	Node Attribute	title ID
	PERSON_BUSINESS_TITLE_DETAIL	47	Other Attribute	title description ID
	PERSON_COMPANY	34	Other Attribute	company ID
	PERSON_DEPTNAME	319	Node Attribute	department description ID
	PERSON_JOB_CODE	13	Other Attribute	job code ID
	PERSON_JOB_FAMILY	65	Other Attribute	job family ID
	PERSON_LOCATION	1	Other Attribute	region ID

(*continued*)

Table 2. (*continued*)

Subject	Attribute name	The number of the attribute	Attribute type	Description
	PERSON_MGR_ID	1397	Node Attribute	manager ID
	PERSON_ROLLUP_1	12	Other Attribute	user grouping ID
	PERSON_ROLLUP_2	106	Other Attribute	user grouping ID
	PERSON_ROLLUP_3	12	Other Attribute	user grouping ID
Resource	RESOURCE_ID	861	Required Attribute	The ID of the resource
	ACTION	2	Other Attribute	The access request is allowed or denied
	WRITE	2	Other Attribute	operation is write
	READ	2	Other Attribute	operation is read
	Execute	2	Other Attribute	operation is execute

5.1 Access Control Knowledge Graph Construction

Based on the dataset introduced in Sect. 4.1, this experiment constructs an access control knowledge graph using the steps in Algorithm 1, and the main process and intermediate knowledge graph construction results are summarized in Table 3.

Finally, this experiment uses the processed data set to build an access control knowledge graph, and the structure of the map is shown in Fig. 1. A rounded rectangle represents a type of node, and an arrow represents the relationship between nodes. There are bold label names for nodes or relationships in the rectangles, and the numbers below the label names indicate the number of nodes or relationships. In addition, the rectangle below the rectangle represents the attributes in the node or relationship.

5.2 Example of Using the Access Control Knowledge Graph

After constructing the access control knowledge graph in this experiment, you can use the cypher statement of the neo4j platform to perform various queries and processing on the constructed knowledge graph. The specific cypher query statement of an access control strategy based on this graph in this experiment is:

Table 3. The construction process of access control knowledge graph

step	Created node	Created property	Created relationship
Step 1	Resource	RESOURCE_ID	Null
	User	PERSON_ID, PERSON_BUSINESS_TITLE_DETAIL, PERSON_COMPANY, PERSON_JOB_CODE, PERSON_JOB_FAMILY, PERSON_LOCATION, PERSON_ROLLUP_1, PERSON_ROLLUP_2, PERSON_ROLLUP_3	
	Manager	MGR_ID	
	Title	PERSON_TITLE	
	Department	PERSON_DEPTNAME	
Step 2	Null	ACTION, WRITE, READ, Execute	access_control
		Null	has_manager
		Null	has_title
		Null	has_department

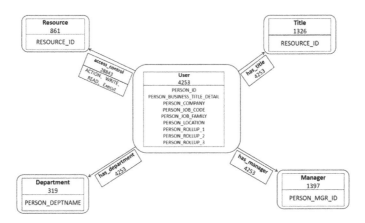

Fig. 1. Access control knowledge graph structure constructed by Algorithm 1

MATCH (u:User)-[:access_control]->(r:Resource),
(u:User)-[:has_title]->(t:Title),
(u:User)-[:has_manager]->(m:Manager),
(u:User)-[:has_department]->(d:Department)
RETURN u, r, t, m, d

After this statement is queried, it is displayed on the neo4j platform as shown in Fig. 2. This statement can query which department the user belongs to, which manager he belongs to and what his position is. There can be multiple relationships between the user and resource access because if a person performs different operations on the same resource, different authorizations will be generated. result.

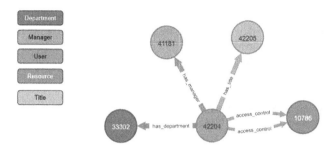

Fig. 2. Cypher statement query results of an access control policy based on this knowledge graph

In addition, for different nodes in the figure, you can also expand the nodes. For example, if you expand for a user node, you can directly query which nodes the user has access control relationships with, and if you expand for a resource node, you can directly query whether the resource node can which user objects are given access. Figure 3 shows an example of expanding a user node.

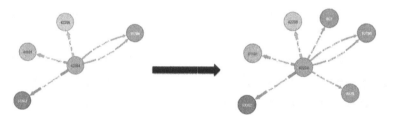

Fig. 3. An example of expanding user nodes in the knowledge graph

Therefore, for a single access control statement in the text, as shown in Fig. 2, the position is 42205, the department is 33302, and the user with the ID 42204 of the manager 41181 can use the graphical interface to express the specific access control of the 10786 resource. Come out, more intuitive.

6   Conclusion

This paper proposes an algorithm for constructing an access control knowledge graph from user attributes and resource attributes. The knowledge graph can present the graphical data form of access control policy rules, showing the relationship between various types of nodes. Compared with access control policies expressed in text form, this graphical representation is more intuitive. At the same time, combined with the Cypher statement on the NEO4J platform, specific access control policies can be traversed.

In future research, experiments will further explore the possibility of using graph structures to detect and resolve conflict strategies, as well as whether the features of graphs can be utilized to complete more access control related work. In addition, further research can be conducted on the application of the strategy set after conflict resolution.

Acknowledgments. This work was supported by grants from the Guangdong Province-Foshan Joint Fund Project No.2022A1515140096.

References

1. Ge, Y.F., Orlowska, M., Cao, J., Wang, H., Zhang, Y.: MDDE: multitasking distributed differential evolution for privacy-preserving database fragmentation. VLDB J. 1–19 (2022). https://doi.org/10.1007/s00778-021-00718-w
2. Rasool, R.U., Ashraf, U., Ahmed, K., Wang, H., Rafique, W., Anwar, Z.: Cyberpulse: a machine learning based link flooding attack mitigation system for software defined networks. IEEE Access 7, 34885–34899 (2019). https://doi.org/10.1109/ACCESS.2019.2904236
3. Wang, H., Sun, L.: Trust-involved access control in collaborative open social networks. In: 2010 Fourth International Conference on Network and System Security, pp. 239–246 (2010). https://doi.org/10.1109/nss.2010.13
4. Chen, Z.G., Zhan, Z., Wang, H., Zhang, J.: Distributed individuals for multiple peaks: a novel differential evolution for multimodal optimization problems. IEEE Trans. Evol. Comput. 24, 708–719 (2020). https://doi.org/10.1109/tevc.2019.2944180
5. Servos, D., Osborn, S.L.: Current research and open problems in attribute-based access control. ACM Comput. Surv. (CSUR) 49(4), 1–45 (2017). https://doi.org/10.1145/3007204
6. Verizon: Data Breach Investigations Report. Technical report, Verizon (2020). https://enterprise.verizon.com/resources/reports/2020-data-breach-investigations-report.pdf
7. Cheng, K., et al.: Secure k-NN query on encrypted cloud data with multiple keys. IEEE Trans. Big Data 7, 689–702 (2021). https://doi.org/10.1109/tbdata.2017.2707552
8. Zhang, J., et al.: On efficient and robust anonymization for privacy protection on massive streaming categorical information. IEEE Trans. Dependable Secure Comput. 14, 507–520 (2017). https://doi.org/10.1109/tdsc.2015.2483503
9. Hu, V.C., Ferraiolo, D., Kuhn, R., et al.: Guide to attribute based access control (ABAC) definition and considerations (draft). NIST Spec. Publ. 800(162), 1–54 (2013)
10. Contu, R., Kavanagh, K.M.: Market Trends: Cloud-Based Security Services Market, Worldwide (2014)
11. Wng, L., Wijesekera, D., Jajodia, S.: A logic-based framework for attribute based access control. In: Proceedings of the 2004 ACM Workshop on Formal Methods in Security Engineering, pp. 45–55. ACM (2004)
12. Zhang, X., Li, Y., Nalla, D.: An attribute-based access matrix model. In: Proceedings of the 2005 ACM Symposium on Applied Computing, pp. 359–363. ACM (2005)
13. Rubio-Medrano, C.E., D'Souza, C., Ahn, G.J.: Supporting secure collaborations with attribute-based access control. In: 9th IEEE International Conference on Collaborative Computing: Networking, Applications and Worksharing, pp. 525–530. IEEE (2013)
14. Ferraiolo, D., Gavrila, S., Jansen, W.: Policy Machine: Features, Architecture, and Specification, NIST Interagency/Internal Report (NISTIR), National Institute of Standards and Technology, Gaithersburg, MD (2015). https://doi.org/10.6028/NIST.IR.7987r1
15. Jahid, S., Gunter, C.A., Hoque, I., Okhravi, H.: MyABDAC: compiling XACML policies for attribute-based database access control. In: Proceedings of the First ACM Conference on Data and Application Security and Privacy, pp. 97–108. ACM (2011)

16. Li, J.: Research on ontology-based ABAC model modeling and security policy optimization methods. Shanghai Jiao Tong University (2019)
17. Pina Ros, S., Lischka, M., Gómez Mármol, F.: Graph-based XACML evaluation. In: Proceedings of the 17th ACM Symposium on Access Control Models and Technologies, pp. 83–92. ACM (2012)
18. Jin, Y., Kaja, K.: XACML implementation based on graph databases. In: CATA, pp. 65–74 (2019)
19. Ahmadi, H., Small, D.: Graph model implementation of attribute-based access control policies. arXiv preprint arXiv:1909.09904 (2019)
20. You, M., Yin, J., Wang, H., et al.: A knowledge graph empowered online learning framework for access control decision-making. World Wide Web **26**(2), 827–848 (2023)

Cyberspace Anonymity

Simulation of Mixmining Reward Parameters for the Nym Mixnet

Harry Halpin[(✉)]

Nym Technologies SA, Place Numa-Droz 2, 2000 Neuchâtel, Switzerland
harry@nymtech.net

Abstract. We focus on analyzing the use of tokenized cryptoeconomics to provision anonymity to determine if it is economically sustainable from a long-term perspective. This paper explores early design decisions of how the blockchain-enabled Nym network uses a tokenized incentive scheme to create a decentralized mix network. The initial inflationary pool of tokens is given by a mixmining pool. We present a simulated economic model that, under certain assumptions, determines under what conditions the token-based inflation can be economically sustainable for the mix network. We show an exponential rate of inflation is suitable. In conclusion, we note the next steps for research at the intersection of privacy and cryptoeconomics.

Keywords: incentives · mix networks · simulation · economics · blockchain

1 Introduction

Anonymity is a public good that can only technically be achieved by *hiding in a crowd*. The Nym network provides a decentralized protocol for provisioning network-level anonymity as a multi-sided platform between services and users, where a decentralized collection ("crowd") of nodes (servers) – a *mix network* – provisions privacy for individual users [7]. Yet how can we assemble a collection of nodes to supply privacy to users?

All actors in the ecosystem need to have incentives to maintain the collective protection of anonymity on the level of the transfer of bytes, which Nym accomplishes via the NYM token. However, the cost of running such nodes over long periods of time needs to be estimated to determine the minimum reward distribution of the NYM token from both an inflationary token pool, which is called the "mixming pool" in the Nym mix network, and fees such that provisioning privacy is economically viable. The precise values and distributions of these parameters were unknown at the time of these simulations, although since then the Nym mixnet has used an exponential decay function in its rewards [13], as validated by these simulations.

After briefly reviewing the intersection of anonymous communication networks and economics in Sect. 2, the design choices of the Nym network are given

© The Author(s), under exclusive license to Springer Nature Singapore Pte Ltd. 2024
G. Wang et al. (Eds.): UbiSec 2023, CCIS 2034, pp. 363–379, 2024.
https://doi.org/10.1007/978-981-97-1274-8_24

in Sect. 3. Then we analyze the network's assumptions and token economics in Sect. 4, and finally we outline the mix network can be sustainable under various growth models in Sect. 4.3. The limitations and future directions for the blockchain-based Nym cryptoeconomics are sketched in Sect. 5. It should be noted that this simulation work was done prior to the game-theoretic analysis and simulations done by Nym Technologies, and so is a useful prelude to that work [13].

2   Background

Anonymous communication networks (ACNs) are networks that can send messages in an unlinkable manner between a sender and receiver [24]. Anonymous communication networks currently fall into a few major research strands. Invented by Chaum [7], a *mix network* (mixnet) is a network whose goal is to mix, or 'shuffle,' messages in such a way that the sender and receiver of a message are unlinkable with respects to third-party adversaries that can observe the entire network [24]. The Java Anonymous Proxy mixnet system had an early version of centralized Chaumian e-cash [9] for payments [5]. *DC-nets* ("dining cryptographer network") used secure multi-party computation to provide superior information-theoretic anonymity but at increased computational cost [8], but there has been a dearth of work on incentives and economics for DC nets and other forms of MPC-based anonymity systems and no actual deployments. Onion-routing systems wrapped messages in layers of encryption and passed them between independent nodes, leading to efficient anonymity in front of less powerful local adversaries [26]. The onion-routing system Tor ("The Onion Router") is the primary anonymity network used at the present moment, with over 2 million daily active users [15].[1] However, Tor does not have a sustainable internal economic model or payments from users, and instead relies on volunteers to run the nodes and supply privacy for free, with core development work funded by government and research grants. In the first proposal to add reputation to Tor, volunteers who ran their own high capacity relays would receive corresponding preferential treatment for their own traffic [22], but this approach fatally allows their own traffic to be more easily de-anonymized. Later work featured relay-specific *BRAIDS* "tickets" distributed by a central bank allowed users to reward nodes for providing a high class of throughput [19], a design that was decentralized in *LIRA* [20].

Interestingly enough, economic analysis of anonymity showed that payment by users was economically rational and that it was also rational for users who would pay for anonymity to desire a large amount of non-paying users to provide cover traffic [1]. This research was continued by the U.S. government sponsors of Tor [21], as a Tor-specific fungible currency was thought of as a possible alternative to non-fungible reputation systems. Payment for routing by users of anonymous packets was put forward in the *PAR* system using Chaumian e-cash [3], but it was not implemented due to the inherent expense and centralization of

---

[1] https://metrics.torproject.org/userstats-relay-country.html.

Chaumian e-cash. *X-Pay* demonstrated that micropayments could be done on a "hop by hop" basis, but the system required that each Tor relay act honestly in relaying payment to the next hop [10]. A better option was put forward to pay only the first hop into the Tor network, and then distribute if the traffic was correctly delivered [23]. Using Bitcoin could even be indirectly used for payment without de-anonymizing the user by having the user put in proof-of-work solutions for hash puzzles directly in the onion-routed traffic at each layer [6]. These proposals were rejected by the Tor project as it was considered adding payments, including payments based on reputation, would cause unknown and possibly harmful changes to their current community of volunteer relay operators, although Tor relay operators still have difficulty in terms of economic sustainability [18]. Currently a "proof of work" system similar to Hashcash is implemented by Tor to defend against denial-of-service attacks, although it is not used for payments [4].[2]

3 Nym: A Continuous-Time, Stratified Mixnet

3.1 Technical Design

Due to space limitations, only a short summary of the design of Nym is presented here. The full design can be referenced in the Nym whitepaper.[3] Similar to Tor, mix networks are composed of multiple *mix nodes* that relay the messages to each other before they exit the network. To achieve anonymity that withstands global network adversaries, mix nodes perform three necessary operations before sending the message to the next mix node that are not performed by Tor:

1. Mix nodes *cryptographically transform equal-sized messages* to achieve *bitwise unlinkability*, meaning that input and output messages cannot be correlated based on their size or content; in other words, inputs and outputs are unlinkable based on their binary representations.[4]
2. Equally importantly, mix nodes *reorder and alter the flow of messages* using a *mixing strategy* so that inputs cannot be correlated to outputs based on their order or time of arrival and exit to and from the mix node.
3. Mix networks may use *cover traffic*, traffic which is generated in order to increase the anonymity set and provide unobservability so an adversary cannot tell when a user is using the mix network.

---

[2] https://blog.torproject.org/introducing-proof-of-work-defense-for-onion-services/.

[3] https://nymtech.net/nym-whitepaper.pdf.

[4] There are two kinds of mix networks in terms of the type of application they are designed for and the cryptographic primitive they use to transform messages: *re-encryption mixnets* are designed for electronic voting applications where assuring a zero-knowledge proof of shuffling is considered the most important, while *decryption mixnets* are commonly used for anonymous messaging and general-purpose communications as they can withstand messages being dropped. Nym is a decryption mix network, so henceforth we will only refer to this family of mix networks.

4. Mix networks connect mix nodes using particular topologies that may have different structures and so can add to the anonymity given by a particular mixing strategy.

Nym uses the Sphinx as its packet format like Mixminion [11] (to achieve unlinkability between constant-sized packets) and like Loopix [25] uses a continuous ("stop and go") mixing strategy based on a memoryless Poisson process, as well as a stratified topology. This design appears to provide reasonable anonymity and performance trade-offs, as shown by prior research [12]. The primary difference between Nym and all other mixnet designs is that Nym is focussed on a dynamic network where the number of mix nodes can be increased or decreased to meet demand. Thus, where Nym adds new features to Loopix are that Nym uses a blockchain maintained for validators serving to maintain the consensus of the mix nodes and other nodes in the network, replacing the static PKI of Loopix and that Nym features an economic model based on a token that should allow the number of mix nodes to match dynamic changes in demand. The intuition is that when the demand for privacy-enhanced bandwidth increases, the supply of mix nodes increases, so that Nym itself functions as a multi-sided market.

3.2 NYM Token

In order to decentralize the mixnet and allow it to serve as a multi-sided market to provision privacy with an adequate quality of service, the NYM token is introduced to the previously non-incentivized Loopix design [25]. The NYM token (called "NYM" in uppercase to distinguish it from the Nym mixnet) is required to participate in the mix network by all actors. The purpose of NYM is to incentivize participation by nodes, and also helps to avoid network abuse by malicious actors [16]. For example, the requirement to pledge NYM tokens to join the network as a mix node prevents zero-cost sybil attacks and so preserves the reliability and availability of the network.

The goal of the mix network is to provide the highest possible quality of service and privacy given a set of users, service providers, and mix nodes. *Quality of service* is defined as minimizing the number of packets dropped, so that the amount of packets sent into the network do not exceed the *capacity* of the mix nodes. We define *privacy* in terms of the *anonymity* that can be measured by the entropy of a given packet in the face of a global passive adversary that can observe all network traffic [14].[5]

From a legal standpoint, the **NYM token** functions as both a *utility* token and a *staking* token. The NYM token is a utility token insofar as possession of a certain amount of NYM by users is required to gain access to the Nym network. The amount of token that is deposited by a user (or a service provider on behalf of a user) to use the Nym network is called a **fee**. In order to prevent these

---

[5] It should be noted that Tor is not amenable to measurement via entropy, and so the more users Tor has – unlike Nym – there is no increase in anonymity in terms of entropy in Tor [26].

fees from de-anonymizing users, the fees are recorded as unlinkable anonymous credentials by gateways [17].

The Nym network functions over **epochs**, which is both the periods of time over which a mix nodes are organized into a single topology and over which mix nodes have their performance measured and fees are collected.[6] The precise length of an epoch is a trade off between concern for an attacker compromise and latency delays caused by the network reorganization (as establishing a new topology requires computation). At the end of an epoch, mix nodes and validators may be added and the assignment of mix nodes to layers may change. From a security perspective, at the end of an epoch the network is forward secure as keys are rotated and derived for mix nodes.

The NYM token may come from a **mixmining** pool, which the part of reserves that provide the inflation of NYM to distribute to mix nodes even if there are no fees. Note this inflation is from a finite supply and so the NYM token is ultimately deflationary. The use of these mixmining rewards is because mix nodes may be needed to be online even if there are no fees for a period of time in order for the network to be assembled and thus capable of handling user traffic when it does arrive. Various inflation rates are for the release of the mixmining pool to mix nodes are studied in Sect. 4. There is also a more general **reserve** that includes both the mixmining pool and the fees taken from usage of the mixnet to reward nodes. The full details of Nym's microeconomics, including Nash equilibria and simulations, are given in other work [13]. In this work, what we do here is simulate a pricing model and more dynamic assumptions in order to determine the distribution for the inflationary rewards studied in more detail in [13]. Given these elements, it is straightforward to define NYM's pricing, although without any speculative aspect.

$$P_t = P_{t\text{-}1} * [1 + \epsilon_t] \tag{1}$$

where

$$\epsilon_t = \frac{D_t/P_{t\text{-}1}}{D_{t\text{-}1}/P_{t\text{-}1}} - \frac{CS_t}{CS_{t\text{-}1}} \tag{2}$$

and where

$$D_t = F_t + I_t + OC_t \tag{3}$$

with D_t = USD market demand, P_t = NYM price, F_t = USD network fees, I_t = USD value of inflation from mixmining pool, OC_t = USD operating costs, CS_t = available circulating NYM supply.

Consequently, while fees paid by users remain low or near zero at launch, the NYM price at any given epoch t is a function of the percent change in mixing power provided by the supply side, the percentage change in mixmining rewards, and the price of NYM in the previous epoch. The system is designed to provide sufficiently high mixmining rewards at market launch to ensure network operators are able to make a profit in the absence of sufficient demand.

---

[6] The actual period over which nodes are reimbursed (with inflation) is one or more epochs.

In the bootstrapping phase of the network, there is an implied cost, which is given by the rewards of the mixmining pool distributed to the potential mix nodes even if they are not currently mixing. So the price of NYM is the *current utility value* as a function of the mix nodes used to mix packets in any given epoch t and by the demand for the service (via credentials) given by F. If there is no demand due to a lack of services using Nym, the number of active mix nodes will dynamically be a function of I and the current NYM price.

4   Token Simulations

The NYM token dynamics need to be played out on a larger scale: Could the addition of a blockchain-based token lead to a sustainable mixnet in the long-term, such as a decade? We define *sustainable* when the income generated for operators of mix nodes at least covers their operational costs and even produces a profit. The primary variable that can be controlled is the distribution, such as an exponential or linear distribution, of the rewards from the mixmining pool.

In order to answer the question of what inflation rate allows the mixnet to be sustainable, we need to make a long-term economic simulation that builds in changes to the price of the token at launch, the decrease in hardware costs over time, and so on. This model will in turn be based on a number of assumptions – input parameters – on the size of the potential market for privacy-enhanced internet usage and the growth of this market. The model works by using the input values on operating costs given in Table 1 and the assumptions on user demand (in Sect. 4.3), while varying the distribution of inflation rewards from the mixmining pool, to produce a new set of outputs per epoch (defined as a month) as per Table 2. The calculations to determine if the income of a node is sustainable are done via the equations given for the NYM token in Sect. 3.2, with each epoch resulting in a new state change based on the prior epoch. Analysis of the simulation results can then determine which of the inflation distribution schedules are suitable for long-term financial sustainability.

The input parameters for the macroeconomic simulation are summarized in Table 1, with a focus on operating costs. The token parameters are fairly arbitrary, but are taken to be representative of the market in 2020. The total valuation of the Nym network was given to be 300 million, with approximately one-third sold to investors (who are assumed to have a monthly vesting schedule for two years and divest of all tokens each month) and another one-third left for mixmining rewards, with 10% put on the market in an initial token sale (the remaining 20% are to put in the reserve). The NYM token itself was set to .3 cents with 90% of the token given to investors being staked.

In Sect. 4.1, we provide an explanation of the estimation of the initial parameters that come from a reference mix node, as well as bandwidth pricing for supply in Sect. 4.2 using the VPN market as a comparable for demand. Given a model of user growth in Sect. 4.3, we can compare the ability of a number of mixmining inflation distributions in Sect. 4.4 to cover costs and become profitable for mix nodes over a time-span of a decade in Sect. 4.5.

Table 1. Input parameters of simulation

Name	Definition	Justification	Initial Value	State Change
Token Parameters				
NYM Price	USD	300 mil. valuation	.30	Equation in Sect. 3.2
Target Staked	% NYM staked	Security parameter	.33%	Corrupt Layer
Total supply	# NYM tokens	Arbitrary	1 billion	Burn-and-mint
Investors Staked	% NYM staked	Sect. 4	90%	constant
Delegators staked	% NYM staked	Sect. 4	80%	constant
Reference Mix Node				
Node capacity	MBs	Running 10%	12.5	See cost decrease
Mix node cost	USD	Sect. 4.1	30	−20%
Mix nodes	#	3 layers min	27	Match demand
Avg. Node PM	%	Sect. 4.1	20%	Constant
Private Bandwidth Market				
GBs per user	GBs	Sect. 4.2	8.3	+30%
Monthly Fee	USD	Sect. 4.2	4.0	−10%

4.1   Reference Mix Node

The first step is to calculate the approximate supply-side costs of privacy in a mix network in order to estimate the price per packet. These assumptions come from estimates of hardware and bandwidth costs in order to create a cost estimate for a *reference mix node*. Some of the constraints on how many nodes also come from our routing topology, as the minimum amount of mix nodes for reasons of reliability is 9 mix-nodes, arranged in three layers with three nodes in each layer. Given the size of the community however, it may be more realistic to assume thirty nodes (10 nodes per layer) at launch. Each single mix-node is assumed to have access to a fiber optic line with 125 Megabytes per second (MB/s) maximum capacity, which is roughly equivalent to an average Ethernet 1 Gigabit/second connection (1000 MBs/8). However, the throughput of user traffic should not be at maximum all the time, as internet traffic is bursty. Thus, the real capacity per mix node is then 125 KBs per second, which is equivalent (with Sphinx packets being 4Kb) to 31 Sphinx packets per second. The cost of a mix node is assumed to be 30 CHF per month with a 20% annual linear decline in price.[7] From these assumptions, one can estimate the average PP should be

---

[7] There will be vast differences between geographical locations for fiber optic access (https://blog.cloudflare.com/the-relative-cost-of-bandwidth-around-the-wo rld/), but 30 CHF month seems to be a conservative estimate, given historical data from servers from relatively cheap servers such as VPS9 in Germany (https:// www.vps9.net/germany-vps to more expensive servers in Singapore (https://www. ovhcloud.com/en-sg/vps/.) Although a linear decreasing in price for bandwidth seems surprising, it is a long-term trend given ubiquitous fiber optic cable that seems to hit a limit in innovation, as per https://www.statista.com/statistics/616210/ average-internet-connection-speed-in-the-us/.

cost per kilobyte per second, multiplied by 4 (the size of Sphnix packet), which is a PP of .000000456 cents per Sphinx packet.

Although secondary to mix nodes in Nym, we also estimate the costs of validators needed to maintain the blockchain. We assume the usage of Cosmos with Tendermint consensus at launch and so a minimum of seven validators is needed [2], with the required 99% up-time (unlike mix-nodes, which can go off-line more often at the cost of having their stake slashed). Given the interest in Nym, a more realistic number is 21 validators at launch. A linear monthly growth rate of .2% is to be expected such that 100 validators (near the theoretical maximum for Tendermint) is reached after one decade of operation. Validators also have a high variation in cost, due to the possibility of using secure hardware and other advanced features, we estimate that the monthly cost is 1000 CHF with the same 20% annual linear decline in price as assumed by validators.[8] Note that unlike other tokens or cryptocurrencies, Nym is not aiming for maximum decentralization but for high quality of service, and Tendermint's limit of 100 validators is acceptable as the validators do not need to grow with user demand for privacy-enhanced bandwidth, but merely serve as a reliable bulletin board for the pledging and rewarding of mix nodes in NYM.

4.2   Private Bandwidth Market Assumptions

In terms of estimating demand, it is difficult to estimate NYM usage in the future as currently there is no large for-scale generic markets for privacy-enhanced, much less anonymous, internet usage. The primary service similar comparable is Tor, but Tor does not have paying users and so cannot be used as a model for historical comparison. However, VPNs are a possible market comparable, as they have paying customers. In 2020, VPNs typically cost between 8 to 12 CHF per month, depending on the precise VPN provider used and a large market of over 25 billion CHF with a compound annual growth rate of 12%.[9] Approximately one fourth of internet users (1 billion users) have used a VPN, and approximately one-third use it due to personal or work-related privacy concerns, as opposed purely for changing jurisdictions to stream video (which is approximately half of VPN usage.[10] If we take the price of a VPN as a starting point for what users are willing to pay and launch a comparable product, then cost per GB of bandwidth using a VPN is approximately 25 cents per month,[11] with a 16% decrease in price annually.[12] As shown by Table 1, although payment for VPN-like services varies

---

[8] These estimates come from discussions with a wide variety of staking services for Tendermint-based blockchains, ranging from Bison Trails to P2P Validator.

[9] As per Global Market Insights: https://www.gminsights.com/industry-analysis/virtual-private-network-vpn-market.

[10] See https://www.statista.com/statistics/306955/vpn-proxy-server-use-worldwide-by-region/.

[11] See Burniske's INET model assumptions: https://docs.google.com/spreadsheets/d/1ng4vv3TUE0DoB12diyc8nRfZuAN13k3aRR30gmuKM2Y/edit#gid=1912132017.

[12] See https://www.telegeography.com/press/press-releases/2015/09/09/ip-transit-prices-continue-falling-major-discrepancies-remain/index.html.

wildly per geolocation, we can nonetheless make a coarse-grained estimate of user demand in terms of payment for access and the amount of average bandwidth a user will consume.

To think in terms of global internet traffic that can potentially be made private, in 2016 Cisco released that annual IP traffic was 212,000,000,000 giga-bytes[13] with a compound annual growth rate (CACR) of 24%, leading to 2,837,056,512,000 gigabytes in 2020.[14] The question is then what percentage of IP address would be possibly addressed by Nym at full market penetration? Assuming that one quarter of global IP traffic requires a VPN-like system and that one third of that traffic requires privacy, then we can conservatively assume approximately 3.3% of internet traffic could use the advanced privacy technology developed by Nym. However, we will assume that modest market penetration will require .1% of this, leading to 94,568,550,400 GBs of usage per month in total.[15]

4.3   User Growth Models

User growth is very difficult to predict, and so in order to determine if our model is sustainable we will need to determine under what user growth models the Nym network becomes sustainable. We test linear, logistic, and bilogistic usage growth curves in our simulation.

1. **Linear:** $f(x) = U_s + \beta U_s t$
   where U_s = Number of users at market launch, t = Current epoch and β = Monthly growth rate
2. **Logistic:** $f(t) = \dfrac{U_s}{1 + \frac{(U_f - U_s/2)}{U_s/2} * e^{\beta \cdot t}}$
   where U_s = Number of users at market launch, U_f = Number of users at full market penetration, t = Current epoch, and β = Growth rate constant.
3. **Bilogistic:** User growth can also characterized by a bilogistic curve, i.e., two logistic growth pulses over time. The first logistic curve models the initial "take off" once product-market fit is discovered, and the second logistic curve models the slower penetration of the market. The equation for this *sequential logistic* model is as follows:

$$f(t) = \frac{U_m}{1 + \frac{(U_m - U_s/2)}{U_s/2} * e^{\beta_1 t}} + \frac{U_f - U_m}{1 + \frac{U_f - U_m - U_s/2}{U_s/2} * e^{\beta_2 t}}$$

where U_s = Number of users at market launch, U_m = Number of users at modest market penetration, U_f = Number of users at full market penetration,

---

[13] http://www.cisco.com/c/en/us/solutions/collateral/service-provider/visual-networking-index-vni/vni-hyperconnectivity-wp.html.

[14] This is approximately inline with current statistics: https://www.statista.com/statistics/267202/global-data-volume-of-consumer-ip-traffic/ that has 2.12 EB with a 27% CACR.

[15] Note that in terms of comparables, Tor provides 25 GBs for a minimum of 2 million users consistently ass given at https://metrics.torproject.org/bandwidth.html.

t = Current epoch, β_1 = Initial growth rate constant, and β_2 = Long term growth rate constant.

4.4 Mixmining Rewards Models

As given in Sect. 3.2, rewards distribution is composed of the sum of mixmining rewards and user fees paid to the network. An ideal inflationary emission schedule for mixmining would allow nodes to maintain their preferred profit rate (PM) and at least their break-even point at network launch. Therefore, one empirical question in terms of sustainability is how to design a mixmining inflation schedule that provisions privacy even in the absence of widespread usage until eventually fees from users take over.

Mixmining rewards can be emitted either via a linear or exponential reward rate: Which rate is optimal? One of the design choices that our model needs to solve is what distribution the reward rate should take. Note the mixmining release schedule is deflationary, as the rewards are sourced from a reserve pool of tokens that are held out of circulation and distributed as rewards for participation by network operators, and the release of tokens from the mixmining pool can be considered the inflation rate of the NYM token.

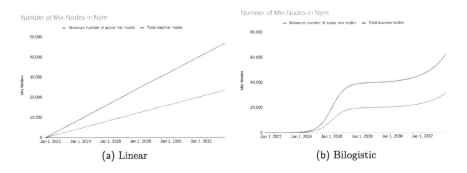

(a) Linear   (b) Bilogistic

Fig. 1. Growth of Mixnodes

The mixmining release schedule is:

1. **Linear:** A simple linear reward rate can be modelled as follows:

$$f(x) = x \cdot \gamma \cdot (1 - \tau) \cdot t \tag{4}$$

where x = Total tokens staked by delegators and pledged by nodes, γ = Mixmining reward rate in epoch 0, τ = Rate of decay and t = Current epoch
2. **Exponential:** An exponent can be added to the linear reward rate to produce:

$$f(x) = x \cdot \gamma \cdot (1 - \tau)^t \tag{5}$$

where variables are defined as above.

Table 2. Output parameters of simulation

Name	Value
Mix nodes	
Active Mixnodes	#
Inactive Mixnodes	#
NYM Supply	
Total Delegated Tokens	NYM
Total Publicly Circulating Tokens	NYM
Monthly Mixmining Reward Budget	NYM
Reward Pool Composition	
Total Fees	NYM
Monthly-Mixmining Reward Budget	NYM
Total Rewards	NYM
Percentage Returns	
Total Returns Per Month	%
Mixmining Rewards per Month	%

4.5   Growth and Inflation Model Validation

Using the assumptions outlined earlier as inputs, each of the user growth models was ran in combination with each of the inflation distributions models to determine which models produced sustainable outcomes. Parameters in the model were stepped through from $0 \leq 1$ in steps of .001, namely β for growth modes and α, β for reward rate models.[16] Inactive nodes were assumed to be needed at least to match the number of active nodes, although future work should fine-tune this parameter. The results for a decade of operation are given for the number of mix nodes, the supply of NYM, percentage of returns for mix nodes, and reward pool compositions. The output for each of the combinations of user growth rate and inflation rate in terms of linear, exponential and bilogistic distributions were graphed and analyzed to determine if they were economically sustainable.

It should be noted that some simulated models were simply not functional and so are not shown in detail. Linear inflation models were unable to meet mix node costs with logistic or bilogistic user growth, and so "fell off a cliff" when the inflation ended. On the other hand, logistic user growth models were typically not suitable for exponential or linear inflation except as the growth would often be too high or too late for the inflation. However, the following combinations of growth models and inflation seemed to be the most plausible:

---

[16] A full exploration of this work would require a very large appendix, which for the sake of brevity we have not included as the vast majority of models were not sustainable.

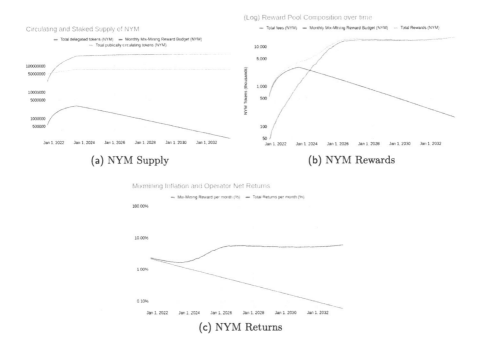

Fig. 2. Bilogistic Growth and Exponential Inflation Simulation Results

– **Linear Growth** and **Exponential Inflation** in Fig. 1a, Fig. 3a, Fig. 3b, and Fig. 3c with a linear growth rate of $\beta = 2500$ and inflation $\tau = .01$.
– **Bilogistic Growth** and **Exponential Inflation** in Fig. 1b, Fig. 2a, Fig. 2b, and Fig. 2c with a short-term growth rate of $\beta_1 = .19$ and a long-term growth rate of $\beta_2 = .066$. Inflation was found to be more suitable at $\tau = .025$ than .01.
– **Bilogistic Growth** and **Linear Inflation** in Fig. 4a, Fig. 4b, and Fig. 4c and with a short-term growth rate of $\beta_1 = .19$ and a long-term growth rate of $\beta_2 = .066$ and inflation $\tau = .01$.

The optimal models for user growth in terms of sustainability were either logistic or bilogistic. In linear growth models, it can be observed in Fig. 3a that after an initial jump in usage the entire network ends up stabilizing, which may seem appealing. However, as shown in Fig. 4b, the exponential decreasing rewards end up sustaining the network, not the fee-based growth. In other words, with long-tailed exponential inflation, a network with only linear user growth can perpetuate but ultimately ends up simply recycling the inflation, and so if the inflation runs out, the network dies. However, if the growth is small, the inflation can last more than a decade. This macroeconomic behavior seems vaguely analogous to Bitcoin.

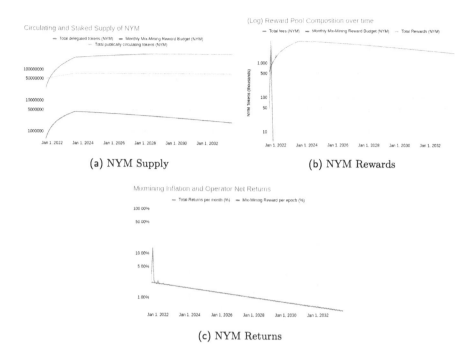

(a) NYM Supply

(b) NYM Rewards

(c) NYM Returns

Fig. 3. Linear Growth and Exponential Inflation Simulation Results

Under a logistic user growth model, the minimum growth rate needed was $\beta = 0.08$. Under a perhaps more realistic bilogistic model, $\beta_1 \geq 0.21$ and $\beta_2 \geq 0.025$ were more appropriate, allowing growth to start in the first wave of adoption, but scale at a slower rate once the user growth had already taken off. In bilogistic models, the growth rate can be smaller than in logistic models insofar as a relatively large amount of usage has been accumulated before the second logistic curve starts growth. Recall that the mixnet could not support only linear growth, as the inflationary mix-mining rewards would simply run out at some point, causing all nodes to leave as there would not be enough rewards, and simply increasing β under non-logistic growth models lead to delaying an inevitable network collapse. However, the more optimistic bilogistic or logistic user growth models would always allow user fees to take over from inflationary rewards approximately at the end of the second year of the operation of the mix net as shown in Fig. 2b. This allows a steady growth that results in reasonable returns as shown in Fig. 2c. This result unsurprisingly shows that blockchain systems do require inflation, but that inflation from a finite pool cannot be used to support a crypto-network with no usage forever. Tokenized blockchains like Nym must, similar to traditional startups, maintain a high growth rate in order to function.[17]

---

[17] Somewhat surprisingly this result shows that constant or no growth (such as in Tor) would not support tokenization.

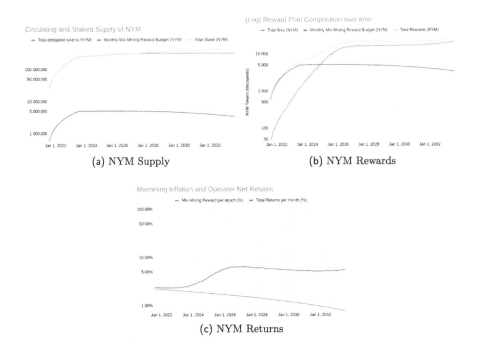

Fig. 4. Bilogistic Growth and Linear Inflation Simulation Results

However, one surprise is that a bilogistic growth model also can be dealt with by a linear inflation model. A linear inflation model delays the inflection point where fees take over from inflation approximately a year, as given in Fig. 4b; the lack of inflation hampers the growth of mix nodes to deal with the push in demand. Nonetheless, the rewards end up being comparable over time as with exponential inflation as given in Fig. 4c and Fig. 2c, which is logical given that the inflation is always eventually marginal given usage fees in networks with (bi)logistic growth. In terms of mixmining, either linear or exponential inflationary rewards would suit a sustainable mixnet, although there seem slight advantages to the exponential reward model in terms of increasing profit for early mix nodes and preparing the network for possible higher growth. For linear inflationary rewards, it is better if there is no expectation of massive growth in the short-term and thus tokens need to be conserved for future usage. In both models, the initial inflation per annum can be set reasonably to 15%, but a 10% inflation is also suitable. Both simply manage to allow sustainability to be reached after two to three years, and the difference between the two is fairly negligible.

Under logistic or bilogistic user growth with any reasonably parameterized exponential or linear inflation scheme, the reward schedule can match the underlying costs of the mix nodes and validators and so provide a sustainable mix net. This is accomplished at the onset of the network via rewards from the mixmining pool, but according to our model is no longer needed when user fees are expected to overtake mixmining rewards about two years after the network launch at earliest. As demand for private internet traffic is expected to continue to increase, the simulation shows that in order to meet demand with logistic growth over ten years, a total of 90,328 mix nodes are needed. Even with the more realistic bilogistic user growth, approximately 31 thousand mix nodes will be needed.

5   Conclusion

The Achilles heel of privacy-enhancing technologies like anonymous communication networks has been the need for expensive computation to hide private data, and tokenization finally allows for it be paid for. As our cryptoeconomic analysis showed, if NYM is considered a cryptoasset that allows this productive computation to become profitable, then mix networks should be a realistic possibility. In the long-term, our simulation-based analysis shows that, with exponential distribution parameters for mixmining rewards, NYM tokens can be used to subsidize the growth of a mix network to provision anonymity to a substantial portion of the world's message-based internet traffic, given a realistic bilogistic user growth rate. One actionable insight is that the design of the Nym mixnet should adopt the parameters recommended in this study for the inflation pool and reward distribution. The exponential distribution parameter selected in these experiments was used in both further more thorough economic simulations of Nym [13] and in the actual network launch itself.

Our model makes a number of simplifying assumptions and does not inspect all possibilities. In particular, the macroeconomics did not explore the various different kinds of long-term inflation rates (tail inflation and so on) and also did not inspect the effect of various kinds of initial token allocations. A different division of the initial tokens, as given by a fair launch for example, could lead to different results in the simulation and this should be explored for other tokens. The reference node model here was substantially changed in the finalized simulation work on Nym [13]. Pricing is likely to be effected by speculation, and this is not taken into account. For example, user demand may also be more bursty as demand is based on particular apps (and so large amounts of users) adopting Nym at distinct intervals. Even within an epoch, the usage of the mix network may itself be bursty. A model with per-node memory, such as an agent-based model, would allow a more fine-grained analysis of the impact of assumptions and parameters.

Although we have used as our case study a particular system, the Nym mixnet, the model given could be abstracted to other systems, including existing popular ACNs like the Tor network as well as work on other types of tokenized ACNs. Lastly, we will need to see how the cryptoeconomics behaves in the wild in terms of real users and mix nodes via careful data collection and analysis. It is all-too-human behavior that will be the judge of any economic model.

Acknowledgments. The author would like to thank Evelyn Hytopoulos for her work on the simulations, as well as Claudia Diaz and Aggelos Kiayias for discussions.

References

1. Acquisti, A., Dingledine, R., Syverson, P.: On the economics of anonymity. In: Wright, R.N. (ed.) FC 2003. LNCS, vol. 2742, pp. 84–102. Springer, Heidelberg (2003). https://doi.org/10.1007/978-3-540-45126-6_7
2. Amoussou-Guenou, Y., Del Pozzo, A., Potop-Butucaru, M., Tucci-Piergiovanni, S.: Dissecting tendermint. In: Atig, M.F., Schwarzmann, A.A. (eds.) NETYS 2019. LNCS, vol. 11704, pp. 166–182. Springer, Cham (2019). https://doi.org/10.1007/978-3-030-31277-0_11
3. Androulaki, E., Raykova, M., Srivatsan, S., Stavrou, A., Bellovin, S.M.: PAR: payment for anonymous routing. In: Borisov, N., Goldberg, I. (eds.) PETS 2008. LNCS, vol. 5134, pp. 219–236. Springer, Heidelberg (2008). https://doi.org/10.1007/978-3-540-70630-4_14
4. Back, A.: Hashcash-a denial of service counter-measure (2002)
5. Berthold, O., Federrath, H., Köpsell, S.: Web MIXes: a system for anonymous and unobservable internet access. In: Federrath, H. (ed.) Designing Privacy Enhancing Technologies. LNCS, vol. 2009, pp. 115–129. Springer, Heidelberg (2001). https://doi.org/10.1007/3-540-44702-4_7
6. Biryukov, A., Pustogarov, I.: Bitcoin over Tor isn't a good idea. In: IEEE Symposium on Security and Privacy, pp. 122–134 (2015)
7. Chaum, D.: Untraceable electronic mail, return addresses, and digital pseudonyms. Commun. ACM **24**(2), 84–88 (1981)
8. Chaum, D.: The dining cryptographers problem: unconditional sender and recipient untraceability. J. Cryptol. **1**(1), 65–75 (1988)
9. Chaum, D., Fiat, A., Naor, M.: Untraceable electronic cash. In: Goldwasser, S. (ed.) CRYPTO 1988. LNCS, vol. 403, pp. 319–327. Springer, New York (1990). https://doi.org/10.1007/0-387-34799-2_25
10. Chen, Y., Sion, R., Carbunar, B.: XPay: practical anonymous payments for tor routing and other networked services. In: Proceedings of the Workshop on Privacy in the Electronic Society, pp. 41–50 (2009)
11. Danezis, G., Dingledine, R., Mathewson, N.: Mixminion: design of a type III anonymous remailer protocol. In: 2003 Symposium on Security and Privacy, pp. 2–15. IEEE (2003)
12. Das, D., Meiser, S., Mohammadi, E., Kate, A.: Anonymity trilemma: strong anonymity, low bandwidth overhead, low latency-choose two. In: 2018 IEEE Symposium on Security and Privacy (SP), pp. 108–126. IEEE (2018)
13. Diaz, C., Halpin, H., Kiayias, A.: Reward sharing for mixnets. Cryptoeconomic Syst. **2**(1) (2022)
14. Díaz, C., Seys, S., Claessens, J., Preneel, B.: Towards measuring anonymity. In: Dingledine, R., Syverson, P. (eds.) PET 2002. LNCS, vol. 2482, pp. 54–68. Springer, Heidelberg (2003). https://doi.org/10.1007/3-540-36467-6_5
15. Dingledine, R., Mathewson, N., Syverson, P.: Tor: the second-generation onion router. In: USENIX Security Symposium, pp. 303–320 (2004)
16. Douceur, J.R.: The Sybil attack. In: Druschel, P., Kaashoek, F., Rowstron, A. (eds.) IPTPS 2002. LNCS, vol. 2429, pp. 251–260. Springer, Heidelberg (2002). https://doi.org/10.1007/3-540-45748-8_24
17. Halpin, H.: Nym credentials: decentralizing identity with privacy using blockchains. In: IEEE Cryptovalley Conference. Springer (2020)
18. Huang, H.-Y., Bashir, M.: The onion router: understanding a privacy enhancing technology community. Proc. Assoc. Inf. Sci. Technol. **53**(1), 1–10 (2016)

19. Jansen, R., Hopper, N., Kim, Y.: Recruiting new Tor relays with BRAIDS. In: Proceedings of the ACM Conference on Computer and Communications Security, pp. 319–328 (2010)
20. Jansen, R., Johnson, A., Syverson, P.: Lira: lightweight incentivized routing for anonymity. Technical report, Naval Research Lab (2013)
21. Johnson, A., Jansen, R., Syverson, P.: Onions for sale: putting privacy on the market. In: Sadeghi, A.-R. (ed.) FC 2013. LNCS, vol. 7859, pp. 399–400. Springer, Heidelberg (2013). https://doi.org/10.1007/978-3-642-39884-1_36
22. Ngan, T.-W., Dingledine, R., Wallach, D.S.: Building incentives into Tor. In: Sion, R. (ed.) FC 2010. LNCS, vol. 6052, pp. 238–256. Springer, Heidelberg (2010). https://doi.org/10.1007/978-3-642-14577-3_19
23. Palmieri, P., Pouwelse, J.: Paying the guard: an entry-guard-based payment system for Tor. In: Böhme, R., Okamoto, T. (eds.) FC 2015. LNCS, vol. 8975, pp. 437–444. Springer, Heidelberg (2015). https://doi.org/10.1007/978-3-662-47854-7_26
24. Pfitzmann, A., Köhntopp, M.: Anonymity, unobservability, and pseudonymity—a proposal for terminology. In: Federrath, H. (ed.) Designing Privacy Enhancing Technologies. LNCS, vol. 2009, pp. 1–9. Springer, Heidelberg (2001). https://doi.org/10.1007/3-540-44702-4_1
25. Piotrowska, A.M., Hayes, J., Elahi, T., Meiser, S., Danezis, G.: The Loopix anonymity system. In: USENIX Security Symposium, pp. 1199–1216 (2017)
26. Syverson, P., Tsudik, G., Reed, M., Landwehr, C.: Towards an analysis of onion routing security. In: Federrath, H. (ed.) Designing Privacy Enhancing Technologies. LNCS, vol. 2009, pp. 96–114. Springer, Heidelberg (2001). https://doi.org/10.1007/3-540-44702-4_6

Blockchain-Based Privacy-Preservation Platform for Data Storage and Query Processing

Michael Mireku Kwakye[1,2](✉) and Ken Barker[2]

[1] Fort Hays State University, Hays, KS 67601, USA
m_mirekukwakye@fhsu.edu
[2] University of Calgary, Calgary, AB T2N 1N4, Canada
{michael.mirekukwakye,ken.barker}@ucalgary.ca

Abstract. Privacy-preservation policies are guidelines and recommendations formulated to protect data provider's private data in data repositories. Previous privacy-preservation methodologies have addressed privacy in which data are permanently stored in repositories and disconnected from changing data provider privacy preferences. This occurrence becomes evident as data moves to another data repository. Moreover, the ability of data providers to flexibly update or change their privacy preferences when it is required is a known challenge. Hence, the need for data providers to control their existing privacy preferences due to data usage changes continues to remain a problem. This paper proposes a blockchain-based methodology/framework for privacy preservation of data provider's private and sensitive data. The research proposes to tightly couple data provider's private attribute data element to privacy preferences and data accessor data elements into a privacy tuple. The implementation presents a framework of tightly-coupled relational database and blockchains. This delivers a secure, tamper-resist-ant, and query-efficient platform for management and query processing of data provider's private data. The evaluation analysis from the implementation offers a validation based on the query processing output of privacy-aware queries on the privacy infrastructure.

Keywords: Data privacy · Privacy model · Privacy infrastructure · Privacy-preserving databases · Blockchains

1 Introduction

Privacy-preservation in data repositories is a fundamental and necessary requirement in the processing of personalized, private data across varied data management areas. The concept of preserving privacy in data stores outlines methodologies and implementations that help protect data provider's private and sensitive data; during data storage, management, and query processing (*i.e.*, access and disclosure) in the data stores. In practical terms, the discussion and applications of privacy concepts has significant influences in different domains, such

G. Wang et al. (Eds.): UbiSec 2023, CCIS 2034, pp. 380–400, 2024.
https://doi.org/10.1007/978-981-97-1274-8_25

as, legal frameworks, healthcare management, and government data platforms, amongst others. The emergence of multiple diverse data collection points across different application domains allow the processing of large data volumes on data providers. Most especially, associated transactions from collected data provider's private, sensitive data through Point-of-Contacts user interface platforms opens up important requirements for storage and management of these data.

Consider the application domain of a healthcare system where patient healthcare records are collected and maintained for healthcare service delivery. The primary source of data is from the patient and so we classify the patient as the data provider. Different forms of data are collected from the data providers. These collected data may be hypothetically categorized as less-sensitive, medium-sensitive, and highly-sensitive. The categorization of these collected data defines an efficient specification of privacy preferences for related data of the same sensitivity level. The varied data forms enable efficient methods for storage, management, and disclosure of related patient private, sensitive data items. The healthcare system presents different categories of data collectors or service providers (*i.e.*, clinicians, lab analysts, *etc.*) who collect disparate data items at separate stages of healthcare delivery. Moreover, we identify data accessors who are designated as individuals (or groups) that request data access and process the collected data. In some instances, data collectors become data accessors due to their work needs and responsibilities.

Processing massive data volumes demands enhanced operational efficiency, performance, and optimal service delivery for both data and service providers (and third-party data accessors). Within the healthcare domain, where private data management is vital, issues of information security and trust between parties involved in service delivery must be adequately addressed. This motivates the need to secure data access and authenticate users on data management systems. Hence, demand for efficient data privacy merits better privacy-preservation policies and methodologies to address service delivery on these data processing platforms.

Previous privacy-preservation methodologies address privacy for data permanently stored in repositories – sometimes called "data-at-rest". Data provider privacy preferences are rarely considered and addressed (especially, as the data moves to another data repository or third-party data accessor) [1]. Two main problems arise. First, with the persistence of these static data in data repositories, data providers or data collectors infrequently or minimally respond to or are alerted to changes in data provider privacy preferences. Second, inability of data providers to flexibly update or change their existing privacy preferences when desired, or when data usage changes.

This paper addresses a blockchain-based privacy-preservation platform for data storage and query processing for data provider's private, sensitive data. The technical contribution involves an approach that offers control on the usage of private, sensitive data by data providers, data collectors, and/or permitted third-party data accessors. The novel concept adopts a formal contextualized privacy ontology; which is foundational to the methodology. Additionally, the approach adopts to tightly couple and encapsulate attribute data, data provider privacy preferences, and data accessor's profile. This is implemented using object-oriented methods. The technological framework of the approach involves coupling both data platforms of blockchains and relational database. The paper is organized as follows: in Sect. 2, we discuss background studies regarding data privacy models, privacy ontologies, blockchains and relational databases. Section 3 discusses key contributions and methodology overview for a privacy model framework. Section 4 discusses the implementation of the proposed research methodology, and Sect. 5 discusses the evaluation and analysis of the results from the implementation procedures performed. Section 6 summarizes our contributions and discusses open issues and future work.

2   Background Research

Privacy preservation approaches provide useful outcomes and/or results in policies, techniques, algorithms, and useful knowledge in securing data provider's private data in data repositories. Several data privacy-preservation approaches have been addressed and proposed by researchers in the data privacy domain. The development of privacy-preserving anonymization methods prevents disclosure of private, sensitive information of persons in published data. One early study on privacy-preserving anonymization methods is provided by Sweeney's *k-anonymity* [2]. There has been a succession of other approaches that seek to address the weaknesses in earlier methods. These models and methodologies are presented in different anonymization techniques (such as, generalization and suppression [2,3], randomization/data perturbation [4], and data swapping [5]).

Privacy ontologies form the structure and model for most contextbased privacy policy formulation. Ontologies formalize diverse preferences, unique attributes, and distinct rules for managing, processing, and modelling privacy policies. Several research efforts have investigated ontologies, and these studies define and describe how ontologies are used in modelling real-world scenarios and application domains. Bawany and Shaikh [6] model a data privacy ontology for various ubiquitous computing platforms. Their research work defines ontology semantic constructs (of *data*, *producer*, and *consumer*) and predicates for privacy preservation of data throughout its life cycle.

The research paradigm of *contextual integrity* (formalized by Nissenbaum *et al.* [7,8]), focus on context-specific viewpoints, such as, *role, temporal norms, value,* and *transmission principle,* among others; to ensure integrity of information flow. These viewpoints provide further insights and perspectives to modelling of privacy ontologies and frameworks. The proposition by Nissenbaum seek to outline different context-based privacy norms adopted in virtual communities and data processing paradigms. Subsequently, Jafari *et al.* [9] investigate purpose-based privacy policies and modelling to formulate workflow models which are used as frameworks for privacy policies. Their studies address different insights and motivations behind *purposes* for application domains.

The study of better privacy-preserving polices, and privacy-aware database models have garnered interest in the research community since the seminal work on *Hippocratic databases* [10]. Agrawal *et al.* [10] outline and address several principles for protecting data stored in database management systems. Moreover, the authors propose an architectural design framework (in terms of privacy metadata schema, privacy policy schema, privacy authorization schema, *etc.*). Further studies by Barker *et al.* [11] seek to outline a privacy taxonomy for the collection, sharing, and disclosure of private data stored in repositories. The authors develop a privacy taxonomy to define parameters for a privacy policy while protecting the data provider's personalized information. Barker's [12] conceptual approach to privacy protection addresses the need to identify trade-off between maximizing data utility and optimum privacy in data repositories. His study proposes a conceptual approach where data provider consents to privacy policies or changes in existing policies with the service provider.

Blockchains offer secured, tamper-resistant, and immutable framework for data processing. These platforms provide a better "database" framework for processing private, sensitive data provider's data. A number of studies have investigated a background framework and design of blockchains data platform. These studies outline unique benefits of offering data verifiability, identity, immutability, encryption, and decentralization [13]. Notable research combining the merits of both blockchains and big data database platforms is addressed by McConaghy *et al.* [14]. In their studies, the authors simulate coupling distributed, decentralized blockchains and big data database systems.

Prominent research works by Daidone *et al.* [15], Fernandez *et al.* [16], and Griggs *et al.* [17] present important methodologies and outcomes with regard to the adoption of blockchains to facilitate preservation of data provider's private data. Daidone *et al.* [15] propose a blockchain-based privacy enforcement architecture where users can define how their data are collected and managed; and ascertain how these data are used without relying on a centralized manager. Their methodology adopts a blockchain to perform privacy preferences' compliance checks in a decentralized fashion on IoT devices; whiles ensuring the correctness of the process through smart contracts. Fernandez *et al.* [16] propose a cloud-IoT architecture, called *Data Bank*, that aims at protecting users' sensitive data by allowing them to control which kind of data is transmitted by their devices. Their architecture consists of several layers of IoT objects, web and mobile applications, and a cloud layer for enforcement and access control. Griggs *et al.* [17] propose a healthcare blockchain system for secure automated remote patient monitoring. In their approach, the research outlines using blockchain-based smart contracts to facilitate secure management of medical sensors.

Previous research has found some methods of protecting data provider's private and sensitive information. However, a better blockchain-based approach to efficiently manage and control data access, availability, and usage of data provider's private, sensitive data stored in relational databases is still a problem. This is because of: (1) the absence of an expressive privacy model and/or ontology model, (2) lack of an adaptable privacy infrastructure and architectural platform, (3) lack of adoption of an expressive and robust private blockchain platform, and (4) minimal degree of data protection provided by data collectors (*i.e.*, service providers). Moreover, the ability to ensure data integrity and data monitoring to changes to data provider's privacy preferences for data use by data collectors/accessors (and consenting third-party accessors) continue to remain a challenge. A formulated methodology in which there is tight-coupling of private, sensitive data, with contextualized data provider privacy preferences, and data accessors' profile has not been addressed yet. Furthermore, a technology that couples blockchains and relational database management system is yet to be devised. This coupling approach will enable the storage of data provider's privacy preferences on their private, sensitive information in a completely tamper-resistant, immutable, and untrusted platform.

3   Proposed Privacy Model and Infrastructure

We describe and discuss details of our proposed privacy model and infrastructure. The model offers an effective integration of system components to provide a platform where data provider's information and transaction data are collected, processed, and managed by data collectors and/or accessors.

3.1   Methodology Overview

The detailed outline of the methodology is as follows: (1) formulation of a formal contextualized and usable privacy ontology; (2) tight-coupling of data elements (attribute data, data accessor profile, and privacy preferences); (3) tight-coupling of decentralized blockchains and a relational database; (4) query processing required for proposed methodology; and (5) encryption approaches on system architecture of (blockchains and relational database). Each of these system components and methodologies work together to provide privacy-preservation in a privacy-aware data platform.

The overall procedure for the methodology involves the following steps: data elements collection, binding data elements into a privacy tuple, applying a hash function to the privacy tuple, storing the hashed privacy tuple on the blockchains, storing data provider data and transactional data in the relational database, and executing queries against privacy-aware stored data with reference to privacy tuples. First, privacy-related personal data values are collected from the data provider through Point-of-Contact user interfaces. Devices designated as Point-of-Contact interfaces for data collection are portable mobile devices and personal computing platforms. The privacy-related data values may come from biographical, demographic, financial, and healthcare information data. Additionally, other application domain transaction data are collected.

The data provider agrees to the privacy policy preferences needed to access data utility services by the data collector (or service provider). Once the data elements are collected, attribute meta-data (from the private, sensitive data) is extracted and bound together with data provider's privacy preferences data (from the privacy policy) and data accessor profiling data, to form a *privacy tuple*. The privacy tuple is hashed, saved, and permanently stored on the

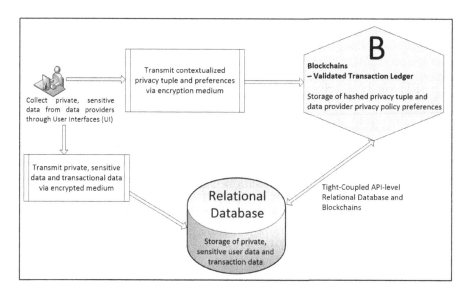

Fig. 1. System Methodology Overview and Architecture

blockchain platform, while the collected data provider private data and transactional data are stored in the relational database. The transmission of hashed privacy tuples and raw data provider private data to the blockchain platform and relational database, respectively, are facilitated through encrypted data communication channels that exist between the system components: relational database, blockchain platform, and user interfaces.

During query processing, hashed privacy tuples are retrieved from the blockchains. These hashed privacy tuples are verified against the privacy tuples stored in the relational database (to check for data integrity). In cases where there is data inconsistency in the verification process of the hashed privacy tuples from the blockchains to the privacy tuples retrieved from the relational database, the query is aborted or otherwise the overall query retrieval process is allowed to proceed. Based on the data value composition in the privacy tuples, all privacy preferences (which are outlined in the privacy policy and) related to the attribute data to be queried are enforced. The query parsing process is subsequently allowed, and the required privacy-aware data records are then retrieved and provided to the requesting data accessor. Figure 1 provides a general overview of the methodology.

3.2   Formal Contextualized Privacy Ontology

The overall methodology approach formulates a contextualized privacy ontology with unique semantics and properties for privacy preservation. This privacy ontology serves as a basis to formalize the privacy model for data processing. Moreover, the formal contextualized privacy ontology becomes the foundation for the design of all entities and predicates in the data privacy-preservation process. This is necessary as the privacy ontology offers a modelling framework for procedural activities and semantics for private, sensitive data and querying processing by data collectors and third-party data accessors.

In the formulated privacy ontology, entity classes, sub-classes, their respective attributes, and associated properties are classified to handle prevalent privacy-related scenarios in privacy-preserving data management. One important aspect that must be considered in a formal contextualized privacy ontology is the need to address semantics in the ontology. To this end, the formulated privacy ontology model details and defines language structure, semantic knowledge, and formalisms of the entities. These modelling semantics handle privacy and data protection authorizations of related *contextual privacy norms* and *perspectives* (of *when*, *who*, *why*, *where*, and *how*). Moreover, the formal contextualized privacy ontology addresses sensitive data provider data usage and authorizations.

In the formulated privacy ontology, we designate the primary (*root*) entity item as the *AttributeDataValue*. This is because each attribute data has unique privacy policy for data storage and retrieval. The *AttributeDataValue* entity has three sub-entity classes; namely, *DataProvider*, *DataCollector*, and *DataPrivacyPolicy*. Figure 2 illustrates a summarized description of the formal contextualized ontology. The *DataProvider* sub-entity describes all information regarding the data provider, (for example, patient requesting healthcare service). This sub-entity has a predicate class, *DataProviderType*, which details data on the various forms of persons who serve as the primary source of data. The instantiated values (within healthcare application domain) for this predicate class are *Patient* and *PatientLegalRepresentative*; where *Patient* identifies with the patient who requests for medical service and offers the necessary data for service delivery. The *PatientLegalRepresentative* is a legal representative for the patient, in cases where the patient is a minor or does not have the capacity to offer requested data. This individual may be a parent, family representative, or a close friend.

The *DataCollector* sub-entity describes the individuals who collect and store data on data subjects (*i.e.*, data providers). This sub-entity also has a predicate class as *DataCollectorType*, which has instantiated values as *ClinicalNurse*, *LaboratoryAnalyst*, and *ClinicalPhysician* in a healthcare system.

The *DataPrivacyPolicy* sub-entity is the most expressive sub-class of the *AttributeDataValue* class. It describes all aspects of the privacy policy on each attribute data value; which has been fully authorized by the data provider and validated by the data collector. We model this entity class based on prior research work of Barker *et al.* [11] on privacy taxonomy for data privacy policies. The *DataPrivacyPolicy* class incorporates other sub-classes which are called, *PurposeUsePrivacyPolicy* (data use), *VisibilityPrivacyPolicy* (data accessibility), *GranularityPrivacyPolicy* (data precision), and *RetentionPrivacyPolicy*, amongst others. Each of these entities describe different aspects of the privacy policy and offer unique modelling semantics for preserving data provider's private and sensitive data.

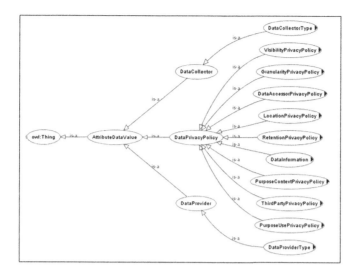

Fig. 2. Formal Contextualized Privacy Ontology Model

3.3   Tight-Coupling of Data Elements

The data coupling component of the overall approach combines three data elements (namely, attribute meta-data, data provider privacy preferences data, and data accessor data) into a privacy tuple to be stored in the blockchains. In this approach, we bind all data provider's data elements for data privacy-preservation. This binding enables data retrieval or query processing on the attribute data to be dependent on the privacy preferences and data accessor profiles specified in the privacy policy and agreed upon by the service provider.

The *attribute data (d_i)* identifies each data provider private, sensitive attribute data collected from or provided by the data provider; as part of service account creation, personal biographical, demographic, and healthcare information, or data transactions performed by the data provider. Forms of attribute data collected are *birth date, phone number*, and *home address*, amongst others. In terms of the data provider privacy preferences, forms of data values collected are *purpose, granularity (data precision), visibility (data accessibility), retention duration, effective date, third-party data accessor*, and *purpose contextual norms* (of *when, who, why, where*, and *how*).

It will be noted that these contextual privacy preferences are outlined based on the formal contextualized privacy ontology, which models and defines the overall contextualized data provider's privacy. A data provider *privacy preferences data (p_i)* is generated based on the data values extracted from the data provider's privacy preferences in the privacy policy.

Access to the underlying data values stored in the relational database is controlled and granted to data accessors with assigned access privileges. The assignment involves setting up different access levels, in accordance with the privacy policy statements. The determination of the data accessor profiling is based on factors and semantics, such as, *user role, data permission level*, and *data sensitivity level*, amongst others. A *data accessor profile data (u_i)* is generated to uniquely identify and grant access to which types of attribute data the data accessors can query or retrieve information.

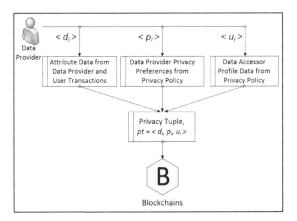

Fig. 3. Tight-coupling of Data Elements into Privacy Tuple

The three data elements (*i.e.*, attribute data, data provider's privacy preference data, and data accessor data) are bound together to constitute the *privacy tuple*, $pt = <d_i, p_i, u_i>$. Hence, this privacy tuple is always preserved and respected whenever an attribute data value is to be retrieved from the relational database repository. The descriptive illustration of the tight-coupling of data elements is illustrated in Fig. 3.

3.4   Tight-Coupling of Relational Database and Blockchains

The data storage mechanism is based on the principle of coupling different database platforms: namely, relational database and blockchain platform. The reason for this approach is to maximize the merits of managing and processing transaction data from each of the data platforms. The relational database offers a scalable, high throughput, and efficient querying engine to meet expected high data processing needs.

Conversely, the blockchain platform offers decentralized data control that is tamper-resistant and immutable for the protection of privacy-related data values. Additionally, the decentralized control of the blockchains offers efficient change request and approval (from service providers and data providers). The blockchains offers a platform that can be used to facilitate privacy audit procedures for data provider privacy preferences.

One key advantage for the incorporation of the blockchains in the privacy model is the ability to provide a platform for all data accessors (data and service providers) to agree on the state and value of data stored. Additionally, the blockchain platform provides an infrastructure platform to effect efficient changes

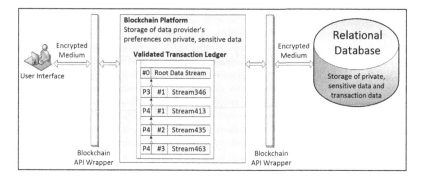

Fig. 4. Architecture of Tight-Coupling of Relational Database and Blockchains

to privacy-related data values. The tight-coupling approach also enables either input of data provider and service provider in the agreement of the parameters for privacy policies; thereby ensuring access consistency for all data accessors in a reliable data provider privacy and identity management.

The high-level methodology is, as follows: the entire set of data values (on data provider personalized information and transaction data) are collected and stored in the relational database. Moreover, an instance of the integrated privacy tuple data is stored in the relational database. On the blockchains, another instance of the tightly-coupled privacy tuple and privacy preferences (which is subsequently hashed) are stored. Figure 4 illustrates the proposed architecture of the relational database and blockchain. With this data platform integration, every data retrieval request from the relation database is authenticated and authorized from the blockchain platform (through its related transaction ledger). This establishes the tight-coupling approach of the integrated data platform, and no other data retrieval (on the relational database) is performed independent of the blockchain. Furthermore, any form of data transfer (query requests and results) between the data repositories is completed in a secured, tamper-resistant access-controlled protocol.

3.5   Query Processing on Proposed Methodology

The proposed methodology takes query requests to the relational database by first mediating them to the blockchains platform before delivering query results. We describe this procedure as privacy-aware; as the query data elements and the expected query data results or tuples are accessed and verified through the privacy preferences of the data provider. The query request is first transmitted to the privacy-aware query analyser. The privacy-aware query analyser parses the query, identifies and extracts attribute data (regarding the requested query) that needs to be accessed for data retrieval. The privacy-aware query attribute data are then transmitted to the blockchains.

At the blockchains, the data provider's transaction ledger data stream needed for data retrieval is identified. The blockchain platform traverses through the

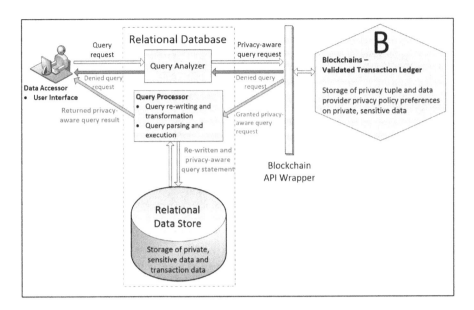

Fig. 5. Query Processing on Relational Database and Blockchains

transaction data stream to access the most recent privacy tuple transaction data item block. Transaction data item block corresponding to privacy tuple is subsequently accessed and retrieved. This data item contains recent data provider privacy policy preference's tuple (on attribute meta-data, contextualized privacy preferences data value, data accessor value, and other privacy preferences). The blockchain API delivers retrieved data items (in its hashed form) to the privacy-aware query processor.

At the query processor, the privacy-aware query is rewritten and transformed. Data items consisting of privacy policy preferences are verified against the retrieved hashed data values from the blockchain. In cases where there is data inconsistency between both data item values, the query is denied and aborted. By data inconsistency, we identify that the hashed data values stored in the blockchain is different from data values retrieved from the relational database. Upon valid consistency check on data item values, the query processor grants access for query processing and data retrieval. The privacy preferences on each data attribute are used to rewrite or transform the privacy-aware query to conform to the current context based on data provider preferences in the privacy policy. The privacy-aware query processor uses the privacy-aware rewritten query statement to generate expected query result or data instance tuples. Consequently, data instance tuples regarding the attribute data are retrieved and presented to the data accessor through user interfaces.

In summary, the blockchain platform acts as a privacy-aware data access control and query analysing medium to the underlying relational database. Hence, whenever a data accessor wants to query or retrieve data values in the underlying relational database, access is routed to the blockchains before privacy-aware data values stored in the relational database are retrieved and presented to the data accessor. Figure 5 illustrates the implementation of the query processing architecture for accessing data provider private, sensitive data from the relational database repository.

4   Research Implementation

We implement the research methodology by modelling, designing and developing different system components. These are privacy ontology, user interfaces, relational database, and blockchains platform.

4.1   Privacy Ontology Formulation and System Modelling

In terms of the formal contextualized privacy ontology, we model and design several entities, sub-classes and their predicate classes. Each entity contributes to the overall modelling of the privacy policy regarding a particular data attribute or category of attribute data. We implement privacy ontology modelling using Protégé Semantic Web Ontology [18] application tool.

We modelled and designed the user interfaces using Unified Modelling Language (UML) use case diagrams. Use case diagrams show interactions between the system and its environment. We developed and programmed the user interfaces using PHP (PHP: Hypertext Preprocessor) web development tool.

4.2   Relational Database Design

We adopt MySQL DBMS as the relational database. The database platform provides functionality for data storage, management, query processing, and native data objects, such as, tables, indexes, and stored procedures. Additionally, the platform provides data processing on data provider biographical and demographic information and other entities.

Three different databases are created in the relational database integration. These are *user_admin, tunote_ppdb,* and *tunote_data_provider*. The *user_admin* database serves to process and store data on system user login details and access privileges. This database contains 2 relational tables. The second database, *tunote_ppdb*, processes and stores data on data provider privacy policy preferences, such as, *attribute category data, data accessor profiles,* and *granularity privacy,* amongst others. The database contains 16 relational tables. The third database, *tunote_data_provider*, processes and stores content data relating to data provider information, physician information, healthcare requisition details, and medical consent details. The database contains 9 relational tables, such as, *data_provider, privacy_consent,* amongst others. The query processing functionality (which involves the query analyzer, processor, and execution) of the system is implemented using a stored procedure database object. The stored procedure acts as a privacy-aware API over the database to process and execute queries. The stored procedure accepts parameters in the form of data provider privacy preferences object identifier values. The output from the stored procedure is a set of privacy-aware data tuples based on the input parameters.

4.3 Blockchains Design, Data Communication, and Encryption

We adopt a blockchain platform to offer authentication and authorize query processing on data provider private and transaction data, respectively. We employ MultiChain blockchain platform [19]; which is a robust platform for private blockchain development. MultiChain blockchain is an open-source,"off-the-shelf" platform for creation and deployment of private blockchains, either within or between organizations. We created a *chain* transaction ledger and a number of data streams. Data streams are append-only, on-chain lists of data - where the *key-value* retrieval capability makes store and query functionality extremely easy. For each data stream, we create validated transaction data block (associated to a privacy tuple). A transaction data block is appended to first data stream or any other related data stream (in the list of data streams created on the chain). Thus, the privacy tuples stored as transaction blocks become valid data and are always accessed during query processing. Storing data on the blockchain involves the process of *publishing* data.

Data communication between the blockchains and/or relational database and user interfaces is facilitated using an API wrapper. The blockchain API wrapper is implemented in PHP programming platform. Data communication between system components are facilitated using encrypted channels. The adopted encryption algorithm provide *confidentiality* of the data message's contents, *verifies* the data message's origin, and provides proof that a data message's contents have not changed since it was sent (*i.e.*, *integrity*). Hence, the encrypted communication medium sufficiently reduces (or best case prevents) any form of attack, data loss, or data leakage as data moves between the system components [20].

5 Evaluation and Results Analysis

We evaluate and analyse the output from the proposed privacy infrastructure based on the propositions discussed in Sect. 3 and implementation procedures discussed in Sect. 4.

5.1 Privacy Infrastructure Security Assessment

We discuss the privacy infrastructure systems security overview in terms of the defences it offers for data provider's private data and overall data processing for data accessors. We discuss these assessment based on the following: *confidentiality*, *integrity*, and *availability*.

We address *confidentiality* in which the privacy infrastructure protects private data from unauthorized access using defined data provider privacy policy preferences saved on the blockchain platform. Moreover, the composition of the privacy tuple authorizes data access to each defined accessor based on privacy preferences. In terms of *integrity*, our proposed methodology offers a framework where private, sensitive data and the preferences defined on them are protected from deletion or modification from unauthorized individuals. Our assessment ensures that changes to privacy preferences stored in the blockchain platform is completed in "consensus" or agreement by both data provider and data collector.

We address security assurance of *availability* based on the tight-coupling of data storage and processing platforms. The architecture and configuration of the blockchain nodes offer functional transaction ledgers and data streams that ensure controlled data throughput to the API and relational database. The relational database is configured with stable query analyzers and processors to parse and execute query statements; and to deliver data values to data accessors.

5.2   Query Processing and Response Time Analysis

We analyze query processing rate on the privacy model system implementation to evaluate the effectiveness of running data queries. The data storage and query processing is done on a single computing machine with eight logical processor(s), 3.6 GHz processing speed, and 16 GB of RAM, and 900 GB of disk storage capacity. We identify three different types of queries(on data provider demographic data, healthcare data, and consent witness data), and discuss the results output from running these queries. Each query presents a unique set of attribute data elements, as well as different set of data provider privacy preferences. We run random independent queries for both privacy-aware and native queries for each query type.

5.3   Query 1: Data Provider Demographic Data

Suppose we want to retrieve data values on data provider demographic information. The attribute data elements from which the query transaction is performed, include: *Street Name, City, Province, Postal Code, Original Province,* and *Phone Number, etc.* The result of query processing rate for data provider demographic information is illustrated in Fig. 6. The privacy-aware queries and native queries are designated with blue and orange colouring, respectively.

Results Analysis and Discussion. In Fig. 6, we observe an increase in query processing time for the privacy-aware queries in comparison to native queries. This is expected because of the added activity of privacy-aware query parsing, processing, and execution which leads to an increase in query data retrieval load or query cost. From the query results, we realize the highest and lowest query processing time for native queries are 19.01 ms (milli seconds) and 11.52 ms (milli seconds), respectively. Moreover, an average query processing time of 13.37 ms is attained. In terms of privacy-aware query processing, we attain highest and

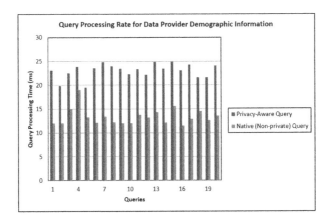

Fig. 6. Query Processing Rate for Data Provider Demographic Data

lowest query processing time of 24.86 ms and 19.48 ms, respectively. We also record an average privacy-aware query processing time of 22.99 ms.

We observe privacy overhead cost of 41.85% for privacy-aware query processing. This is indicative of the varied number of demographic attribute data and the instance data stored on these attribute data. More importantly, we analyze the privacy preference parameters of data information privacy with instance data representation of: *'Level-4: Restricted'*, granularity privacy with instance data representation of: *'Specific: Specific data item is accessed. A query for data item returns actual data value'*, visibility privacy with instance data representation of: *'Third-Party Allied Health Access: Data accessible to parties not covered by explicit agreement with House'*, and purpose privacy with instance data representation of: *'Reuse-Same: Data used for same purpose and multiple times'*. This analysis by the privacy-aware query analyzer increases the query overhead cost for the overall query processing. Based on the query response times attained from both privacy-aware and native query processing, we determine that query processing on the proposed privacy model architecture is efficient, and there is safe, cost-effective data retrieval on the overall architecture.

5.4 Query 2: Data Provider Healthcare Data

Suppose we want to retrieve data values on data provider healthcare information. The attribute data elements from which the query transaction is performed, include: *Personal Health Number, Medical Record Number, Chart Number, Personal Care Physician Name*, and *Dentist Physician Name, etc.* The result of query processing rate for data provider healthcare information is displayed in Fig. 7. The privacy-aware queries and native queries are designated with blue and orange colouring, respectively.

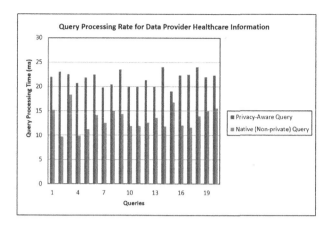

Fig. 7. Query Processing Rate for Data Provider Healthcare Data

Results Analysis and Discussion. Similar to *Query 1*, *Query 2* also shows an increase in the query processing time for the privacy-aware queries in comparison to the native queries. In terms of native (non-private) query processing, we attain highest and lowest query processing time of 18.38 ms and 9.74 ms, respectively. We also record an average query processing time of 13.38 ms. Regarding privacy-aware query processing, we note that the highest and lowest query processing time are 23.97 ms and 19.03 ms, respectively. Moreover, an average privacy-aware query processing time of 21.67 ms is attained.

In terms of privacy overhead query cost, we observe 38.26% for privacy-aware query processing in relation to native (non-private) query processing. It will be noted that data provider healthcare information processed here involve unique set of privacy-aware attribute data, which are not many in comparison to demographic data in *Query 1*. Moreover, the privacy overhead query cost is attributed to data provider privacy preference parameters of data information privacy with instance data representation of: *'Level-3: Confidential'*, granularity privacy with instance data representation of: *'Partial: Partial or altered and non-destructive data values returned to accessor'*, visibility privacy with instance representation value of: *'Third-Party Allied Health Access: Data accessible to parties not covered by explicit agreement with House'*, and purpose privacy with instance data representation of: *'Reuse-Selected: Data used for primary purpose for which data'*. Finally, we note that query response times attained from both privacy-aware and native query processing determine that proposed privacy model architecture offers an efficient platform for processing data provider private information.

5.5   Query 3: Data Provider Consent Witness Data

Suppose we want to retrieve data values on data provider health information. The attribute data elements from which the query transaction is performed, include: *Witness Last Name, Witness First Name, Witness Phone Number, Witness Street, Witness City, Witness Province,* and *Witness Postal Code, etc.* The result of query processing rate for data provider consent witness information is displayed in Fig. 8. The privacy-aware queries and native queries are designated with blue and orange colouring, respectively.

Results Analysis and Discussion. We observe that query processing rate is in the same range of query response time as the preceding queries. Similar to preceding queries (*i.e., Query 1* and *Query 2*), there is an increase in query processing time on privacy-aware queries in comparison to native (non-private) queries. From the query results, we note that the highest and lowest query processing time for native queries are 12.57 ms (milli seconds) and 9.15 ms (milli seconds), respectively. Moreover, an average query processing time of 10.28 ms is attained. In terms of privacy-aware query processing, we attain the highest and lowest query processing time of 21.85 ms and 16.71 ms, respectively. We also record an average query processing time of 18.24 ms.

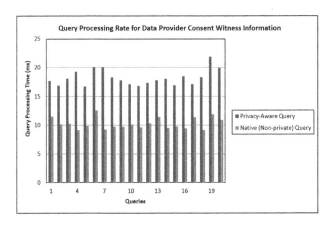

Fig. 8. Query Processing Rate for Data Provider Consent Witness Data

We observe privacy overhead cost of 43.65% for privacy-aware query processing. This is attributed to data retrieval that involves greater number of attribute data elements in comparison to queries *Query 1* and *Query 2*. Moreover, the privacy-aware query parsing and analyzes involving these attribute data contribute to the increase in privacy query overhead cost. An analysis on the data provider privacy preferences indicate parameters of data information privacy with instance data representation of: *'Level-2: Internal Use'*, granularity privacy with instance data representation of: *'Existential: Information released to indicate the existence of data in repository, not actual data values'*, visibility privacy with instance data representation of: *'House: Data accessible to everyone who collects, access, and utilize the data'*, and purpose privacy with instance data representation of: *'Reuse-Selected: Data used for primary purpose for which data'*. We determine that based on the query response times attained from both privacy-aware and native query processing, the proposed privacy model offers an efficient platform for data provider privacy-aware query processing.

5.6 Average Query Processing and Privacy Overhead Cost Analysis

We compute average query processing rate for all three queries and analyse the query response time for each query form. We note that there is a considerable increase in the query response time for privacy-aware queries in relation to native queries. This is mainly attributed to privacy overhead cost from privacy-aware query parsing, analyzes, and execution.

Table 1. Summary of Average Query Response Time and Privacy Overhead Cost

Queries	Average Query Response Time (ms)		
	Native (Non-private) Query	Privacy-Aware Query	Privacy Overhead Cost
Query 1: Data Provider Demographic Data	13.37	22.99	9.62 (41.85%)
Query 2: Data Provider Healthcare Data	13.38	21.67	8.29 (38.26%)
Query 3: Data Provider Consent Witness Data	10.28	18.24	7.96 (43.65%)
All Queries	12.34	20.96	8.62 (41.25%)

Table 1 illustrates the average query response time and their respective privacy overhead cost. Here, we note that queries, *Query 1* (Data Provider Demographic Data), *Query 2* (Data Provider Health Data), and *Query 3* (Data Provider Consent Witness Data) deliver privacy overhead query response time of 9.62 ms, 8.29 ms, and 7.96 ms, respectively. Moreover, an average privacy overhead cost of 8.62 ms (milli seconds) is realized for all queries processed. These privacy overhead query response times translate into 41.85%, 38.26%, and 43.65% for queries: *Query 1*, *Query 2*, and *Query 3*, respectively. We note an average of 41.25% privacy overhead query cost for all queries processed. We illustrate the average query processing time and privacy overhead cost for all queries in Fig. 9.

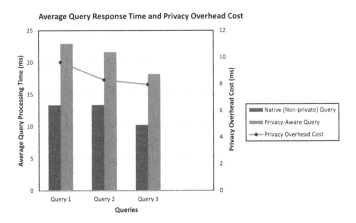

Fig. 9. Average Query Processing Time and Privacy Overhead Cost

In general, we note that the average privacy overhead query cost is relatively very low. This indicates an effective privacy-aware query processing platform from the privacy model and infrastructure; and infers an optimum run of privacy-aware queries in comparison to native queries. A review of attained privacy overhead query cost indicates that the proposed privacy model and infrastructure, and resultant privacy overhead query cost does not excessively or negatively impact on overall query transaction processing. Hence, we establish that the proposed privacy model offers an efficient, reliable, and robust framework for privacy-aware query processing on data provider private and transaction data stored in the blockchains and relational database, respectively.

6   Conclusion

This paper presents a blockchain-based privacy-preservation platform for data storage and query processing. The research addresses the need for a practical approach to protect data provider's private and sensitive data using immutable, tamper-resistant data platforms.

The adopted privacy model offers an effective integration of data repository components to provide a data platform where data provider's private data and transaction data are proficiently collected, processed, and managed by data collectors. The overall approach formulates a contextualized privacy ontology with unique semantics and properties for privacy preservation. We implement tight-coupling of three data elements (namely, attribute meta-data, data provider privacy preferences data, and data accessor data) into a *privacy tuple*; to be stored in the blockchains. Moreover, we implement tight-coupling of relational database and blockchains platforms. The key reason for this approach is to maximize the merits from all data management platforms. We discuss that the adopted

methodology approach and evaluation results attained validate a better approach for managing data provider's private, sensitive data in comparison to other
approaches. Our evaluation and result analysis establishes a robust implementation of privacy model and infrastructure. The privacy model offers a secured,
immutable, and efficient privacy-aware query processing platform.

We envision some areas of open issues and future work. In terms of some
open issues, we address the choice of private blockchain adopted for the privacy
model architecture. It must be noted that different (private) blockchain platforms
characterises distinct and peculiar functionalities for data storage and retrieval.
Regarding future work, we anticipate the execution of complex relational *join*
queries on data provider data. Relational *join* queries will improve the overall
query processing experience on the tightly-coupled data repository platforms.

References

1. Zakerzadeh H., Aggarwal, C.C., Barker, K.: Privacy-preserving big data publishing.
   In: Proceedings of the 27th International Conference on Scientific and Statistical
   Database Management (SSDBM 2015), La Jolla, CA, USA, pp. 1–11 (2015)
2. Sweeney, L.: k-anonymity: a model for protecting privacy. Internat. J. Uncertain.
   Fuzziness Knowl.-Based Syst. **10**(5), 557–570 (2002)
3. Machanavajjhala, A., Gehrke, J., Kifer, D., Venkitasubramaniam, M.: l-diversity:
   privacy beyond k-anonymity. In: 22nd International Conference on Data Engineering, Atlanta, Georgia, USA, p. 24 (2006)
4. Dwork, C.: Differential privacy. In: Bugliesi, M., Preneel, B., Sassone, V., Wegener,
   I. (eds.) ICALP 2006. LNCS, vol. 4052, pp. 1–12. Springer, Heidelberg (2006).
   https://doi.org/10.1007/11787006_1
5. Fienberg, S.E., McIntyre, J.: Data swapping: variations on a theme by Dalenius
   and Reiss. In: Domingo-Ferrer, J., Torra, V. (eds.) PSD 2004. LNCS, vol. 3050,
   pp. 14–29. Springer, Heidelberg (2004). https://doi.org/10.1007/978-3-540-25955-
   8_2
6. Bawany, N. Z., Shaikh, Z. A.: Data privacy ontology for ubiquitous computing.
   Int. J. Adv. Comput. Sci. Appl. **8**(1) (2017)
7. Barth, A., Datta, A., Mitchell, J.C., Nissenbaum, H.: Privacy and contextual
   integrity: framework and applications. In: IEEE Symposium on Security and Privacy (S&P 2006), pp. 184–198, Berkeley, California, USA (2006)
8. Nissenbaum, H.: Privacy in Context - Technology, Policy, and the Integrity of Social
   Life, pp. 1–288, I–XIV. Stanford University Press (2010). ISBN 978-0-8047-5237-4
9. Jafari, M., Safavi-Naini, R., Fong, P.W.L., Barker, K.: A framework for expressing
   and enforcing purpose-based privacy policies. ACM Trans. Inf. Syst. Secur. **17**(1),
   1–31 (2014)
10. Agrawal, R., Kiernan, J., Srikant, R., Xu, Y.: Hippocratic databases. In: 28th
    International Conference on Very Large Data Bases (VLDB 2002), pp. 143–154,
    Hong Kong, China (2002)
11. Barker, K., et al.: A data privacy taxonomy. In: Sexton, A.P. (ed.) BNCOD 2009.
    LNCS, vol. 5588, pp. 42–54. Springer, Heidelberg (2009). https://doi.org/10.1007/
    978-3-642-02843-4_7
12. Barker, K.: Privacy protection or data value: can we have both? In: Kumar, N.,
    Bhatnagar, V. (eds.) BDA 2015. LNCS, vol. 9498, pp. 3–20. Springer, Cham (2015).
    https://doi.org/10.1007/978-3-319-27057-9_1

13. Baskaran, H., Yussof, S., Rahim, F.A.: A survey on privacy concerns in blockchain applications and current blockchain solutions to preserve data privacy. In: Anbar, M., Abdullah, N., Manickam, S. (eds.) ACeS 2019. CCIS, vol. 1132, pp. 3–17. Springer, Singapore (2020). https://doi.org/10.1007/978-981-15-2693-0_1
14. McConaghy, T., et al.: BigchainDB: a scalable blockchain database. White paper. ascribe GmbH, Berlin, Germany (2016)
15. Daidone, F., Carminati, B., Ferrari, E.: Blockchain-based privacy enforcement in the IoT domain. IEEE Trans. Dependable Secure Comput. **19**(6), 1–1 (2022)
16. Fernandez, M., Jaimunk, J., Thuraisingham, B.: Privacy-preserving architecture for cloud-IoT platforms. In: IEEE International Conference on Web Services (ICWS 2019), Milan, Italy, pp. 11–19 (2019)
17. Griggs, K.N., Ossipova, O., Kohlios, C.P., Baccarini, A.N., Howson, E.A., Hayajneh, T.: Healthcare blockchain system using smart contracts for secure automated remote patient monitoring. J. Med. Syst. **42**(7), 130 (2018)
18. Stanford Center for Biomedical Informatics Research. Protégé Semantic Web Ontology. https://protege.stanford.edu. Accessed 26 Sept 2023
19. MultiChain Blockchain Platform. https://www.multichain.com. Accessed 26 Sept 2023
20. Ghosh, S.S., Parmar, H., Shah, P., Samdani, K.: A comprehensive analysis between popular symmetric encryption algorithms. In: 1st International Conference on Data Science & Analytics (IEEE Punecon 2018), Pune, India, pp. 1–7 (2018)

Is It Really You Who Forgot the Password? When Account Recovery Meets Risk-Based Authentication

Andre Büttner[1]([envelope]) [iD], Andreas Thue Pedersen[1] [iD], Stephan Wiefling[2] [iD], Nils Gruschka[1] [iD], and Luigi Lo Iacono[3] [iD]

[1] University of Oslo, Oslo, Norway
{andrbut,nilsgrus}@ifi.uio.no
[2] swiefling.de, Sankt Augustin, Germany
ubisec23@swiefling.de
[3] H-BRS University of Applied Sciences, Sankt Augustin, Germany
luigi.lo_iacono@h-brs.de

Abstract. Risk-based authentication (RBA) is used in online services to protect user accounts from unauthorized takeover. RBA commonly uses contextual features that indicate a suspicious login attempt when the characteristic attributes of the login context deviate from known and thus expected values. Previous research on RBA and anomaly detection in authentication has mainly focused on the login process. However, recent attacks have revealed vulnerabilities in other parts of the authentication process, specifically in the account recovery function. Consequently, to ensure comprehensive authentication security, the use of anomaly detection in the context of account recovery must also be investigated.

This paper presents the first study to investigate risk-based account recovery (RBAR) in the wild. We analyzed the adoption of RBAR by five prominent online services (that are known to use RBA). Our findings confirm the use of RBAR at Google, LinkedIn, and Amazon. Furthermore, we provide insights into the different RBAR mechanisms of these services and explore the impact of multi-factor authentication on them. Based on our findings, we create a first maturity model for RBAR challenges. The goal of our work is to help developers, administrators, and policy-makers gain an initial understanding of RBAR and to encourage further research in this direction.

Keywords: Risk-Based Account Recovery · RBAR · Authentication · Account Security · Online Services

1 Introduction

Passwords are still the pre-dominant authentication method for online services, even for services that give access to confidential data or financial resources [14, 31]. However, attacks on password authentication can be automated—e.g., credential stuffing using leaked passwords—and therefore scaled with little effort.

G. Wang et al. (Eds.): UbiSec 2023, CCIS 2034, pp. 401–419, 2024.
https://doi.org/10.1007/978-981-97-1274-8_26

This makes account takeover attacks on password-protected online services very lucrative for hackers [3]. As a countermeasure, more and more services offer multi-factor authentication (MFA) as an extension to password authentication. In this case, the user has to give additional proof of their identity, e.g., by entering a code from a one-time password (OTP) app or a text message (SMS). However, the additional step makes the authentication process more cumbersome and increases the risk of account lockouts in case the additional token gets lost [30].

The idea of risk-based authentication (RBA) [12,14,38] is to balance security and usability. Here, the online service only requests additional authentication steps or blocks a client when it detects suspicious behavior. RBA does this by analyzing a set of feature values (e.g., location, browser, or login time) during the login process [14,38].

A general problem with authentication is that the user might lose access to the authentication method—in the case of password authentication, this means primarily forgetting the password. In such a case, the user has to pass the *account recovery* process to regain access to their account. The process often involves sending a password reset link or an OTP to a pre-configured email address or phone number. If the required authentication (e.g., ownership of a phone, login to the email account) is weaker than the primary authentication, account recovery puts the overall account security at risk [27,29].

A high and common threat to account recovery mechanisms via email is when an attacker gains access to the corresponding email account, e.g., via credential stuffing [2,33]. The recent FBI cybercrime report [11] shows that compromised email addresses and phishing attacks are very popular attacks with potentially high financial loss for the hacked victims. Therefore, it is very important for online services to secure account recovery, for example, with MFA or RBA. So far, risk-based mechanisms have mostly been studied in the context of login authentication. However, we observed that mechanisms similar to RBA are also used for account recovery.

We define *Risk-Based Account Recovery* (RBAR)[1] as a dynamic account recovery process on online services. It was indicated that such a method is used at a large online service [7], but beyond that, RBAR and its appearances in the wild have not been publicly investigated yet. This is, however, important as it has the potential to protect a large number of users from account recovery attacks immediately. To learn about the current use of RBAR, we address the following research questions in this paper:

RQ1: Do RBA-instrumented online services also use RBAR mechanisms?
RQ2: What RBAR challenges are used in practice?
RQ3: Are different RBAR challenges required when setting up MFA?

Contributions. This paper presents the first scientific insight into using RBAR in practice. We performed an exploratory analysis of RBAR behavior at Google

---

[1] To the best of our knowledge, there is no standard term for it yet.

and a systematic experiment on four other popular online services. We verified RBAR at three of the five services. The analysis also included the influence of MFA configurations and different (virtual) locations. The main contributions achieved from these activities are the following:

- Identification of RBAR at popular online services
- A maturity model for different RBAR mechanisms

The remainder of this paper is structured as follows. Section 2 provides an overview of related work. In Sect. 3, we describe details behind how RBAR works. Section 4 explains the methodology of our experiments. The findings of the two experiments are described in Sects. 5 and 6, respectively. Our overall results are discussed in Sect. 7. Section 8 summarizes our work and suggests possible future work.

2   Related Work

Most of the previous work on account recovery considered it a static mechanism. For instance, a lot of research focused on different additional authentication challenges for recovery that can be solved easily by legitimate users but not by potential attackers. Examples include cryptographic keys [9], delegated account recovery [20,22], dynamic security questions [1,19], and email address or phone number verification [26]. While these works do not address risk-based use cases, we argue that such methods would be beneficial in conjunction with a risk analysis of the user context.

Further research evaluated online services in the wild. Li et al. [23] studied the account recovery mechanisms of 239 popular online services in 2017 and 2019. They found that most of them implemented email address or mobile phone verification as a recovery mechanism. Amft et al. [6] conducted a large-scale study investigating which recovery methods are usually deployed in conjunction with MFA methods. They unveiled that website documentation usually does not correspond with the actual recovery procedure, showing the lack of transparency in account recovery. We confirm this as we analyzed the documentation of the services we tested for any references to RBAR, which in most cases were absent (see Sect. 7).

The only indication of risk-based recovery mechanisms we found in literature was mentioned by Bonneau et al. [7], where they noted that Google performed a *"risk analysis"* for account recovery. However, they did not further investigate how it works or what mechanisms are applied depending on the risk scenario.

Research on RBA is especially relevant for our work as it provides us with methods to analyze and develop risk-based systems. For example, Wiefling et al. [38] studied RBA re-authentication mechanisms on five popular online services. They found that most online services used email verification to re-authenticate users. Gavazzi et al. [14] leaned on this work to identify that more than 75% of the 208 studied online services do not use any form of RBA. While the research in this field only addresses plain user authentication, our work extends it by

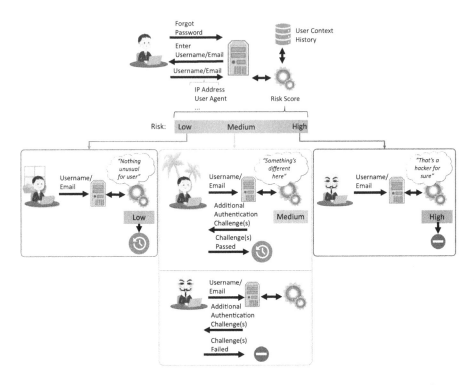

Fig. 1. Overview of the RBAR procedure (based on RBA illustration in [35])

showing that the methods used in RBA research can be equally applied in the context of account recovery. Consequently, we used the insights from prior work on RBA as a basis to study the use of RBAR on Google and other online services.

3   Risk-Based Account Recovery

Since there is no official description of RBAR yet, we describe its basic concept. Based on our observations on online services and previous knowledge in the related RBA field [36,38], RBAR works as follows (see Fig. 1):

A user typically starts an account recovery process, e.g., by clicking *"forgot password"* at the online service's login form. After that, the user is asked to enter the username or email used for the account to recover. While submitting this identifier, the user also submits additional feature data that is available in the current context to the online service, e.g., IP address or user agent string. Based on this information, RBAR compares these values with the user context history and calculates a risk score. The user context history contains feature values of past user actions, like previous legitimate logins that might have been validated by RBA mechanisms [37] before. The risk score is then classified into low, medium, and high risk. Based on the risk, the online service performs different actions.

At a *low* risk, the feature values likely belong to the legitimate user, and the online service proceeds with the account recovery process (e.g., verify email address). A *medium* risk occurs if the user's feature values deviate from the expected values. The online service then introduces additional authentication challenges that require more user effort (e.g., solving a CAPTCHA or answering questions related to the account). After successfully solving these challenges, the online service proceeds with the account recovery process. A *high* risk means that the online service suspects that the user is likely targeted by a hacking attempt. The online service might block the account recovery process in these cases. However, to avoid locking out legitimate users trying to recover their accounts, this possibility has to be carefully selected by the online service.

4 Methodology

We investigated the research questions by conducting two experiments. Prior research has indicated that Google applies risk-based decision-making for account recovery [7], making it a suitable candidate for our first experiment. Therefore, we conducted an exploratory experiment on Google. We created test cases with different account setups, i.e., different authentication and recovery factor combinations. These were then tested with different user features to see how these could affect the recovery procedure. The study considered two RBA features, as suggested in Wiefling et al. [38]: known/unknown browser and known/unknown IP address. A *known* browser is the one that was used before to sign in to Google, i.e., it has stored cookies from prior sessions. The *unknown* browser was tested using the browser's incognito mode to have a clean browser session without previously set cookies. The IP address feature was varied by using a VPN connection to be able to study the uncertain area of medium to high risk scores [38]. By comparing the recovery procedures of the different features for each test case, we identified the mechanisms used for RBAR. The test cases and the final results are given in Sect. 5.

For the second experiment, we developed an improved and more systematic approach. As the experiment required manual effort, we limited the number of tested services to the following services that are known to use RBA [14,38]:

- LinkedIn (linkedin.com)
- Amazon (amazon.com)
- GOG (gog.com)
- Dropbox (dropbox.com)

The experiment was composed of three phases. First, we prepared user accounts for each service. Afterward, we checked whether any of the online services indicated RBAR behavior. Finally, since LinkedIn clearly turned out to implement

RBAR, we analyzed if RBAR on LinkedIn is influenced by the MFA settings (as was the case with Google). More details on the steps and the results are presented in Sect. 6.

5   Experiment 1: RBAR Use by Google

In the first experiment, we investigated previous assumptions [7] on whether Google used RBAR and identified features that might have an influence on the RBAR behavior. We describe the experiment and its results in the following.

5.1   Preparation

The exploratory experiment on Google was conducted between October 2021 and March 2022. We set up four Google user accounts that were created at intervals of several weeks to mitigate being detected as a researcher. Based on the visible feedback from the online service, we assume that we remained under the respective detection thresholds. In order to test the use of RBAR on Google, we defined the test cases based on the authentication and recovery factors offered in the Google account settings. At the time of the study, Google provided the following factors:

– **Main authentication:** password, sign in by phone
– **Secondary authentication:** Google prompt, phone call or text message, backup codes, security key, authenticator app
– **Recovery factors:** email, phone

The experiment on Google covered every possible single-factor authentication (SFA) account setup and eight MFA account setups. Each account setup was tested with all four RBA feature combinations. For each combination, all possible recovery options were explored.

5.2   Results

The study found that Google used RBAR for both SFA and MFA account setups. This became clear as using an unknown browser and/or an unknown IP address increased the difficulty of recovering the account compared to using a known browser and IP address. This was indicated by requiring additional authentication factors, recovery options that were made unavailable, or an extra prompt like asking for the phone number of a registered phone.

Recovery Without MFA Enabled. Table 1 lists a few examples[2] of the tests from studying SFA account recovery that clearly show the different recovery procedures based on RBA features. One can observe that in cases where an unknown browser was used for recovery, Google initially asked for an old password that

---

[2] All results for the tests on Google are published on https://github.com/AndreasTP/GoogleAccountRecovery.

Table 1. Examples for Google account recovery without MFA enabled

Recovery factor	Phone signed in	Known browser	Known IP	Recovery procedure
None	○	●	●	Recovery not possible
None	●	●	●	1. Google prompt
None	●	○	○	1. Enter old password 2. Google prompt (two steps)
Email	○	●	●	1. Verify account email
Email	○	○	●	1. Enter old password 2. Verify account email

● = *Feature present,* ○ = *Feature not present*

the user could remember. This was not the case when using a known browser and a known IP address. The recovery procedure continued the same way, even if this step was skipped.

When a phone was signed in to the same Google account, this phone was prompted with a button showing *"Yes, it's me"*. Users had to click this button to confirm the ownership of the account. This behavior changed when trying to recover the account from an unknown browser and an unknown IP address. In this case, Google also showed a two-digit number on the recovery web page and presented a dialogue with three number options on the phone. Users then had to select the correct number on the phone to proceed with the recovery.

Recovery With MFA Enabled. Table 2 shows some of the results that indicated obvious differences when trying to recover an account with a phone number configured for MFA. Note that in the given examples, we omitted the step of verifying access to the actual Google account email address to see what alternatives would be offered. When the recovery was performed from a known browser, it was sufficient to verify the phone that was set up for MFA by entering an OTP code that was sent to the phone via text message. Afterward, Google provided the user with an option to register and verify a new email address. A password reset email was sent to the newly registered email after 48 h. In the meantime, the (legitimate) account owner got notifications about the ongoing recovery attempt. This allowed them to stop the procedure in case they did not request the recovery. However, this recovery option was not available when using an unknown browser. In that case, the user needed access to both the phone number and the email address registered on the actual Google account. This highlights how much RBAR features can impact the user's chance of a successful recovery.

The last example in Table 2 shows a recovery procedure when using both an unknown browser and an unknown IP address. In this case, the user was first asked to enter the phone number used for MFA before actually verifying the ownership of this phone number.

Table 2. Examples for Google account recovery with phone (text message) enabled for MFA

Recovery factor	Known browser	Known IP	Recovery procedure
None	●	●/○	1. Verify MFA phone 2. ~~Verify account email~~ 3. Verify new email → Reset email after 48 h
None	○	●	1. Verify MFA phone 2. ~~Verify account email~~ → Recovery not possible
None	○	○	1. Enter MFA phone number 2. Verify MFA phone 3. ~~Verify account email~~ → Recovery not possible

● = Feature present, ○ = Feature not present, ~~XXX~~ = Step omitted

Further Observations. Also, we observed that when failing a recovery, Google revealed some information on how its RBAR mechanism might work. The message displayed to the user on a failed recovery attempt suggested using a known device and Wi-Fi during recovery (see Fig. 2).

However, during the study, we experienced that the recovery process could change from one day to another. This was true despite using the same account, having the same recovery options configured, and using the same browser and IP address. For instance, a recovery procedure that earlier gave access to the account after 48 h through a password reset email ended in a failed recovery. An authentication factor that could previously be used to help recover an account was occasionally removed as a recovery option. This suggests that Google uses more RBAR features than the two tested in this study. Nonetheless, we confirm the assumption in prior work that Google implements a risk assessment in its recovery [7].

6   Experiment 2: RBAR Use by Other Services

The second experiment focused on online services that are known to use RBA [38] and investigated whether and how they also use some form of RBAR. We describe the experiment and its results below.

6.1   Preparation

For this experiment, we began by setting up user accounts for all four online services (see Sect. 4). Testing account recovery with personal accounts is not ideal since there is always the risk that accounts will be locked out or disabled entirely. However, RBA is oftentimes triggered only for legitimate accounts with a certain history of activity [38]. This makes sense from a technical perspective,

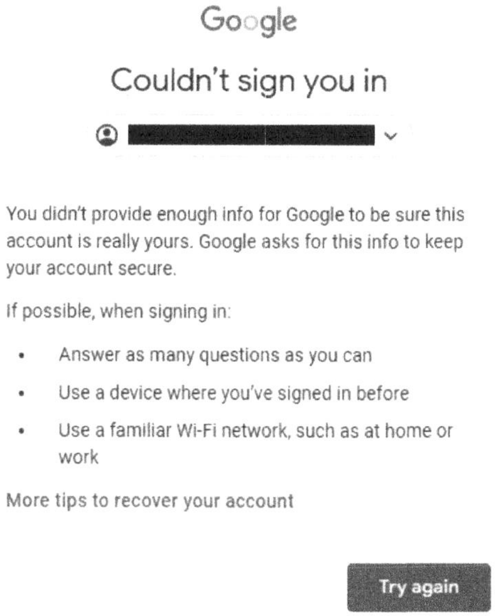

Google

Couldn't sign you in

You didn't provide enough info for Google to be sure this account is really yours. Google asks for this info to keep your account secure.

If possible, when signing in:

- Answer as many questions as you can
- Use a device where you've signed in before
- Use a familiar Wi-Fi network, such as at home or work

More tips to recover your account

Try again

Fig. 2. Message shown when failing Google's account recovery using an unknown browser and an unknown IP address. It reveals information that might give indications of their inner RBAR workings.

as such algorithms need a certain amount of training data from the legitimate user to work correctly [37]. Therefore, we created four new test accounts for each of the services. These accounts were set up with the most basic settings, i.e., with a password and one email address. To avoid bias, we made sure to create and use new email addresses on general-purpose email providers not linked to universities for each account. In addition, we were able to provide one old account for each service, some of which were either personal or created in previous studies.

A training was conducted in which the test accounts were logged in more than 20 times within a time period of about 1.5 months (December 2022–January 2023). We based the number of logins on Wiefling et al.'s study [38]. Furthermore, it was ensured that the logins for each account were performed with a similar context, i.e., from the same browser and the same IP location. Also, logins from university IP addresses were avoided since experience has shown that online services might recognize these IP addresses and block accounts to prevent systematic analyses of their services. For reproducibility, we documented the context before each account login. We did this by recording all information from the IP address and HTTP header and the browser's internal JavaScript functions, as in related work [36].

Table 3. Account recovery procedures for a normal and suspicious user context for the different test accounts of each online service

Online Service	Account	User context	
		Normal	Suspicious
Amazon	A1, A2, A4, A6*	EC	EC
	A3, A1†	CA → EC	CA → EC
	A5*	EC	<u>CA</u> → EC
Dropbox	D1 – D4, D5*	EL	EL
GOG	G1 – G4, G5*	CA → EL	CA → EL
LinkedIn	L1 – L4, L5*	EC	<u>CA</u> → EC

EC = Email (Code), EL = Email (Link), CA = CAPTCHA, * = Old account, † = Experiment repeated, <u>XXX</u> = Additional step*

6.2 Identifying RBAR Usage

After training the test accounts, we analyzed whether the online services actually use RBAR mechanisms. As in related work by Wiefling et al. [38] and Gavazzi et al. [14], this was tested by discovering differences in two distinct user contexts: *normal* and *suspicious*. This time, we considered a normal user to perform the account recovery from the same browser and IP location as in the training phase. In contrast, the suspicious user performs account recovery from a Tor browser. Web services can typically recognize Tor browser clients by the IP address of the exit nodes or by other browser features. Moreover, using a Tor browser is often considered suspicious [38]. We expected this to increase the likelihood of triggering risk-based mechanisms, if any, and compared to the first experiment on Google, where the Tor browser was not used. Note that we only considered differences that occurred after starting the recovery procedure for a specific account, e.g., after entering an email address. Any differences beforehand would not be relevant as it would mean that it is independent of the history of a user account.

Experimental Procedure. For this within-group experiment, account recovery was performed twice for each test account on different days at the end of January 2023, once with a normal user context and once with a suspicious user context, in varying orders, to avoid bias. This means we performed two account recoveries with all provided accounts. In the case of Amazon, we repeated the experiment with one of the new accounts and another old account due to inconsistent results, as described in more detail below.

Results. Table 3 summarizes the recovery procedures for each online service and account. Overall, the presentation of a CAPTCHA was the only noticeable difference that was found. The CAPTCHAs in the table are underlined in those cases where they appeared only in the suspicious user context. Note that Amazon uses its own AWS WAF CAPTCHA [5], while GOG uses the Google reCAPTCHA v2 [17] and LinkedIn appears to use a custom CAPTCHA implementation. Dropbox did not use any CAPTCHA within our experiments.

For **Amazon**, in three cases, only an OTP code sent via email was requested. Afterward, the password could be changed. For one of the new test accounts (A3), Amazon first requested a CAPTCHA before the email OTP code, but for both normal and suspicious contexts. For the old account (A5), there was an actual difference as the CAPTCHA was only displayed in the suspicious context. Because of this inconsistent behavior, we did an additional test with A1, which this time required solving a CAPTCHA for both user contexts, similar to A3. Furthermore, we included a test with another personal account (A6) that was actively used to check if the behavior was related to the account age or activity. This time, no CAPTCHA had to be solved. Consequently, the risk assessment was more complex and could not be easily reproduced with our experimental setup.

Dropbox only requested the verification of the email address through a link before the password could be changed. This was the same for all user accounts, including the old one, and for both user contexts.

For **GOG**, a CAPTCHA had to be solved before verifying the email address through a link and finally changing the password. This was again equal for all accounts and both normal and suspicious user contexts.

LinkedIn was the only online service that consistently showed a different behavior depending on the context. For a normal user context, the email address had to be verified by an OTP code before the password could be changed. However, when performing recovery from a suspicious user context, a CAPTCHA had to be solved, sometimes multiple times.

In summary, Amazon and LinkedIn used RBAR, while Dropbox and GOG have not indicated any risk-based behavior during recovery. The only challenge that was shown depending on the user context was a CAPTCHA. The results for Amazon, however, were inconsistent for the different accounts. It was decided not to do a deeper analysis here, as the experimental setup clearly did not consider enough context parameters to simulate both a normal and a suspicious user context reliably. Yet, we conclude that Amazon must have used some form of RBAR. For LinkedIn, on the other hand, the RBAR behavior could clearly be reproduced with all accounts. Thus, we conducted a second experiment on LinkedIn using the newly created test accounts, as described in the subsequent section.

6.3 Analyzing the Influence of MFA Settings on Account Recovery on LinkedIn

In Sect. 5, we showed that Google implements RBAR by incorporating different authentication mechanisms that are set up as MFA factors in a user account. Since we could prove that LinkedIn also provides some form of RBAR, we conducted another experiment to determine whether LinkedIn used any other RBAR challenges beyond the CAPTCHA.

Table 4. Account recovery procedures for a normal and suspicious user context for the different LinkedIn account setups

#	Recovery		MFA		User context	
	Second Email	Text (SMS)	Auth. App	Text (SMS)	Normal	Suspicious
1	●	○	○	○	EC1 | EC2	<u>CA</u> → EC1 | EC2
2	○	●	○	○	EC1 | P1	<u>CA</u> → EC1 | P1
3	○	○	●	○	EC1 → AU	<u>CA</u> → EC1 → AU
4	○	○	○	●	EC1 → P2	<u>CA</u> → EC1 → P2
5	●	○	●	○	EC1 | EC2 → AU	<u>CA</u> → EC1 | EC2 → AU
6	●	●	○	●	EC1 | EC2 → P2	<u>CA</u> → EC1 | EC2 → P2
7	○	●	○	●	EC1 → P2	<u>CA</u> → EC1 → P2
8	○	●	●	○	EC1 | P1 → AU	<u>CA</u> → EC1 | P1 → AU

● = Feature present, ○ = Feature not present, EC1 = Primary Email (Code),
EC2 = Secondary Email (Code), P1: Recovery Phone (SMS Code),
P2 = MFA Phone (SMS Code), AU = Authenticator App, CA = CAPTCHA,
| = Alternative <u>XXX</u> = Additional step

Experimental Procedure. For this experiment, we changed the authentication and recovery options in the LinkedIn test accounts. At the time of this experiment (January–February 2023), LinkedIn provided the following authentication and recovery methods:

- **Main authentication:** password
- **Secondary authentication:** phone (SMS), authenticator app
- **Recovery factors:** email address, phone (SMS)

We tested the effects of all possible combinations of these methods. In addition, LinkedIn also offered a non-digital recovery method requiring the user to submit a copy of a government-issued ID. As this would have revealed the experimenters' identities, we did not include this method in the experiment. Similar to Google, the expected outcome for LinkedIn was that different authentication factors would be requested in a suspicious user context.

Results. Table 4 shows the results for the different tested account setups. Note that in setups 1, 2, 5, 6, and 8, there are two possibilities for receiving the verification code: as an alternative to the primary email address, the secondary email address or the phone number could be entered (indicated by the "|" symbol). LinkedIn allows configuring the same phone number as a second authentication factor and as a recovery method. In fact, when enabling the phone number for MFA, the same number is activated automatically for recovery by phone. However, in such cases, using the phone for account recovery does not make much sense as only a single factor (ownership of the SIM card) is required for resetting the password and logging in afterward, which contradicts the idea of *multi*-factor authentication. In these cases, i.e., setups 6 and 7, we only received an inaccurate error message (see Fig. 3). We filed a bug report for this to LinkedIn on February

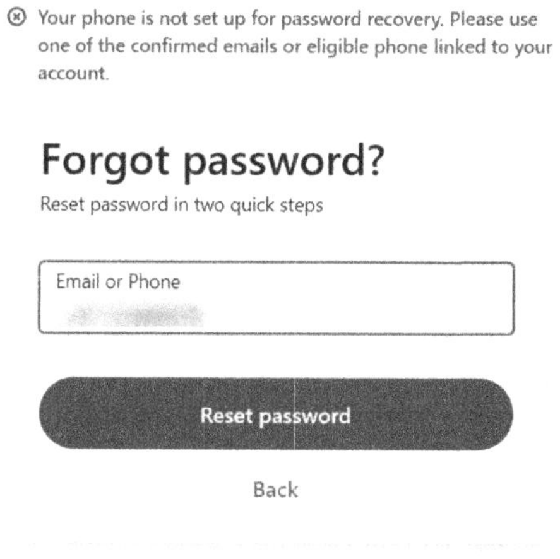

⊗ Your phone is not set up for password recovery. Please use one of the confirmed emails or eligible phone linked to your account.

Forgot password?

Reset password in two quick steps

Email or Phone

Reset password

Back

Fig. 3. Error message for phone recovery, when also Text Message MFA is activated

Table 5. Number of CAPTCHA iterations for different (pretended) locations for account recovery on LinkedIn

CAPTCHA iterations	Location of Tor exit
1	Sweden, Poland, United Kingdom, *Mexico*
2	United Kingdom, Germany
3	3× USA, *Czech Republic*
5	USA, Canada, *Netherlands*

24, 2023. However, the response from LinkedIn (one day later) indicated that it will not be fixed anytime soon unless it gets noticed by several other users.

The experiments show that the behavior when configuring further recovery or authentication methods is identical to the base setup. The only difference in the account recovery procedure for all setups was the initial CAPTCHA shown in the suspicious user context. Apart from that, the account recovery procedure always started with the verification of the primary email address or phone number by an OTP code, followed by the verification of the MFA method if one was activated.

Variation of CAPTCHA Iterations. In addition to our main results, we observed that the number of iterations of the CAPTCHA on LinkedIn varied in different experiments between 1 and 5. When mapping the number of iterations to the pretended location (i.e., the location of the Tor exit node), an interesting correlation showed up (see Table 5). The normal usage location for all accounts was in Europe, and when the pretended location was also in Europe (just another country), 1 or 2 repetitions of the CAPTCHA were required. In cases where the suspicious location was on a different continent, 3 or 5 repetitions were needed. However, there were also cases (marked in italics) where this was not true. Nonetheless, it indicates that LinkedIn's RBAR might give different suspicious risk classifications that are reflected in the number of CAPTCHA iterations. It also seems that the location is one important feature. Further experiments are needed to analyze to what extent other features are included.

7   Results and Discussion

In our exploratory study on Google and the follow-up experiment with other online services, we confirmed that several online services apply RBAR to a certain degree. In this section, we describe the results of the experiments with regard to the research questions. Furthermore, we summarize the results in a maturity model that we propose for RBAR implementations. Finally, we outline the limitations of our experiments and discuss further aspects of RBAR usage in practice.

7.1   Experiment Results

Within the scope of our experiments, we observed that Google implements RBAR in quite a sophisticated manner. It showed different authentication methods depending on the account setup and the user context. Dropbox and GOG did not apply any risk-based mechanisms during account recovery. Amazon actually indicated the use of RBAR, however, by assessing context information that was not considered by our two different user contexts. In some tests, a CAPTCHA had to be solved, while in others, it was not required. LinkedIn clearly behaved differently in a suspicious user context. When trying to recover an account from a Tor browser, LinkedIn showed a CAPTCHA challenge before entering an email verification code. In contrast to Google, however, the RBAR for LinkedIn did not involve MFA settings in a user account.

With regard to **RQ1**, we conclude that there are online services that use RBA, which also use RBAR—including Google, Amazon, and LinkedIn—but not all of them. To answer **RQ2**, the challenges we found on Google include pre-configured MFA methods (e.g., phone number) and questions requiring background knowledge (e.g., old passwords). On LinkedIn and Amazon, we only observed a CAPTCHA challenge in connection with RBAR. Concerning **RQ3**, we found that the MFA settings influenced the recovery procedure on Google only, while LinkedIn did not vary RBAR challenges depending on any configured MFA methods.

7.2   Maturity Model

Based on our results and inspired by [30], we propose a maturity model that ranks the different RBAR challenges by difficulty for an attacker (see Table 6). Due to the nature of RBAR, the model only considers the measures used in connection with a risk assessment. It describes the additional security gain in case the primary recovery factor (e.g. email address), if any, has already been

Table 6. Maturity model with maturity levels, mapping of RBAR challenges to the tested services and possible attacks against these challenges

Maturity	RBAR challenge	Identified on	Possible attacks
3	Pre-configured MFA	Google	Physical attack, malware [8]
2	Background knowledge	Google	OSINT, leaked passwords, phishing [1,19]
1	CAPTCHA	LinkedIn, Amazon	Manual recovery, CAPTCHA bypass algorithm [21,32]
0	None	Dropbox, GOG	n/a

compromised. Thus, no RBAR at all is considered the least mature as it does not involve any risk assessment and does not provide additional measures. Showing a CAPTCHA is ranked as level 1 as it can prevent automated attacks. Yet an attacker might bypass it or manually exploit account recovery. Background questions are ranked as level 2 as they require an attacker to gather knowledge of a victim. However, it also increases only the cost of the attack. MFA methods that are pre-configured in an account are considered the most mature as they require more sophisticated methods or even physical access for a successful attack.

The model can be used, e.g., to assess the security of an RBAR implementation. Online services can also use such a model for their RBAR implementations to enable certain challenges with a higher maturity ranking at higher risk scores. Note that the model is only one possible way to assess RBAR. It might be different if other types of RBAR challenges are used that were not discovered within our study.

7.3 Comparison with Official Documentation

To the best of our knowledge, the experiments showed for the first time that Amazon, LinkedIn, and Google use RBAR. To compare our findings with the public communications of the online services, we took their official documentation into consideration [4,10,15,18,25]. Interestingly, none of the RBAR-instrumented online services mentioned that they change the account recovery behavior based on contextual information collected during the recovery process [4,18,25]. Only Google hinted that users should possibly use a familiar device and location [18]. However, they did not mention why users should do this, i.e. because they use RBAR. Our results show that the account recovery mechanisms of these online services seem to do more to protect their users than what is officially communicated to them.

Trying to hide implemented security mechanisms from the user base has already been observed in the related case of RBA [16] and other research on account recovery [6]. We do not consider this a good practice, as it follows the anti-pattern of *"security by obscurity"*. Users also tend to get frustrated when they experience security barriers that were not communicated to them beforehand [34]. Beyond that, attackers are known to adapt to obscured security mechanisms [28,33]. We assume that public RBAR research, to increase the body of knowledge, will increase the overall adoption of online services and enable a large user base to be protected with RBAR following the principle of *"good security now"* [13].

7.4   Ethics

We only tested account recoveries with accounts owned by the researchers, i.e., we did not try to exploit the recovery of other users' accounts. Also, since we conducted manual tests, we did not create high traffic on the online services that could have affected other users.

While it could be reasoned that our findings are helpful for attackers, we argue that they are more valuable to the public. As the gained knowledge helps researchers and online service providers to get an understanding of how RBAR works, this can support the development of more secure and usable account recovery mechanisms.

7.5   Limitations

Beyond Google, only four online services were analyzed in terms of RBAR. This was mainly due to the lack of any automatism for training user accounts and testing account recovery, therefore requiring manual effort to conduct our experiments. Nevertheless, as mentioned before, these services have been carefully selected as they are known to use RBA [38].

We could not find any RBAR mechanisms in Dropbox and GOG. Due to the nature of a black-box test, we do not know the implementation details of the tested online services. Thus, there is always uncertainty involved. Nevertheless, we are confident that the accounts were sufficiently trained—especially since we also tested older accounts—and tested with the highest risk possible [38].

7.6   RBAR

Attackers may abuse account recovery to circumvent authentication. Hence, the security of account recovery is as essential as the security of login authentication. Previous research showed that email addresses often become a single point of failure [23,24]. RBAR might be an advantageous way to increase the difficulty of a successful account takeover by incorporating additional authentication methods, as with RBA. At the same time, it may reduce the burden on legitimate users and increase their chances of recovering an account.

The RBAR used by Google is quite different from LinkedIn. Google uses additional authentication methods, while LinkedIn just requires a suspicious user to solve an additional CAPTCHA. This CAPTCHA actually only reduces the risk of automated attacks by making it more costly for an attacker. In general, CAPTCHAs mainly increase friction for users [39]. It may be an improvement to use a risk score to decide if a CAPTCHA should be solved, compared to, e.g., GOG, where a CAPTCHA is shown to all users. However, the security gain is insignificant since researchers have already demonstrated attacks against Google's widely known reCAPTCHA [21,32]. Moreover, this does not prevent targeted attacks. We argue that if a service already implements a risk assessment in its account recovery, it should even go further and include actual authentication methods. In the case of LinkedIn, it could, for instance, request the verification of another recovery email or phone if set up.

8 Conclusion

Account recovery mechanisms remain a relevant entry point for account takeover attacks [27,29]. Online services should strengthen their account recovery with additional security mechanisms, like risk-based account recovery (RBAR), to protect their users.

In this paper, we investigated the use of RBAR in practice. We described the concept behind RBAR and conducted two experiments to learn about if and how online services use it. The results show that Google, Amazon and LinkedIn used RBAR. However, their implementations differed widely in suspicious contexts, from asking users for background knowledge or pre-configured MFA methods (Google) to showing a CAPTCHA challenge (Amazon and LinkedIn). Based on our results, we proposed a maturity model that researchers or service providers can use to assess the security of RBAR systems or guide in implementing RBAR.

Following this first systematic analysis of RBAR, future work can extend our proposed model with other RBAR challenges. Furthermore, it can be studied what features specifically trigger RBAR challenges. As there seems to be a tendency to include risk-based decision-making into account recovery, there should be a comparison of RBA and RBAR and how they can complement each other in authentication systems as a whole.

Acknowledgments. Stephan Wiefling did this research while working at H-BRS University of Applied Sciences.

References

1. Addas, A., Salehi-Abari, A., Thorpe, J.: Geographical security questions for fallback authentication. In: PST 2019. IEEE (2019). https://doi.org/10.1109/PST47121.2019.8949063
2. Akamai: Credential Stuffing: Attacks and Economies. [state of the internet]/security **5**(Special Media Edition) (2019). https://web.archive.org/web/20210824114851/https://www.akamai.com/us/en/multimedia/documents/state-of-the-internet/soti-security-credential-stuffing-attacks-and-economies-report-2019.pdf
3. Akamai: Loyalty for Sale - Retail and Hospitality Fraud. [state of the internet]/security **6**(3) (2020). https://web.archive.org/web/20201101013317/https://www.akamai.com/us/en/multimedia/documents/state-of-the-internet/soti-security-loyalty-for-sale-retail-and-hospitality-fraud-report-2020.pdf

4. Amazon: Reset Your Password (2023). https://web.archive.org/web/20210918230138/https://www.amazon.com/gp/help/customer/display.html?nodeId=GH3NM2YWEFEL2CQ4

5. Amazon Web Services Inc: What is a CAPTCHA puzzle? (2023). https://docs.aws.amazon.com/waf/latest/developerguide/waf-captcha-puzzle.html

6. Amft, S., et al.: Lost and not found: an investigation of recovery methods for multi-factor authentication. arXiv:2306.09708 (2023)

7. Bonneau, J., Bursztein, E., Caron, I., Jackson, R., Williamson, M.: Secrets, lies, and account recovery: lessons from the use of personal knowledge questions at Google. In: WWW 2015. ACM (2015). https://doi.org/10.1145/2736277.2741691

8. Campobasso, M., Allodi, L.: Impersonation-as-a-service: characterizing the emerging criminal infrastructure for user impersonation at scale. In: CCS 2020. ACM (2020). https://doi.org/10.1145/3372297.3417892

9. Conners, J.S., Zappala, D.: Let's authenticate: automated cryptographic authentication for the web with simple account recovery. In: WAY 2019 (2019)

10. Dropbox: Change or reset your Dropbox password (2023). https://web.archive.org/web/20230518113022/https://help.dropbox.com/security/password-reset

11. Federal Bureau of Investigation: Internet Crime Report 2022 (2023). https://web.archive.org/web/20230311011752/, https://www.ic3.gov/Media/PDF/AnnualReport/2022_IC3Report.pdf

12. Freeman, D., Jain, S., Dürmuth, M., Biggio, B., Giacinto, G.: Who are you? A statistical approach to measuring user authenticity. In: NDSS 2016. Internet Society (2016). https://doi.org/10.14722/ndss.2016.23240

13. Garfinkel, S.L.: Design principles and patterns for computer systems that are simultaneously secure and usable. Ph.D. thesis, Massachusetts Institute of Technology (2005)

14. Gavazzi, A., et al.: A study of multi-factor and risk-based authentication availability. In: USENIX Security 2023. USENIX Association (2023)

15. GOG: How do I reset my password? (2023). https://web.archive.org/web/20230317223608/, https://support.gog.com/hc/en-us/articles/212185409-How-do-I-reset-my-password-?product=gog

16. Golla, M.: I had a chat about RBA with @Google in April 2016. the short story: "RBA is an arms race, and we are not revealing any details that could potentially help attackers" (2019). https://web.archive.org/web/20210812104239/, https://twitter.com/m33x/status/1120979096547274752

17. Google: reCAPTCHA v2 | Google Developers (2021). https://developers.google.com/recaptcha/docs/display

18. Google: Tips to complete account recovery steps (2023). https://web.archive.org/web/20230422113749/https://support.google.com/accounts/answer/7299973

19. Hang, A., De Luca, A., Hussmann, H.: I know what you did last week! Do you?: Dynamic security questions for fallback authentication on smartphones. In: CHI 2015. ACM (2015). https://doi.org/10.1145/2702123.2702131

20. Hill, B.: Moving account recovery beyond email and the "secret" question. In: Enigma 2017. USENIX Association (2017)

21. Hossen, M.I., et al.: An object detection based solver for Google's image reCAPTCHA v2. In: RAID 2020. USENIX Association (2020)

22. Javed, A., Bletgen, D., Kohlar, F., Dürmuth, M., Schwenk, J.: Secure fallback authentication and the trusted friend attack. In: ICDCSW 2014. ACM (2014). https://doi.org/10.1109/ICDCSW.2014.30

23. Li, Y., Chen, Z., Wang, H., Sun, K., Jajodia, S.: Understanding account recovery in the wild and its security implications. IEEE TDSC **19**(1) (2020). https://doi.org/10.1109/TDSC.2020.2975789

24. Li, Y., Wang, H., Sun, K.: Email as a master key: analyzing account recovery in the wild. In: INFOCOM 2018. IEEE (2018). https://doi.org/10.1109/INFOCOM.2018.8486017

25. LinkedIn: Password Reset Basics (2023). https://web.archive.org/web/20221229120339/, https://www.linkedin.com/help/linkedin/answer/a1382101

26. Markert, P., Golla, M., Stobert, E., Dürmuth, M.: Work in progress: a comparative long-term study of fallback authentication. In: USEC 2019. Internet Society (2019). https://doi.org/10.14722/usec.2019.23030

27. Microsoft Detection and Response Team: DEV-0537 criminal actor targeting organizations for data exfiltration and destruction (2022). https://www.microsoft.com/security/blog/dev-0537

28. Milka, G.: Anatomy of account takeover. In: Enigma 2018. USENIX Association (2018)

29. MITRE Corporation: CWE-640: Weak Password Recovery Mechanism for Forgotten Password (2021). https://cwe.mitre.org/data/definitions/640.html

30. Pöhn, D., Gruschka, N., Ziegler, L.: Multi-account dashboard for authentication dependency analysis. In: ARES 2022. ACM (2022)

31. Quermann, N., Harbach, M., Dürmuth, M.: The state of user authentication in the wild. In: WAY 2018 (2018). https://wayworkshop.org/2018/papers/way2018-quermann.pdf

32. Sukhani, K., Sawant, S., Maniar, S., Pawar, R.: Automating the bypass of image-based captcha and assessing security. In: ICCCNT 2021. IEEE (2021). https://doi.org/10.1109/ICCCNT51525.2021.9580020

33. Thomas, K., et al.: Data breaches, phishing, or malware?: Understanding the risks of stolen credentials. In: CCS 2017. ACM (2017). https://doi.org/10.1145/3133956.3134067

34. Wiefling, S., Dürmuth, M., Lo Iacono, L.: More than just good passwords? A study on usability and security perceptions of risk-based authentication. In: ACSAC 2020. ACM (2020). https://doi.org/10.1145/3427228.3427243

35. Wiefling, S., Dürmuth, M., Lo Iacono, L.: Verify it's you: how users perceive risk-based authentication. IEEE Secur. Priv. **19**(6) (2021). https://doi.org/10.1109/MSEC.2021.3077954

36. Wiefling, S., Dürmuth, M., Lo Iacono, L.: What's in score for website users: a data-driven long-term study on risk-based authentication characteristics. In: Borisov, N., Diaz, C. (eds.) FC 2021. LNCS, vol. 12675, pp. 361–381. Springer, Heidelberg (2021). https://doi.org/10.1007/978-3-662-64331-0_19

37. Wiefling, S., Jørgensen, P.R., Thunem, S., Lo Iacono, L.: Pump up password security! evaluating and enhancing risk-based authentication on a real-world large-scale online service. ACM TOPS **26**(1) (2023). https://doi.org/10.1145/3546069

38. Wiefling, S., Lo Iacono, L., Dürmuth, M.: Is this really you? An empirical study on risk-based authentication applied in the wild. In: Dhillon, G., Karlsson, F., Hedström, K., Zúquete, A. (eds.) SEC 2019. IAICT, vol. 562, pp. 134–148. Springer, Cham (2019). https://doi.org/10.1007/978-3-030-22312-0_10

39. Yan, J., El Ahmad, A.S.: Usability of CAPTCHAs or usability issues in CAPTCHA design. In: Proceedings of the 4th symposium on Usable privacy and security, pp. 44–52 (2008)

A Unified Knowledge Graph to Permit Interoperability of Heterogenous Digital Evidence

Ali Alshumrani[1,2]([✉]) [iD], Nathan Clarke[1] [iD], and Bogdan Ghita[1] [iD]

[1] Centre for Cyber Security, Communications and Network Research (CSCAN),
University of Plymouth, Plymouth, UK
{ali.alshumrani,n.clarke,bogdan.ghita}@plymouth.ac.uk
[2] Department of Information Systems, Umm Al-Qura University,
Makkah, Saudi Arabia

Abstract. The modern digital world is highly heterogeneous, encompassing a wide variety of communications, devices, and services. This interconnectedness generates, synchronises, stores, and presents digital information in multidimensional, complex formats, often fragmented across multiple sources. When linked to misuse, this digital information becomes vital digital evidence. Integrating and harmonising these diverse formats into a unified system is crucial for comprehensively understanding evidence and its relationships. However, existing approaches to date have faced challenges limiting investigators' ability to query heterogeneous evidence across large datasets. This paper presents a novel approach in the form of a modern unified data graph. The proposed approach aims to seamlessly integrate, harmonise, and unify evidence data, enabling cross-platform interoperability, efficient data queries, and improved digital investigation performance. To demonstrate its efficacy, a case study is conducted, highlighting the benefits of the proposed approach and showcasing its effectiveness in enabling the interoperability required for advanced analytics in digital investigations.

Keywords: Digital Forensics · Investigation · Cybercrime · Evidence Harmonisation · Interoperability · Ontology · Knowledge Graph

1 Introduction

The widespread use of digital devices and internet services has increased the quantity and diversity of digital evidence [1]. This explosive growth has given rise to an unprecedented deluge of digital data, with daily volumes exceeding 2.5 quintillion bytes [2]. The surge in technology has not only transformed our daily lives but has also led to a corresponding surge in criminal activities, necessitating an increased demand for digital forensic services [3]. Digital evidence, once primarily associated with cybercrime, now plays a pivotal role in investigating traditional criminal cases, with approximately 90% of criminal investigations encompassing a digital footprint [4].

G. Wang et al. (Eds.): UbiSec 2023, CCIS 2034, pp. 420–435, 2024.
https://doi.org/10.1007/978-981-97-1274-8_27

However, the investigation of digital evidence has become increasingly challenging due to the sheer volume of data scattered across various evidence sources [5]. Each source has its unique file formats, structures, and schemes, creating a tapestry of heterogeneity and inconsistency in the nature of complex evidence. The complexity of integrating and unifying complex evidence effectively has significantly impacted digital forensics. The inherent heterogeneity and inconsistency in this data create a significant hurdle in achieving interoperability across digital sources [6]. Achieving interoperability across this diverse digital landscape necessitates the harmonisation and unification of these heterogeneous data types, a task that traditionally demands substantial effort and relies on leveraging a multitude of tools and methods [6–8]. This need arises because traditional forensic tools, which are often tailored to specific technologies or platforms, tend to yield fragmented evidence. Consequently, in its isolated form, each piece of evidence requires manual examination and analysis to outline a comprehensive and correlated narrative [8]. This manual intervention is time-consuming, error-prone, a cognitively taxing burden on investigators, and wholly inadequate to cope with the voluminous evidence encountered in contemporary digital environments [9].

In response to these challenges, the modern paradigm of evidence investigation requires a robust data harmonisation method capable of seamlessly integrating isolated evidence footprints into a unified system [8]. Arguably, combining and representing heterogeneous data within a unified framework can address multiple challenges. These include tackling data heterogeneity and inconsistency, enhancing data automation, enabling advanced data correlation and visualisation across evidence resources, all while reducing the need for manual examination. This approach can also be instrumental in addressing other critical issues, such as anti-forensics techniques. For instance, unifying and cross-matching data from system-related events like web browser activity with network traffic logs can reveal whether a suspect is utilising some form of incognito function on the web browser to conceal their search history. Furthermore, the automated harmonisation, consolidation, and uniform structuring of evidence data can enhance the efficiency of digital investigations [7].

Therefore, this study proposes the adoption of a Unified Metadata Graph Model (UMGM) as a solution to address the interoperability and harmonisation challenges posed by heterogeneous digital evidence. The proposed approach offers a standardised and unified methodology for representing fragmented and isolated evidence, regardless of its diverse sources or formats. By leveraging the power of graph database structures, this approach seamlessly integrates and harmonises evidence based on their associated metadata attributes, thereby enabling the potential for cross-platform interoperability within the realm of heterogeneous evidence. Furthermore, the adoption of the data graph database facilitates the unified knowledge representation of evidence data, capturing intricate relationships among entities, attributes, and events. Incorporating this proposed method empowers investigators with advanced query capabilities, interactive data refinement, and streamlined evidence analytics across the entire spectrum of evidence objects.

In the subsequent sections, Sect. 2 explores existing research on data ontologies and graphs and their applicability in achieving interoperability of heterogeneous digital evidence. Section 3 outlines the methodology and implementation of the unified system architecture, detailing its functionalities and features. In Sect. 4, a hypothetical case study is conducted to illustrate the effectiveness of the proposed approach. Finally, in Sect. 5, the findings are summarised, and promising directions for future research are outlined.

2   Literature Review

Data ontology holds a pivotal position within the semantic web, offering a formalised and standardised definition of concepts, relationships, and properties that characterise evidence-related information. The adoption of data ontology within the realm of digital evidence has been the subject of many studies. Authors in [10] developed a Digital Evidence Semantic Ontology (DESO) to index and classify evidence artefacts, focusing primarily on their discovery locations. To gauge the effectiveness of DESO, they undertook a case study that examined evidence from two distinct computer systems and USB memory devices. The findings from this study indicated that the approach mainly identified artefacts by their location, overlooking related properties. Moreover, the technique employed for data correlation based on relevance was not adequately detailed, leading to the method's suboptimal utilisation, as it was heavily reliant on the expertise of the digital examiner. In a related study, [11] introduced the Semantic Analysis of Digital Forensic Cases (SADFC) system. This system was designed to reconstruct and analyse timelines relevant to evidence incidents. It employs the Ontology for the Representation of Digital Incidents and Investigations (ORD2I) as a formal logical language, capturing the semantics of concepts and relationships within digital evidence and thereby facilitating knowledge representation. To assess the proposed approach, the authors conducted experiments with an experimental malware dataset, which included browser-related data, such as browsing histories and downloaded files. The experiments showcased SADFC's ability to effectively extract knowledge from file system artefacts, conduct data analysis, and address queries. However, it is noteworthy that SADFC faces challenges in the seamless integration, analysis, and validation of complex evidence, especially when dealing with a vast volume of heterogeneous data without human intervention.

Seeking to standardise the representation of data objects and relationships to enhance correlation among evidence sources, [12] leveraged the capabilities of the Cyber Observable eXpression (CybOX) schema and the Unified Cyber Ontology (UCO) to develop an ontology named Digital Forensic Analysis eXpression (DFAX). DFAX enhances CybOX's functionalities by offering a more detailed depiction of forensic-relevant information, covering activities executed by both subjects and forensic examiners. It also incorporates UCO's general abstractions to represent concepts that span the cyber domain, thereby facilitating more advanced forensic analysis. This initiative laid the groundwork for the introduction of the Cyber-investigation Analysis Standard Expression (CASE) ontology [13]. Developed in collaboration with the UCO ontology, CASE consistently represents constructs across various cyber-centric domains, enhancing interoperability among different evidence domains. However, while these systems primarily focus on consolidating and formatting evidence data to facilitate its exchange across a broad spectrum of cyber-related domains, they do not address the essential need to harmonise evidence data in a standardised and unified manner. Such harmonisation would enable the application of advanced data correlation methods and more effective searching of the evidence data.

In research conducted in [14], introduced an Event-based Forensic Integration Ontology for Online Social Networks (EFIOSN) as a formal knowledge model for constructing and automating evidence analysis. The application of this model was demonstrated through a theoretical case study involving a defamation attempt on the Twitter platform. The study utilised timeline analysis based on temporal activity patterns to establish the sequential order of evidence-related events. The findings revealed that EFIOSN successfully identified associations and similarities among potential events, serving as an initial step for further investigation and forming direct evidence. However, it is important to note that the proposed model assumes the ontology's adequacy in capturing all pertinent aspects of online social network data, indicating that the completeness and comprehensiveness of the ontology may not be sufficient. In a further effort to semi-automate network packet analysis, [15] proposed a Packet Analysis Ontology (PAO) with the intention of providing a formal representation of concepts and properties related to packet analysis. To assess the effectiveness of this ontology, a case study was conducted using honeypot data, which simulates critical infrastructure containing Supervisory Control and Data Acquisition (SCADA) components. The ontology was applied to capture data semantics based on Wireshark frames, including packet frame numbers, timestamps, source and destination IP addresses, protocol numbers, and frame length values. The results demonstrated that the proposed system achieved a broader concept and role semantics range compared to similar studies with similar objectives. However, inherent limitations of this approach include its restriction to capturing data aligned with Wireshark frames only and its scalability mechanisms for validating, interacting with, and refining the captured data. These limitations may impede the ability to perform complex analyses and obtain desired results.

In a subsequent study, [16] introduced ForensicFlow system. This system built upon the Web Ontology Language (OWL), a semantic web technology, is designed to facilitate knowledge integration and enable semantic querying of data relationships using a query language known as SPARQL Protocol and Resource Description Framework (RDF) Query Language (SPARQL). For their experimental setup, the researchers conducted a case study focused on a ransomware attack scenario. This scenario involved various digital artefacts, including memory dumps and a disk image of a Windows operating system. The proposed ontology was instantiated by analysing these artefacts and querying Windows

Prefetch data using SPARQL. This process successfully revealed two suspicious events and their dependencies. However, it's worth noting that the system's scope is confined to specific high-level events within the operating system. This limitation may hinder its applicability in more intricate cases. Additionally, the system lacks automated data validation capabilities, which could affect its robustness when handling large volumes of related data.

In the context of utilising data graph databases to automate digital forensic analyses, [17] proposed a CyGraph system for capturing data relationships across various network and host source entities, thereby facilitating cybersecurity analytics and the visual representation of security events. The efficacy of this system was assessed via a case study, which encompassed an attack scenario executed on several internally vulnerable host systems. This case study underscored the system's proficiency in executing data queries and visually mapping potential attack patterns. However, the system's scalability is primarily confined to the predefined data graph model, which is predominantly designed for network-oriented environments. In a parallel vein, [18] proposed a Property Graph Event Reconstruction (PGER) system with an emphasis on data normalisation and correlation. During the evaluation, researchers applied the PGER to a sample dataset containing events from web browsing, downloaded files from various web browser applications, document application events, and other system-related events. The system demonstrated the ability to index traversal and discover adjacent node entities to some extent, defining high-level rules through a combination of terms. However, it did present limitations in providing a holistic abstraction, given that the expert rules formulated within the system did not encapsulate all system events.

Whilst the aforementioned studies undeniably provide pivotal advancements in the field, there remain areas that necessitate further improvements. The scalability of current methodologies requires enhancement, particularly in terms of harmonising diverse data types, refining data relationships, optimising intelligent data querying mechanisms, and fostering sophisticated cross-data analytics. A considerable limitation of ontological studies lies in their circumscribed scope, which solely maps data relationships pertinent to specific technological objects. This constraint implies that such methodologies are relegated to identifying and extracting data that aligns with their predefined classifications. Ontological studies frequently concentrate on discrete subsets of digital traces, whilst failing to encompass the full spectrum of relevant evidence information. Their predominant reliance on specific types of data analysis, such as timeline analysis, may inadvertently introduce constraints, potentially limiting the effectiveness and scalability of investigations. Conversely, studies employing graph-based approaches demonstrate the potential to capture data relationships and perform data queries, yet they encounter limitations concerning the level of abstraction and interpretability of heterogeneous events. While these approaches have enhanced data model scalability and query efficiency, further research is crucial to devise a comprehensive solution addressing the challenges of data heterogeneity and interoperability within a consistent, interactive framework. The development of more advanced

and robust tools that adeptly integrate, harmonise, and analyse intricate relationships within heterogeneous evidence will enable investigators to query, navigate, refine, and define the evidence more efficiently, leading to more effective
forensic investigations.

3 Unified Metadata Graph Model

The UMGM introduces a structured framework, divided into three pivotal
phases, that is aimed at effectively integrating, harmonising, and unifying diverse
data objects. The first phase lays the foundation, focusing on the extraction and
ingestion of evidence metadata, ensuring all essential data is captured and ready
for processing. The second phase delves into metadata harmonisation and unification, which is further categorised into two subphases: metadata integration
and mapping; and knowledge validation and enrichment. The third phase shifts
the focus towards extracting actionable insights, concentrating on conducting
advanced analytics across the resultant homogeneous data, aiding investigators
in discerning significant patterns and conclusions. Figure 1 provides a general
overview of the system's workflow process, demonstrating a visual representation of the methodological progression. The subsequent sections will delve
deeper, elucidating the objectives associated with each phase within the UMGM
framework.

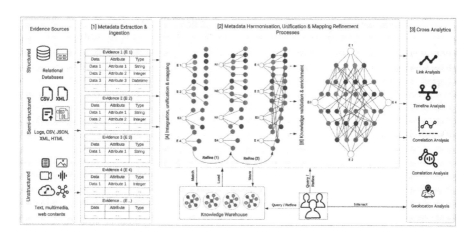

Fig. 1. A generic workflow of the unified metadata graph model.

3.1 Metadata Extraction and Ingestion

The metadata extraction and ingestion process is designed to capture and incorporate relevant attributes from various forms of evidence. This evidence encompasses structured data from relational databases, semi-structured formats such

as logs, CSV, JSON, XML, and HTML from web applications and configuration files, as well as unstructured data including text documents, multimedia files, and dynamic web content. Given the extensive range of data sources, the resulting metadata can represent a myriad of types. These may consist of attributes like usernames, timestamps, file sizes, geolocation data, MIME types, email IDs, phone numbers, IP addresses, and network protocols, among other significant properties. This phase subsequently processes these multi-dimensional attributes, transmitting and adapting them into the system for subsequent analyses and operations.

3.2   Metadata Harmonisation, Unification, and Mapping Refinement Processes

During this phase, the extracted metadata attributes are defined, integrated, and transformed into a standardised, unified graph database format. This transformation ensures the harmonisation of metadata from various data sources into a consistent structure, highlighting the advantages of using a graph database. The main components of this unified data graph structure include nodes, properties, and relationships. Nodes represent individual data entities, with each node corresponding to specific metadata that provides detailed insights about the associated data properties. Properties offer further specific information related to each node. Relationships define the connections, associations, or dependencies among nodes, capturing the intricate structure and semantics between data entities. Presenting data in this manner facilitates a holistic understanding of evidence attributes, their characteristics, and relationships. This structure notably enables efficient cross-querying and exploration of evidence connections. As a result, investigators gain a comprehensive view of metadata-associated properties from multiple evidence data sources. They can also effectively utilise cross-search functionalities to retrieve and refine evidence attribute relationships. These objectives are achieved through two specific sub-phases, which will be outlined in the subsequent sections.

Unification, Mapping, and Refinement Process: This process harmonises heterogeneous evidence efficiently. It standardises and aligns metadata attributes using predefined data model characteristics from the knowledge warehouse. Investigators then actively engage with evidence entities and relationships, which sheds light on interdependencies and associations. The unified system retrieves metadata attributes from extracted and ingested metadata, and this raw data undergoes automatic refinement based on predefined criteria matched with the knowledge warehouse. The first refinement stage, represented as 'Refine 1', establishes initial relationships between instances, enhancing data coherence and structure. The refined metadata is then made available to investigators for further enhancement. In the second refinement stage, denoted as 'Refine 2', investigators identify and establish new relationships between instances, as depicted in Fig. 1. This iterative process of refining and enhancing data enables investigators to gain insights into the interconnectedness and dependencies among entities, thus supporting a more comprehensive and accurate digital investigation. It addresses discrepancies and conflicts in metadata, promoting data interoperability and consistency. Additionally, it reveals connections across diverse evidence sources, offering a panoramic evidence perspective.

Knowledge Validation and Enrichment: The knowledge validation and enrichment phase builds upon previously refined metadata relationships. It further involves human interaction and validation mechanisms to ensure the accuracy and reliability of the generated models of evidence metadata. Investigators actively engage in this phase to validate and identify areas for potential enhancement, thereby further enriching the evidence. By leveraging the defined data relationships, investigators retrieve additional relevant data based on the newly established connections. Moreover, investigators verify the accuracy, completeness, and reliability of the harmonised metadata through this knowledge validation process, ensuring the integrity of the evidence and its associated relationships. Knowledge enrichment plays a vital role in this phase, involving the integration of additional contextual or domain-specific knowledge into the metadata. This process enhances the richness and implications of the evidence, providing a holistic perspective on related evidence and a more comprehensive understanding of the case. This ensures a well-informed approach before proceeding with cross-data analytics, making the digital forensics investigation more effective and accurate.

3.3   Cross Evidence Analytics

The cross-analytic phase equips investigators with the capability to apply various evidence-analytical techniques to the harmonised and enriched knowledge graph, aiding in identifying patterns and correlations across evidence sources. This facilitates the determination of critical evidence. The system's interactive data exploration functionalities allow for the retrieval and visual representation of predefined data models. This enables investigators to review, exclude or focus on specific nodes, add information, and update changes for further analysis. Specifically, the system supports Link Analysis, identifying relationships between entities; Timeline Analysis, showcasing events chronologically; Correlation Analysis, assessing relationships among data points; and Geolocation Analysis, analysing the geographical data associated with evidence. Moreover, built-in queries offer searches based on attributes such as username, timeline frame, geolocation, email ID, IP address, and keyword search. The system also suggests visualisation types and allows combining methods within one interface, enhancing evidence analysis. Advanced analytics enhance the efficiency of forensic investigations. The system's capabilities facilitate a comprehensive exploration of evidence data, bolstering overall investigative outcomes.

4 Use Case Evaluation

This section presents a hypothetical data leakage case study that showcases the practical application and capabilities of the proposed system. The aim is to demonstrate how the unified knowledge graph model can formalise and streamline the investigation process by seamlessly integrating and analysing evidence from diverse sources. The case study revolves around an intricate investigation scenario that involves multiple sources of evidence. Through the application of the unified knowledge graph model, this illustrative case study highlights the effectiveness and efficiency of the approach in addressing the challenges posed by heterogeneous evidence in digital forensics investigations.

4.1 Crime Scenario Overview

Corporation AIxz specialises in developing Artificial Intelligence (AI) models for financial institutions. These highly valuable models are securely stored in a dedicated cloud server, which can only be accessed through a limited list of static IP addresses within the corporation's local network. However, on May 19_{th} 2022, an incident of data leakage occurred involving an unauthorised transfer of a highly confidential AI model to an external source. In response to this breach, the corporation's digital investigation team swiftly initiated an initial examination of the internal network to determine the source of the breach. During the initial investigation, the team identified a high volume of encrypted traffic originating from various internal IP addresses. Thus, based on this determination, they uncovered compelling evidence implicating several systems connected to employees named Alex, Bill, Lisa, and Abby, as well as an unidentified IP address associated with an unrecognised host system. Recognising the seriousness of the situation, the team promptly seized several digital resources, as indicated in Table 1, for further analysis and investigation to identify the insider(s) responsible for the breach.

Table 1. Summary of the seized digital sources.

Evidence	Description
Network logs	An initial collection of network traffic logs covering the past 30 days
Computers	Several Windows operating systems
Memory artefacts	A collection of computers' volatile memory artefacts
Servers	Several internal server logs, including Syslog, Email, DNS, and web application servers
Cloud storage	A dedicated cloud storage logs for storing the developed AI models
Firewall logs	An initial collection of perimeter firewall logs covering the past 30 days

4.2 Investigation Objectives

The primary objective of this investigation was to analyse the seized evidence and determine the responsibility of the identified suspects for the leakage of the AI model. Consequently, the following investigative questions were postulated:

1. Investigate whether the identified suspects were involved in transmitting the AI model.
2. Investigate the origin of the unidentified IP and analyse patterns and anomalies across the seized evidence.
3. Conduct link analysis across all potential data objects and identify relationships among the identified pieces of evidence.
4. Based on data harmonisation results, perform timeline visualisation analysis and highlight the potential patterns or anomalies of evidence events chronologically.

4.3   Investigation Workflow

This subsection outlines the sequential phases of the proposed system in investigating the data leakage case study.

Metadata Extraction: In the context of the seized evidence sources mentioned in Table 1, a crucial step in the proposed system's investigation process is the identification and extraction of the relevant metadata attributes. Table 2 provides illustrative examples of these evidence metadata attributes, encompassing memory, network logs, cloud data, and Syslog attributes. These metadata attributes correspond to the extracted artefacts that hold the utmost relevance to the investigation.

Table 2. A simplified example of evidence metadata attributes.

(a) Sample memory artefacts.

Process Name	Protocol	Local IP Address	Foreign Address	State	CPU Time	Elapsed Time
Putty	TCP	10.0.0.20:52814	10.0.0.100:ssh	Established	0:00:11.812	0:08:58.851

(b) Sample network PCAP logs.

Timestamp	Source MAC	Destination MAC	Source IP	Destination IP	Source Port	Destination Port	Protocol	Host
18/5/2022 10:10:05	Ff:df:f9:c4:94:ac	24:d4:4b:8e:02:86	10.0.0.20	10.0.0.100	52814	22	SSHv2	System1
18/5/2022 10:10:40	Ff:df:f9:c4:94:ac	24:d4:4b:8e:02:86	10.0.0.20	10.0.0.100	49130	443	HTTPS	System1
18/5/2022 10:55:12	98:0c:b9:99:3f:5b	—	10.0.0.15	93.125.188.220	49190	443	HTTPS	—

(c) Sample cloud metadata attributes.

File Name	File Size	Created By	Created Timestamp	Accessed By	Accessed Timestamp
FinAI.h5	4.2 GB	AIxz	20/04/2022 13:20:22	Alex@AIxz.ai	18/5/2022 10:10:40

(d) Sample syslog server events.

Device Name	IP Address	Event Type	Created Timestamp	Accessed By	Accessed Timestamp
Perimeter firewall	10.0.0.200	Logon	20/04/2022 13:20:22	Alex	18/5/2022 10:20:20

Table 2a provides a sample of memory logs detailing a network connection established using a "Putty" application. These logs were generated from a host system with an IP address of 10.0.0.20 via port number 52814. They include information about the connection state, CPU time, and elapsed time. In the context of the collected network PCAP (Packet Capture), Table 2b shows a sample view of the extracted logs containing timestamps, MAC and IP addresses, ports, protocol, and the hosts involved in the communication. It provides information about network traffic events and their corresponding details. Furthermore, Table 2c provides information about cloud sample events. It indicates the creation timestamps of the model, includes the model named "FinAI.h5", and specifies its size as 4.2 GB. Finally, Table 2d showcases sample events captured by the Syslog server, highlighting attributes such as device name, event type, creation timestamp, and the individual who accessed the device. These logs refer to a login attempt on the perimeter firewall, specifying the source IP address, accessing user name, and the relevant timestamps.

Notably, the examination of these multitudes of metadata attributes using traditional methodologies necessitates investigators to transition between an array of tools and techniques each tailored to specific data types. For instance, when analysing the metadata illustrated in Tables 2a to 2d investigative teams would typically employ distinct specialised tools and manual methodologies for each data source. They commonly employ tools like Volatility or Rekall for memory dump analysis and Wireshark or TCPdump for inspecting network packets. Furthermore, they might manually cross-reference access logs or employ dedicated tools to investigate event logs found in Syslog and cloud data records. Whilst the unified knowledge graph seeks to thoroughly extract, examine, and harmonise diverse metadata types into a unified graph database, thus enabling interactive refinement by investigators and ensuring compatibility with heterogeneous digital evidence. Through the proposed approach, investigators can explore interconnected metadata attributes, effectively identifying correlations and patterns that may have been overlooked in traditional investigations. Furthermore, the graph's query and refinement features provide a more streamlined and intuitive method for extracting information, reducing the reliance on disparate tools and manual efforts. The following subsection will demonstrate how these diverse metadata attributes are effectively harmonised and mapped, highlighting the efficiency of the proposed model in facilitating comprehensive digital evidence investigations.

Metadata Mapping Process: The process of mapping, validating, and enriching metadata involves applying various transformations and enhancements to the extracted metadata. This metadata mapping process includes mapping, refining, and enriching the represented nodes and metadata attributes to establish evidence relationships. As a result, it establishes connections and relationships among metadata entities, capturing dependencies, associations, and interdependencies among different metadata attributes. To illustrate the metadata harmonisation process descriptively, Fig. 2 presents six subfigures. These subfigures depict the interactive workflow of initiating, refining, and querying metadata relationships among various entities, such as memory artefacts, network logs, and web browser data. The process begins with the unified system retrieving and defining metadata attributes within the data graph structure, as shown in sub-figure 'A' of Fig. 2. Subsequently, sub-figure 'B' illustrates the process of establishing cross-relationships among evidence entities based on their metadata types. During this stage, investigators interactively draw dashed black lines to establish the initial cross-matching between instances. The metadata initiated in sub-figure 'C' is then made available for investigators to review, edit, reject, or confirm. In this example, the investigative team rejects unnecessary nodes, such as the 'URL' node highlighted in the red dashed circle. They also reject the red dashed line linking two port numbers of entities associated with 'net' and 'm' nodes, as it is not relevant to the investigation. Subsequently, the outcome of the interactive engagement with the retrieved data modules is depicted in sub-figure 'D'. Lastly, the last two subfigures, sub-figure 'E' and sub-figure 'F' illustrate the outcomes of the cross-evidence query feature. For instance, the investigative team executes two queries based on cross-matching evidence timestamps and cross-matching IP addresses of entities, respectively.

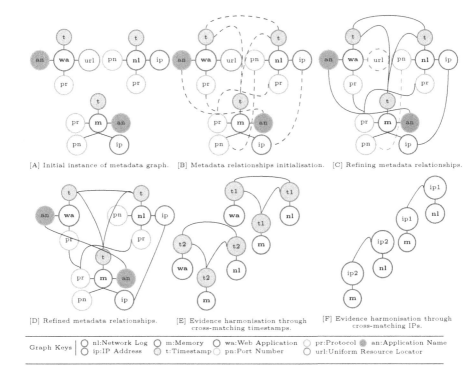

Fig. 2. An exemplary depiction of the metadata harmonisation process.

Building upon the aforementioned process, Fig. 3 illustrates the final result of the data harmonisation process, detailing potential evidence pertinent to this case study and addressing the first investigative question Q 1.. This visual representation implicates the suspect, Alex, in the leakage of the AI model. Distinct colours in the figure denote various attributes and entities: red nodes highlight timestamp events; orange nodes signify the AI model's size attribute; green nodes are events associated with suspect Alex; while light black nodes portray the primary data objects, illustrating the connections between network elements. Green lines mark positive matches between related entities. Notably, the red rectangle labelled with the initial 'A' pinpoints metadata attributes of the origin of the unidentified IP, addressing the second investigative question Q 2.. Overall, this figure elucidates the intricate interconnectedness and dependencies among different entities, offering a comprehensive view of the case study, and providing insight into the answer to investigative question Q 3..

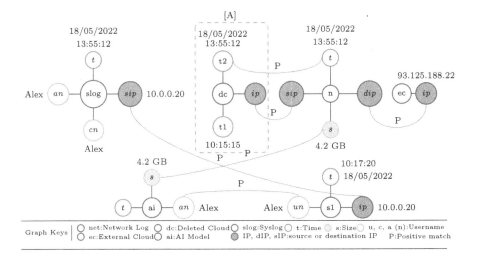

Fig. 3. A brief illustration of the metadata harmonisation case study results.

Cross Analytics: The proposed system's cross-analytics capabilities present a broad spectrum of analysis options. These options operate seamlessly across harmonised evidence, enhancing comprehensive digital forensics investigations. This study, however, emphasises the cross-timeline analysis to outline chronological events, thereby addressing Q 4. across the harmonised evidence demonstrated in the Fig. 3.

Cross-Timeline Analysis: This form of analysis aims to construct a chronological representation of incident-related events. It aids in establishing timelines for activities and pinpointing relationships, dependencies, anomalies, and sequential temporal events. Pertaining to this case study, Table 3 delineates details of harmonised timeline events linked to the potential data of the case. It encapsulates data related to the evidence, focusing on specific aspects, especially events connected to the leaked 'FinAI.h5' model, as well as the origins of these timestamp events. In parallel, Fig. 4 visually showcases these timeline events, tracing the entire life cycle of the 'FinAI.h5' model from its creation and deployment to the final moment of leakage.

Table 3. Summary of the harmonised timestamp events.

Date	Time	Timestamp Attribute	Category	Type	Attribute	Value	Metadata Source
20/04/2022	13:20:22	Created	Development	AI model	Model name	FinAI.h5	File system
20/04/2022	14:40:45	Created	Security	Access permission	Username	Alex	Cloud monitoring alert
18/05/2022	10:10:05	Accessed	Connection	SSH	Username	Alex	Memory
18/05/2022	10:15:15	Created	Deployment	Cloud server	Username	Alex	Cloud monitoring alert
18/05/2022	10:20:20	Created	Security	Logged in	Username	Alex	Syslog server
18/05/2022	10:55:12	Created	Network	Transmission	IP	10.0.0.15	Network logs

Fig. 4. Timeline analysis of the harmonised timestamp events.

The timeline analysis, as illustrated in Fig. 4, began with the creation and deployment of the 'FinAI.h5' model on AIxz's primary cloud server on April 20_{th}, 2022, at 13:20:22. Shortly after, at 14:40:45, the Cloud monitoring system logged a security event, granting full access permissions to an employee named Alex. On May 18_{th}, 2022, at 10:10:05, Alex leveraged his privileges and accessed the system via Secure Socket Shell (SSH). By 10:15:15, a new cloud server had been deployed, and the AI model was duplicated. At 10:20:20, a syslog event captured Alex accessing the perimeter firewall and establishing a new policy rule that allowed file transfer from the internal server 10.0.0.15 to external networks. The timeline analysis of the network traffic revealed that on May 18_{th}, 2022, at 11:33:10, a file approximately the size of the AI model was transferred to an external IP address. This in-depth timeline analysis offers insights into the sequence of events, highlighting potential security breaches and suspicious activities.

5   Conclusion

In the realm of digital forensics investigations, the harmonisation of heterogeneous evidence and the incorporation of advanced cross-data analytics are becoming paramount. This study proposes a novel approach to confront the challenges inherent to data heterogeneity and interoperability within digital evidence. The research findings underscore the UMGM's efficacy in seamlessly integrating and harmonising diverse evidence data. A key feature of the system is its capability to capture intricate relationships of digital evidence across diverse formats. By unifying different evidence formats, it enables cross-data queries and facilitates cross-analysis across evidence. It also empowers investigators to navigate and refine interconnected evidence pieces, enhancing cross-platform interoperability. The conducted case study further validates the proposed approach and highlights its benefits. Through the unified approach, investigators could streamline their workflows, reduce manual efforts in correlating pieces of information, and improve the accuracy and speed of evidence analysis. Future research will focus on enhancing the UMGM's scalability for handling larger and more complex datasets. Additionally, efforts will be directed towards integrating machine learning algorithms into the system to automate advanced evidence analytics.

References

1. Vincze, E.A.: Challenges in digital forensics. Police Pract. Res. **17**(2), 183–194 (2016)
2. Namjoshi, J., Rawat, M.: Role of smart manufacturing in industry 4.0. Mater. Today: Proc. **63**, 475–478 (2022)
3. Casey, E.: The chequered past and risky future of digital forensics. Aust. J. Forensic Sci. **51**(6), 649–664 (2019)
4. Miller, C.M.: A survey of prosecutors and investigators using digital evidence: a starting point. Forensic Sci. Int.: Synergy **6**, 100296 (2023)
5. Lillis, D., Becker, B., O'Sullivan, T., Scanlon, M.: Current challenges and future research areas for digital forensic investigation. arXiv preprint arXiv:1604.03850 (2016)
6. Rahman, H., Hussain, M.I.: A comprehensive survey on semantic interoperability for internet of things: state-of-the-art and research challenges. Trans. Emerg. Telecommun. Technol. **31**(12), e3902 (2020)
7. Mohammed, H., Clarke, N., Li, F.: Automating the harmonisation of heterogeneous data in digital forensics. In: ECCWS 2018, 17th European Conference on Cyber Warfare and Security, pp. 299–306 (2018)
8. Alshumrani, A., Clarke, N., Ghita, B.: A Unified Forensics Analysis Approach to Digital Investigation. Academic Conferences International Ltd. (2023)
9. Casino, F., et al.: Research trends, challenges, and emerging topics in digital forensics: a review of reviews. IEEE Access **10**, 25464–25493 (2022)
10. Brady, O., Overill, R., Keppens, J.: DESO: addressing volume and variety in large-scale criminal cases. Digit. Invest. **15**, 72–82 (2015)
11. Chabot, Y., Bertaux, A., Nicolle, C., Kechadi, T.: An ontology-based approach for the reconstruction and analysis of digital incidents timelines. Digit. Invest. **15**, 83–100 (2015)
12. Casey, E., Back, G., Barnum, S.: Leveraging CybOX™ to standardize representation and exchange of digital forensic information. Digit. Invest. **12**, S102–S110 (2015)

13. Casey, E., Barnum, S., Griffith, R., Snyder, J., van Beek, H., Nelson, A.: The evolution of expressing and exchanging cyber-investigation information in a standardized form. In: Biasiotti, M.A., Mifsud Bonnici, J.P., Cannataci, J., Turchi, F. (eds.) Handling and Exchanging Electronic Evidence Across Europe. LGTS, vol. 39, pp. 43–58. Springer, Cham (2018). https://doi.org/10.1007/978-3-319-74872-6_4

14. Arshad, H., Jantan, A., Hoon, G.K., Abiodun, I.O.: Formal knowledge model for online social network forensics. Comput. Secur. **89**, 101675 (2020)

15. Sikos, L.F.: Knowledge representation to support partially automated honeypot analysis based on Wireshark packet capture files. In: Czarnowski, I., Howlett, R.J., Jain, L.C. (eds.) Intelligent Decision Technologies 2019. SIST, vol. 142, pp. 345–351. Springer, Singapore (2020). https://doi.org/10.1007/978-981-13-8311-3_30

16. Chikul, P., Bahsi, H., Maennel, O.: An ontology engineering case study for advanced digital forensic analysis. In: Attiogbé, C., Ben Yahia, S. (eds.) MEDI 2021. LNCS, vol. 12732, pp. 67–74. Springer, Cham (2021). https://doi.org/10.1007/978-3-030-78428-7_6

17. Noel, S., Harley, E., Tam, K.H., Limiero, M., Share, M.: CyGraph: graph-based analytics and visualisation for cybersecurity. Handb. Stat. **35**, 117–167 (2016)

18. Schelkoph, D.J., Peterson, G.L., Okolica, J.S.: Digital forensics event graph reconstruction. In: Breitinger, F., Baggili, I. (eds.) ICDF2C 2018. LNICST, vol. 259, pp. 185–203. Springer, Cham (2019). https://doi.org/10.1007/978-3-030-05487-8_10

SMARPchain: A Smart Marker Based Reputational Probabilistic Blockchain for Multi-agent Systems

Chin-Tser Huang[1]([✉])(iD), Laurent Njilla[2](iD), Matthew Sharp[1](iD), and Tieming Geng[1](iD)

[1] Department of Computer Science and Engineering, University of South Carolina, Columbia, SC 29208, USA
huangct@cse.sc.edu, {mpsharp,tgeng}@email.sc.edu
[2] Air Force Research Laboratory, Rome, NY, USA
laurent.njilla@us.af.mil

Abstract. Designed as a distributed data storage system, blockchain employs a consensus mechanism to validate the addition of new data blocks while saving the need for mediation by a centralized server. However, when the blockchain technology is applied in decision-making applications, the consensus mechanism requires the decision to be deterministic, which will ignore different recommendations made by multiple agents and may put the computing system at risk. In this paper, we propose and develop SMARPchain, a paradigm of reputational probabilistic blockchain which is based on smart markers. The distinguishing characteristic of our SMARPchain approach is that it enables multiway branching which allows the result produced by each agent to be kept on the blockchain as a branchchain. Moreover, SMARPchain computes a probabilistic score on each branchchain based on the associated agent's reputation to help the decision maker reach an informed decision. SMARPchain satisfies three desirable requirements of recognizability, compatibility, and authenticability, and evaluation results show that SMARPchain will enhance the security and robustness of multi-agent decision making systems with acceptable overhead.

Keywords: Probabilistic Blockchain · Smart Marker · Multiway Branching · Multi-agent System · Decision Making

1 Introduction

Blockchain technology aims to provide a viable solution for maintaining a public distributed database of transactions, where the information is stored in blocks that are cryptographically chained. Blockchain technology spans uses like cryptocurrency, inventory and supply chain management, digital ID, wealth inheritance and transfer, smart city services, etc. An integral component of the blockchain technology is the consensus protocol [6], which ensures the consistency

G. Wang et al. (Eds.): UbiSec 2023, CCIS 2034, pp. 436–449, 2024.
https://doi.org/10.1007/978-981-97-1274-8_28

of the blockchains maintained by distributed nodes. As blockchain gradually finds new applications in multi-agent decision-making and risk assessment systems [1] such as machine learning [3] and intrusion detection systems [11], the need for majority consensus can pose problems. If only the majority view is accepted, valid minority opinions are discarded, possibly leading to flawed decisions.

We introduce SMARPchain, which is a reputational probabilistic blockchain using smart markers for multiway branching. Unlike existing solutions which mainly focus on majority consensus or summaries, SMARPchain retains all agent results and tags them with dynamic scores based on the agent's historical accuracy.

The key contributions of SMARPchain are threefold. First, SMARPchain enables the storage of all results generated by each agent by branching the chain into multiple branchchains, which avoids missing any useful insights not included in the majority consensus. Second, SMARPchain keeps the results generated by each agent in previous tasks, which allow for finer-grained evaluation of each agent's previous performance. Third, SMARPchain calculates and assigns to each branchchain a dynamic probabilistic score, which gives the user some information about the reliability level of each agent's previous performance and allows the user to make a wise, informed decision on which agent's result should be adopted for the current task.

The remainder of this paper is organized as follows. In Sect. 2, we give an overview of related work on probabilistic blockchain and its applications. In Sect. 3, we provide the background information about smart markers, which is the underlying technology used in this work. In Sect. 4, we present the details of SMARPchain design and discuss several unique advantages of SMARPchain in comparison with other methods. In Sect. 5, we describe a prototype implementation of our design and evaluate its performance. In Sect. 6, we conduct some experiments to verify the efficiency of our design. Finally, we conclude the paper and discuss future work in Sect. 7.

2   Related Work

In this section, we briefly review the recent works in three directions: 1) probabilistic blockchains, 2) multi-agent systems based on blockchain, and 3) probabilistic applications of the blockchain.

Probabilistic blockchains were first proposed by Salman et al. [12], these blockchains foster collaborative decision-making. Traditional blockchains verify transactions and fetch transaction statuses but lack mechanisms for global consensus. Salman's model incorporates probabilistic data to facilitate this. Potential uses span intrusion detection systems, recommendation systems, and reinforcement learning. Salman et al. also added a reputation framework to enhance decision-making, but it's off-chain, potentially allowing malicious manipulation since it lacks blockchain's security.

Yang et al. [15] suggested a blockchain framework for meme propagation in social networks. This model examines: a) influential features like agent weight, b) semantic features including user/message counts, and c) network attributes like meme popularity. Liang et al. [10] integrate blockchain and multi-agent systems for IoT-based intrusion detection. Feng et al. [4] introduced a dynamic multi-agent hierarchical consensus model to minimize communication costs and efficiently tally votes. In [9], researchers combined multi-agent systems with smart contracts, leading to a protocol for autonomous business activities and UAV experimentation.

Ecole Polytechnique and IBM Research [8] provided a Bitcoin Blockchain probabilistic model, emphasizing five features that aid in model selection and subsequent AI training. Chatterjee et al. [2] designed a game on blockchain using a probabilistic smart contract to produce trustworthy pseudorandom numbers. Jeong and Ahn [7] crafted a blockchain approach using probabilistic stochastic weighting for cloud user information management, ensuring data integrity during edits.

3   Background of Smart Markers

This section delves into *smart markers*, a core technology in our study. Introduced in our earlier research [5], smart markers enable branching in blockchains, allowing blocks to hold one-to-many dependencies. They signal when the blockchain diverges and later, when it converges. Traditional blockchains might temporarily branch, but eventually, only the longest branch persists for system integrity. Smart markers can be seamlessly integrated into blockchain systems because they are designed to satisfy the following three requirements. The first is *recognizability*: smart markers are inserted into a blockchain at the points where branching and merging occurs, and blockchain users can easily recognize smart marker blocks because of a unique pattern contained in the header of marker blocks. The second is *compatibility*: smart markers are stored as marker blocks which share compatible structure as normal blocks and can be conveniently inserted into blockchains. The third is *authenticability*: marker blocks are authenticatable to prevent malicious users from inserting forged smart markers to cause disruption in the validation process.

Marker blocks, like regular blocks, have a similar structure to fit seamlessly into existing blockchain systems. For instance, Bitcoin's block components include a magic number, block size, header, transaction count, and transaction list. Marker blocks retain this structure with slight adjustments: they have a fixed size, are absent transaction data, and have an authentication digital signature. Their headers, like standard blocks, reference the preceding block's cryptographic hash.

In smart marker-utilizing blockchains, branching marker count doesn't always equal merging marker count. Every branch uses a branching marker, but some might end without merging, marked with a terminal marker. All branches, termed *branchchains*, retain their transaction histories and are not pruned.

All additional data needed to identify the smart markers are stored in the block header. The "type" field in the header is used to indicate the type of block, in which 0 stands for a regular block, 1 for a branching marker block, 2 for a merging marker block, and 3 for a terminal marker block.

4 Design

In this section, we will introduce the design of our SMARPchain approach. In order that SMARPchain can achieve the goals of providing the decision maker with comprehensive results produced by all the agents and helping it reach an informed decision, we need to overcome the following three research challenges:

1. How to reliably maintain all results on the chain without relying on off-chain processing?
2. How to reliably maintain the reputation of each agent in terms of evaluating each agent fairly while avoiding missing any useful insights?
3. How to maintain the freshness and timeliness of each agent's reputation and influence?

To address these challenges, SMARPchain uses three novel features that will be explained in more detail shortly:

1. We use *smart markers* to allow the multiway branching and merging of branchchains. We accomplish this by inserting a branching marker block before the first block of each agent's branchchain and inserting a merging marker block of a branchchain after the associated agent has finished the exploration work on an assigned task.

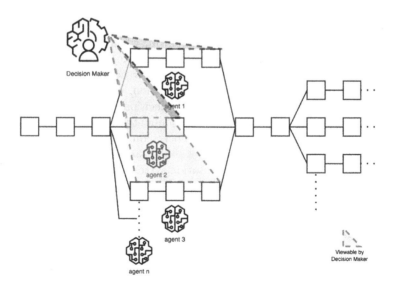

Fig. 1. System Structure of SMARPchain.

2. We design SMARPchain to use *probabilistic branchchains*. Each probabilistic branchchain is associated with one unique agent and stores the completed results of that agent on an assigned task. The reputation of each agent is maintained on the branching and merging markers which enclose the corresponding branchchain as a probabilistic score. Multi-way branching enabled by smart markers can support an unbounded number of agents and probabilistic branchchains.
3. SMARPchain uses a *confidence variable* to allocate higher influence to the more recent branchchains, while reducing the influence of earlier branchchains. The confidence variable allows the agent's probabilistic score and reputation to recover from past mistakes, while promoting reliable work and activity.

We introduce the SMARPchain framework, designed to create a probabilistic blockchain model that facilitates multiway branching in multi-agent systems. This model uses a dynamic score reflecting each agent's performance and reliability in the system. Using an agent's historical performance, we can execute decision-making or AI feature extraction. Thanks to smart markers, SMARPchain can simultaneously store and display multiple data branches, allowing agents employing various machine learning or deep learning algorithms to work collaboratively on distinct branchchains within the same blockchain.

Figure 1 depicts the system structure with a blockchain branching into three branchchains, showing the design's flexibility to support numerous branches. Each branchchain can employ varied data structures and algorithms or AI models. A decentralized autonomous organization (DAO) decision maker oversees the system, signaling the most trusted branchchain. Our design is flexible and does not have limit on which reputation formulation mechanism to use. Currently, we use Fine-Grained Rated Proportional Multi-Configurable EWA (FGRPMC-EWA) as the reputation mechanism, which is inspired by RPMC-EWA as described in [13]. The FGRPMC-EWA equation (Eq. 1) promotes timely correct answers, adjusts penalties based on answer accuracy, and ensures fairness among branchchains. Branchchain reputation, encompassing agent reputation and their data, fluctuates based on decision accuracy and timeliness. With FGRPMC-EWA, SMARPchain predominantly accepts valid results and dismisses untrustworthy ones, ensuring blockchain integrity and incentivizing agent trustworthiness. SMARPchain's reliability stems from *retaining* previous minority results, creating a robust reputation system. We introduce a confidence variable to decrease older branchchains' influence, ensuring the newest and most reputable branchchains exert the most control, thereby motivating consistent, trustworthy agent behavior. Compromised agents' impact is minimized by diluting aged branchchains' influence, emphasizing the need for consistent, dependable work to build reputation.

Our method retains the typical blockchain block structure for *compatibility* with standard blockchains, as illustrated in Fig. 2. Block headers contain the previous hash and timestamp. Standard block bodies store the transaction history, while marker blocks' headers feature a field with the branchchain agent's past probabilistic score. Their bodies embed a digital signature authenticating the agent associated with the branchchain. Each branchchain chronicles an agent's task progression. In SMARPchain, we utilize smart markers for probabilistic branchchain creation. These branchchains coexist within SMARPchain and aren't pruned. Tasks, such as intrusion detection or facial recognition AI tasks, are termed *exploration work*. For concurrent task exploration by multiple agents, a branching marker is added to SMARPchain, marking the start point for each agent's branchchain. Each agent independently completes the task, logging results in their branchchains. As different agents may employ varied algorithms or AI models, branchchain results may differ in trustworthiness. We allocate a probabilistic score to each result, reflecting its reliability based on prior trustworthiness and recent results. This is depicted in Fig. 3. An agent's initial trustworthiness score is 0.5, on a 0.0 (least trustworthy) to 1.0 (most trustworthy) scale. Post exploration, branchchains merge using a merging marker, culminating in a unified blockchain, as seen in Fig. 4. Enclosed by branching and merging markers, users can identify individual branchchains and associate results with respective agents.

While the multiway exploration work by the agents is ongoing, the decision maker will see multiple probabilistic branchchains coexisting in the SMARPchain network and will have access to each agent's intermediate results. No agent is perfect. Agents execute exploration work based on their configured models and algorithms, with output accuracy fluctuating due to ever-changing real-time scenarios. This accuracy is documented on their branchchains, thus they are "probabilistic branchchains". Our method attaches a probabilistic score to a branchchain's branching marker, as illustrated in Fig. 3. This score, paired in the subsequent merging marker, is then available for the next exploration round post-evaluation.

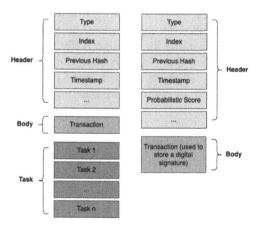

Fig. 2. Structure of a block. The left side represents a regular block while the right side represents a smart marker block.

Each exploration work round involves only a single branching level, not multi-level. This method offers advantages over the one in [12], where all agents must finish before summarizing the work. In our approach, the decision maker doesn't await synchronization to view exploration results. Agents might finish at varying times, evident from the differing block counts in each agent's branchchain in Fig. 3. Upon an agent's completion, its results are accessible to the decision maker, aiding comprehensive decision-making.

The reputation $R_{i,t}$ of an agent i at task t is defined as:

$$R_{i,t} = \frac{\begin{cases} 0.5: & if\ t{=}0\ (i.e.,\ first\ task); \\ [(\alpha\frac{p}{p+n}+(1-\alpha)(2R_{i,t-1}-1)](1-\frac{w_{i,t}}{bx_t}): & if\ correct\ decision; \\ [\beta\frac{-n}{p+n}+(1-\beta)(2R_{i,t-1}-1)](\gamma): & if\ wrong\ decision\ and\ 0\%{<}RSD{<}20\%; \\ \beta\frac{-n}{p+n}+(1-\beta)(2R_{i,t-1}-1): & if\ wrong\ decision\ and\ RSD{>}20\%; \end{cases}}{2}+0.5 \quad (1)$$

where α and β are configurable parameters between 0 and 1, p is the number of correct decisions (i.e., equal to the decision chosen by the decision maker), n is the number of incorrect decisions, and $w_{i,t}$ is the work time taken by agent i on completing task t. We incorporate the work time with the principle that the faster an agent comes to the correct answer, the more it is rewarded. In Eq. (1), we take the original positive reward amount and decrease it by a small ratio which is $w_{i,t}$ divided by the product of a configurable variable b and x_t which is the time required for the slowest agent to finish its work on task t. Decreasing the reward based on time ensures that the agents will attempt to complete the task with their best effort in terms of time. Furthermore, our system more finely tunes the reward and detriment to the reputation of the agents. We consider the deviation from the answer chosen by the decision maker when deciding to adjust the reputation of agents. The lesser the deviation from the chosen answer, the less the reputation will be damaged. This way if an agent is not acting maliciously but just makes a slight error, its reputation will be less affected. We finely tune the amount of penalty applied by multiplying the relative standard deviation (RSD) by a configurable γ penalty for different RSDs. If the deviation is between 0%–5% no penalty is applied. For 5%–10% deviation, γ penalty is applied; for 10%–20% deviation, $2 * \gamma$ penalty is applied; if the deviation is above 20% the maximum penalty is applied. In our case, we set γ to be 0.25. This ensures that

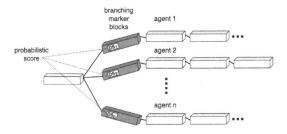

Fig. 3. Branching of the Blockchain into Probabilistic Branchchains

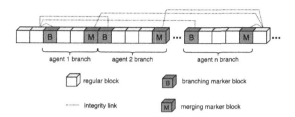

Fig. 4. Linear Storage Structure of SMARPchain

small mistakes impact the reputation less, while larger deviations are penalized more. Every agent's reputation is initialized to the neutral score of 0.5.

Before the decision maker follows the longest continuous path of reputable branchchains to make an informed decision, a confidence variable is applied to the probability of all branchchains. This confidence variable is designed to decay over time which will give the older branchchains, whether they be malicious or not, less of an influence on the decision maker. The confidence variable is set to be 50% of the distance of a branchchain from the most recent n branchchains. For example, for a chain of 20 branchchains where n is set to 5, then the latest 5 branchchains are unaffected by the confidence variable and the confidence applied to the 7th branchchain in the chain (i.e., the 2nd branchchain before the most recent 5 branchchains) would be $1 - (0.5 * 2/15)$. The confidence variable ensures that reputation scores reflect the most recent performance to maintain the freshness of the reputation. The addition of the confidence variable aims to motivate all agents to consistently contribute good work because past high reputation will wear down over time. The confidence variable prevents outdated information from significantly impacting an agent's reputation, promoting a more accurate representation of the current abilities and strengths of the agent. Moreover, the confidence variable will strengthen the protection against Sybil attacks, since an attacker will have to spend more resources more frequently to retain its influence.

4.1   Advantages

The unique advantages of the SMARPchain can be summarized as follows:

1. *SMARPchain maintains the minority results on branchchains.* Our design allows for the storage of branchchains generated by minority agents that would normally be pruned on standard blockchain systems. These minority findings allow the decision maker a more comprehensive dataset for use as reference.
2. *SMARPchain allows for real-time updates throughout the exploration work.* Agents can append blocks to their own branchchain when they are performing their exploration work. When an agent finishes the exploration work on the current task, its branchchain is completed and tagged with a probabilistic score according to the evaluation of the reliability of its results. The decision

maker and other users can see the trustworthiness of a branchchain from the previous task and use these intermediary results as they see fit.

3. *SMARPchain allows for a more comprehensive record of all agents on the blockchain.* Each agent's probabilistic scores are updated after every exploration task. A history of the results is recorded for every agent in the agent's branchchains.

4.2 Concerns and Mitigation

With every new design there are potential risks and concerns. In this subsection, we will discuss possible issues people may raise about SMARPchain and how they can be overcome or mitigated.

Performance. Performance is a concern when maintaining larger blockchains, since more data needs to be stored and processed. SMARPchain's performance depends on its data structures, hardware, and network. With its branchchains allowing varied data structures and AI models for the same task, users should strategically allocate computer resources for optimal performance. Enhancements can also be achieved through caching and data pre-processing to minimize real-time processing demands.

Security. Security is a central theme for blockchain technology. SMARPchain utilizes cryptographic hash functions for block integrity and timestamps for consistent temporal branching. Leveraging smart markers, SMARPchain inherits recognizability, compatibility, and authenticity [5]. It operates on a probabilistic blockchain with a reputation system to verify block reliability over time. Storing minority results, SMARPchain defends against collusion attacks and identifies malicious behaviors from previously trusted agents.

Decentralization. Decentralization is another essential and desirable property of the blockchain technology. By enabling agents to independently conduct exploration without a central authority, decentralization is enhanced. With a decentralized decision-making platform, users or AI can influence branchchain selection post-exploration. Keeping minority results ensures all agents contribute to their branchchains, bolstering system robustness. By dispersing the power of reputable branchchains, we curtail undue influence across the entire SMARPchain, preventing dominance by any single group.

Fairness. Ensuring blockchain fairness boosts participation in exploration. SMARPchain's retention of minority results and inclusion of their agents in future explorations offers enhanced fairness over traditional blockchains. Branchchain reputation varies with performance, and by restricting influence calculation to the latest n blocks, we curb undue dominance by any block or group over time.

As the above discussion shows, we have considered various possible issues when it comes to the implementation and operation of SMARPchain, and our design has already addressed or mitigated many of these concerns.

5 Implementation

We developed a prototype of SMARPchain using Node.js, which implements the blockchain in four modules: node module, task module, blockchain module, and the DAO module.

The node module manages the peer-to-peer communication which enables the broadcasting and synchronization of blocks. The node module is implemented with the WebSocket protocol library. Each node can be both a server and a client at the same time to enable nodes to be interconnected. These nodes host the individual agents for use on the branchchains. The task module generates tasks and assigns them to each participating agent. Tasks have a dictionary data structure where each task is identified with a unique ID. The blockchain module generates the genesis block, appends blocks to the blockchain and branchchains, validates each block, and forwards interim answers to the DAO module. Each agent can generate multiple blocks on the agent's branchchain during exploration work. Since the agents will be running different algorithms or AI models, the number of blocks produced by each agent may differ. The DAO module collects the intermediate results from the blockchain module to allow the decision maker to make informed decisions. After the exploration work is finished by each agent, the DAO module updates the agent's probabilistic score. The consensus mechanism is used to process the agreement on transactions. We have chosen DPoS as the concensus mechanism for our design. DPoS uses delegates to collect all transactions, validate new blocks, and achieve the concensus. We choose DPoS for its ability to work robustly and continuously with limited computational resources.

To enact our prototype, we add the agent's probabilistic score as a percentage into the header of the branching marker blocks, as seen in Fig. 2. This percentage is a variable number within the range between 0 and 1, where 0 means not trusted at all and 1 means completely trusted. As each task is performed, these numbers are dynamically adjusted based on previous performance. The design of our prototype has no limit on the number of agents and is only hampered by the amount of available computing resources. The prototype is limited by the speed at which the reputation can be gathered through traversing the many branchchains. However, the user can limit the consumed resources by only traversing the last n branchchains for their more current reputation in the SMARPchain. Thus the speed of which the user gathers information from a SMARPchain can be increased and decreased by increasing and decreasing n respectively.

During exploration work, the decision maker can either monitor agents' intermediate results or wait until all agents complete their tasks. The decision maker then computes a score using the reputation of the last n agents in the branchchains. This score stems from the agent's average accuracy in their branchchain during the work, adjusted by the branchchain's reputation from prior tasks. We've developed a prototype supporting several decision-making modes, as follows:

1. In the *dictator* mode, the decision maker selects which branchchain to use. This choice is based on averaging the last n scores to ensure fairness. Alternatively, a weighted average can emphasize recent reputations in the branchchain. After obtaining percentages from agents, we compute the branchchain's mean percentage, minimum, maximum, mode, standard deviation from the mean, and modified z-score. Using this data, the decision maker determines the optimal branchchain for the subsequent task.
2. A *grassroots* mode, where the users other than the decision maker may decide if a specific branchchain is preferred for a specific task. In this mode, each user can choose a branchchain and vote on a ranking. This ranking is summed and added to the probabilistic score for the block or branchchain.
3. A *hybrid* mode, where the votes of the users are weighted when the decision maker is calculating the best branchchain.

We used an Intel Core i7-8700 CPU, with 16GB RAM, and a GeForce RTX 2070 to set up an environment for testing our DAO. To test the accuracy of our model we created an AI model, which was trained with different classifiers including a kNN, a SVM and a RF, each running on their own branchchain to determine their effect on the accuracy of the decision maker's ability to choose the highest rated branchchain. To find the optimal settings for the SVM we tested linear, polynomial, and radial basis function kernels. The optimal settings, taken as output from the training tests, were set at $c = 20$ (regularization parameter), $Q - value = 0.1$ and the kernel set to radial basis function (RBF). For the kNN, the value of k was found to be 19 as the optimal parameter. A number of trees were tested to find out the optimal settings for the RF, ranging from 50 to 200. We selected 60 as the optimal value resultant from the tested trees. This model was then trained on 800 different iterations of our SMARPchain prototype. Each blockchain differed in size and number of branchings and mergings. We tested the model on 200 of these prototype iterations and were able to achieve up to 98% accuracy when choosing the best branchchain for the current task after following all the previously chosen branchchains starting from the genesis block.

The use cases of this technology can include implementing multiple cryptographic hashing algorithms inside of each branchchain, thus the security of the hashing can be enhanced. This is due to an attacker needing to compromise multiple diverse algorithms in order to successfully attack the blockchain, rather than just a single algorithm. Another use case example could be the secure storing and management of private keys. Each branchchain within the blockchain can utilize different key management systems on each branchchain, making it more difficult for attacks to find a single weakness within the system. The use cases of SMARPchain are not limited to the area of security; this technology could be used to audit other systems using different techniques or applying the same technique to different sets of data on each branchchain. For example, in any industry where goods need to be tracked, applying SMARPchain by utilizing diverse algorithms or AI models within each branchchain can provide a higher level of protection against fraudulent activity. These multiple branchchains can improve the overall accuracy and reliability of the tracked information as it can be validated by multiple independent systems.

6   Evaluation

In this section, we present an analysis of the performance of SMARPchain's exploration work. For simplicity and without loss of generality, we established the SMARPchain network on one machine such that network transmission delay on the data synchronization is excluded and only the exploration work is measured. We execute and measure the overhead time on the gathering of the weighted reputations of the branchchains after exploration work has completed. We test 1,000 rounds and take the average of the elapsed time. The sizes of the tested SMARPchains (approximate number of blocks in the blockchain) are set to be 500, 1K, 5K, 10K, 50K, and 100K, and the elapsed time is shown in Table 1.

Table 1. Overhead time used

Size	500	1K	5K	10K	50K	100K
Time (ms)	2.15	5.70	22.54	60.36	421.59	1567.08

From the results, we can see that the running time increases roughly proportional with the number of blocks in the blockchain network. We notice that the time used on a much larger blockchain network that contains 100K blocks is less than two seconds (keeping in mind that this simulation excludes the transmission time and network delay). Therefore, the results show that our framework is both practical and scalable.

Table 2. Accuracy of Decision Maker During Sybil Attack

Sybil branches (%)	0	5	10	15	20	25
Accuracy (%)	99.87	99.65	99.27	98.52	98.13	97.33

Next, we evaluate the robustness of SMARPchain against collusion attacks such as Sybil attacks, in which a malicious entity controls numerous fake identities with an aim to sway the reputation system. To simulate a Sybil attack we conducted an experiment by tagging raising percentages of branchchains as malicious throughout the entire SMARPchain. We ran the experiment using 10,000 chains of 10,000 branchchains, where malicious agent's branchchains were tagged evenly throughout the entire SMARPchain from the genesis block to the end of the chain. For simplicity without loss of generality, we assume each branchchain contains only one block. The objective was to see how accuracy is affected as the proportion of malicious agent branchchains in the SMARPchain increases. In our experiment we introduced a configurable confidence variable that exponentially influences the impact of previous branchchains on the final results, with decreasing weight assigned to the older branchchains. We set the confidence variable to evenly decrease influence on previous branchchains in the direction from the last n branchchain added to the SMARPchain backward to the genesis block. We set n to 1,000, which means all agents' last 1,000 branchchains added to the SMARPchain have full influence. We incrementally increased the percentage of malicious agent branchchains in the SMARPchain from 5% to 25% percent while monitoring the accuracy levels. Our findings, as seen in Table 2, show that even with 25% malicious agent branchchains, the SMARPchain only has an additional 2.67% loss in accuracy when compared to a non-malicious one. The results show that the confidence variable was critical in reducing the influence of malicious agent branchchains in the system. By assigning a lower confidence to older branchchains, we ensure a greater emphasis on the more recent branchchains, which have higher likelihood of being current. This confidence-based evaluation mechanism employed by SMARPchain achieves its effectiveness by minimizing the impact of the compromised branchchains, although it could not entirely eliminate the inaccuracy.

7   Conclusion

In multi-agent systems, it is essential to have easy access to comprehensive results from all agents for decision-making. However, current probabilistic blockchain solutions, constrained by the no-branching rule, capture the majority view. We introduce SMARPchain, leveraging smart markers to document each agent's outcomes on a branchchain, while also assigning a dynamic score indicating result reliability based on historical performance. Compared to existing models, SMARPchain offers distinct advantages, and our simulation confirms its practicality and resilience against collusion attacks.

Future enhancements for SMARPchain include data sharding [14]. By segmenting data, transaction verification becomes more efficient, strengthening the system against malicious agents. Given SMARPchain's design to retain both majority and minority views, sharding can decentralize the system further, making it tougher for colluding parties to dominate.

Acknowledgments. This work is supported by the Summer Faculty Fellowship Program (SFFP) with the Information Assurance Branch of the AFRL, Rome, NY and the Information Institute (II). Any opinions, findings, and conclusions or recommendations expressed in this material are those of the authors and do not necessarily reflect the views of the Air Force Research Laboratory.

References

1. Cerf, M., Matz, S., Berg, A.: Using blockchain to improve decision making that benefits the public good. Front. Blockchain **3**, 13 (2020)
2. Chatterjee, K., Goharshady, A.K., Pourdamghani, A.: Probabilistic smart contracts: Secure randomness on the blockchain. In: 2019 IEEE International Conference on Blockchain and Cryptocurrency (ICBC), pp. 403–412. IEEE (2019)
3. Chen, F., Wan, H., Cai, H., Cheng, G.: Machine learning in/for blockchain: future and challenges. Can. J. Stat. **49**(4), 19 (2021)
4. Feng, L., Zhang, H., Chen, Y., Lou, L.: Scalable dynamic multi-agent practical byzantine fault-tolerant consensus in permissioned blockchain. Appl. Sci. **8**(10), 1919 (2018)
5. Geng, T., Njilla, L., Huang, C.T.: Smart markers in smart contracts: enabling multiway branching and merging in blockchain for decentralized runtime verification. In: Proceedings of 2021 IEEE Conference on Dependable and Secure Computing (DSC 2021), pp. 1–8 (2021). https://doi.org/10.1109/DSC49826.2021.9346270
6. Huang, C.T., Njilla, L., Geng, T.: Consensus of whom? A spectrum of blockchain consensus protocols and new directions. In: 2019 IEEE International Smart Cities Conference (ISC2), pp. 1–8. IEEE (2019)
7. Jeong, Y.S., Ahn, B.T.: An efficient management scheme of blockchain-based cloud user information using probabilistic weighting. J. Supercomput. **77**(4), 3339–3358 (2021)
8. Jourdan, M., Blandin, S., Wynter, L., Deshpande, P.: A probabilistic model of the bitcoin blockchain. In: Proceedings of the IEEE/CVF Conference on Computer Vision and Pattern Recognition Workshops (2019)
9. Kapitonov, A., Lonshakov, S., Krupenkin, A., Berman, I.: Blockchain-based protocol of autonomous business activity for multi-agent systems consisting of UAVs. In: 2017 Workshop on Research, Education and Development of Unmanned Aerial Systems (RED-UAS), pp. 84–89. IEEE (2017)
10. Liang, C., et al.: Intrusion detection system for the internet of things based on blockchain and multi-agent systems. Electronics **9**(7), 1120 (2020)
11. Meng, W., Tischhauser, E.W., Wang, Q., Wang, Y., Han, J.: When intrusion detection meets blockchain technology: a review. IEEE Access **6**, 10 (2018)
12. Salman, T., Jain, R., Gupta, L.: Probabilistic blockchains: a blockchain paradigm for collaborative decision-making. In: 2018 9th IEEE Annual Ubiquitous Computing, Electronics & Mobile Communication Conference (UEMCON), pp. 457–465. IEEE (2018)
13. Salman, T., Jain, R., Gupta, L.: A reputation management framework for knowledge-based and probabilistic blockchains. In: 2019 IEEE International Conference on Blockchain (Blockchain), pp. 520–527. IEEE (2019)
14. Wang, G., Shi, Z.J., Nixon, M., Han, S.: SoK: sharding on blockchain. In: AFT 2019, pp. 41–61. Association for Computing Machinery, New York (2019). https://doi.org/10.1145/3318041.3355457
15. Yang, F., Qiao, Y., Wang, S., Huang, C., Wang, X.: Blockchain and multi-agent system for meme discovery and prediction in social network. Knowl.-Based Syst. **229**, 107368 (2021)

Automatically Inferring Image Base Addresses of ARM32 Binaries Using Architecture Features

Daniel Chong[(⊠)], Junjie Zhang, Nathaniel Boland, and Lingwei Chen

Department of Computer Science and Engineering, Wright State University,
Dayton 45435, USA
{chong.8,junjie.zhang,boland.5,lingwei.chen}@wright.edu

Abstract. We designed an innovative method, namely *iBase*, which automatically infers the image base address of an ARM32 binary by statistically, structurally, and semantically correlating the absolute and the relative addresses contained in the binary. *iBase* exploits ARM32's architecture features, and hence it is immune to variances introduced by software development and compilation. In addition, *iBase* is parameter-free and it requires no manual configuration. We implemented *iBase* and performed evaluation using 20 ARM32 binaries. Our evaluation results have shown that *iBase* successfully detects base addresses for all of them and outperforms start-of-the-art tools including `Ghidra` and `Radare2`.

Keywords: Reverse Engineering · Image Base Address · Microcontrollers · Binary Analysis · Embedded Systems

1 Introduction

Software reverse engineering occupies a critical role in mitigating threats to the Internet of Things (IoT). Specifically, it enables a variety of security tasks such as malware analysis, vulnerability detection, and binary optimization. Effective software reverse engineering usually relies on the correct identification of the image base address (a.k.a., the base address) of an analyzed binary, which refers to the lowest virtual address from which this binary is loaded into the memory. Image base addresses are indispensable to disassemble and emulate binaries, which, for example, will need them to determine the correct destination addresses of branch instructions. While the base address is readily available for a binary compiled for debugging, it is commonly concealed in a binary for release, especially for firmware binaries [1,2] used for IoTs, whose auxiliary information has been extensively stripped away to reduce their footprints in memory and ROM. Therefore, it is a highly-demanded but challenging task to accurately identify the image base addresses of IoT firmware binaries.

A few attempts [3–5] have been made towards this objective. Specifically, Skochinskey et al. [3] proposed to leverage jump tables, string tables, and initialization code to infer the base address. Unfortunately, this method requires a reverse engineer to manually identify one or more of these structures within the binary. Alternatively, Zachry Basnight et al. [4] proposed to use immediate values in instructions. The immediate values are offset by candidate image base values. If the offset value points to a structure such as the beginning of a string, it is considered to be a match. Therefore, a high match percentage indicates a high likelihood of the candidate being the correct image base. Nevertheless, this method requires the candidate image addresses to be manually identified and it requires significant time to complete the analysis. Zhu et al. [5,6] devised an automated method to determine the base addresses of binaries compiled to the ARM architecture, which reportedly host approximately 63% of embedded systems. Unfortunately, this method relies on the accurate identification of function entry tables (FETs) [5] or function entry addresses [6], which limit its practical applicability. On the one hand, the method [5] is inapplicable to binaries without FETs and those with undetectable FETs; the FET identification process used by this method is sensitive to manually-configured parameters. On the other hand, compiler optimizations and architecture variety makes it challenging to detect function entry addresses.

In this paper, we present an innovative method, namely *iBase*, which automatically infers the image base address of an ARM32 binary. Same as existing work [3–6], *iBase* focuses on binaries compiled for the 32-bit ARM architecture (a.k.a ARM32), a leading target architecture used by an enormous number of high-profile binaries. However, fundamentally different from these existing methods that rely on software-specific heuristics, *iBase* exploits architecture features that are inherent to all ARM32 binaries. As a consequence, *iBase* is immune to variances introduced by software development and compilation. In addition, *iBase* is parameter-free and it requires no manual configuration. We have implemented *iBase* in Python and performed evaluation using 20 real-world ARM32 binaries. Our evaluation results have demonstrated that *iBase* successfully detects base addresses for all of them and outperforms start-of-the-art tools including `Ghidra` [7] and `Radare2` [8]. To summarize, our work has made the following novel contributions.

- We have designed a novel, parameter-free method to automatically infer image base addresses of stripped ARM32 binaries.
- We have implemented a system, namely *iBase*, and we plan to publish its source code once the paper is accepted.
- We have evaluated our system using 20 binaries and accomplished a high accuracy with negligible performance overhead.

The rest of the paper is organized as follows. Section 2 discusses the related work. The system design is presented in Sect. 3. Section 4 organizes the evaluation results including effectiveness and performance. Section 5 discusses the potential future work and Sect. 6 concludes.

2   Related Work

Image bases are essential for reverse engineering [9]. They are indispensable for disassembling [10] and emulating [11] stripped binaries, exemplified by those binaries extracted from IoT devices. A few methods [3–5] have been proposed. Skochinskey et al. [3] use four software features including self-relocating code, the initialization code, jump tables, and string tables. Unfortunately, while parts of this method can be automated, this method relies heavily upon the engineer's ability to identify these code structures and does not yield a final, definitive value.

Basnight et al. described another method for image base determination called the "load immediate instructions trick" [4]. In this method, all load register (LDR) instructions referencing immediate (i.e. absolute) values are collected. These references are then offset by candidate image base addresses to see which candidate correctly aligns the references with target data such as strings or function entries. A fundamental limitation of this method is that a reverse engineer needs to manually determine the candidates of image addresses. In addition, the "load immediate instructions" technique is a brute force method and requires significant time to complete.

Zhu et al. proposed an automated detection method that relies on the identification of function entry tables (FETs) to determine the image base of a binary file [5]. It first identifies FETs. Then the lowest and highest addresses contained in the FET are used in conjunction with the size of the binary file to calculate the range of the image base. The algorithm sequentially applies each candidate image base value to the FET addresses and attempts to match the function prologue with the newly-offset address. The number of matched function addresses is recorded. The candidate address where the percentage of matched function entry addresses exceeds a threshold is considered the true image base. However, despite the fact that this method is automated and its detection result is conclusive, it has a few fundamental limitations. First, if the source code's author does not implement an array of function pointers, there will not be FETs present within the binary, and the algorithm will fail. Additionally, the threshold which determines the success or failure of a candidate image base must be configured by the user. Therefore, the user must interpret the results of this algorithm and use these interpretations to modify the threshold parameter to correctly arrive at a final value. Zhu et al. also proposed an alternative solution [6] to detect base address using function address rather than FETs. Nevertheless, similar to [5], this method leverages software heuristics. Specifically, it is based on the observation that ARM binaries often load function addresses into registers with the LDR instruction. it also needs to assess whether a candidate base address results in points to correct function prologues. Unfortunately, these software heuristics can be easily subverted by compiling optimization or obfuscation [12]. For example, a compiled binary does not have to use the LDR instruction to load function addresses, and therefore this method will not be able to obtain a data set of addresses; a binary may not necessarily follow a specific function prologue pattern [13], making it extremely challenging to detect functions' entry addresses.

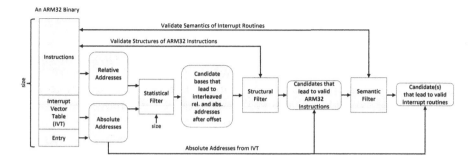

Fig. 1. The Architectural Overview of *iBase*

3 System Design

iBase focuses on inferring the base address by statistically, structurally, and semantically correlating the absolute and the relative addresses contained in an ARM32 binary, where these addresses are partially manifested by ARM32's architecture specifications. Specifically, *iBase* exploits the following three of ARM32's architectural features:

- Entry Point: the entry point, a.k.a the initial value of the program counter, is the address of the first instruction to be executed. The entry point of an ARM32 binary is stored in the second dword of this binary (i.e., with the address of 0x00000004), where a dword contains 4 bytes. The entry point is an absolute address.
- Interrupt Vector Table (IVT): the IVT immediately follows the second dword and starts from 0x00000008. This table is a list of addresses for all of the interrupt service routines. All these addresses are absolute addresses. Yet, the size of the IVT is unknown.
- Instruction Section: the instruction section, which is a sequence of instructions, immediately follows IVT. The starting address of the instruction section is not manifested in the binary. Since IVT's size is unknown, the starting address of the instruction section is also unknown. Both absolute and relative addresses are used in this section, but they are distinguishable based on their associated instructions.

The architectural overview of *iBase* is presented in Fig. 1. Specifically, *iBase* derives both absolute and relative addresses from an ARM32 binary. It then infers candidate image base addresses by statistically correlating absolute and relative addresses. *iBase* further filters out irrelevant candidate image base addresses using structural analysis and finally detects the actual image base address using lightweight semantic analysis.

3.1   Retrieving Absolute and Relative Addresses

Both the entry point and addresses contained in the IVT are absolute addresses. Comparatively, certain instructions such as branch statements in the instruction section use relative addresses. We can therefore efficiently parse the entry point, the interrupt vector table, and branch statements to retrieve absolute and relative addresses. Nevertheless, the IVT's size varies for different binaries but it is not manifested in the binary. Therefore, the ending address of the IVT, and thus the starting address of the instruction section, are unknown.

In order to address this challenge, we leverage the entry point (denoted as $entry$) and the size of the binary (denoted as $size$). We use S_{abs} to denote the set of absolute addresses, where $S_{abs} = \{entry\}$. Specifically, after a binary is loaded into the memory, the highest possible address of a byte in the binary is $entry + size$; similarly, the lowest possible one is $entry - size$. In other words, when this binary is loaded into the memory, it will reside in the range of $R_{mem} = [entry - size, entry + size]$. It is worth noting that this range is also applicable to absolute addresses in IVT. $iBase$ therefore enumerates each dword denoted as dw starting from 0x00000008. If dw resides in the range (i.e., $entry - size \le dw \le entry + size$), it will be identified as an absolute address in IVT and added to $S_{abs} = S_{abs} \cup \{dw\}$, and $iBase$ will proceed to the next word. When $iBase$'s enumeration reaches the first dword in the instruction, because the literal value of an instruction has no intrinsic meaning, the dw value is highly likely to exceed the upper bound of this range (i.e., $dw > entry + size$). In other words, a binary value indicating an address must fall within a certain range because the literal value of the dword is an address; however, a binary value indicating an instruction is uninhibited by this constraint as its literal value has no meaning. Therefore, when $iBase$ encounters a dw where $dw > entry + size$, it stops the enumeration and considers this dword as the first dword of the instruction section. This enumeration process will lead to a set of absolute addresses, which is denoted as S_{abs}.

Once the enumeration stops, $iBase$ starts to disassemble instructions. The disassembling continues sequentially until either the end of the binary is reached or a disassembling attempt fails. $iBase$ only concerns branch instructions that use relative addresses as arguments, ignoring those using registers as arguments. This step will lead to a set of relative addresses, denoted as S_{rel}.

3.2   Inferring Candidate Base Addresses

After $iBase$ identifies S_{abs} and S_{rel}, it will leverage them to derive the range of the image base addresses, denoted as R_{base}. We denote the minimal and the maximal values in S_{abs} as $min(S_{abs})$ and $max(S_{abs})$, respectively. We will then have $base + size \ge max(S_{abs})$. This indicates that when the binary is loaded into the memory with the image base address of $base$, the maximal absolute address can never exceed $base + size$. Similarly, we will have $min(S_{abs}) \ge base$ to ensure $min(S_{abs})$ is accessible when the binary is loaded. Therefore, we can infer that $base \in R_{base} = [max(S_{abs}) - size, min(S_{abs})]$.

Given the range of *base*, we can further derive a set of candidate *base* values. Our method takes advantage of ARM32's two architecture specifications, where i) the image base address is always aligned with the address of a memory page [14] and ii) the page size is typically 1KB or 4KB. Therefore, we use a finer granularity of 1KB as the page size (i.e., $page\_size = 1$KB). Specifically, *iBase* derives a set of candidate image bases as $S_{base} = \{addr~\&~\neg(page\_size - 1) \mid max(S_{abs}) - size \leq addr \leq min(S_{abs})]\}$.

3.3 Statistically Filtering

iBase next filters out invalid image base values from S_{base} using statistical analysis. Such analysis leverages our observation that absolute addresses, after the correct image base address is subtracted, should be interleaved with relative addresses. Specifically, we can use a candidate image, say $base_i \in S_{base}$, and then subtract it from all absolute addresses in S_{abs}, resulting in S'_{abs}. If $base_i$ is likely to be a reasonable image base, values in S'_{abs} should be very close to those in S_{rel} (i.e., values from these two sets are interleaved); otherwise, values from S'_{abs} and S_{rel} are likely to disperse, introducing outliers.

In order to quantitatively assess this observation, we have leveraged interquartile range (IQR) [15], an efficient, parameter-free method to statistically detect outliers. Algorithm 1.1 presents how *iBase* integrates S_{base}, S_{rel}, and S_{abs} to filter out irrelevant values from S_{base}. Our algorithm joins S'_{abs} and S_{rel} and then applies IQR to detect outliers. Specifically, if an outlier is detected, S'_{abs} and S_{rel} are not considered to be sufficiently interleaved and the corresponding $base_i$ is discarded; otherwise, S'_{abs} and S_{rel} are considered to be sufficiently close to each other and the corresponding $base_i$ is preserved.

```
 1  Validate-Distance(combined_set):
 2      quartile_1 = median(combined_set.first_half)
 3      quartile_3 = median(combined_set.second_half)
 4      iqr = quartile_3 - quartile_1
 5      upper_limit = quartile_3 + iqr * 1.5
 6      lower_limit = quartile_1 - iqr * 1.5
 7      for a in combined_set:
 8          if a > upper_limit or a < lower_limit:
 9              return False
10      return True
11
12  Statistic-Filter(candidates, abs, rel):
13      for c in candidates:
14          combined_set = rel
15          for r in abs:
16              combined_set.append(r - c)
17          if Statistic-Filter(combined_set) == False:
18              candidates.remove(c)
19      return candidates
```

Listing 1.1. Statistically Filtering

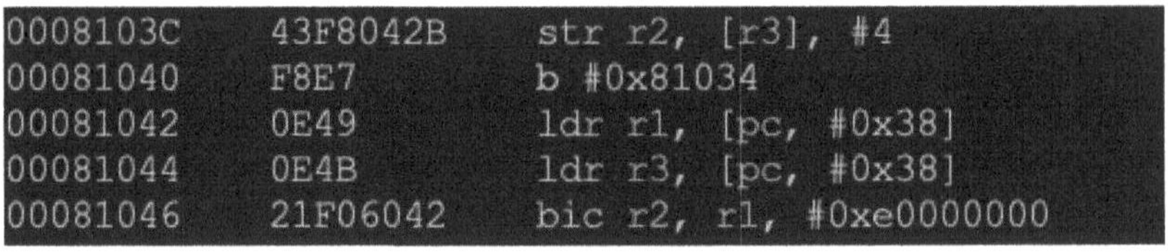

```
0008103C    43F8042B    str  r2, [r3], #4
00081040    F8E7        b #0x81034
00081042    0E49        ldr  r1, [pc, #0x38]
00081044    0E4B        ldr  r3, [pc, #0x38]
00081046    21F06042    bic  r2, r1, #0xe0000000
```

Fig. 2. A disassembled ARM32 binary snippet whose instruction size is 1 or 2 bytes

3.4 Structurally Filtering

After removing invalid candidates of base addresses using the statistical filter, *iBase* conducts additional filtering using ARM32's instruction sizes. Specifically, instructions in ARM32 can only be 1 or 2 bytes long [16]. Figure 2 presents a disassembled ARM32 binary snippet, whose instructions are either 1 or 2 bytes.

Our algorithm of structurally filtering is presented in Listing 1.2. Specifically, *iBase* offsets each absolute address (i.e., abs_j) by a candidate base (i.e., $base_i$). This results in an address (i.e., $abs_j - base_i$) that should point to an instruction in the binary. If this candidate base, $base_i$, is correct, $abs_j - base_i$ should always point to the beginning of a 2-byte instruction or that of a 1-byte instruction. Therefore, if $abs_j - base_i$ points to the middle of a 2-byte instruction, $base_i$ will be considered as an invalid candidate base and hence filtered out.

```
 1  Validate-Inst(absolute, base):
 2      for a in absolute:
 3          address = a - base
 4          instruction = binary_code[address]
 5          if instruction == None:
 6              return False
 7      return True
 8
 9
10  Structural-Filter(candidates, absolute):
11      for c in candidates:
12          if Validate-Inst(absolute, c) == False:
13              candidates.remove(c)
14      return candidates
```

Listing 1.2. Structurally Filtering

3.5 Semantically Filtering

iBase next performs lightweight semantic analysis for each candidate image base address that survives both the statistical and structural filters. It leverages the nature of an interrupt event and the expected semantics to process it. Specifically, an interrupt event is unpredictable since it is typically triggered by an external event. In the event of an interrupt, a context switch is triggered. For an ARM32 system, the context switch involves five steps. First, the current instruction finishes executing. Next, registers R0, R1, R2, R3, R12, the link register (LR), the program counter (PC), and the program state register (PSR) are pushed onto the stack. Third, LR is set to a special value which tells the processor how many values to pop from the stack when returning to normal execution. Fourth, the interrupt program state register (IPSR) is set to the number of the triggered interrupt. Finally, the PC is loaded with the interrupt vector [17].

Notably, while the register values are saved, the registers themselves are not initialized to specific values. Therefore, when the routine that handles this interrupt begins, registers are in undetermined states (e.g., they can contain arbitrary values written by other routines). In other words, it is unreasonable to directly read a register, particularly a general purpose input/output (GPIO) register, since its value can be arbitrary. Specifically, it would be illegitimate if an instruction uses a register for arithmetic, comparison, and addressing without firstly loading its value from the memory. Comparatively, it would be valid if the routine starts with pushing registers' values onto the stack (i.e., to restore registers after this routine completes). ARM32 supports 232 possible machine instructions. Therefore, it is expensive to track system states after the execution of each instruction and then determine an illegitimate instruction. *iBase* mitigates this challenge by only investigating the first instruction in the routine.

Specifically, *iBase* parses the first instruction in the routine and extracts its opcode. It classifies an instruction as arithmetic, comparison, branching, modifying, loading (or storing), or stack control based on the opcode extracted from this instruction. For example, an instruction will be considered an arithmetic instruction if its opcode is adc, add, mul, rsb, rsc, sbc, sdiv, udiv, or sub; one will be considered as a comparison instruction if its opcode is cmp or cmn; it will be considered as a branch instruction if its opcode is b, or cbz. If the first instruction in the routine is an arithmetic, comparison, branching, modifying, or loading (or storing) instruction and it uses a register as its operand, it will be considered illegitimate; if the first instruction in the routine is a stack control instruction but it is not push, it will be considered illegitimate.

Algorithm 1.3 presents how *iBase* leverages such analysis to identify the final candidate(s). Specifically, for each candidate base address (i.e., $base_i$), *iBase* subtracts it from each absolute address (i.e., abs_j) derived from the interrupt vector table to get an offset value (i.e., $abs_j - base_i$). It then attempts to disassemble the instruction with this offset in the binary, which will be the first instruction of an interrupt routine if the selected image base address is correct. If this instruction contains the illegitimate use of any register, the selected candidate image base address will be eliminated.

```
1  Validate-Prologue(absolute, base):
2      for a in absolute:
3          address = a - base
4          interrupt_first_instruction = binary_code[address]
5          if is_illegal_reg_usage(interrupt_first_instruction
       ):
6              return False
```

```
 7          else:
 8              return True
 9
10  Semantic-Filter(candidates, absolute):
11      for c in candidates:
12          if Validate-Prologue(absolute, c) == False:
13              candidates.remove(c)
14      return candidates
```

Listing 1.3. Semantically Filtering

4 Evaluation

Since the manufacturer of a microcontroller determines the exact value of the image base for a binary to be executed in this microcontroller, we have used PlatformIO, an embedded development tool [18] that is capable of compiling binaries for different microcontrollers. We developed a program and compiled its source code into both a stripped binary and a binary of executable and linking format (ELF) for each microcontroller: the ELF binary contains the image base and therefore offers the ground-truth information; the stripped binary does not have such information but is commonly encountered for reverse engineering. We totally generate 20 elf-stripped pairs, where each pair of binaries are for an ARM32 microcontroller with a distinct manufacturer. We use *iBase* to infer the image base of a stripped binary and validate the result using the ground-truth image base derived from its ELF counterpart. Since none of the existing methods [3–6] publishes its tool, we cannot experimentally compare them with *iBase*. We also exclude IDA since its free version only works with PE files and not stripped binaries (i.e., .bin files). We compare *iBase* with two state-of-the-art reverse engineering tools including Ghidra and Radare2. The experiments were conducted on a workstation with Intel Core i7 with 32 GB RAM.

Table 1 presents the evaluation results, including the number of absolute addresses, the number of relative addresses, the inferred range of the image base, the number of image base candidates after the statistical, structural, and semantic filters, the running time measured in seconds, and the validation result using the available ground truth. The detection results of Ghidra and Radare2 are presented in the last two columns. As shown by the evaluation results, *iBase* has successfully detected image base addresses in all tested binaries, with a negligible running time of less than 1 s. Comparatively, Ghidra and Radare2 fail to detect all of them.

Table 1. Detection Accuracy and System Performance

Microcontroller	Abs.	Rel.	Range of Base Addresses	Stat.	Struc.	Semantic	Runtime (s)	iBase	Ghidra	Radare2
TI MSP-EXP432401R	3	2362	0x0000000 - 0x0002800	10	5	1 (0x0000000)	0.16	Yes	No	No
Arduino Due	16	818	0x007C400 - 0x0080800	17	2	1 (0x0080000)	0.07	Yes	No	No
NXP LPC1768	45	838	0x0000C00 - 0x0004000	13	1	1 (0x0004000)	0.11	Yes	No	No
Black STM32F407VE	30	1010	0x7FFD800 - 0x8001400	15	1	1 (0x8000000)	0.06	Yes	No	No
Black F407VG	30	1010	0x7FFD800 - 0x8001400	15	1	1 (0x8000000)	0.06	Yes	No	No
STM32duino	3	1097	0x7FFA800 - 0x8000000	22	16	1 (0x8000000)	0.09	Yes	No	No
Blue STM	30	1010	0x7FFD800 - 0x8001400	15	1	1 (0x8000000)	0.07	Yes	No	No
Olimex F103	18	940	0x7FFD800 - 0x8001000	14	2	1 (0x8000000)	0.05	Yes	No	No
Microduino32	18	499	0x8003400 - 0x8005000	7	1	1 (0x8005000)	0.03	Yes	No	No
BlackPill STM32F401CC	21	571	0x7FFeC00 - 0x8001000	9	1	1 (0x8000000)	0.04	Yes	No	No
NXP LPC1769	45	1056	0x0000000 - 0x0004000	16	1	1 (0x0004000)	0.07	Yes	No	No
Adafruit Feather	30	1010	0x7FFD800 - 0x8001400	15	1	1 (0x8000000)	0.06	Yes	No	No
ST STM32F0308DISCOVERY	16	1104	0x7FFDC00 - 0x8001400	14	4	1 (0x8000000)	0.10	Yes	No	No
Olimex Olimexino-STM32F03	24	1083	0x7FFD800 - 0x8001800	16	1	1 (0x8000000)	0.06	Yes	No	No
STM3210C-EVAL	2	333	0x7FFEC00 - 0x8000000	5	4	1 (0x8000000)	0.02	Yes	No	No
STM32F103C4	16	927	0x7FFDC00 - 0x8001000	13	2	1 (0x8000000)	0.05	Yes	No	No
STM32F446RE	30	1101	0x7FFD800 - 0x8001800	16	1	1 (0x8000000)	0.06	Yes	No	No
STM32F7508	2	340	0x7FFEC00 - 0x8000000	4	1	1 (0x8000000)	0.02	Yes	No	No
SparkFun SAMD51	11	528	0x0001800 - 0x0004000	10	2	1 (0x0004000)	0.04	Yes	No	No
STM32F103R4	16	927	0x7FFDC00 - 0x8001000	13	2	1 (0x8000000)	0.05	Yes	No	No

7. Eagle, C., Nance, K.: The Ghidra Book: The Definitive Guide. No Starch Press, San Francisco (2020)
8. Ni, Z., Li, B., Sun, X., Chen, T., Tang, B., Shi, X.: Analyzing bug fix for automatic bug cause classification. J. Syst. Softw. **163**, 110538 (2020)
9. Slowinska, A., Stancescu, T., Bos, H.: Howard: a dynamic excavator for reverse engineering data structures. In: NDSS (2011)
10. Du, Y., et al.: Learning symbolic operators: a neurosymbolic solution for autonomous disassembly of electric vehicle battery. arXiv preprint arXiv:2206.03027 (2022)
11. Zheng, Y., Davanian, A., Yin, H., Song, C., Zhu, H., Sun, L.: FIRM-AFL: high-throughput greybox fuzzing of IoT firmware via augmented process emulation. In: USENIX Security Symposium, pp. 1099–1114 (2019)
12. Kruegel, C., Robertson, W., Valeur, F., Vigna, G.: Static disassembly of obfuscated binaries. In: USENIX security Symposium, vol. 13, p. 18 (2004)
13. Shin, E.C.R., Song, D., Moazzezi, R.: Recognizing functions in binaries with neural networks. In: 24th {USENIX} Security Symposium ({USENIX} Security 2015), pp. 611–626 (2015)
14. ARM paging (2019). https://wiki.osdev.org/ARM_Paging
15. Identifying outliers: IQR method (2022). https://online.stat.psu.edu/stat200/lesson/3/3.2
16. ARM. ARM Architecture Reference Manual (2005)
17. Valvano, J., Yerraballi, R.: Embedded Systems - Shape The World, 5th edn. Jonathan Valvano, Texas (2014)
18. Platoformio (2014). https://docs.platformio.org/en/latest/
19. Ben-Gal, I.: Outlier detection. In: Data Mining and Knowledge Discovery Handbook, pp. 131–146 (2005)
20. Pang, G., Shen, C., Cao, L., Van Den Hengel, A.: Deep learning for anomaly detection: a review. ACM Comput. Surv. (CSUR) **54**(2), 1–38 (2021)

Author Index

© The Editor(s) (if applicable) and The Author(s), under exclusive license
to Springer Nature Singapore Pte Ltd. 2024
G. Wang et al. (Eds.): UbiSec 2023, CCIS 2034, pp. 463–464, 2024.
https://doi.org/10.1007/978-981-97-1274-8

Printed in the United States
by Baker & Taylor Publisher Services